Overtime

America's Aging Workforce and the Future of Working Longer

EDITED BY
Lisa F. Berkman

AND
Beth C. Truesdale

UNIVERSITY PRESS

OXFORD
UNIVERSITY PRESS

Oxford University Press is a department of the University of Oxford. It furthers
the University's objective of excellence in research, scholarship, and education
by publishing worldwide. Oxford is a registered trade mark of Oxford University
Press in the UK and certain other countries.

Published in the United States of America by Oxford University Press
198 Madison Avenue, New York, NY 10016, United States of America.

© Oxford University Press 2022

All rights reserved. No part of this publication may be reproduced, stored in
a retrieval system, or transmitted, in any form or by any means, without the
prior permission in writing of Oxford University Press, or as expressly permitted
by law, by license, or under terms agreed with the appropriate reproduction
rights organization. Inquiries concerning reproduction outside the scope of the
above should be sent to the Rights Department, Oxford University Press, at the
address above.

You must not circulate this work in any other form
and you must impose this same condition on any acquirer.

Library of Congress Cataloging-in-Publication Data
Names: Berkman, Lisa F., editor. | Truesdale, Beth C., editor.
Title: Overtime : America's aging workforce and the future of working longer /
edited by Lisa F. Berkman and Beth C. Truesdale.
Other titles: Overtime (Berkman) | America's aging workforce and the
future of working longer
Description: New York, NY : Oxford University Press, [2022] |
Includes bibliographical references and index.
Identifiers: LCCN 2022012699 (print) | LCCN 2022012700 (ebook) |
ISBN 9780197512067 (hardback) | ISBN 9780197512081 (epub) |
ISBN 9780197512098
Subjects: MESH: Aged | Workforce—trends | Socioeconomic Factors |
United States
Classification: LCC HB849.41 (print) | LCC HB849.41 (ebook) |
DDC 304.6—dc23/eng/20220613
LC record available at https://lccn.loc.gov/2022012699
LC ebook record available at https://lccn.loc.gov/2022012700

DOI: 10.1093/oso/9780197512067.001.0001

This material is not intended to be, and should not be considered, a substitute for medical or other professional
advice. Treatment for the conditions described in this material is highly dependent on the individual
circumstances. And, while this material is designed to offer accurate information with respect to the subject
matter covered and to be current as of the time it was written, research and knowledge about medical and health
issues is constantly evolving and dose schedules for medications are being revised continually, with new side
effects recognized and accounted for regularly. Readers must therefore always check the product information
and clinical procedures with the most up-to-date published product information and data sheets provided by
the manufacturers and the most recent codes of conduct and safety regulation. The publisher and the authors
make no representations or warranties to readers, express or implied, as to the accuracy or completeness of this
material. Without limiting the foregoing, the publisher and the authors make no representations or warranties as
to the accuracy or efficacy of the drug dosages mentioned in the material. The authors and the publisher do not
accept, and expressly disclaim, any responsibility for any liability, loss, or risk that may be claimed or incurred as
a consequence of the use and/or application of any of the contents of this material.

9 8 7 6 5 4 3 2 1

Printed by Sheridan Books, Inc., United States of America

Contents

Acknowledgments   vii
About the Editors and Contributors   xi

Is Working Longer in Jeopardy?   1
Lisa F. Berkman and Beth C. Truesdale

PART ONE   Who Has a Job? Labor Trends from Commuting Zones to Countries

1. When I'm 54: Working Longer Starts Younger Than We Think   27
   Beth C. Truesdale, Lisa F. Berkman, and Alexandra Mitukiewicz

2. The Geography of Retirement   49
   Courtney C. Coile

3. The European Context: Declining Health but Rising Labor Force Participation among the Middle-Aged   69
   Axel Börsch-Supan, Irene Ferrari, Giacomo Pasini, and Luca Salerno

4. Planning for the "Expected Unexpected": Work and Retirement in the United States after the COVID-19 Pandemic Shock   91
   Richard B. Freeman

PART TWO   What's the Fit? Workers and Their Abilities, Motivations, and Expectations

5. The Link between Health and Working Longer: Disparities in Work Capacity   113
   Ben Berger, Italo López García, Nicole Maestas, and Kathleen J. Mullen

6. The Psychology of Working Longer — 138
Margaret E. Beier and Meghan K. Davenport

7. Forecasting Employment of the Older Population — 155
Michael D. Hurd and Susann Rohwedder

PART THREE   **Lived Experience: The Role of Occupations, Employers, and Families**

8. Dying with Your Boots On: The Realities of Working Longer in Low-Wage Work — 177
Mary Gatta and Jessica Horning

9. Ad Hoc, Limited, and Reactive: How Firms Respond to an Aging Workforce — 196
Peter Berg and Matthew M. Piszczek

10. How Caregiving for Parents Reduces Women's Employment: Patterns across Sociodemographic Groups — 213
Sean Fahle and Kathleen McGarry

PART FOUR   **Politics and Policy: Where Population Aging Meets Rising Inequality**

11. Working Longer in an Age of Rising Economic Inequality — 237
Gary Burtless

12. How Does Social Security Reform Indecision Affect Younger Cohorts? — 254
John B. Shoven, Sita Nataraj Slavov, and John G. Watson

13. The Biased Politics of "Working Longer" — 276
Jacob S. Hacker and Paul Pierson

14. What Is the Way Forward? American Policy and Working Longer — 301
Lisa F. Berkman, Beth C. Truesdale, and Alexandra Mitukiewicz

Index — 323

Acknowledgments

This book grew from the collective thinking of many close friends and colleagues. First, we acknowledge the superb and enlightened leadership of Kathleen Christensen, who led the Alfred P. Sloan Foundation's decade-long research program on working longer that created networks of researchers and sparked this book. Kathleen was essential as she supported the broad, interdisciplinary thinking that pushed us all to think beyond the narrow financial issues of retirement and to embrace questions about the dignity and meaning of work, how families affect and were affected by working longer, the intersection between work and health issues that older workers face, and how older adults continue to contribute in meaningful ways to their society.

The Advisory Board of the Working Longer program at Sloan inspired much of our thinking. We especially want to thank David Wise, who calmly, in his inimitable fashion, asked the killer, hardest questions of us. In one of our final meetings for the program, David asked a question that gave birth to the idea for this book. He said: What about all the older people we are not counting in our employment statistics? What about all the middle-aged people who are not counted in unemployment statistics because they have left the labor force? Surely, we don't anticipate that we will bring those people back into the workforce at 62 or 65 to work even longer? The day David Wise made that comment was the start of the Stanford Institute for Economic Policy Research (SIEPR) Working Longer Conference, led by John Shoven, another key player in this volume. During that conference we started to flesh out the idea for the volume. Many of the people we wanted to write chapters were in the room that day. We also wanted to look more widely for a truly interdisciplinary group of authors who could bring new perspectives. Lively conversations followed, and the book was born. Kathleen Christensen found support from Sloan for the book, and we were on.

Funding for this book was predicated on the idea that good things happen when people meet and talk and then write and again meet and discuss. Sloan generously funded us to gather the authors in person for two meetings to improve our ideas together and create more connections among the chapters. Intense meetings at the Harvard Center for Population and Development Studies and engaged conversations between the meetings strengthened the links among chapters and created opportunities for critical review. This was especially important because our authors included experts in economics, sociology, psychology, organizational behavior, political science, and epidemiology, whose different disciplines helped to expand our collective thinking. Again, we thank Kathleen Christensen and Jeffrey Cunningham for the support of these activities and their understanding of the ways in which the volume was greatly strengthened by the conversations.

An important part of Sloan's mission has been to expand the community of research on work and aging. Thus, we invited senior scholars to recruit colleagues and junior scholars to coauthor chapters in the volume. The more junior authors in this volume inherit the job of moving the field forward.

We deeply thank all the authors for their generous engagement and participation in the entire project as well as for their insightful chapters. They also read our introductory and closing policy chapters and provided enormously helpful feedback. They corrected errors, added nuance, and made us think harder. They agreed with some of our ideas and disagreed with others, and we are grateful for both. We thank all our contributors: Margaret E. Beier, Peter Berg, Ben Berger, Axel Börsch-Supan, Gary Burtless, Courtney C. Coile, Meghan K. Davenport, Sean Fahle, Irene Ferrari, Richard B. Freeman, Mary Gatta, Jacob S. Hacker, Jessica Horning, Michael D. Hurd, Italo López García, Nicole Maestas, Kathleen McGarry, Alexandra Mitukiewicz, Kathleen J. Mullen, Giacomo Pasini, Paul Pierson, Matthew M. Piszczek, Susann Rohwedder, Luca Salerno, John B. Shoven, Sita Nataraj Slavov, and John G. Watson. Their contributions have made this volume greater than the sum of its parts.

The Harvard Center for Population and Development Studies has been a home to this project in both the intellectual and emotional sense. Our Center has strived to be a deeply collaborative home to intellectual discourse across many disciplines and perspectives. It is dedicated to understanding population dynamics and to producing new knowledge that can help to reduce economic, social, and health inequities. Lesley Harkins organized events, communicated with authors, and helped prepare the entire manuscript for publication; Laura Price, Rob Correia, and Claudette Agustin kept the logistics running beautifully; and many colleagues provided stimulating conversations and moral support. Alexandra Mitukiewicz contributed stellar data skills, writing, policy insights, and unstinting good humor, first as a research assistant and then as a coauthor. We are fortunate to have had the chance to work with this outstanding team.

At Oxford University Press, Chad Zimmerman recognized the value of this book even before our ideas were fully formed. We could not have proceeded without his support of our proposal. We are grateful to Sarah Humphreville and Emma Hodgdon, who became our editors midway through and shepherded the book all the way through peer review and production. Oxford University Press has supported work in the interdisciplinary areas of health equity and social determinants of health for decades. We appreciate OUP's ongoing commitment to work in this area.

Truesdale is grateful to the W.E. Upjohn Institute for Employment Research for supporting her work on this volume in its later stages. When she moved from Harvard to the Upjohn Institute, she gained a wonderful new set of colleagues whose deep understanding of labor markets was matched only by the warmth of their welcome. The Institute has proved to be an ideal place to study the cross-currents of work, aging, and retirement in America.

Finally, we thank our teachers and our students: all those whose curiosity has inspired us to learn more about the world we inhabit and to share what we have learned. You are too many to list here, but you know who you are. And we thank our families. We hope our children (Erin and Leah) and grandchildren (Klara, Elio, Amalia, and Ezra) grow up in a world where good jobs are plentiful and security in old age is assured.

—Lisa F. Berkman and Beth C. Truesdale

About the Editors and Contributors

Editors

Lisa F. Berkman is the Director of the Harvard Center for Population and Development Studies (HCPDS) and the Thomas D. Cabot Professor of Public Policy, Epidemiology, and Global Health and Population at the Harvard T. H. Chan School of Public Health. Her research focuses on identifying and developing solutions for inequalities in health related to work conditions and social policy, socioeconomic status, and social networks and isolation.

Beth C. Truesdale is a Research Fellow at the W.E. Upjohn Institute for Employment Research and a visiting scientist at the Harvard Center for Population and Development Studies. Her research focuses on inequalities in work and aging, the future of retirement, and the effects of social institutions and public policies on Americans' well-being. She holds a PhD in sociology from Harvard University.

Contributors

Margaret E. Beier is a Professor of Industrial and Organizational Psychology at Rice University in Houston, Texas. Her research examines the influence of individual differences in age, gender, abilities, and motivation as related to success in educational and organizational environments. In particular, she examines the cognitive, attitudinal, and motivational determinants of job and training performance, job choice and retirement, and the influence of these factors on lifelong development and learning. Her work has been funded by the National Science Foundation (NSF), and she is a fellow of the Society for Industrial and Organizational Psychologists (SIOP) and a fellow of the Association for Psychological Science (APS).

Peter Berg is Professor of Employment Relations and Director of the School of Human Resources and Labor Relations at Michigan State University. His research interests include work-life flexibility policies and practices, the implications of an aging workforce for organizations, and international comparisons of working time.

Ben Berger is a PhD Candidate in Public Policy at the Harvard Kennedy School of Government and a National Science Foundation Graduate Research Fellow. He studies how public policy shapes the diffusion of scientific breakthroughs and adoption of innovative health care technologies.

Axel Börsch-Supan is the Director of the Munich Center for the Economic of Aging at the Max-Planck-Society. He is also Professor of Economics at the Technical University of Munich and a NBER Research Associate in Cambridge, Massachusetts. He leads the Survey of Health, Ageing and Retirement in Europe (SHARE). His research is about population aging, retirement, saving, pensions, and health at older ages.

Gary Burtless is a Senior Fellow (Emeritus) in Economics at the Brookings Institution in Washington, DC. He graduated from Yale College and earned his PhD in economics at M.I.T. His research focuses on aging, saving, labor markets, income distribution, social insurance, and the behavioral effects of government policy. He is coauthor of, among other books, *Growth with Equity: Economic Policymaking for the Next Century* (1993) and *Can America Afford to Grow Old? Paying for Social Security* (1989). Burtless has also written many scholarly and popular articles on the economic effects of Social Security, public welfare, unemployment insurance, and taxes.

Courtney C. Coile is a Professor of Economics at Wellesley College and a Research Associate of the National Bureau of Economic Research, where she serves as codirector of the NBER Retirement and Disability Research Center and Codirector of the International Social Security project. Her research focuses on the economics of aging and health, with particular interests in retirement decisions and public programs used by older and disabled populations.

Meghan K. Davenport is a Graduate Student at Rice University pursuing her PhD in Psychological Sciences with a focus on Industrial-Organizational Psychology. Her research focuses on the psychology of workplace aging, with a specific focus on motivation, personality, and learning across the lifespan.

Sean Fahle is a Research Fellow in the Department of Economics at the University of Tübingen. Previously, he worked as an Assistant Professor of Economics at the State University of New York at Buffalo. His research centers on the microeconomic behavior of households, particularly their decisions concerning savings, long-term care, intergenerational transfers, and labor supply. He holds a PhD in Economics from the University of California, Los Angeles.

Irene Ferrari is an Assistant Professor in the Economics Department of University Ca' Foscari of Venice. She holds a PhD in economics from the University of Bologna. Previously, she was a Postdoctoral Researcher at the Max Planck Institute for Social Law and Social Policy—Munich Center for the Economics of Aging. Her research interests lie in the fields of labor economics, economics of aging, policy evaluation, and household finance. In her research she uses survey data, mostly from the Survey of Health, Ageing and Retirement in Europe (SHARE), as well as large administrative datasets.

Richard B. Freeman holds the Herbert Ascherman Chair in Economics at Harvard University. He is a Research Associate at the NBER, Faculty Codirector of the Labor and Worklife Program at the Harvard Law School, and Coeditor of the *Journal of Participation and Employee Ownership* (JPEO). His research interests include the job market for scientists and engineers; the transformation of scientific ideas into innovations; Chinese and Korean labor markets; the effects of AI and robots on the job market; and forms of labor market representation and employee ownership.

Mary Gatta is an Associate Professor of Sociology at City University of New York (Guttman). Her research focuses on policy and programs that can improve job quality and economic security for marginalized workers. She has written on workplace flexibility for low-wage workers, the experiences of women navigating public workforce systems, and older workers and retirement insecurity. She holds a PhD in Sociology from Rutgers University.

Jacob S. Hacker is Stanley Resor Professor of Political Science at Yale University. An expert on American governance, he is the author or coauthor of more than a half-dozen books, numerous journal articles, and a wide range of popular writings. His latest book, written with Paul Pierson, is *Let Them Eat Tweets: How the Right Rules in an Age of Extreme Inequality*. He is a member of the American Academy of Arts and Sciences and the American Academy of Political and Social Science and was awarded the Robert Ball Award of the National Academy of Social Insurance in 2020.

Jessica Horning is currently a Data Associate with the Tahirih Justice Center, a nonprofit immigration law firm, and previously worked at Wider Opportunities for Women on issues surrounding economic security. Her research has focused on economic security for families, women, and elders, which has spanned issues surrounding the labor market, safety net programs, and retirement supports.

Michael D. Hurd is a Senior Principal Researcher at RAND, Director of the RAND Center for the Study of Aging, and a member of the NBER. His research interests include retirement, pensions, Social Security, the determinants of consumption and saving, the economic effects of the Great Recession, the cost of dementia, the lifetime use of nursing homes, survey methods, and the properties and uses of subjective probabilities. He is a coinvestigator of the Health and Retirement Study.

Italo López García is an Economist at the RAND Corporation, a Research Fellow of the Institute for the Study of Labor (IZA), and a Professor at the Pardee RAND Graduate School. His research interests include labor economics and development economics, with a focus on the study of the determinants of human capital investments over the life cycle.

Nicole Maestas is an Associate Professor of Health Care Policy at Harvard Medical School and a Research Associate of the National Bureau of Economic Research (NBER), where she directs the NBER's Retirement and Disability Research Center. Her research investigates work capacity among older individuals and people with disabilities, working conditions in the American labor force, the Medicaid and Medicare programs, and the opioid epidemic.

Kathleen McGarry is a Professor of Economics at the University of California, Los Angeles. Her research focuses on the economic aspects of aging with particular attention paid to public and private transfers, including the transfer of resources within families. She has studied issues related to health insurance, long-term care insurance, and medical expenditures as well as the role played by families in providing insurance and supporting their least well-off members. She is a coinvestigator for the Health and Retirement Study and a research associate at the NBER.

Alexandra Mitukiewicz is a PhD Candidate in Sociology and Social Policy at Harvard University. Her research centers on labor market inequality and policy, with a focus on aging and work, and work-family policy.

Kathleen J. Mullen is a Senior Economist and the Director of the RAND Center for Disability Research. Her research addresses intersections between health and work, including the effects of health on employment and the role of job demands and working conditions in determining health status and labor force participation, particularly at older ages. She holds a PhD in Economics from the University of Chicago.

Giacomo Pasini is a Professor in Econometrics at Ca' Foscari University of Venice, Italy. After obtaining a PhD in Economics in Venice, he moved to Utrecht for a postdoc period. He had visiting appointments at Stanford, Harvard Center for Population and Development Studies, Goethe University of Frankfurt, Groningen University, and University of St. Gallen. His research interests are in economics of aging, health economics, and household finance.

Paul Pierson is the John Gross Professor of Political Science at the University of California at Berkeley and Director of the Berkeley Center for the Study of American Democracy. His teaching and research areas include the fields of American politics and public policy, comparative political economy, and social theory.

Matthew M. Piszczek is an Assistant Professor of Management in the Mike Ilitch School of Business at Wayne State University with a PhD in Industrial Relations and Human Resources from Michigan State University. His research focuses on work-life and age-related human resource management practices and their implications for employers and employees.

Susann Rohwedder is a Senior Economist at RAND and Associate Director of the RAND Center for the Study of Aging. Her research focuses on the economics of aging in the areas of household consumption and saving behavior, financial security of households, retirement, long-term care, the prevalence and cost of dementia, and individuals' expectation formation. She holds a PhD in Economics from University College London.

Luca Salerno is a Researcher at the Munich Center for the Economics of Aging of the Max Planck Institute for Social Law and Social Policy. His research interests focus on social policy and health developments. He is currently pursuing his PhD at the Technical University of Munich.

John B. Shoven is the Trione Director of the Stanford Institute for Economic Policy Research and the Charles R. Schwab Professor of Economics at Stanford. He is also a Senior Fellow at the Hoover Institution and a Research Associate of the National Bureau of Economic Research. He specializes in public finance and corporate finance and has published on Social Security, health economics, corporate and personal taxation, mutual funds, pension plans, economic demography, and applied general equilibrium economics.

Sita Nataraj Slavov is a Professor at the Schar School of Policy and Government at George Mason University, a Research Associate at the National Bureau of Economic Research, and a nonresident senior fellow at the American Enterprise Institute. She has previously served as a Senior Economist specializing in public finance issues at the White House's Council of Economic Advisers and a member of the 2019 Social Security Technical Panel on Assumptions and Methods. Her research focuses on public finance and the economics of aging, including issues relating to older people's work decisions, Social Security, and tax reform.

John G. Watson is a Lecturer in Finance at the Stanford Graduate School of Business. His current research focuses on life-cycle models and what they tell us about preparing for our retirement years. He holds a PhD in Mathematics from Rensselaer Polytechnic Institute.

Is Working Longer in Jeopardy?

Lisa F. Berkman and Beth C. Truesdale[1]

1. Introduction

Worldwide, aging populations are one of humanity's greatest accomplishments—and one of our greatest challenges. As longevity has risen and fertility has fallen, older adults make up a larger portion of populations. Without a doubt, societies can reap more benefits from older people's contributions than they did in previous generations. At the same time, this demographic transition changes everything—including how nations navigate work and retirement.

On average, Americans live much longer and healthier lives than they did 50 years ago and substantially longer than when Social Security was created in the 1930s. Many policymakers and academics think it is logical—almost inevitable—that Americans will spend more of these years in the paid labor force.[2]

Working longer, it is argued, is a win-win-win solution for society, employers, and workers. Working longer and delaying retirement could cut the cost of Social Security for an aging population; provide a bigger pool of experienced labor; and shore up individuals' financial security. In particular, longer life expectancies mean that Americans need income to support more years of life, and working longer is a commonly proposed solution. Some research even suggests that working longer leads to better health in older age by helping adults maintain cognitive skills and social networks. The idea that longer lives should translate naturally and seamlessly into longer *working* lives has become the mainstream policy position in America and in many wealthy nations.[3]

The purpose of this book is to examine the viability of this working-longer framework.

This volume emerged as an idea during conversations at the Alfred P. Sloan Foundation's Working Longer Initiative. Near the end of a 10-year run of this advisory group's meetings, we started to question exactly *who we were counting* in labor and employment statistics—or more precisely, *who we were leaving out*. In thinking about working-longer ideals, we began to examine the pitfalls as well as the promises. For older Americans, what were the challenges and barriers to working longer? Were major trends in the United States making working longer an easier and more attractive pathway—or just the opposite?

We soon realized that some of the basic assumptions underpinning working-longer policy solutions—including the tacit assumptions that almost everyone is still employed in the run-up to traditional retirement years and can delay retirement if they so choose—are incorrect. It rapidly became clear to us that many Americans left the active labor force in their 50s or even earlier. Many more struggled to remain in. Adults who are neither in paid work nor looking for jobs are typically excluded from formal unemployment statistics. Likewise, they are typically excluded from conversations about working longer.

What are the implications for working-longer policies if a large number of Americans are no longer in paid employment by the time they are in their early 60s? As we started to explore this question, several other concerning patterns became clear. Large and persistent inequalities in health, family dynamics, and jobs between groups defined by socioeconomic position (SEP), race/ethnicity, and gender cast into doubt the idea that working longer is a simple solution to American labor force, retirement, and productivity issues. In addition, changes during the past three to four decades to health, family dynamics, and jobs, as well trends in public policy, suggested that working longer might become difficult for a growing segment of Americans. We outline these four domains briefly here before unpacking the evidence below.

First, social and economic inequality has increased over the past four decades, creating large divides between college graduates and those without college degrees in terms of opportunities, earnings, and the capacity to work longer. Although average working conditions improved steadily during much of the twentieth century, these trends have become less clear in recent decades. Among low- and even middle-income workers, many jobs feature difficult working conditions, few benefits, instability, and stagnating wages. In the context of large inequalities, policies that cater to the needs of the "average" American may be a poor fit for substantial sections of the population.

Second, health inequalities between richer and poorer Americans are large and have grown in tandem with rising economic inequality. Important sections of the generations in their 40s and 50s today may not actually be as healthy as earlier cohorts were. Steady improvements in life expectancy have stagnated or reversed. Indeed, among adults under age 65, mortality rates *increased* slightly in the late 2010s among all race/ethnic groups (Woolf and Schoomaker 2019). As life expectancy has continued to rise in other developed nations, the United States has slid down the rankings. In short, trends toward better health for all sociodemographic groups in the United States can no longer be taken for granted.

Third, family dynamics have altered enormously in recent decades. Rates of fertility, marriage, divorce, single parenthood, multigenerational households, and same-sex relationships have changed over time. Patterns of geographic mobility and immigration have also shifted. Many middle-aged adults, especially women, now combine paid work with major caregiving responsibilities for younger and older generations. Taken together, these changes mean that the traditional vision of retirement—a male breadwinner retiring on a solid pension from a career job—is the exception, not the rule.

Finally, from the 1980s onward, the role of American government has changed. Many risks have increasingly been cast as a matter of personal rather than public responsibility, weakening the government's capability to respond to the needs of an aging population. Tax cuts, policies that undermine labor unions, weak enforcement of rules that protect workers, increased political polarization, and the rising political clout of the very wealthy have combined to put an aging workforce into a precarious position. These issues are not merely a matter for individuals to respond to by themselves. Population aging is a matter of demography; our response to it is a matter of politics and policy.

The stresses faced by so many Americans are partly a function of trying to continue to work in the paid labor force while facing difficult job conditions, health problems, or caregiving needs while lacking the protection and support that only robust democratic governments can provide. Growing older in America is, for many, a hard path to travel.

These long-term trends suggested serious challenges to the working-longer policy framework even before the COVID-19 pandemic, which exacerbated existing inequalities in employment, health, and family life. We see this as a pivotal moment to jettison old projections based on assumptions that may have been reasonable in the mid-twentieth century but are now outdated. It is time to explore more deeply what current patterns can tell us about new policy solutions that would benefit Americans in the decades to come. For America to be resilient to demographic, economic, and political challenges, we must understand the conditions that influence participation in the paid workforce and the conditions that produce exits from the workforce.

In the face of both population aging and rising inequality, what is the future of working longer?

* * *

Our introduction to this volume is divided into two parts. In the first section, we outline trends in American demographics, health, family dynamics, jobs, and politics in some depth, because the evidence in these five areas—well-known to researchers in those areas but often neglected in the working-longer conversation—is a key motivation for this book.

Then we turn to the new frontiers of research on aging, work, and retirement. To generate a well-rounded picture of the promises and pitfalls of the working-longer policy solution, we asked experts to examine the evidence in their fields and to fill gaps in that evidence. The core of the book comprises 13 chapters, drawing on expertise from investigators in economics, sociology, psychology, organizational behavior, political science, and epidemiology. In the second section of this chapter, we describe what they uncovered. The final chapter in this volume describes a policy framework integrating the domains of work and retirement, which we argue flows from the evidence developed in this book.

We carry two themes throughout this book: (a) the consequences of large and growing economic and social inequalities and (b) changes across generations or birth cohorts, especially considering the circumstances of middle-aged adults now in their "prime" working years.

The theme of social and economic inequality is important because averages hide huge differences across social, demographic, and economic groups—differences that shape our capacity to work, the skills and resources we have, the discrimination and other challenges we face, and the benefits that may accrue to us for working longer. For instance, raising the Social Security retirement age reduces lifetime benefits for everyone, both low and high earners, but it falls hardest on the most disadvantaged groups, who are more likely to have poor health or physically demanding jobs that make it difficult to delay claiming. Yet early claiming locks in lower monthly benefits for life.[4] As we discuss opportunities for working longer, it is as important to understand the *population distribution* of resources, abilities, and opportunities as it is to understand overall *average population trends*. We can't understand the future of working longer without understanding American inequality.

The theme of changes across cohorts is important because the experiences of today's middle-aged Americans differ from the experiences of today's retirees. As we discuss below, substantial sections of the generations now in middle age are facing more precarious jobs, greater caregiving responsibilities, no better health, and a less responsive federal government than their counterparts at or beyond traditional retirement ages. For the purpose of this book, we focus on the current and next generations of older Americans. While conditions in early life clearly shape work opportunities and well-being at older ages, our emphasis in this volume is on what we as a society can do in the next two to three decades. Because everyone who will be 60 by 2050 is currently more than 30 years old, we focus on conditions and policies that affect adults.

Our bottom line is that if we as a society want to make working longer a healthy reality for many Americans, we need to address the issues facing young and middle-aged workers now. We must build in policies to level the social and economic playing field that is tilted against disadvantaged Americans and put in place policies that improve both working lives today and retirement security for these Americans in 20 or 30 years. Long-term policies that invest in the future should go along with redistributive policies that support the immediate needs of older workers and retirees. We will need viable options for those who cannot work longer to be economically secure and socially engaged in their communities. And we should not give up on the idea that all Americans deserve a stable retirement after a lifetime of work.

2. Five American Dilemmas
2.1. Demographics: From a Pyramid to a Pillar
Changing age distributions are a crucial backdrop to working-longer policies. For most of recorded history, populations, both globally and nationally, could be drawn as a pyramid: many infants and young children at the base, tapering gradually to very few older people at the top. During the twentieth century, global mortality rates at all ages improved dramatically. When the odds of children surviving into adulthood improved, fertility rates decreased. As fertility fell and longevity rose, the classic demographic pyramid was reshaped into something more like a pillar.

As an indicator of population aging, demographers commonly compare the proportion of people aged 65 and older to the proportion under age 5. As Figure I.1 shows, in the United States, the older group outnumbered the younger group for the first time in the 1960s. Worldwide, the crossover took place in 2018. United Nations projections, shown by the dotted lines, suggest the proportion of older adults will continue to rise sharply during the next three decades.

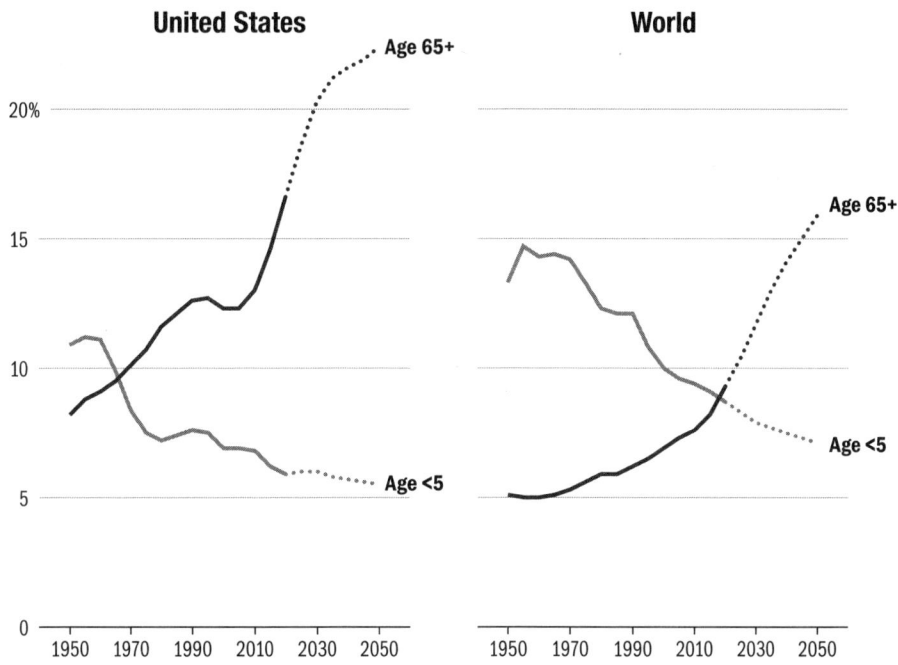

FIGURE I.1 Aging populations, 1950–2050
Population estimates for older adults (ages 65+) and young children (under age 5). Dotted lines indicate future projections.
Source: United Nations, Department of Economic and Social Affairs, Population Division (2019). World Population Prospects 2019, custom data acquired via website (https://population.un.org/wpp/).

Population aging has changed the ratio of people in the paid labor force to retirees. In the United States in 1950, there were 14 people of traditional retirement age (65 and older) per 100 people of working age (between ages 20 and 64). By 2015, that age ratio had changed to 25 per 100. Similarly, from 1950 to 2015, the ratio changed from 6 to 10 in India, from 9 to 15 in China, from 13 to 31 in Spain, and from 16 to 35 in Germany (OECD 2017, table 5.5). Most nations are aging; while there are exceptions among lower-income countries, they are few and decreasing in number.

For retirement systems, these changing ratios pose a financial challenge. U.S. Social Security is largely a pay-as-you-go program—that is, today's workers and employers pay taxes into the program, while benefits flow out to today's retirees. Working longer is often framed as a response to the issue of funding public pensions such as Social Security. If the problem is that Americans are living longer and Social Security has to pay for more years of retirement, then one plausible solution is to raise the full retirement age (FRA). When the FRA rises, workers must either wait longer to claim benefits or lock in lower monthly payments for life. Under legislation enacted in 1983, the FRA is gradually increasing from age 65 to age 67; some proposals call for raising the FRA to 70 or beyond. Raising the retirement age reduces the total benefits paid to each retiree and cuts the cost of Social Security.

While Americans are being asked to work longer to shore up Social Security in an aging society, their *capacity* to work longer rests on three areas we discuss next: their health, their family dynamics, and the future of work.

2.2. U.S. Population Health: Rising Inequalities, Stalling Averages

One of the key premises underlying the working-longer ideal is that Americans are living *healthier* as well as *longer* lives. The increase in life expectancy since Social Security was implemented means that more people need income for more years of life. This fact leads to one argument for working longer: if people live longer because they are healthier, some fraction of the increased life expectancy can be spent working in order to finance a longer retirement. If 70 is truly the new 60, perhaps delaying retirement for a few more years should not be too difficult. Because this premise is so fundamental, we devote extra attention to U.S. population health.

Inequalities and trends in health are important for the future of working longer because poor health is one of the main reasons that people retire earlier than they planned. Despite large bodies of research on American health trends and long-standing knowledge that poor health is a major driver of workforce exit (e.g., Bound et al. 1999), the evidence on trends and patterns has rarely been used to query the future of the working-longer policy solution.

2.2.1. Socioeconomic and Racial/Ethnic Inequalities in Health

Average rates of poor health, disability, and mortality hide large, persistent, and in some cases widening inequalities by social and economic disadvantage in the United States. Individuals who have less formal education, earn lower wages, or who are Black or Hispanic tend to experience much worse health than those who are more advantaged.

Mortality gaps by socioeconomic position (SEP) are large. As Figure I.2 shows, in 2014, 40-year-old men with incomes in the top quartile could expect to live to about age 87, while those with incomes in the bottom quartile could expect to live to about age 77 (Chetty et al. 2016). These inequalities have increased over time. Better-educated and higher-income Americans have continued to make modest gains in life expectancy. Depending on the time period and the definition of the group, those with the least education and income have experienced minimal improvements, stagnation, or absolute worsening of mortality rates (Meara, Richards, and Cutler 2008; Chetty et al. 2016).

Racial and ethnic differences in mortality are also large and are not completely accounted for by differences in education or income (Olshansky et al. 2012). For most of the past century, mortality rates remained 1.2 to 1.5 times higher among Black adults than among white adults, even as mortality improved in absolute terms among both groups (Levine et al. 2001). Compelling evidence suggests that racism and discrimination at the structural, cultural, and individual levels disadvantage members of racial/ethnic minority groups, especially Black Americans, and have done so for hundreds of years (Williams, Lawrence, and Davis 2019). Racism has serious consequences for health. Large bodies of research document structural racism within housing, labor, education, health care, and other major social systems, which combine to perpetuate racial inequities in health.

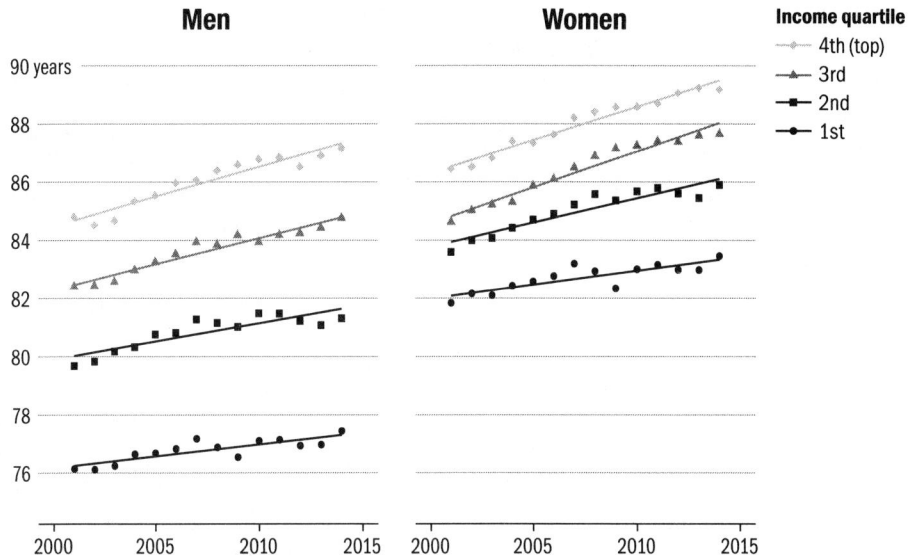

FIGURE I.2 Rising inequalities in life expectancy by income quartile, 2001–2014
Expected age at death for 40-year-olds
Source: Chetty et al. 2016, data from https://opportunityinsights.org/data/ (Table: "Income and Life Expectancy: Data for Figures, Tables, and Numbers in Text of JAMA Manuscript").

In the past two decades, inequalities in death rates between racial and ethnic groups remained large, while average improvements stalled. These trends were especially notable among middle-aged adults. Figure I.3 illustrates death rates between 2000 and 2017 among Black, white, and Hispanic adults aged 45 to 64. Among adults under age 65, mortality rates *increased* slightly in the late 2010s among all race/ethnic groups (Woolf and Schoomaker 2019).

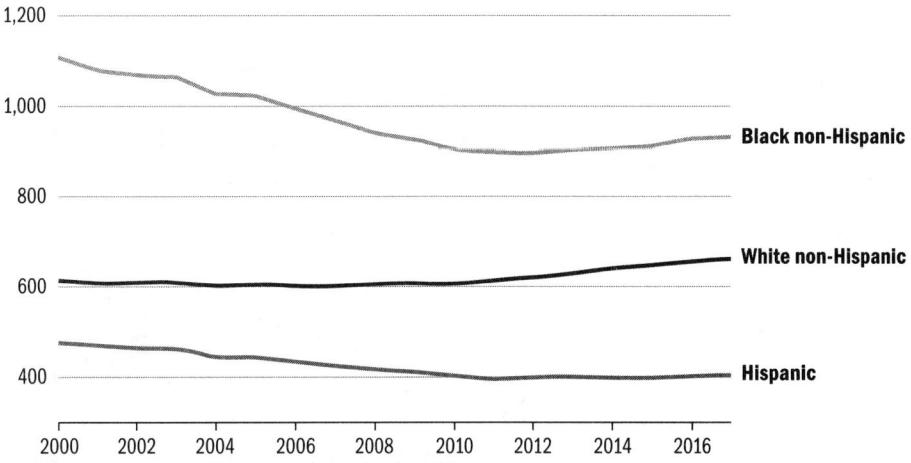

FIGURE I.3 Middle-aged mortality rates, 2000–2017
Age-specific death rates among U.S. adults ages 45 to 64, by race and ethnicity (per 100,000 population).
Source: CDC Data Brief 342, "Mortality Trends by Race and Ethnicity: Data Table for Figure 3," https://www.cdc.gov/nchs/data/databriefs/db342_tables-508.pdf

Functional ability and disability rates vary across racial/ethnic and socioeconomic groups as well. Rates of several disability outcomes are roughly 1.5 to 2 times higher among Black adults than among white adults. The largest inequalities occur between ages 50 and 69, precisely the years that are targeted by working-longer policies (Nuru-Jeter, Thorpe, and Fuller-Thomson 2011). Disability rates declined among both Black and white adults for several decades in the late twentieth century, but the trends have reversed in the past 10 to 20 years (Freedman and Spillman 2016). Some of the racial/ethnic differences reflect lifelong economic disadvantage, including limited educational opportunities, but differences persist even when controlling for socioeconomic resources. Inequalities in health are likely to translate into inequalities in work capacity.

2.2.2. Slowdowns in Population Health Improvements

Continued improvements in U.S. population health are not a given, as trends in mortality rates and life expectancies demonstrate. As Figure I.4 shows, average mortality rates, which declined steadily over most of the past century in the United States, have shown smaller decreases in the past decade. U.S. life expectancy rose from 69.9 years in 1960 to a peak of 78.9 years in 2014. The rate of increase flattened around 2010 and life expectancy actually fell in the years after 2014.

The United States has been virtually alone among developed nations in these concerning trends in life expectancy and mortality. Figure I.4 also shows how, beginning in the 1980s, the United States fell from the middle of the international rankings to virtually the bottom. By the early 2000s, the United States ranked last among 22 high-income countries in life expectancy at birth, and the gap has only widened in recent years.

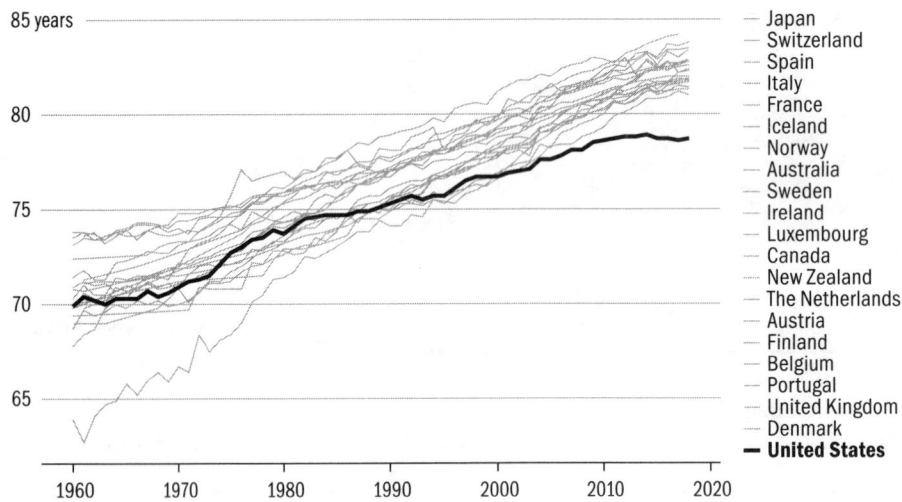

FIGURE I.4 Life expectancy at birth in 22 OECD countries, 1960 to 2018
Country names are in order of life expectancy in 2018
Source: OECD (2021).

A major contributor to stalling and falling U.S. life expectancy has been a rise in cause-specific mortality rates among adults aged 25 to 64 years that began in the 1990s, with alarming increases in midlife deaths from drug overdoses, suicides, and noninfectious diseases among middle-aged adults of all racial groups (Woolf and Schoomaker 2019). Rising midlife mortality bodes ill for the health of those cohorts as they age.

2.2.3. Trends in Middle-Aged Health

We see similar trends across cohorts when we turn to other health measures. Morbidity (physical and mental illness), functional limitations (difficulty with physical tasks), and disability (needing help with daily activities) are critical measures of health limitations that may affect work capacity.

In terms of morbidity, health improvements cannot be taken for granted among younger cohorts. Cohorts now between ages 40 and 65 in the United States have, by and large, not experienced the declines in disease that earlier cohorts experienced. Depending on the disease and the age group, some studies show improvements; others show a stagnation in morbidity rates; others show actual increases in disease (Crimmins et al. 2019). Overall, rates of good self-rated health have declined among adults in the run-up to retirement (Zack et al. 2004; Soldo et al. 2007). Trends in obesity (a risk factor for many diseases as well as back and joint pain, which are in turn risk factors for work disability) likewise suggest that younger cohorts will not fare as well as their predecessors (Martin et al. 2009).

While functional limitations and disability are challenging to measure consistently over time, in many ways these aspects are the most important for understanding whose health interferes with paid work. Using multiple waves of the National Health Interview Surveys, Zajacova and Montez (2018) report a sizeable increase in the prevalence of both functional limitations and disability between 2002 and 2016 among American men and women aged 45–64—prime age for labor force participation. They find that despite some positive changes, such as increased educational attainment and falling rates of smoking, deteriorating economic conditions have contributed to worsening health.

Worsening health among today's middle-aged men and women is a particular concern. Their comparatively poor function argues for deep consideration of how they will continue to participate in the paid labor force and how the United States will need to plan for their financial security as they age.

* * *

We spend time discussing health trends and social and economic inequalities in health in the introduction because longer, healthier lives have been one of the major premises of working-longer ideals. Many observers have assumed that longer lives and better health make working longer a simple path toward improving older individuals' financial security, providing employers with a bigger pool of experienced workers, and shoring up Social Security by increasing the Full Retirement Age.

What we have revealed in this section is that while Americans have gained life expectancy and health in many ways since 1950, there is reason to be concerned that along several dimensions the health of today's working cohorts is no better, and perhaps worse, than that of today's older Americans. Chapter 5 by Berger and colleagues and Chapter 6 by Beier and Davenport suggest that most Americans will retain the health they need to do paid work throughout their 60s. But an important minority, who are disproportionately disadvantaged, will not. Socioeconomic, racial, and ethnic differences are large, persistent, and in some cases widening for many important outcomes, including mortality, disability, and morbidity. These inequalities suggest that we need solutions for work and retirement that meet the needs of Americans with a very wide set of health conditions in middle and older ages.

2.3. Changing Family Compositions and Dynamics

When Social Security and employer-based retirement plans were developed in the United States in the mid-twentieth century, the modal American family consisted of a breadwinner husband and a homemaker wife (Waite and Nielsen 2001). With stay-at-home wives caring for both children and elders, it was conceivable that men could work until traditional retirement ages without experiencing conflict between their paid employment and family caregiving needs. Even in the mid-twentieth century, however, there was a wide variety of family compositions, especially among more economically disadvantaged families, immigrants, and families of color. America's retirement systems were not designed with the full range of household configurations in mind.

Over time, American families became increasingly diverse and increasingly pressured. Today, in the face of stagnant or falling wages and rising costs of housing, health care, and education, a full-time homemaker is, for most families, an unaffordable luxury. At the same time, increases in life expectancy among the older generation have meant that more middle-aged adults have elderly family members who require help with basic day-to-day activities. Falling fertility has meant that there are fewer siblings to share eldercare responsibilities. After World War II, U.S. women had an average of 3.6 children, compared to 1.8 in 2020, one of the lowest rates on record (Our World in Data, n.d.). As Fahle and McGarry point out in Chapter 10, in the mid-2010s, roughly one in five adults ages 45 to 54 and one in four adults ages 55 to 64 were providing care to elderly family members.

U.S. policies have not kept pace with these changes. Unlike almost all other industrialized nations, the United States lacks national standards on paid family leave. Existing laws on unpaid family leave cover only about 60 percent of workers. Compared to higher earners, lower-income workers are less likely to have access to paid leave, less likely to be eligible for unpaid leave, and less likely to be able to afford to take unpaid leave even when they are eligible for it (AEI-Brookings 2017). The conflict between caregiving and paid work for many middle-aged adults, especially women, is substantial. With these shifts in family circumstances, the need to develop policies that dial down the tensions between work and family obligations is center stage.

2.4. Changes in the Nature of Work

We now turn our attention to a core question: if Americans are working longer, what's the nature of work available to them?

There are some reasons to think that trends in working conditions would facilitate working longer. First, many jobs have become less physically demanding and less dangerous.

Better regulation of physical hazards has cut the number of recorded work-related deaths, illnesses, and injuries dramatically: worker deaths declined by about 2.5 times between 1970 and 2019, and worker injuries and illnesses declined by nearly 4 times (U.S. Department of Labor, n.d.). Second, the labor market increasingly rewards social skills. Between 1980 and 2012, the proportion of U.S. jobs requiring high levels of social interaction grew by nearly 12 percentage points (Deming 2017). Because both knowledge and emotional experience tend to improve with age while physical ability declines, as Beier and Davenport note in Chapter 6, these shifts should benefit older workers. Finally, advances in work-from-home technology could open up possibilities for workers with disabilities and remove geographic constraints.

But other trends in working conditions are more concerning. Indeed, the fundamental organization of employment has changed for many Americans, especially those in lower- and middle-wage jobs and in many sectors, including service and industrial occupations. The economy has become increasingly "fissured": jobs that in the mid-twentieth century were part of large corporations—ranging from hotel housekeeping to IT support—have been broken off through subcontracting, outsourcing, and franchising (Weil 2014). These disconnects reduce large firms' responsibilities to their workers, increase health and safety risks, and eliminate job ladders that once allowed employees to work their way up within firms. Part of the trend toward new organizational structures is a rise in "gig" work in which the worker is an independent contractor with no benefits or investment from the firm that profits from their labor.

As employers pared back their responsibilities to their workers, many jobs became worse in various ways (Kalleberg 2011; Osterman 2020). Despite rising GDP, real wages stagnated over the last 50 years for low- and middle-wage workers; employer-based defined benefit pensions and other benefits eroded; and employment became increasingly precarious and insecure. Although many changes have been worst for workers without a college degree, there is increasing evidence that the modern organization of work puts unsustainable stress even on workers who are highly educated and well-paid (Kelly and Moen 2020).

Physically and psychologically difficult working conditions are widespread and damaging, including for older workers. While there is little information on trends in work stress over time, in 2014, some 44 percent of workers ages 58 and older were employed either in physically demanding jobs (involving, for example, a lot of time standing, lifting, bending, kneeling, or crouching) or in difficult working conditions (such as extreme temperatures or hazardous equipment) (Bucknor and Baker 2016). The rise of remote work during the COVID-19 pandemic did not benefit workers like these, whose jobs require physical presence. Stressful jobs, lack of schedule control, and limited worker "voice" in shaping the working environment contribute to poor mental and physical health, including a range of cardiovascular and metabolic conditions (Lovejoy et al. 2021). Badly paid jobs that feature high stress, high turnover, and few benefits are unlikely to pave a healthy path toward working longer.

Among the forces that have shaped changes in wages and working conditions, declines in union membership stand out. In the private sector, 16.8 percent of workers were union members in 1983; by 2015, the figure was only 6.7 percent (Dunn and Walker 2016). Because unions tend to improve wages and working conditions both by direct negotiation with employers and by advocacy for better labor laws, their decline has left workers increasingly vulnerable.

The end result of trends in work, as the MIT initiative Inventing the Organizations of the 21st Century (1999) puts it, is that our current organization of economic activity is not achieving what we humans really want. Rather, it is socially, economically, and environmentally untenable and leads to increasing gaps between the "haves" and "have-nots" within countries and around the world.

Over recent decades, jobs and workplaces themselves have changed in important ways. Some of these changes have the potential to create better jobs for older workers and optimize the skills and resources they have; others create further challenges for older workers and make it harder for them to remain in the labor force. And for some changes that are still unfolding—such as climate change, technological changes, and geographic shifts in the location of jobs—the likely impact on working longer is not clear.

2.5. Changes in the Role of American Government

We have discussed trends in demography, health, family, and jobs in the United States. All of these are influenced by and interwoven with trends in politics and policy that are frequently missing from the working-longer discussion.

The past century has seen a contest in the United States between two visions of the purpose of government: one that believes that "government is the problem" and that America will flourish when individuals bear responsibility for their own fates; and one that believes that government should work in creative tension with markets to address problems that can only be fixed at a national scale (Cox Richardson 2020). The latter vision—that the job of government is to help ordinary Americans—underpinned much federal policy under governments of both parties from the Great Depression through the 1970s. It operated, however, under an incomplete vision of who counted as "ordinary Americans," focusing more on the needs of U.S.-born white men than on other groups.

It is in this context that Social Security, the backbone of retirement in the United States, was born. In 1934, President Franklin D. Roosevelt, responding to high poverty rates among elderly Americans, introduced an "economic security proposal based on social insurance rather than welfare assistance" (Social Security Administration n.d.). When the Social Security Act was signed into law in 1935, it covered about half of the jobs in the United States, but excluded agricultural and domestic occupations disproportionately filled by Black workers. Overall, 65 percent of Black workers and 27 percent of white workers were not covered (DeWitt 2010). The program expanded in 1939 to cover benefits for workers' dependents and survivors, and again in the 1950s to cover agricultural and domestic occupations.

For many years, Social Security has provided a predictable retirement income for millions of older Americans. Only 3 percent of U.S. adults age 60 and over never receive Social Security benefits (Center for Budget and Policy Priorities 2020). Although benefits are modest—in 2020, the average Social Security retirement benefit was just over $1,500 a month, or about $18,000 a year, replacing about 40 percent of preretirement earnings (Center for Budget and Policy Priorities 2020)—Social Security is the main source of income for the majority of older Americans today, making it America's biggest antipoverty program by far (Fox 2020).

In spite of the importance of the program, Social Security is in difficulty. In fact, that was a central reason for developing this volume. Current estimates suggest that the combined Social Security trust funds will be able to pay scheduled benefits until 2034. At that point, if Congress does nothing, revenues will cover only 78 percent of promised benefits (Social Security Administration 2021). As Shoven and colleagues point out in Chapter 12, uncertainty about the future of Social Security is itself a problem for workers. This crisis has been decades in the making: policymakers have been aware of the coming shortfall for many years.

Why has Congress not reformed funding for Social Security in recent years? It is a highly popular program. In a 2014 survey for the National Academy of Social Insurance (NASI), 69 percent of Republicans and 84 percent of Democrats agreed that it was critical to preserve Social Security benefits for future generations even if it meant increasing Social Security taxes paid by working Americans; even more agreed that top earners should pay more to support Social Security (Walker, Reno, and Bethell 2014). One might think that ensuring the program's stability would be an easy win for lawmakers looking to please their constituents.

But updating Social Security—like updates in many other domains—has been stymied by changes in the role of government. In the Reagan era, the trajectory of American politics shifted sharply. While the American welfare state has remained relatively intact, there has been a marked "privatization of risk" as a result of changes in work, family, and employment-based benefits alongside relative stagnation in social protections (Pierson 1994; Hacker and Pierson 2016). Perhaps not coincidentally, the rising inequalities in health, family life, and jobs that we described above took place in tandem with these trends in the role of government.

Retirement security is a systemic problem as well as an individual one. Because Social Security benefits are modest, Americans need private retirement savings in order to maintain their standard of living in retirement. However, policy choices have created a system in which private pension savings are largely attached to employers. While employer-based pensions have provided secure retirements for some, especially higher-income workers, they have left many Americans behind. About half of all American workers do not participate in any employer-based retirement plan—a number that has not changed much during the past three decades (Center for Retirement Research at Boston College n.d.). The result is that many older adults do not have enough savings to maintain their standard of living in retirement. Continuing to work for pay is often the only practical way for Americans to improve their economic situation as they age.

It is easy to think of these issues narrowly as problems with the American retirement system. But a view of the broader political landscape suggests that retirement problems are just one facet of a "great risk shift." As Hacker (2019) argues, the past four decades have seen a major shift of economic risk—including the risk of being poor in old age—from government and business onto American families and individuals. For the policy solutions we need to improve health, work, and retirement to be implemented, we need a well-organized government that cares about the social situation of its citizens.

2.6 And Then There Was COVID-19

The COVID-19 pandemic exacerbated the deep fault lines in American society, cutting across the domains of health, family, jobs, and politics that are so critical in the working-longer story. As Freeman points out in Chapter 4, the pandemic was a discontinuity that amplified the need to question our forecasts for working longer.

During the pandemic, going to work in person became an existential threat in the most literal sense. In the United States, workers in agriculture, food service, warehouses, construction, and transportation died at especially high rates (Y.-H. Chen et al. 2021). These "frontline" jobs, which typically lacked paid sick leave, were concentrated among workers without college degrees. COVID-19 mortality rates were 1.3 times higher among Black Americans than among white Americans, and five times higher among those without high school diplomas than among college graduates (J. T. Chen et al. 2021). Rates of job loss also illustrate the pandemic's unequal effects, with bigger losses and slower recoveries among disadvantaged groups.

Losing a job can have serious consequences for older workers. Coile and colleagues (2014) found that experiencing a recession in one's late 50s led not only to reduced employment but also to reduced health care coverage and lower longevity. Moreover, the COVID-19 recession increased inequalities in working longer: among adults in their late 50s and early 60s, those without college degrees were more likely to retire early, while college graduates were more likely to delay retirement (Davis et al. 2021). This pattern echoes the rising inequality in retirement ages between higher- and lower-SEP groups that took place in the Great Recession of 2008 (Coile and Levine 2010).

In addition to affecting older workers, the pandemic may have longer-term effects on today's middle-aged cohorts. Job losses among prime-age workers matter for working longer and retirement security because midlife career interruptions often change employment trajectories permanently. As Freeman shows in Chapter 4, employment dropped by 12 percent among men and 18 percent among women in the early months of the pandemic. A year later, many had not come back (Kochhar and Bennett 2021). It is also clear that a nontrivial minority of people who have had the virus experience serious symptoms that affect their work capacity for months and perhaps years (Powell 2021).

The pandemic intensified the paradox of working longer: those who need to work for more years because they lack retirement security are often those least able to do so.

3. New Knowledge about Working Longer

We organized this volume to examine the working-longer framework—the idea that longer lives should translate naturally and seamlessly into longer *working* lives.

As we looked at the evidence outlined above on trends in demographics, health, family dynamic, work, and the role of government, it was clear that there was ample reason to reexamine the working-longer ideal. But it was equally clear that we needed new evidence on working longer that paid attention to both (a) the consequences of large and growing economic and social inequalities and (b) changes across generations or birth cohorts, especially considering the circumstances of middle-aged adults now in their prime working years.

We recruited authors from several disciplines to provide evidence about the feasibility of working longer and potential solutions to the challenges we have outlined above. Economists have been at the core of the working-longer conversation, and their valuable perspectives are represented in several chapters. We also draw on experts in sociology, psychology, organizational behavior, political science, and epidemiology, who bring different and complementary perspectives. This section summarizes the new knowledge laid out in this volume.

3.1. Who Has a Job? Labor Trends from Commuting Zones to Countries

We open with four chapters that delve into who is working and who is not. These chapters describe patterns of employment across cohorts, ages, and geographies in the United States, and compare U.S. trends to those in European countries. Then, having clarified trends in the past, we consider how those past trends can (or can't) be used to forecast the future.

In Chapter 1, "When I'm 54: Working Longer Starts Younger Than We Think," Beth C. Truesdale, Lisa F. Berkman, and Alexandra Mitukiewicz bring Americans who are out of the labor force in late middle age back into the working-longer conversation. They find that working longer is not as straightforward as many people in the policy arena may assume. Employment rates are much lower among disadvantaged groups over the entire life course, but they drop by about 20 percentage points among *all* groups between ages 50 and 60. Working longer is concentrated among those have continuous employment during their 50s, but only about half of American adults—disproportionately male, white, and college-educated—are continuously employed in their 50s.

While much of the working-longer conversation focuses on increasing employment beyond age 65 or 70, these results suggest that difficulties with working longer begin a decade or more earlier. Policies that improve the quality and consistency of employment in late middle age could improve more Americans' chances of working longer.

As Courtney C. Coile points out in Chapter 2, "The Geography of Retirement," geography is an important dimension of disparities in work and retirement. In 2018, employment rates among adults in their 60s differed across commuting zones (CZs) by more than 20 percentage points. Regional patterns—higher employment rates in the middle of the country and the Northeast, and lower employment rates in Appalachia and the South—have not changed much in the past three decades. Some of this variation is due to differences in composition. For instance, people with college degrees, who are more likely to have jobs than those with less education, push the overall employment rate up wherever they cluster. But much of the variation is not simply an aggregate of individual characteristics. CZs with lower rates of working longer seem to have been left behind more generally.

A geographic lens suggests a way forward for policy. Importantly, employment rates for prime-age workers and older workers are strongly correlated across CZs; employment rates among more and less educated adults are also strongly correlated. It seems likely that places that are good for the employment chances of lower-income older adults tend to be good for employment across the board. Place-based policies that improve conditions in low-employment CZs could benefit workers of all ages and socioeconomic levels.

Axel Börsch-Supan, Irene Ferrari, Giacomo Pasini, and Luca Salerno bring an international view to the question of who has a job in Chapter 3, "The European Context: Declining Health but Rising Labor Force Participation among the Middle-Aged." In the United States, health and employment trends have moved in tandem: both have stalled or fallen among middle-aged adults. How does Europe compare? Börsch-Supan and colleagues find that health and employment trends have moved in *opposite* directions in Europe in the past two decades. Health stagnated or declined among middle-aged Europeans, especially among disadvantaged men, while employment rates continued to rise.

The international perspective shows how financial incentives in public pension systems profoundly influence overall rates of employment at older ages. While individuals who experience poor health are much more likely to leave the labor force than those in good health, country-specific institutions appear to be even more powerful than population health in shaping average employment rates. Compared to the United States, European countries have much more generous public pension systems, allowing people to retire earlier and with higher benefits. Retirement ages also tend to be less variable in Europe, with both lower rates of early exit from the labor force and lower rates of delayed retirement than in the United States Against a European background of relatively good population health and relatively early retirement ages, Börsch-Supan and colleagues argue, negative trends in health may not have much effect on overall rates of working longer in Europe.

Richard B. Freeman, in Chapter 4, "Planning for the 'Expected Unexpected': Work and Retirement in the United States after the COVID-19 Pandemic Shock," turns to the question of what happens when the past is not a good guide to the future. Most projections of retirement and working longer are based on extrapolations from past trends, assuming that the future will be a more or less smooth continuation of the past. As Freeman points out, however, the world also changes "through unforeseeable shocks that upend the 'best-laid schemes o' mice and men.'"

COVID-19 is the archetype of an unexpected shock. The pandemic precipitated the fastest loss of jobs and the biggest spike in workers seeking unemployment insurance in U.S. history. And it created a new form of labor market inequality between white-collar workers who can work from home and blue-collar and service workers whose jobs require them to work in person—a new division that mapped on to long-standing inequalities by gender, race/ethnicity, and education. Workers over age 65 lost jobs more rapidly, and regained them more slowly, than middle-aged workers. The policy response mattered, for better and worse: although labor policy did less to prevent job loss in the United States compared to many OECD countries, massive U.S. rescue packages temporarily reduced rates of poverty and sped recovery.

The big lesson from the pandemic, Freeman argues, is that planning for the future of work and retirement should consider "expected unexpected" shocks from the natural world. Planning should incorporate both the natural and social sciences, including investigations into human behavior in response to shocks as well as strategies to improve the effectiveness of private and public organizations.

3.2. What's the Fit? Workers and Their Abilities, Motivations, and Expectations

In the second set of chapters, we asked three teams of scientists to think more deeply about issues of person/environment fit—that is, how the abilities, expectations, and motivations of workers match the work environment as they grow older.

Ben Berger, Italo López García, Nicole Maestas, and Kathleen Mullen examine the fit between Americans' functional abilities and the demands of occupations in Chapter 5, "The Link between Health and Working Longer: Disparities in Work Capacity." The fundamental insight is that occupations demand dozens of different cognitive, sensory, physical, and psychomotor abilities—ranging from selective attention and near vision to static strength—and if we match the abilities individuals say they have to the demands of occupations in the U.S. economy, we get a measure of individuals' work capacity. Berger and colleagues find that work capacity declines only modestly with age, at least between age 25 and age 71. This suggests that most Americans retain the health-related abilities they need to hold *some* job as they get older, although adults in physically demanding jobs may not be able to transfer easily to other jobs if their physical abilities diminish with age.

Inequalities in work capacity, especially by education, are concerning. Health-related differences between college graduates and nongraduates translate into substantial inequalities in work capacity—inequalities that grow with age. And consistent with other research that shows worsening health among middle-aged Americans, Berger and colleagues find that younger cohorts of white Americans have lower work capacity than older white Americans, which may bode ill for working longer in the future.

An important question is what motivates older adults to stay in the workforce. Margaret E. Beier and Meghan K. Davenport explore this question in Chapter 6, "The Psychology of Working Longer." As they explain, the fit between a person and their environment is one of the keys: what seem like individual choices to work or retire are actually embedded in the context of the job, the organization, and the broader society. These contexts influence individuals' skills, perceptions of their abilities, and their motivations. As a result, the environment that organizations create for older workers can have a big effect on their decisions to work longer.

The lifespan perspective that Beier and Davenport use sheds light on how people's skills, abilities, and motivations develop continually across the life course. On average, a slight decline with age in work-related reasoning abilities is offset by gains in knowledge, which is good news for working longer. But there is also enormous heterogeneity in patterns of growth and decline. Individuals' desire to work longer is affected by their future time perspectives (that is, whether they perceive their future time in the work context as limited or expansive), their working conditions, and changes in their level of job satisfaction. The psychological perspective emphasizes how Human Resources practices that improve older workers' experiences are likely to benefit workers of all ages.

If we want to know whether Americans in upcoming cohorts are likely to work longer, there's really no substitute for asking them what they expect to do. This is the approach Michael D. Hurd and Susann Rohwedder take in Chapter 7, "Forecasting Employment of the Older Population." Hurd and Rohwedder use individuals' subjective probability of working longer to forecast future trends in working longer. Using long-run panel data from the Health and Retirement Study, they first describe the solid link between subjective probabilities of working and actual employment rates. Having validated that association, they forecast the probability that men and women at younger ages will continue to work at older ages. This approach is a good way to make predictions that do not simply extrapolate from past trends.

The forecast is not rosy. In fact, individuals' expectations suggest that the employment rate for 70-year-olds in the early 2030s will be lower than it was in 2016, reversing the long-term trend toward higher rates of working longer. Hurd and Rohwedder predict that declines in late-life employment will occur across almost all subpopulations, perpetuating large disparities by gender, race/ethnicity, and education. Their results suggest that it is problematic to assume that rates of working longer in America will continue to rise.

3.3. Lived Experience: The Role of Occupations, Employers, and Families

In the third set of chapters, we examine employment in the context of two vital institutions—the family and the workplace—and how they shape older workers' opportunities to work longer.

Some work sectors, especially those that feature low pay, few formal benefits, and little job security, make working longer particularly challenging—and yet these sectors also do the least to prepare workers for a financially secure retirement. In Chapter 8, "Dying with Your Boots On: The Realities of Working Longer in Low-Wage Work," Mary Gatta and Jessica Horning chronicle the experiences of older workers.

Restaurant work is an important example of low-wage service industries that represent a growing portion of the U.S. economy. Qualitative interviews with older adults who have spent their working lives in the restaurant industry make it clear that many of these workers love their jobs but struggle to stay employed as they age. Ageism, changes in restaurant ownership, and injuries at work combine with intense physical job demands to precipitate job loss. Workers patch together strategies to try to stay employed longer and to supplement their low incomes—but these creative strategies are not always enough to make ends meet. There is only so much that workers can do because the entire sector is predicated on precarious, low-paid, and sometimes off-the-books labor. Gatta and Horning pair individuals' stories with quantitative data that show that, compared to a benchmark of basic economic security, workers who worked a full-time minimum wage job their entire careers cannot ever afford to retire on Social Security alone.

Much has been written advising employers how to retain experience and talent by making their workplaces more attractive to older workers. But we know much less about what employers actually do—and even whether they actually *want* to retain older workers. Peter Berg and Matthew M. Piszczek tackle these questions in Chapter 9, "Ad Hoc, Limited, and Reactive: How Firms Respond to an Aging Workforce." The picture that emerges from survey data and in-depth interviews at manufacturing firms in the United States and Germany is that retaining older workers is, by and large, not a priority for employers. Firms may make ad hoc arrangements to retain older workers with particularly essential skills, but these efforts are neither systematic nor motivated by a desire to create a more age-diverse workforce. In some cases, Berg and Piszczek find, firms actively push older workers (especially lower-wage workers whose skills are more easily replaced) out of the workforce.

National differences in midlevel institutions such as corporations matter, however. Partly because groups that represent workers' interests—trade unions and works councils—are much stronger in Germany than in the United States, Germany's social policy has been more encouraging of phased retirement plans and alternative paths to retirement than has the United States. These findings suggest that a resurgence in worker voice in the United States could lead to policies that support both individuals who want to work longer and those who want to retire.

The family is also an important institution that affects working longer, as Sean Fahle and Kathleen McGarry describe in Chapter 10, "How Caregiving for Parents Reduces Women's Employment: Patterns across Sociodemographic Groups." Nearly 70 percent of elderly individuals will need help with daily tasks such as bathing and eating at some point in their lives. Paid-for eldercare—whether institutional or home care—is expensive. Except for adults with extremely limited finances, paid care is not covered by Medicare or Medicaid. As a result, much of the care for frail older adults is provided by their adult children, especially their daughters.

When it comes to caregiving, differences across sociodemographic groups are particularly complex. Women with more education, better jobs, and greater economic resources are slightly more likely to be caregivers than their less-advantaged counterparts. This is partly because higher-SEP women are simply more likely to have living parents. But even among women with living parents, higher-SEP women are more likely to be caregivers, perhaps enabled by greater resources and more flexible jobs. However, when women with lower levels of education and non-white women provide care for parents, they are likely to report many more hours spent in caregiving.

Across sociodemographic groups, women who were caregivers were less likely to be employed, worked fewer hours, and earned less—even years after the caregiving was over. Unless America dramatically transforms the way eldercare is provided, unpaid caregiving for parents will continue to reduce the possibilities for women to work longer.

3.4. Politics and Policy: Where Population Aging Meets Rising Inequality

Our final set of chapters addresses questions of national policy. Social Security and private pensions are rightly prominent in the discussion about the financial security of older Americans. In addition, a broader view of national politics sheds important light on why U.S. policies have not been more responsive to the needs of older Americans.

In Chapter 11, "Working Longer in an Age of Rising Economic Inequality," Gary Burtless examines the collision of two important trends: population aging and rising economic inequality. Over the past five decades, economic well-being improved among Americans age 65 and older: "poverty rates fell, median incomes rose, and the income gap between adults under age 65 and those over age 65 shrank." Even toward the bottom of the income distribution, the finances of older adults have improved over time. Social Security, Medicare, and other safety net programs are key to the financial well-being of retirees, especially lower-income adults.

At the same time, rising inequality among working-age Americans has been reflected in rising inequality among older Americans. While Social Security reduces income inequality among older adults (and helps to make economic inequality smaller among over-65s than under-65s), incomes from workplace pensions and savings increase old-age earnings inequality. And trends toward working longer also increase economic inequality among older Americans because working longer is concentrated among adults with higher levels of education—that is, those who would have been affluent even without later retirement.

The importance of Social Security is also clear in Chapter 12, "How Does Social Security Reform Indecision Affect Younger Cohorts?" As John B. Shoven, Sita Nataraj Slavov, and John G. Watson explain, the Social Security trust fund will be depleted in the early 2030s, necessitating some change to policy either at or before that date. The reform options are relatively straightforward and include a range of tax increases and benefit cuts.

Policymakers can act now, deciding what changes to taxes and benefits will go into effect in the future. Alternatively, they can delay action, waiting until the last moment to decide what changes to make. Delaying action has real costs to young and middle-aged workers, who must plan for retirement without knowing what set of reforms will be adopted. These workers would value having accurate information about what the future holds for Social Security.

Shoven and his colleagues calculate the value of advance knowledge of future Social Security reforms to young and middle-aged workers. They find values can be quite large, in some cases equivalent to two months of earnings. Thus, policymakers inflict real costs on workers by delaying action. Unlike the cost of Social Security benefit cuts or tax increases, which are unavoidable given the system's finances, the cost of policy indecision is avoidable.

Many chapters in this book document the difficulties faced by older Americans. Compared to older adults in other developed nations, Americans tend to receive less generous pension benefits, die earlier, and are more likely to have to work to support themselves after age 65. They are also more likely to live in poverty. In Chapter 13, "The Biased Politics of 'Working Longer,'" Jacob S. Hacker and Paul Pierson look for broader reasons that the United States has fallen behind. Why have politicians not done more to address the needs of older Americans?

This is a puzzle partly because older adults tend to be central to electoral politics—compared to younger adults, they are more organized, more engaged, and more likely to vote for the Republican Party, which has dominated national politics for most of the past three decades. Indeed, American social policy has tended to be relatively generous to older adults, and American voters, including Republicans, generally support measures to reduce economic insecurity. But the historical influence of older voters has not helped them gain more protective social and economic policies in recent years.

Hacker and Pierson argue that we need to look away from voters, whose influence in policymaking is often limited, toward organized political actors such as political parties. Growing inequality has resulted in a shift in power toward businesses and the wealthy, which pushes policy toward the right. Older Americans have suffered—as have many other vulnerable groups—from a political economy that has prevented a wide range of existing protections from being updated to meet new needs.

3.5. What Is the Way Forward?

Finally, in Chapter 14, "What Is the Way Forward? American Policy and Working Longer," we set out policy proposals that emerge from this new research. We note that the diversity of the American workforce and inequalities in actual working conditions call for a set of policy responses suited to the varied experiences of Americans in different social, economic, and health circumstances. We argue that policies affecting *work*—those that shape labor markets for workers of all ages—must be considered in tandem with policies affecting *retirement*. Working longer is an important but incomplete response to population aging.

This framework demonstrates that a broad range of policies rightfully belong in the working-longer conversation. In the broadest sense, investments in population health and well-being—including poverty reduction and education from childhood onward—could be working-longer policies. However, there are many opportunities to intervene beyond the early years. Because our time horizon for this volume is the next two to three decades, we focus our policy proposals on the needs of today's middle-aged Americans, who are the retirees of the future, as well as today's older adults. Our final chapter highlights specific policies to improve the well-being of Americans as they work and retire—policies that can help the United States to meet the challenges of an aging society.

Notes

1. We thank all the contributors to this volume for reading and commenting on this chapter. We also thank Alexandra Mitukiewicz for valuable research assistance.
2. By "Americans," we mean U.S. residents, including non-U.S. citizens.
3. Ghilarducci (2021) describes the emergence of the "Working Longer Consensus" across the OECD.
4. While delayed claiming of Social Security results in higher *monthly* benefits, delayed claiming may actually decrease *lifetime* benefits for lower-SEP workers. Lower life expectancies among lower-SEP groups mean that many individuals do not live long enough to recoup the benefits foregone by delayed claiming (Ghilarducci, Moore, and Webb 2018).

References

AEI-Brookings. 2017. "Paid Family and Medical Leave: An Issue Whose Time Has Come." Working Group on Paid Family Leave. Washington, DC: AEI-Brookings. https://www.brookings.edu/wp-content/uploads/2017/06/es_20170606_paidfamilyleave.pdf.

Bound, John, Michael Schoenbaum, Todd R. Stinebrickner, and Timothy Waidmann. 1999. "The Dynamic Effects of Health on the Labor Force Transitions of Older Workers." *Labour Economics* 6 (2): 179–202. https://doi.org/10.1016/S0927-5371(99)00015-9.

Bucknor, Cherrie, and Dean Baker. 2016. "Still Working Hard: An Update on the Share of Older Workers in Physically Demanding Jobs." Washington, DC: Center for Economic and Policy Research. https://cepr.net/images/stories/reports/still-working-hard-2016-03.pdf.

Center for Budget and Policy Priorities. 2020. "Policy Basics: Top Ten Facts about Social Security." Center on Budget and Policy Priorities. August 13, 2020. https://www.cbpp.org/research/social-security/top-ten-facts-about-social-security.

Center for Retirement Research at Boston College. n.d. "Pension Participation of All Workers, by Type of Plan, 1989–2016." Accessed September 30, 2021. https://crr.bc.edu/wp-content/uploads/2015/10/Pension-coverage.pdf.

Chen, Jarvis T., Christian Testa, Pamela D. Waterman, and Nancy Krieger. 2021. "Intersectional Inequities in COVID-19 Mortality by Race/Ethnicity and Education in the United States, January 1, 2020–January 31, 2021." *Harvard Center for Population and Development Studies Working Paper* 21 (3).

Chen, Yea-Hung, Maria Glymour, Alicia Riley, John Balmes, Kate Duchowny, Robert Harrison, Ellicott Matthay, and Kirsten Bibbins-Domingo. 2021. "Excess Mortality Associated with the COVID-19 Pandemic among Californians 18–65 Years of Age, by Occupational Sector and Occupation: March through October 2020." PLoS ONE 16(6): e0252454. https://doi.org/10.1371/journal.pone.025245.

Chetty, Raj, Michael Stepner, Sarah Abraham, Shelby Lin, Benjamin Scuderi, Nicholas Turner, Augustin Bergeron, and David Cutler. 2016. "The Association Between Income and Life Expectancy in the United States, 2001–2014." *JAMA* 315 (16): 1750–1766. https://doi.org/10.1001/jama.2016.4226.

Coile, Courtney C., and Phillip B. Levine. 2010. *Reconsidering Retirement: How Losses and Layoffs Affect Older Workers*. Washington, DC: Brookings Institution Press. http://muse.jhu.edu/book/356.

Coile, Courtney C., Phillip B. Levine, and Robin McKnight. 2014. "Recessions, Older Workers, and Longevity: How Long Are Recessions Good for Your Health?" *American Economic Journal: Economic Policy* 6 (3): 92–119. https://dx.doi.org/10.1257/pol.6.3.92.

Cox Richardson, Heather. 2020. *How the South Won the Civil War: Oligarchy, Democracy, and the Continuing Fight for the Soul of America*. New York: Oxford University Press.

Crimmins, Eileen M., Yuan S. Zhang, Jung Ki Kim, and Morgan E. Levine. 2019. "Changing Disease Prevalence, Incidence, and Mortality among Older Cohorts: The Health and Retirement Study." *The Journals of Gerontology: Series A* 74 (S1): S21–S26. https://doi.org/10.1093/gerona/glz075.

Davis, Owen, Bridget Fisher, Teresa Ghilarducci, and Siavash Radpour. 2021. "The Pandemic Retirement Surge Increased Retirement Inequality." Status of Older Workers Report Series. New York: Schwartz Center for Economic Policy Analysis at the New School for Social Research. https://www.economicpolicyresearch.org/jobs-report/the-pandemic-retirement-surge-increased-retirement-inequality.

Deming, David J. 2017. "The Growing Importance of Social Skills in the Labor Market." *The Quarterly Journal of Economics* 132 (4): 1593–1640. https://doi.org/10.1093/qje/qjx022.

DeWitt, Larry. 2010. "The Decision to Exclude Agricultural and Domestic Workers from the 1935 Social Security Act." *Social Security Bulletin* 70 (4): 49–68. https://www.ssa.gov/policy/docs/ssb/v70n4/v70n4p49.html.

Dunn, Megan, and James Walker. 2016. "Union Membership In The United States." U.S. Bureau of Labor Statistics. https://www.bls.gov/spotlight/2016/union-membership-in-the-united-states/pdf/union-membership-in-the-united-states.pdf.

Fox, Liana. 2020. "The Supplemental Poverty Measure: 2019." Current Population Reports. Washington, DC: U.S. Census Bureau. https://www.census.gov/content/dam/Census/library/publications/2020/demo/p60-272.pdf.

Freedman, Vicki A., and Brenda C. Spillman. 2016. "Active Life Expectancy in the Older US Population, 1982–2011: Differences between Blacks and Whites Persisted." *Health Affairs* 35 (8): 1351–1358. https://doi.org/10.1377/hlthaff.2015.1247.

Ghilarducci, Teresa. 2021. "Making Old People Work: Three False Assumptions Supporting the 'Working Longer Consensus.'" *Politics & Society* 49 (4): 549–574. https://doi.org/10.1177/0032329220987084.

Ghilarducci, Teresa, Kyle Moore, and Anthony Webb. 2018. "The Inequitable Effects of Raising the Retirement Age on Blacks and Low-Wage Workers." Policy Note Series. Schwartz Center for Economic Policy Analysis and Department of Economics: The New School for Social Research. http://www.economicpolicyresearch.org/resource-library/research/the-inequitable-effects-of-raising-the-retirement-age-on-blacks-and-low-wage-workers.

Hacker, Jacob S. 2019. *The Great Risk Shift: The New Economic Insecurity and the Decline of the American Dream*. 2nd ed. New York: Oxford University Press.

Hacker, Jacob S., and Paul Pierson. 2016. *American Amnesia: How the War on Government Led Us to Forget What Made America Prosper*. New York: Simon & Schuster.

Kalleberg, Arne L. 2011. *Good Jobs, Bad Jobs: The Rise of Polarized and Precarious Employment Systems in the United States, 1970s to 2000s*. New York: Russell Sage Foundation.

Kelly, Erin L., and Phyllis Moen. 2020. *Overload: How Good Jobs Went Bad and What We Can Do about It*. Princeton, NJ: Princeton University Press.

Kochhar, Rakesh, and Jesse Bennett. 2021. "U.S. Labor Market Inches Back from the COVID-19 Shock, but Recovery Is Far from Complete." https://www.pewresearch.org/fact-tank/2021/04/14/u-s-labor-market-inches-back-from-the-covid-19-shock-but-recovery-is-far-from-complete/.

Levine, Robert S., James E. Foster, Robert E. Fullilove, Mindy T. Fullilove, Nathaniel C. Briggs, Pamela C. Hull, Baqar A. Husaini, and Charles H. Hennekens. 2001. "Black-White Inequalities in Mortality and Life Expectancy, 1933–1999: Implications for Healthy People 2010." *Public Health Reports* 116 (5): 474–483. https://www.ncbi.nlm.nih.gov/pmc/articles/PMC1497364/.

Lovejoy, Meg, Erin L. Kelly, Laura D. Kubzansky, and Lisa F. Berkman. 2021. "Work Redesign for the 21st Century: Promising Strategies for Enhancing Worker Well-Being." *American Journal of Public Health* 111 (10): 1787–1795. https://doi.org/10.2105/AJPH.2021.306283.

Martin, Linda G., Vicki A. Freedman, Robert F. Schoeni, and Patricia M. Andreski. 2009. "Health and Functioning Among Baby Boomers Approaching 60." *The Journals of Gerontology Series B: Psychological Sciences and Social Sciences* 64B (3): 369–377. https://doi.org/10.1093/geronb/gbn040.

Meara, Ellen, Seth Richards, and David Cutler. 2008. "The Gap Gets Bigger: Changes in Mortality and Life Expectancy by Education, 1981–2000." *Health Affairs* 27 (2): 350–360. https://doi.org/10.1377/hlthaff.27.2.350.

MIT 21st Century Manifesto Working Group. 1999. "What Do We Really Want? A Manifesto for the Organizations of the 21st Century." Sloan School of Management, MIT. http://ccs.mit.edu/papers/pdf/wp032manifesto21C.pdf.

Nuru-Jeter, Amani M., Roland J. Thorpe, and Esme Fuller-Thomson. 2011. "Black-White Differences in Self-Reported Disability Outcomes in the U.S.: Early Childhood to Older Adulthood." *Public Health Reports* 126 (6): 834–843. https://doi.org/10.1177/003335491112600609.

OECD. 2017. "Old-Age Dependency Ratio." In *Pensions at a Glance 2017: OECD and G20 Indicators*. Paris: OECD: 122–123. https://www.oecd-ilibrary.org/social-issues-migration-health/pensions-at-a-glance-2017/old-age-dependency-ratio_pension_glance-2017-22-en.

OECD. 2021. "Life Expectancy at Birth (Indicator)." https://doi.org/10.1787/27e0fc9d-en.

Olshansky, S. Jay, Toni Antonucci, Lisa Berkman, Robert H. Binstock, Axel Boersch-Supan, John T. Cacioppo, Bruce A. Carnes, et al. 2012. "Differences In Life Expectancy Due to Race and Educational Differences Are Widening, and Many May Not Catch Up." *Health Affairs* 31 (8): 1803–1813. https://doi.org/10.1377/hlthaff.2011.0746.

Osterman, Paul, ed. 2020. *Creating Good Jobs: An Industry-Based Strategy*. Cambridge, MA: MIT Press.

Our World in Data. n.d. "Children per Woman." https://ourworldindata.org/grapher/total-fertility-rate-by-development-level-including-un-projections-through-2100.

Pierson, Paul. 1994. *Dismantling the Welfare State?: Reagan, Thatcher and the Politics of Retrenchment*. Cambridge: Cambridge University Press.

Powell, Alvin. 2021. "A pandemic that endures for COVID long-haulers." *Harvard Gazette*, April 13, 2021. https://news.harvard.edu/gazette/story/2021/04/harvard-medical-school-expert-explains-long-covid/.

Social Security Administration. n.d. "Historical Background and Development of Social Security." https://www.ssa.gov/history/briefhistory3.html.

Social Security Administration. 2021. "2021 OASDI Trustees Report." Washington, DC. https://www.ssa.gov/OACT/TR/2021/index.html.

Soldo, Beth J., Olivia S. Mitchell, Rania Tfaily, and John F. McCabe. 2007. "Cross-Cohort Differences in Health on the Verge of Retirement." In *Redefining Retirement: How Will Boomers Fare?*, edited by Brigitte Madrian, Olivia S. Mitchell, and Beth J. Soldo, pp. 138–158. New York: Oxford University Press.

U.S. Department of Labor. n.d. "Commonly Used Statistics." Occupational Safety and Health Administration. https://www.osha.gov/data/commonstats.

Waite, Linda J., and Mark Nielsen. 2001. "The Rise of the Dual-Earner Family, 1963–1997." In *Working Families: The Transformation of the American Home*, edited by Rosanna Hertz and Nancy L. Marshall. pp. 23–41. Berkeley, CA: University of California Press.

Walker, Elisa A., Virginia P. Reno, and Thomas N. Bethell. 2014. "Americans Make Hard Choices on Social Security." Washington, DC: National Academy of Social Insurance. https://www.nasi.org/research/report-americans-make-hard-choices-on-social-security-a-survey-with-trade-off-analysis/.

Weil, David. 2014. *The Fissured Workplace: Why Work Became so Bad for so Many and What Can Be Done to Improve It*. Cambridge, MA: Harvard University Press.

Williams, David R., Jourdyn A. Lawrence, and Brigette A. Davis. 2019. "Racism and Health: Evidence and Needed Research." *Annual Review of Public Health* 40 (1): 105–125. https://doi.org/10.1146/annurev-publhealth-040218-043750.

Woolf, Steven H., and Heidi Schoomaker. 2019. "Life Expectancy and Mortality Rates in the United States, 1959–2017." *JAMA* 322 (20): 1996–2016. https://doi.org/10.1001/jama.2019.16932.

Zack, Matthew M., David G. Moriarty, Donna F. Stroup, Earl S. Ford, and Ali H. Mokdad. 2004. "Worsening Trends in Adult Health-Related Quality of Life and Self-Rated Health—United States, 1993–2001." *Public Health Reports* 119 (5): 493–505. https://doi.org/10.1016/j.phr.2004.07.007.

Zajacova, Anna, and Jennifer Karas Montez. 2018. "Explaining the Increasing Disability Prevalence among Mid-Life US Adults, 2002 to 2016." *Social Science & Medicine* 211 (August): 1–8. https://doi.org/10.1016/j.socscimed.2018.05.041.

PART I

Who Has a Job?

Labor Trends from Commuting

Zones to Countries

When I'm 54

Working Longer Starts Younger Than We Think

Beth C. Truesdale, Lisa F. Berkman, and Alexandra Mitukiewicz[1]

1. Introduction

Most research on retirement decisions begins by focusing on men and women who are in paid employment in their late 50s and early 60s. By definition, those who are already out of work in their early to mid-50s are excluded: we cannot observe retirement decisions among those who have no job from which to retire. However, focusing on those who remain in the labor force as they age leaves substantial gaps in our understanding of the limits of working longer as a solution to the challenge of aging populations faced by the United States and other developed nations. We bring those who are out of the labor force during late middle age—who are unlikely to be candidates for working longer, that is, working past the Social Security earliest eligibility age of 62—back into view.

If the fraction of the adult *population* that can realistically work longer is substantially smaller than the fraction of *workers* that can realistically work longer, our view of the working longer ideal may be too rosy. In addition, because members of disadvantaged groups are disproportionately likely to be out of employment in middle age, trends toward working longer may further increase social inequalities in work, income, and well-being at older ages.

Individuals who are out of the labor force in late middle age are invisible in the usual unemployment statistics, just as they are invisible in many discussions about working longer. In 2018, the unemployment rate among American adults ages 55 to 59 years was only 2.9 percent, slightly lower than the 3.3 percent unemployment rate among 25- to 54-year-olds. However, those figures set aside the 28 percent of 55- to 59-year-olds who were not in the labor force—a number that is much higher than the 18 percent of 25- to 54-year-olds who were not in the labor force (U.S. Bureau of Labor Statistics 2019). Employment exit in late middle age can be permanent, because many factors, including age discrimination, make it difficult for older Americans to get new jobs after they have been out of work (Johnson and Mommaerts 2011).

During the past 20 years, labor force participation rates have fallen among both men and women during their prime working years, even as they have risen among both men and women at older ages. The bodies of research examining these two trends have been largely separate. We argue that they should be linked, as employment earlier in life is likely to affect one's options for employment later in life. We examine working longer using a life course perspective. Understanding connections across the life course sheds light on the timing of potential policy interventions.

We focus on who is left out of the working-longer conversation by examining differences in employment across and within cohorts. We use the 1962 to 2019 waves of the Current Population Survey (CPS) to describe employment rates across the life course. We then turn to the 1992 to 2018 waves of the Health and Retirement Study (HRS) to investigate employment stability among individuals in their 50s and how employment stability during one's 50s relates to employment beyond age 62, the earliest age of eligibility for Social Security retirement benefits. We examine changes across birth cohorts as well as inequalities by gender, race, and education within cohorts. By understanding who is (and who is not) working across the life course now, we can better understand what working longer might mean for future cohorts.

Our results suggest that working longer is not as straightforward as many people in the policy arena may assume.[2] We find that consistent employment in one's 50s is an important precursor of employment beyond age 62. Yet employment rates and patterns in one's 50s are highly heterogeneous. We show that employment rates are much lower among disadvantaged groups over the entire life course, and they drop sharply among *all* sociodemographic groups—by about 20 percentage points—between ages 50 and 60. We find that only about half of Americans are continuously employed during the decade before age 62, while a third have intermittent employment patterns and 15 percent never worked for pay during those years.

We find that employment stability in late middle age is strongly related to working longer. Some 80 percent of those continuously employed in their 50s are employed at some point between ages 62 and 66, compared to 35 percent of those in the intermittent group and only 4 percent of those who were not working in their 50s.

We find that inequalities in employment rates and employment stability within cohorts are much greater than changes across cohorts, especially across the past two or three decades. While there are stark differences in employment patterns by education, gender, and race, it is employment stability in one's 50s that predicts whether someone works longer, even when sociodemographic, health, and other characteristics are taken into account.

There are strong social gradients, especially by education, in the proportion of those who are never employed in their 50s. This group of individuals—who are largely invisible in the working-longer discussion precisely *because* they are not working during their 50s—are disproportionately non-white, women, and those without college degrees. Disability is an important reason people in this group are not employed. Among those consistently out of the workforce in their 50s, about 60 percent of men and 27 percent of women received Social Security Disability Insurance (SSDI) benefits.

There is a silver lining to these otherwise sobering results. We find that the experience of employment at some point during the life course is nearly universal. In the HRS, less than

1 percent of men and less than 4 percent of women say they have never worked for pay. Even among those not working in the run-up to traditional retirement ages, the large majority last worked at some point after age 40. As a result, there may be many missed opportunities to retain people in the labor force earlier in life.

Bringing people who are out of employment in their 50s into the working-longer debate has implications for policy. Policy recommendations to support working longer, such as job flexibility (e.g., Moen 2016; Maestas et al. 2018), often focus on the needs and preferences of older workers, which may be quite different than the needs and preferences of those who are not employed in late middle age. Working longer is concentrated among those who are continuously employed during their 50s. A renewed focus on employment in late middle age suggests a much broader range of policies to support working longer, as we discuss in the final chapter in this volume. In terms of life course perspectives, our results are in line with social trajectory models, suggesting that interventions to improve employment stability among middle-aged Americans could support working longer.

2. Employment across the Life Course

At its most fundamental, a life course approach pays attention to the connections between different phases of life, acknowledging that events and contexts in a given phase may have consequences years or even decades later (Elder, Johnson, and Crosnoe 2003). We examine working longer using a life course perspective. This perspective is useful for research on working longer because employment patterns in prime age and in the run-up to retirement, as well as other experiences, likely shape individuals' decisions and options to work and retire.

Life course research suggests three different, but not mutually exclusive, pathways by which experiences earlier in life affect well-being later in life (Berkman and Kawachi 2014). First, in a *sensitive period* model, exposure to a risk has especially serious long-term consequences if the exposure takes place during a particular phase of life, and intervention later in life may not be successful. Second, in a *cumulative disadvantage* model, early-life experiences put individuals on a track either toward or away from future risks, and the effect of experiences on well-being adds up or compounds over time. Third, in a *social trajectory* model, early-life experiences make exposure to certain risks in adulthood more or less likely, but it is the adult exposures that directly affect well-being. Each of these three pathways has implications for the timing of policy interventions in people's lives.

We use a life course perspective to connect two large bodies of research that have been mostly separate. An influential line of research examines the motivations for older workers' retirement decisions, typically excluding adults who were out of employment in their 50s. This research often uses longitudinal data on adults in their 50s and 60s to investigate the reasons that individuals transition from employment to retirement, including Social Security benefits, individual wealth, health and health insurance, career histories, spouses' retirement decisions, and labor demand (e.g., Han and Moen 1999; Warner, Hayward, and Hardy 2010; Coile 2015). Because this research investigates why, when, and how older adults retire, researchers usually focus on adults who had a job or were in the labor force at the start of the window of observation and follow them over time to examine retirement behavior. Some important studies narrow the selection further; for instance, Cahill, Giandrea, and Quinn (2006) study retirement patterns among older Americans who recently worked full-time in career jobs. This line of research, which has been central to the working-longer conversation, sets aside adults who worked for pay intermittently or not at all in their 50s.

To be clear, some research on retirement does include all older adults, regardless of their employment or labor force status. This subset of research uses cross-sectional data to count those who are out of the labor force at older ages (e.g., Burtless and Quinn 2002; Coile 2019; Abraham, Hershbein, and Houseman 2021), but the nature of the data makes it impossible to observe how individuals' experiences evolve across substantial sections of the life course.

Distinct from the retirement research, another large body of research is focused on changes in labor force participation among men and women in prime ages, conventionally defined as ages 25 to 54. Among prime-age men, rates of labor force participation have declined substantially since the 1960s, especially among men with less than a college degree. This decline is attributed, in part, to increasingly unstable employment that leads men to cycle in and out of the labor force (Coglianese 2018; Binder and Bound 2019). Women's employment patterns are very different than men's because women are more likely to take time out of work for childrearing. Among prime-age women, rates of labor force participation have increased since the 1960s and have stagnated in recent years (U.S. Department of Labor n.d.). This research on prime-age workers is relevant to the working-longer discussion because individuals who are out of the labor force in their late 40s and early 50s are likely to retire several years earlier than their counterparts who are in the labor force in midlife (Ciecka and Skoog 2017).

Less research focuses on labor force participation and employment during the decade before age 62, the Social Security Earliest Eligibility Age. This decade bridges the age brackets customarily studied in research on retirement decisions and research on prime-age work. Even less work investigates the conditions that shape employment in one's 50s in a life course context that takes account of employment both earlier and later, or examines differences in employment by race and education as well as by gender. Investigating heterogeneities is important because averages can obscure substantial variation. For example, variability in the timing of men's retirement increased substantially in the United States in the last third of the twentieth century, even as average retirement ages first fell and then rose (Han and Moen 1999). Around the turn of the twenty-first century, the modal age of men's retirement was 62, but more than three-quarters of male retirements took place "off time" in Social Security terms, either earlier than age 62 or later than age 65 (Warner, Hayward, and Hardy 2010). Focusing on heterogeneities in employment patterns during one's 50s should provide a more complete perspective on working longer as the outcome of events and contexts earlier in life.

3. Data and Methods

In order to bring those who are not working during their 50s back into the working longer discussion, we investigate (a) employment rates across the life course, (b) employment stability among individuals in the decade before the Social Security Earliest Eligibility Age of 62 (for brevity, "the 50s"), and (c) how individuals' employment stability during those years relates to working beyond age 62. We examine changes across birth cohorts as well as heterogeneity by gender, race, and education within cohorts.

We focus on employment (having paid work) rather than labor force participation (either having paid work or actively seeking it). For many questions, the distinction makes little difference, and many studies of retirement behavior focus on labor force participation because they are interested in the larger group of individuals who intend to work or are working rather than the slightly smaller group of those who are working for pay at a given moment. However, labor force participation rates can understate the actual size of inequalities in working because *both* labor force nonparticipation *and* unemployment rates tend to be higher among disadvantaged groups than among advantaged groups. Labor force participation rates also neglect de facto unemployment among "discouraged workers" who would like to work but are not actively seeking employment, including individuals who have been forced to retire earlier than they would wish. In addition, several important outcomes related to working longer—including one's Social Security benefits and one's ability to save for retirement—are based not on individuals' labor force history but on their employment history. We therefore focus on employment.

To address the three questions above, we use two sources of data.

3.1. Current Population Survey

First, for a broad overview of employment rates across cohorts and across the life course, we use the 1962 through 2019 waves of the Annual Social and Economic Supplement of the Current Population Survey (CPS-ASEC) (Flood et al. 2020). Conducted by the U.S. Census Bureau and the Bureau of Labor Statistics, the CPS is a large, nationally representative cross-sectional survey that is the main source of U.S. federal statistics on employment. The definition of employment includes "any work at all for pay or profit." This includes self-employment, which is particularly important at older ages (Abraham, Hershbein, and Houseman 2021).

To compare employment rates across cohorts, we construct synthetic cohorts for individuals who were born in 1930 through 1969. For instance, the 1930 birth cohort includes those who turned 25 in 1955, those who turned 26 in 1956, and so on. In the most recent data (2019), individuals born in the 1930s and 1940s were older than 70; those born in the 1950s were in their 60s; and those born in the 1960s were in their 50s.

After examining trends by birth cohort, we pool the 1930–1959 cohorts to increase sample size and present employment rates across the life course within groups defined by educational attainment, race, and gender. Finally, we examine trends in education-based inequalities in employment over time.

3.2. Health and Retirement Study

Next we turn from population employment *rates* to individual employment *patterns*. Employment patterns during the run-up to the Social Security Earliest Eligibility Age, age 62, may tell us a great deal about the fraction of these cohorts who are likely to be candidates for working longer. We use longitudinal data from the Health and Retirement Study. The HRS is a nationally representative biennial study of Americans over age 50. For our analysis we use the RAND version of the HRS, a merged and cleaned version of the dataset, supplemented with RAND's version of the raw public-use HRS files (the RAND HRS Fat Files). We use all waves of data currently available, spanning 1992 to 2018. Since 1992, additional cohorts have been added to the study every six years, creating a multicohort panel design.[3]

We examine individual employment patterns between ages 51 and 61 (for brevity, "the 50s"), as well as the association between employment patterns in one's 50s and employment later in life, that is, working between ages 62 and 66. We use data on two cohorts: the HRS Original Cohort, born between 1936 and 1941; and the War Babies, born between 1942 and 1947.[4] Members of these cohorts were ages 51 to 56 at first interview and are interviewed every two years. Both cohorts have aged past age 66, allowing us to examine how employment patterns in the run-up to the Social Security Earliest Eligibility Age relate to working between ages 62 and 66. We select those individuals who were present at the first interview for their cohort and who reported their employment status (employed or not employed) in at least three interviews between ages 51 and 61 and reported their employment status in at least one interview between ages 62 and 66.[5]

Our dependent variable, working longer, is a dichotomous variable equal to one if an individual is employed during at least one interview between ages 62 and 66 and equal to zero if not employed.

Our independent variable, employment stability, is the portion of time an individual is employed during the years between their first interview between ages 51 and 56, and their last interview before age 62. For each respondent in our sample we divide the number of interviews they were employed over the total number of interviews when they reported their employment status between ages 51 and 61 ("the 50s"). To allow the relationship between employment stability during one's 50s and working longer to be nonlinear, we create mutually exclusive categories:

- Steady Out: Never employed in one's 50s.[6]
- Intermittent
  - Low intermittent: employed more than 0 and less than 50 percent of one's 50s.
  - Medium intermittent: employed more than 50 and less than 80 percent of one's 50s.
  - High intermittent: employed more than 80 and less than 100 percent of one's 50s.
- Steady In: Always employed during one's 50s.

We estimate linear probability models to examine the association between employment stability during the 50s and working longer (reporting employment at some point between ages 62 and 66). We first estimate the bivariate regression of working longer on employment stability. Then we evaluate whether other factors help explain this association, controlling for sociodemographic characteristics, employment history, wealth, and health.[7]

We control for the following sociodemographic characteristics: respondent's educational attainment (less than high school, high school diploma or GED, some college, or college degree), race (white, Black, or other race), gender, marital status (married or partnered at first interview vs. not married or partnered), birth cohort (HRS Original Cohort or War Babies), age at first interview, nativity status (born in the United States or born outside the United States), and region of residence at first interview (one of nine Census Bureau–designated divisions).

We next control for individuals' pension coverage, employment history, and wealth. Pension provision is likely to affect retirement timing (Coile 2015). We include a dichotomous variable equal to one if a respondent, at first interview, has a pension from their current or previous two jobs and equal to zero if the respondent is not covered by a pension. Because employment history earlier in life is likely associated with both employment in one's 50s and working longer, we control for the percent of respondent's lifetime spent working at first interview (the number of self-reported years of previous employment divided by the respondent's age at first interview). Greater wealth may enable earlier retirement (Coile 2015), so we also include a measure of household net worth percentile at the first interview.

Finally, we control for health characteristics because poor health is strongly associated with early retirement (Bound et al. 1999). Following Cutler et al. (2011), we control for individuals' baseline health status and changes in their health during their 50s. We include five measures of baseline health status: the respondent's number of (1) major and (2) minor health conditions at first interview,[8] and the respondent's number of difficulties with (3) activities of daily living (ADLs), (4) instrumental activities of daily living (IADLs), and (5) other functional limitations at second interview.[9] We include two measures of health shocks: whether a respondent reports (1) a new major health condition or (2) a new minor health condition during their 50s.

We consider our results in light of life course models. If variables that represent experiences relatively early in life (such as educational attainment) largely explain the association between employment stability and working longer, such a result would suggest that late childhood or early adulthood is a *sensitive period* for social processes that lead jointly to employment stability and to working longer. If *cumulative disadvantage* is at work, we would expect the combination of early-life experiences (such as educational attainment) and midlife experiences that are shaped by early-life experiences (such as health and work history before one's 50s) to explain much of the association between employment stability and working longer. Finally, if employment stability in one's 50s is robustly related to working longer even after we take earlier experiences into account, such a result would suggest a *social trajectory* model in which early-life experiences (such as educational attainment) shape individuals' employment stability during their 50s, but employment stability itself shapes further later-life employment.

We also we take a closer look at the group of people who never worked in their 50s (the Steady Outs). We examine what proportion of this group receive SSDI benefits, which is an important consideration because few people who meet the stringent qualifications for disability benefits ever make a long-term return to the workforce (Liu and Stapleton 2010). We also examine when Steady Outs last worked using work history data.

4. Results
4.1. Current Population Survey: Employment Rates

We begin with an overview of employment rates over the life course. Many of the stylized facts in this section will be familiar to researchers studying work and retirement, but they are not often visualized as trends across the life course within birth cohorts. Figure 1.1 shows how employment rates have changed for cohorts born between 1930 and 1969. Among men, rates of employment during prime ages, 25 to 54, have fallen consistently from cohort to cohort. Among women, rates of prime age employment rose dramatically from the cohorts born in the 1930s to the cohorts born in the 1950s, but stalled or fell among the cohort born in the 1960s. The effect of the Great Recession is clearly visible: children of the 1960s were aged 39 to 48 in 2008. Among both men and women, employment rates dropped substantially for adults in the 1960s birth cohorts in their 40s.

Compared to falling or stalling employment rates from cohort to cohort during prime ages, cohort trends are noticeably different among older adults. Above age 60, rates of employment rise from cohort to cohort at older ages among both men and women. Despite the rise in employment at older ages, only a minority of adults are still employed after age 65. Rates of employment at age 65 are below 50 percent among men and 40 percent among women even in recent cohorts.

Next, we examine how employment rates change across the life course among different sociodemographic groups. As Figure 1.2 shows, education-related inequalities in employment are large across the life course among both men and women. Notably, although less educated groups start from a lower base, employment rates fall rapidly among all groups between ages 50 and 60. For instance, among men, employment rates fall between ages 50 and 60 from roughly 94 to 74 percent among those with college degrees, from 86 to 63 percent among those with high school diplomas, and from 73 to 50 percent among those without high school diplomas. There are similar decreases among women. In absolute terms, the drop is similar across subgroups, approximately 20 percentage points.

Figure 1.3 shows differences within education groups by race, focusing on white and Black adults. Among men, there are notable disparities in employment rates between Black and white respondents with the same educational attainment. It is striking that employment rates for Black men with a college degree are almost identical to those of white men with a high school degree, while employment rates of Black men with a high school degree are almost identical to those of white men without a high school degree. Among women, however, racial differentials are reversed. Black women have a higher rate of employment than white women at each education level early in the life course. Later in the life course, the racial gaps close, although the educational gaps do not.

Finally, we examine how disparities in employment rates have changed over time. As Figure 1.4 shows, absolute disparities in employment rates by education rose between the 1960s and 2019 in both late middle age (ages 50 to 61) and at older ages (ages 62 to 70) among both men and women. Increasing inequalities are especially notable among those in the younger age group. Among men in late middle age, inequalities increased because employment rates fell faster among less educated groups than among college graduates.

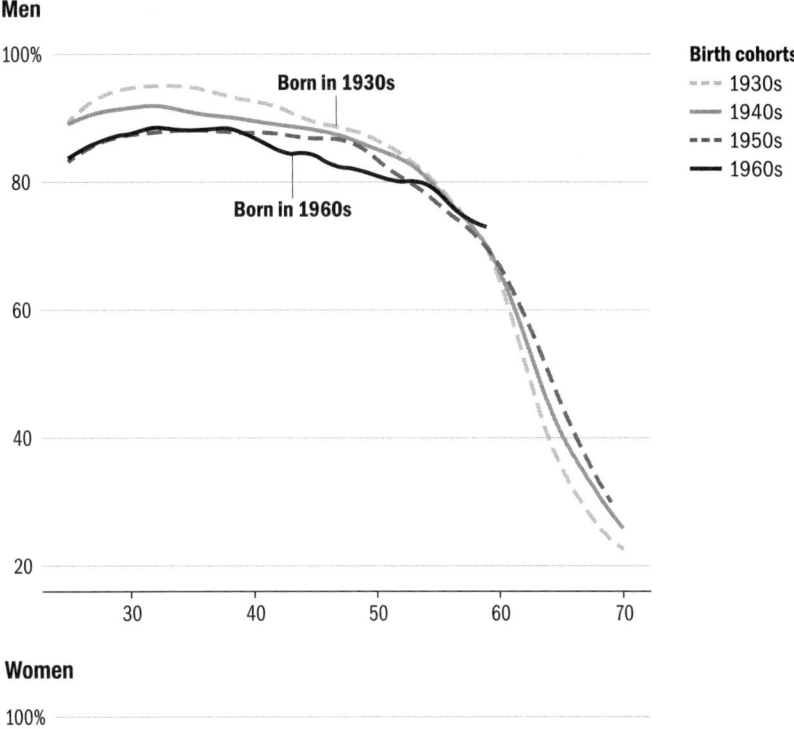
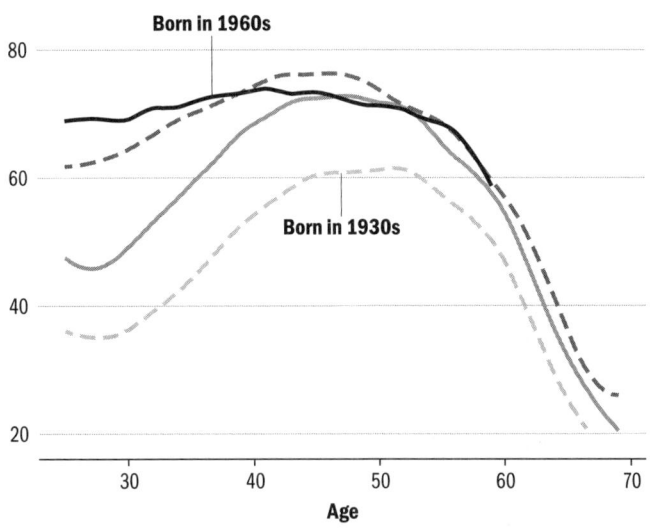

FIGURE 1.1 Across cohorts, employment rates are rising at older ages but stalling or falling during prime ages
Employment rates ages 25 to 70, by birth cohort
Note: Data from the 1962-2019 waves of the Current Population Survey (CPS).

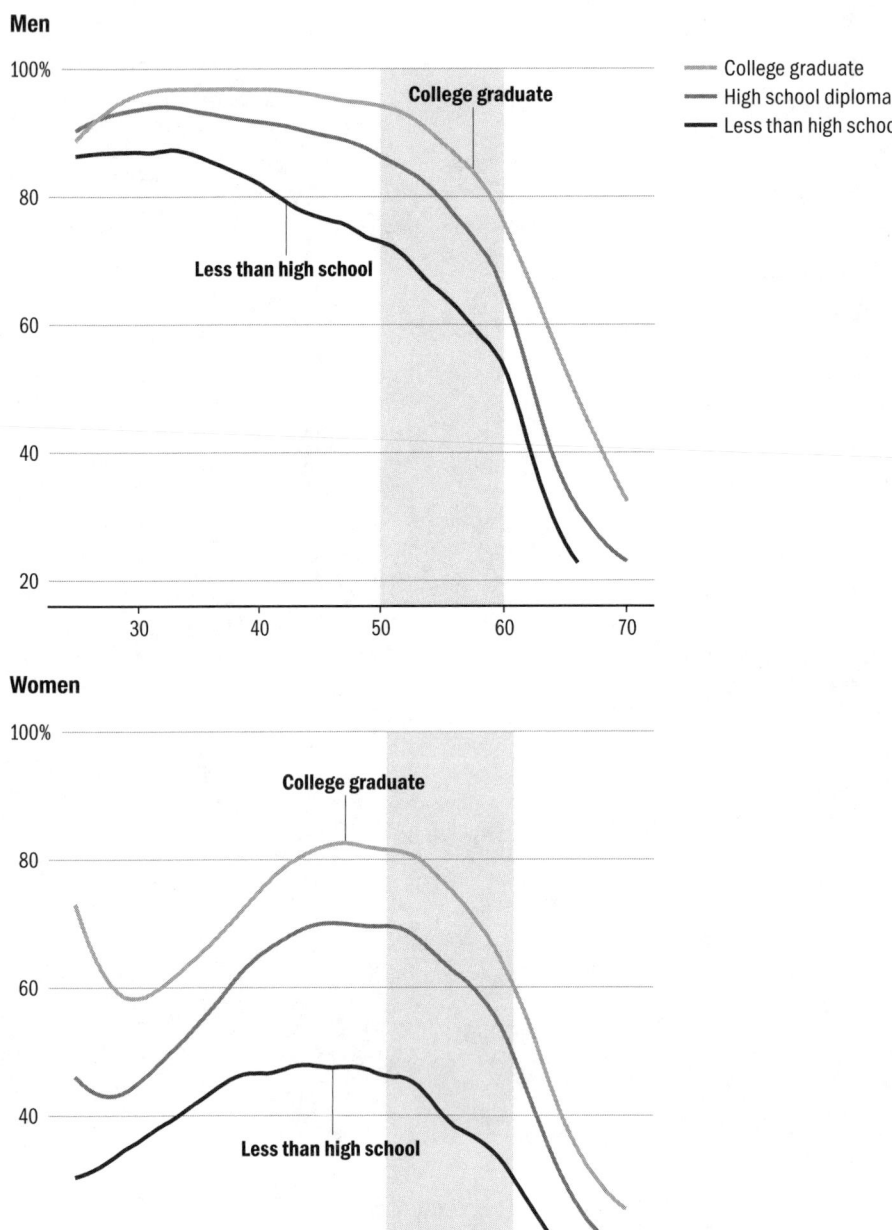

FIGURE 1.2 Employment rates by gender and education across the life course
Grey shading shows the fall in employment rates between ages 50 and 60
Note: Data from the Current Population Survey (CPS), pooled 1930–1959 birth cohorts. Loess smoother applied.

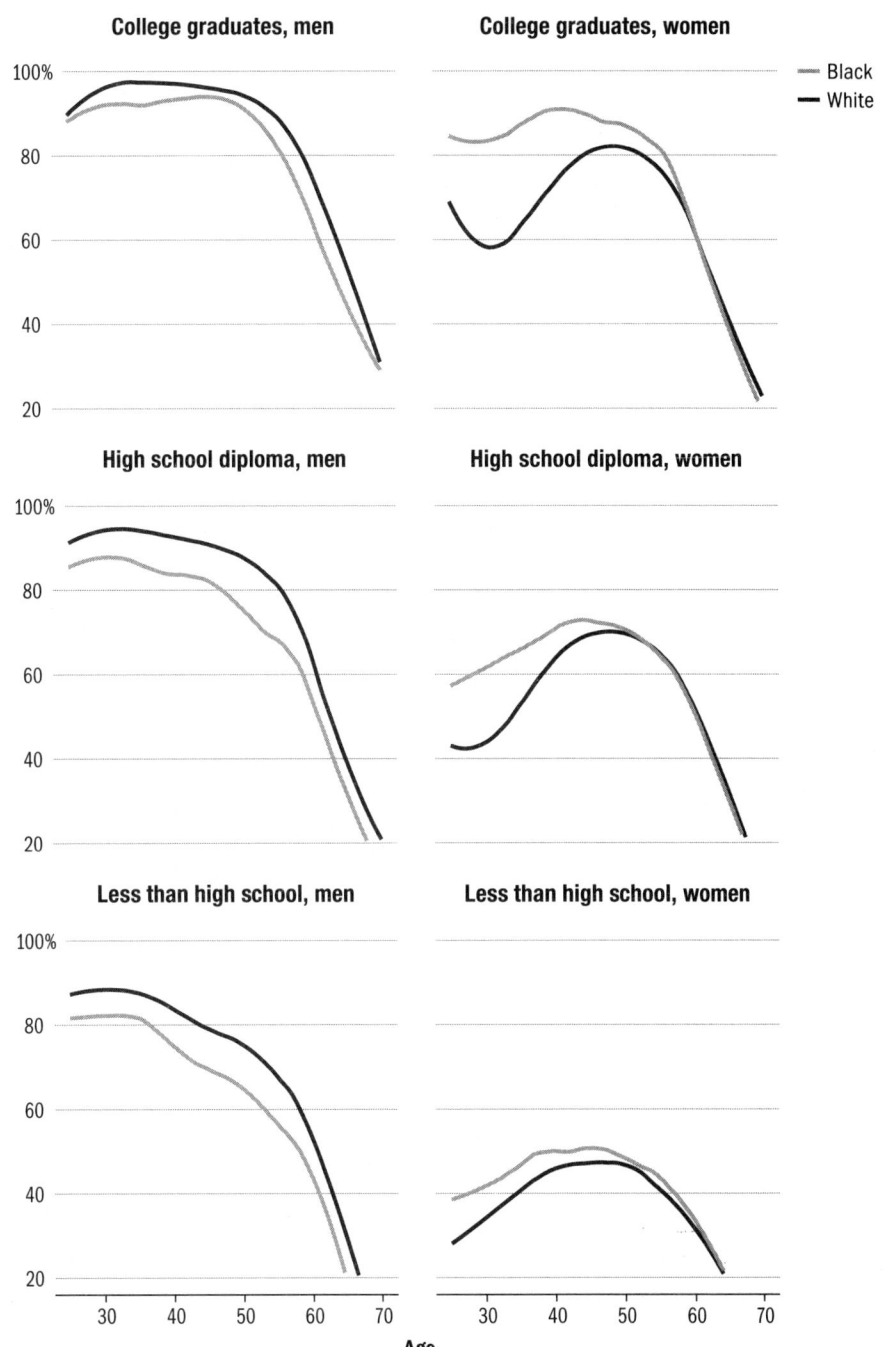

FIGURE 1.3 Employment rates by gender, race, and education across the life course
Note: Data from the Current Population Survey (CPS), pooled 1930-1959 birth cohorts. Loess smoother applied.

Among women in late middle age, inequalities increased because employment rates rose faster among more educated women than among those with less than a high school degree. In the older age group, among men, absolute disparities have remained relatively steady as employment rates fell and then rose among all educational groups. Among older women, absolute disparities fell, then rose, mostly driven by changes in employment rates among more-educated women. However, especially in the past two to three decades, the picture is chiefly of large and persistent education-based disparities in both age groups, with inequalities between educational groups greater than changes across cohorts.

Proponents of working longer frequently point out that Americans are increasingly delaying retirement. However, Figure 1.4 allows us to consider these trends over a longer timeframe than we were able to see in Figure 1.1. The cohorts born between the 1930s and the 1950s, who are depicted in Figure 1.1, reached retirement age between the 1990s and the 2010s. These cohorts saw a trend toward later retirement among both men and women. Figure 1.1 shows the trend across cohorts; Figure 1.4 shows the trend across time. Between the 1990s and the 2010s, employment rates rose among older men and women in all educational

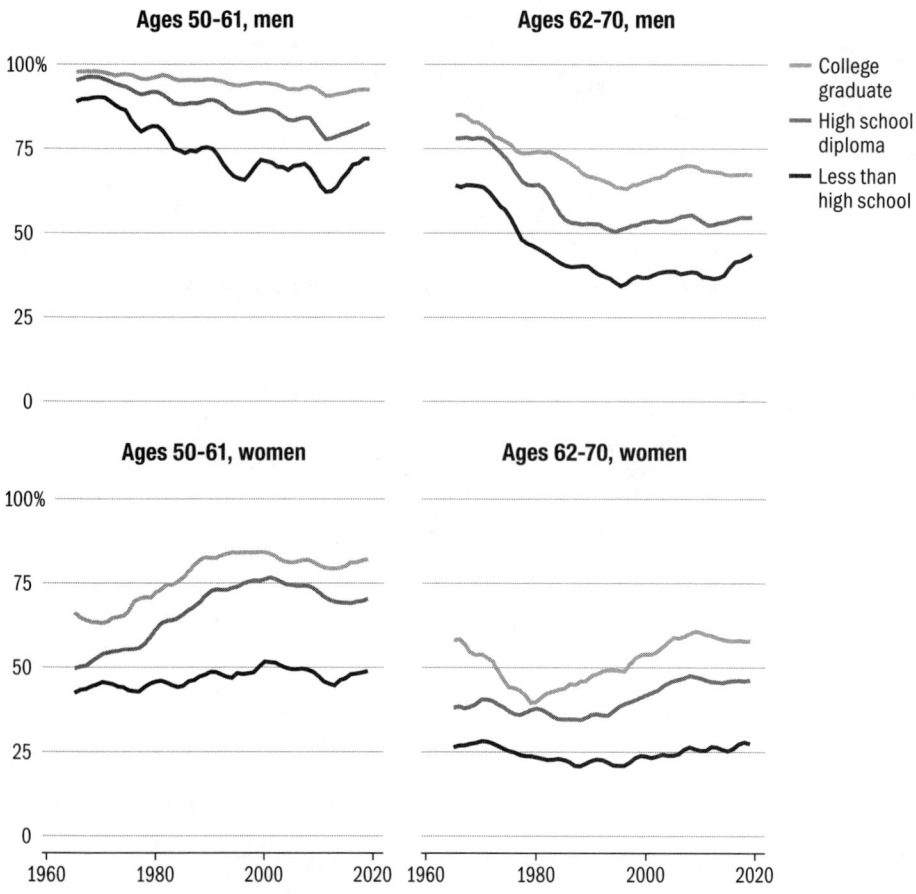

FIGURE 1.4 Employment rates by gender, education, and age, 1962–2019
Note: Data from the Current Population Survey (CPS), three-year rolling averages.

groups. However, among men, the rise in employment rates at older ages from the 1990s to the 2010s was much smaller than the fall from the 1960s through the 1980s. Among women, the peak in rates of working longer in the 2010s only just exceeded rates of working longer around 1960.

In summary, although rates of employment at older ages have risen across recent cohorts, the cohorts now in their 40s and 50s are approaching retirement with lower employment rates than the cohorts now in their 60s and 70s, which may mean that fewer members of younger cohorts are in a good position to work longer. Changes in employment rates across recent cohorts are relatively small, however, compared both to the historical record and to inequalities within cohorts. There is a great deal of heterogeneity by race and education in employment rates across the entire life course, with especially large inequalities by education. A life course perspective suggests that social inequalities in working longer are likely linked to social inequalities earlier in the life course.

4.2. Health and Retirement Study: Employment Stability

4.2.1. Descriptive Results

We turn next to the results of our analysis of the HRS data, which allow us to examine how employment patterns over a decade are associated with the likelihood of working longer. Employment patterns during one's 50s may be important in part because they predict who is likely to be a candidate for working longer and who is not. The HRS data are well suited to investigating this because the study interviews a nationally representative sample of American adults starting between ages 51 and 56 and following up every two years. Table A1 in Truesdale et al. (2021) contains full descriptive statistics.

As Figure 1.5 shows, based on HRS data, 52 percent of adults worked throughout their 50s, whereas the rest were not consistently employed. About 15 percent of adults never worked during their 50s and the remaining 34 percent experienced intermittent employment. That is,

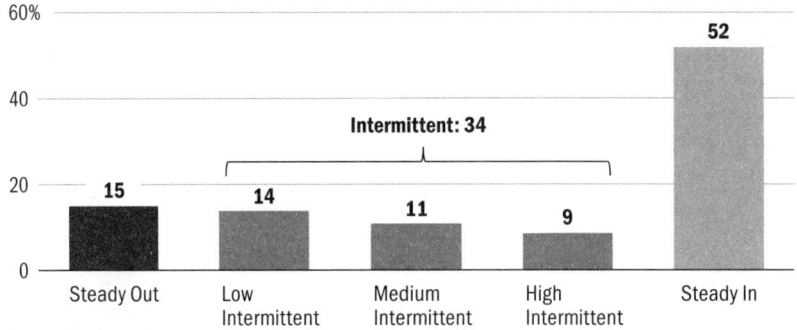

FIGURE 1.5 Employment stability between ages 51 and 61
As reported by U.S. adults born between 1936–1947
Note: Weighted samples from the Health and Retirement Study (HRS). Percentages may not sum to 100 due to rounding. Employment stability categories are defined by the proportion of interviews between ages 51 and 61 at which individuals report employment: Steady Outs (never employed); Low Intermittent (more than 0 and less than 50 percent); Medium Intermittent (more than 50 and less than 80 percent); High Intermittent (more than 80 and less than 100 percent); Steady In (always employed).

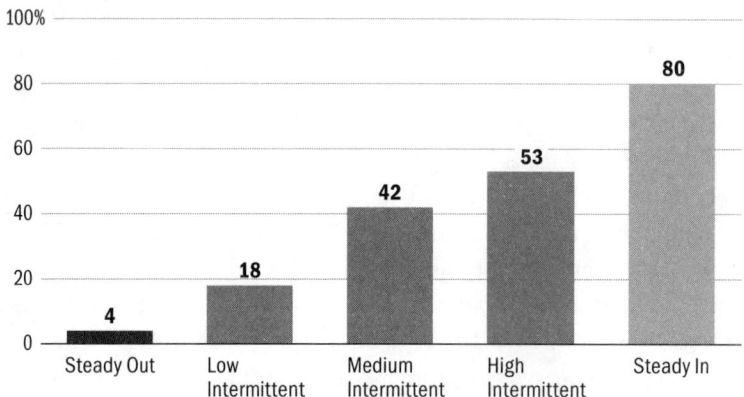

FIGURE 1.6 Likelihood of working longer rises with employment stability in one's 50s
Percent of U.S. adults who work between ages 62 and 66, by employment stability between ages 51 and 61
Note: Weighted samples from the Health and Retirement Study (HRS).

roughly half of Americans approached the earliest eligibility age for Social Security without a consistent employment history over the previous decade.

In terms of working longer, we find that slightly more than half of adults (54 percent) worked between ages 62 and 66. Figure 1.6 shows how the likelihood of working longer is stratified by employment stability in one's 50s. Of Steady Ins (those steadily employed in their 50s), 80 percent worked longer; by contrast, only 4 percent of Steady Outs (those never employed in their 50s) were employed at some point between ages 62 and 66. Of those with intermittent employment, 35 percent worked longer, ranging from 18 percent among those in the Low Intermittent category to 53 percent among those in the High Intermittent category.

When we examine the overlap between employment stability in one's 50s and working longer, we find that only 42 percent of American adults were *both* continuously employed during their 50s (Steady Ins) *and* employed at some point between ages 62 and 66. That is, the common perception of solid employment up to retirement is a reality only for a minority of Americans.

Next we examine differences by education, gender, and race. Rates of continuous employment are far lower among disadvantaged groups. As Figure 1.7 shows, both the Steady In and Steady Out employment categories are highly stratified by education. Only 36 percent of those without a high school degree reported continuous employment during their 50s (Steady Ins), compared to 65 percent of college graduates. Conversely, only 6 percent of college graduates reported never being employed during their 50s (Steady Outs), compared to 32 percent of those without a high school diploma. The intermittent categories were somewhat more similar across educational groups, although compared to college graduates, those without a high school diploma were about twice as likely to have a Low Intermittent employment pattern and half as likely to have a High Intermittent pattern.

Employment stability is also stratified by race and gender, but these disparities are substantially smaller than disparities by education. As Figure 1.8 shows, women were more

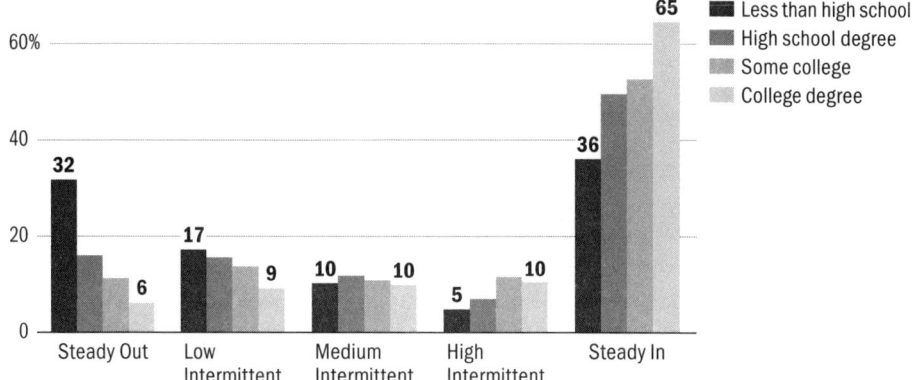

FIGURE 1.7 Employment stability between ages 51 and 61, by educational attainment.
Note: Weighted samples from the Health and Retirement Study (HRS). Percentages may not sum to 100 due to rounding.

likely than men to be in the Steady Out or Low Intermittent categories, and less likely to be in the Steady In category. Similarly, Black adults were more likely than white adults to be in the Steady Out or Low Intermittent categories, and less likely to be in the Steady In category.

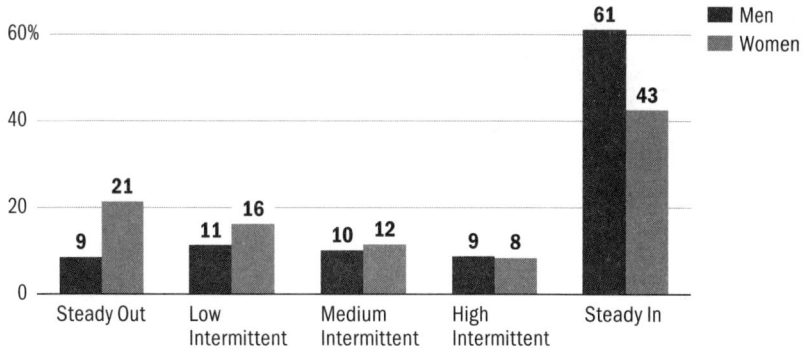

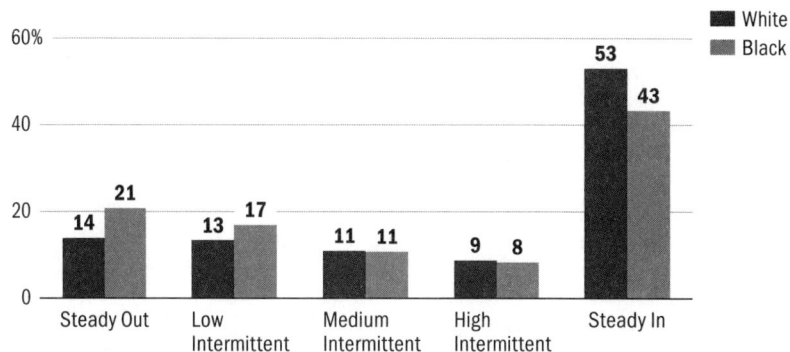

FIGURE 1.8 Employment stability between ages 51 and 61, by gender and by race
Note: Weighted samples from the Health and Retirement Study (HRS). Percentages may not sum to 100 due to rounding.

In summary, based on HRS data, only about half of adults were consistently employed (Steady Ins) during their 50s; the other half were not employed at least some of the time. These averages mask large differences by race, gender, and especially by education. In descriptive terms, employment stability in one's 50s is strongly related to working longer in one's 60s.

4.2.2. Regression Results

We turn to regression analysis to investigate what other factors might account for the bivariate association between employment stability in one's 50s and working longer. Figure 1.9 shows the key results (coefficients are available in Table A2 in Truesdale et al. [2021]). Overall, employment stability in one's 50s is strongly associated with working between ages 62 and 66, and this association changes very little when we control for sociodemographic, employment, wealth, and health characteristics.

The bivariate regression of working longer on employment patterns in one's 50s (Model 1) shows the marked increase in the probability of working longer with more stable employment patterns in one's 50s, as seen in Figure 1.6. The predicted probability of working longer does not change much when sociodemographic characteristics are added in Model 2, employment history and wealth variables are added in Model 3, and health status variables are added in Model 4. Nor does the proportion of variance explained (R^2) change much as we add an increasingly rich set of control variables: it increases from 0.37 in Model 1 to 0.39 in Model 4. Employment patterns in the decade prior to traditional retirement ages are strong predictors of whether individuals work for pay during their 60s.

Together, the descriptive results and regression models using the HRS suggest that there is a social gradient in employment stability in one's 50s, which translates into a strong social gradient in the likelihood of working longer. These results are most consistent with social trajectory life course models. That is, it appears that factors such as educational attainment

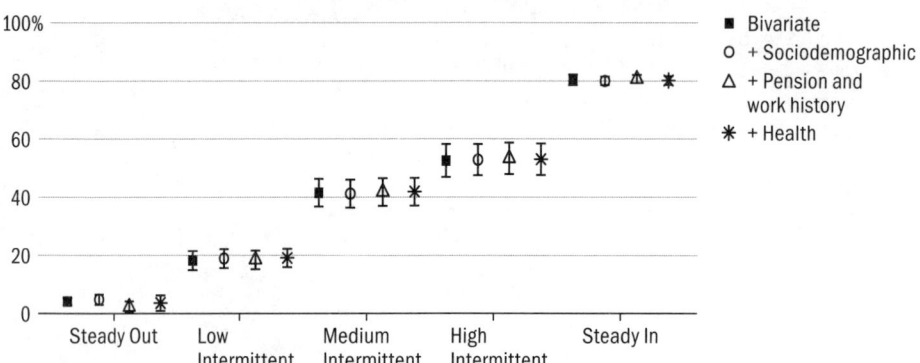

FIGURE 1.9 Likelihood of working longer rises with employment stability in one's 50s
Predicted probability of working between ages 62 and 66, by employment stability between ages 51 and 61
Note: Predicted probabilities from linear probability models, holding all other variables at their mean. Data from the Health and Retirement Study (HRS). Employment stability categories are defined by the proportion of interviews between ages 51 and 61 at which individuals report employment: Steady Outs (never employed); Low Intermittent (more than 0 and less than 50 percent); Medium Intermittent (more than 50 and less than 80 percent); High Intermittent (more than 80 and less than 100 percent); Steady In (always employed). Working longer means reporting employment at least once between ages 62 and 66.

influence individuals' employment stability during their 50s, but employment stability itself shapes further later-life employment.

4.3. Steady Outs: Work History and Disability

Finally, we investigate the group of men and women who have not been employed between ages 51 and 61, those we call Steady Outs, in more detail. The possibility that initiatives targeting this group could result in substantially higher rates of employment at older ages may depend both on whether disabilities prevent them from working and on the length of time since they were last employed.

Receipt of federal disability benefits is an important indicator of work-related health and disability. We compare the proportion of men and women in each employment pattern who report ever receiving SSDI, between ages 51 and 61. Although some disability benefit recipients have some work capacity (Liebman 2015), receipt of benefits indicates a high level of impairment. Workers do not qualify if it is "possible for [them] to do work which exists in the national economy," even if such work does not exist in the local area or there are no job openings.[10]

In this section, we use HRS data on the HRS Original, War Babies, and Early Baby Boomers cohorts, all of whom were older than age 61 by the 2018 survey. HRS Original respondents were born between 1936 and 1941; War Babies were born between 1942 and 1947; and Early Baby Boomers were born between 1948 and 1953.[11]

In total, only about 10 percent of interviewees report ever receiving SSDI in their 50s. Figure 1.10 shows the distribution by gender, cohort, and employment stability. Among male Steady Outs, around 60 percent in all three cohorts received SSDI. Among female Steady Outs, the proportion of disability recipients rises with more recent cohorts from 22 percent to 37 percent, reflecting the increase in women's eligibility for SSDI benefits as more women accrue the work history needed to qualify (Liebman 2015). Approximately 13 percent of both women and men with intermittent employment in their 50s report receiving SSDI at some

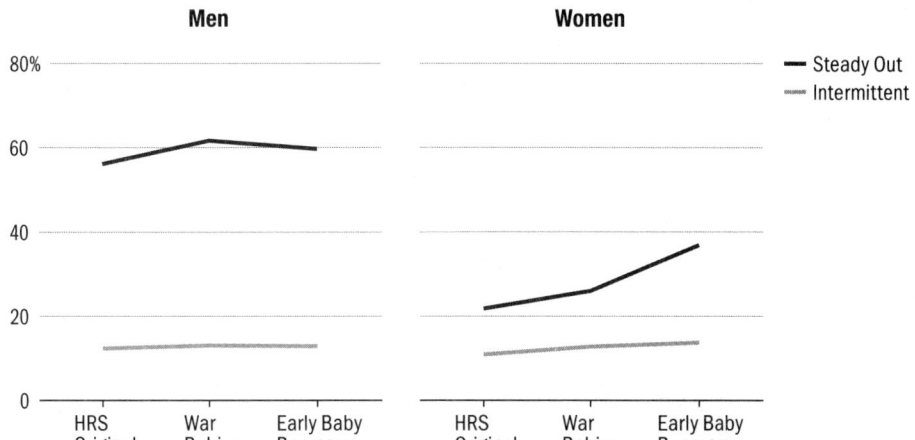

FIGURE 1.10 Federal disability benefit receipt, by birth cohort and employment stability
Percent who report ever receiving Social Security Disability Insurance (SSDI) benefits between ages 51 and 61.
Note: Weighted samples from the Health and Retirement Study (HRS). Birth cohorts: HRS Original, 1936–1941; War Babies, 1942–1947; Early Baby Boomers, 1948–1953.

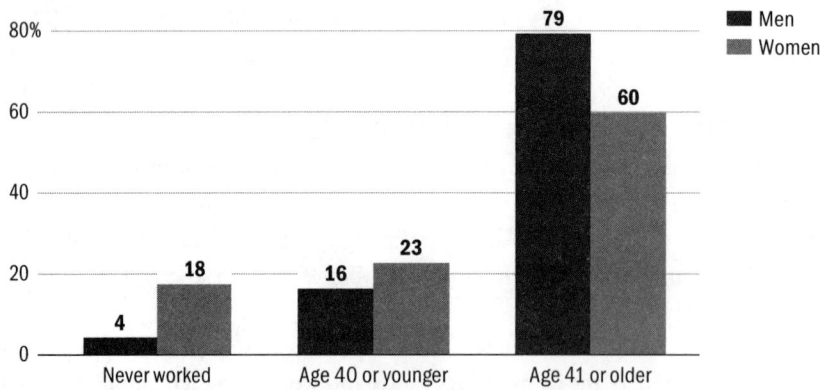

FIGURE 1.11 Ages at which Steady Outs last worked
Note: Weighted samples from the Health and Retirement Study (HRS). Percentages may not sum to 100 due to rounding.

point, a number that does not change much across cohorts. Among both men and women, fewer than 1 percent of Steady Ins report receiving disability benefits, so we omit them from the graph.

The high proportion of Steady Outs who receive disability benefits suggests that many Steady Outs are unlikely to be candidates for working longer because their health severely limits the work they can do. By contrast, the relatively low proportion of people with intermittent employment patterns who receive disability benefits suggests that work disability is not the main reason for intermittent employment in one's 50s, although it is a contributor. To understand why people experience intermittent employment in their 50s, future research should consider alternative explanations such as caregiving responsibilities, precarious jobs, and age discrimination (see Chapter 8 by Gatta and Horning, Chapter 9 by Berg and Pisczcek, and Chapter 10 by Fahle and McGarry).

We also examine the work histories of those who were Steady Out during their 50s. Employment policy solutions for this group may depend on whether a large fraction have never worked for pay, have some work experience many years ago, or have recently worked. Figure 1.11 shows the results. Among both men and women, a substantial majority of those who are never employed in their 50s say they have had a job after age 40. Only 18 percent of female Steady Outs and 4 percent of male Steady Outs say that they have never been employed. Among all adults, 0.4 percent of men and 3.7 percent of women say they have never worked. This suggests that some experience of paid employment may be closer to universal than is commonly recognized, and it could provide a basis for intervention earlier in the life course.[12]

5. Discussion

This chapter aims to bring those who are not employed during their 50s back into the working-longer discussion and to situate this pivotal decade in the context of employment both earlier and later in life. A life course perspective has informed our work. We examine both changes across birth cohorts and heterogeneity by gender, race, and education within cohorts, finding that heterogeneity within cohorts is much greater than changes across recent cohorts. We first describe population trends using the Current Population Survey. Then, using the Health and Retirement Study, we find that the large majority of people who work longer (defined as employed at some point between ages 62 and 66) are those who were continuously employed during their 50s. The likelihood of working longer is strongly associated with employment stability in one's 50s, even when we take sociodemographic characteristics, pensions, wealth, work history, and health conditions into account.

We find that a substantial proportion of Americans are unlikely to be strong candidates for working longer. Continuous employment during one's 50s is a strong predictor of working longer, yet only about half of Americans—about 61 percent of men and 43 percent of women—are in continuous employment during their 50s. In other words, for many Americans, difficulties with working longer appear to start not in the mid- to late 60s but a decade or more earlier. Working longer starts younger than we might think.

There are strong social gradients, especially by education, in employment rates across the life course. Likewise, we find strong social gradients in the proportion of people in their 50s who are in continuous employment (Steady Ins) or continuous nonemployment (Steady Outs). About two-thirds of college graduates are continuously employed during their 50s, compared to 36 percent of those without a high school diploma. Only 6 percent of college graduates never work for pay in their 50s, compared to about a third of those without a high school degree. Among those who were continuously not employed, about 60 percent of men and 27 percent of women received SSDI benefits at some point during their 50s, suggesting that many of those who have left employment before their 50s have impairments that limit their capacity to work.

Changes *during* one's 50s are more similar across sociodemographic groups, however. Although disadvantaged groups start from a much lower base, employment rates fall by about 20 percentage points among *all* groups between ages 50 and 60. Similarly, roughly a third of all sociodemographic groups experience some sort of intermittent employment pattern during their 50s. These results resemble Maestas's (2010) finding that there is little socioeconomic gradient to "unretirement." Future research needs to examine the reasons that Americans experience intermittent employment during their 50s.

Most of our findings are concerning news for prospects of working longer. However, our examination of work histories before the early 50s suggests reasons for optimism and a potential focus for policy solutions. Less than 1 percent of men and 4 percent of women say they had never worked for pay. Even among those who are not employed during the run-up to traditional retirement ages, a large majority say they last worked after age 40. Some experience of paid work appears to be nearly universal. As a result, there may be many missed opportunities to retain people in the labor force earlier in life.

From a policy perspective, a key reason to favor working longer is that continued employment may improve the financial well-being of individuals and their families, supplementing income from Social Security, pensions, and personal retirement savings. Our results show that the most vulnerable groups—those who are most likely to lack adequate retirement income—are least likely to have steady employment in their 50s that could provide a foundation for working longer in their 60s. As it currently stands, working longer is not a realistic cure for retirement insecurity for many Americans.[13]

In order to succeed, interventions must be targeted toward moments where change is possible. Our findings, seen with a life course perspective, are most consistent with social trajectory models. That is, factors such as educational attainment shape individuals' employment stability during their 50s, but employment stability during one's 50s itself shapes further later-life employment. Our results suggest that policies geared toward improving the quality and consistency of employment earlier in the life course, especially among disadvantaged groups, may increase rates of working longer. We return to policy opportunities for improving prospects for working longer in the final chapter in this book.

Notes

1. We gratefully acknowledge comments from fellow participants. We thank Courtney Coile and Gary Burtless for helpful feedback and J. L. Herrera for valuable research assistance. This research was supported by the Alfred P. Sloan Foundation and by the National Institute on Aging of the National Institutes of Health under Award Number P30AG024409. The content is solely the responsibility of the authors and does not necessarily represent the official views of the National Institutes of Health.
2. For a discussion of the working longer policy consensus, see Ghilarducci (2021).
3. The HRS is sponsored by the National Institute on Aging (grant number NIA U01AG009740) and is conducted by the University of Michigan.
4. The complete HRS Original Cohort includes individuals born between 1931 and 1941, who were between ages 51 and 61 at the first interview. Because we are interested in employment patterns in the run-up to the Social Security Earliest Eligibility Age, we restrict the sample to those who were ages 51 to 56 at the first interview to match the sampling design of the War Babies cohort and subsequent cohorts.
5. Results are substantively similar when we include only those who reported their employment status every wave between ages 51 and 61.
6. We use employment status at the time of the interview. We may miss short employment and nonemployment spells between survey waves, which occur every two years. Because the first interview takes place between ages 51 and 56, the longest period of time we call "the 50s" includes ages 51 to 61, while the shortest includes ages 56 to 61. As mentioned earlier, we limit our sample to individuals who reported their employment status in at least three interviews between ages 51 and 61.
7. We estimate linear probability models for the sake of interpretability. Our conclusions do not change when we use logistic regression.
8. *Major health conditions* is a count of up to five conditions a respondent reports at first interview: heart condition, lung condition, cancer, stroke, and psychiatric diagnosis. *Minor health conditions* is a count of up to three conditions a respondent reports at first interview: arthritis, hypertension or high blood pressure, and diabetes. Our results do not change when we treat these as dichotomous variables (any condition or no condition).
9. *ADLs* include bathing, dressing, eating, getting out of bed, and walking to the other side of the room. *IADLs* include using a phone, managing money, and taking medications. *Other functional limitations* include sitting for two hours; getting up from a chair after sitting for long periods; lifting or carrying weights over 10 pounds; stooping; kneeling; or crouching; reaching arms above shoulder level; pushing or pulling large objects; and picking up a dime from the table. For comparability across waves, we use data on these questions from wave 2 and beyond because the question wording changed substantially between the first and second waves. Our results do not change when we treat these as dichotomous variables (any difficulty or no difficulty).
10. For federal disability qualifications, see https://www.ssa.gov/OP_Home/cfr20/404/404-1566.htm.

11. As mentioned earlier, the complete HRS Original Cohort includes individuals born between 1931 and 1941, who were between ages 51 and 61 at the first interview. We again restrict the sample to those who were ages 51 to 56 at the first interview to match the sampling design of the War Babies cohort and subsequent cohorts.
12. If the HRS is biased toward healthier individuals with more employment history, these figures may underestimate the experience of never working in the U.S. noninstitutionalized civilian population. However, our figures are of a similar magnitude as those of Scott and Hatalla (1990), who find that only 2.1 percent of a small sample of college-educated women who were born around 1937 (overlapping with the HRS Cohort) had never been employed 25 years after graduation.
13. Some proponents argue that working longer will boost national income by increasing labor supply among older workers. However, those who leave the workforce at earlier ages are disproportionately those with less education and lower wages. Thus, increasing labor force participation rates among older low-wage workers is likely to have only modest effects on national income.

References

Abraham, Katharine G., Brad Hershbein, and Susan N. Houseman. 2021. "Contract Work at Older Ages." *Journal of Pension Economics & Finance* 20 (3): 426–447. https://doi.org/10.1017/S1474747220000098.

Berkman, Lisa F., and Ichiro Kawachi. 2014. "A Historical Framework for Social Epidemiology." In *Social Epidemiology*, edited by Lisa F. Berkman, Ichiro Kawachi, and M. Maria Glymour, 1–16. Oxford: Oxford University Press.

Binder, Ariel J., and John Bound. 2019. "The Declining Labor Market Prospects of Less-Educated Men." *Journal of Economic Perspectives* 33 (2): 163–190. https://doi.org/10.1257/jep.33.2.163.

Bound, John, Michael Schoenbaum, Todd R. Stinebrickner, and Timothy Waidmann. 1999. "The Dynamic Effects of Health on the Labor Force Transitions of Older Workers." *Labour Economics* 6 (2): 179–202. https://doi.org/10.1016/S0927-5371(99)00015-9.

Burtless, Gary, and Joseph F. Quinn. 2002. *Is Working Longer the Answer for an Aging Workforce?* Boston, MA: Center for Retirement Research at Boston College. https://crr.bc.edu/wp-content/uploads/2002/12/ib_11_508x.pdf.

Cahill, Kevin E., Michael D. Giandrea, and Joseph F. Quinn. 2006. "Retirement Patterns from Career Employment." *The Gerontologist* 46 (4): 514–523.

Ciecka, James E., and Gary R. Skoog. 2017. "Expected Labor Force Activity and Retirement Behavior by Age, Gender, and Labor Force History." *Statistics and Public Policy* 4 (1): 1–8. https://doi.org/10.1080/2330443X.2017.1358125.

Coglianese, John. 2018. "The Rise of In-and-Outs: Declining Labor Force Participation of Prime Age Men." Working Paper. http://econweb.umd.edu/~davis/eventpapers/CoglianeseRise.pdf.

Coile, Courtney C. 2015. "Economic Determinants of Workers' Retirement Decisions." *Journal of Economic Surveys* 29 (4): 830–853. https://doi.org/10.1111/joes.12115.

Coile, Courtney C. 2019. "Working Longer in the United States: Trends and Explanations." In *Social Security Programs and Retirement around the World: Working Longer*, edited by Courtney C. Coile, Kevin Milligan, and David A. Wise, 299–324. Chicago: University of Chicago Press. https://www.nber.org/chapters/c14052.

Cutler, David M., Ellen Meara, and Seth Richards-Shubik. 2011. "Health Shocks and Disability Transitions Among Near-Elderly Workers." *Boston College Retirement Research Center Working Paper*, no. 11–08. http://crr.bc.edu/wp-content/uploads/2011/08/Health-Shocks.pdf.

Elder, Glen H., Jr., Monica Kirkpatrick Johnson, and Robert Crosnoe. 2003. "The Emergence and Development of Life Course Theory." In *Handbook of the Life Course*, edited by Jeylan T. Mortimer and Michael J. Shanahan, 3–19. New York: Kluwer Academic/Plenum.

Flood, Sarah, Miriam King, Renae Rodgers, Steven Ruggles, and J. Robert Warren. 2020. *Integrated Public Use Microdata Series, Current Population Survey: Version 8.0* [Dataset]. Minneapolis, MN: IPUMS. https://doi.org/10.18128/D030.V8.0.

Ghilarducci, Teresa. 2021. "Making Old People Work: Three False Assumptions Supporting the 'Working Longer Consensus.'" *Politics & Society* 49 (4): 549–574. https://doi.org/10.1177/0032329220987084. Accessed on June 03, 2022.

Han, Shin-Kap, and Phyllis Moen. 1999. "Clocking Out: Temporal Patterning of Retirement." *American Journal of Sociology* 105 (1): 191–236. https://doi.org/10.1086/210271.

Health and Retirement Study. RAND HRS Longitudinal File 2018 (V1); RAND HRS 1992 Fat File (V1B); RAND HRS 1998 Fat File (V2C) public use dataset. Produced and distributed by the University of Michigan with funding from the National Institute on Aging (grant number NIA U01AG009740). Ann Arbor, MI (2021, 1992, 1998).

Johnson, Richard W., and Corina Mommaerts. 2011. "Age Differences in Job Loss, Job Search, and Reemployment." The Program on Retirement Policy Discussion Paper 11–01. Washington, DC: The Urban Institute. https://www.urban.org/research/publication/age-differences-job-loss-job-search-and-reemployment

Liebman, Jeffrey B. 2015. "Understanding the Increase in Disability Insurance Benefit Receipt in the United States." *Journal of Economic Perspectives* 29 (2): 123–150. https://doi.org/10.1257/jep.29.2.123.

Liu, Su, and David Stapleton. 2010. "How Many SSDI Beneficiaries Leave the Rolls for Work? More Than You Might Think." Disability Policy Research Brief 10–01. Mathematica Policy Research. https://www.ssa.gov/disabilityresearch/documents/TTW5_Brief_2_DIcohort_REV2.pdf.

Maestas, Nicole. 2010. "Back to Work: Expectations and Realizations of Work after Retirement." *Journal of Human Resources* 45 (3): 718–748. https://doi.org/10.3368/jhr.45.3.718.

Maestas, Nicole, Kathleen J Mullen, David Powell, Till von Wachter, and Jeffrey B. Wenger. 2018. "The Value of Working Conditions in the United States and Implications for the Structure of Wages." NBER Working Paper 25204. Cambridge, MA: National Bureau of Economic Research.

Moen, Phyllis. 2016. *Encore Adulthood: Boomers on the Edge of Risk, Renewal, and Purpose.* New York: Oxford University Press.

RAND HRS Longitudinal File 2018 (V1); RAND HRS 1992 Fat File (V1B); RAND HRS 1998 Fat File (V2C). Produced by the RAND Center for the Study of Aging, with funding from the National Institute on Aging and the Social Security Administration. Santa Monica, CA (February 2021, June 2004, April 2013).

Scott, Judith, and Josie Hatalla. 1990. "The Influence of Chance and Contingency Factors on Career Patterns of College-Educated Women." *The Career Development Quarterly* 39 (1): 18–30. https://doi.org/10.1002/j.2161-0045.1990.tb00231.x.

Truesdale, Beth C., Lisa Berkman, and Alexandra Mitukiewicz. 2021. "When I'm 54: Working Longer Starts Younger Than We Think." Harvard Center for Population and Development Studies Working Paper Series 21 (9). https://cdn1.sph.harvard.edu/wp-content/uploads/sites/2623/2021/12/21_Truesdale_HCPDS-Working-paper_Vol-21-no-9_Final2.pdf.

U.S. Bureau of Labor Statistics. 2019. "Employment Status of the Civilian Noninstitutional Population by Age, Sex, and Race." https://www.bls.gov/cps/aa2018/cpsaat03.htm.

U.S. Department of Labor. n.d. "Labor Force Participation Rate of Women by Age." https://www.dol.gov/agencies/wb/data/lfp/women-by-age.

Warner, David F., Mark D. Hayward, and Melissa A. Hardy. 2010. "The Retirement Life Course in America at the Dawn of the Twenty-First Century." *Population Research and Policy Review* 29 (6): 893–919. https://doi.org/10.1007/s11113-009-9173-2.

2

The Geography of Retirement

Courtney C. Coile[1]

1. Introduction

Americans are working longer, responding to a changing retirement landscape in which people are living longer and facing more responsibility to plan for their own retirement (Munnell 2015; Coile 2019). Several studies suggest that working longer is the best means of raising one's standard of living in retirement (Bronshtein et al. 2019; Munnell, Hou, and Sanzenbacher 2019). People for whom working longer is not feasible or desirable may face an increased risk of financial insecurity and poverty in old age.

Geography is a natural lens though which to explore the heterogeneity in work at older ages, given regional disparities in prime-age employment. Regional income convergence has slowed or reversed after decades of progress (Moretti 2011; Ganong and Shoag 2017; International Monetary Fund 2019), leading to a "hardening" of regional differences in the employment of prime-age individuals (Austin, Glaeser, and Summers 2018) and renewed interest in the potential of place-based policies to address these differences (Neumark and Simpson 2015; Bartik 2020). Relatedly, there are large geographic differences in the receipt of Social Security Disability Insurance (SSDI) benefits (McVicar 2006; Coe et al. 2011; Gettens, Lei, and Henry 2016). Place-based factors, including local economic conditions, contribute to these regional disparities, as areas facing more import competition, occupational polarization, or unemployment experience lower wages, lower labor force participation, and higher SSDI receipt (Autor and Duggan 2003; Autor, Dorn, and Hanson 2013; Autor 2019). Long-term impacts of childhood neighborhood characteristics on adult economic outcomes (Sharkey 2016; Chetty and Hendren 2018a, 2018b) also point to an effect of place on employment. The COVID-19 pandemic raised questions about whether geographic differences in job characteristics such as the ability to work remotely (Althoff et al. 2021) may lead to disparate labor market impacts.

There is mounting evidence of the role of place in health as well (Macintyre, Ellaway, and Cummins 2002; Deryugina and Molitor 2021). The life expectancy of low-income individuals differs substantially across cities and states, and these differences are correlated with local area characteristics and policies (Chetty et al. 2016; Montez et al. 2020). Mortality among those displaced by Hurricane Katrina is strongly influenced by mortality rates in the areas to which they moved (Deryugina and Molitor 2018), and Medicare beneficiaries who move are similarly influenced by location (Finkelstein, Gentzkow, and Williams 2019). Given the importance of health considerations in retirement decisions (French and Jones 2017), these studies provide further motivation for examining retirement through a geographic lens.

The role of place may be characterized as being due to a combination of compositional and contextual factors. The former refers to the attributes of the local population, such as their level of education, while the latter refers to features of place that are not directly related to individual characteristics; it is often treated as the residual after accounting for compositional factors. Some critics have suggested that this distinction may be less useful than it seems, as some individual characteristics may be affected by place and represent intermediate outcomes that should not be treated as confounding factors (Macintyre, Ellaway, and Cummins 2002).

While there is a substantial literature examining retirement decisions (as discussed in Coile [2018]), little attention has been paid to the role of geography. Regional disparities in prime-age employment could foreshadow disparities at older ages, or geographic disparities in employment might be smaller at older ages. Characteristics like education are strongly correlated with individual retirement behavior (Burtless 2013), suggesting that compositional factors could contribute to regional disparities in retirement. Contextual factors such as the strength of local labor markets may also have an important impact on employment at older ages, particularly given that older workers are less geographically mobile than younger workers and that geographic mobility has declined over the past two decades; these factors might matter even more for less educated workers, who are relatively less mobile (Childers et al. 2019). The magnitude of geographic differences in older age employment as well as the extent to which they are explained by compositional versus contextual factors is not currently well understood.

This study aims to begin to fill this gap by exploring geographic differences in employment at older ages. We first document the magnitude of geographic differences in employment rates and in the change in employment over time. Our key measure of geography is commuting zones (CZs), aggregations of counties that are defined by commuting patterns, and our primary data come from the U.S. Census and the American Community Survey (ACS). Second, we examine the characteristics of areas with high and low employment rates, supplementing our main data with six additional sources. Third, we estimate regression models of CZ-level employment rates on demographics, education, health, economic conditions, and other local factors, in order to evaluate the relative importance of these factors in explaining geographic differences in employment. Finally, we explore spatial cross-correlations of employment across demographic groups and with SSDI receipt, to see if areas with low rates of employment at older ages tend to be the same across age and education groups and the same as areas with high SSDI receipt.

We find large differences across U.S. CZs in employment rates at older ages—a gap of about 20 percentage points between areas at the 90th and 10th percentiles of employment. We also find that low-employment areas are different from high-employment areas, with a less educated and more diverse population, more low-wage jobs and import competition from China, poorer health outcomes and health care access, lower government spending, and more income inequality. Although these correlations are not necessarily causal, these factors collectively can explain about four-fifths of the geographic variation in employment at older ages. Lastly, we find that places with low employment at older ages tend to have low employment at younger ages, low employment of both less and more educated older workers, and high rates of SSDI receipt. Our findings suggest that place-based factors likely affect employment at older ages and that place-based strategies merit further study as a potential means of redressing retirement inequities.

2. Data and Methods

The primary data source for this project is the U.S. Census and American Community Survey (ACS).[2] These data contain large samples—5 percent of the U.S. population in the public Census data and 1 percent in the annual ACS—and geographic identifiers, enabling the construction of employment rates by location and the merger of these data with other location-specific data. The geographic unit for this analysis is the CZ, a measure of local labor markets developed by Tolbert and Sizer (1996) based on 1990 commuting patterns. CZs are aggregations of counties, defined such that most commuting activity occurs within rather than across CZs. The United States has 741 CZs, as compared to over 3,000 counties, and these CZs collectively provide full coverage of the country, including rural areas (Chetty et al. 2016).

Constructing CZ-level data in the Census/ACS requires several steps. First, employment rates within each public use microdata area (PUMA) are constructed from individual-level data. PUMAs are geographic areas with a population size of 100,000 to 200,000 that lie within state boundaries and consist of contiguous counties or census tracts; there are 2,378 in the United States. We use PUMAs rather than counties for this step because PUMAs are available for all Census/ACS households. Next, PUMAs are matched to CZs using a crosswalk provided by Autor, Dorn, and Hanson (2013; hereafter "ADH"). As a single PUMA may be part of multiple CZs, the match is made on a probabilistic basis, using information from the crosswalk.[3] Finally, employment rates within CZs are created from the PUMA-level data with CZ identifiers.[4]

The years for the analysis are 1990, 2000, 2007, and 2018, chosen to span a period in which labor force participation rates at older ages were rising and to provide observations about one decade apart. We use 2007 data rather than 2010 in order to avoid the effects of the Great Recession and focus on long-term trends. To boost sample size, "2007" data combine data from the 2006, 2007, and 2008 ACS, and "2018" data combine data from the 2017, 2018, and 2019 ACS. Using four years of data and aggregating to the CZ-level results in a sample of about 3,000 CZ-year observations. As employment rates differ substantially by age and sex, we calculate rates separately by sex and five-year age groups for ages 55 to 74. In some cases, we focus on a 10-year group, ages 60 to 69, to streamline the presentation of results.

We supplement the Census/ACS data with location-related data from six other sources.[5] We use four sources of county-level data: unemployment rates from the Bureau of Labor

Statistics, mortality data from the Center for Disease Control and Prevention's WONDER database (for year 2000 and later), employment by industry from Eckert et al. (2021) based on the U.S. Census Bureau's County Business Patterns data, and SSDI receipt rates from Moore (2021) based on Social Security Administration data. These sources are aggregated to CZ-level using the ADH county-to-CZ crosswalk and county population weights. We also use two sources of CZ-level data: data on exposure to China imports from ADH and a large set of CZ-level covariates from the Health Inequality Project (HIP). The ADH data are available for 2000 and 2007 only, and the HIP data, which come from different sources representing different years, are not available over time.

Before moving to the analysis, it is worth considering whether migration could influence the results. Retirement could increase the probability of migration, as some retirees may move to be closer to family or have a lower cost of living. Such migration would tend to raise the employment rate in the origin location and lower it in the destination, potentially leading to incorrect inferences about the role of area characteristics in old-age employment. However, the evidence suggests that migration at older ages is limited—less than 2 percent of individuals age 55 to 69 moved within the last year and less than 5 percent moved within the last 5 years, with migration unrelated to the unemployment rate in the original location (Coile, Levine, and McKnight 2014). We conclude that migration is unlikely to have a major impact on the results below.

3. Analysis
3.1. Geographic Differences in Employment at Older Ages

The first goal of this analysis is to document geographic differences in employment at older ages. We begin, in Figure 2.1, by displaying the pattern of male employment rates across CZs in the contiguous United States in 1990 (panel A) and 2018 (panel B), as well as the changes in employment between these two years (panel C). We focus on ages 60 to 69, the range during which most retirement occurs. Several findings emerge from these graphs. First, there is considerable heterogeneity in retirement rates across CZs, with clear regional patterns. Focusing first on 1990, many of the highest-employment CZs are in the middle of the country in a swath running from the upper Midwest down into Texas, in a corridor along the northeast and southeast coast, and in the northern Rocky Mountains. A band of low-employment CZs runs from Appalachia into Arkansas and Louisiana; the Southwest and northernmost Midwest are other areas of low employment. Despite these clear regional patterns, there are also many cases where adjacent CZs have employment rates that differ by more than 10 percentage points (indicated on the graph as being more than one shade apart).

Second, there is a clear trend toward working longer, as evident in the darker grays in panel B relative to panel A. The employment rate for men ages 60 to 69 rises by nearly 10 percentage points over this three-decade period, from 40.2 percent to 49.8 percent. Many of the regional patterns evident in 1990 remain visible in 2018. Consistent with this, the correlation between 1990 and 2018 employment is 81 percent.

Panel A: Employment rate, 1990

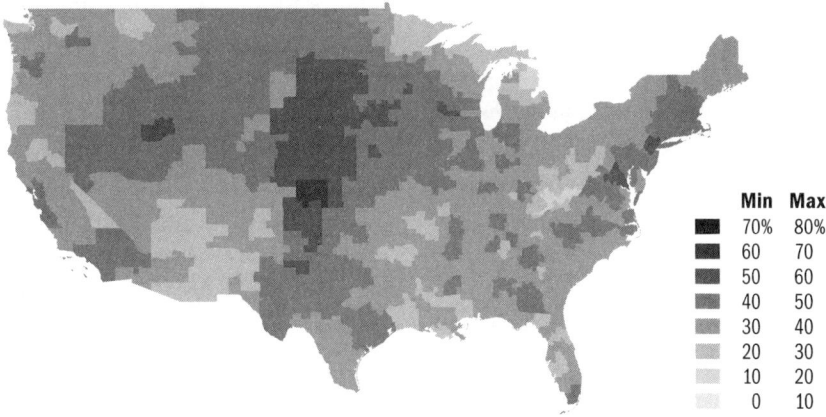

Panel B: Employment rate, 2018

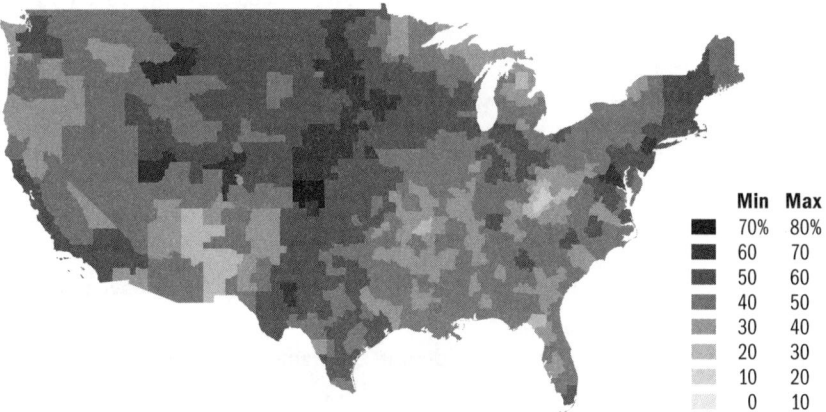

Panel C: Change in employment rate, 1990 to 2018

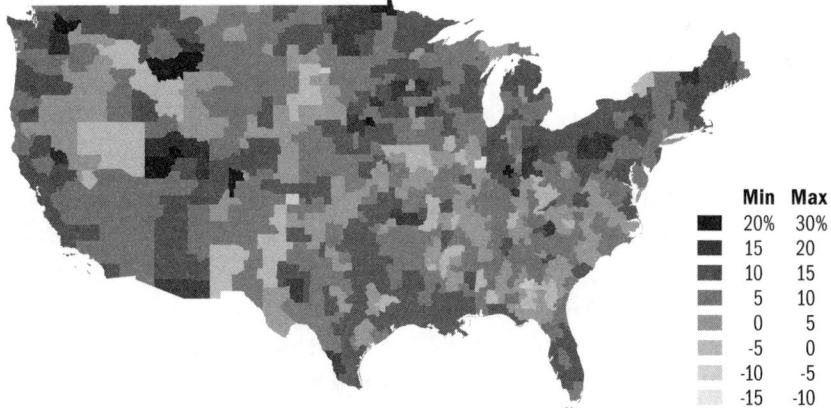

FIGURE 2.1 Employment rate of men ages 60–69 by commuting zone, 1990 and 2018

Third, as seen in panel C, there is substantial heterogeneity in the change in employment over time and not much of a regional pattern in this measure. The correlation between the 1990 employment rate and employment growth over the next three decades is −20 percent, indicating that high-employment CZs experience somewhat slower employment growth on average. The negative correlation suggests some tendency toward geographic convergence in men's employment rates at older ages over time, although the high correlation between 1990 and 2018 also points to a high degree of stability in geographic disparities. These patterns are broadly consistent with those for men ages 55 to 59 and 70 to 74 (not shown).

Figure 2.2 shows the data for women. In 1990, there are higher employment rates in the middle of the country and in the Northeast and lower employment rates in Appalachia and into the South, as for men. The differences in employment rates across CZs for women are somewhat smaller than for those for men (reflected in the use of fewer shades of gray). By contrast, a comparison of 1990 and 2018 indicates that the trend of increased employment over time is stronger for women. The employment rate rises by 15 percentage points over this period, from 25.5 to 40.4 percent. The correlation between 1990 and 2018 employment rates is 72 percent. As before, there are no strong regional patterns when it comes to changes in employment over time. The correlation between the 1990 employment and the change in employment over time is essentially zero.

Figure 2.3 provides the distribution of employment rates for the age 60 to 69 group, by year and sex. These figures exclude CZs where fewer than 100 observations were used to compute the employment rate, to minimize the impact of sampling variation. The differences in employment rates across CZs are large—for men, the difference in employment rates for CZs at the 90th versus the 10th percentile of the distribution is 22 percentage points in both 1990 and 2018, while for women the 90-10 difference is 13 points in 1990 and 18 points in 2018. The increase in working longer is evident in the rightward shift of the distribution between 1990 and 2018, particularly for women. The lower panels display the distribution of changes in employment between the two periods. There is substantial variation across CZs in the change in employment between 1990 and 2018, with a 90-10 difference of 13 percentage points for both men and women. Overall, the key conclusions that emerge from these figures are that there is substantial geographic heterogeneity in employment and in the change in employment over time, even as the graphs provide clear evidence of the trend toward working longer.

3.2. Characteristics of Low- and High-Employment Areas

The next logical question is to ask: what are the characteristics of CZs with low and high employment rates at older ages? To explore this, we first classify CZs into quartiles based on their employment rate, comparing within the same sex, age group, and year. In Table 2.1, we present the mean characteristics of CZs in the lowest and highest quartile of employment, as well as the ratio of low-to-high mean values and an indicator of whether the ratio is statistically different from 1. We examine all factors for which we have data, including demographic and economic variables as well as the large set of (non-time-varying) CZ-level characteristics from HIP. While this analysis is purely descriptive, it may nonetheless provide some indication of characteristics that could influence employment rates at older ages.

Panel A: Employment rate, 1990

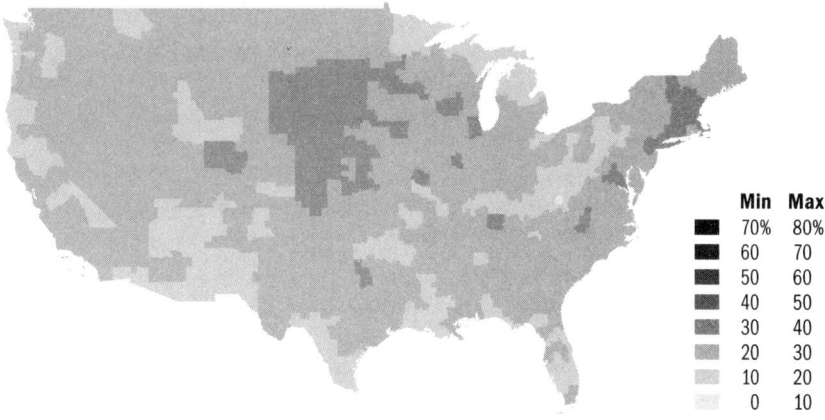

Panel B: Employment rate, 2018

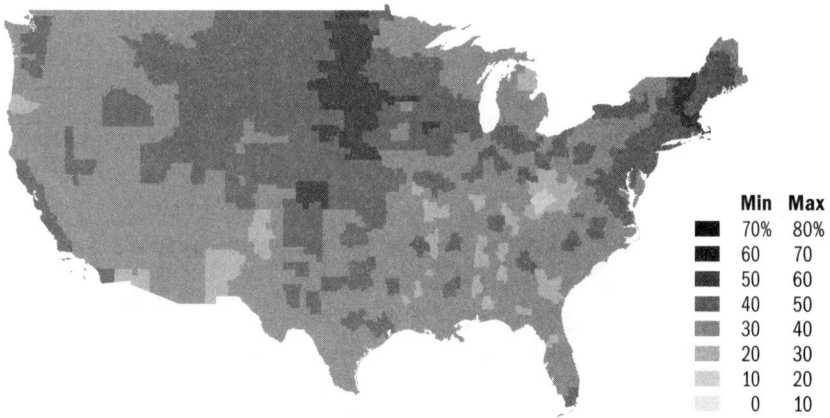

Panel C: Change in employment rate, 1990 to 2018

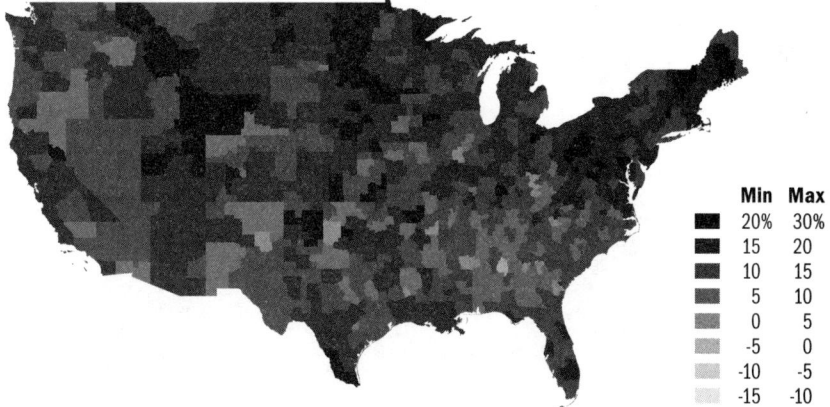

FIGURE 2.2 Employment rate of women ages 60–69 by commuting zone, 1990 and 2018

Panel A: Distribution of employment rates

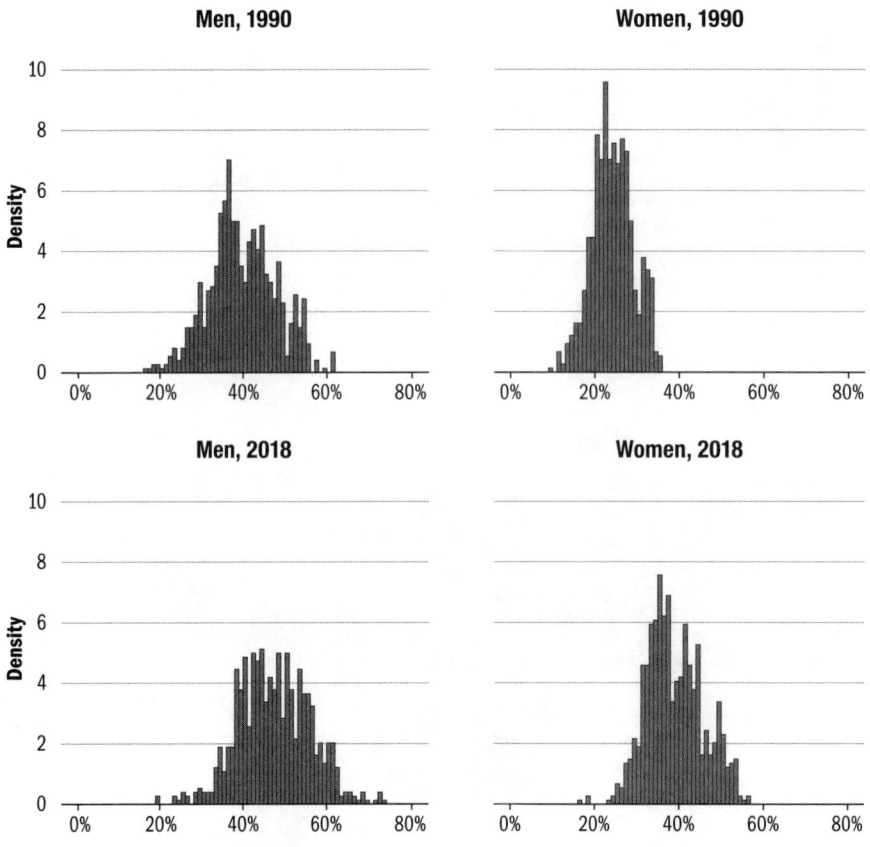

Panel B: Distribution of changes in employment rates, 1990 to 2018

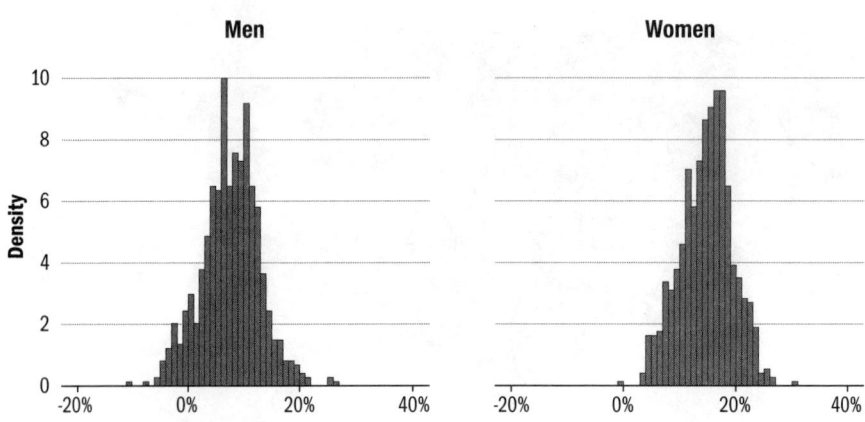

FIGURE 2.3 Commuting zone employment rates among adults ages 60–69, 1990 to 2018

TABLE 2.1 Characteristics of commuting zones with low versus high employment rates, 1990–2018

Characteristic	Low-employment-rate CZs (1st quarter)	High-employment-rate CZs (4th quarter)	Low/high ratio	Significant difference?
DEMOGRAPHIC				
Married	67.8%	71.5%	95%	Yes
Race: White	87.5%	92.1%	95%	Yes
Race: Black	7.6%	2.2%	349%	Yes
Race: Asian	0.6%	1.4%	44%	Yes
Race: Other	4.3%	4.3%	100%	No
Hispanic	5.2%	3.5%	145%	Yes
Citizen	98.5%	98.6%	100%	No
Veteran	24.8%	23.8%	104%	Yes
Education: < High school	26.5%	18.3%	145%	Yes
Education: High school	41.6%	43.6%	95%	Yes
Education: Some college	16.9%	19.1%	88%	Yes
Education: College	14.9%	18.9%	79%	Yes
Population	4,663	7,038	66%	Yes
ECONOMIC				
SSDI beneficiaries	5.2%	3.0%	173%	Yes
Unemployment rate	6.0%	3.7%	162%	Yes
Employment rate: 10-year lag	56.3%	68.7%	82%	Yes
Industry shares				
Agriculture, forestry, fishing	1.0%	0.4%	270%	Yes
Mining	2.2%	1.6%	137%	Yes
Utilities	1.1%	1.2%	91%	Yes
Construction	5.7%	5.6%	102%	Yes
Manufacturing	17.7%	14.1%	126%	Yes
Wholesale trade	3.6%	6.1%	59%	Yes
Retail trade	17.3%	16.8%	103%	Yes
Transportation/warehousing	3.4%	3.5%	97%	Yes
Information	1.7%	2.3%	75%	Yes
Finance and insurance	3.5%	4.8%	73%	Yes
Real estate	1.2%	1.1%	110%	Yes
Professional, scientific, technical	2.8%	3.2%	88%	Yes
Management of companies	0.8%	1.0%	84%	Yes
Administrative and support	3.4%	2.8%	123%	Yes
Educational services	1.4%	1.8%	77%	Yes
Health care/social assistance	16.1%	16.6%	97%	Yes
Arts, entertainment, recreation	1.3%	1.4%	90%	Yes
Accommodation and food service	11.1%	10.6%	105%	Yes
Other services	4.4%	4.9%	90%	Yes
Public administration	0.2%	0.3%	66%	Yes

(continued)

TABLE 2.1 Continued

Characteristic	Low-employment-rate CZs (1st quarter)	High-employment-rate CZs (4th quarter)	Low/high ratio	Significant difference?
China imports/worker: lagged	0.9	0.5	191%	Yes
China imports/worker: change	2.2	1.4	157%	Yes
HEALTH OUTCOMES AND BEHAVIORS				
Mortality rate (ages 55–74)	1.7%	1.3%	123%	Yes
Current smoker (Q1)	29.1%	26.0%	112%	Yes
Current smoker (Q4)	13.2%	11.4%	115%	Yes
Obesity rate (Q1)	31.6%	28.7%	110%	Yes
Obesity rate (Q4)	23.9%	22.6%	106%	Yes
Exercise rate (Q1)	59.2%	63.4%	94%	Yes
Exercise rate (Q4)	84.3%	86.2%	98%	Yes
HEALTH CARE				
Uninsured	20.0%	17.3%	116%	Yes
Medicare spending per enrollee ($)	9,442	8,549	110%	Yes
Mortality: 30-day heart attacks	0.169	0.162	105%	Yes
Mortality: 30-day pneumonia	0.110	0.111	99%	Yes
Mortality: 30-day heart failure	0.128	0.117	110%	Yes
Mortality: 30-day hospital (index)	0.860	0.346	249%	Yes
Ambulatory care (index)	−0.479	0.020	—	Yes
Primary care (1 or more visit)	80.4%	79.8%	101%	Yes
Diabetic care: Eye exam	63.7%	70.4%	91%	Yes
Diabetic care: Hemoglobin	82.6%	83.9%	98%	Yes
Diabetic care: Lipids	77.9%	75.5%	103%	Yes
Mammogram	61.8%	64.9%	95%	Yes
Ambulatory care/sensory conditions	83.4	64.2	130%	Yes
INEQUALITY AND SOCIAL COHESION				
Income segregation	0.033	0.032	102%	No
Segregation of affluence	0.034	0.034	98%	No
Segregation of poverty	0.030	0.029	107%	Yes
Racial segregation	0.124	0.110	113%	Yes
Gini Index (bottom 99%)	0.324	0.263	123%	Yes
Poverty rate	17.3%	12.6%	137%	Yes
Top 1% income share	10.6%	10.2%	104%	Yes
Middle class	52.4%	59.7%	88%	Yes
Absolute upward mobility	41.8%	48.4%	86%	Yes
Social Capital Index	−0.448	1.166	—	Yes
Religious (%)	49.1%	62.9%	78%	Yes
OTHER FACTORS				
Change in population (1980–2000)	16.6%	4.5%	372%	Yes
Migration inflow	1.7%	1.3%	124%	Yes

TABLE 2.1 Continued

Characteristic	Low-employment-rate CZs (1st quarter)	High-employment-rate CZs (4th quarter)	Low/high ratio	Significant difference?
Migration outflow	1.6%	1.6%	103%	Yes
Population density	62.0	84.2	74%	Yes
Commute < 15 minutes	42.1%	54.9%	77%	Yes
Mean household income ($)	30,306	34,163	89%	Yes
Median house value ($)	106,516	109,103	98%	Yes
School expenditure/student ($)	5,711	6,442	89%	Yes
Student/teacher ratio	17.1	15.2	112%	Yes
Test score (income adj.)	−2.8	3.9	—	Yes
Crime rate	0.007	0.005	128%	Yes
Local government expenditure ($)	2,112	2,524	84%	Yes
Local tax rate	2.0%	2.8%	72%	Yes
Tax progressivity	0.757	1.026	74%	Yes

Notes: CZs are sorted into quartile of employment rate by year, age group, and sex. Population is the number of people in the CZ–year–age group–sex cell. Employment rate (10-year lag) is the employment rate for workers in the same birth cohorts 10 years earlier. China imports per worker is the value (in dollars) either 10 years ago or the change over the past 10 years; data are available for 2000 and 2007 only. Mortality rate is deaths per 100,000 population at ages 55 to 74 (both sexes); data are available from 2000 on. Variables listed under Health Outcomes and Behaviors, Health Care, Inequality and Social Cohesion and Other Factors come from the Health Inequality Project (Chetty et al. 2016) and are time invariant; for more details on these variables, see eTable 3 in the appendix of Chetty et al. 2016. CZ, commuting zone; SSDI, Social Security Disability Insurance.

Turning to Table 2.1, we first examine demographic characteristics. Low-employment CZs have about 3.5 times as many Black residents and 1.5 times as many Hispanic residents as a share of the older population, as compared to high-employment CZs. Low-employment CZs have nearly 1.5 times as many high school dropouts and 0.8 times as many college graduates. Low-employment CZs tended to be smaller, with an average population about two-thirds the size of that in high-employment CZs.

Moving on to economic variables, we first look at SSDI receipt. This association should be interpreted with particular caution, as SSDI may be affected by or jointly determined with employment. Nonetheless, it is interesting to note the strong relationship—low-employment CZs have 1.7 times as many SSDI disabled worker beneficiaries as a share of the adult working-age population as high-employment CZs, 5.2 percent versus 3.0 percent. The average unemployment rate in low-employment CZs is 1.6 times that in high-employment CZs. This effect is partly mechanical, since a weakening of the labor market will normally lead to both higher unemployment and lower employment. However, this correlation is also consistent with the interpretation that poor labor market conditions contribute to low employment rates at older age, particularly given that there are large, persistent differences in unemployment rates across local labor markets (Lkhagvasuren 2012). CZs with lower employment for a given year, age, and sex group tended to have lower employment of the same birth cohort 10 years earlier.

Compared to high-employment CZ, low-employment CZs have a larger share of employment in agriculture, forestry, and fishing, mining, manufacturing, and administrative support and a smaller share of employment in wholesale trade, public administration, finance and insurance, information, educational services, management of companies, and professional, scientific, and technical services. Broadly speaking, industries overrepresented in low-employment CZs are more likely to feature blue-collar, lower- or middle-wage jobs while industries overrepresented in high-employment CZs are more likely to feature white-collar, higher-wage jobs. A final set of economic variables are the China imports data from ADH. Low-employment CZs were affected 1.5 to 2 times as much by imports from China as were high-employment CZs.

Next, we move to health and health care factors, mindful that except for mortality, the remaining variables are only available for a single point in time and reflect values for the entire population. The mortality rate among individuals ages 55 to 74 is 23 percent higher in low-employment CZs, 1.7 versus 1.3 percent. Individuals in low-employment CZs have modestly higher rates of obesity and smoking and lower rates of exercise. There are also differences in interactions with the health care system. Individuals in low-employment CZs are 16 percent more likely to be uninsured and 30 percent more likely to be hospitalized with conditions that might have been preventable with more primary care (ambulatory care-sensitive). They have lower rates of mammography and some kinds of diabetes care, higher mortality rates after an inpatient hospital stay, and higher Medicare spending per enrollee.

Turning to social factors, low-employment CZs have more poverty, inequality, and racial segregation. They have lower population density and shorter commutes, as well as lower income, fewer religious residents, higher crime, lower government spending, and less progressive taxation.

Overall, while it is important to interpret the differences by employment rate quartile shown in this table as descriptive, they paint a picture in which low-employment CZs have more Black and Hispanic residents and individuals with less education; have higher rates of SSDI receipt; have been more subject to import shocks and have lower employment rates at younger ages; have more employment in industries characterized by blue-collar, middle- or lower-wage jobs; have fewer healthy residents who receive lower quality health care; and have residents who face more inequality and have lower levels of local government spending.

3.3. Explanations for Geographic Differences

We turn to our final key question: how much of the geographic differences in employment can be explained by demographic, education, health, economic, and other local factors? To provide some evidence on this, we run population-weighted regressions examining the relationship between the variables from Table 2.1 and employment rates at older ages in our sample of CZ-year observations for 1990, 2000, 2007, and 2018. We run regressions separately by five-year age group and sex, as work at older ages differs substantially across groups. We estimate these models using labor force participation rates rather than employment rates—while continuing to use the term employment in the text—to avoid a mechanical connection between the unemployment rate and employment. We exclude SSDI from the model because it may be affected by or jointly determined with employment but revisit the spatial cross-correlation of employment and SSDI below.

Our primary purpose is to estimate the relative importance of different groups of variables in explaining differences in employment across CZs. To do so, we employ a method introduced by Fields (2003) and used more recently by Jusot, Tubeuf, and Trannoy (2013). In this approach, the model-explained variance—the share of differences in CZ-level employment that can be explained by all of the variables in the model—is decomposed into the share that can be explained by each group of variables. We choose this approach over adding variables to the model and calculating the incremental variation explained because the results of the latter depend on the order in which variables are added. Given our focus, we report only the share of the model-explained variance (not total variance) in employment explained by different groups of variables and do not report regression coefficients.

In the top section of Table 2.2, we show that the economic variables—including the unemployment rate, the employment rate of the same cohort 10 years earlier, and the industry share and China import variables—are jointly responsible for one-quarter of the model-explained variance for men and one-fifth of the variation for women in both age groups. We also re-estimate the model excluding lagged employment, which might be influenced by education or demographics; doing so reduces the estimate only slightly for all groups except for women 65 to 69, for whom the contribution of economic factors drops by half, consistent with a bigger role for cohort effects in explaining older women's employment.

The importance of time trends also differs by sex. The year variables explain less than 10 percent of model-explained variance for men, versus over one-third for women age 60 to 64 and over one-quarter for women 65 to 69. Education is important for both sexes, explaining 10 to 15 percent of geographic differences in employment; for women ages 65 to 69, the effect is twice as large. Demographic characteristics explain 6 to 12 percent of the variation in employment for men but none for women, while mortality has little explanatory power for either sex. The few negative values indicate that if one were to predict CZ-level employment based on those variables alone, the predicted employment rates would be negatively correlated with the employment rates predicted using a model with all of the variables.

The HIP variables collectively explain 40 to 50 percent of the model-explained variation for men. Dividing these into categories, the "other" variables in Table 2.1, which include items like local government spending, house values, and population density, explain 24 to 30 percent of the model-explained variation, while the inequality variables explain 12 to 19 percent and the health and health care variables explain 1 to 8 percent, depending on the age group. For women, these variables collectively explain about 30 percent of the variation in employment rates, with the "other" and inequality factors responsible for the bulk of the explained variation and the health/health care factors adding little. Overall, the model explains 80 to 90 percent of the total variation in employment across CZs for both men and women, leaving 10 to 20 percent that might be due to a role of place not captured by the model or to random variation.

In the lower section of Table 2.2, we repeat this variance decomposition exercise, substituting indicator variables for the 741 CZs for the HIP variables. As the HIP variables are time-invariant, their effect is now subsumed within the effect of the CZ variables. More generally, the CZ variables capture the effect of any CZ-level factors that are constant over time. For example, to the extent that economic factors vary across CZs but do not vary much within a CZ over time, the role of economic factors in explaining differences in employment will mostly be attributed to the CZ variables. In this analysis, the economic factors contribute

TABLE 2.2 Variance in employment rates explained by commuting zone characteristics

Characteristic	Share of model-explained variance			
	Men 60–64 years	Men 65–69 years	Women 60–64 years	Women 65–69 years
MODEL A: CZ CHARACTERISTICS				
Year	9%	8%	37%	27%
Demographic	6%	12%	−1%	−1%
Education	14%	10%	13%	26%
Economic	25%	27%	20%	20%
Mortality	−4%	2%	2%	1%
HIP: Health/health care	8%	1%	3%	−2%
HIP: Inequality	19%	12%	14%	8%
HIP: Other	24%	30%	13%	22%
Adjusted R-squared	81%	79%	88%	84%
MODEL B: CZ FIXED EFFECTS				
Year	11%	12%	42%	30%
Demographic	7%	5%	4%	0%
Education	8%	1%	5%	18%
Economic	−3%	0%	−1%	−2%
Mortality	2%	15%	10%	7%
CZ fixed effects	75%	67%	41%	47%
Adjusted R-squared	90%	88%	89%	88%

Note: Results from population-weighted regressions on year–CZ–age group–sex cells, for years 1990, 2000, 2007, and 2018. Adjusted R-squared reflects the share of the total variation in CZ-level employment (here defined as labor force participation) explained by the model. CZ, commuting zone, HIP, Health Inequality Project.

to the model-explained variance only to the extent that changes in economic factors over time within a CZ are correlated with changes in the employment rate over time.

The difference between these two models is striking. The effect of economic factors is wiped out—or more precisely, now operates through the CZ variables—and the role of education and demographic factors is also diminished. Time factors remain important, being responsible for about 10 percent of the model-explained variance for men and 30 to 40 percent for women. The CZ variables explain two-thirds to three-quarters of the variation for men, up from half in the case of the HIP variables that they replace; for women, the CZ variables explain 40 to 50 percent of the model-explained variance, up from 30 percent. The share of the total variation in CZ-level employment explained by the model is generally 5 to 10 percent higher than in the previous model for both men and women, leaving 10 percent unexplained.

What conclusions can be drawn from this decomposition exercise? Economic factors like industry share and Chinese import competition help to explain geographic differences in employment at older ages for men and women ages 60 to 64, while their effect is smaller for women ages 65 to 69. A comparison of the two models indicates that the persistent differences in economic factors across places matter far more than changes in these factors over time. Education is important in explaining geographic variation in employment rates for both sexes, while demographic and health factors are less important. A broad set of social and other characteristics of the local area such as inequality and governmental resources also play an important role. Finally, cohort effects and time trends help explain differences in older women's employment across time and space because essentially all CZs saw increases in women's employment rates between 1990 and 2018.

3.4. Correlation in Geographic Patterns of Employment by Education and Age

Finally, we examine the spatial cross-correlation between the employment rates of various demographic groups. We first ask whether areas with low employment for older people tend to have low (or high) employment for young people. This question is of interest given the "lump of labor" fallacy, which suggests that higher employment at older ages may reduce employment opportunities for younger workers, a theory with little empirical support (Munnell and Wu 2012). We also examine whether areas with low employment for less educated older people tend to have low employment for more educated older people. Finally, we explore whether areas with low employment for older people tend to have high SSDI receipt. We use a simple descriptive analysis in which CZs are sorted into quartiles based on each outcome and the distribution of CZs across the two quartile measures is reported in a cross-tabulation. If the two outcomes are unrelated, CZs would be distributed equally across all cells in a given row.

The top section of Table 2.3 shows the distribution of CZs by quartile of older employment (ages 60 to 69) and prime-age employment (age 25 to 54). There is a clear tendency for CZs to be in the same quartile for both measures. For example, among CZs in the lowest quartile of older male employment, 62 percent are in the lowest quartile of prime-age male employment; similarly, 66 percent of CZs in the highest quartile of older male employment are in the highest quartile of prime-age male employment. Values for women are nearly identical.

In the middle section, we find a strong relationship between the employment rate of older less educated individuals (high school graduate or less) and the employment rate of older more educated individuals (some college or more). Among CZs in the lowest quartile of employment for less educated individuals, 55 and 50 percent are in the lowest quartile of employment for more educated individuals for men and women, respectively. Among CZs in the highest quartile of employment for the less educated, 63 and 55 percent are in the highest quartile of employment for the more educated.

Finally, the lower section shows a strong negative relationship between the employment rate of less educated older individuals and the rate of SSDI receipt in the working-age population. We focus on less educated adults because they are more likely to receive SSDI than more educated adults (Coile 2015). Among CZs in the lowest quartile of employment for less educated older men, 53 percent are in the highest quartile of SSDI receipt; for women, this value is 50 percent. Similarly, among CZs in the highest quartile of employment for less educated men, 49 and 46 percent are in the lowest quartile of SSDI receipt for men and women, respectively.

TABLE 2.3 Share of commuting zones by employment rate and SSDI quartile

Quartile of CZ employment rate: Age 60–69	Share in quartile of CZ employment rate: Age 25–54				Share in quartile of CZ employment rate: Age 25–54			
	Lowest	2nd	3rd	Highest	Lowest	2nd	3rd	Highest
	Men				Women			
Lowest	62.1%	27.2%	10.2%	0.5%	61.6%	26.3%	9.5%	2.6%
2nd	24.6%	40.6%	27.7%	7.2%	30.1%	40.8%	22.8%	6.2%
3rd	11.4%	21.0%	41.1%	26.6%	8.4%	25.6%	40.5%	25.5%
Highest	2.2%	11.1%	21.1%	65.7%	0.3%	6.9%	27.1%	65.8%

Quartile of CZ employment rate: Less education	Share in quartile of CZ employment rate: More education				Share in quartile of CZ employment rate: More education			
	Lowest	2nd	3rd	Highest	Lowest	2nd	3rd	Highest
	Men				Women			
Lowest	55.0%	27.4%	13.6%	4.0%	50.4%	29.4%	14.7%	5.5%
2nd	29.9%	35.8%	27.3%	7.0%	31.3%	33.3%	25.0%	10.4%
3rd	13.4%	24.7%	35.8%	26.1%	13.1%	25.4%	32.3%	29.1%
Highest	2.0%	12.0%	23.2%	62.7%	6.0%	11.1%	28.0%	55.0%

Quartile of CZ employment rate: Less education	Share in quartile of SSDI beneficiaries				Share in quartile of SSDI beneficiaries			
	Lowest	2nd	3rd	Highest	Lowest	2nd	3rd	Highest
	Men				Women			
Lowest	5.3%	12.7%	29.3%	52.8%	10.6%	13.6%	26.2%	49.5%
2nd	13.6%	21.5%	31.9%	33.0%	16.1%	22.6%	29.3%	32.0%
3rd	32.6%	32.2%	24.2%	11.0%	28.1%	30.6%	27.5%	13.8%
Highest	49.1%	33.6%	14.9%	2.5%	45.8%	33.3%	17.2%	3.7%

Notes: CZs are sorted into quartile of employment rate by year, sex, and education group for workers age 60–69; more educated is some college or more, and less educated is high school or less. SSDI quartile is computed similarly but does not vary by education. Values on the table are the share of CZ-year observations in each quartile. CZ-year values based on fewer than 100 sample observations are excluded from the analysis. Diagonals are shaded to highlight the main relationships. CZ, commuting zone; SSDI, Social Security Disability Insurance.

In sum, there is a high degree of spatial cross-correlation in employment across age and education groups. This suggests that factors such as those explored in the Table 2.2 analysis may exert a common influence on the employment of different groups. That is, places where older adults—or less educated older adults specifically—are less likely to be employed also tend to be places where younger adults and more educated older adults are less likely to be employed and where there is more use of disability benefits.

4. Discussion

This chapter has examined the role of geography in employment at older ages. We have several major findings. First, we find that geographic differences in employment at older ages are large—in 2018, the employment rate at ages 60 to 69 in CZs at the 90th percentile of the distribution was 22 percentage points higher than the rate in CZs at the 10th percentile for men and 18 points higher for women. There are clusters of higher employment in particular regions, particularly the Midwest down to Texas, the northeast and southeast coast, and the northern Rocky Mountains, but there are also numerous instances of large differences in employment in adjacent CZs. Changes over time in employment are large, heterogeneous in magnitude, and less likely to be regionally concentrated.

Second, we show that there are significant differences in the characteristics of CZs with low and high employment rates. Low-employment CZs tend to have a less educated and more racially and ethnically diverse older population. They have been more affected by imports from China, have more jobs in traditionally blue-collar, lower-wage industries, and have higher rates of SSDI. Low-employment CZs have higher mortality, poorer health behaviors, and lower rates of health insurance. They also have more income inequality, less social cohesion, and lower government spending. It is important to note that these correlations do not establish causality.

Regression analysis confirms that these factors collectively can explain about four-fifths of the geographic variation in employment at older ages. Economic factors and education are important explanatory variables, while demographic and health factors are less important. Other place-level characteristics, including inequality and other factors like government resources, collectively account for 30 to 50 percent of the model-explained variation. Time trends and cohort effects not captured by changes in the other variables are important, particularly for women. Finally, spatial cross-correlations indicate that places that have low employment rates at older ages tend to have low rates at younger ages, have low employment among the less educated and more educated alike, and have high rates of SSDI receipt.

In sum, it seems clear that place does affect employment at older ages. These findings may be viewed in the context of other recent work highlighting large regional disparities in prime-age employment and the role of economic factors in these disparities. Collectively, this evidence has led some analysts to suggest that it may be time to challenge the conventional wisdom that "relief is best targeted towards poor people, not poor places" and reconsider place-based policies (Austin, Glaeser, and Summers 2018). While these policies most often taken the form of state and local tax incentives designed to promote local job growth (Bartik 2020), some analysts have proposed new infrastructure investments like high-tech hubs across the country (Gruber and Johnson 2019), which could serve as the modern equivalent of earlier investments like the federal highway system or Tennessee Valley Authority. Analysts and policymakers may wish to more carefully consider these and other policies that aim to assist individuals in low-employment areas with an eye to meeting the needs of workers of all ages.

Notes

1. Helpful comments from *Overtime* project organizers and fellow participants are gratefully acknowledged. The author thanks Timothy Moore for sharing data on Social Security Disability Insurance beneficiaries and David Dorn and his coauthors, Fabian Eckert and his coauthors, and the Health Inequality Project for generously making their data available to other researchers.
2. These data are accessed via www.ipums.org (Flood et al. 2018).

3. ADH crosswalks are available at https://www.ddorn.net/data.htm (cw_puma1990_czone.dta; cw_puma2000_czone.dta; cw_puma2010_czone.dta) (Dorn, n.d.). We first create 100 identical observations for each PUMA in the Census/ACS data. We also expand the crosswalk to have 100 observations for each PUMA, where the number of each PUMA's observations assigned to each CZ matches reflect the probabilities provided in the crosswalk. When the two datasets are merged, CZs are matched to Census/ACS PUMA-level observations in these same proportions. Note that a single CZ can also include multiple PUMAs, but this is easily handled in the matching process.
4. In the collapsing of individual-level data to PUMA means and of (duplicated) PUMA-level means data to CZ-level data, person weights are applied. An example of the process of mapping counties and PUMAs into CZs is available in the appendix of Coile (2021).
5. The sources of these data are as follows: unemployment rate: https://www.bls.gov/lau/data.htm (U.S. Bureau of Labor Statistics, n.d.); mortality (multiple cause of death files): https://wonder.cdc.gov/mcd-icd10.html (Centers for Disease Control and Prevention, n.d.); employment by industry (efsy_panel_naics.csv): http://www.fpeckert.me/cbp/ (Eckert et al. 2021); SSDI rates (data provided by Timothy Moore (2021)); China imports (workfile_China.dta from Autor-Dorn-Hanson-ChinaSyndrome-FileArchive.zip): https://www.ddorn.net/data.htm (Dorn, n.d.); CZ-level covariates (health_ineq_online_table10.dta): https://healthinequality.org/data/; ADH county to CZ crosswalk (cw_cty_czone.dta): http://www.ddorn.net/data.htm (Dorn, n.d.). Mortality data (crude mortality rate) are for ages 55–74, both sexes; three years of data are aggregated (1999–2001, 2006–2008, and 2017–2019) to improve precision; data from 1999 to 2001 are used for 1990 as mortality data are not available before 1999. The employment-by-industry data are available through 2016 only, so 2016 values are used for the 2018 observations in the analysis. China import data are available for 2000 and 2007 only, so data for 2000 are used for 1990 and data for 2007 are used for 2018.

References

Althoff, Lukas, Fabian Eckert, Sharat Ganapati, and Conor Walsh. 2021. "The Geography of Remote Work." Working Paper 29181. NBER Working Paper Series. Cambridge, MA: National Bureau of Economic Research. https://doi.org/10.3386/w29181.

Austin, Benjamin, Edward Glaeser, and Lawrence Summers. 2018. "Jobs for the Heartland: Place-Based Policies in 21st-Century America." *Brookings Papers on Economic Activity* (vol. 2018, no. 1), Spring: 151–255. https://doi.org/10.1353/eca.2018.0002.

Autor, David H. 2019. "Work of the Past, Work of the Future." *AEA Papers and Proceedings* 109 (May): 1–32. https://doi.org/10.1257/pandp.20191110.

Autor, David H., David Dorn, and Gordon H. Hanson. 2013. "The China Syndrome: Local Labor Market Effects of Import Competition in the United States." *American Economic Review* 103 (6): 2121–2168. https://doi.org/10.1257/aer.103.6.2121.

Autor, David H., and Mark G. Duggan. 2003. "The Rise in the Disability Rolls and the Decline in Unemployment." *The Quarterly Journal of Economics* 118 (1): 157–206. https://doi.org/10.1162/00335530360535171.

Bartik, Timothy J. 2020. "Using Place-Based Jobs Policies to Help Distressed Communities." *Journal of Economic Perspectives* 34 (3): 99–127. https://doi.org/10.1257/jep.34.3.99.

Bronshtein, Gila, Jason Scott, John B. Shoven, and Sita Nataraj Slavov. 2019. "The Power of Working Longer." *Journal of Pension Economics & Finance* 18 (4): 623–644. https://doi.org/10.1017/S1474747219000088.

Burtless, Gary. 2013. "Can Educational Attainment Explain the Rise in Labor Force Participation at Older Ages?" Issue Brief #13-13. Chestnut Hill, MA: Center for Retirement Research at Boston College. https://crr.bc.edu/briefs/can-educational-attainment-explain-the-rise-in-labor-force-participation-at-older-ages/.

Centers for Disease Control and Prevention. n.d. "Multiple Cause of Death, 1999–2019." https://wonder.cdc.gov/mcd-icd10.html.

Chetty, Raj, and Nathaniel Hendren. 2018a. "The Impacts of Neighborhoods on Intergenerational Mobility I: Childhood Exposure Effects." *The Quarterly Journal of Economics* 133 (3): 1107–1162. https://doi.org/10.1093/qje/qjy007.

Chetty, Raj, and Nathaniel Hendren. 2018b. "The Impacts of Neighborhoods on Intergenerational Mobility II: County-Level Estimates." *The Quarterly Journal of Economics* 133 (3): 1163–1228. https://doi.org/10.1093/qje/qjy006.

Chetty, Raj, Michael Stepner, Sarah Abraham, Shelby Lin, Benjamin Scuderi, Nicholas Turner, Augustin Bergeron, and David Cutler. 2016. "The Association Between Income and Life Expectancy in the United States, 2001–2014." *JAMA* 315 (16): 1750–1766. https://doi.org/10.1001/jama.2016.4226.

Childers, Chandra, Ariane Hegewisch, Tanima Ahmed, and Amy Burnett Cross. 2019. "Geographic Mobility, Gender, and the Future of Work." Research Report IWPR #C487. Washington, DC: Institute for Women's Policy Research. https://iwpr.org/iwpr-issues/employment-and-earnings/geographic-mobility-gender-and-the-future-of-work/.

Coe, Norma B., Kelly Haverstick, Alicia H. Munnell, and Anthony Webb. 2011. "What Explains State Variation in SSDI Application Rates?" Working Paper WP #2011-23. Chestnut Hill, MA: Center for Retirement Research at Boston College. https://crr.bc.edu/working-papers/what-explains-state-variation-in-ssdi-application-rates/.

Coile, Courtney C. 2015. "Disability Insurance Incentives and the Retirement Decision: Evidence from the United States." In *Social Security Programs and Retirement Around the World: Disability Insurance Programs and Retirement*, edited by David A. Wise, 45–80. Chicago: University of Chicago Press. https://doi.org/10.7208/chicago/9780226262604.003.0001.

Coile, Courtney C. 2018. "The Demography of Retirement." In *Future Directions for the Demography of Aging: Proceedings from a Workshop*, edited by Mark D. Hayward and Malay K. Majmundar, 217–248. Washington, DC: The National Academies Press. https://doi.org/10.17226/25064.

Coile, Courtney C. 2019. "Working Longer in the United States: Trends and Explanations." In *Social Security Programs and Retirement around the World: Working Longer*, edited by Courtney C. Coile, Kevin Milligan, and David A. Wise, 299–324. Chicago: University of Chicago Press. https://www.nber.org/chapters/c14052.

Coile, Courtney C. 2021. "The Geography of Retirement." NBER Working Paper Series. Cambridge, MA: National Bureau of Economic Research. http://www.nber.org/papers/w29433.

Coile, Courtney C., Phillip B. Levine, and Robin McKnight. 2014. "Recessions, Older Workers, and Longevity: How Long Are Recessions Good for Your Health?" *American Economic Journal: Economic Policy* 6 (3): 92–119. https://dx.doi.org/10.1257/pol.6.3.92.

Deryugina, Tatyana, and David Molitor. 2018. "Does When You Die Depend on Where You Live? Evidence from Hurricane Katrina." Working Paper 24822. NBER Working Paper Series. Cambridge, MA: National Bureau of Economic Research. https://doi.org/10.3386/w24822.

Deryugina, Tatyana, and David Molitor. 2021. "The Causal Effects of Place on Health and Longevity." Working Paper 29321. NBER Working Paper Series. Cambridge, MA: National Bureau of Economic Research. https://doi.org/10.3386/w29321.

Dorn, David. n.d. "Data Page." https://www.ddorn.net/data.htm.

Eckert, Fabian, Teresa C. Fort, Peter K. Schott, and Natalie J. Yang. 2021. "Imputing Missing Values in the US Census Bureau's County Business Patterns." Working Paper w26632. Cambridge, MA: National Bureau of Economic Research. https://doi.org/10.3386/w26632.

Fields, Gary S. 2003. "Accounting for Income Inequality and Its Change: A New Method, With Application to the Distribution of Earnings in the United States." In *Worker Well-Being and Public Policy (Research in Labor Economics, Vol. 22)*, edited by Solomon W. Polachek, 1–38. Bingley: Emerald. https://doi.org/10.1016/S0147-9121(2003)22.

Finkelstein, Amy, Matthew Gentzkow, and Heidi L. Williams. 2019. "Place-Based Drivers of Mortality: Evidence from Migration." Working Paper 25975. NBER Working Paper Series. Cambridge, MA: National Bureau of Economic Research. https://doi.org/10.3386/w25975.

Flood, Sarah, Miriam King, Renae Rodgers, Steven Ruggles, and J. Robert Warren. 2018. "Integrated Public Use Microdata Series, Current Population Survey: Version 6.0." Dataset. Minneapolis, MN: IPUMS. https://doi.org/10.18128/D030.V6.0.

French, Eric, and John B. Jones. 2017. "Health, Health Insurance, and Retirement: A Survey." Working Paper 17–03. Working Paper Series. Richmond, VA: Federal Reserve Bank of Richmond. https://doi.org/10.21144/wp17-03.

Ganong, Peter, and Daniel Shoag. 2017. "Why Has Regional Income Convergence in the U.S. Declined?" *Journal of Urban Economics* 102 (November): 76–90. https://doi.org/10.1016/j.jue.2017.07.002.

Gettens, Jack, Pei-Pei Lei, and Alexis Henry. 2016. "Accounting for Geographic Variation in DI and SSI Participation." DRC Working Paper 2016-03. Washington, DC: Mathematica Center for Studying Disability Policy. https://mathematica.org/publications/accounting-for-geographic-variation-in-di-and-ssi-participation.

Gruber, Jonathan, and Simon Johnson. 2019. *Jump-Starting America: How Breakthrough Science Can Revive Economic Growth and the American Dream*. New York: Public Affairs.

International Monetary Fund. 2019. "World Economic Outlook, October 2019: Global Manufacturing Downturn, Rising Trade Barriers." Washington, DC: International Monetary Fund. https://www.imf.org/en/Publications/WEO/Issues/2019/10/01/world-economic-outlook-october-2019.

Jusot, Florence, Sandy Tubeuf, and Alain Trannoy. 2013. "Circumstances and Efforts: How Important Is Their Correlation for the Measurement of Inequality of Opportunity in Health?" *Health Economics* 22 (12): 1470–1495. https://doi.org/10.1002/hec.2896.

Lkhagvasuren, Damba. 2012. "Big Locational Unemployment Differences Despite High Labor Mobility." *Journal of Monetary Economics* 59 (8): 798–814. https://doi.org/10.1016/j.jmoneco.2012.10.004.

Macintyre, Sally, Anne Ellaway, and Steven Cummins. 2002. "Place Effects on Health: How Can We Conceptualise, Operationalise and Measure Them?" *Social Science & Medicine* 55 (1): 125–139. https://doi.org/10.1016/S0277-9536(01)00214-3.

McVicar, Duncan. 2006. "Why Do Disability Benefit Rolls Vary Between Regions? A Review of the Evidence from the USA and the UK." *Regional Studies* 40 (5): 519–533. https://doi.org/10.1080/00343400600757635.

Montez, Jennifer Karas, Jason Beckfield, Julene Kemp Cooney, Jacob M. Grumbach, Mark D. Hayward, Huseyin Zeyd Koytak, Steven H. Woolf, and Anna Zajacova. 2020. "US State Policies, Politics, and Life Expectancy." *The Milbank Quarterly* 98 (3): 668–699. https://doi.org/10.1111/1468-0009.12469.

Moore, Timothy. 2021. "Disability Benefit Receipt by State and County, 1970–2018: Description and Dataset." Personal communication.

Moretti, Enrico. 2011. "Local Labor Markets." In *Handbook of Labor Economics*, edited by David Card and Orley Ashenfelter, Vol. 4, Part B, 1237–1313. North Holland: Elsevier. https://doi.org/10.1016/S0169-7218(11)02412-9.

Munnell, Alicia H. 2015. "The Average Retirement Age: An Update." Issue Brief 15-4. Chestnut Hill, MA: Center for Retirement Research at Boston College. https://crr.bc.edu/briefs/the-average-retirement-age-an-update/.

Munnell, Alicia H., Wenliang Hou, and Geoffrey T. Sanzenbacher. 2019. "How Would More Saving Affect the National Retirement Risk Index?" Issue Brief 19-16. Chestnut Hill, MA: Center for Retirement Research at Boston College. https://crr.bc.edu/briefs/how-would-more-saving-affect-the-national-retirement-risk-index/.

Munnell, Alicia H., and April Yanyuan Wu. 2012. "Will Delayed Retirement by the Baby Boomers Lead to Higher Unemployment Among Younger Workers?" Working Paper 2012-2022. Chestnut Hill, MA: Center for Retirement Research at Boston College. https://crr.bc.edu/working-papers/will-delayed-retirement-by-the-baby-boomers-lead-to-higher-unemployment-among-younger-workers/.

Neumark, David, and Helen Simpson. 2015. "Place-Based Policies." In *Handbook of Regional & Urban Economics*, edited by Gilles Duranton, J. Vernon Henderson, and William C. Strange, 5: 1197–1287. Amsterdam: Elsevier. https://doi.org/10.1016/B978-0-444-59531-7.00018-1.

Sharkey, Patrick. 2016. "Neighborhoods, Cities, and Economic Mobility." *RSF: The Russell Sage Foundation Journal of the Social Sciences* 2 (2): 159–177. https://doi.org/10.7758/rsf.2016.2.2.07.

Tolbert, Charles M., and Molly Sizer. 1996. "U.S. Commuting Zones and Labor Market Areas: A 1990 Update." Economic Research Service Staff Paper 9614. Washington, DC: Rural Economy Division, Economic Research Service, U.S. Department of Agriculture. https://usa.ipums.org/usa/resources/volii/cmz90.pdf.

U.S. Bureau of Labor Statistics. n.d. "Featured LAU Searchable Databases." Local Area Unemployment Statistics. https://www.bls.gov/lau/data.htm.

3

The European Context
Declining Health but Rising Labor Force Participation among the Middle-Aged

Axel Börsch-Supan, Irene Ferrari, Giacomo Pasini, and Luca Salerno[1]

1. Introduction

This chapter is motivated by the concern that negative trends in both health and employment among middle-aged Americans may put trends toward working longer in jeopardy. Indeed, both health and labor force participation in the United States have stalled or fallen among middle-aged adults. To understand the potential future of working longer in America, this contribution compares trends in health and employment in Europe with those in the United States.

At the individual level, people who experience a health shock or chronic ill health are much more likely to leave the labor force than people who remain in good health. Applying the same logic to countries, we might expect that if health declines within a population, labor force participation rates would also decline; and that countries with poor population health would have lower labor force participation rates than those with better population health. However, international comparisons are more complex because country-specific factors, especially health, labor market policies, and retirement policies, may drive trends in different directions.

In fact, Europe is different from the United States in many respects. On the one hand, almost all EU countries feature a higher life expectancy (OECD 2019b), higher healthy life expectancy, and better health in general (Avendano et al. 2009; Avendano and Kawachi 2014) than the United States, potentially due to universal health insurance in Europe (Bloom, Khoury, and Subbaraman 2018). On the other hand, labor force participation at older ages is much lower in Europe than in the United States. There is a large body of evidence linking the strong financial incentives for early retirement in most European countries to low rates of labor force participation among older adults (Gruber and Wise 2004). The reduction of these incentives in the late 1990s and early 2000s reverted the trend toward earlier retirement in

Europe and led to a strong increase of old-age employment (Börsch-Supan and Coile 2020, Forthcoming). From a health point of view, this increase was possible since the health capacity to work longer was plentiful in Europe for cohorts approaching retirement in the early 2000s (Wise 2017).

This paper addresses two key questions. First, will this health capacity remain or will Europe experience a trend similar to the United States in that today's middle-aged cohorts have worse health than earlier cohorts? We use panel data for eight EU countries and Switzerland from the Survey of Health, Ageing and Retirement in Europe (SHARE) to measure health by age and cohort, stratifying by education and wealth. We find that health has improved among Europeans over the age of 65, but at best it has stagnated among middle-aged Europeans. Moreover, the number of health problems has increased sharply across cohorts among men in the bottom half of their country's educational and wealth distributions, thus increasing health disparities between more- and less-advantaged men. While most of these increased health deficits are not necessarily life-threatening, such as anxiety or lack of concentration, our findings contradict the folklore in Europe and earlier scientific studies which claim that medical progress keeps improving health in Europe for all socioeconomic groups in all cohorts.[2]

The second key question is whether employment of middle-aged individuals in Europe faces a declining trend similar to that in the United States. We use data from the European Labor Force Survey and aggregated by Eurostat to create a pseudo-panel for the same countries as in the first part. We do not find any evidence for a reduction of middle-aged employment in Europe, opposite to the trend in the United States.

Both findings fit well with the results by Coile et al. (2017) that health trends have very little predictive value for employment trends in Europe. While health is a significant determinant of labor force participation in a cross-section within each country, health explains neither the cross-national differences in old-age labor force participation nor its trajectory over time. Financial incentives by far dominate all other potential explanations, including health.

We draw two policy conclusions. First, for Europe, although it is concerning that health has declined among disadvantaged middle-aged men and stagnated for the rest, this trend in health is unlikely to have much impact on future rates of employment at older ages. Second, for America, the European experience suggests that institutional and economic factors such as the financial incentives in public pension systems are likely to be more important than population health for overall rates of working longer.

2. Institutional and Health Background: United States and Europe

Public pension systems are much larger in Europe than in the United States. They are 15.6 percent of GDP in Italy, 15.0 percent in France, 12.3 percent in Spain, and 10.3 percent in Germany, to take the four largest European economies, as compared to only 5.2 percent in the United States (European Commission 2018). This is due not only to older populations in Europe but also to greater generosity in terms of benefits and eligibility. The net replacement rate for an average worker (i.e., the after-tax pension benefit of average workers divided by their previous after-tax earnings) is 51.9 percent in Germany, 73.6 percent in France, 83.4 percent in Spain, and 91.8 percent in Italy, compared to 49.4 percent in the United States (OECD 2019a). Likewise, the effective retirement age[3] among men is 64.0 years in Germany, 63.3 years in Italy, 62.1 years in Spain, and 60.8 years in France, as compared to 67.9 years in the United States (OECD 2019a). This greater generosity now holds in spite of a string of pension reforms all across the EU that has increased the financial incentives to work longer (Börsch-Supan and Coile 2020). The studies in Börsch-Supan and Coile (Forthcoming) show that these reforms were very effective in increasing the average exit age from the labor force. Accompanying reforms also targeted disability insurance more narrowly, most effectively by abandoning access to disability insurance for labor market rather than health reasons. Some countries reduced the replacement rate of public pensions, but not all. Many countries actually increased the benefits for poor and/or disabled individuals.

A second large institutional difference relevant for this paper is the fact that all EU countries have universal health insurance that residents do not lose in case of unemployment or nonemployment. In addition, the European income support systems in the case of unemployment or poverty are more generous than in the United States. France spends 9.3 percent of GDP on such social support systems, Spain 7.1 percent, Germany 6.7 percent, and Italy 5.6 percent, as compared to only 3.3 percent in the United States (OECD 2019c).

As Avendano et al. (2009) show, most indicators of health exhibit a gradient from the European Union (highest) to the United Kingdom (middle) to the United States (lowest). All-cause-mortality is 833 deaths per 100,000 population in the United States, 763 in the United Kingdom, and only 698 in the four largest EU countries (OECD 2019b). Healthy life expectancy, defined as the absence from functional limitations in everyday life, decreases from 73.0 years in the four largest EU countries to 71.9 years in the United Kingdom and only 68.5 years in the United States (World Health Organization 2019). Not only the levels but also the dynamics of health are different. Between 2012 and 2018, life expectancy at birth increased in the four largest EU countries by more than 1.5 years, all but stagnated in the United Kingdom, and decreased in the United States by about 9 months.

3. Measuring Health and Employment with the SHARE Data

Health is not straightforward to measure, especially in an internationally comparable context and as trends over time. While mortality is commonly used to compare health across countries, mortality rates may not capture changes in work-related health since many chronic conditions are not life-threatening but make working harder, especially in occupations that require manual labor. Similarly, poor mental health may interfere with paid employment even if it does not result in death. We therefore construct a health deficiency index that covers a wide variety of physical and mental conditions that may impede working longer. We follow the approach proposed by Mitnitski, Mogilner, and Rockwood (2001), which has been applied to internationally comparable data by Abeliansky and Strulik (2019). Essentially, the health deficit index is the number of health deficits which an individual has relative to the possible number of health deficits that are measured in the data:

$$\text{Health Deficit Index} = \frac{\Sigma(x_i)}{n} \qquad (1)$$

where $x_i \in [0,1]$ denotes health measure i and n the number of health measures.[4]

We base our analyses on the Survey of Health, Ageing and Retirement in Europe (SHARE) since it includes a wide range of micro-data on socioeconomic status, social and family networks, and health across European countries. SHARE Release 7.0.0 provides a multidisciplinary and cross-national database with currently about 140,000 individuals aged 50 or older in 28 countries. A detailed description can be found in in Börsch-Supan et al. (2013).

For the analysis of health trends, we define middle-aged as age 50–64. For comparison, we also provide some evidence for the 65–85 group. Because we require a large time horizon to distinguish between age and cohort effects, we include only those SHARE countries that delivered data in all seven survey waves. These are Austria (N = 15,267, M = 6,914),[5] Belgium (N = 23,671, M = 12,481), Denmark (N = 14,730, M = 7,884), France (N = 19,482, M = 10,062), Germany (N = 17,390, M = 8,793), Italy (N = 19,743, M = 8,856), Spain (N = 20,214, M = 8,632), Sweden (N = 16,295, M = 6,469), and Switzerland (N = 12,069, M = 5,828).

Data on 52 health deficits are available in all seven waves of SHARE. Abeliansky and Strulik (2019), who also use SHARE data, choose 38 items, including 4 items which were not available in all waves. They explain their choice by claiming that these represent aging-related health deficits. We deviate from their approach for three reasons. First, in order to avoid selectivity bias, we do not include the four items that are available only in the earlier waves of SHARE (see Börsch-Supan et al. 2020, Table A.7).[6] Second, for reasons of parsimony, we want to include only those items that add explanatory power and avoid too much multicollinearity. Third, we want to include only those items that are related to work ability. We accomplish the last two aims simultaneously by using the Least Absolute Shrinkage and Selection Operator (Lasso) technique, a method for selecting and fitting covariates in a regression model predicting labor force participation. Lasso seeks regression coefficients that minimize the residual sum of squares like ordinary least squares. In addition, it penalizes the number of covariates to obtain a more parsimonious model which, in general, will have better out-of-sample prediction accuracy.[7] This procedure leads to the exclusion of only one of the 52 available variables, showing that most of the items matter for labor force participation. A detailed list of the variables used is included in the working paper version of this chapter (Börsch-Supan et al. 2020). We refer to our index as the MEA (Munich Center for the Economics of Aging) health deficit index.

Since not only health levels but also health trends may differ according to socioeconomic status, we stratify the analysis of age and cohort-specific health deficits by educational attainment and by wealth. This reduces confounding since education has been increasing steadily for the birth cohorts considered. We split the sample into higher- and lower-educated depending on the median of each cohort's education years. Wealth of the household in which the respondent lives is measured as the household's total net worth variable contained in the fully imputed version of the SHARE dataset.[8] We split the sample into higher- and lower-wealth, based on the median wealth of each cohort. For both education and wealth, medians are calculated separately by country, sex, interview year, and cohort.

For the analysis of employment, we define middle-aged as age 50–59. We compare the employment of middle-aged adults with older individuals (age 60–74) and younger (age 25–34). Employment data by age and year were taken from Eurostat, file "Employment rates by sex, age and educational attainment level" [lfsa_ergaed] for the eight EU countries and Switzerland as retrieved in January 2020 and published in December 2019. The data were aggregated by Eurostat from its Labor Force Surveys. We converted these data into a pseudo-panel by age and cohort.

4. Health Trends among Middle-Aged Adults in Europe

We first investigate whether Europe is experiencing a similar trend as the United States in that younger cohorts have worse health than their predecessors. We start by describing overall changes in health across cohorts. We then provide a more formal analysis using regression, which delivers significance levels for the cohort trends, permits stratification by wealth, education, and sex, and allows us to investigate which specific health deficits changed across cohorts.

4.1. Basic Descriptive Findings

Among middle-aged Europeans, health appears to have declined across cohorts. Figure 3.1 shows the smoothed age profiles of the MEA health deficit index by cohort, averaged over the nine countries in our sample, for individuals of age 50–64.[9] Because SHARE data are collected only since 2004, we cannot observe the entire age span for all cohorts. The youngest cohorts (1960–1964) contain only relatively young individuals, while the individuals from the oldest cohorts (1940–1944) cannot be younger than 59 years. Thus, we cannot compare these cohorts to each other without additional assumptions, in this case the identifying assumption that period (time) effects are zero.[10] However, even if we restrict ourselves to comparing only overlapping cohorts, the younger cohorts have more health deficits than the oldest cohort, and certain older cohorts are healthier than the subsequent cohorts. Generally, there seems not to be much of a difference between the younger cohorts, with the 1955–1959 and 1960–1964 cohorts standing out as the cohorts with the highest health deficit index. Considering the very narrow scale on the vertical axis, however, the difference across cohorts is not very large.

Worsening health among recent cohorts in middle age is in stark contrast to the trends among earlier cohorts at older ages (Figure 3.2). Among the older individuals, the younger the cohort, the fewer health deficits individuals have at a specific age. It suggests that much of the recent improvement in health happened at a relatively old age, while individuals in working age were either unaffected or even worse off. Notably, the scales on the vertical axes of Figure 3.1 and Figure 3.2 are different, meaning that the apparent declines in health

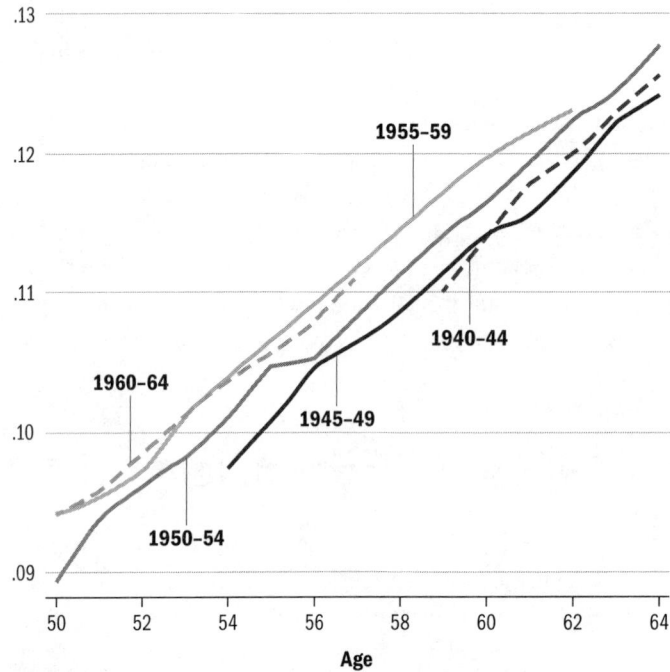

FIGURE 3.1 Health deficit index by birth cohort for Europeans ages 50–64
Source: SHARE Waves 1–7.

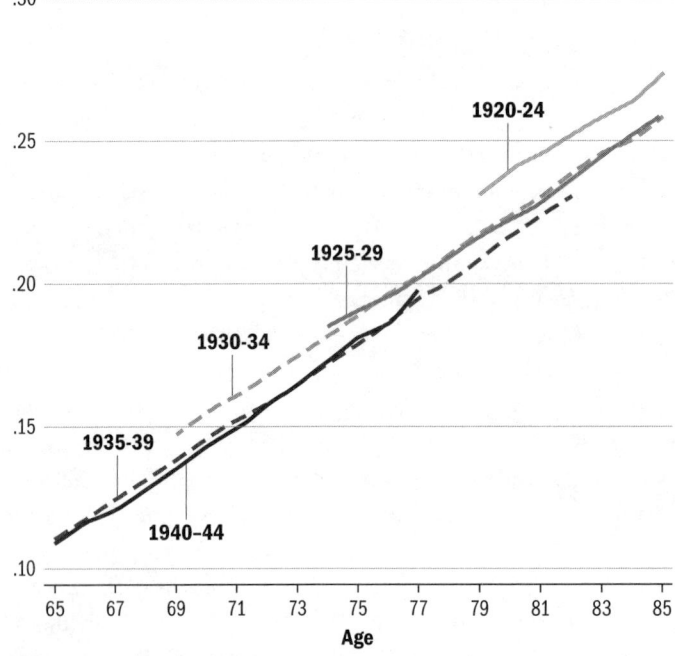

FIGURE 3.2 Health deficit index by birth cohort for Europeans ages 65–85
Source: SHARE Waves 1–7.

among middle-aged Europeans may be smaller than the improvements in health among older Europeans.

The findings of Figure 3.1 contradict the folklore and earlier scientific studies that claim that medical progress keeps improving health in Europe. Abeliansky and Strulik (2019) find an improvement of health over the entire age range of 50–85. They do not, however, stratify by age, and their analysis suffers from selectivity bias as shown by Börsch-Supan, Ferrari, and Salerno (2021), which results in an overly optimistic picture for individuals in middle age. The difference in trends between Figure 3.1 and Figure 3.2 suggest that there is important heterogeneity by age in European health trends that has been previously neglected.

4.2. Regression Analyses

The graphs in Figure 3.1 and Figure 3.2 provide suggestive descriptive evidence. In order to establish whether the observed cohort differences in health are statistically significant, and to stratify the results by education and wealth, we provide a more formal analysis by running regressions of the health deficit index on the year of birth, holding age constant. The identifying assumption is (as before) the absence of period effects. Year-of-birth effects are parametrized as fixed effects; this allows us to present the corresponding coefficients in a graph. Since the health deficit index has a skewed empirical distribution, we use a log-linear relationship.

Specifically, we use the following regression models:

$$\ln(Health\ Index_i) = r + \alpha * age_i + \sum_{t=1}^{T-1} \gamma_t * yrbirth_{it} + country_i + \overline{age}_i + \epsilon_i \qquad (2)$$

where i represents the individual, age represents the age at the interview, $yrbirth$ is a set of year-of-birth fixed effects, t refers to the year of birth, $country$ are the country fixed effects, $\overline{(age)}$ the country-specific means of age, and ϵ is the error term.[11]

We estimate the models separately by gender as we found large differences between women and men. We also present results stratified by educational background and by wealth in order to examine whether socioeconomic inequalities in health have changed across birth cohorts. Regression results including the coefficients of the year-of-birth dummies are relegated to the working paper version of this chapter (Börsch-Supan et al. 2020). Figures 3.3 to 3.7 present the coefficients on the year-of-birth dummies graphically. The omitted year of birth is always 1953.

As Figure 3.3 shows, there is no clear cohort trend in health among women, but there is a worsening trend among men. In the left-hand panel, compared to women born in 1953, those born in 1941 have a 3.4 percent higher health deficit index, and those born in 1964 have a 4.7 percent higher index. A Wald test shows no statistically significant difference between the 1941 and the 1964 cohorts.[12]

The right panel of Figure 3.3 shows the cohort coefficients for men. Health deficits stay relatively constant across cohorts for males born until 1957. After that, however, the more recent cohorts face more health deficits. While men who were born in 1941 have a 7.2 percent lower health deficit index than those born in 1953, the 1964 cohort has a 2.4 percent higher

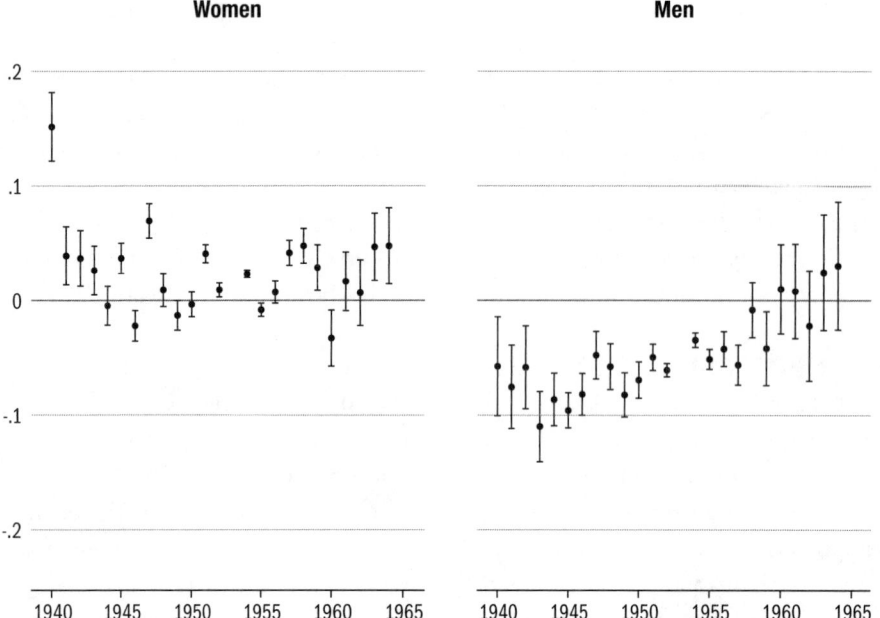

FIGURE 3.3 Cohort changes in the health deficit index by gender among Europeans ages 50–64
Source: SHARE Waves 1-7. Units are percentage differences of the health index (equation 1).

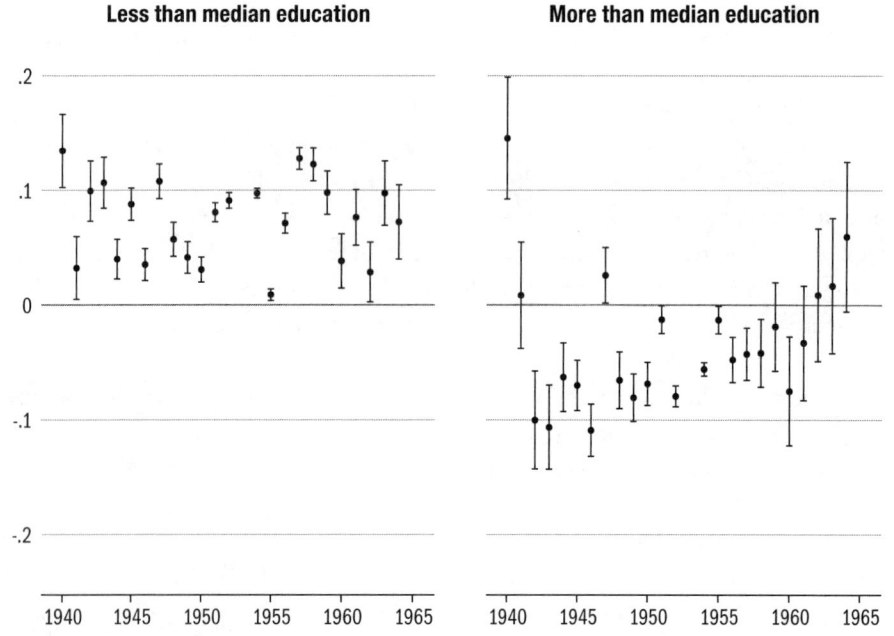

FIGURE 3.4 Cohort changes in the health deficit index by education among European women ages 50–64
Source: SHARE Waves 1–7

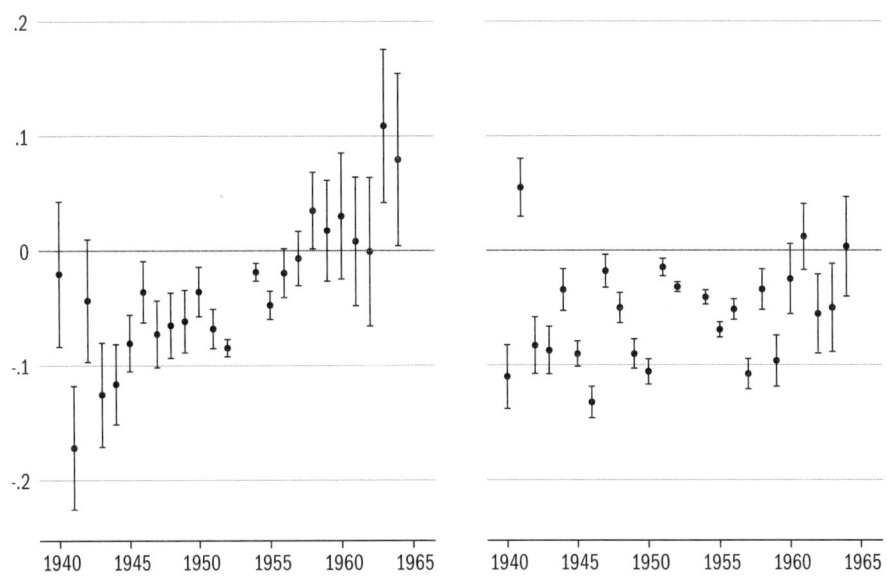

FIGURE 3.5 Cohort changes in the health deficit index by education among European men ages 50–64
Source: SHARE Waves 1–7.

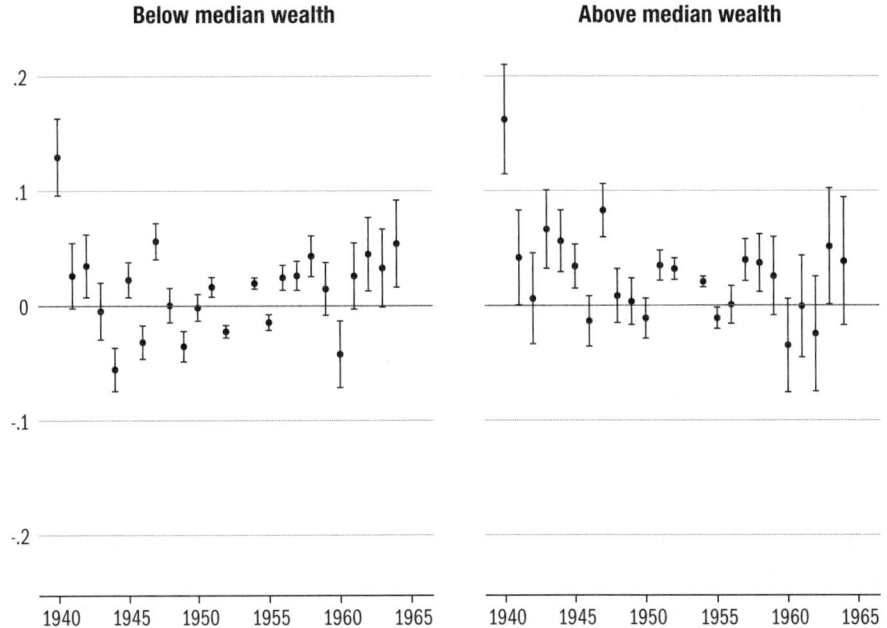

FIGURE 3.6 Cohort changes in the health deficit index by wealth among European women ages 50–64
Source: SHARE Waves 1–7.

78 | OVERTIME

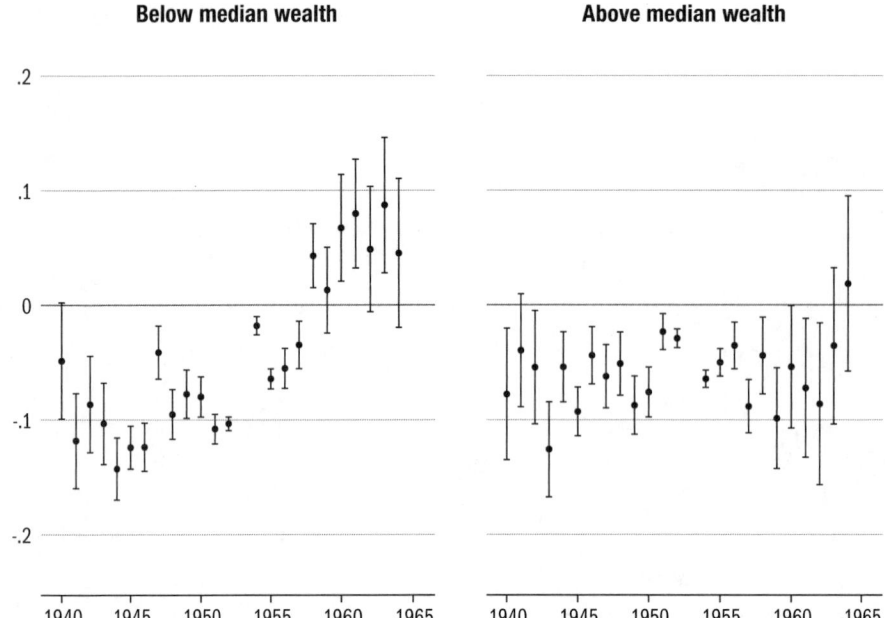

FIGURE 3.7 Cohort changes in the health deficit index by wealth among European men ages 50–64
Source: SHARE Waves 1–7.

health deficit index than the 1953 cohort. The difference between the 1941 and 1964 cohorts is statistically significant ($p < .05$).

When we stratify by sex and education (Figures 3.4 and 3.5), we see a clearly worsening trend in health among less-educated men. The trends are more ambiguous among the other sociodemographic groups, although there is some suggestion of a worsening trend among more-educated women.

In Figure 3.4, among women with less education, there is no clear trend across cohorts. However, among women with more education, more recent cohorts face somewhat higher health deficits than earlier cohorts, and the difference between the 1942 and 1963 cohorts is statistically significant ($p < .05$). As we would expect, women with more education tend to enjoy better health than those with less education: the mean health deficit index is 0.113 for women with more education and 0.14 for those with less education. Hence, health disparities between women of different educational backgrounds decreased because more-educated women's health declined.

Figure 3.5 suggests that less-educated men have become less healthy across cohorts, while there is no clear trend in health among men with more education. Compared to men born in 1953, those born in 1943 had a health deficit index 11.8 percent lower, while those born in 1964 had a health deficit index 8.3 percent higher, and the difference between the 1943 and 1964 cohorts is statistically significant ($p < .01$). The mean health deficit index is 0.085 for men with more education and 0.106 for those with less education. Hence, health disparities between men of different educational backgrounds increased because less-educated men's health declined.

When we stratify by sex and wealth, the clearest trend is the worsening health among less-wealthy men. In Figure 3.6, there is no noticeable relationship between the health deficit index and the year of birth among women with either higher or lower levels of education, and the differences between earlier and later cohorts are not statistically significant.

For men, Figure 3.7 suggests that there are neither statistically significant health improvements nor declines over time among wealthier men. Among men with less household wealth, however, health deficits increase sharply across cohorts. The mean health deficit index is 0.083 for wealthier men and 0.11 for those with less wealth. Thus, health disparities between more-wealthy and less-wealthy men increased across cohorts. The clear trend observed for less-wealthy men can be also seen when looking at the percentage changes. Men born in 1941 have 11.2 percent fewer deficits than those born in 1953, while those born in 1964 have 4.6 percent more deficits. This remarkable difference is statistically significant ($p < .001$).

From the perspective of work-related health conditions, it may matter which health deficits improved and which deteriorated across cohorts. We therefore divide the 51 health deficits into four categories: difficulties with activities of daily living (ADLs) or instrumental activities of daily living (IADLs) such as walking, sitting, or lifting; diagnosed illnesses; mental health; and other issues. We ran probit regressions of each binary health deficit item on age and cohort (entering age and cohort as continuous variables). Detailed results are relegated to the working paper version of this chapter (Börsch-Supan et al. 2020). A positive coefficient on the cohort variable indicates that the health deficit has become more prevalent for younger cohorts. We find that most of the measures of functional health (ADLs and IADLs, mobility) either improved or did not change. Among the diagnosed illnesses, heart attacks, cancers, and hypertension became less prevalent among younger cohorts; only lung diseases increased. However, mental health issues (including depression, trouble sleeping, irritability, and fatigue) became more prevalent among younger cohorts, as did symptoms that may be related to mental health problems (including falls, fear of falls, dizziness, and fainting).

The increase of mental health conditions among younger cohorts is a trend that is reflected in the reasons individuals apply for disability insurance. For instance, in Germany, mental health disorders, especially depression, make up the largest group of conditions among workers who receive disability insurance benefits (Deutsche Rentenversicherung 2019). People with generalized anxiety disorder (GAD) and major depressive episodes (MDE) have the lowest employment rates among French males (Barnay and Defebvre 2016). This parallels the United States, where anxiety and depression are major causes of work disability.

5. Employment Trends of the Middle-Aged in Europe

We next examine whether employment among middle-aged individuals has been falling in Europe, as it has been in the United States.

Employment of older individuals in Europe declined steadily throughout most of the twentieth century. In 1900, labor force participation at 65 was well above 50 percent in Britain, Germany, and France, while by 1995 it had declined to 4 percent in Germany, 5 percent in France, and 15 percent in Britain (Costa 1998; Coile, Milligan, and Wise 2017). One reason for this secular development was the introduction of public pension programs that permitted retirement without the risk of poverty. Starting in the 1970s, early retirement and disability programs in many European countries allowed even middle-aged workers to leave the labor force (Börsch-Supan and Schnabel 1998; Milligan and Wise 1999).

Employment trends among older adults changed direction in the late 1990s, as shown in Figure 3.8. Employment rates among men age 60 to 74 rose in all EU countries between the late 1990s and 2018, with growth rates varying from 6.4 percent in Sweden to 26.1 percent in the Netherlands (Coile, Milligan, and Wise 2017). Growth rates were almost twice as large for women. The main drivers were changes in the incentives to work longer, which significantly increased since the 1990s (Börsch-Supan and Coile Forthcoming) and the rise in female labor force participation at all ages.

In contrast to the United States, employment has risen among middle-aged adults in Europe in recent decades. Figure 3.8 shows the uninterrupted increase in European middle-aged employment (age 45–54) since the late 1980s for women and about 1996 for men. In Europe, employment rates among middle-aged and older individuals are also strongly positively correlated both across countries (Figure 3.9, $R^2 = 76\%$ for men and $R^2 = 54\%$ for women). Among middle-aged workers, the Great Recession did not make a substantial dent in employment, as it did among younger adults (age 25–34). As of the time of this writing, it is unclear whether the economic downturn following the COVID-19 pandemic will have a differential effect on the employment of younger and older individuals. Early in the pandemic, the employment effects were mild for all age groups since most European countries

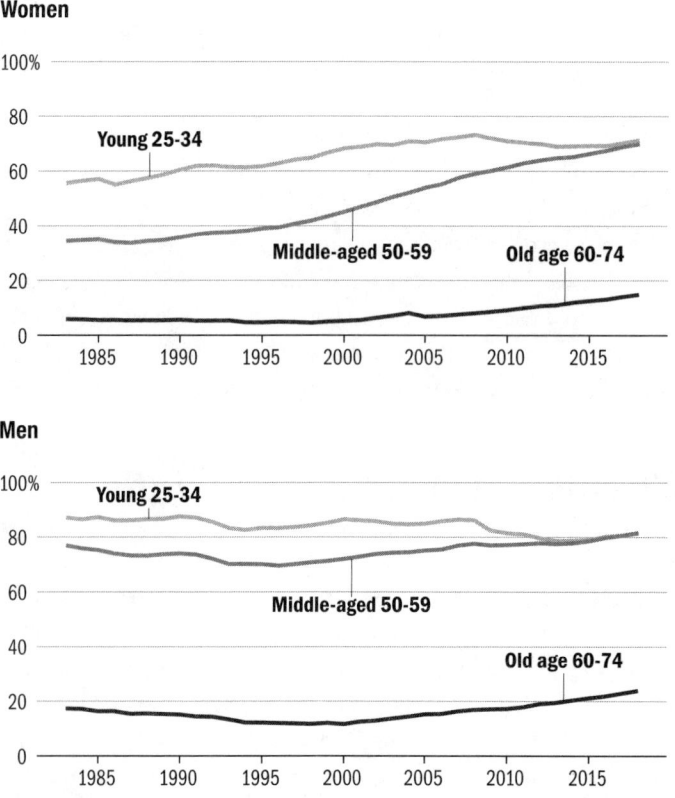

FIGURE 3.8 Employment rates by age in eight European countries, 1983–2018
Source: Eurostat, includes Belgium, Demark, France, Germany, Italy, Netherlands, Spain, and United Kingdom.

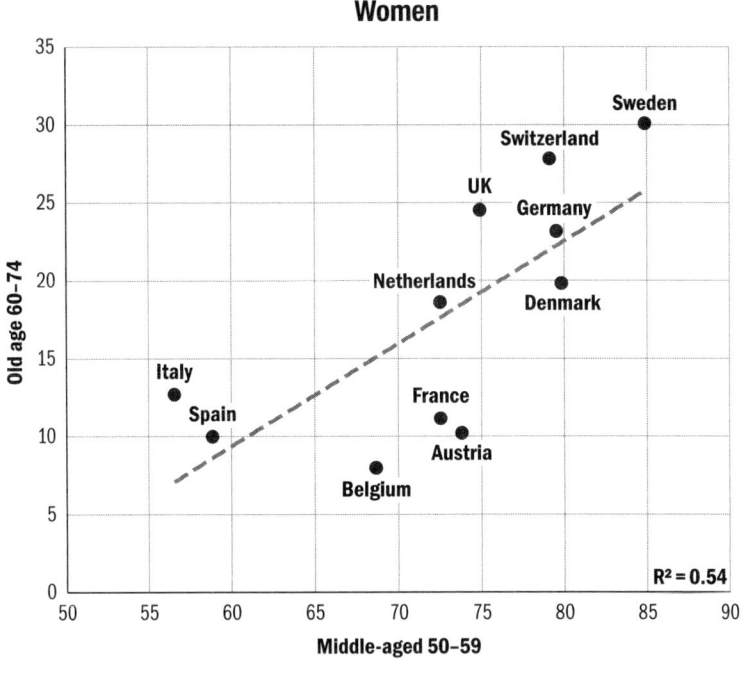

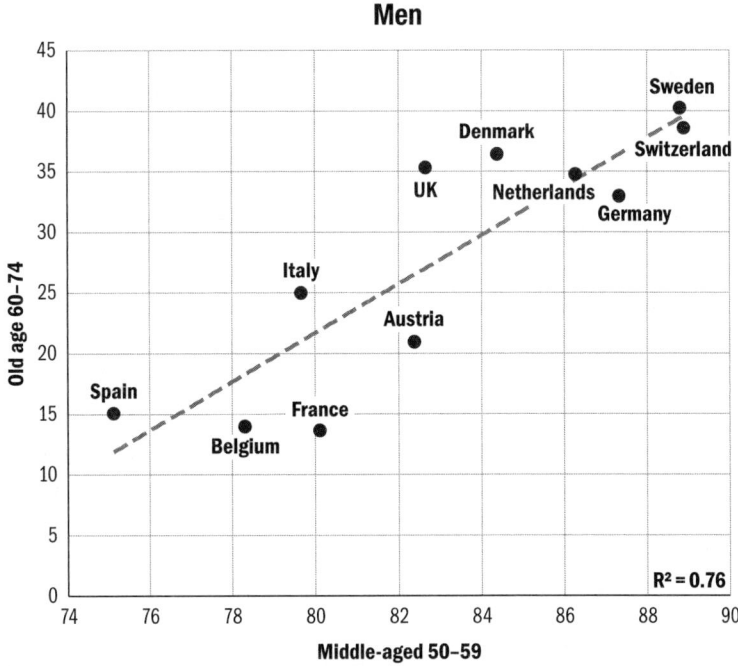

FIGURE 3.9 Employment rates of middle-aged vs. older individuals by country, 2018
Source: Eurostat.

made heavy use of "short-time employment aid" to prevent mass unemployment like that experienced in the United States.

To study the cohort tends in more detail and separately for each country, we converted the Eurostat employment data for each country into a pseudo-panel by age and cohort.

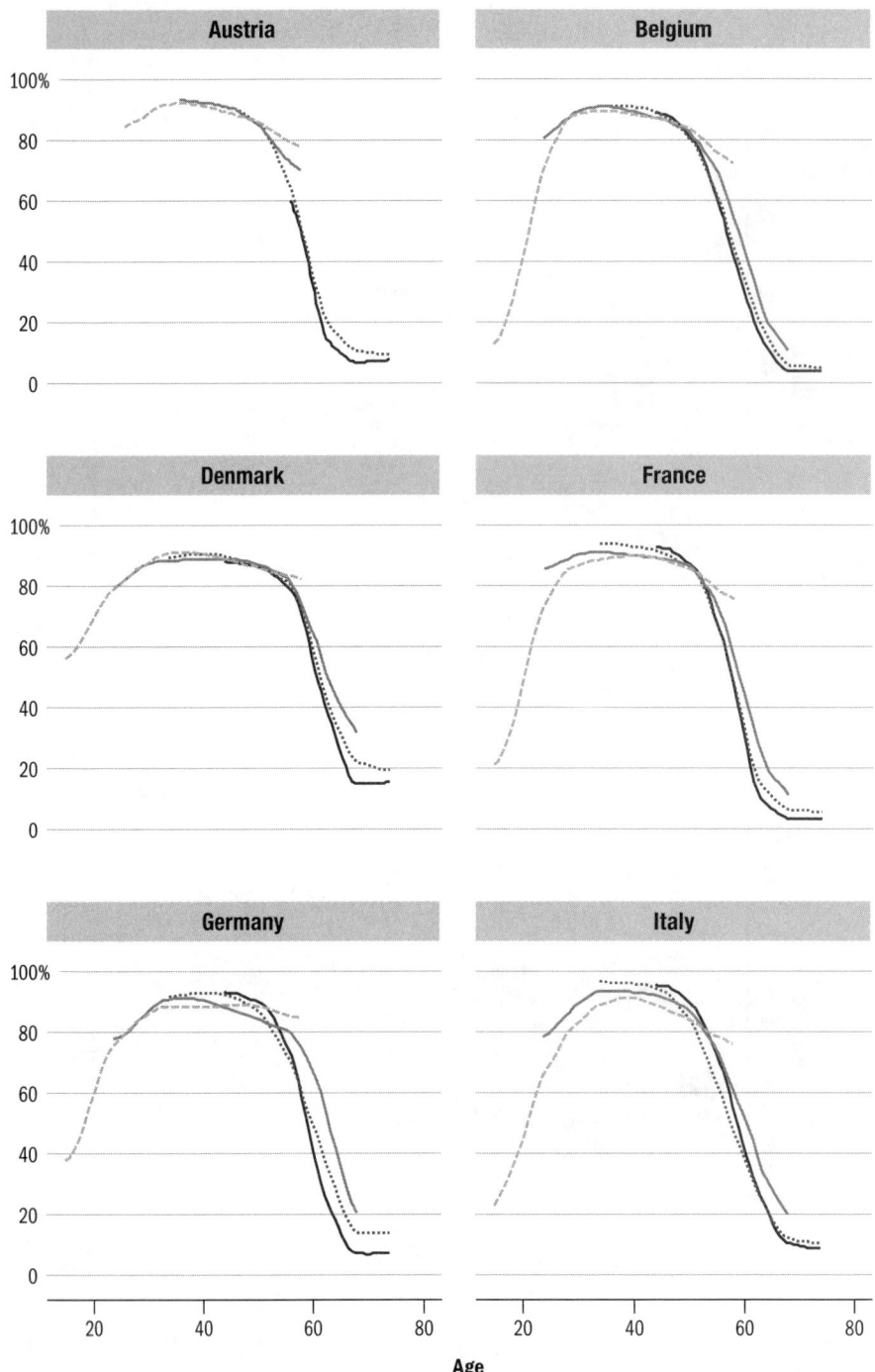

FIGURE 3.10 Employment rates by age and year of birth, men, ages 15–74
Source: Eurostat.

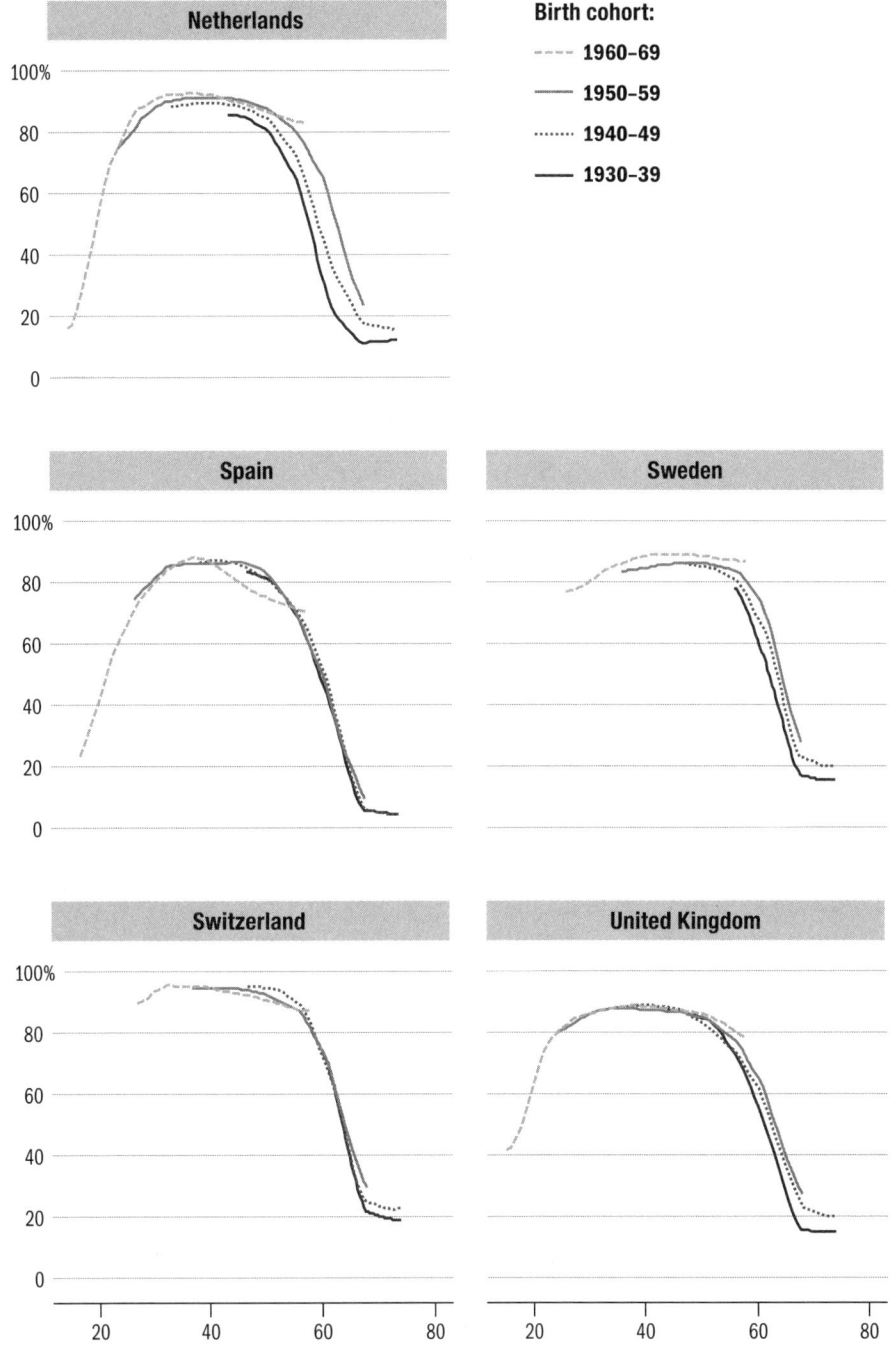

FIGURE 3.10 Continued

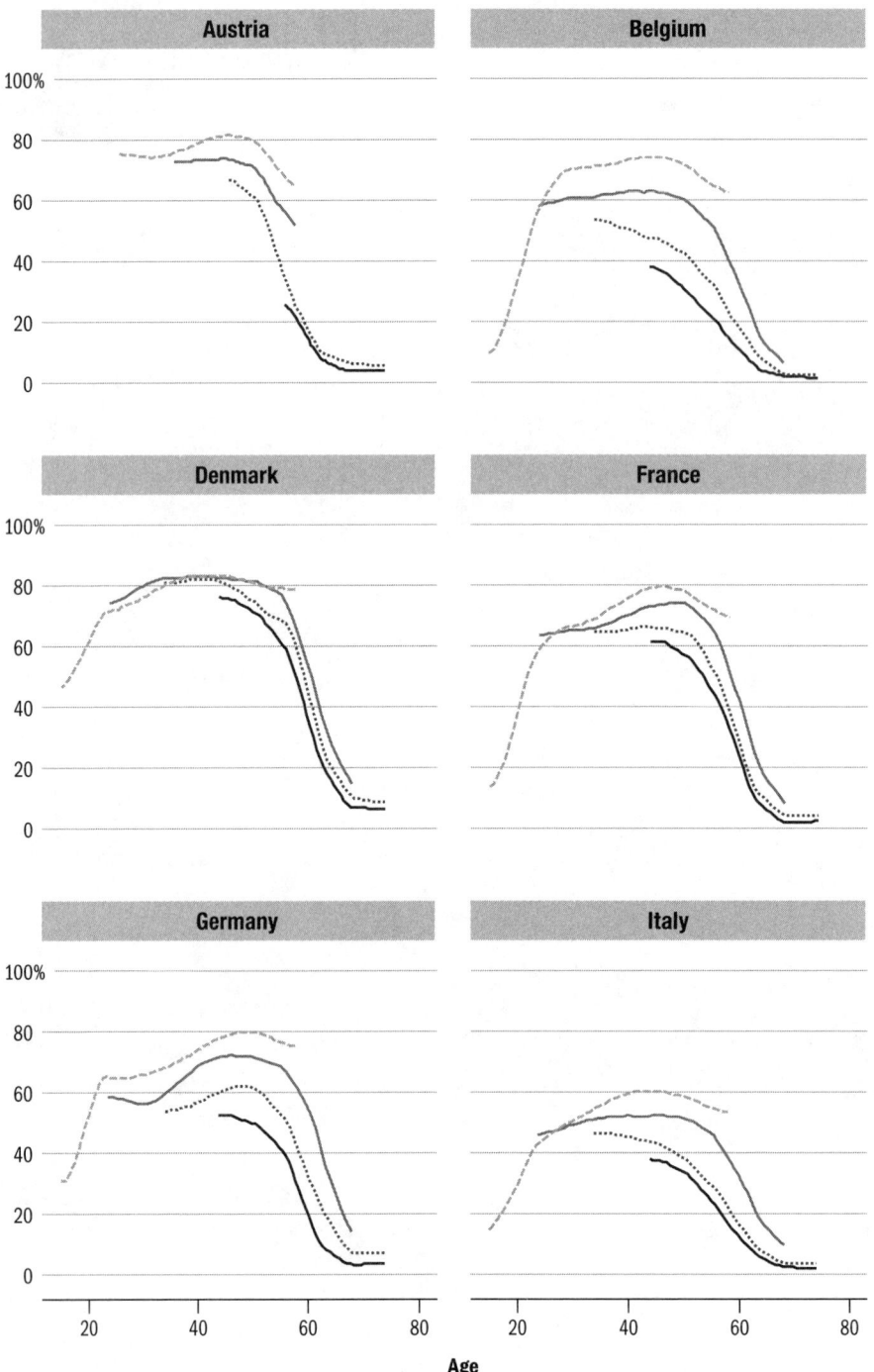

FIGURE 3.11 Employment rates by age and year of birth, women, ages 15–74
Source: Eurostat.

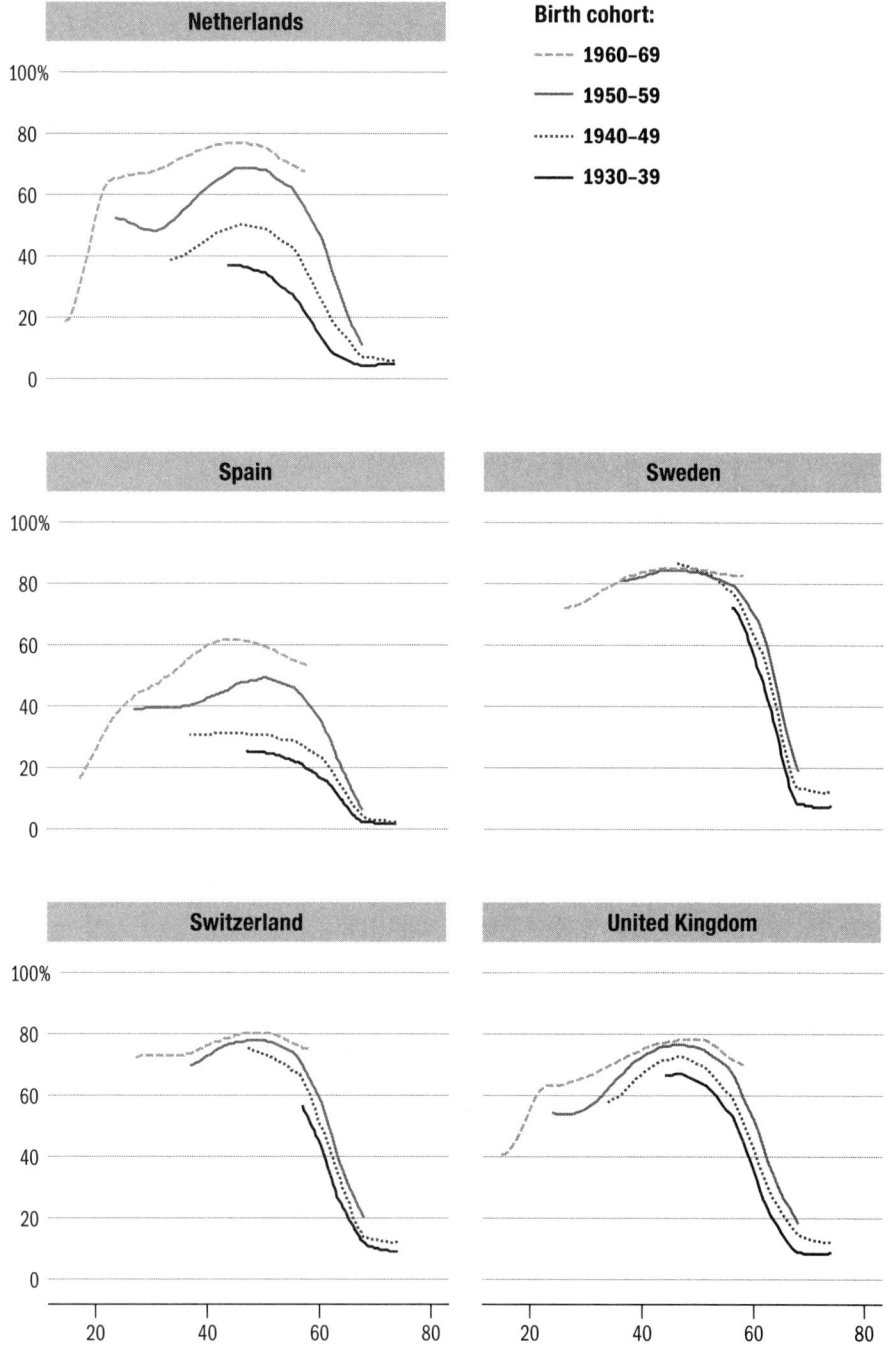

FIGURE 3.11 Continued

Figures 3.10 and 3.11 present the results. For men, none of the cohort differences is significant. If there is an observable trend at all, it is negative in Italy and Spain, probably reflecting the effects of the Great Recession, and positive in the Netherlands, Sweden, and the United Kingdom. For women, there are large cohort differences in almost every country, all pointing to consistently rising employment rates.

6. The Link between Health and Employment

Finally, we link both parts of the paper by discussing whether health trends have predictive value for labor force participation trends in Europe.

In the United States, middle-aged adults, especially those with lower levels of education and income, have experienced both worsening health and falling employment rates. These trends may bode ill for working longer as today's middle-aged American cohorts approach retirement age. In Europe, the situation is somewhat different. Although health has deteriorated markedly among middle-aged men in the bottom half of their country's education and wealth distributions (Section 3), employment rates have not fallen (Section 4). In Europe, there is at best a weak correlation between health and employment trends. This is in strong contrast to the findings for the United States in this volume.

That changes in population health have little predictive power for the development of employment over time in recent Europe is not a new insight. While health is a significant determinant of labor force participation in a cross-section within each country, health explains neither the cross-national differences in old-age labor force participation nor its trajectory within countries over time (Coile, Milligan, and Wise 2017). Similarly, across European countries, there is no correlation between early retirement and health, but there is a strong relation between early retirement and the generosity of disability benefits (Wise 2012). The U-shaped development of employment rates among middle-aged and older men visible in Figure 3.8 can be well explained by the change of economic incentives, particularly the financial incentives of public pension systems and the eligibility for disability insurance benefits (Börsch-Supan and Coile 2020, Forthcoming), but not by health and similar slow-moving determinants considered by Coile, Milligan, and Wise (2017).

There are numerous reasons for retiring early, and poor health may be one of them, but both our findings and those of other researchers suggest it cannot be the main reason. The country chapters in Wise (2017) use SHARE microdata comparable to those we use in Section 3 to investigate the relation between health and employment. The authors simulate employment rates at age 55 to 59 given the observed health conditions in the sample. In all countries, the actual share working is much smaller than predicted. In other words, the correlation between population health and labor force participation is at most weak among adults in their late 50s in Europe.

7. Conclusions

We used European microdata from SHARE to study the evolution of health and employment of middle-aged individuals over time. While health in Europe improved between 2004 and 2018 among older adults (age 65–85), we find the opposite among middle-aged adults (age 50–64). More recent cohorts of middle-aged individuals experienced a stalling health trend relative to earlier cohorts, and health has worsened among less-educated and less-wealthy men. In this respect, Europe seems to experience negative developments similar to those in the United States. Most of the health deficits that have increased during our sample period are mental health issues (such as depression, sleeping problems, irritability, and fatigue) or could be related to mental health problems (such as falls, fear of falls, dizziness, and faints). Life-threatening illnesses (such as heart attacks, cancers, and hypertension) have become less prevalent for younger cohorts.

In terms of employment, however, Europe is different than the United States. We do not find any sign that employment rates of middle-aged individuals are stagnating or falling. Rather, employment has increased steadily since the late 1990s.

We thus do not find any correlation between health and employment trends. This is in line with the work by the International Social Security Project (Wise 2012) which shows that, while bad health is a predictor for detachment from the labor force within each country, neither trends over time nor cross-national differences in labor force participation across Europe can be explained by differences in health.

It is too early to conclude what stalling health trends among middle-aged cohorts imply for old-age labor force participation in 10 or 15 years, that is, whether Europe will experience a revival of early retirement in the years to come as today's middle-aged cohorts reach retirement age. However, based on the evidence that health is not a main driver of employment rates at older ages in Europe, we argue that economic considerations, such as public pension and disability insurance policies, are likely to continue to have a greater influence on rates of early retirement. Relative to the United States, the health advantage of Europeans is still large, and the worsening health conditions among middle-aged Europeans are less severe than those of their U.S. peers.

Notes

1. This paper uses data from all SHARE Waves (DOIs: 10.6103/SHARE.w1.700 through 10.6103/SHARE.w7.700). The SHARE data collection has been primarily funded by the European Commission through the FP5 (QLK6-CT-2001-00360), FP6 (SHARE-I3: RII-CT-2006-062193, COMPARE: CIT5-CT-2005-028857, SHARELIFE: CIT4-CT-2006-028812), FP7 (SHARE-PREP: N°211909, SHARE-LEAP: °227822, SHARE M4: N°261982), and Horizon 2020 (SHARE-DEV3: GA N°676536, SERISS: GA N°654221) and by DG Employment, Social Affairs & Inclusion. Additional funding from the German Ministry of Education and Research, the Max Planck Society for the Advancement of Science, the U.S. National Institute on Aging (U01_AG09740-13S2, P01_AG005842, P01_AG08291, P30_AG12815, R21_AG025169, Y1-AG-4553-01, IAG_BSR06-11, OGHA_04-064, HHSN271201300071C) and from various national funding sources is gratefully acknowledged (see www.share-project.org).
2. See Abelianski and Strulik (2019) for a review of previous studies and their own study.

3. More precisely: the average effective labor market exit age. This OECD concept measures the average age at which individuals of a synthetic cohort leave the labor force, conditional that they have worked at age 40.
4. If there were missing values for some of the variables used, we reduced the denominator by the corresponding number of missing variables. The health index is thus always relative to the number of available health measures.
5. N corresponds to the number of observations from that country in our extended sample (i.e., women and men from age 50–85). Most of the empirical part refers to the subsample of middle-aged individuals (age 50–64) with size M.
6. These are asthma, arthritis, pain in back/knees/hips/joints, and walking speed.
7. Lasso penalizes the sum of the regression coefficients in absolute size by setting some of the coefficients to zero This reduces the variance of the predicted values (Tibshirani 1996; James et al. 2013). We choose the penalty parameter by cross-validation, that is, by using the penalty parameter with the largest out-of-sample prediction accuracy.
8. The multiple imputation algorithm uses the conditional specification approach of Van Buuren et al. (2006). We use the average calculated from all five available imputations. A detailed description of the imputation method in SHARE can be found in De Luca, Celidoni, and Trevisan (2015) and De Luca and Rossetti (2019). An evaluation of the method of multiple imputations in longitudinal wealth data can be found in Westermeier and Grabka (2016).
9. In order to smooth the lines, we ran regressions of health on age and included cohort-dummies and country-dummies. We then predicted the health deficit index for individuals and took the average over countries to present them together in one graph.
10. This assumption can be justified by the fact that population health is changing only very slowly except for pandemics or sudden jumps in medical technology. We subsume the slow and steady improvement of medical technology as a cohort effect.
11. Including individuals' age mean allows us to account for the correlation at the individual level of unobserved heterogeneity with time-changing covariates. The constant r refers to the fact that health deficits grow exponentially with age akin to the Gompertz law of mortality, where $exp(r)$ describes the base rate of growth.
12. We use 1941 rather than 1940, the first available cohort, because the coefficient on the 1940 cohort seems to be an outlier. We proceed like this whenever the coefficient of the youngest or oldest cohort is very different from the others.

References

Abeliansky, Ana Lucia, and Holger Strulik. 2019. "Long-Run Improvements in Human Health: Steady but Unequal." *The Journal of the Economics of Ageing* 14: 100189. https://doi.org/10.1016/j.jeoa.2019.01.003.

Avendano, Mauricio, M. Maria Glymour, James Banks, and Johan P. Mackenbach. 2009. "Health Disadvantage in US Adults Aged 50 to 74 Years: A Comparison of the Health of Rich and Poor Americans with That of Europeans." *American Journal of Public Health* 99 (3): 540–548. https://doi.org/10.2105/AJPH.2008.139469.

Avendano, Mauricio, and Ichiro Kawachi. 2014. "Why Do Americans Have Shorter Life Expectancy and Worse Health Than Do People in Other High-Income Countries?" *Annual Review of Public Health* 35 (1): 307–325. https://doi.org/10.1146/annurev-publhealth-032013-182411.

Barnay, Thomas, and d'Eric Defebvre. 2016. "Quelles Trajectoires De Santé Des Seniors Après La Retraite? L'effet Des Conditions De Travail Et De Vie." Paris Chaire Transitions démographiques, transitions économiques. http://tdte.fr/article/show/quelles-trajectoires-de-sante-des-seniors-apres-la-retraite-l-effet-des-conditions-de-travail-et-de-vie.

Bloom, David E., Alexander Khoury, and Ramnath Subbaraman. 2018. "The Promise and Peril of Universal Health Care." *Science* 361 (6404): eaat9644. https://doi.org/10.1126/science.aat9644.

Börsch-Supan, Axel, Martina Brandt, Christian Hunkler, Thorsten Kneip, Julie Korbmacher, Frederic Malter, Barbara Schaan, Stephanie Stuck, and Sabrina Zuber. 2013. "Data Resource Profile: The Survey of Health, Ageing and Retirement in Europe (SHARE)." *International Journal of Epidemiology* 42 (4): 992–1001. https://doi.org/10.1093/ije/dyt088.

Börsch-Supan, Axel, and Courtney C. Coile, eds. 2020. *Social Security Programs and Retirement around the World: Reforms and Retirement Incentives.* National Bureau of Economic Research Conference Report. Chicago: University of Chicago Press.

Börsch-Supan, Axel, and Courtney C. Coile, eds. Forthcoming. *Social Security and Retirement Programs Around the World: Microestimates of Reforms and Retirement Incentives.* Chicago: University of Chicago Press.

Börsch-Supan, Axel, Irene Ferrari, Giacomo Pasini, and Luca Salerno. 2020. "Is Working Longer in Jeopardy? Health and Labor Force Participation of Middle-Aged Europeans." *SSRN Electronic Journal.* MEA Discussion Paper No. 04-2020. https://doi.org/10.2139/ssrn.3586427.

Börsch-Supan, Axel, Irene Ferrari, and Luca Salerno. 2021. "Long-Run Health Trends in Europe." *The Journal of the Economics of Ageing* 18: 100303. https://doi.org/10.1016/j.jeoa.2020.100303.

Börsch-Supan, Axel, and Reinhold Schnabel. 1998. "Social Security and Declining Labor-Force Participation in Germany." *The American Economic Review* 88 (2): 173–178. https://www.jstor.org/stable/116914.

Coile, Courtney C., Kevin Milligan, and David A. Wise. 2017. "Introduction." In *Social Security Programs and Retirement around the World: The Capacity to Work at Older Ages*, edited by David A. Wise. National Bureau of Economic Research Conference Report. Chicago: University of Chicago Press, pp. 1–33. https://press.uchicago.edu/ucp/books/book/chicago/S/bo25527519.html.

Costa, Dora L. 1998. "The Evolution of Retirement: Summary of a Research Project." *The American Economic Review* 88 (2): 232–236. https://www.jstor.org/stable/116925.

De Luca, Giuseppe, Martina Celidoni, and Elisabetta Trevisan. 2015. "Item Nonresponse and Imputation Strategies in Share Wave 5." In *SHARE Wave 5: Innovations & Methodology*, edited by Frederic Malter and Axel Börsch-Supan, 85–100. Munich: Munich Center for the Economics of Ageing at the Max Planck Institute for Social Law and Social Policy. http://www.share-project.org/fileadmin/pdf_documentation/Method_vol5_31March2015.pdf.

De Luca, Giuseppe, and Claudio Rossetti. 2019. "Weights and Imputations." In *SHARE Wave 7 Methodology: Panel Innovations and Life Histories*, edited by Michael Bergmann, Annette Scherpenzeel, and Axel Börsch-Supan, 167–189. Munich: Munich Center for the Economics of Ageing at the Max Planck Institute for Social Law and Social Policy.

Deutsche Rentenversicherung. 2019. "Versichertenbericht 2019." Berlin. https://www.deutsche-rentenversicherung.de/SharedDocs/Downloads/DE/Statistiken-und-Berichte/Berichte/versichertenbericht_2019.html.

European Commission. 2018. "The 2018 Ageing Report: Economic & Budgetary Projections for the 28 EU Member States (2016–2070)." Institutional Paper 079. Luxembourg: Publications Office of the European Union. https://doi.org/10.2765/615631.

Gruber, Jonathan, and David A. Wise, eds. 2004. *Social Security Programs and Retirement Around the World: Micro-Estimation.* National Bureau of Economic Research Conference Report. Chicago: University of Chicago Press.

James, Gareth, Daniela Witten, Trevor Hastie, and Robert Tibshirani, eds. 2013. *An Introduction to Statistical Learning: With Applications in R.* Springer Texts in Statistics 103. New York: Springer. https://www.statlearning.com/.

Milligan, Kevin, and David A. Wise. 1999. *Social Security and Retirement around the World.* Edited by Jonathan Gruber and David A. Wise. National Bureau of Economic Research Conference Report. Chicago: University of Chicago Press. https://press.uchicago.edu/ucp/books/book/chicago/S/bo3632903.html.

Mitnitski, Arnold B., Alexander J. Mogilner, and Kenneth Rockwood. 2001. "Accumulation of Deficits as a Proxy Measure of Aging." *The Scientific World Journal* 1 (Article ID 321027): 323–336. https://doi.org/10.1100/tsw.2001.58.

OECD. 2019a. *Pensions at a Glance 2019: OECD and G20 Indicators.* Paris: OECD. https://doi.org/10.1787/b6d3dcfc-en.

OECD. 2019b. "Life Expectancy at Birth." http://doi.org/10.1787/27e0fc9d-en.

OECD. 2019c. *Society at a Glance 2019: OECD Social Indicators*. Paris: OECD. https:/doi.org/10.1787/soc_glance-2019-en.

Tibshirani, Robert. 1996. "Regression Shrinkage and Selection Via the Lasso." *Journal of the Royal Statistical Society: Series B (Methodological)* 58 (1): 267–288. https://doi.org/10.1111/j.2517-6161.1996.tb02080.x.

Van Buuren, S., J. P. L. Brand, C. G. M. Groothuis-Oudshoorn, and D. B. Rubin. 2006. "Fully Conditional Specification in Multivariate Imputation." *Journal of Statistical Computation and Simulation* 76 (12): 1049–1064. https://doi.org/10.1080/10629360600810434.

Westermeier, Christian, and Markus M. Grabka. 2016. "Longitudinal Wealth Data and Multiple Imputation: An Evaluation Study." *Survey Research Methods* 10 (3): 237–252. https://doi.org/10.18148/srm/2016.v10i3.6387.

Wise, David A., ed. 2012. *Social Security Programs and Retirement around the World: Historical Trends in Mortality and Health, Employment, and Disability Insurance Participation and Reforms*. National Bureau of Economic Research Conference Report. Chicago: University of Chicago Press. https://press.uchicago.edu/ucp/books/book/chicago/S/bo13948236.html.

Wise, David A., ed. 2017. *Social Security Programs and Retirement around the World: The Capacity to Work at Older Ages*. National Bureau of Economic Research Conference Report. Chicago: University of Chicago Press.

World Health Organization. 2019. "Global Health Estimates: Life Expectancy and Leading Causes of Death and Disability." https://www.who.int/data/gho/data/themes/mortality-and-global-health-estimates.

4

Planning for the "Expected Unexpected"

Work and Retirement in the United States after the COVID-19 Pandemic Shock

Richard B. Freeman

1. Introduction

The best-laid schemes o' Mice an' Men / Gang aft agley.
—Robert Burns, 1785

Most analyses of work and retirement and of the private and public investments that finance retirement are rooted in extrapolations of ongoing demographic, economic, and technological trends, and increasingly of predictions of global warming as well.

The main demographic trend affecting work and retirement in America is greater longevity. Longer lives flatten the age structure of the population and raise the number of retirees per worker,[1] threatening the financial viability of pay-as-you-go Social Security systems.

The main economic trend affecting work and retirement is the slow growth of real earnings, decoupled from productivity and accompanied by high and rising inequality. Continual indexing of Social Security can maintain retirees' living standards but requires higher taxes if earnings are relatively stagnant.

The main technological trend affecting work is the inexorable advance of artificial intelligence (AI) robotics that creates better machine substitutes for human workers and concurrent digitalization of work, which allows new software to spread automation from blue-collar to white-collar work, with the potential for increased productivity and earnings.

The main climate trend is global warming, which may create a tipping-point disaster that permanently alters the Earth's geology and ecosystems, endangering the "natural capital" of soil, air, water, and living things that helps create productive economies.

The unexpected COVID-19 disaster reminds us, however, that the world does not change solely through ongoing or expected trends that we can build into our future plans.

Richard B. Freeman, *Planning for the "Expected Unexpected"* In: *Overtime*. Edited by: Lisa F. Berkman and Beth C. Truesdale, Oxford University Press. © Oxford University Press 2022. DOI: 10.1093/oso/9780197512067.003.0005

The world also changes through unforeseeable shocks that upend the "best-laid schemes o' Mice an' Men."

Building on the impact of the COVID experience on the labor market and economy, I argue that realistic planning for the future of work must go beyond analyzing ways to respond to foreseeable demographic, economic, technological, and climate trends. Realistic planning must also assess ways to respond to unexpected shocks from the natural world, building the *expected unexpected* into our plans for the future, despite the uncertainty about the timing and form of those shocks.

My analysis begins by documenting the unexpected disaster that the pandemic wreaked on employment in March–April 2020, the partial recovery of employment through spring 2021, and government efforts to find the most efficacious path to a healthy recovery. I argue that the pandemic recession should be seen not as a once-in-a-century rare event to be put into history books per the 1918 flu pandemic, but as a wake-up call to a future of discontinuous shocks from the natural world, and to the need to plan for such shocks.

2. The COVID-19 Pandemic's Impact on Labor Markets

> Unimagined just a few short months ago, the ongoing COVID-19 pandemic has upended our entire planet, quickly challenging past assumptions and future certainties . . . possibly ushering in a new epoch of pandemics.
> —MORENS AND FAUCI (2020)

COVID-19 hit the United States in March 2020. The lesson from China and the European Union, which experienced COVID-19 cases first, was that quick decisive action was critical to control the virus. The United States responded slowly and indecisively. After denying the problem, President Trump favored, then opposed, public health recommendations, declared he was in charge, then abdicated responsibility to state governments, and blamed the Obama Administration, Democratic governors, World Health Organization, and China for the explosion of cases and deaths. After pushing for warp-speed development of a vaccine, the president switched gears to propose untested medicines, bleach, sunlight, and miracles as cures.

By the end of the first year of the pandemic, the United States accounted for 19.1 percent of the cumulated world deaths from COVID-19—4.4 times our share of the world's population,[2] despite being the world leader in health spending and biomedical research.[3]

To slow the spreading disease, states and localities introduced *nonpharmaceutical interventions*: wearing masks; social distancing; staying at home; self-quarantining; and isolating vulnerable groups. In March and April 2020, much of the country shut down businesses deemed not essential and introduced stay-at-home policies for residents. Combined with public fear of infections, this produced a discontinuous shrinkage of economic activity that showed up in the greatest loss of jobs in the shortest period in U.S. history. As illustrated in Figure 4.1, the ratio of employment to the civilian population aged 16+ fell by a bit under

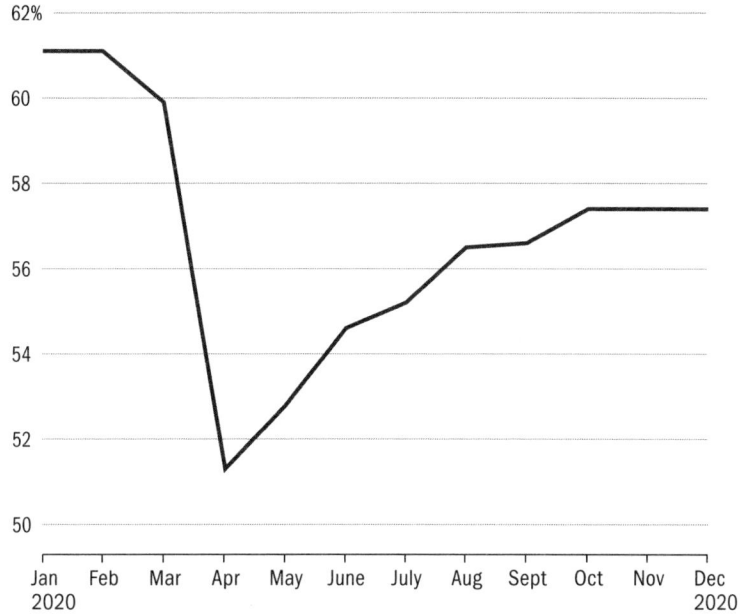

FIGURE 4.1 U.S. employment to population ratio in 2020
Source: U.S. Bureau of Labor Statistics, Employment-Population Ratio [EMRATIO], retrieved from FRED, Federal Reserve Bank of St. Louis; https://fred.stlouisfed.org/series/EMRATIO, May 24, 2021.

10 percentage points from 61.1 in prepandemic February 2020 to 51.3 in April 2020. The actual number employed (not seasonally adjusted) dropped by 24.7 million in the Current Population Survey of households (which includes the self-employed), and by 20.7 million in the Current Employment Statistics survey of establishments (limited to workers employed by firms).[4]

The loss of jobs was concentrated in a set of industries that normally experience only modest cyclic job losses. Table 4.1 shows the change in employment in major industries from pre-COVID-19 February 2020 to the trough of job loss in April 2020, and the recovery through September 2020 measured by employment relative to the February 2020 level. Ratios below 1.00 imply employment below February 2020 employment. One minus the ratio is the percentage change in employment from its prepandemic February level.

The pandemic recession job loss by industry diverges greatly from job loss in previous recessions. Employment nearly halved from February 2020 to April 2020 in traditionally acyclic leisure and hospitality industries while falling much less in traditionally highly cyclic manufacturing and construction. Job loss was minimal in finance, professional services, and the federal government, as digitalization of white-collar work and the Internet permitted widespread work from home.

The massive job loss in the pandemic added to an ongoing twenty-first-century trend in U.S. employment that has arguably received less attention than it deserves: the country's fall from being one of the top advanced countries in employment per person of working age to a much lower position in country rankings. In the 1990s, the United States was hailed for its great success in creating jobs. Many analysts credited its high employment rate to an

TABLE 4.1 Level of employment by industry relative to February 2020, ordered by loss of employment through September 2020

Industry	Feb. 2020, number employed (000s)	April 2020 employment relative to Feb. 2020	Sept. 2020 employment relative to Feb. 2020
Leisure and hospitality	16,264	0.52	0.81
Mining and logging	700	0.92	0.88
Education and health	24,711	0.89	0.89
Other services	5,889	0.78	0.92
Local government	14,844	0.95	0.92
Information	2881	0.90	0.93
Durable manufacturing	8,036	0.88	0.95
Professional and business services	21,246	0.94	0.95
Transportation and warehousing	5,610	0.89	0.96
Nondurable manufacturing	4,759	0.91	0.97
State government	5,105	1.01	0.98
Finance	8,797	0.97	0.99
Utilities	544	0.99	0.99
Construction	7,276	0.89	1.02
Federal government	2,848	1.01	1.10

Source: Data for industry from Current Employment Statistics. U.S. Bureau of Labor Statistics, https://www.bls.gov/webapps/legacy/cesbtab1.htm.

"employment at will" job system that allowed firms to change employment quickly with little role for the social dialogue among firms, unions, and governments that most advanced countries used to govern the labor market. At the end of the twentieth century, the United States' 0.74 employment rate of adults aged 15 to 64 led all advanced countries, except for lightly populated Norway (0.78) and Denmark (0.76) (OECD 2021).

However virtuous employment-at-will may be in booming times, the Great Recession and ensuing recovery revealed its deficiencies when the economy weakens. In the Great Recession, the United States lost a greater fraction of jobs than most other countries and had a relatively slow job recovery as well, which dropped the United States' employment rate to the middle of the pack, where it remained through the pandemic recession and recovery. In the first quarter of 2021, the United States' employment-to-population ratio was 0.69—five points lower than in 2000—behind the rates of Switzerland (0.80), Germany (0.76), Norway (0.74), Denmark (0.74), Sweden (0.76), Canada (0.72), the United Kingdom (0.75), Australia (0.74), and New Zealand (0.74), and marginally above Ireland (0.68) (OECD 2021).

The flip side of the huge job loss was the greatest increase in workers seeking unemployment insurance (UI) in U.S. history. As illustrated in Figure 4.2, the number of job losers making new UI claims jumped from less than 0.3 million in the week of March 14 to 3 million in the following week. Over the next two weeks, the number of new claimants jumped

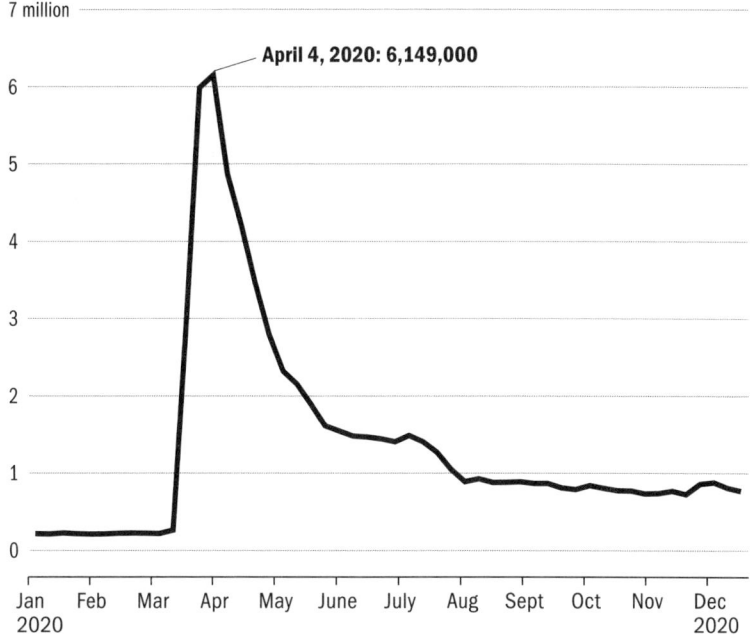

FIGURE 4.2 U.S. workers losing jobs who made an initial unemployment claim, 2020
Source: U.S. Employment and Training Administration, Initial Claims [ICSA], retrieved from FRED, Federal Reserve Bank of St. Louis; https://fred.stlouisfed.org/series/ICSA, May 24, 2021.

again to 6 million. Most firms told laid-off workers they would be recalled when the economy returned to normal, so that over three-quarters of job losers expected a quick recall with only a short need for UI support (Long and Guskin 2020).

With prescience that the pandemic recession created greater need for financial support for workers and their families than a normal recession, in March 2020 Congress enacted the Coronavirus Aid, Relief, and Economic Security Act (CARES), which boosted UI and gave cash payments to individuals and families.[5] Many states placed a moratorium on the eviction of tenants who could not pay rent during the crisis. This was followed by a federal moratorium (O'Connell 2021; USAGov 2021). Absent CARES, the concentration of job loss among lower-paid workers would have increased poverty and inequality. But the wages of many low-paid job losers were so low that the emergency support gave them higher incomes than their normal work, which reduced poverty and inequality, albeit briefly (Cortes and Forsythe 2020; Han, Meyer, and Sullivan 2020a; Parolin et al. 2020). Congress also enacted a Paycheck Protection Program to loan funds to small businesses for payroll and other costs, with unclear effects on jobs.

In May 2020, as the number of cases and deaths from COVID-19 fell, states and localities lifted or loosened stay-at-home policies and allowed more businesses to operate. Employment increased greatly through June and July. Many firms rehired their laid-off workers, which fed President Trump's "gut" feeling that the economy was heading for a rapid V-shaped recovery.[6] But the disruption of economic activity was too great to reverse direction and return to full employment within a few weeks. June and July's rapid job growth decelerated in fall 2020 while the numbers of jobless and those on UI remained high. In early October 2020, more than 9.6 million people received state UI payments—six to seven times as many as had been on UI a year earlier. Even as employment grew, layoffs continued at a high rate, producing roughly three-quarters of a million UI initial claimants per week in October.

Six months later, in April 2021, newspapers headlined the "good news" that initial claimants dropped to 613,000 per week (U.S. Department of Labor 2021). But the good news was relative to the April 2020 collapse. A year after the pandemic recession the April 2021 number of claimants was still three times the April 2019 number and close to the peak monthly number of claimants in the Great Recession.[7] Throughout summer and fall of 2021, the number of unemployment claimants greatly exceeded prepandemic levels and the employment-population ratio remained about 2 percentage points below its prepandemic level.

Employment did not bounce back as rapidly as it had fallen in part because economies are intertwined networks of firms and consumers in which activities in one sector or area propagate to other sectors and areas, albeit with lags. Firms that cut activities in April 2020 purchased fewer intermediate goods and services from suppliers, who in turn reduced purchases from their suppliers, and so on along the supply chain. Loss of sales forced suppliers and suppliers of suppliers to lay off workers. The job losers spent less on goods and services, shrinking economic activity further. Indoor venues where proximity of customers could readily spread the disease such as restaurants and sporting and artistic events suffered loss of revenues that forced many to close.

At the state level, the interconnection of economic activities across geographic areas spread the economic effects of the pandemic even to states with relatively few COVID-19 cases in the first wave of the pandemic. A case in point is Iowa, whose state government rejected policies to fight the disease by significantly restricting economic behavior. The state government refused to lock down businesses and forbid local governments from mandating masks.[8] Still Iowa suffered major job losses. In fall 2020, UI claims were three times their pre-COVID-19 levels, while employment was 4.1 percent lower in February 2021 than in February 2020 (Iowa Workforce Development 2021a, 2021b).

3. A New Inequality

The pandemic created a *new form of labor market inequality* that threatens to keep inequality in the United States high:[9] inequality by collar and place of work—between primarily white-collar workers able to work from home and blue-collar and service workers whose jobs required them being proximate to other workers or customers at a work site.

Table 4.2 documents the new form of inequality in terms of the proportion of workers who worked from home due to the pandemic, as given by the Current Population Survey from May 2020 through the following year, for the nine major nonagricultural occupational categories in U.S. statistics, and for farming, fishery, and forestry occupations as well.

TABLE 4.2 Level of employment by occupation relative to February 2020, ordered by percentage of workers working from home

Occupation (number employed in 000s)	Percent working from home because of COVID-19 (avg., May 2020–April 2021)	April 2020 employment relative to Feb. 2020	Sept. 2020 employment relative to Feb. 2020
WHITE-COLLAR OCCUPATIONS			
Management, business, and financial (27,926)	42.8	0.95	0.96
Professional (38,218)	41.9	0.91	0.94
Office and administrative support (16,225)	26.5	0.88	0.96
Sales (15,069)	18.8	0.81	0.84
BLUE-COLLAR AND SERVICE OCCUPATIONS			
Installation, maintenance, and repair (4,922)	4.8	0.85	0.95
Service (26,223)	4.6	0.69	0.89
Production (8,344)	4.3	0.76	0.92
Construction and extraction (8,154)	3.1	0.80	0.99
Transportation and material moving (11,793)	2.6	0.79	0.89
Farming, fishery, and forestry (1,144)	1.6	0.94	0.84

Source: Percent of employed working from home: Gould and Kandra (2021), Figure D. Employment relative to Feb. 2020: U.S. Bureau of Labor Statistics, Employment by occupation, from Current Population Survey, https://www.bls.gov/webapps/legacy/cpsatab13.htm.

Column 1 shows the proportion of employed workers who reported that *they worked from home for pay as a result of the pandemic* as a 12-month average between May 2020 and April 2021. The work-from-home figures are based on questions that the Bureau of Labor Statistics added to the Current Population Survey (CPS) on the impact of the pandemic on work from home. Over the entire period, 43 percent of employed managers, 42 percent of professionals, 27 percent of office and administrative support, and 19 percent of sales workers reported that they were working from home compared to less than 5 percent of workers in other primarily blue-collar and service occupations.

Column 2 records employment at the bottom of the recession in April 2020 relative to the February 2020 prepandemic baseline. It shows a massive loss of jobs in blue-collar and service occupations with minimal possibility to work-from-home compared to minimal job losses in the white-collar occupations where employees could shift to work from home. Finally, Column 3 shows employment in September 2020, after the summer recovery, relative to the February prepandemic baseline. Despite a large jump in blue-collar and service occupation jobs in June, July, and August, the ratios of employment in those occupations relative to the February baseline remained below the comparable ratios for the white-collar jobs.

To what extent, if at all, is the shift of work from the workplace to homes likely to persist? Before the pandemic, fewer than one in ten workers worked from home, so the pandemic increased work from home by over three-fold. In the recovery from May

2020 to April 2021, the proportion of employed workers reporting working from home halved from 36 percent (May) to 18 percent (April), suggesting that absent another epidemic outbreak, any "new normal" would be below the May peak but still noticeably above the 10 percent prepandemic level (Gould and Kandra 2021). If the rate of decline in the number of workers reporting working from home due to the pandemic continues for another two to three years, at (say) 10 percent of actual employment, and the 10 percent or so working from home for reasons other than the pandemic remains roughly stable, on the order of one-fifth of the workforce might work from home in the future. Indicative of the potential future response of major firms to work from home, in 2021 the CEO of IBM declared a long-term strategy of "hybrid remote work for most employees post the pandemic" (Sonnemaker 2021)—a strategy which reversed IBM's 2017 rejection of work from home, which itself ended nearly 20 years of IBM using work from home to save money on office space and commuting time (Kessler 2017).

4. Education, Gender, Race/Ethnicity, and Age: Demographics of Pandemic Job Loss and Recovery

Because the demographic characteristics of workers vary across occupations, the differing rates of pandemic job losses and recovery job gains among occupations impacted workers differently by demography. Table 4.3 shows the monthly employment pattern of workers by education, gender, race/ethnicity, and age from February 2020 to the March and April 2020 loss of jobs through the summer-fall recovery—all measured relative to the February base.

Job loss by education was qualitatively similar to job losses in previous recessions, with persons with the least education having the biggest percentage loss of employment and those with bachelor's degrees or more having the smallest percentage job loss. From February to April 2020, employment dropped by 21 percent for workers with less than four years of high school, by 13 percent for high school graduates, and by 15 percent for persons with some college education, compared to a 7 percent drop for workers with a bachelor's degree or more. The data for the summer-fall recovery show commensurately greater job gains for the biggest job-losing groups, but with none of the demographic groups fully regaining February employment. The main reason for the variation in job losses was the concentration of the less educated in blue-collar and service jobs with little option for work from home compared to the concentration of bachelor's degree or higher workers in management and professional jobs, where work from home substituted for working in an office.

Job loss by gender, by contrast, diverged from that in previous recessions. In most recessions, men experience greater job loss than women because men are more likely than women to work in highly cyclic industries such as manufacturing and construction. In the February to April pandemic recession, employment fell more for women (18 percent) than for men (12 percent), due primarily to the concentration of women in service-sector and retail occupations and industries that require workers to interact with other workers and

TABLE 4.3 Level of employment relative to February 2020 by demographic group

	Feb. 2020, number employed (000s)	\multicolumn{6}{c}{Employment compared to Feb. 2020}
		March	April	May	June	July	Aug.
\multicolumn{8}{c}{EDUCATION*}
Less than high school	8,670	0.97	0.79	0.79	0.83	0.79	0.87
High school diploma	34,793	0.96	0.87	0.83	0.88	0.88	0.89
Some college	36,061	0.99	0.85	0.88	0.88	0.85	0.92
Bachelor's degree or more	59,411	1.00	0.93	0.94	0.96	0.96	0.98
\multicolumn{8}{c}{GENDER}
Male	83,047	0.98	0.88	0.89	0.89	0.93	0.95
Female	74,970	0.98	0.82	0.85	0.92	0.93	0.91
\multicolumn{8}{c}{RACE/ETHNICITY}
White	121,929	0.99	0.85	0.88	0.92	0.93	0.94
Black	19,530	0.97	0.83	0.85	0.87	0.88	0.90
Hispanic	28,311	0.97	0.80	0.82	0.88	0.88	0.91
Asian	18,327	0.97	0.82	0.82	0.85	0.89	0.91
\multicolumn{8}{c}{AGE}
16–19	5,012	0.96	0.63	0.75	0.97	1.07	1.01
20–24	14,069	0.94	0.71	0.75	0.83	0.86	0.89
25–54	101,152	0.99	0.87	0.89	0.91	0.91	0.93
55 and older	37,784	0.98	0.85	0.87	0.90	0.91	0.93
65 and older	10,847	0.94	0.78	0.81	0.85	0.94	0.89

* For persons aged 25 and older.

Source: U.S. Bureau of Labor Statistics, The employment situation of the population, from Historical Data Table A-9, Selected Employment Indicators, https://www.bls.gov/webapps/legacy/cpsatab9.htm.

The 65 and older figures are the sum of those employed with a disability and with no disability, U.S. Bureau of Labor Statistics, Employed—With No Disability, 65 Years and over, and Employed—With a Disability, 65 Years and over [LNU02075379 and LNU02075600], retrieved from FRED, Federal Reserve Bank of St. Louis; https://fred.stlouisfed.org/series/LNU02075379 and https://fred.stlouisfed.org/series/LNU02075600, May 24, 2021.

customers, compared to men working in managerial and professional jobs, where digitalization of work and internet connections allowed for extensive work from home.

The employment of female workers was also impacted by the increase in demand for household production activities stemming from the closure of schools and daycare centers. The historic role of women in caring for children placed a dual demand on their time that pulled some working mothers from the labor force and reduced the productivity of many others, who kept working but had to care for their children while working from home.[10] In the recovery many faced difficult work-life balance decisions when firms reopened offices and sought to restore traditional work times.

The last section in Table 4.3 distinguishes people by age. In the first months of the pandemic, COVID-19 endangered the health of older people the most. The likelihood of being infected, sick, or dying rose monotonically with age. A jarring number of deaths occurred in nursing homes, which were unprepared for the pandemic. By fall 2020, however, the infection rate among older adults fell below the average (Monod et al. 2021), in large part because the medical system, the elderly and their families, and nursing homes had adopted nonpharmaceutical interventions that kept the elderly from interacting with persons with the disease. If they got the disease, however, older persons still had high mortality.

Job losses, by contrast, were largest for younger workers. This happened in part because most firms use "last in, first out" layoff practices, which protect workers with seniority over recent hires, who tend to be disproportionately young. This was also due in part because the collapse of new hires in the pandemic reduced employment for the young, as those graduating high school and college could not find their first job as had earlier cohorts of new graduates. To add to the employment problem of younger persons, jobs which normally hire young workers offer relatively few opportunities to work from home (Chen and Munnell 2020). From February 2020 to April 2020, employment fell by 37 percent for persons aged 16–19 and 29 percent for those aged 20–24 compared to 13 percent for workers 25–54 and 15 percent for those aged 55 and older. Among older workers, however, those aged 65 and over lost jobs more rapidly than those 25–54, possibly because they chose early retirement in a collapsing job market.

In the fall recovery the youngest had the largest gains in employment, while older workers had smaller gains. This fits with past experience. Once unemployed, workers over 65 tend to take more time to find new employment than younger workers (Neumark, Burn, and Button 2019). In the Great Recession, job losers aged 55 to 64 were the group most likely to exit the labor force, probably via early retirement (Farber 2017). Retirements increased during the pandemic as well (Kolko 2021), reducing the number of older workers.

Finally, the concentration of job losses by occupation, industry, and demography combined to produce greater job losses among lower-paid than higher-paid workers, which would have devastated their incomes absent the emergency government programs. Indeed, the CARES unemployment benefits offset these losses from March 2020 to July 2020 enough to reduce poverty a bit. When a politically divided Congress chose not to extend the benefits after July, however, the lower-paid workers suffered and the rate of poverty rose (Han, Meyer, and Sullivan 2020b).[11]

5. Recovery, Recovery, My ~~Kingdom~~ Presidency for a Rapid Recovery

In summer 2020, rapid return to full employment seemed unlikely. The Congressional Budget Office's Economic Forecast expected that unemployment would not fall to 5 percent or below until approximately 2027 and that real GDP would not regain its pre-COVID-19-level per capita until 2023 (CBO, July 2020).[12] Foroni, Marcellino, and Stevanović's (2020) review of other forecasting and now-casting models showed that they concurred that the country faced a slow, painful recovery. None of these models built into their forecasts the rapid development of vaccines nor the possibility of further positive or negative shocks to the economy. All were influenced by the slow recovery from the Great Recession and the inability of the Democrats and Republicans to come together on an aggressive recovery policy.

What a difference an election can make! The 2020 elections changed the presidency and control of the Senate and opened the door to more activist economic policies that could speed up the recovery. Newly elected President Biden proposed a $1.9 trillion American Rescue Plan Act (ARPA) of short-run direct relief to families and workers still impacted by the COVID-19 crisis. Like the CARES bill which Congress supported almost unanimously, ARPA sought to maintain living standards for primarily low-income groups. In contrast to CARES, however, ARPA was passed in March 2021 by Democratic legislators over unanimous Republican opposition. Taking account of the passage of ARPA, the likely vaccination of millions in spring and summer 2021 and the possibility that Congress would support some form of long-term investment program on infrastructure, the CBO changed its projections. The 2021 CBO projection anticipated the unemployment rate dropping to 5.0 percent in 2022—five years *earlier* than its 2020 projection—and remaining below 5 percent thereafter; and real GDP per capita regaining its prepandemic level by the end of 2021 (CBO, July 2021, table 2).

Even a strong recovery, however, would leave serious economic problems: a labor participation rate below its pre-COVID level, reflecting the impact of the disease on the longer-term health of those afflicted, and changed attitudes toward work and looking for work. The Bureau of Labor Statistics reported in fall of 2021 that 7.9 percent of people who were not in the labor force but said that they wanted to work were prevented from looking for a job because of the COVID-19 pandemic (U.S. Bureau of Labor Statistics 2021). These COVID-19-related problems combined with the trend in the ratio of workers to retirees raised new questions about the viability of the Social Security system and of extant work-longer/retire-later policies to maintain the system.

6. Social Security and Work-Longer/Retire-Later Policies

Social Security is the centerpiece of U.S. retirement. About 90 percent of retirees receive Social Security, and 57 percent of retirees receiving Social Security rely on it as their major source of retirement income (Brenan 2019). As a tool for reducing poverty, Social Security has been extraordinarily successful, reducing elderly poverty to the lowest rate among age groups (Engelhardt and Gruber 2004; Li and Dalaker 2021, figure 4.2).

Social Security is a pay-as-you-go intergenerational transfer system in which retiree benefits come largely from the tax payments of existing workers. The viability of the system is thus highly dependent on intergenerational demographic and economic factors. When Social Security gains more in taxes than it pays out, the money is invested in interest-bearing Treasury securities held by the Social Security Trust Fund. When the current workforce pays less in Social Security taxes than the benefits promised to retirees, Social Security taps the Fund to meet the shortfall. From the latter part of the twentieth century to 2020, population aging forced Social Security to withdraw money from the Fund to make payments to existing retirees. Prior to the pandemic the rate of withdrawal was sufficiently large that the agency expected the Fund to deplete entirely by 2035.

Three policy tools exist to deal with the problems of funding retirement in an aging population. The first is to tax existing workers to pay for the increasing number of aged retirees. The second is to reduce the benefits going to retirees. The third and generally preferred way involves policies that encourage or force older workers to work longer and retire later. People who work longer and retire later pay more tax money into Social Security funds and take less money out (OECD 2019). Someone who works an additional five years will, for example, pay Social Security taxes into the Social Security Trust Fund for those five years, and, assuming a given life span, take five years less of benefits. The United States and other governments have accordingly adopted various policies to get older persons to work more before retiring, including to work partially after claiming Social Security (Farrell 2019).[13] To deal with the depleting fund in the 1980s Congress legislated gradual increases in the full retirement age for persons born in and after 1960 from age 65 to 67 and smaller increases for persons born earlier. Incentivized to work two or so extra years, Americans aged 55 and older increased their labor participation by about 10 percentage points from 1989 to 2018 (Baily and Harris 2019). This raised the average age of retirement from 64.2 to 67.9 years for men and from 63.4 to 66.5 years for women between 2003 and 2018 (OECD n.d.). Partial work has become common as well. Upward of 45 percent of Social Security recipient "units" (individuals and married couples) aged 62–64 reported that earnings from employment constituted nearly one-fourth of their total income (Morrissey 2011). Pfau, Tomlinson, and Vernon (2019) simulated the best strategy for older workers to maximize their wealth and found that most can improve their well-being by delaying retirement and working smartly within the rules of the Social Security earnings test.

A working-longer/retiring-later strategy succeeds, however, only if older workers can maintain employment. In the Great Recession and ensuing sluggish recovery, job-related problems impelled many workers to choose early retirement. Slightly over half of the retirees who retired early reported doing so because they had employment-related problems: job loss (23 percent), organizational changes at their place of employment (15 percent), or unhappiness with their job (13 percent). An additional 9 percent said they retired due to a retirement incentive or buyout. Once unemployed, moreover, older workers are more likely to stay in the labor force than other unemployed workers, seemingly to stave off early retirement (Burtless 2016).

During the pandemic 15 percent of employers reported increases in the number of employees withdrawing from their defined contribution plans and 12 percent reported an increase in employees taking plan loans.[14] These behaviors could push the workers to work longer and delay retirement to rebuild their pension wealth if the recovery continues strong and employees can readily find jobs. The strong recovery notwithstanding, however, the U.S. Treasury predicted in 2021 that the Social Security Trust Fund will run out of money by 2033 – two years earlier than expected before the pandemic hit. This prediction is based not only on the shrinkage of the labor force and early retirements but also on an expected 1 percent slower growth of productivity per year. Absent improved productivity and employment the United States will likely face retirement funding problems in little over a decade (Franck 2021), even without any future pandemic shock or other adverse event.

7. Conclusion: Planning Work and Retirement for Future Unexpected Shocks

Plans are worthless, but planning is everything.
—Dwight D. Eisenhower, quoting an old Army aphorism

Prior to COVID-19, future-of-work analyses focused on extrapolations of demographic, economic, and technological trends, and increasingly on projections of global warming as well (ILO 2018). Analyzing the effects of expected developments on work and retirement is a sine qua non for planning for the future. But the impact of COVID-19 on work shows that realistic planning must also take into account potential unexpected shocks from the natural world (or elsewhere) that can "gang aft agley" our "best-laid schemes."

How can society plan for unexpected future shocks? If something is unexpected, doesn't that mean it comes as a surprise for which one cannot by definition plan?

The answer to this seeming conundrum lies in the distinction between *unexpected unexpected* events and *expected unexpected* events. It is near impossible to plan for the unexpected unexpected since no one has an inkling of its nature, timing, whatever. But it is possible to plan for expected unexpected shocks by analyzing the ways a "shock" may come and impact work and retirement, even when the timing and detailed characteristics of the shock are unpredictable.

The insurance industry, indeed, is based on the expected unexpected—the car crash, fire, surprise illness—that has some probability of occurring with a range of destructive effects based on earlier similar events. Around the world, defense and security agencies plan for unexpected attacks which may or may not occur in any given period. They try to figure out the capability of possible enemies and ways to respond to possible attacks through war game scenarios and exercises. The expected unexpected may take a different form than the scenarios planned, but per the Eisenhower quote, the exercise of planning may itself improve the ability to deal with unexpected twists and turns.

The COVID-19 "attack" on humanity that upended economies and employment offers an example of an expected unexpected shock for which analysts of work and retirement (and in most other areas of social and economic decision-making) did not plan. We have built up a stock of knowledge about the COVID-19 virus and about ways to protect persons against it. We know that the virus will mutate quickly and suspect that a successful mutant form will be less harmful to us than the forms that surfaced in 2020–2021, but we cannot be sure that a more harmful variant is not coming down the pike. Similarly, per Fauci and Morens's coming "new epoch of pandemics," we can expect attacks from other viruses,[15] though we have little clue as to which virus will cause a crisis and when that would be. The story for contagious diseases from bacteria is the same. Bacterial antibiotic resistance is growing, but we cannot predict which bacteria will mutate enough to negate our current medicines nor when such a mutation will occur.

Although the science is different, we face a similar problem in the battle against global warming. Our knowledge of climate change is limited to knowing that we will face unexpected shocks of some sort from continued warming, without any surety of the specifics of the shocks. There is growing evidence that we should expect more extreme weather events—fire, floods, storms—and growing concerns that we may face a potential turning point disaster to the environment that will degrade natural capital and thus our productive ability. But we have no reliable prediction of the specifics. In the economic world, financial crises are the archetypal expected unexpected disaster, as the 2007 implosion of Wall Street reminded us.

What lessons can we draw from the unexpected COVID-19 shock to the job market and economy for planning for the future of work and retirement? What types of policies might we study further as part of our planning process?

I draw four interrelated lessons from the pandemic and our responses to it.

The first lesson is that it almost surely will pay off for the United States and other countries to improve the knowledge base of what expected unexpected shocks can do to us. Cutler and Summers (2020) estimated that U.S. losses from the pandemic in lives, GDP, and damage to health were on the order of $16.9 trillion.[16] This is an amount that easily justifies sizable increases in R&D spending to study the shocks we may face in the future and to plan to deal with those shocks. While positive returns from greater R&D (itself an investment in an expected unexpected) cannot be guaranteed, high stakes justify more spending than low stakes even if only a small share of projects yield fruit. And it is reasonable to expect positive benefits from more research spending on COVID-19, and by extension other possible unexpected disasters. The avalanche of COVID-19 studies that the disease unleashed (Else 2020) shows that biological and medical scientists can shift their research programs quickly to learn about a new enemy. The rapid development of vaccines, which culminated a "25-year journey" working out a messenger RNA strategy (Collins 2021) and "extraordinary multidisciplinary effort" (Fauci 2021) supports greater R&D to reduce the possible losses from the next contagious disease shock, be it viral or bacterial.

The second lesson is that increased spending should extend to social and behavioral sciences. Part of the huge loss in the pandemic was due to socially deleterious human behavior – persons unwilling to undertake nonpharmaceutical interventions such as wearing a mask, social distancing, and so on, or to take protective vaccines. Unwillingness to follow the science may be greater in the United States than in other countries, but opposition to vaccines and mask-wearing in many other countries suggests that many people distrust the expertise of scientists and public health officials around the world, weakening our ability to fight the virus.[17] Accordingly, part of any increase in R&D budgets should go to studies of ways to convince people to follow the science, ranging from social psychology analyses of how "gut intuitions" and moral values influence responses to expert advice (Tavernise 2021), to economic studies of responses to monetary and nonmonetary incentives, to sociology studies of the transmission of information and imitation in networks, to education studies of science teaching, and to marketing/communication studies of consumers' responses to advertising.

The third lesson is that we need to improve the efficacy of social institutions and organizations designed to protect us in several areas. On health, the COVID Tracking Project estimated that over 34 percent of all U.S. COVID-19 deaths occurred among the less than 1 percent of the population in nursing homes and other long-term-care facilities (Curiskis et al. 2021). Early in the COVID-19 outbreak the General Accountability Office (GAO) asked the Department of Health and Human Services to "develop a strategy to capture more complete COVID-19 data in nursing homes retroactively back to January 1, 2020" (Dicken 2021), which at a minimum would prepare those institutions to react more quickly than in 2020. In economic policy, the failure of Florida's unemployment insurance computer system to get money to claimants during the pandemic was an institutional failure of the first order, which the Governor claimed was due to his predecessor rigging the UI system with pointless roadblocks so that people would give up trying to get their money (Wamsley 2020).[18] Research into the effectiveness of all types of organizations responsible for others—schools, daycares, nursing homes, health care systems, and local and state government emergency help agencies—in the COVID-19 crisis should concentrate on helping them respond better to the next crisis shock, whatever form it takes.

A November 2021 editorial in *Science* (Proctor and Geng 2021) captures this lesson succinctly: "COVID-19 has shown the world that 'knowing what to do' does not ensure 'doing what we know.' It demonstrates that intervention discovery is the start, not the end, of the scientific journey." The editorial calls for the National Institutes of Health (NIH) to create an office of implementation research, but as the problem goes beyond the biomedical area that is NIH's forte, any such program should involve more government agencies and publicly concerned groups.

My fourth lesson is that planning for social problems likely to be impacted by future expected unexpected shocks, such as work and retirement, needs greater use of two research tools: "societal exercises" to test the effectiveness of organizations to respond to crisis; and computer simulations of policies or mixes of policies that can only be examined online. Israel's November 11, 2021, nationwide drill / war game to prepare for the next possible battle against COVID-19 exemplifies what can be done in societal exercises to prepare for an expected unexpected disaster of a particular kind. Recognizing the value in closely monitoring the situation and preparing for a worst-case scenario, Israel posited an attack by "omega," a more lethal coronavirus mutant, and tested the response of organizations and people to policy interventions ranging from monitoring omega's spread, to lockdowns that would slow its spread, to providing economic support for affected workers and their families (Ackerman 2021). Facing an entirely different expected unexpected shock, NASA's Jet Propulsion Lab Center for Near Earth Objects tested the response of its decision-makers to a hypothetical asteroid crashing into Earth. NASA forced its team to decide in a short time span on actions to minimize damage from the asteroid crash, and to react to new information coming in at different times (Dvorsky 2021).

The other way to plan for expected unexpected shocks is to develop online simulation models. Such models can combine many determinants with different response parameters to get a wider picture of possible outcomes than in a single societal drill. They can also pinpoint key parameters to which analysts should give greater attention. In the case of future work and retirement, simulations could help assess interactions among the determinants of change—for example, how a new contagious disease shock, which almost surely will depress demand for labor and shift work to homes, might operate in conjunction with extreme weather events, which increase demand for labor, first by emergency workers, and then for construction labor to rebuild infrastructure.

To update Eisenhower's paean to planning, while social exercises and simulations of the future of work and retirement are unlikely to fit the next expected unexpected shock that strikes us, the act of simulating may be indispensable to improving decisions to address that shock.

Notes

1. In 1960, the ratio of U.S. persons aged 25 to 61 to those aged 62 and over was 3.8, giving a large number of workers to pay taxes for retirees. In 2020, the ratio was 2.3. The decline in the ratios requires a rise in taxes or fall in benefits to stabilize pay-as-you-go Social Security. See Urban Institute, Age Distribution of the Population, 1950–2060, https://www.urban.org/sites/default/files/2015/10/09/t2_age_distribution.pdf
2. See Statista (n.d.). The spread of the disease to Brazil and India subsequently reduced the U.S. share of COVID-19 cases and deaths, but it did not wipe away the horrific performance of the United States in 2020, when many other countries did so much better in controlling the disease.
3. In 2016, the United States spent about 8.5 percent of its GDP on health out of public funds, about the same as the average of other comparable countries, but had much higher private spending of 8.8 percent of GDP compared to 2.7 percent on average for other nations. The United States leads the world in biomedical research because the National Institutes of Health has the largest research budget.
4. U.S. Bureau of Labor Statistics, All Employees, Total Nonfarm [PAYNSA], retrieved from FRED, Federal Reserve Bank of St. Louis; https://fred.stlouisfed.org/series/PAYNSA; and Employment Level [LNU02000000], retrieved from https://fred.stlouisfed.org/series/LNU02000000l; November 23, 2021.
5. CARES provided UI in excess of normal UI; new benefits to self-employed and other workers outside the state-run program; and one-time payments of $1,200 per adult and $500 per child to most households.
6. Trump expressed his feelings in April (https://www.nbcnews.com/politics/donald-trump/trump-predicting-rapid-economic-recovery-experts-say-it-s-not-n1184496) and May (https://nypost.com/2020/05/18/trump-predicts-v-shaped-coronavirus-recovery-as-stocks-soar/).
7. U.S. Employment and Training Administration, Initial Claims [ICSA], retrieved from FRED, Federal Reserve Bank of St. Louis; https://fred.stlouisfed.org/series/ICSA, May 24, 2021.
8. On April 3, 2020, Iowa Governor Reynolds argued that the measures taken, including closing schools and some businesses, were equivalent to a mandatory shelter-in-place or stay-at-home directive. On July 7, 2020, Governor Reynolds indicated that local governments could not implement mask requirements because they were not consistent with her public health disaster proclamation. "Covid-19 Pandemic in Iowa," https://en.wikipedia.org/wiki/COVID-19_pandemic_in_Iowa, accessed May 25, 2021.
9. The United States stands atop income inequality among advanced countries with levels comparable to those in less developed countries. World Bank (https://data.worldbank.org/indicator/SI.POV.GINI) and OECD data (https://data.oecd.org/ inequality/income-inequality.htm) show the United States with the highest Gini coefficient among high-income countries.

10. For the demands on mothers more broadly, see Agovino (2020) and Cooper (2020).
11. See povertymeasurement.org/COVID-19-poverty-dashboard for poverty trends.
12. These estimates are from Table 1 in Congressional Budget Office (2020), with unemployment in annual averages and real GDP based on changes in annual levels.
13. Social Security allows beneficiaries below full retirement age to earn a certain amount with no reduction in benefits while allowing beneficiaries at or above full retirement age to have unlimited earned income with full benefits.
14. The CARES Act allowed retirees to withdraw up to a set amount from private pensions without the 10 percent early withdrawal penalty, allowed employers to increase the amount workers could borrow from their pension fund, and allowed employees to delay payments for loans received.
15. That 2000–2020 experienced six zoonotic viral attacks on humans—SARS-CoV in 2003, MERS-CoV in 2012, Chikungunya (2014), Zika (2015), H1N1 "swine" flu (2009), and Ebola (2014–2020), in addition to SARS-CoV-2—gainsays any notion that there is little or no chance of another pandemic in our lifetimes.
16. This is their sum from a Congressional Budget Office (2020) estimate that the pandemic recession cost the United States on the order of $7.6 trillion, value-of-life estimates that the near half a million deaths (at the time of their study but higher since) cost $4.4 trillion, and estimates of health costs to persons afflicted by the virus of $4.9 trillion.
17. Government mandates in particular areas that forced people to change behavior—*vide* closing of restaurants and bars—seemed necessary to convince them the viral threat was real enough to change their behavior (Freeman and Li 2022). This is particularly important for the United States, where death rates exploded compared to Australia, Germany, Singapore, and South Korea in part because the United States reacted the slowest in mandating behavioral changes (Sebenius and Sebenius 2020). Experimentation with fines or rewards may also be valuable in finding the path to following public health advice (Madani 2021).
18. In March 2021 it was estimated that fixing and maintaining the Florida computer system would cost up to $244 million (Lyons 2021).

References

Ackerman, Gwen. 2021. "Israel Holds 'War Games' to Prepare for More Lethal Covid Strain." *Bloomberg*, November 11, 2021. https://www.bloomberg.com/news/articles/2021-11-11/israel-holds-war-games-to-prepare-for-more-lethal-covid-strain.

Agovino, Theresa. 2020. "Double Duty Takes a Toll on Working Mothers." SHRM, December 2, 2020. https://www.shrm.org/hr-today/news/hr-magazine/winter2020/pages/the-plight-of-the-working-mother.aspx.

Baily, Martin Neil, and Benjamin H. Harris. 2019. "Working Longer Policies: Framing the Issues." Economic Studies at Brookings. Washington, DC: Brookings Institution. https://www.brookings.edu/research/working-longer-policies-framing-the-issues/.

Brenan, Megan. 2019. "More Nonretired Americans Expect Comfortable Retirement." Gallup. June 18, 2019. https://news.gallup.com/poll/258320/nonretired-americans-expect-comfortable-retirement.aspx.

Burtless, Gary. 2016. "Labor Force Dynamics in the Great Recession and Its Aftermath: Implications for Older Workers." Working Paper CRR WP 2016-1. Chestnut Hill, MA: Center for Retirement Research at Boston College. https://www.brookings.edu/research/labor-force-dynamics-in-the-great-recession-and-its-aftermath-implications-for-older-workers/.

Chen, Anqi, and Alicia H. Munnell. 2020. "Can Older Workers Work from Home?" Center for Retirement Research at Boston College. https://crr.bc.edu/wp-content/uploads/2020/06/IB_20-9.pdf.

Collins, Francis S. 2021. "COVID-19 Lessons for Research." *Science* 371 (6534): 1081–1081. https://doi.org/10.1126/science.abh3996.

Congressional Budget Office. 2020. "An Update to the Economic Outlook: 2020 to 2030." https://www.cbo.gov/publication/56465.

Congressional Budget Office. 2021. "The 2021 Long-Term Budget Outlook." 56977. Washington, DC: Congress of the United States. http://www.cbo.gov/publication/56977.

Cooper, Marianne. 2020. "Mothers' Careers Are at Extraordinary Risk Right Now." *The Atlantic*, October 1, 2020. https://www.theatlantic.com/family/archive/2020/10/pandemic-amplifying-bias-against-working-mothers/616565/.

Cortes, Guido, and Eliza Forsythe. 2020. "Impacts of the Covid-19 Pandemic and the CARES Act on Earnings and Inequality." Upjohn Institute Working Paper 20-332. Kalamazoo, MI: W.E. Upjohn Institute for Employment Research. https://doi.org/10.17848/wp20-332.

Curiskis, Artis, Conor Kelly, Erin Kissane, and Kara Oehler. 2021. "What We Know—and What We Don't Know—About the Impact of the Pandemic on Our Most Vulnerable Community." The COVID Tracking Project. March 31, 2021. https://covidtracking.com/analysis-updates/what-we-know-about-the-impact-of-the-pandemic-on-our-most-vulnerable-community.

Cutler, David M., and Lawrence H. Summers. 2020. "The COVID-19 Pandemic and the $16 Trillion Virus." *JAMA* 324 (15): 1495–1496. https://doi.org/10.1001/jama.2020.19759.

Dicken, John E. 2021. "Covid-19 In Nursing Homes: HHS Has Taken Steps in Response to Pandemic, but Several GAO Recommendations Have Not Been Implemented." GAO-21-402T. U.S. Government Accountability Office Testimony Before the Committee on Finance, U.S. Senate. Washington, DC: U.S. Government Accountability Office. https://www.gao.gov/products/gao-21-402t.

Dvorsky, George. 2021. "The Asteroid Impact Simulation Has Ended in Disaster." *Gizmodo*, April 30, 2021. https://gizmodo.com/the-asteroid-impact-simulation-has-ended-in-disaster-1846800347.

Else, Holly. 2020. "How a Torrent of Covid Science Changed Research Publishing—in Seven Charts." *Nature* 588 (7839): 553. https://doi.org/10.1038/d41586-020-03564-y.

Engelhardt, Gary V., and Jonathan Gruber. 2004. "Social Security and the Evolution of Elderly Poverty." Working Paper 10466. Working Paper Series. Cambridge, MA: National Bureau of Economic Research. https://doi.org/10.3386/w10466.

Farber, Henry S. 2017. "Employment, Hours, and Earnings Consequences of Job Loss: US Evidence from the Displaced Workers Survey." *Journal of Labor Economics* 35 (S1): S235–S272. https://doi.org/10.1086/692353.

Farrell, Chris. 2019. "8 Policy Changes to Let Older Workers Work Longer." *Forbes*, March 24, 2019. https://www.forbes.com/sites/nextavenue/2019/03/24/8-policy-changes-to-let-older-workers-work-longer/?sh=7beb970f4d94.

Fauci, Anthony S. 2021. "The Story Behind COVID-19 Vaccines." *Science* 372 (6538): 109. https://doi.org/10.1126/science.abi8397.

Foroni, Claudia, Massimiliano Marcellino, and Dalibor Stevanović. 2020. "Forecasting the COVID-19 Recession and Recovery: Lessons from the Financial Crisis." Working Paper 2468. Frankfurt, Germany: European Central Bank. https://www.ecb.europa.eu/pub/pdf/scpwps/ecb.wp2468~068eec9e3e.en.pdf.

Franck, Thomas. 2021. "Social Security Trust Funds Now Projected to Run out of Money Sooner than Expected Due to Covid, Treasury Says." CNBC. August 31, 2021. https://www.cnbc.com/2021/08/31/social-security-trust-funds-set-to-be-depleted-sooner-than-expected.html.

Freeman, Richard B., and Grace Li. 2022. "Protective Behavior in the COVID-19 Pandemic: The Surprising Effect of Interrupted Personal Plans." Manuscript in Process.

Gould, Elise, and Jori Kandra. 2021. "Only One in Five Workers Are Working from Home Due to COVID: Black and Hispanic Workers Are Less Likely to Be Able to Telework." *Economic Policy Institute* (blog). June 2, 2021. https://www.epi.org/blog/only-one-in-five-workers-are-working-from-home-due-to-covid-black-and-hispanic-workers-are-less-likely-to-be-able-to-telework/.

Han, Jeehoon, Bruce D. Meyer, and James X. Sullivan. 2020a. "Income and Poverty in the COVID-19 Pandemic." Working Paper 27729. Working Paper Series. National Bureau of Economic Research. https://doi.org/10.3386/w27729.

Han, Jeehoon, Bruce D. Meyer, and James X. Sullivan. 2020b. "Real-Time Poverty Estimates During the COVID-19 Results Through September 2020." COVID-19 Income and Poverty. PovertyMeasurement.org. http://povertymeasurement.org/wp-content/uploads/2021/01/Real-time-Poverty-Estimates-through-September-2020.pdf.

ILO. 2018. *World Employment Social Outlook 2018: Greening with Jobs*. Geneva: International Labour Office. https://www.ilo.org/weso-greening/documents/WESO_Greening_EN_web2.pdf.

Iowa Workforce Development. 2021a. "Current Employment Statistics." 2021. https://www.iowaworkforcedevelopment.gov/current-employment-statistics.

Iowa Workforce Development. 2021b. "Unemployment Insurance Statistics." 2021. https://www.iowaworkforcedevelopment.gov/unemployment-insurance-statistics.

Kessler, Sarah. 2017. "IBM, Remote-Work Pioneer, Is Calling Thousands of Employees Back to the Office." *Quartz*, March 21, 2017. https://qz.com/924167/ibm-remote-work-pioneer-is-calling-thousands-of-employees-back-to-the-office/.

Kolko, Jed. 2021. "In Reversal, Retirements Increased during the Pandemic." *The New York Times*, May 12, 2021. https://www.nytimes.com/2021/05/12/upshot/retirements-increased-pandemic.html.

Li, Zhe, and Joseph Dalaker. 2021. "Poverty among the Population Aged 65 and Older." R45791, Version 6. Washington, DC: Congressional Research Service. https://crsreports.congress.gov/product/pdf/R/R45791/6.

Long, Heather, and Emily Guskin. 2020. "Over 33 Million Americans Lost Their Job during the Pandemic. 77 Percent Believe They'll Get It Back, Post-Ipsos Poll Finds." *Washington Post*, May 7, 2020. http://www.washingtonpost.com/business/2020/05/07/nearly-80-percent-laid-off-workers-believe-they-will-return-their-old-job-post-ipsos-poll-finds/.

Lyons, David. 2021. "Florida Unemployment System Overhaul Could Cost $244M." *GovTech*, March 2, 2021, sec. Budget & Finance. https://www.govtech.com/budget-finance/Florida-Unemployment-System-Overhaul-Could-Cost-244M.html.

Madani, Doha. 2021. "States Are Introducing Vaccine Lotteries—Some with Multimillion-Dollar Prizes—to Combat Slowing Vaccination Rates." NBC News. May 20, 2021. https://www.nbcnews.com/news/us-news/states-are-introducing-vaccine-lotteries-some-multimillion-dollar-prizes-combat-n1268048.

Monod, Mélodie, Alexandra Blenkinsop, Xiaoyue Xi, Daniel Hebert, Sivan Bershan, Simon Tietze, Marc Baguelin, et al. 2021. "Age Groups That Sustain Resurging COVID-19 Epidemics in the United States." *Science* 371 (6536): eabe8372. https://doi.org/10.1126/science.abe8372.

Morens, David M., and Anthony S. Fauci. 2020. "Emerging Pandemic Diseases: How We Got to COVID-19." *Cell* 182 (5): 1077–1092. https://doi.org/10.1016/j.cell.2020.08.021.

Morrissey, Monique. 2011. "The Myth of Early Retirement." Issue Brief 319. Washington, DC: Economic Policy Institute. https://www.epi.org/publication/myth-early-retirement/.

Neumark, David, Ian Burn, and Patrick Button. 2019. "Is It Harder for Older Workers to Find Jobs? New and Improved Evidence from a Field Experiment." *Journal of Political Economy* 127 (2): 922–970. https://doi.org/10.1086/701029.

O'Connell, Ann. 2021. "Emergency Bans on Evictions and Other Tenant Protections Related to Coronavirus." Nolo.Com. October 1, 2021. https://www.nolo.com/evictions-ban.

OECD. 2019. *Working Better With Age*. Ageing and Employment Policies. Paris: OECD Publishing. https://doi.org/10.1787/c4d4f66a-en.

OECD. 2021. "Employment Rate (Indicator)." OECD Data. 2021. https://doi.org/10.1787/1de68a9b-en.

OECD. n.d. "Ageing and Employment Policies—Statistics on Average Effective Age of Retirement." Data Set. Paris, France. Accessed October 18, 2021. https://www.oecd.org/els/emp/average-effective-age-of-retirement.htm.

Parolin, Zachary, Megan Curran, Jordan Matsudaira, Jane Waldfogel, and Christopher Wimer. 2020. "Monthly Poverty Rates in the United States during the COVID-19 Pandemic." Poverty and Social Policy Working Paper. New York: Center on Poverty and Social Policy. https://static1.squarespace.com/static/5743308460b5e922a25a6dc7/t/5f87c59e4cd0011fabd38973/1602733471158/COVID-Projecting-Poverty-Monthly-CPSP-2020.pdf.

Pfau, Wade, Joe Tomlinson, and Steve Vernon. 2019. "Viability of the Spend Safely in Retirement Strategy." Schaumburg, IL: Society of Actuaries. https://www.soa.org/globalassets/assets/files/resources/research-report/2019/viability-spend-safely.pdf.

Proctor, Enola K., and Elvin Geng. 2021. "A New Lane for Science." *Science* 374 (6568): 659. https://doi.org/10.1126/science.abn0184.

Sebenius, Isaac, and James K. Sebenius. 2020. "How Many Needless Covid-19 Deaths Were Caused by Delays in Responding? Most of Them." *Stat News* (blog). June 19, 2020. https://www.statnews.com/2020/06/19/faster-response-prevented-most-us-covid-19-deaths/.

Sonnemaker, Tyler. 2021. "IBM's CEO Predicts a Hybrid Remote-Work Model for 80% of Employees Post-Pandemic." *Business Insider*, March 31, 2021. https://www.businessinsider.com/ibm-ceo-hybrid-remote-work-for-most-employees-post-pandemic-2021-3.

Statista. n.d. "Coronavirus Deaths Worldwide by Country." Accessed April 20, 2021. https://www.statista.com/statistics/1093256/novel-coronavirus-2019ncov-deaths-worldwide-by-country/.

Tavernise, Sabrina. 2021. "Vaccine Skepticism Was Viewed as a Knowledge Problem. It's Actually about Gut Beliefs." *The New York Times*, April 29, 2021. https://www.nytimes.com/2021/04/29/us/vaccine-skepticism-beliefs.html.

U.S. Bureau of Labor Statistics. 2021. "People Not Looking for Work Because of COVID-19." November 12, 2021. https://stats.bls.gov/opub/ted/2021/people-not-looking-for-work-because-of-covid-19.htm.

U.S. Department of Labor. 2021. "Unemployment Insurance Weekly Claims." News Release USDL 21-1859-NAT. Washington, DC: US Department of Labor, Employment and Training Administration. https://oui.doleta.gov/press/2021/041521.pdf.

USAGov. 2021. "Disaster Financial Assistance with Food, Housing, and Bills." August 2021. https://www.usa.gov/disaster-help-food-housing-bills.

Wamsley, Laurel. 2020. "Gov. Says Florida's Unemployment System Was Designed to Create 'Pointless Roadblocks.'" *NPR*, August 6, 2020. https://www.npr.org/sections/coronavirus-live-updates/2020/08/06/899893368/gov-says-floridas-unemployment-system-was-designed-to-create-pointless-roadblock.

PART II

What's the Fit?

Workers and Their Abilities, Motivations, and Expectations

5
The Link between Health and Working Longer
Disparities in Work Capacity

Ben Berger, Italo López García, Nicole Maestas, and Kathleen J. Mullen[1]

1. Introduction

As workers age, they become increasingly likely to experience serious health problems that may interfere with their ability to continue working. Fortunately, over the last century, improvements in population health and life expectancy have reduced the likelihood of illness and disability in older age (Vaupel 2010; Crimmins 2015), at the same time as employment at older ages has become increasingly common (Cahill, Giandrea, and Quinn 2016). However, recent research has revealed troubling trends in health and life expectancy among middle-aged Americans (Woolf et al. 2018; Woolf and Schoomaker 2019; Case and Deaton 2020; Case, Deaton, and Stone 2020), which raise the question of whether gains in functional capacity and employment will persist among future cohorts of older Americans.

Health problems among middle-aged cohorts today may portend rising rates of work disability among future older Americans. But the extent to which this occurs depends on how health conditions impact the specific functional abilities needed to meet job demands. For health conditions that can be effectively managed through treatment, there may be little effect on functioning or job performance—or at least a delayed effect. The ways in which various health conditions affect functional abilities are not well understood, especially for individuals who are or could possibly be in the labor force. One promising avenue for research is to investigate the intersection between the "supply" of functional abilities in the population and the demand for functional abilities by U.S. employers.

Health-related functional abilities are "enduring attributes of the individual that influence [work] performance" (O*NET Resource Center 2019). As defined by O*NET, a U.S. government database of occupational information, these attributes comprise the cognitive, physical, psychomotor, and sensory dimensions of ability that individuals can use to accomplish work. While these abilities are persistent, they are not innate; they depend directly on health. For instance, the sensory ability *Near Vision*—the ability to "see details at close range"—may deteriorate from the visual complications of diabetes. Degenerative joint disease may erode *Static Strength*—the ability to "exert maximum muscle force to lift, push, pull or carry objects." Mental health impairments can reduce *Selective Attention*—the ability to "concentrate on a task over a period of time without being distracted." In other words, adverse health events reduce functional abilities, limiting the activities individuals can comfortably perform in the workplace.

Occupations themselves demand different levels of functional abilities. Surgeons and jewelers may need a high level of *Arm-Hand Steadiness*, but lawyers and retail salespeople may not. This interaction of an individual's health-related functional abilities with occupational demands produces what we term *work capacity*, the individual's set of *potential* occupations and associated earnings given their current functional abilities.

We use new measures of individual work capacity to characterize the interaction between health-related functional abilities and occupational demands, both in the population overall and across different population groups. Our study of functional abilities differs sharply from previous research because we explicitly consider how individuals' functional abilities interface with the economy's occupational demands. Specifically, we investigate how health-related functional abilities map to the ability requirements of different occupations in the U.S. economy by combining new survey data with information from the Occupational Information Network (O*NET) database. O*NET is the definitive source for detailed information about occupational requirements for all occupations in the national economy.

We then compare average work capacity across different groups to assess how work capacity varies by age cohort, gender, race/ethnicity, and education in the United States. Identification of disparities in work capacity across demographic groups are of first-order importance because they may contribute to disparities in realized employment and income. If many Americans, especially those in disadvantaged groups, are unable to work longer because poor health undermines the functional abilities they need to do their jobs, or if their health constrains them to a narrow set of occupations, then policies that reduce health disparities may increase the proportion who are healthy enough to work longer. Large bodies of research document significant health disparities along demographic lines, stemming not from innate differences but from the unequal distributions of societal advantages and disadvantages groups face. These disparities may thus propagate to differences in the comparative functional abilities and work capacity of U.S. adults.

Black adults in particular face structural racism in their daily lives which adversely impacts health by limiting access to and quality of health care, manifesting unjust risks to personal and community health, and causing psychosocial trauma and chronic stress (Bailey et al. 2017). These health disparities may then be reflected in reduced functional abilities and greater limitations on labor market opportunities. For instance, significant disparities in diabetes prevalence exist between non-Hispanic white and Black adults (Centers for Disease Control and Prevention 2020). Diabetes itself may cause vision loss, cognitive impairment, and reduced mobility, and racial disparities in access to quality health care and opportunities for intensive physical activity may further exacerbate disparities in functional abilities (Rejeski et al. 2012; Newhall et al. 2016). Racial discrimination itself has been shown to provoke a stress response. Exposure to repeated stress from racial discrimination may worsen mental health and affect cognitive functional abilities (Berger and Sarnyai 2015). Understanding how these health disparities affect the relative occupational opportunities and challenges faced by different groups is key to determining how policy encouraging adults to work longer will heterogeneously impact Americans.

We find that cognitive abilities are the most important determinant of potential occupations and earnings, with a one standard deviation increase in self-reported cognitive abilities associated with an increase of 126 potential occupations (out of 936 possible occupations) and an increase of $35,000 in maximum potential earnings. Sensory abilities have a smaller but economically meaningful association with potential occupations and earnings. A one standard deviation increase in physical abilities is associated with an additional 35 potential occupations, most of which do not require a college degree. Since physically demanding jobs tend to be low-paying, there is little association between physical abilities and potential earnings.

Average functional abilities decline somewhat with age, led by significant declines in physical and psychomotor abilities; however, potential occupations and earnings fall only modestly. This suggests that many adults maintain the functional abilities to work at least into their late 60s, although older adults who can no longer work their physically demanding jobs may nonetheless face significant barriers to new employment in the form of educational requirements, costs to acquire new skills, and discrimination.

We do observe differences by gender and race/ethnicity in self-reported functional abilities, but these differences are small compared to real-world differences in earnings, suggesting that health is not a major driver of gender- and race-related earnings gaps. Education-related gaps in functional abilities are substantially larger and more economically consequential than gaps by either gender or race/ethnicity. College graduates report significantly higher functional abilities than nongraduates across all ability domains, including physical abilities. This leads to an average difference in maximum potential earnings of over $34,000. This is consistent with extensive research on educational disparities in health (see e.g., Montez et al. 2019, for an overview).

Finally, we consider how potential earnings vary across cohorts by gender, educational attainment, and race. We find that middle-aged white respondents have *lower* potential earnings than white respondents ages 62–71. The reverse is true for middle-aged Black respondents, who have substantially higher potential earnings than older Black respondents. Our evidence suggests that health may be a bigger barrier to work at older ages for white Americans now in middle age than it has been for white Americans now at retirement age. We also find that potential earnings decline with age more slowly among college graduates than nongraduates. We suggest that this may be due in part to the deleterious effects of physically demanding and hazardous jobs that are disproportionately held by nongraduates, but many factors that jointly determine education and health may be at play.

Overall, our analysis indicates that health is an important determinant of ability to work as people age; that disparities in health translate to diminished labor market opportunities for those with less education; and that worse health among younger cohorts of white Americans may reduce their ability to work up to and past traditional retirement ages.

2. Data

Previous research on the links between health and work capacity has been constrained by the lack of data that use the same measures to rate (a) individuals' functional abilities and (b) the functional abilities required for various occupations. We use new data collected specifically to fill this gap. To measure work capacity, we combine data from two sources: the American Work Capacity and Abilities Survey (López García, Maestas, and Mullen 2019) and the Occupational Information Network (O*NET). The American Work Capacity and Abilities Survey (AWCAS) collected data on self-assessed abilities from participants in the RAND American Life Panel (ALP), a nationally representative (when weighted), probability-based panel of individuals age 18 or older who are regularly interviewed over the internet for scientific research purposes. AWCAS was fielded between July and September 2018 to 2,829 subjects, of whom 2,355 (83 percent) completed the survey. Respondents were asked to rate their level of ability for 52 different abilities, collectively intended to provide a comprehensive picture of individuals' functional ability along cognitive, psychomotor, physical, and sensory dimensions. The 52 abilities in AWCAS correspond exactly to the abilities used by O*NET to classify occupations in the U.S. economy. Raked sampling weights were created to match the 2018 Current Population Survey.[2]

O*NET is a database maintained by the Bureau of Labor Statistics that comprehensively rates and classifies all occupations in the national economy in terms of required abilities, skills, knowledge, and other characteristics.[3] For each occupation, eight O*NET labor analysts rate the *level* of each ability needed to perform the occupation's tasks on a scale from 0 to 7. The required level of any given ability for any given occupation is the average of the eight analyst ratings. The O*NET analysts also evaluate the *importance* of each ability to the occupation on a scale of 1 to 5.

To standardize ability assessment across occupations, O*NET assigned level anchors to particular numbers in each ability scale. Each anchor has an example of a job-related activity that could be done at that level of ability. For example, the ability *Stamina* has anchors at levels 1, 4, and 6, corresponding to the activities "Walk a mile," "Climb 6 flights of stairs," and "Run 10 miles," respectively. *Reaction Time* has anchors at levels 4 and 6, corresponding to being able to "Throw a switch when a red warning light goes off" and to "Hit the brake when a pedestrian steps in front of the car." *Number Facility* has anchors at levels 1, 3, and 5, corresponding to "Add 2 and 7," "Balance a checkbook," and "Compute the interest payment that should be generated from an investment." See Table 5.1 for a complete list of all O*NET abilities.

A key difference between AWCAS and the O*NET ability data is that AWCAS measures individuals' reported abilities while O*NET measures occupations' required abilities. Specifically, AWCAS asked survey respondents to rate their level of each ability, while O*NET

TABLE 5.1 O*NET abilities and estimated population means using the AWCAS sample

	Ability	Mean	Description
		COGNITIVE ABILITIES	
1	Oral comprehension	4.99	The ability to listen to and understand information and ideas presented through spoken words and sentences.
2	Written comprehension	5.03	The ability to read and understand information and ideas presented in writing.
3	Oral expression	4.88	The ability to communicate information and ideas in speaking so others will understand.
4	Written expression	4.55	The ability to communicate information and ideas in writing so others will understand.
5	Fluency of ideas	4.52	The ability to come up with a number of ideas about a topic (the number of ideas is important, not their quality, correctness, or creativity).
6	Originality	4.19	The ability to come up with unusual or clever ideas about a given topic or situation, or to develop creative ways to solve a problem.
7	Problem sensitivity	4.85	The ability to tell when something is wrong or is likely to go wrong. It does not involve solving the problem, only recognizing there is a problem.
8	Deductive reasoning	4.46	The ability to apply general rules to specific problems to produce answers that make sense.
9	Inductive reasoning	4.49	The ability to combine pieces of information to form general rules or conclusions (includes finding a relationship among seemingly unrelated events).
10	Information ordering	4.12	The ability to arrange things or actions in a certain order or pattern according to a specific rule or set of rules (e.g., patterns of numbers, letters, words, pictures, mathematical operations).
11	Category flexibility	4.55	The ability to generate or use different sets of rules for combining or grouping things in different ways.
12	Mathematical reasoning	3.76	The ability to choose the right mathematical methods or formulas to solve a problem.
13	Number facility	4.37	The ability to add, subtract, multiply, or divide quickly and correctly.
14	Memorization	3.99	The ability to remember information such as words, numbers, pictures, and procedures.
15	Speed of closure	4.22	The ability to quickly make sense of, combine, and organize information into meaningful patterns.
16	Flexibility of closure	4.43	The ability to identify or detect a known pattern (a figure, object, word, or sound) that is hidden in other distracting material.
17	Perceptual speed	4.14	The ability to quickly and accurately compare similarities and differences among sets of letters, numbers, objects, pictures, or patterns. The things to be compared may be presented at the same time or one after the other. This ability also includes comparing a presented object with a remembered object.

(continued)

TABLE 5.1 Continued

	Ability	Mean	Description
18	Spatial orientation	3.75	The ability to know your location in relation to the environment or to know where other objects are in relation to you.
19	Visualization	4.55	The ability to imagine how something will look after it is moved around or when its parts are moved or rearranged.
20	Selective attention	4.45	The ability to concentrate on a task over a period of time without being distracted.
21	Time sharing	4.46	The ability to shift back and forth between two or more activities or sources of information (such as speech, sounds, touch, or other sources).
	PSYCHOMOTOR ABILITIES		
22	Arm-hand steadiness	4.65	The ability to keep your hand and arm steady while moving your arm or while holding your arm and hand in one position.
23	Manual dexterity	4.74	The ability to quickly move your hand, your hand together with your arm, or your two hands to grasp, manipulate, or assemble objects.
24	Finger dexterity	4.57	The ability to make precisely coordinated movements of the fingers of one or both hands to grasp, manipulate, or assemble very small objects.
25	Control precision	4.26	The ability to quickly and repeatedly adjust the controls of a machine or a vehicle to exact positions.
26	Multi-limb coordination	4.32	The ability to coordinate two or more limbs (for example, two arms, two legs, or one leg and one arm) while sitting, standing, or lying down. It does not involve performing the activities while the whole body is in motion.
27	Response orientation	4.65	The ability to choose quickly between two or more movements in response to two or more different signals (lights, sounds, pictures). It includes the speed with which the correct response is started with the hand, foot, or other body part.
28	Rate control	4.39	The ability to time your movements or the movement of a piece of equipment in anticipation of changes in the speed and/or direction of a moving object or scene.
29	Reaction time	5.62	The ability to quickly respond (with the hand, finger, or foot) to a signal (sound, light, picture) when it appears.
30	Wrist-finger speed	4.71	The ability to make fast, simple, repeated movements of the fingers, hands, and wrists.
31	Speed of limb movement	5.09	The ability to quickly move the arms and legs.
	PHYSICAL ABILITIES		
32	Static strength	4.67	The ability to exert maximum muscle force to lift, push, pull, or carry objects.
33	Explosive strength	3.99	The ability to use short bursts of muscle force to propel oneself (as in jumping or sprinting), or to throw an object.
34	Dynamic strength	4.27	The ability to exert muscle force repeatedly or continuously over time. This involves muscular endurance and resistance to muscle fatigue.
35	Trunk strength	4.46	The ability to use your abdominal and lower back muscles to support part of the body repeatedly or continuously over time without "giving out" or fatiguing.

TABLE 5.1 Continued

	Ability	Mean	Description
36	Stamina	3.86	The ability to exert yourself physically over long periods of time without getting winded or out of breath.
37	Extent flexibility	4.78	The ability to bend, stretch, twist, or reach with your body, arms, and/or legs.
38	Dynamic flexibility	4.05	The ability to quickly and repeatedly bend, stretch, twist, or reach out with your body, arms, and/or legs.
39	Gross body Coordination	4.18	The ability to coordinate the movement of your arms, legs, and torso together when the whole body is in motion.
40	Gross body equilibrium	3.99	The ability to keep or regain your body balance or stay upright when in an unstable position.
	SENSORY ABILITIES		
41	Near vision	4.51	The ability to see details at close range (within a few feet of the observer).
42	Far vision	4.57	The ability to see details at a distance.
43	Visual color Discrimination	4.36	The ability to match or detect differences between colors, including shades of color and brightness.
44	Night vision	4.41	The ability to see under low light conditions.
45	Peripheral vision	4.10	The ability to see objects or movement of objects to one's side when the eyes are looking ahead.
46	Depth perception	4.15	The ability to judge which of several objects is closer or farther away from you, or to judge the distance between you and an object.
47	Glare sensitivity	4.17	The ability to see objects in the presence of glare or bright lighting.
48	Hearing sensitivity	3.89	The ability to detect or tell the differences between sounds that vary in pitch and loudness.
49	Auditory attention	4.60	The ability to focus on a single source of sound in the presence of other distracting sounds.
50	Sound localization	5.06	The ability to tell the direction from which a sound originated.
51	Speech recognition	4.73	The ability to identify and understand the speech of another person.
52	Speech clarity	4.81	The ability to speak clearly so others can understand you.

Notes: N = 2,222. AWCAS sample of respondents from ALP. Abilities measured on a scale from 0 to 7. Means are sample-weighted to approximate population average. AWCAS, American Work Capacity and Abilities Survey. O*NET, Occupational Information Network. ALP, American Life Panel.

tasked analysts with evaluating the level of each ability needed to perform each occupation.[4] Critically, AWCAS and O*NET measure the exact same abilities using the exact same scales.

Nonetheless, an important limitation of our approach is that the individual functional abilities elicited by the AWCAS are self-reported. Self-reported data are subjective in nature and thus prone to known and unknown response biases. We discuss one particular form of bias below. At the same time, in comparison with objective ability assessments, self-reports are less costly to elicit and respondents' own views of their abilities likely influence their occupational and employment choices in important ways.

Additionally, we use data from AWCAS on demographics, including age, gender, race, ethnicity, education, and self-reported health, as well as earnings data from the 2018 American Working Conditions Survey (Maestas et al. 2018), which was fielded to American Life Panel respondents in the same year as AWCAS and contains additional data for a majority of its respondents. Of the 2,355 total respondents, we conduct analysis on a main sample of 2,222 respondents, omitting respondents who responded too quickly or too repetitively; respondents who did not report their age, race/ethnicity, education, or their level of ability for any of the 52 abilities; and respondents younger than 25.

Finally, we link the O*NET abilities data to wage data from the May 2018 release of the Occupational Employment Statistics (OES) published by the Bureau of Labor Statistics (U.S. Bureau of Labor Statistics 2018). The OES data contain estimates of mean and median earnings nationwide for each occupation at the six-digit SOC level. After merging the two datasets, there are 936 occupations with both abilities data from O*NET and wage data from OES.

3. Summarizing Functional Abilities

We begin by summarizing functional ability levels as measured in the AWCAS data. Table 5.1 presents the 52 O*NET abilities, their definitions, and their AWCAS sample means, the latter obtained by averaging over all individuals in the sample. Across the different measures of ability, average ability is generally between levels 4 and 5 (on a scale from 0 to 7). Note that ability levels may not be directly comparable across different functional abilities because their interpretations are relative to ability anchors, as described above.

Next, to evaluate overall functional ability, we construct within-person averages of self-reported ability over all of the individual's 52 O*NET ability scores and for the subset of abilities belonging to each ability domain—cognitive, psychomotor, physical, and sensory. We then investigate average functional abilities by gender, race/ethnicity, education, and age cohort. As the ability distributions in Figure 5.1 show, men report higher ability levels than women, college graduates report higher ability levels than nongraduates, and younger age cohorts report slightly higher abilities than older age cohorts. By race, while the distributions of abilities reported by white and Black respondents are centered about the same location, Black respondents are more likely to report ability profiles in the extremes—a greater fraction report either low or high average abilities compared to white respondents. We explore these differences in detail below.

4. Measuring Work Capacity

Next we examine how individuals' health-related functional abilities interact with occupational requirements to determine work capacity. We consider two definitions of work capacity: (a) the size of an individual's potential occupation set and (b) their maximum and median potential earnings. We also explore how education constrains potential occupations and earnings.

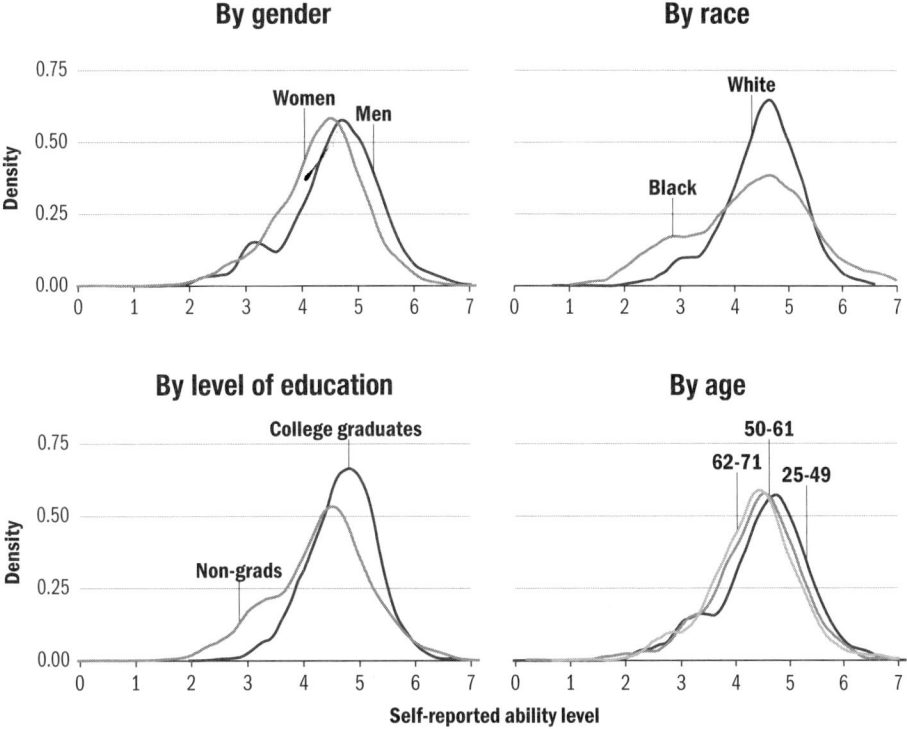

FIGURE 5.1 **Distribution of average self-reported ability**

First, we combine individuals' reported abilities with occupational ability requirements from O*NET in order to define a set of potential occupations for each individual. For an occupation to qualify as one of an individual's potential occupations, each of the individual's reported O*NET ability levels must either meet or exceed the required level for the occupation, or otherwise be relatively unimportant for the occupation.[5] Specifically, we measure occupation-specific work capacity OWC as:

$$OWC_{i,j} = \prod_{\substack{k=1 \\ \{k:IM_{j,k} \geq 3.0\}}}^{K} 1(\theta_{i,k} \geq c_{j,k}), \tag{1}$$

where $\theta_{i,k}$ is an individual i's level of ability k, and $c_{j,k}$ is the level of k needed to perform occupation j, as determined by the average level assigned by the O*NET raters. If $\theta_{i,k} \geq c_{j,k}$, for all k abilities that are important for performing occupation j (i.e., abilities with O*NET importance rating $IM_{j,k} \geq 3.0$), then $OWC_{i,j} = 1$; otherwise, $OWC_{i,j} = 0$. This definition of occupation-specific work capacity is strict, since if an individual is missing even one important ability, they are not credited with the potential occupation.[6] Note that here potential occupations are based solely on individuals' functional abilities and their match with current occupational requirements, and not on other factors that may be vital in qualifying for jobs such as education, acquired skills, or knowledge.

Once we obtain the individual's occupation-specific work capacity for every occupation, we define total work capacity *WC* as their total number of potential occupations:

$$WC_i = \sum_{j=1}^{J} OWC_{i,j}, \qquad (2)$$

This definition of work capacity sheds light on whether health-related functional abilities are an important limiting factor for working longer. However, individuals with all the necessary functional abilities will nonetheless be excluded from particular jobs for many reasons, such as education, experience, social networks, discrimination, geography, and economic conditions. While we cannot examine all the factors that prevent adults from gaining suitable employment, we do examine a major one: educational attainment. To examine the degree to which education requirements might constrain an individual's potential occupation set, we also compute the number of potential occupations for the subset of occupations requiring a high school degree or less, a baccalaureate degree, or an advanced degree (all of which sum to equation (2)).[7]

Figure 5.2 shows the sample distribution of individuals' counts of potential occupations out of 936 possible detailed occupations recorded in O*NET. The maximum number of potential occupations in the AWCAS sample is 936 and the minimum is 1. Most individuals have many potential occupations; however, there is a large share of individuals with fewer than 50 potential occupations. This is a consequence of the all-or-nothing nature of equation (1). If these individuals were credited with occupations for which they were only partially qualified (possessing, say, nine out of ten required abilities), then the mass would disperse to the right, as shown by López García, Maestas, and Mullen (2019). Missing abilities may limit

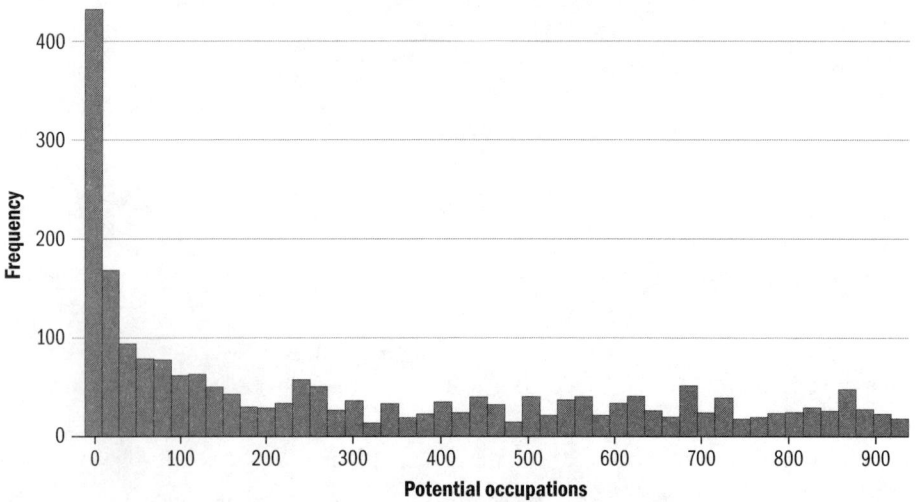

FIGURE 5.2 Sample distribution of the number of potential occupations

prospects more on the hiring margin than the exit margin; while employers might be reluctant to hire individuals with missing abilities into an occupation that requires those abilities, employers are required by law to provide reasonable accommodations to job incumbents who lose abilities (i.e., who become disabled).

Our second approach to work capacity considers potential earnings. We first compute each occupation's median annual earnings (top-coded at $208,000). We then construct each individual's *maximum potential earnings* as the maximum over all potential occupations' median earnings and *median potential earnings* as the median over all potential occupations' median earnings.

Figure 5.3 depicts the sample distribution of potential earnings using both the maximum and median potential earnings measures. Individuals' maximum potential earnings have a population-weighted median of $80,200, and median potential earnings have a median of $34,170. In contrast, median observed earnings are $30,000 ($48,000 among workers and zero among nonworkers). The fact that the median of maximum potential earnings is more than twice as high as observed median earnings indicates that some in the United States are earning far less than their potential (if functional abilities were the only limiting factor). There are many possible reasons for this discrepancy. People may face barriers to obtaining more lucrative occupations such as discrimination or costly educational requirements and certification. Some occupations pay a premium in part because they involve a hazardous or unpleasant work environment, leading many people to accept lower earnings at a safer or more pleasant job. People also may accept lower earnings because they prefer a particular line of work. Finally, some people choose not to work at all. Altogether there are numerous reasons that individuals might earn significantly less than their potential.

Table 5.2 summarizes the relationship between the four classes of abilities and individuals' work capacity, revealing which abilities drive differences in work capacity. For all measures of work capacity, higher average cognitive and sensory abilities are associated with

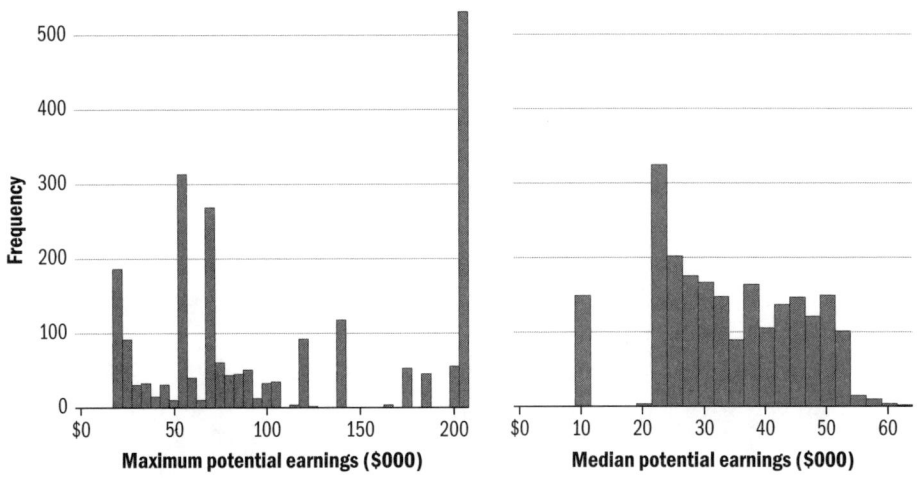

FIGURE 5.3 Sample distribution of potential earnings measures

TABLE 5.2 Relationship between average abilities and work capacity

	Outcome: Number of potential occupations by required education level				Outcome: Potential earnings	
	(1)	(2)	(3)	(4)	(5)	(6)
	All education levels	No bachelor's degree required	Bachelor's degree required	Advanced degree required	Maximum	Median
Average of self-assessed cognitive ability scores (standardized)	125.66***	55.79***	46.93***	22.93***	35,176.01***	6,174.54***
	(12.45)	(7.16)	(4.24)	(1.99)	(2,738.40)	(474.77)
Average of self-assessed physical ability scores (standardized)	35.21***	27.99***	5.55	1.68	1,900.41	−156.38
	(9.53)	(5.41)	(3.32)	(1.48)	(2164.48)	(372.43)
Average of self-assessed psychomotor ability scores (standardized)	2.69	12.79	−7.33	−2.77	1,947.25	943.01
	(13.91)	(8.41)	(4.47)	(2.02)	(3,168.99)	(683.20)
Average of self-assessed sensory ability scores (standardized)	85.01***	61.09***	18.77***	5.15**	18202.46***	3321.09***
	(11.29)	(6.78)	(3.71)	(1.66)	(2553.84)	(460.98)
R^2	0.57	0.57	0.47	0.45	0.59	0.68
Observations	2,222	2,222	2,222	2,222	2,222	2,222
Mean of dependent variable	300	210	65	24	110,176	34,870
Total number of occupations in O*NET	936	525	260	151		

Notes: Explanatory variables are standardized to have mean zero and standard deviation 1. Potential occupations are determined only by individuals' abilities, excluding their level of education and other required skills. Occupations requiring a bachelor's degree include jobs that also require an additional certification. All regressions are survey-weighted. Standard errors are in parentheses. O*NET, Occupational Information
* p<0.05, ** p<0.01, *** p<0.001

higher work capacity. A one standard deviation increase in self-assessed cognitive ability increases the average individual's number of potential occupations by 126 (out of 936 possible occupations), leading to an increase in maximum potential earnings of $35,176 and in median potential earnings of $6,175. Sensory abilities also have a meaningful association with work capacity, with a one standard deviation increase increasing the average individual's number of occupations by 85, maximum potential earnings by $18,203, and median potential earnings by $3,321.

Physical abilities have a weaker association with the number of potential occupations, with a one standard deviation increase increasing the number of potential occupations by 35. This is driven almost entirely by the effect of physical abilities on the number of potential occupations that do not require a college degree (Column 2). Among people without a college degree, low levels of physical ability (such as a deterioration in strength, stamina, or flexibility that comes with age) substantially limit the number of available occupations. Among people with a college degree, who tend to work in occupations that are not physically demanding, physical ability scarcely affects the number of potential occupations (Columns 3 and 4). Consequently, as shown in Columns 5 and 6, because occupations that do not require a college degree tend to be low-paying, increases in physical ability have no effect on potential earnings. Average self-reported psychomotor ability has no significant effects on work capacity using either the number of potential occupations or potential earnings.

We next investigate which specific abilities are most important for driving differences in potential earnings. Figure 5.4 displays the association of individual abilities with maximum potential earnings by reporting the t-statistics from a regression of maximum potential earnings on each ability. The abilities most associated with maximum potential earnings are cognitive abilities (problem sensitivity, inductive reasoning, memorization, selective attention), certain sensory abilities (near vision, speech recognition, and speech clarity), and the psychomotor ability of control precision.

If the number of potential occupations is a reasonable measure of work capacity, we would expect it to be positively associated with many labor outcomes. In analyses not shown, we find that both observed earnings and employment rates are higher on average for those with a larger potential occupation set.

5. Work Capacity by Demographic Groups

Next, we examine how the interaction of functional abilities with occupational demands varies by age cohort, gender, education, and race/ethnicity.

5.1. Work Capacity by Age Cohort

As Table 5.3 shows, the average score for all functional abilities declines only slightly across age cohorts, from 4.523 for the youngest cohort to 4.326 for the oldest cohort. Declines are minimal for the cognitive, psychomotor, and sensory ability domains, and slightly larger (though still modest in magnitude) for physical abilities. The work capacity measures show similar patterns by age cohort. The set of potential occupations is largest among those ages

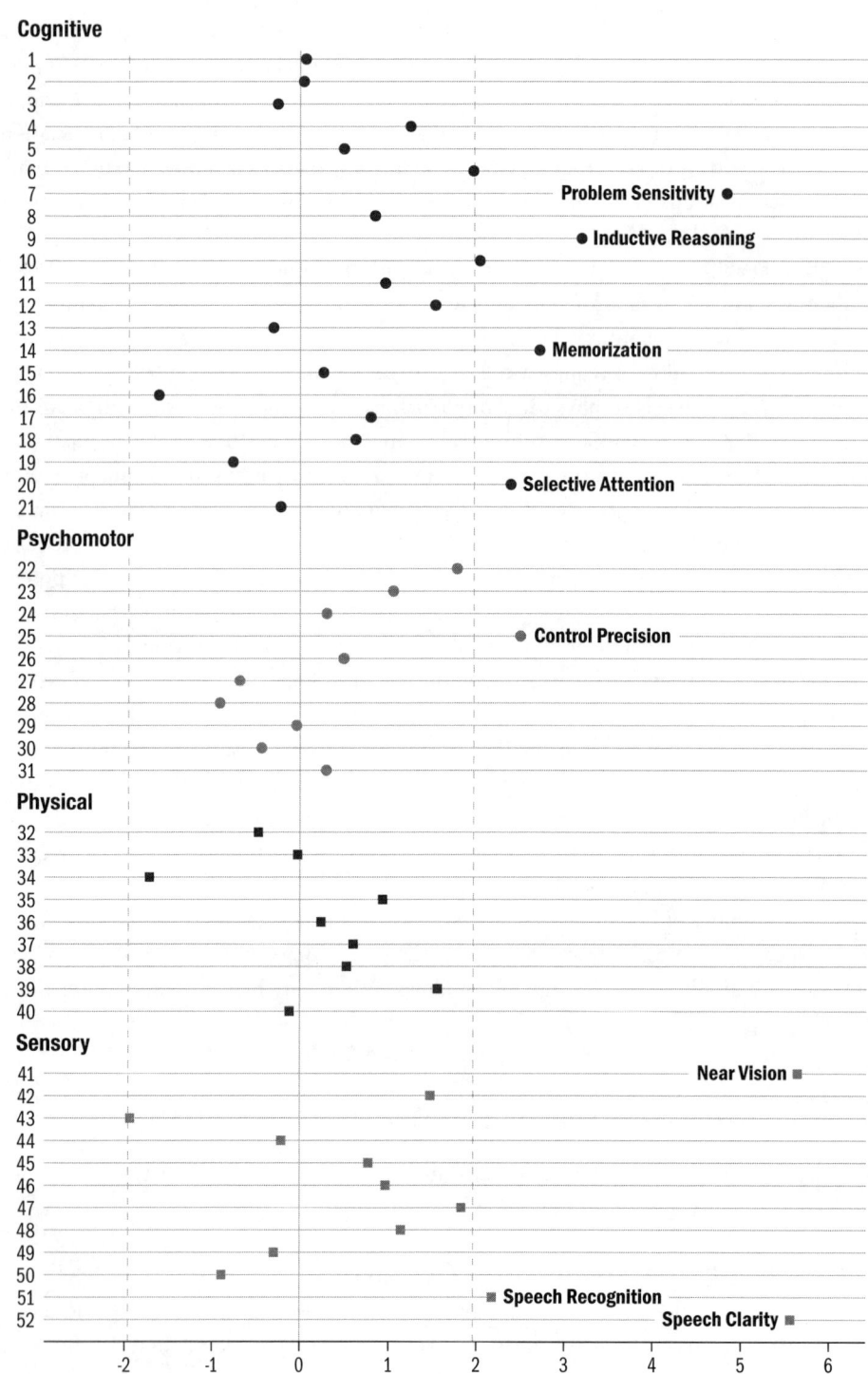

FIGURE 5.4 Association of abilities with maximum potential earnings
Reported t-statistics from the regression of maximum potential earnings on each of the 52 O*NET abilities

TABLE 5.3 Average abilities and work capacity by age cohort

	(1) Age 25–49	(2) Age 50–61	(3) Age 62–71
Average of self-assessed ability scores	4.523	4.380	4.326
	(0.055)	(0.042)	(0.042)
Average of self-assessed cognitive ability scores	4.453	4.368	4.376
	(0.059)	(0.048)	(0.045)
Average of self-assessed physical ability scores	4.436	4.129	3.859
	(0.057)	(0.053)	(0.055)
Average of self-assessed psychomotor ability scores	4.736	4.687	4.608
	(0.063)	(0.045)	(0.047)
Average of self-assessed sensory ability scores	4.533	4.333	4.352
	(0.064)	(0.050)	(0.045)
Number of potential occupations	318.9	275.9	276.1
	(16.6)	(13.9)	(14.2)
Number of potential occupations not requiring a bachelor's degree	224.3	193.7	190.5
	(10.9)	(9.2)	(9.0)
Number of potential occupations requiring only a bachelor's degree	69.0	59.8	62.7
	(4.5)	(3.9)	(4.1)
Number of potential occupations requiring an advanced degree	25.7	22.3	22.9
	(1.9)	(1.7)	(1.8)
Maximum potential earnings	114,460	104,519	105,315
	(4,136)	(3,458)	(3,271)
Median potential earnings	35,298	34,119	34,643
	(802)	(598)	(553)
Observations	780	767	675

Notes: Number of potential occupations is out of 936 occupations possible. Standard errors are in parentheses.

25–49 (319), declines by 13.5 percent among those ages 50–61 (276), and holds steady at that level through ages 6–71. The modest decline in physical abilities observed between middle and older age is not large enough to reduce the set of potential occupations.

Table 5.3 also shows how education requirements constrain potential occupations sets. Of 276 potential occupations on average for the middle-aged cohort, 70 percent do not require a college degree, 22 percent require a college degree (but no more), and 8 percent require an advanced degree. In other words, holding functional abilities constant, the potential occupation set of a middle-aged individual without a college degree would be 31 percent larger if they had a college degree and 42 percent larger if they had an advanced degree. Education constraints are of similar magnitude among the younger and older age cohorts.

Lastly, we consider median and maximum potential earnings. Potential earnings from individuals' median potential occupation average $35,298 among the youngest cohort and are only slightly lower (and not significantly so) among the middle-aged and older cohorts. Similarly, maximum potential earnings exhibit a modest and marginally significant ($p < 0.10$) decline with age ($114,460 on average for the younger cohort and roughly $105,000 for the middle-aged and older cohorts).

5.2. Work Capacity by Gender

Table 5.4 reveals that women report lower levels of ability than men overall and across all ability domains. The difference is especially notable for physical ability, where women report a level of 3.995 on average while men report an average score of 4.528, a difference of over

TABLE 5.4 Average abilities and work capacity by gender

	(1) Men	(2) Women	(3) Difference
Average of self-assessed ability scores	4.579	4.331	−0.248
	(0.061)	(0.031)	(0.069)
Average of self-assessed cognitive ability scores	4.500	4.341	−0.159
	(0.066)	(0.035)	(0.074)
Average of self-assessed physical ability scores	4.528	3.995	−0.532
	(0.059)	(0.039)	(0.071)
Average of self-assessed psychomotor ability scores	4.817	4.593	−0.224
	(0.070)	(0.036)	(0.079)
Average of self-assessed sensory ability scores	4.559	4.346	−0.213
	(0.071)	(0.035)	(0.079)
Number of potential occupations	339.0	264.2	−74.8
	(18.2)	(10.4)	(21.0)
Number of potential occupations not requiring a bachelor's degree	237.7	184.9	−52.8
	(12.0)	(6.7)	(13.7)
Number of potential occupations requiring only a bachelor's degree	73.9	57.7	−16.2
	(5.0)	(2.9)	(5.8)
Number of potential occupations requiring an advanced degree	27.3	21.5	−5.8
	(2.1)	(1.3)	(2.4)
Maximum potential earnings	114,071	106,639	−7,433
	(4,418)	(2,702)	(5,179)
Median potential earnings	35,568	34,236	−1,332
	(894)	(437)	(995)
Observations	915	1,307	

Notes: Number of potential occupations is out of 936 occupations possible. Standard errors are in parentheses.

half a standard deviation. As a result, women have fewer potential occupations for all levels of education requirements. However, this difference has little effect on potential earnings because (as shown in Table 5.2) physical ability does not correlate with potential earnings. The statistical equality of *potential* earnings between men and women suggests that the *observed* male-female earnings gap arises from factors other than functional abilities or their interaction with occupational requirements.

The differences in reported abilities between men and women are also consistent with bias from overconfidence among men (or underconfidence among women). The use of anchors in the O*NET ability scale is intended to guard against this type of bias by relating ability levels to concrete tasks individuals should be able to perform at each level. However, if male overconfidence bias contributes to the male-female ability gap, our key finding that potential earnings are not statistically different between men and women would either hold or we would find that women have higher potential earnings than men after accounting for overconfidence bias. Moreover, overconfidence and underconfidence may themselves affect observed labor outcomes; that is, while they do not change individuals' actual abilities, they may impact the occupations individuals feel they have the abilities to do and thus employment and income.

5.3. Work Capacity by Education

Differences in functional abilities and, consequently, in work capacity, are especially large across education groups. As shown in Table 5.5, college graduates report higher ability scores than non–college graduates, overall and by domain. The difference is especially pronounced for cognitive and physical abilities. Nongraduates have 138 (35 percent) fewer potential occupations than college graduates. The occupational penalty for not having a college degree is large; holding their abilities fixed, the potential occupation set of a nongraduate would increase by 50 occupations (27 percent) if they had a college degree. Further, both maximum and median potential earnings are lower for non–college graduates by 26 and 17 percent, respectively. Lastly, in analyses not shown, we find that 40 percent of the potential occupations of college graduates are expected to grow rapidly in the next several years or have large numbers of job openings,[8] compared to approximately 35 percent among non–college graduates.

5.4. Work Capacity by Race and Ethnicity

Table 5.6 examines functional abilities and work capacity by race/ethnicity. Due to small sample sizes for other groups, we focus on Black, white, and Hispanic adults. Black respondents report statistically equivalent ability scores compared to whites on average, and for cognitive and physical abilities. In contrast, they tend to report lower psychomotor and sensory abilities. Hispanic respondents similarly report statistically equivalent ability scores compared to whites on average, and for physical and psychomotor abilities, but report lower scores in the cognitive and sensory domains. These disparities in functional abilities translate into disparities in potential occupations. Compared to whites, Black adults have 16 percent fewer potential occupations while Hispanic adults have 22 percent fewer. The occupational penalty for not having a college degree is slightly higher for Blacks compared to whites, but slightly lower for Hispanics—a college degree increases the number of potential occupations by 31 percent among white adults, by 35 percent among Black adults, and by 28 percent among Hispanic adults. In terms of potential earnings, white adults have higher median (and maximum) potential earnings than Black[9] and Hispanic adults—at $36,065, $32,057, and $33,433, respectively.

TABLE 5.5 Average abilities and work capacity by Education

	(1) College graduates	(2) Nongraduates	(3) Difference
Average of self-assessed ability scores	4.688	4.319	−0.369
	(0.027)	(0.047)	(0.054)
Average of self-assessed cognitive ability scores	4.720	4.251	−0.469
	(0.031)	(0.050)	(0.059)
Average of self-assessed physical ability scores	4.456	4.135	−0.321
	(0.037)	(0.051)	(0.063)
Average of self-assessed psychomotor ability scores	4.863	4.610	−0.253
	(0.031)	(0.055)	(0.063)
Average of self-assessed sensory ability scores	4.659	4.332	−0.327
	(0.029)	(0.055)	(0.063)
Number of potential occupations	389.0	251.1	−137.9
	(13.5)	(13.3)	(19.0)
Number of potential occupations not requiring a bachelor's degree	258.7	183.5	−75.2
	(7.9)	(9.1)	(12.0)
Number of potential occupations requiring only a bachelor's degree	93.4	50.2	−43.2
	(4.2)	(3.5)	(5.5)
Number of potential occupations requiring an advanced degree	36.9	17.5	−19.4
	(1.9)	(1.4)	(2.4)
Maximum potential earnings	132,337	98,082	−34,256
	(2,920)	(3,389)	(4,473)
Median potential earnings	39,208	32,502	−6,707
	(444)	(653)	(790)
Observations	1,088	1,134	

Notes: Number of potential occupations is out of 936 occupations possible. Standard errors are in parentheses.

The white-Black and white-Hispanic potential earnings gaps are at 11 percent and 7 percent, respectively. In analyses not shown, we find that the potential occupation sets of Black adults (based solely on reported functional abilities) contain substantially more occupations that require little experience or formal training[10] compared to those of white adults, and, to a lesser degree, Hispanic adults; similarly, the potential occupation sets of Black adults have a smaller share of growing occupations, compared to white and Hispanic adults.

Lastly, it bears noting that these gaps in *potential* earnings are smaller than *observed* earnings gaps. For example, Black men earn 22 percent less than white men, while Black women earn 11.7 percent less than white women, holding constant education, experience,

TABLE 5.6 Average abilities and work capacity by race

	(1) Non-Hispanic White	(2) Non-Hispanic Black	(3) Hispanic
Average of self-assessed ability scores	4.516	4.285	4.373
	(0.035)	(0.134)	(0.069)
Average of self-assessed cognitive ability scores	4.475	4.335	4.297
	(0.037)	(0.153)	(0.078)
Average of self-assessed physical ability scores	4.293	3.998	4.242
	(0.042)	(0.153)	(0.069)
Average of self-assessed psychomotor ability scores	4.776	4.453	4.690
	(0.045)	(0.139)	(0.076)
Average of self-assessed sensory ability scores	4.539	4.272	4.340
	(0.036)	(0.129)	(0.081)
Number of potential occupations	319.8	267.9	250.1
	(12.3)	(31.1)	(23.1)
Number of potential occupations not requiring a bachelor's degree	224.6	179.4	181.7
	(7.9)	(20.7)	(15.1)
Number of potential occupations requiring only a bachelor's degree	70.0	62.7	50.5
	(3.5)	(8.0)	(6.6)
Number of potential occupations requiring an advanced degree	25.2	25.8	18.0
	(1.5)	(3.6)	(2.7)
Maximum potential earnings	114,147	105,596	102,562
	(2,915)	(8,659)	(5,824)
Median potential earnings	36,065	32,057	33,433
	(507)	(1,714)	(903)
Observations	1,495	254	242

Notes: Number of potential occupations is out of 936 occupations possible. Standard errors are in parentheses.

metro status, and region of residence (Wilson and Rodgers 2016). This suggests that disparities in functional ability may explain some but not all of the observed race-earnings gaps.

6. Work Capacity across Cohorts by Gender, Race, and Education

Although work capacity in aggregate declines modestly across age cohorts (see Table 5.3), it is nonetheless possible that health problems among specific demographic groups within these cohorts may portend rising rates of work disability among future older Americans in these groups. In this section, we investigate the age cohort patterns in work capacity—as summarized by potential earnings—within gender, race, and education groups.

Beginning with gender, Table 5.7 shows that maximum potential earnings for men decline slightly across age cohorts. In sharp contrast, potential earnings for women are U-shaped—that is, *lower* for middle-aged women than for their older (and younger) counterparts. This pattern reflects earlier onset of health problems for today's middle-aged women.

Table 5.8, which compares potential earnings by both age cohort and race, shows that changes across cohorts in potential earnings differ sharply between Black and white respondents. Although white and Black respondents' maximum potential earnings are similar among the young and middle-aged groups, they diverge at older ages. Maximum potential earnings drop substantially from the middle-aged cohort to the oldest cohort among Black respondents, contrasting with the small but *positive* difference for white respondents.

These differing potential earnings trajectories are consistent with cohort trends in health. Table 5.9 shows that while both groups report very good or excellent health about 47 percent of the time within the youngest cohort, white respondents report very good or excellent health at a rate 2.5 times higher than Black respondents in the age 62–71 cohort. As in the case of potential earnings, the oldest white respondents report very good or excellent health more frequently than middle-aged white respondents, but the oldest Black respondents report poorer health on average than middle-aged Black adults. These contrasting Black-white cohort-age trajectories likely reflect the very different life experiences of

TABLE 5.7 Average potential earnings by age and gender

	(1) Men	(2) Women	(3) Difference
Maximum potential earnings			
Age 25–49	116,897	112,125	–4,772
	(7,236)	(4,266)	(8,400)
Age 50–61	114,102	96,723	–17,379
	(5,856)	(3,913)	(7,043)
Age 62–71	105,314	105,316	2
	(4,571)	(4,658)	(6,526)
Median potential earnings			
Age 25–49	35,650	34,962	–688
	(1,490)	(673)	(1,635)
Age 50–61	35,750	32,792	–2,958
	(988)	(712)	(1,218)
Age 62–71	35,073	34,255	-818
	(796)	(768)	(1,106)
Observations		915	1,307

Notes: Standard errors are in parentheses.

TABLE 5.8 Average potential earnings by age and race

	(1) White Non-Hispanic	(2) Black Non-Hispanic	(3) Difference
Maximum potential earnings			
Age 25–49	121,326	109,312	−12,014
	(5,338)	(13,673)	(14,678)
Age 50–61	103,632	112,420	8,788
	(3,769)	(12,429)	(12,988)
Age 62–71	112,319	78,026	−34,293
	(3,649)	(9,060)	(9,767)
Median potential earnings			
Age 25–49	37,156	32,091	−5,065
	(955)	(2,712)	(2,875)
Age 50–61	34,436	33,678	−758
	(603)	(2,248)	(2,328)
Age 62–71	35,827	28,828	−6,999
	(592)	(2,126)	(2,207)
Observations	1,495	254	

Notes: Standard errors are in parentheses.

Black and white Americans. For Black respondents, they may reflect the cumulative effects of structural racism, which has barred many Black Americans from quality education and health care, among other things, throughout their lives. In contrast, economic disadvantage has come relatively recently to white Americans (particularly the less educated), resulting in today's middle-aged cohorts exhibiting worse health than middle-aged cohorts of the past (Case and Deaton 2020; Case, Deaton, and Stone 2020).

TABLE 5.9 Percent of respondents reporting very good or excellent health

	(1) White Non-Hispanic	(2) Black Non-Hispanic
Age 25–49	47.3	46.7
	(3.7)	(8.2)
Age 50–61	42.3	28.3
	(3.0)	(6.1)
Age 62–71	53.9	21.5
	(2.7)	(7.8)
Observations	1495	254

Notes: Standard errors are in parentheses.

TABLE 5.10 Average potential earnings by age and education

	(1) College graduates	(2) Nongraduates	(3) Difference
Maximum potential earnings			
Age 25–49	133,890	102,903	−30,987
	(4,617)	(5,696)	(7,332)
Age 50–61	130,689	93,785	−36,904
	(3,810)	(4,516)	(5,909)
Age 62–71	129,562	90,402	−39,160
	(3,677)	(4,481)	(5,797)
Median potential earnings			
Age 25–49	39,456	32,825	−6,631
	(687)	(1,122)	(1,316)
Age 50–61	38,779	32,207	−6,572
	(632)	(783)	(1,006)
Age 62–71	38,943	31,998	−6,945
	(634)	(755)	(986)
Observations	1,088	1,134	

Notes: Standard errors are in parentheses.

Table 5.10 displays potential earnings by age cohort and education level. Although college graduates have higher potential earnings than non–college graduates in every cohort, the trajectories differ within educational groups. Maximum potential earnings hold steady across age cohorts among college-educated respondents but decline across cohorts among non–college graduates, amplifying inequalities by education in the older cohorts. Our finding above of opposing age-cohort trajectories in work capacity for Black respondents versus whites suggests that the aggregate age-education patterns likely mask important differences by race.

7. Discussion and Conclusions

Our findings suggest that differences in functional ability will influence to whom the burdens and benefits of working longer accrue. While functional ability declines across age cohorts, potential earnings decline only modestly, suggesting that the current cohort of older individuals maintains the ability to work into their late 60s and early 70s. However, declines in physical ability may still disrupt some workers' abilities to do their (physically demanding) jobs as they age—a burden which likely falls primarily on non–college graduates who, as we have shown, have fewer potential occupations and lower potential earnings than graduates. Furthermore, the potential occupations of non–college graduates are more concentrated in occupations that are not expected to grow in the future. By contrast, while the existence of differences in reported functional ability by race and gender has sizeable effects on potential occupations, differences in potential earnings are modest. This suggests that differences in functional abilities can explain only part of the observed gender- and race-related gaps in earnings, implying that factors other than functional abilities play larger roles.

Finally, considering how work capacity evolves across cohorts for different groups is crucial to understanding the heterogeneous impacts of working longer both for Americans now at traditional retirement ages and for younger cohorts as they age. While our study is the first to collect nationally representative data on individuals' functional abilities on the same scale that O*NET uses to evaluate occupational demands, its cross-sectional design limits us from making definitive statements about the evolution of individuals' work capacity because we do not observe those individuals' abilities at multiple points in time. However, we observe interesting cross-sectional patterns across cohorts that suggest how work capacity may evolve. Middle-aged white respondents have lower potential earnings and report worse health than whites ages 62–71. As these respondents age, their work capacity will decline and thus they may face more difficulties with employment than older-age white individuals do today. The opposite is true for middle-aged Black respondents, who have substantially greater work capacity than Black respondents in the oldest cohort. We also find that gaps in potential earnings between college graduates and nongraduates are large and increase with age, suggesting that declining health and functional abilities disproportionately constrain the capacity of those with less education to work longer.

Notes

1. We thank Lisa Berkman, Beth Truesdale, Kathleen McGarry, Jonathan Skinner, and attendees of *America's Aging Workforce and the Challenge of Working Longer* authors' conferences, Stockholm University Swedish Institute for Social Research's Workshop on Diversity and Workplace Inclusion, Stanford University Institute for Economic Policy Research's Working Longer and Retirement Conference, the Tufts University Department of Economics Seminar, and the Michigan State University Department of Economics Applied Economics Seminar for helpful feedback. Michael Jetsupphasuk provided outstanding research assistance. This research was supported by the National Institute on Aging (R01AG056239) and the Alfred P. Sloan Foundation.
2. The raking procedure is described here: https://www.rand.org/research/data/alp/panel/weighting.html.
3. O*NET uses the Standard Occupational Classification (SOC) system to catalog occupations at a detailed, six-digit level. Six-digit occupations are narrowly defined to include workers who perform similar job tasks. O*NET further subdivides certain six-digit occupations (approximately 6 percent) to an eight-digit level using its O*NET-SOC taxonomy (which is identical to the SOC taxonomy for six-digit occupations that are not further subdivided). The O*NET-SOC taxonomy also includes some new occupations that have not yet been added to the SOC. We use the O*NET 23.3 Database (May 2019 Release) (O*NET Resource Center 2019), which contains 773 six-digit SOC occupations and 967 O*NET-SOC occupations (which encompass the 773 SOC occupations). This data release is based on the 2010 version of the SOC system. The database includes an additional 136 six-digit SOC occupations for which data are not collected. These include military occupations and occupations in the catch-all category "All Other" that are not classified elsewhere.
4. Additionally, while AWCAS self-ratings are in discrete increments between 1 and 7, O*NET ratings are averages of eight occupational analysts' judgments and therefore often take decimal values.

5. We also do not require individuals to exceed the levels of 153 ability-occupation pairs that O*NET analysts recommend suppressing due to the high variance of the analysts' required level ratings. Requiring these abilities for occupations does not substantially change any of our results.
6. López García, Maestas, and Mullen (2019) present formulations of the measure that are less strict, giving partial credit in cases where respondents lack the complete set of abilities required in determining potential occupation sets.
7. We determine required level of education by using data from O*NET on incumbents' assessments of required education. For each occupation, we choose the level of education most frequently reported by incumbents as required. In the event of a tie, we choose the lower level of education.
8. Occupations expected to grow rapidly in the next several years or have large numbers of job openings are assigned a "Bright Outlook" designation by O*NET.
9. The Black-white difference seems to be driven by the oldest Black respondents (see Table 5.8).
10. Such occupations are assigned to Job Zone 1 by O*NET. The five O*NET Job Zone designations tier occupations by level of required preparation (e.g., work experience, education and training), with level 1 indicating the least preparation required and level 5 the most.

References

Bailey, Zinzi D., Nancy Krieger, Madina Agénor, Jasmine Graves, Natalia Linos, and Mary T. Bassett. 2017. "Structural Racism and Health Inequities in the USA: Evidence and Interventions." *The Lancet* 389 (10077): 1453–1463. https://doi.org/10.1016/S0140-6736(17)30569-X.

Berger, Maximus, and Zoltán Sarnyai. 2015. "'More Than Skin Deep': Stress Neurobiology and Mental Health Consequences of Racial Discrimination." *Stress* 18 (1): 1–10. https://doi.org/10.3109/10253 890.2014.989204.

Cahill, Kevin E., Michael D. Giandrea, and Joseph F. Quinn. 2016. "Evolving Patterns of Work and Retirement." In *Handbook of Aging and the Social Sciences* (8th ed.), edited by Linda K. George and Kenneth F. Ferraro, 271–291. San Diego: Academic Press. https://doi.org/10.1016/B978-0-12-417 235-7.00013-5.

Case, Anne, and Angus Deaton. 2020. *Deaths of Despair and the Future of Capitalism*. Princeton, NJ: Princeton University Press.

Case, Anne, Angus Deaton, and Arthur A. Stone. 2020. "Decoding the Mystery of American Pain Reveals a Warning for the Future." *Proceedings of the National Academy of Sciences* 117 (40): 24785–24789. Retrieved from https://doi.org/10.1073/pnas.2012350117, June 1, 2022.

Centers for Disease Control and Prevention. 2020. "National Diabetes Statistics Report 2020. Estimates of Diabetes and Its Burden in the United States." CS 314227-A. Washington, DC: US Department of Health and Human Services. https://www.cdc.gov/diabetes/pdfs/data/statistics/national-diabetes-statistics-rep ort.pdf.

Crimmins, Eileen M. 2015. "Lifespan and Healthspan: Past, Present, and Promise." *The Gerontologist* 55 (6): 901–911. https://doi.org/10.1093/geront/gnv130.

López García, Italo, Nicole Maestas, and Kathleen Mullen. 2019. "Latent Work Capacity and Retirement Expectations." Working Paper MRDRC WP 2019-400. Ann Arbor: Michigan Retirement and Disability Research Center, University of Michigan. https://doi.org/10.2139/ssrn.3489371.

Maestas, Nicole, Kathleen J. Mullen, David Powell, Till von Wachter, and Jeffrey B. Wenger. 2018. "The American Working Conditions Survey Data." Data Set. Santa Monica, CA: RAND Corporation. https://alpdata.rand.org/index.php?page=data&p=showsurvey&syid=503.

Montez, Jennifer Karas, Anna Zajacova, Mark D. Hayward, Steven H. Woolf, Derek Chapman, and Jason Beckfield. 2019. "Educational Disparities in Adult Mortality across U.S. States: How Do They Differ, and Have They Changed Since the Mid-1980s?" *Demography* 56 (2): 621–644. https://doi.org/10.1007/s13 524-018-0750-z.

Newhall, Karina, Emily Spangler, Nino Dzebisashvili, David C. Goodman, and Philip Goodney. 2016. "Amputation Rates for Patients with Diabetes and Peripheral Arterial Disease: The Effects of Race and Region." *Annals of Vascular Surgery* 30 (January): 292–298. https://doi.org/10.1016/j.avsg.2015.07.040.

O*NET Resource Center. 2019. "Data Dictionary—O*NET 23.3 Database: Abilities." Data Dictionary. Raleigh, NC: National Center for O*NET Development. https://www.onetcenter.org/db_releases.html.

Rejeski, W. Jack, Edward H. Ip, Alain G. Bertoni, George A. Bray, Gina Evans, Edward W. Gregg, Qiang Zhang, and Look AHEAD Research Group. 2012. "Lifestyle Change and Mobility in Obese Adults with Type 2 Diabetes." *The New England Journal of Medicine* 366 (13): 1209–1217. https://doi.org/10.1056/NEJMoa1110294.

U.S. Bureau of Labor Statistics. 2018. "May 2018 National Occupational Employment and Wage Estimates." Occupational Employment and Wage Statistics. https://www.bls.gov/oes/2018/may/oes_nat.htm#00-0000.

Vaupel, James W. 2010. "Biodemography of Human Ageing." *Nature* 464 (7288): 536–542. https://doi.org/10.1038/nature08984.

Wilson, Valerie, and William M. Rodgers III. 2016. "Black-White Wage Gaps Expand with Rising Wage Inequality." Washington, DC: Economic Policy Institute. https://www.epi.org/publication/black-white-wage-gaps-expand-with-rising-wage-inequality/.

Woolf, Steven H., Derek A. Chapman, Jeanine M. Buchanich, Kendra J. Bobby, Emily B. Zimmerman, and Sarah M. Blackburn. 2018. "Changes in Midlife Death Rates Across Racial and Ethnic Groups in the United States: Systematic Analysis of Vital Statistics." *BMJ* 362 (August): k3096. https://doi.org/10.1136/bmj.k3096.

Woolf, Steven H., and Heidi Schoomaker. 2019. "Life Expectancy and Mortality Rates in the United States, 1959–2017." *JAMA* 322 (20): 1996–2016. https://doi.org/10.1001/jama.2019.16932.

6
The Psychology of Working Longer

Margaret E. Beier and Meghan K. Davenport

1. Introduction

Why do some people work at older ages, while others do not? Answers to this question often focus on economic and social realities such as job availability, financial insecurity, family commitments, and worker health. But these explanations, while important, tell only part of the story. People make decisions about working longer for many reasons not explained by economic and social realities. Some people, for example, may feel motivated to continue using their skills and abilities to contribute to society in a meaningful way; others may see their work as an opportunity to learn new things or to stay socially connected. This chapter presents a psychological perspective on working longer. In contrast to economic and sociological perspectives, psychological perspectives take a person-centric view of individual behaviors and consider contextual factors in terms of their influence on individual skills, attitudes, and motivation.

In this chapter, we make four main arguments. First, decisions to work longer are a function of a continuous developmental process of growth and decline, which is highly variable from person to person. Second, person and environment factors shape decisions to work or to retire through their influences on skills, perceptions of one's ability to work, and motivation to work. Third, environmental features that affect individual development and decisions to work longer operate at the level of the job, the organization, and the broader sociocultural context. Because other chapters cover the larger sociocultural context, we focus mainly on organization and job-related factors. Finally, organizations can influence individuals' decisions to work longer by modifying the work environment.

The influence of context on decisions to work longer is particularly salient given the global impact of the COVID-19 pandemic. In the United States, for example, 7 percent (or 2.9 million) of workers ages 55 to 70 exited the labor force during the first three months of the pandemic (March to June 2020) compared with 4.8 percent of workers ages 18 to 54. While all workers are vulnerable to job elimination, layoffs, and a dwindling job market in

precarious times, health concerns among older workers accelerated their exit fro.
force and inhibited their reentry. By June 2020, 38 percent of the older workers v
labor market gave up looking for work and officially retired (Papadopoulos et al.
the face of such extreme historical events, particularly when work is hard to find reg,
individual behavior, it is perhaps useful to ask about the importance of psychologica.
for predicting decisions to work longer or to retire. We assert that it is crucial to understand how the psychology of working longer is influenced by cultural and environmental characteristics against such a stark backdrop. In a global crisis, keeping one's current job, finding bridge employment, or starting a new job may depend on an individual's motivation and ability to overcome extreme obstacles to persevere.

We take a lifespan perspective to examine the psychology of working longer, which emphasizes the continuous, lifelong process of growth and loss influenced by individual and contextual factors (Baltes 1987). The continuity of the lifespan perspective contrasts with life-stage models, which delineate discrete normative life stages (e.g., young adulthood, middle age, old age). Because lifespan theories consider aging a continuous process, they do not identify a set age at which people become "older." One person at age 50 may resemble a typical 70-year-old in abilities and motivation, while another may resemble a typical 30-year-old (Hertzog et al. 2008). Although below we describe normative trends in ability and motivation, individuals' experiences may differ greatly from these averages.

The chapter is organized in three parts. First, we present a model that incorporates theory and research on the person and environmental factors influencing decisions to work longer. We then link elements of our model to human resource (HR) practices that have been effective for engaging older workers. We conclude with directions for future research.

2. A Psychological Model of Working Longer

Our model, shown in Figure 6.1, focuses on the psychological determinants of working longer, by which we mean working beyond traditional retirement ages embedded in pension eligibility and cultural norms (e.g., beyond the early 60s in the United States). The model reflects the complex nature of modern retirement, which may include a reduction of responsibility over time, bridge employment, and/or the exploration of a completely new career. Cutting across each of these scenarios are options about the number of hours worked (full-time or part-time) and how these hours are organized (James, Matz-Costa, and Smyer 2016).

At the center of Figure 6.1 are three interrelated psychological factors derived from a person's work history and life experiences that directly influence decisions to continue working: (a) work-related skills, (b) work ability perceptions, which are individuals' perceptions of their capacity to meet job demands and to continue working (McGonagle et al. 2015), and (c) motivation to work (Kanfer, Beier, and Ackerman 2013). These psychological factors are influenced by individual attributes, environmental features, and variables that derive from the cumulative effects of a person's interactions with their environment, called "person-context transaction variables" (Kanfer, Beier, and Ackerman 2013). Transaction variables include work-related goals, a person's perception of time left in life, or "future time

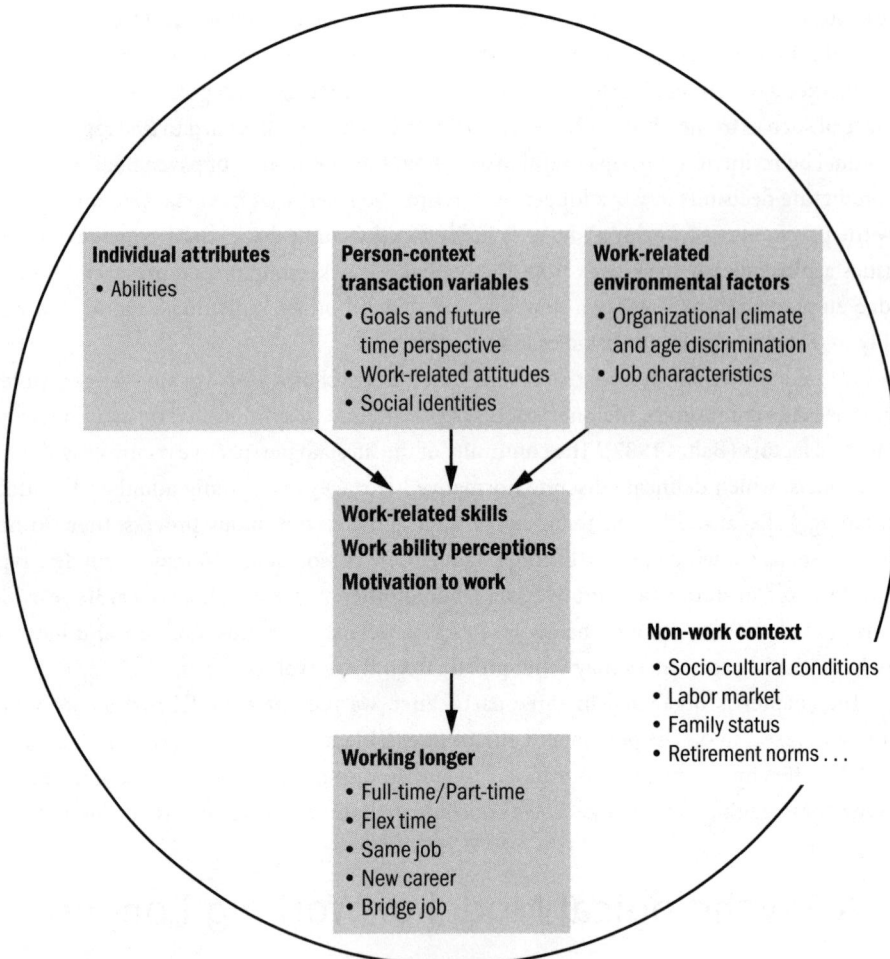

FIGURE 6.1 A model of the antecedents of working longer
The model proposes that individual and environmental factors influence working longer—defined as working past the years normally slated for retirement—through their effect on work-related skills, perceptions of those skills (work ability perceptions), and motivation at work.

perspective" (Kooij et al. 2018), and work-related attitudes. Transaction variables also include social identities, which result from the interaction between individual demographic attributes (e.g., age, race, or gender) and one's cultural context (Tajfel and Turner 2004).

Finally, reflecting the lifespan approach, the model in Figure 6.1 acknowledges that decisions to work longer do not happen in a vacuum. Sociocultural and economic phenomena such as the types of jobs available, family status and caregiving demands, and retirement norms within a community or family influence the psychology of working longer and the contexts in which people work (Kanfer, Beier, and Ackerman 2013). For example, the COVID-19 pandemic influenced decisions to work longer through individual health and wealth considerations, workers' motivation and work ability perceptions, and the availability of different types of work for older workers. Next, we unpack the elements of our model.

2.1. Individual Attributes

Individual attributes are characteristics of people considered largely independent of the environment, such as cognitive abilities and personality traits. We discuss race and gender (which are often considered individual attributes) as person-context transaction variables below because their importance for work and aging is the role they play in the development of social identity. Personality has not been extensively studied in the context of decisions to work longer or to retire, so it is not covered here (although see Staudinger [2020] for a discussion of personality and lifespan development). Here we focus on cognitive abilities because they are relatively stable and less affected by contextual factors than other constructs we examine, but we acknowledge that abilities are affected by environmental factors (e.g., socioeconomic status and educational opportunities; Cottrell, Newman, and Roisman 2015).

2.1.1. Age and Abilities

Psychological theories of workplace aging describe aging as a process of decline and growth (Kanfer and Ackerman 2004). *Decline* refers to well-documented declines in cognitive abilities such as working memory capacity, cognitive processing speed, and short-term memory, which people rely on to solve novel problems. When compared directly in cross-sectional studies, younger adults tend to perform better than older adults on reasoning ability tests, which has been interpreted as evidence of substantial lifespan declines in these abilities. Longitudinal research that examines changes within individuals over time suggests less precipitous declines in these abilities, although declines are still apparent (Schaie 2013). One possible explanation for this tension is that cross-sectional comparisons cannot distinguish between cohort-related changes and age-related changes. For example, graduates entering the workforce in 2020 have grown up with access to smartphones and other technology that may affect how they solve problems.

Cohort effects will also potentially affect a person's decisions to work or to retire. For instance, different histories with technology for 50- and 25-year-olds will make acquiring new technology skills relatively more challenging for the 50-year-old compared to the 25-year-old regardless of ability level. But age-related changes in abilities also play a role. Declines in reasoning abilities will make learning new things more challenging for older learners relative to their younger selves, and perceptions of the amount of effort involved in learning new things affects motivation for engaging in developmental activities (Kanfer and Ackerman 2004).

To understand how reasoning abilities are related to decisions to work or retire, Beier et al. (2020) assessed the effect of fit between job demands and worker abilities (demands-ability fit) for workers over 50 on retirement decisions. They found that when workers' reasoning abilities were matched to, or exceeded, the demands of the job, they were likely to report working longer. However, when the reasoning demands of the job exceeded workers' reasoning abilities, they were likely to retire at earlier ages. These findings reinforce the idea that—because of declining reasoning abilities with age—jobs that tap those abilities will be particularly difficult for older workers.

The decline in reasoning abilities is offset by continuous *growth* in knowledge abilities, defined as the knowledge acquired over the lifespan through formal educational environments and experience (Salthouse 2010). Older adults tend to outperform younger adults on tests of knowledge across academic (history, literature) and nonacademic (current events, technology) domains (Ackerman 2007). In work contexts, age is associated with job knowledge that comes from experience either at a specific job (e.g., an internal client management software) or across different jobs (e.g., project management) (Beier, Young, and Villado 2018). As people age, their growing knowledge compensates for declining reasoning abilities to enable people to tackle job tasks that tend to rely on knowledge gained through experience (Beier, Torres, and Beal 2020). Because job performance is largely a function of knowledge rather than reasoning abilities, older people tend to perform just as well in their jobs as younger people do (Ng and Feldman 2008).

Together, reasoning and knowledge abilities represent the cognitive resources that a person can bring to bear on a given task, and as such, they affect the ease with which someone accomplishes a task. Because they affect task performance, abilities also influence attitudes about the task (e.g., whether or not the task is fun and interesting, whether it can be accomplished with ease) and perceptions about the self (e.g., whether I am skilled or unskilled). Thus, age-related changes in abilities affect decisions to work and to retire through their effect on the development of job-related skills, and through perceptions of work ability and motivation to work (Kanfer and Ackerman 2004).

2.2. Person-Context Transaction Factors

Social scientists often think of goals, attitudes, and social identities as characteristics of individuals. In fact, they are the product of interactions between individuals and their environments. These person-context transaction factors reflect the "cumulative effects that an individual's life and work experiences with his/her environment have on work-related goals and motivation" (Kanfer, Beier, and Ackerman 2013, 259). Person-context transaction variables include health, wealth, and education, which are discussed elsewhere in this volume. Here we focus on variables most pertinent to the psychology of working longer: goals and future time perspectives, job attitudes, and social identities.

2.2.1. Goals and Future Time Perspective

Perceptions of time remaining—called "future time perspectives"—typically change with age and affect goals for working longer (Kanfer and Ackerman 2004). Future time perspectives have been studied relative to time left in life (Carstensen, Isaacowitz, and Charles 1999) and also in relation to an employee's remaining time in the work context (Zacher and Frese 2009). These perspectives are part of socioemotional selectivity theory, which posits that younger people often perceive the future as expansive, so they focus on developing knowledge and skills that will make them successful in the future and focus on growth and achievement-oriented goals. By contrast, older people often perceive time as limited, so they adopt goals that are socioemotionally fulfilling such as developing meaningful relationships (Carstensen, Isaacowitz, and Charles 1999).

Socioemotional selectivity theory predicts that younger workers, who typically have more expansive time perspectives, are likely to value job roles that provide opportunity for growth and achievement (e.g., learning new skills, engaging in stretch assignments, obtaining more pay and promotions), while older workers, who typically have more restricted time perspectives, are likely to have goals related to intrinsic interests and developing relationships with others (e.g., focusing on a pet project, mentoring younger workers). In support of this theory, a longitudinal study of university workers found that an expansive time perspective—not age per se—was the key factor in workers' achievement motivation, growth motives, and motivation to work longer (Kooij, Bal, and Kanfer 2014). Meta-analytic research on workplace goals also shows that work-related goals tend to shift from achievement to socioemotional with age (Kooij et al. 2011).

The negative effect of restricted future time perspectives on achievement goals (Kooij et al. 2011; Kooij, Bal, and Kanfer 2014) might imply that organizations should deny achievement-oriented opportunities to older workers, but this would be a mistake. Due to the age-related variability described earlier, many older workers continue to adopt a relatively expansive future time perspective and achievement goals throughout their careers. Furthermore, denying opportunity to workers solely based on age is not only discriminatory but also illegal in many countries. A more productive interpretation of these findings is that achievement opportunities may be better received by older workers if they are framed in terms that align with older workers' goals. For example, framing an opportunity to learn a new client management software as a way to enable more meaningful connections with customers—rather than as a means to a promotion—might increase some older workers' motivation to learn the software.

As a person-context transaction variable, future time perspective is potentially malleable, which suggests that organizations might be able to facilitate more expansive future time perspectives in their workers (Kooij et al. 2018). Although there is limited research on this topic, we do know that company policies that promote employee growth and development at all ages and perceptions of age-friendly organizational cultures tend to extend occupational future time perspectives, leading to later retirement ages (Zacher and Yang 2016; Korff, Biemann, and Voelpel 2017).

The shift from achievement/growth to socioemotional goals also depends somewhat on occupation. Kooij et al. (2011) found that, as expected, age was negatively related to growth motives among workers in professional nonmanagerial jobs, such as engineers, accountants, and scientists. But age was *positively* related to growth motives for workers in manual jobs, such as factory workers and electricians (i.e., older workers expressed greater growth motives). One possible explanation for this finding is that manual jobs tend to be physically demanding, so workers in these jobs may anticipate the need for skill enhancement and retraining as they grow older. More research is needed to understand the effects of the work context and occupation type on motivational processes such as future time perspectives and worker goals. In general, however, research highlights the potential for organizational policies and job design to extend working lives.

2.2.2. Job Attitudes

Job attitudes are a function of both dispositional and contextual factors. For example, managers will not be surprised that subordinates who are higher in negative affectivity tend to be dissatisfied with their work, and those higher in positive affectivity tend to be more satisfied, regardless of the day, job, or organizational context (Judge and Kammeyer-Mueller 2012). Some job attitudes are more malleable than others, and for job attitudes like job satisfaction, changes may be more important than absolute levels in predicting decisions to work longer (Zacher and Rudolph 2017).

Work centrality, or the extent to which work is central to a person's identity or self-concept (Paullay, Alliger, and Stone-Romero 1994), is not necessarily related to a specific job. Rather, it is a more stable, dispositional, work attitude and tends to be unaffected by organization and job-specific characteristics. People who are higher in work centrality typically intend to work longer and are more likely to return to work after retirement than those for whom work is less central (Armstrong-Stassen and Ursel 2009; Post et al. 2013; Beier, LoPilato, and Kanfer 2018). Although it predicts intentions to work longer, because of its stable nature, there is relatively little an organization can do to change a given worker's level of work centrality.

Although job satisfaction has a dispositional component—those who are more generally dissatisfied are likely to be dissatisfied with their job—job satisfaction is somewhat malleable. Age has a small positive relationship with job satisfaction, defined as a state of contentment with one's job (Judge and Kammeyer-Mueller 2012), and there are many potential reasons for this relationship. Older workers may have had more opportunity over their careers to actively shape their work environments, either through changing those environments or changing how they think about their work, both of which are facets of "job crafting" (Kooij, Tims, and Kanfer 2015). Age is also related to greater sensitivity for positive versus negative stimuli (Mather and Carstensen 2005), suggesting that the positive relationship between age and job satisfaction reflects a tendency for older workers to focus on factors that enhance versus detract from satisfaction (i.e., they are less likely to sweat the small stuff). The positive relationship between age and job satisfaction could also be attributable to selection bias in that those who are more dissatisfied with work are more likely to leave the workforce at earlier ages. The relationship between age and job satisfaction is thus a function of disposition and complex interactions between a worker and his or her work environment over the course of a career.

Job satisfaction appears to have little effect on workers' decisions to retire or keep working, however. When a relationship is found at all, the effects tend to be weaker than the relationships found between job satisfaction and *turnover* intentions (i.e., intentions to leave one job for another; Fisher, Chaffee, and Sonnega 2016). Although job satisfaction may affect both decisions to retire and decisions to change jobs, many other factors influence decisions to exit the workforce completely (e.g., savings, health, family situation) that do not necessarily influence decisions to leave one job for another. However, for older workers who need to remain in the workforce, job attitudes are an important determinant of *how*, not whether, they choose to retire. For instance, job attitudes are positively related to older workers' intention to scale back on job duties but to continue working in the same organization after retirement. Conversely, workers who are less satisfied are more likely to seek postretirement bridge employment outside of their career organizations (Fisher, Chaffee, and Sonnega 2016).

Although absolute levels of job attitudes are only weakly related to retirement and turnover intentions, *changes* in job satisfaction show larger effects (Chen et al. 2011; Zacher and

Rudolph 2017). An example illustrates this point. We might expect two workers ("David" and "Dominique") with the same job satisfaction score (4 on a 5-point scale) both to have relatively low turnover or retirement intentions because their absolute level of job satisfaction is relatively high. However, if David reported a 5 on last year's job satisfaction index, and Dominque a 3, then it is likely that David, whose job satisfaction decreased over the course of a year, would be more likely to want to leave his job than Dominique, whose job satisfaction increased. Thus, in addition to considering who is most and least satisfied among a group of employees, employers should focus on within-person comparisons for predicting who will want to continue working versus retire (Zacher and Rudolph 2017).

2.2.3. Social Identities

Demographic characteristics shape the formation of social identities that provide an orientation for self-reference that affects attitudes and behaviors (Tajfel and Turner 2004). In our model, social identities are the person-context transition variables derived from the interaction of demographic factors within the larger sociocultural context. Although research often focuses on one social identity at a time (such as gender, race, or social class), a single person holds multiple identities and experiences the workplace at the intersection of those identities in ways that overlap, compound each other, and are difficult to disentangle (Crenshaw 1989). Although we know of no research that has directly examined the relationship between social identities and decisions to work longer, research on social identities in the workplace suggests that the more workers report suppressing their identities (e.g., they refrain from talking about their identity and using language, listening to music, or eating food that might be associated with their identities), the more they perceive workplace discrimination, the lower their job satisfaction, and the greater their turnover intentions (Madera, King, and Hebl 2012). It seems likely that older workers' comfort expressing their social identities at work would affect their decisions to work longer in their current organizations.

The role of social identity in workplace aging is a potentially fruitful area of future research. Researchers should focus not only on singular identities but also on their intersection to understand fully how social identity affects decisions to work longer or to retire. The research cited above also highlights the importance of organizational climates where workers feel comfortable in expressing their identities, a topic we turn to next.

2.3. Work-Related Environmental Factors

Environmental factors that influence decisions to work longer operate on many different levels. At the organizational level, messages of support for or discrimination against older workers can be subtle and impactful. While organization-level factors are important, the experience of work is largely a function of the worker's interaction with his or her job, the characteristics of which might facilitate or inhibit working longer.

2.3.1. Organizational Climate and Age Discrimination

Organizational climate is defined as "shared perceptions of and the meaning attached to the policies, practices, and procedures employees experience" (Schneider, Ehrhart, and Macey

2013, 362). Understanding how climate affects individual workers requires analysis at multiple levels from the overall organization to work units. To date, however, very little research has examined the effect of organizational climate on intentions to work longer, and none that we found took a multilevel approach. The research that has been done suggests that, after accounting for health and wealth, older workers tend to want to remain in organizations that promote age-friendly policies (e.g., provide opportunities to mature employees to take on new roles, offer incentives to mentor others) and implement those policies fairly (Armstrong-Stassen and Schlosser 2011). The availability of training and development opportunities is also an important determinant of perceived organizational support, which positively affects intentions to remain working (Armstrong-Stassen and Ursel 2009).

Unsurprisingly, perceived discrimination is an important aspect of an organizational climate, and age discrimination has been studied extensively. Organizational policies that support overt discrimination, such as expressly denying older workers the opportunity to participate in training programs, are increasingly rare due to legal protections. By contrast, subtle discrimination is more common, more ambiguous to the receiver of the discrimination, difficult to detect, and more likely to be internalized (i.e., "Something is wrong with me"). Examples of subtle age-related discrimination are excluding older workers from future planning meetings due to assumptions of impending retirement and giving high-profile assignments to younger workers on the belief that they will benefit more from the exposure. To our knowledge, there is no research on overt versus subtle age discrimination, but studies of racial discrimination suggest that overt and subtle discrimination are equally pernicious and can lead to disengagement from work and decreased well-being, both of which may reduce an individual's desire to work longer (Jones et al. 2016).

Ageist stereotypes are at the root of discrimination and impact how older workers are treated by organizations, coworkers, and managers, as well as how workers see themselves (Posthuma and Campion 2009). Some of the most prevalent age-related stereotypes are that older workers are poor performers, less motivated to work, less willing to participate in training and development activities, more resistant to change, less healthy, less trusting, more vulnerable to work-family imbalance issues, and more likely to leave the organization than are younger adults (Posthuma and Campion 2009; Ng and Feldman 2012). For the most part, empirical research does not support these stereotypes. There is no evidence that older workers are worse performers, less motivated, less willing to change, less healthy, less trusting, or more vulnerable to work-family issues than are younger workers. Empirical support has been found only for a negative relationship between age and motivation for training and development (Ng and Feldman 2012) and a negative relationship between age and performance in workplace training and development activities (Ng and Feldman 2008).

The finding that older workers tend to be less motivated for training and development (Ng and Feldman 2012) aligns with research on future time perspectives discussed above (Kooij et al. 2011). But reduced motivation for training seems contrary to the finding that training and development programs signal organizational support to older workers (Armstrong-Stassen and Ursel 2009). There are many explanations for these seemingly contradictory findings. Perhaps older workers are jaded about the value of organization-sponsored training given negative experiences in the past, although they may see the value of these activities for their colleagues. Or perhaps they have internalized age-related stereotypes about their own ability to learn and develop with age. What is clear is that, even if many older workers do not desire training and development opportunities for themselves, the existence of such opportunities signals an organization's investment in people.

Age-based stereotypes—regardless of their veracity—can affect not only the opportunities older workers receive from their organizations, coworkers, and managers, but it can lead to internalization, and thus perpetuation, of the stereotypes. For instance, older workers who believe they are unable to learn new things may assume that difficulty encountered in training is an uncontrollable byproduct of age instead of something they can change through effort. Such an assumption would create a self-fulfilling prophecy by negatively affecting motivation for, and performance in, training and development activities (Beier, Teachout, and Cox 2012). The internalization of such stereotypes may depend more on individual workers' perceptions of their relative age in the work context than their chronological age (i.e., their age relative to their organization, their work group, or their supervisor; Armstrong-Stassen and Lee 2009). For example, older workers with supervisors perceived to be similar to them in age felt more respected than older workers with supervisors perceived to be younger, and older workers with age-similar work groups felt that they were afforded more tailored training opportunities than older workers with younger or middle-aged work groups. In addition to perceptions of one's own age, attitudes about these perceptions are also important. In a sample of older workers, the negative relationship between perceived organizational age discrimination and workplace engagement was strong when employees thought of themselves as older workers, but close to zero when workers also indicated that they were happy being older (Bayl-Smith and Griffin 2014). Organizations that promote positive attitudes about aging may avoid worker disengagement.

2.3.2. Job Characteristics

Organizational climates can send messages about the value of older workers and influence decisions to work longer, but workers' day-to-day experiences are most influenced by their jobs. Job characteristics—the content, structure, tasks, and activities associated with a job—influence both workers' perceptions that they have the skills to continue working and their motivation to do so. Job design refers to the engineering of a job's characteristics with the goals of facilitating performance and motivating employees. Arguably the most parsimonious and flexible job design model is the Job Demands and Resources (JD-R) model (Demerouti et al. 2001). *Job demands* require physical or mental resources and have physical or psychological costs. Job demands are further divided into *hindrance job demands*, which involve excessive undesirable constraints and interfere with goal achievement, and *challenge job demands*, which cost effort but promote growth and achievement. Time pressure and shift work are examples of hindrance job demands, while "stretch" work assignments that provide a means to develop desired skills are examples of challenge job demands. *Job resources* are aspects of the job that promote personal growth and development and support the achievement of work goals. Examples include supervisor and coworker support, feedback, autonomy over how and when work gets done, and rewards including recognition, promotion, and pay.

Job demands and resources have consequences for health and motivation for workers of all ages. Job demands promote stress, exhaustion, and burnout, while job resources promote job engagement. However, job demands and resources interact such that job resources can buffer the effect of job demands on outcomes like stress and strain. Jobs that offer both challenge demands and resources tend to result in greater worker engagement and better job performance (Bakker and Demerouti 2017). It remains unclear whether jobs high in challenge demands—even if offset by job resources—lead to exhaustion and burnout over an extended period of time, however. Moreover, whether job demands are perceived as hindrances or challenges depends on individuals' perceptions of their own abilities and the work context (Tuckey et al. 2015). In the context of working longer, it is likely that some job demands change from perceived challenge to hindrance as workers age, although there is no research examining the dynamic nature of job characteristics over the career lifespan.

Job demands and resources also affect the development of skills, perceptions of work ability, and motivation to work. Pak et al. (2019) found that physical job demands and unfavorable work times such as shift work—arguably hindrance demands for older workers—were associated with lower work ability perceptions and less motivation to work past traditional retirement ages. By contrast, resources such as job control, skill discretion (e.g., having autonomy over when and how work gets done), and social support from managers and coworkers were associated with higher work ability perceptions and motivation to continue working. Indeed, job demands and resources appear to be more important for motivation and perceptions of work ability among older workers than among younger workers, suggesting that older workers are especially sensitive both to job demands and to resources provided by the jobs. This has important implications for real-world job design interventions, which should focus not only on reducing demands but also on increasing resources for older workers.

3. Organizational Policies to Encourage Working Longer

The aging of the global workforce is focusing attention on how organizational practices motivate workers who are near normative retirement age. These organizational practices are aimed at affecting work-related environmental factors (from Figure 6.1), particularly as related to job characteristics and maintaining or developing work-related skills, work-ability perceptions, and motivation to work. Four bundles of HR practices have been identified (Pak et al. 2019): (a) *maintenance practices* that permit workers to maintain their current level of functioning in the face of new challenges (e.g., flexible schedules), (b) *utilization practices* that help workers return to previous performance levels after a loss by eliminating job demands that can no longer be accomplished and replacing them with tasks that tap different existing skills (e.g., a lateral move), (c) *developmental practices* that help workers reach higher levels of functioning (e.g., organizational training), and (d) *accommodative practices*, in which jobs are organized around a lower level of functioning when maintenance and development are no longer desired or possible (e.g., reduction of physical labor job tasks).

Developmental, maintenance, and accommodation practices were positively related to motivation and work ability perceptions for older workers. There is sparse evidence for the effectiveness of utilization practices to date, but research in this area has only just begun. Notably, the effectiveness of any one of these approaches will depend on the job and preferences of the individual worker.

An important question is whether HR practices should be general or tailored to different age groups. We do not recommend age-related HR practices because of the variability associated with aging (i.e., age-targeted interventions would likely miss their mark for many older workers) and because they may be perceived as discriminatory. However, HR practices that improve older workers' experiences are likely to benefit workers of all ages because they are likely to enhance accessibility. For example, an investment in training modules that adapt to the pace and unique abilities of learners may be undertaken in an effort to facilitate older workers' training success, and such adaptive training would ultimately benefit all workers. A focus on accessibility underscores the idea of universal design (the design of environments for maximum accessibility by people regardless of age, size, ability or disability; Steinfeld and Maisel 2012).

4. Future Research

Many of the factors that influence the psychology of working longer are related to the larger sociocultural context, including labor market conditions and retirement norms. As such, psychologists must collaborate with economists and sociologists to contextualize the study of individual attitudes and behaviors in decisions to work longer. Some examples of these collaborations are already available. For example, in a study of job search and reemployment, Wanberg et al. (2016) reviewed economic data to understand trends in job loss and reemployment for older workers, and also examined individual behaviors associated with successful job search for workers over 50. With an aspiration toward interdisciplinary research, we describe five important areas for future research on the psychology of working longer.

First, most psychological research on working at older ages has focused on the determinants and timing of retirement rather than on working longer (Fisher, Chaffee, and Sonnega 2016). These constructs are related, of course, but they may have different antecedents: one may love working but also be pulled toward retirement by family concerns, for example. Moreover, when we flip the frame from a focus on retirement to working longer, we consider motivation to continue working in an array of modern retirement arrangements, such as bridge jobs, completely new "encore" careers, or part-time or contingency work, before a complete exit from the workforce. Although research has begun to focus on working longer rather than retirement (Kanfer, Beier, and Ackerman 2013), more research should be done to understand the determinants of working longer in general and the myriad ways that workers can continue to engage in work in particular.

Second, more research is needed that recognizes the heterogeneity in the psychological processes leading to working longer. Typically, organizational scientists focus on normative trends in aging and retirement, which treat older workers as a monolithic category. Furthermore, like most research in psychology, retirement research tends to use samples that are largely WEIRD: white, educated, industrialized, rich, and democratic (Henrich, Heine, and Norenzayan 2010). But there are important differences by gender, race, education, occupation, and many other individual and environmental characteristics that influence decisions to work longer or retire. For example, normative goal shifts from achievement to socioemotional are not observed among workers in physically demanding jobs, as described above. Moreover, social identities affect attitudes and retirement behavior based on group norms and interpretations of workplace climate for discrimination based on gender, race, age, and other characteristics. Although little is known about the relationship between social identities and workplace attitudes and behaviors, even less is known about how multiple social identities might interact to influence work-related outcomes in unique ways not captured when considering a single identity at a time.

The importance of heterogeneity is also evident in the tensions in research about training and development activities. The discussion above suggests that the existence of training and development opportunities is important to older workers, even if they choose not to take advantage of them (Armstrong-Stassen and Ursel 2009). Of course, it may be that—on average—older workers are not motivated to engage in development at work, but assuming that this is true for all older workers would be a mistake. Future research could investigate how to increase older workers' motivation for training and development activities. Some interesting questions along these lines include the following: Will increased participation in training and development by older role models increase self-efficacy for older workers? How can training be designed to lead to skill development as well as to fulfill the desire for continuous lifelong learning?

Third, the confluence of technology with the aging workforce has highlighted the importance of lifelong learning for workers to remain engaged. Although scientists have described the types of jobs that will be available in the twenty-first century and how these jobs map to the skills and abilities of older workers (Beier, Torres, and Beal 2020), more research is needed to predict the job characteristics and environmental factors that will be prevalent in the workplace of the future and how to engage older workers in these jobs.

Fourth, future time perspective affects goals for working longer, and it is relatively malleable, suggesting that organizational interventions may be useful. There is some research to suggest that perceptions of opportunities at work are related to occupational future time perspective (Zacher and Frese 2009), but whether interventions that highlight workplace opportunities are effective in expanding workers' future time perspectives is currently unknown. Moreover, we know relatively little about how life circumstances affect future time perspectives generally or occupational future time perspectives, more specifically. A recent meta-analysis suggests that socioeconomic status is positively related to future time perspective and that women have a more expansive future time perspective than men (Kooij et al. 2018). Race and ethnicity were not examined, however, but they could be. It would be interesting to further understand the correlates and determinants of future time perspective, which could provide much-needed information about its development and the conditions that enhance or diminish it.

Fifth, the COVID-19 pandemic has amplified the vulnerabilities that older workers experience when they work longer. Employers may see them as riskier hires and easier targets for layoffs or hour reduction, potentially seeing such discrimination as protective, not problematic, due to concerns about infection (Monahan et al. 2020). Since most research on the work-family interface has focused on young parents, the unique concerns of older workers are not yet understood. For instance, working from home as an older worker might include juggling the logistics of caregiving for an older relative without physical separation between the caregiving space and the workspace, sharing space with adult children who have unexpectedly moved home, or navigating relationships with children who relied on them for supplemental childcare for grandchildren prior to the pandemic. Although some jobs will return to in-person settings after the pandemic, others may remain more flexible about where and when work gets done. Such flexibility could benefit older workers who might otherwise have opted out of the workforce due to caregiving obligations or the strain of working an in-person full-time job during conventional daytime hours. However, some older workers may not want remote jobs, given the relative social isolation that comes with them. Time will tell how the world of work is ultimately shaped by the pandemic, and whether these changes facilitate or inhibit older workers in working longer.

5. Conclusion

Why do some people work longer than others? While retirement is often seen as a numbers-driven decision that people make by balancing the labor market and personal finances, we have argued that it is not so cut and dried. Like any decision made by humans, the decision to work longer or to retire is the result of a dynamic interplay of person and environmental factors that influence skills, self-perceptions, and motivation. Acknowledging these nuances, and embracing the idea that older workers can continue to develop throughout their careers, allows for a less fatalistic approach to working longer, in which organizations can take ownership over what they can do to influence decisions to work longer.

References

Ackerman, Phillip L. 2007. "New Developments in Understanding Skilled Performance." *Current Directions in Psychological Science* 16 (5): 235–239. https://doi.org/10.1111/j.1467-8721.2007.00511.x.

Armstrong-Stassen, Marjorie, and Seung Hwan (Mark) Lee. 2009. "The Effect of Relational Age on Older Canadian Employees' Perceptions of Human Resource Practices and Sense of Worth to Their Organization." *The International Journal of Human Resource Management* 20 (8): 1753–1769. https://doi.org/10.1080/09585190903087156.

Armstrong-Stassen, Marjorie, and Francine Schlosser. 2011. "Perceived Organizational Membership and the Retention of Older Workers." *Journal of Organizational Behavior* 32 (2): 319–344. https://doi.org/10.1002/job.647.

Armstrong-Stassen, Marjorie, and Nancy D. Ursel. 2009. "Perceived Organizational Support, Career Satisfaction, and the Retention of Older Workers." *Journal of Occupational and Organizational Psychology* 82 (1): 201–220. https://doi.org/10.1348/096317908X288838.

Bakker, Arnold B., and Evangelia Demerouti. 2017. "Job Demands–Resources Theory: Taking Stock and Looking Forward." *Journal of Occupational Health Psychology* 22 (3): 273–285. https://doi.org/10.1037/ocp0000056.

Baltes, Paul B. 1987. "Theoretical Propositions of Life-Span Developmental Psychology: On the Dynamics between Growth and Decline." *Developmental Psychology* 23 (5): 611–626. https://doi.org/10.1037/0012-1649.23.5.611.

Bayl-Smith, Piers H., and Barbara Griffin. 2014. "Age Discrimination in the Workplace: Identifying as a Late-Career Worker and Its Relationship with Engagement and Intended Retirement Age." *Journal of Applied Social Psychology* 44 (9): 588–599. https://doi.org/10.1111/jasp.12251.

Beier, Margaret E., Alexander C. LoPilato, and Ruth Kanfer. 2018. "Successful Motivational Aging at Work: Antecedents and Retirement-Related Outcomes." *Work, Aging and Retirement* 4 (2): 213–224. https://doi.org/10.1093/workar/wax034.

Beier, Margaret E., Mark S. Teachout, and Cody B. Cox. 2012. "The Training and Development of an Aging Workforce." In *The Oxford Handbook of Work and Aging*, edited by Walter C. Borman and Jerry W. Hedge, 436–453. New York: Oxford University Press. https://doi.org/10.1093/oxfordhb/9780195385052.013.0138.

Beier, Margaret E., W. Jackeline Torres, and Daniel J. Beal. 2020. "Workplace Aging and Jobs in the Twenty-First Century." In *Current and Emerging Trends in Aging and Work*, edited by Sara J. Czaja, Joseph Sharit, and Jacquelyn Boone James, 13–32. New York: Springer. https://doi.org/10.1007/978-3-030-24135-3_2.

Beier, Margaret E., Wendy Jackeline Torres, Gwenith G. Fisher, and Lauren E. Wallace. 2020. "Age and Job Fit: The Relationship Between Demands–Ability Fit and Retirement and Health." *Journal of Occupational Health Psychology* 25 (4): 227–243. https://doi.org/10.1037/ocp0000164.

Beier, Margaret E., Carmen K. Young, and Anton J. Villado. 2018. "Job Knowledge: Its Definition, Development and Measurement." In *The SAGE Handbook of Industrial, Work and Organizational Psychology: Personnel Psychology and Employee Performance*, edited by Deniz Ones, Neil Anderson, Chockalingam Viswesvaran, and Handan Sinangil, 2nd ed., 3: 279–298. Los Angeles, CA: Sage. https://doi.org/10.4135/9781473914940.

Carstensen, Laura L., Derek M. Isaacowitz, and Susan T. Charles. 1999. "Taking Time Seriously: A Theory of Socioemotional Selectivity." *American Psychologist* 54 (3): 165–181. https://doi.org/10.1037/0003-066X.54.3.165.

Chen, Gilad, Robert E. Ployhart, Helena Cooper Thomas, Neil Anderson, and Paul D. Bliese. 2011. "The Power of Momentum: A New Model of Dynamic Relationships between Job Satisfaction Change and Turnover Intentions." *Academy of Management Journal* 54 (1): 159–181. https://doi.org/10.5465/amj.2011.59215089.

Cottrell, Jonathan M., Daniel A. Newman, and Glenn I. Roisman. 2015. "Explaining the Black–White Gap in Cognitive Test Scores: Toward a Theory of Adverse Impact." *Journal of Applied Psychology* 100 (6): 1713–1736. https://doi.org/10.1037/apl0000020.

Crenshaw, Kimberle. 1989. "Demarginalizing the Intersection of Race and Sex: A Black Feminist Critique of Antidiscrimination Doctrine, Feminist Theory and Antiracist Politics." *University of Chicago Legal Forum* 1989 (1): 139–167. https://chicagounbound.uchicago.edu/uclf/vol1989/iss1/8.

Demerouti, Evangelia, Arnold B. Bakker, Friedhelm Nachreiner, and Wilmar B. Schaufeli. 2001. "The Job Demands-Resources Model of Burnout." *Journal of Applied Psychology* 86 (3): 499–512. https://doi.org/10.1037/0021-9010.86.3.499.

Fisher, Gwenith G., Dorey S. Chaffee, and Amanda Sonnega. 2016. "Retirement Timing: A Review and Recommendations for Future Research." *Work, Aging and Retirement* 2 (2): 230–261. https://doi.org/10.1093/workar/waw001.

Henrich, Joseph, Steven J. Heine, and Ara Norenzayan. 2010. "The Weirdest People in the World?" *Behavioral and Brain Sciences* 33 (2–3): 61–83. https://doi.org/10.1017/S0140525X0999152X.

Hertzog, Christopher, Arthur F. Kramer, Robert S. Wilson, and Ulman Lindenberger. 2008. "Enrichment Effects on Adult Cognitive Development: Can the Functional Capacity of Older Adults Be Preserved and Enhanced?" *Psychological Science in the Public Interest* 9 (1): 1–65. https://doi.org/10.1111/j.1539-6053.2009.01034.x.

James, Jacquelyn Boone, Christina Matz-Costa, and Michael A. Smyer. 2016. "Retirement Security: It's Not Just about the Money." *American Psychologist* 71 (4): 334–344. https://doi.org/10.1037/a0040220.

Jones, Kristen P., Chad I. Peddie, Veronica L. Gilrane, Eden B. King, and Alexis L. Gray. 2016. "Not So Subtle: A Meta-Analytic Investigation of the Correlates of Subtle and Overt Discrimination." *Journal of Management* 42 (6): 1588–1613. https://doi.org/10.1177/0149206313506466.

Judge, Timothy A., and John D. Kammeyer-Mueller. 2012. "Job Attitudes." *Annual Review of Psychology* 63 (1): 341–367. https://doi.org/10.1146/annurev-psych-120710-100511.

Kanfer, Ruth, and Phillip L. Ackerman. 2004. "Aging, Adult Development, and Work Motivation." *The Academy of Management Review* 29 (3): 440–458. https://doi.org/10.2307/20159053.

Kanfer, Ruth, Margaret E. Beier, and Phillip L. Ackerman. 2013. "Goals and Motivation Related to Work in Later Adulthood: An Organizing Framework." *European Journal of Work and Organizational Psychology* 22 (3): 253–264. https://doi.org/10.1080/1359432X.2012.734298.

Kooij, Dorien T. A. M., P. Matthijs Bal, and Ruth Kanfer. 2014. "Future Time Perspective and Promotion Focus as Determinants of Intraindividual Change in Work Motivation." *Psychology and Aging* 29 (2): 319–328. https://doi.org/10.1037/a0036768.

Kooij, Dorien T. A. M., Annet H. De Lange, Paul G. W. Jansen, Ruth Kanfer, and Josje S. E. Dikkers. 2011. "Age and Work-Related Motives: Results of a Meta-Analysis." *Journal of Organizational Behavior* 32 (2): 197–225. https://doi.org/10.1002/job.665.

Kooij, Dorien T. A. M., Ruth Kanfer, Matt Betts, and Cort W. Rudolph. 2018. "Future Time Perspective: A Systematic Review and Meta-Analysis." *Journal of Applied Psychology* 103 (8): 867–893. https://doi.org/10.1037/apl0000306.

Kooij, Dorien T. A. M., Maria Tims, and Ruth Kanfer. 2015. "Successful Aging at Work: The Role of Job Crafting." In *Aging Workers and the Employee-Employer Relationship*, edited by P. Matthijs Bal, Dorien T. A. M. Kooij, and Denise M. Rousseau, 145–161. Cham: Springer International. https://doi.org/10.1007/978-3-319-08007-9_9.

Korff, Jörg, Torsten Biemann, and Sven C. Voelpel. 2017. "Human Resource Management Systems and Work Attitudes: The Mediating Role of Future Time Perspective." *Journal of Organizational Behavior* 38 (1): 45–67. https://doi.org/10.1002/job.2110.

Madera, Juan M., Eden B. King, and Michelle R. Hebl. 2012. "Bringing Social Identity to Work: The Influence of Manifestation and Suppression on Perceived Discrimination, Job Satisfaction, and Turnover Intentions." *Cultural Diversity and Ethnic Minority Psychology* 18 (2): 165–170. https://doi.org/10.1037/a0027724.

Mather, Mara, and Laura L. Carstensen. 2005. "Aging and Motivated Cognition: The Positivity Effect in Attention and Memory." *Trends in Cognitive Sciences* 9 (10): 496–502. https://doi.org/10.1016/j.tics.2005.08.005.

McGonagle, Alyssa K., Gwenith G. Fisher, Janet L. Barnes-Farrell, and James W. Grosch. 2015. "Individual and Work Factors Related to Perceived Work Ability and Labor Force Outcomes." *Journal of Applied Psychology* 100 (2): 376–398. https://doi.org/10.1037/a0037974.

Monahan, Caitlin, Jamie Macdonald, Ashley Lytle, MaryBeth Apriceno, and Sheri R. Levy. 2020. "COVID-19 and Ageism: How Positive and Negative Responses Impact Older Adults and Society." *American Psychologist* 75 (7): 887. https://doi.org/10.1037/amp0000699.

Ng, Thomas W. H., and Daniel C. Feldman. 2008. "The Relationship of Age to Ten Dimensions of Job Performance." *Journal of Applied Psychology* 93 (2): 392–423. https://doi.org/10.1037/0021-9010.93.2.392.

Ng, Thomas W. H., and Daniel C. Feldman. 2012. "Evaluating Six Common Stereotypes About Older Workers with Meta-Analytical Data." *Personnel Psychology* 65 (4): 821–858. https://doi.org/10.1111/peps.12003.

Pak, Karen, Dorien T. A. M. Kooij, Annet H. De Lange, and Marc J. P. M. Van Veldhoven. 2019. "Human Resource Management and the Ability, Motivation and Opportunity to Continue Working: A Review of Quantitative Studies." *Human Resource Management Review* 29 (3): 336–352. https://doi.org/10.1016/j.hrmr.2018.07.002.

Papadopoulos, Michael, Bridget Fisher, Teresa Ghilarducci, and Siavash Radpour. 2020. "Over Half of Unemployed Older Workers at Risk of Involuntary Retirement." Status of Older Workers Report Series.

New York: Schwartz Center for Economic Policy Analysis at The New School for Social Research. https://www.economicpolicyresearch.org/jobs-report/over-half-of-older-workers-unemployed-at-risk-of-involuntary-retirement.

Paullay, Irina M., George M. Alliger, and Eugene F. Stone-Romero. 1994. "Construct Validation of Two Instruments Designed to Measure Job Involvement and Work Centrality." *Journal of Applied Psychology* 79 (2): 224–228. https://doi.org/10.1037/0021-9010.79.2.224.

Post, Corinne, Joy A Schneer, Frieda Reitman, and Dt Ogilvie. 2013. "Pathways to Retirement: A Career Stage Analysis of Retirement Age Expectations." *Human Relations* 66 (1): 87–112. https://doi.org/10.1177/0018726712465657.

Posthuma, Richard A., and Michael A. Campion. 2009. "Age Stereotypes in the Workplace: Common Stereotypes, Moderators, and Future Research Directions." *Journal of Management* 35 (1): 158–188. https://doi.org/10.1177/0149206308318617.

Salthouse, Timothy A. 2010. *Major Issues in Cognitive Aging*. Oxford: Oxford University Press. https://doi.org/10.1093/acprof:oso/9780195372151.001.0001.

Schaie, K. Warner. 2013. *Developmental Influences on Adult Intelligence: The Seattle Longitudinal Study*. 2nd ed. New York: Oxford University Press.

Schneider, Benjamin, Mark G. Ehrhart, and William H. Macey. 2013. "Organizational Climate and Culture." *Annual Review of Psychology* 64 (1): 361–388. https://doi.org/10.1146/annurev-psych-113011-143809.

Staudinger, Ursula M. 2020. "The Positive Plasticity of Adult Development: Potential for the 21st Century." *American Psychologist* 75 (4): 540–553. https://doi.org/10.1037/amp0000612.

Steinfeld, Edward, and Jordana Maisel. 2012. *Universal Design: Creating Inclusive Environments*. Hoboken, NJ: John Wiley & Sons.

Tajfel, Henri, and John C. Turner. 2004. "The Social Identity Theory of Intergroup Behavior." In *Political Psychology: Key Readings*, edited by John T. Jost and Jim Sidanius, 276–293. Hove, England: Psychology Press. https://doi.org/10.4324/9780203505984-16.

Tuckey, Michelle R., Ben. J. Searle, Carolyn M. Boyd, Anthony H. Winefield, and Helen R. Winefield. 2015. "Hindrances Are Not Threats: Advancing the Multidimensionality of Work Stress." *Journal of Occupational Health Psychology* 20 (2): 131–147. https://doi.org/10.1037/a0038280.

Wanberg, Connie R., Ruth Kanfer, Darla J. Hamann, and Zhen Zhang. 2016. "Age and Reemployment Success After Job Loss: An Integrative Model and Meta-Analysis." *Psychological Bulletin* 142 (4): 400–426. https://doi.org/10.1037/bul0000019.

Zacher, Hannes, and Michael Frese. 2009. "Remaining Time and Opportunities at Work: Relationships between Age, Work Characteristics, and Occupational Future Time Perspective." *Psychology and Aging* 24 (2): 487–493. https://doi.org/10.1037/a0015425.

Zacher, Hannes, and Cort W. Rudolph. 2017. "Change in Job Satisfaction Negatively Predicts Change in Retirement Intentions." *Work, Aging and Retirement* 3 (3): 284–297. https://doi.org/10.1093/workar/wax009.

Zacher, Hannes, and Jie Yang. 2016. "Organizational Climate for Successful Aging." *Frontiers in Psychology* 7 (July): 1007. https://doi.org/10.3389/fpsyg.2016.01007.

Forecasting Employment of the Older Population

Michael D. Hurd and Susann Rohwedder

1. Introduction

The aging of the U.S. population is due to individuals living longer, the maturing of the baby boomer generation into retirement age, and a decline in fertility. Reflecting these causes, population aging has led to concerns about the ability of individuals and households to finance a longer retirement period; the ability of the younger workforce to support social programs that benefit the older population; and the ability of employers to find an adequate workforce. Many of the challenges associated with population aging can be ameliorated if individuals work longer. They can increase their retirement wealth both by delaying accessing it and by continuing to save while working. They will continue to pay Medicare taxes and Social Security contributions, supporting the financial stability of those programs. Often, they do not use Medicare because the health care coverage provided by an employer is first payer. And employers find a larger pool of experienced employees.

Indeed, before the COVID-19 pandemic, there was a strong long-term trend toward extended work lives. As shown in Figure 7.1, the rate of working among those over the age of 60 increased for 25 years for both men and women, possibly with a relatively brief interruption associated with the Great Recession. However, employment rates of younger men and women under 60 did not increase nearly as robustly, and in some cases they actually declined. The Great Recession accelerated the decline, and only from the mid-2010s was there some recovery.

In light of the weak trend in employment of both men and women in their late 40s and 50s, it is uncertain whether the trend toward postponed retirement will continue as today's middle-aged cohorts grow older because of the low rates of entry into employment at older ages. We make projections based on novel methods that take advantage of forward-looking data elements from the Health and Retirement Study (HRS). The HRS asks respondents about their subjective probability of working past certain ages (62, 65, and 70). Rather than

Michael D. Hurd and Susann Rohwedder, *Forecasting Employment of the Older Population* In: *Overtime*. Edited by: Lisa F. Berkman and Beth C. Truesdale, Oxford University Press. © Oxford University Press 2022. DOI: 10.1093/oso/9780197512067.003.0008

156 | OVERTIME

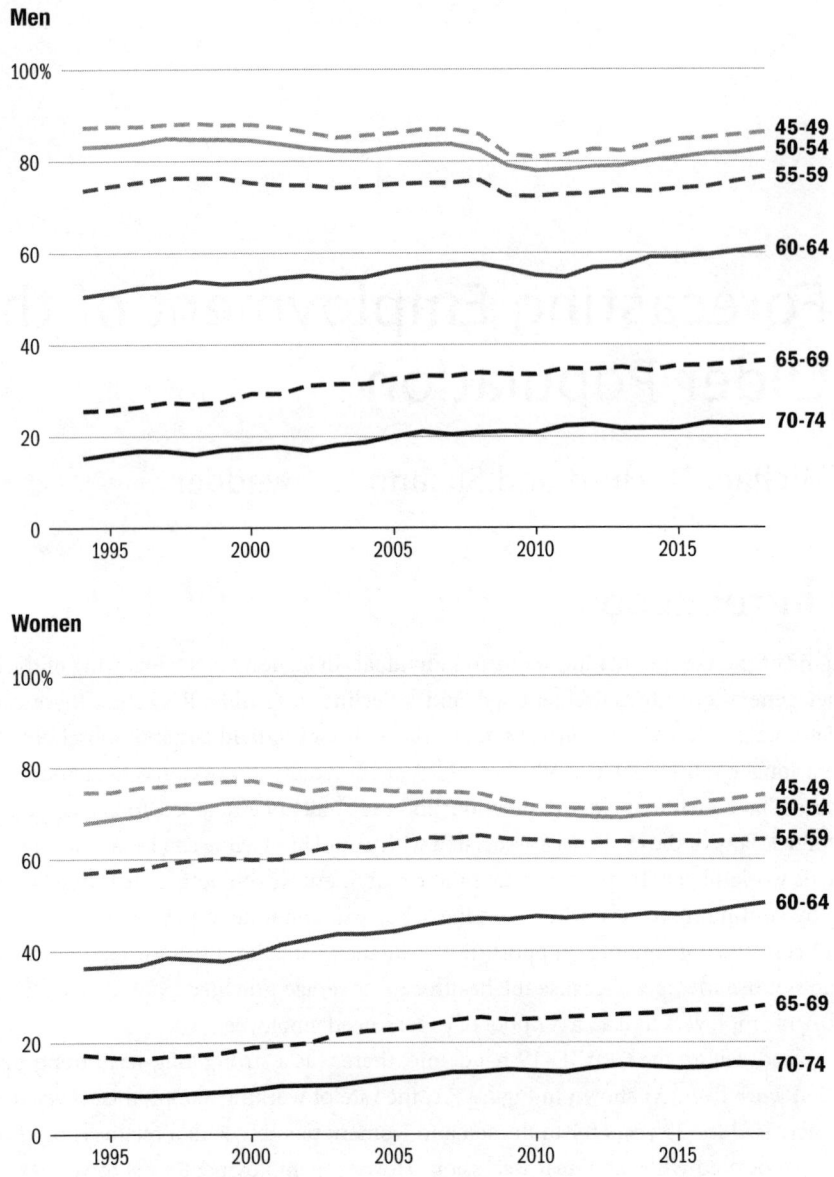

FIGURE 7.1 **Trends in employment by age, 1994–2018**
Source: U.S. Bureau of Labor Statistics. Data Tools, One-screen search, accessed October 30, 2019. https://data.bls.gov/PDQWeb/ce

relying on past trends to project future trends, we use these expectations about how long individuals will work which capture both individual-level heterogeneity and private information which is otherwise not available. We show the trends in this measure over the course of the past two decades and demonstrate that it has predicted actual work outcomes. We use data on these subjective probabilities and on transitions into and out of working to predict the employment rate of the population age 70 or 71 in 2031–2036.[1]

We disaggregate our results by gender, education, and race/ethnicity because the data on predictors of employment such as health show differential trends, leading us to expect differential trends in late-life working by those disaggregates. Further, analyses of inequality often use variation across these categories because of policy or scientific interest, and certainly the variation in the length of work life is an indicator both of the ability to work and of lifetime economic resources.

Our main result is the prediction that the late-life (ages 70–71) employment rate in the early to mid-2030s will be lower by about four percentage points than it was in 2016: the long-term growth in employment will have ended. This decline is consistent with declines in health observed from 1992 to 2016 over five cohorts spaced six years apart. Although we find a decline in late-life employment across almost all subpopulations defined by gender, race/ethnicity, and education, there is variation: relative to their comparison groups, the employment rates of women, of college graduates, and of Blacks (both male and female) will decline the most. Using the forward-looking subjective probabilities matters for these results: based just on past data on transition rates into and out of the labor force used in simulations, the overall level would be about the same as in 2016, and no subpopulation would have an important decline.

The COVID-19 pandemic inflicted a major shock to the labor market. For example, in 2020 the employment rate of men ages 60–64 was 58.9 percent, down from 61.1 percent in 2018; the corresponding rate for women was 47.8 percent, down from 50.4 percent. Our forecasts do not account for the pandemic shock. However, we can imagine permanent changes to the labor market caused by COVID-19 that would change future employment rates. Work might be reduced because of permanent damage to the health of the population as the direct result of COVID-19 infections; permanent reductions in the use of nursing homes which would require more in-home informal care and withdrawal from the labor force by adult caregiving children; and the direct effects of unemployment that, as shown by the 2008 Great Recession, take many years to erase. Several other effects of COVID-19 may increase employment: damaged retirement finances through reduced employment or investment losses; and increased job flexibility such as working from home, which would reduce the fixed costs of working and permit concurrent informal caregiving. With no empirical evidence as to which effects will dominate, we have not attempted to alter our forecasts to accommodate any COVID-19-related changes: our forecasts implicitly assume that over the long run the labor market will return to the long-run dynamic equilibrium path that it was on prior to the shock.

The most notable recent policy changes have operated to encourage working longer, particularly changes in Social Security that led to the increase in the Social Security normal retirement age, the elimination of the earnings test after age 65, and the increase in the delayed retirement credit. It is likely that these policy changes are at least partially responsible for the increases in labor force participation at older ages observed to 2016. However, our results show that if no fresh policies are introduced to encourage later retirement, the trend toward longer work life will cease because of countervailing tendencies such as health. Furthermore, new policy needs to recognize that a one-size-fits-all policy is unlikely to be successful because of the heterogeneity in health and health trends.

2. Data: Health and Retirement Study

The data for our analyses come from the HRS, an ongoing nationally representative longitudinal survey of the U.S. population age 51 or older. It is conducted by the University of Michigan and funded by the National Institute on Aging (grant number NIA U01AG009740) and the Social Security Administration. The initial survey was fielded in 1992, with subsequent panel interviews conducted every two years. Refreshment cohorts of ages 51 to 56 were added to the study every six years in 1998, 2004, 2010, and 2016. The sample size is about 20,000 per wave, with about half age 65 or older. The survey collects a wide range of information about demographics, socioeconomic status, labor market status, health, and vital status. Wherever possible, we use derived variables from the RAND HRS Longitudinal File 2016 (V1).[2]

3. Past Trends in Work at Older Ages

The strong increase in working at older ages coupled with the lack of any strong increase in employment at younger ages suggests that workers in their 60s delayed retirement. That is, successive cohorts of workers entering their 60s reduced their tendency to leave the workforce. Figure 7.2 depicts the retirement hazards of two cohorts in the HRS: one born in 1936 (observed from age 56) and one born in 1941 (observed from age 51). Specifically, the graph shows, by year of age, the probability that, given working for pay at time t, an individual will no longer be working for pay at $t + 2$. The retirement hazards increase with age, and they are similar across the two cohorts except between ages 60 and 65, where the earlier cohort left the labor force at a substantially higher rate. For example, among those age 61 from the 1936 cohort, about 25 percent left employment by the time they were age 63; among those age 61 from the 1941 cohort, just 19 percent left employment by age 63.

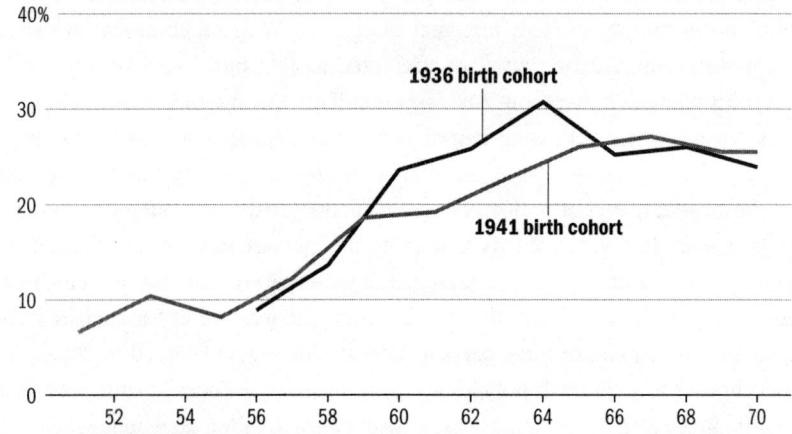

FIGURE 7.2 Retirement hazards for two cohorts, men and women combined
Workers' retirement rate, ages 51 to 70
Notes: Authors' calculations based on HRS. Statistics are weighted.

Across all the cohorts observed in HRS between ages 51 and 79, the declines in the retirement hazards for men were concentrated among those ages 60 to 64 and 75 to 79 (not shown). Among women the retirement hazards decreased in all age bands above 50, with particularly large reductions at ages 60 to 64 and 70 to 74.

3.1. Possible Mechanisms

Several studies have investigated the reasons for the observed increases in labor force participation at older ages with summaries presented by Coile (2015) and Bosworth et al. (2016), among others. The following factors are likely contributors to the observed increase in labor force participation at older ages.

Changing economic incentives associated with public and private pensions. Several rule changes governing the timing and amount of Social Security benefits have been implemented in the past 20 years. The changes included the removal of the Social Security earnings test at ages beyond the Social Security normal retirement age; increased delayed benefit claiming credits; and increases in the Social Security claiming age to qualify for full benefits. Overall, these changes reduced Social Security benefits and discouraged early benefit claiming (Banerjee and Blau 2016). The prevalence of defined benefit pensions, which often provide strong economic incentives to retire at a particular age, has declined. They have been largely replaced by defined contribution pension plans that do not encourage retirement at any particular age.

Increases in education. The fraction of the population with a college degree has increased markedly across cohorts, especially among women. In the HRS, the fraction of 51- to 55-year-old women with a college degree rose from 15 percent in 1992 to 33 percent in 2016. Among men in the same age group, the fraction with a college degree rose from 24 percent in 1992 to 32 percent in 2016. Because college graduates tend to retire at later ages than nongraduates, possibly as a result of more steady jobs and better health, one might predict an increase in delayed retirement (Coile and Levine 2010).

Coordination of retirement with working spouse. With more women working in recent cohorts, more couples must decide whether to coordinate the timing of their retirements. Because husbands tend to be older than their wives, a normal retirement age of the wife will lead to a coordinated later retirement of the husband (Hurd 1990; Coile 2003).

Shift from a manufacturing to a more service-oriented economy. There has been a gradual reduction in physically demanding jobs held by older workers, which would permit more workers to retain their jobs longer. Further, the number of jobs in the service industry has been increasing offering employment opportunities with limited entry skill requirements and part-time options permitting easier transitions from full-time work to part-time. Taken together, these trends may enable individuals in their 60s to work additional years, either in their long-held jobs or by switching to a different job.

Increased longevity. Average life expectancy increased by almost 10 years in the past 60 years. Longer life spans require financing additional years of consumption, which in turn would lead some to work to older ages. It is worth noting that average life expectancy peaked in 2014 and then declined the three following years (Woolf and Schoomaker 2019), so it is unclear whether this factor will continue to be relevant. Also, inequalities in life expectancy

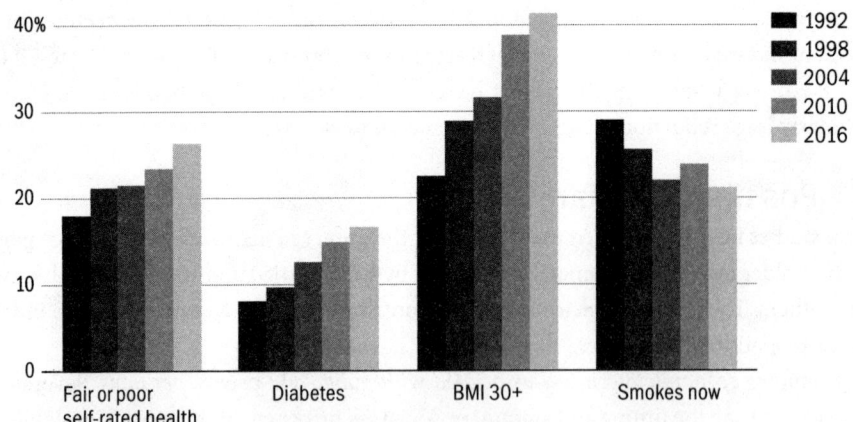

FIGURE 7.3 Health trends among U.S. adults ages 51 to 55, 1992–2016
Notes: Authors' calculations based on HRS. Statistics are weighted.

by education are large and increasing. Adults with more years of education tend to live longer than those with fewer, and between 1990 and 2010 the largest gains in life expectancy accrued to those with more years of education, while life expectancy stalled or declined among less educated groups (Sasson 2016).

Trends in health. Good health reduces the probability of retirement, although the magnitude of the estimated effects is sensitive to specification (Blundell et al. 2017). Healthy life expectancy at age 65 increased by 1.8 years in the United States between 1992 and 2008 (Chernew et al. 2017), while disabled life expectancy fell at age 65 by 0.5 years over the same period. Yet, despite the general trend toward better health at older ages, some indicators point toward worsening health among those in their 50s. Figure 7.3 shows several such health indicators for successive cohorts of 51- to 55-year-olds observed in the HRS. The fraction reporting their health as fair or poor increased with each cohort, from 18 percent in 1992 to 26 percent in 2016. The rate diagnosed with diabetes doubled from 8.1 percent to 16.5 percent, and the fraction of obese almost doubled from 22.5 percent to 41.5 percent. Although the fraction who smoke decreased by 8 percentage points from 1992 to 2016, the overall impression is of worsening health across cohorts, which may reduce or eliminate the trend toward later retirement.

3.2. A More Comprehensive Health Measure

To create a more comprehensive health measure, we constructed an index that combines the information from additional health indicators. The health indicators are measured at ages 51 to 55 in HRS 1992 and 1998, and they are used to predict work status at age 70 or 71, as observed in later waves. Thus, the index is specifically designed to predict future work status but not necessarily other health-related outcomes such as mortality or disease onset, although obviously they would be related. For example, some health conditions may make continued employment difficult, even if they have little effect on the risk of death. Such conditions would be given high weight in an index to predict retirement but low weight in an index to predict mortality. To create the index, we estimated the regression of work status at

70 or 71 on self-rated health, current smoking, BMI ≥ 35, whether a doctor ever diagnosed a heart condition, high blood pressure, diabetes, cancer, lung disease, stroke, or psychological problems, smoking behavior (ever, now), any drinking of alcoholic beverages, experiencing moderate or severe pain, and the subjective probability of living past age 75.

The fitted or predicted values from the regression for each of the five cohorts of adults in the HRS, stratified by gender and education, yield the graph in Figure 7.4. The top line refers to those with a college education, the next lower line to those with some education, and the bottom line to those lacking a high school degree. Education itself was not used as a

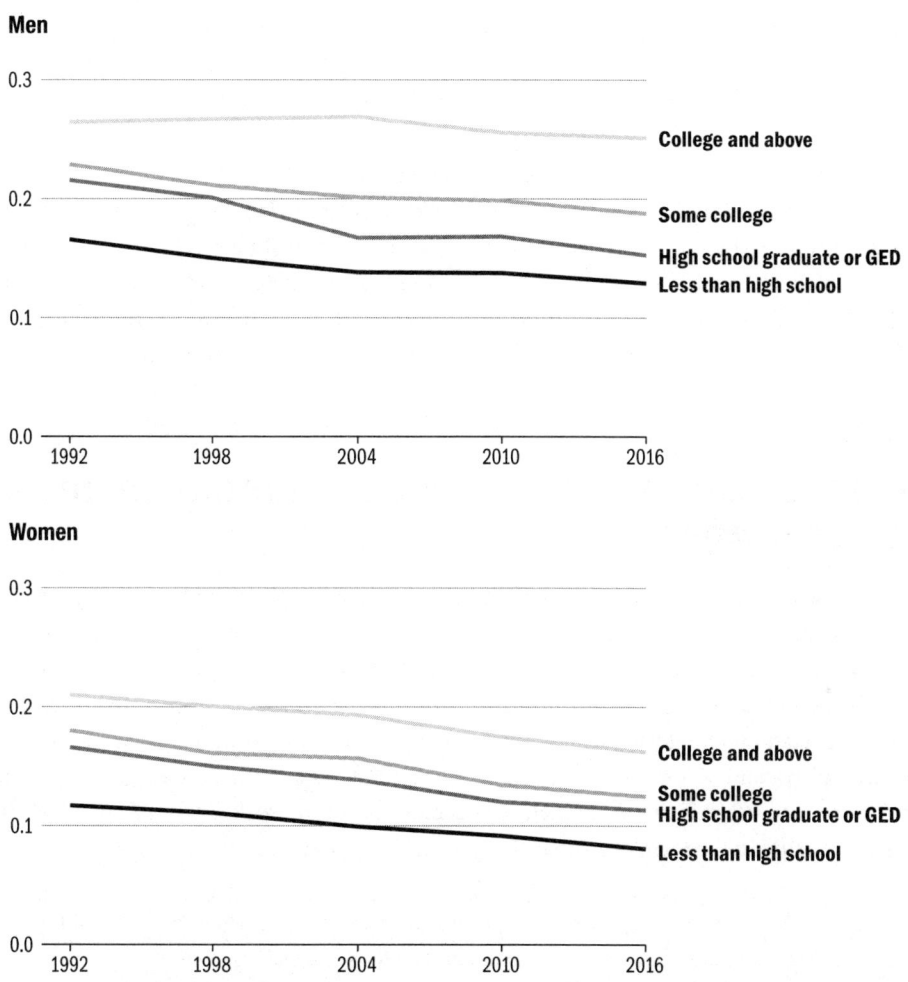

FIGURE 7.4 Trends in health index by education among U.S. adults ages 51 to 55
Notes: Health indicators measured at ages 51 to 55 combined into an index to predict work status at age 70 or 71, based on HRS panel data. Health measures included in the index are self-rated health, current smoking, BMI ≥ 35, whether a doctor ever diagnosed a heart condition, high blood pressure, diabetes, cancer, lung disease, stroke, or psychological problems, smoking behavior (ever, now), drinking any alcohol, experiencing moderate or severe pain, and the subjective probability of living past age 75. Education was not included in the index estimation; instead it is used for stratification after evaluating the health index for the observed values of the health variables. Weighted.

regressor, so the variation across education categories is only due to variation in the health indicators. As would be expected, more educated groups have substantially better health than those with less education. For example, among men in 2004 the difference between the highest and lowest education groups is 0.13; this is approximately the difference in the index that would be predicted by moving from excellent self-rated health to good self-rated health. Across cohorts, the health index declines for all education groups, although among men with college degrees the decline is modest.

Forecasting methods that use past trends in employment rates at older ages to predict future rates would predict a continued increase in the rate of working at ages past 60, as seen in Figure 7.1. Yet the declines in health among recent cohorts across a range of health conditions related to working may halt or reverse trends toward delayed retirement and extended work lives for the upcoming generations of older workers, those in their early 50s in 2016. However, other factors are in operation that could possibly offset the effects of worsening health, most importantly the continuing increase in the Social Security normal retirement age, the age when a worker qualifies for full Social Security benefits. A 53-year-old from the 2004 wave had a normal retirement age of 66, which was reached in 2017; a 53-year-old from the 2010 wave has a normal retirement age of 66 ½, which will be reached in 2023; and a 53-year-old from the 2016 wave has a normal retirement age of 67, which will be reached in 2030. We would expect this progression to cause an increase in the average retirement age. The other contributors toward increasing retirement age mentioned above are likely to have smaller impacts.

4. Forecasting Future Trends in Employment at Older Ages

Forecasting from past trends will, by definition, miss turning points and the ensuing systematic and continuing deviations from trend. An alternative, which we employ, is to ask individuals about their expectations of their future work. The value of this approach is based on the empirical observation that individuals have private information such as their financial situation, expectations about their health, their employers' attitudes toward older workers, their spouses' plans, and so forth which influence their thinking about future employment, and which they can use to summarize their expectations of future work. The HRS survey elicits this expectation in the form of a subjective probability by asking respondents:

> *Thinking about work in general and not just your present job, what do you think the chances are that you will be working full-time after you reach age [x]?*

where the target age [x] is replaced with ages 62, 65, and 70. The question permits the expression of uncertainty which is appropriate or even necessary because whether someone will work in the future depends on many future random events, particularly future health. The responses permit quantification because, if accurate, the average probability in a population will be the average rate of working full-time at the target age. We use this forward-looking information about the subjective probability of working past age 62 and the subjective probability of working past age 70 to forecast the rate of employment at later ages. We refer to the subjective probabilities of working as P62, P65, and P70.

Prior to HRS 2008, P62 and P65 were asked only of those working for pay at the time of interview. Nonworkers were instead asked about the chances of doing any work for pay sometime in the future. In 2012, HRS began to ask about the chances of doing any work for pay after age 70, and the chances of working full-time after age 70.

4.1. Predictive Accuracy of Workers' Expectations

In a static environment, where people have well-formed, rational probability judgments, the average subjective probability should predict the average outcome even if there are deviations at the individual level due to some people overestimating and others underestimating the chances. But changes in the environment at the macro level such as the 2008 Great Recession could intervene between the time of reporting of the expectation and the time the outcome is observed. Then the frequency of the outcome would shift so that the average of the expectations and subsequent outcomes would not match. To assess any such differences, we followed several birth cohorts of respondents, who were asked about P62 and P65 in their early 50s, and have since reached the respective target age. We compare their average subjective probabilities of working with actual work status at age 62 or at age 65 as recorded in later waves of the HRS. P62 predicts future work status well. The average value of P62 reported by workers ages 51 to 55 in HRS 1992 (48.3 percent) is close to the fraction later observed working full-time or part-time at ages 62 or 63 (46.2 percent). Usefully, P62 varies with covariates that are associated with future work status, such as education, health status, and pension characteristics (McGarry 2004; Hurd 2009; Hurd and Rohwedder 2011).

For a more detailed analysis we turn to P65, which is the more relevant target age because recent increases in employment at older ages were more pronounced after age 65 than after age 62 and because the forecast horizon is farther out and closer to age 70.[3] Comparisons of P65 as stated by workers in their early 50s with subsequent full-time work at age 65 or 66 produce a close match in the HRS. As Table 7.1 shows, across all workers ages 51 to 55 at baseline, P65 was 25.7 percent; 22.9 percent of the same individuals were working full-time at age 65 or 66, a difference of 2.6 percentage points. Table 7.1 also shows variation in P65 and actual work status at 65 or 66 by demographic characteristics. Both are higher for men and those with higher education. Differences between expectations and outcomes by subpopulations do not show any marked systematic patterns as the differences are relatively small across the board. These findings suggest that subjective probabilities of working can be useful to predict future employment rates at older ages among cohorts that are in middle age, and that forecasts based on subjective probabilities should be similarly accurate across groups defined by gender, race/ethnicity, and education.

4.2. Trends in Expectations of Working at Older Ages

Figure 7.5 shows the evolution of average P65 in successive cross-sections of 55- to 59-year-old HRS respondents from 1994 to 2016, both workers and nonworkers. For workers, respondent reports of P65 are available for all waves. For nonworkers, P65 is observed from

TABLE 7.1 **Average P65 reported by 51- to 55-year-old workers compared to their actual full-time work status at age 65 or 66 observed in later HRS waves**

		P65	Actual percent working at 65 or 66	Difference (actual – expected)
All		25.7	22.9	–2.6
Gender	Men	30.1	26.9	–3.0
	Women	21.7	19.2	–2.2
Race/ethnicity	White non-Hispanic	26.4	22.8	–3.5
	Black non-Hispanic	20.2	22.9	2.7
	Other non-Hispanic	27.9	25.9	–0.9
	Hispanic	28.1	23.8	–3.8
Education	Less than high school	24.9	20.8	–3.9
	High school graduate	22.1	20.8	–1.1
	Some college	26.7	21.4	–5.0
	College and above	30.8	29.1	–1.7

Notes: N = 3,801. Workers ages 51–55 observed in HRS 1992 or HRS 1998. Longitudinal follow-up in HRS panel to compare expected full-time work after age 65 reported by 51- to 55-year-old workers (P65) to the actual full-time work status of the same individuals. We assess actual work status at age 65 or 66, because HRS interviews are conducted only every other year so that some respondents are interviewed at age 65 and others at age 66. HRS, Health and Retirement Study.

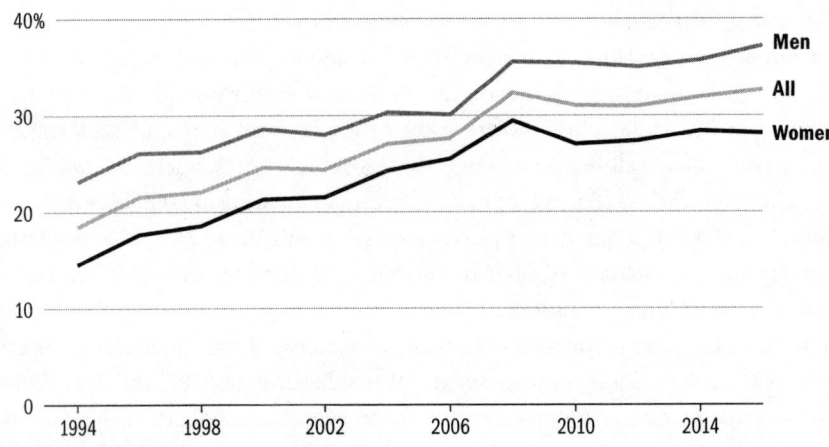

FIGURE 7.5 **Trends in the subjective probability of working after age 65, 1994–2016**
As reported by workers and non-workers ages 55 to 59
Notes: P65, the probability of working full-time after age 65, was not elicited from non-workers prior to 2008, but a similar expectation, the probability of doing any work for pay in the future, was asked starting in 1994. It is highly predictive of individuals returning to the labor force as observed in HRS panel data. Both expectations are available for both workers and non-workers in HRS 2008–2016. Regression analyses confirm a strong correlation of the probability of working in the future with P65 for non-workers in the waves when both expectations are observed. We therefore use a regression-based imputation of P65 for non-workers for HRS waves prior to 2008. Weighted.

2008 onward; for the earlier waves it is imputed using a similar expectations variable (chance of doing any work in the future) that is highly correlated with P65 as observed from 2008. The chosen age band is 55 to 59, so we can use data from every HRS wave (ages 51 to 55 are only fully represented in the HRS when a new refresher cohort is added every six years). Men report a higher average P65 than women by about 10 percentage points. Their respective expectations evolved in almost a parallel fashion, with some narrowing up to 2008 and then some widening by 2016. The P65 of both genders increased between 1994 and 2008 by about 15 percentage points, for men from a level of 23 percent, and for women from a level of 14 percent. That steady increase stalled so that after 2008, P65 was largely flat. In the latest two HRS waves, P65 increased slightly among men, but it is hard to tell whether that indicates a return to further increases in P65. Overall, the past increases in P65 were in accordance with the observed trends in working. The cessation of an increase suggests that the fraction working at older ages will not continue to increase.

4.2.1. Using Subjective Probabilities of Working to Forecast the Fraction Working at Older Ages

To quantify this conjecture, we will compare actual rates of working among 70- or 71-year-olds in 2016 (the "2016 cohort") with simulated rates of working among adults who will reach age 70 or 71 around 2033, and who were in their early 50s in 2016 (the "2033 cohort"). We use two simulation models for the 2033 cohort. In the first, we use the transition rates between working (any work), not working, and dead that we observe in the pooled HRS data between 1992 and 2016 to simulate the path of employment of the 2033 cohort. This first simulation estimates the rates of employment at older ages we would expect for future cohorts if conditions were unchanged from the recent past. In the second simulation, we impose restrictions using P62 and P70. Using the subjective probabilities of working reported by the 2033 cohort when they were ages 51 to 55, we require that the 2033 cohort's rate of working at age 62 or 63 matches P62, and that the cohort's rate of working at age 70 or 71 matches P70. Because our simulations predict "any work," we use the version of P70 that asks about the subjective probability of any work for pay after the age of 70 rather than of full-time work.[4] This second simulation incorporates private information that HRS respondents have about their expectations.

From these trajectories we calculate the expected number of years that individuals would spend working from the initial ages (51–55) to the end of life and how that number would change under the model should P62 and P70 accurately forecast the future rate of working. The change in work years is a good measure of how lifetime employment (and hence earnings) will evolve, whereas the rate of employment at age 70 just measures the rate of working at that age. For example, were a reduction in work life attributable to declining health, the loss of earnings would be a good metric to use, in addition to well-being, to place an overall value on health.

4.2.2. Employment Transitions in the Health and Retirement Study

Because HRS is a biennial survey, we calculate two-year transitions. An alternative is to use smoothness assumptions to interpolate and find one-year transitions. However, transition rates as a function of age are not smooth because of policy; for example, the transition from working to not working spikes at age 62 due to the availability of Social Security benefits. Therefore, we take two-year baseline transitions from observed transition rates in the HRS calculated over 13 waves (or 12 transitions) of HRS from 1992 to 2016. The transitions are from working to working, from working to not working, from working to dead, and from not working to those same states.

The importance of disaggregating by work status is shown in Table 7.2, using 51-year-olds as an example. In the initial wave, on average 75.1 percent of 51-year-olds were working; in the following wave the working rate declined to 73.0 percent. Of those initially working, 91.0 percent were working in the following wave; 8.7 percent were not working and 0.3 percent died. The table shows a strong tendency to remain in the same state. For example, only 19.0 percent of those not working became workers. It is important to include the transition to dead, because mortality differs sharply by work status. Among those age 51 and initially not working, 2.6 percent died by the following wave versus just 0.3 percent among those initially working. The absolute difference by employment status in mortality risk increases from 2.3 percentage points at age 51 to 4 percentage points at age 72 (not shown). If we did not model the higher mortality rate of those not working, that group would become overrepresented over time, biasing downward the predicted rates of working among the living. We estimate similar two-year transition probabilities for initial ages 52, 53, 54, and 55 and so forth up to age 94 or 95.

4.2.3. Simulations

Our first simulation of employment rates for the 2033 cohort begins with their initial rate of employment at ages 51 to 55 in 2016 and uses the transition rates observed between 1992 and 2016 so as to find what we would expect in 2033 if average conditions between 2016 and 2033 were the same as average conditions between 1992 and 2016. For example, for those initially age 51 in HRS 2016, we simulate work status at age 53 by random draws on a trivariate variable with outcomes given by the probabilities of transitions to working, not working, and death. The transition probabilities depend on initial work status. To be able to represent subpopulations, we increased sample size by using those initially ages 51 to 55 in HRS 2016; they will reach age 70 between 2031 and 2035. Those initially age 51, 53, or 55 are forecast to the odd ages up to age 95, and those initially age 52 or 54 are forecast to the even

TABLE 7.2 Transition probabilities (percent) among those initially age 51, estimated over pooled HRS waves 1–13

Status in wave t (age 51)	Status in wave $t + 1$ (age 53)			
	Working (73.0%)	Not working (26.1%)	Died (0.9%)	All
Working (75.1%)	91.0	8.7	0.3	100.0
Not working (24.9%)	19.0	78.5	2.6	100.0

Notes: N = 3,766 observations. Respondents alive in wave $t + 1$ and interviewed. Not interviewed excluded. HRS, Health and Retirement Study.

ages up to age 94. We then combine the trajectories to produce a trajectory by single years of age from age 51 to 94. Because some are forecast to age 70 and some to age 71, we will speak of working to age 70/71. Thus, we interpret the simulated rate of working at 70 or 71 as the rate that would be expected under the average conditions of the 13 waves of the HRS, but possibly modified to account for a different initial mix at ages 51 to 55 between working and not working.

In our second simulation of employment rates for the 2033 cohort, we use the subjective probability of working at later ages. We repeat the simulations but impose two conditions for those initially working: their rate of working at age 62/63 must equal their average stated P62, and their rate of working at age 70/71 must equal their average stated P70. We impose similar conditions for those initially not working. To achieve those constraints, we borrow an idea from population survival analysis. The Cox proportional hazard model is often a good description of how single-year survival rates may be modified by changing a single risk factor. Thus, under a Cox model, if h_t is mortality risk at age t, a risk factor that modifies the risk by θ at age τ will modify all risks by that same factor, that is, the single-year mortality risk will become θh_t for all t. We use this idea to modify the risk of transitioning from working to not working and from not working to working.

We proceeded in two steps. In the first, based on repeated simulations, we found two risk factors, one for the transition from working to not working and the other from not working to working, so that the predicted rate of working at 62/63 matched P62 as stated by workers and by nonworkers ages 51–55 in 2016. In the second, we anchored the trajectories of working and not working at the stated P62 values, and then found two more risk factors to match the predicted rate of working to the average P70, again as stated by workers and nonworkers in 2016. Thus the simulated employment trajectories satisfied the initial conditions (the mix between working and not working at ages 51 to 55), the average P62, the average P70, and the general shape derived from the HRS transition probabilities.

We repeated these calculations for subpopulations. For example, we found from 13 waves of HRS the transition rates of men, both workers and nonworkers, including their transition rates to dead. We simulated their employment trajectories from ages 51 to 55 in HRS 2016 to ages 94/95 with Cox-type adjustments to their transitions rates, so as to match their average stated P62 and P70.

4.2.4. Results

Figure 7.6 shows an example of the first set of simulations. It uses the initial conditions for those age 52 in HRS 2016 and the past transition rates in the HRS, but not P62 or P70. It shows the simulated rate of working of those who, in the simulations, survived. The top line is for those initially working, the bottom line for those initially not working, and the middle line is for all. Among all respondents, 77 percent were working at age 52. With the passage of time, some initially working leave, some initially not working enter, and the overall rate of working declines. Based on the transition rates observed in the HRS, we would forecast that 27 percent of those who survive to age 70 (in 2034) will be working. The rate of working of all those initially 52, not conditioning on survival, would be 21 percent; the difference shows the importance of accounting for mortality.

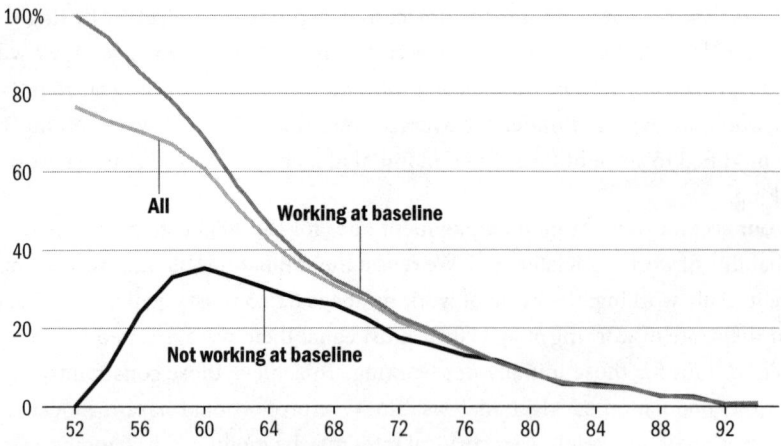

FIGURE 7.6 Simulated rate of working among adults age 52 in 2016
Based on past transition rates, adjusted for survival

We conducted such simulations for the initial ages 51, 52, 53, 54, and 55. Table 7.3 shows for the 2016 cohort, the actual rate of working at ages 70/71; for the 2033 cohort, the predicted rate of working at ages 70/71, simulated from the characteristics of the population ages 51 to 55 in HRS 2016, and the transition rates observed in the HRS but without adjustment to match P62 and P70; and for the 2033 cohort, the stated subjective probability of working past age 70, P70. The rate of working at 70/71 observed in 2016 was 24.8 percent. According to the simulations that use the transitions between working, not working, and dead as observed in 13 waves of HRS, the predicted rate of working at 70/71 (in years 2031–2035) is 24.7 percent among those simulated to survive to that age. The fact that these rates in the first two columns are almost identical is somewhat surprising given the changes in the rates of working (Figure 7.1) and in the retirement hazards (Figure 7.2), but the similarity is at least partially due to our use of transitions averaged over 12 panel changes in the HRS rather than, say, the transitions from the early waves.

Among those interviewed at ages 51 to 55 in 2016, the average subjective probability of working at age 70 was 20.6 percent. This suggests that employment rates at age 70/71 for the 2033 cohort will be somewhat lower than the actual employment rates for the 2016 cohort, as well as somewhat lower than the rate predicted based on past transition probabilities (without adjustment). This conclusion applies qualitatively to most subpopulations: men and women, all education groups except for those not graduating from high school, and all race/ethnic groups. The differences are largest among Black Non-Hispanic men, where the actual rate of working at 70/71 was 30.0 percent for the 2016 cohort compared to P70 expectations of 17.0 percent for the 2033 cohort; and among college graduates, where the actual rate was 38.1 percent for the 2016 cohort compared to P70 of 25.0 percent for the 2033 cohort.

The results in Table 7.3 suggest that, if individuals' own expectations of their likelihood of working at older ages continue to be as good a predictor of population-level employment rates as they have been in the past, rates of working at older ages are unlikely to keep increasing across cohorts and may actually fall.

TABLE 7.3 Percent working at age 70 or 71: Actual rates for the 2016 cohort, simulated rates for the 2033 cohort, and subjective probability for the 2033 cohort

	2016 cohort	2033 cohort (interviewed in 2016 at ages 51 to 55)	
	Actual rate of working at age 70/71 (2016)	Simulated to age 70/71 based on past transition rates in the HRS	Reported subjective probability of working at age 70 (P70)
All	24.8	24.7	20.6
Men	28.7	30.7	24.3
Women	21.1	20.1	17.8
Education			
Less than high school	16.1	15.5	17.3
High school graduate	19.7	21.9	17.0
Some college	20.6	26.5	22.0
College graduate	38.1	36.2	25.0
Race/ethnicity			
White non-Hispanic	25.1	26.0	23.1
Hispanic	24.8	18.7	22.1
Black non-Hispanic	25.0	22.1	15.0
Men	30.0	27.4	17.0
Women	21.5	19.4	13.7

Note: Subjective probability (P70) is calculated over those who survived to age 70/71 in the simulations. The 2016 cohort reached age 70/71 in 2016; the 2033 cohort were ages 51 to 55 in 2016 and will reach age 70/71 between 2031 and 2036. HRS, Health and Retirement Study.

To incorporate individuals' reports of their work expectations into our simulations, we conducted a second set of simulations for the 2033 cohort which matched the predicted rate of working at age 62 to average P62 and the predicted rate of working at age 70 or 71 to average P70. To compare the projected rate of working after the matching with the rate before matching, we use "expected years working or expected work life." By "expected work life" we mean the number of years expected to be worked from age 51 to the end of life (up to age 94). In Figure 7.6, the area under the middle curve is the expected work life of the population conditional on survival to age 94.

The first two columns of Table 7.4 show the expected work life of survivors with and without the adjustment to match P62 and P70. According to these estimates, if those ages 51 to 55 in 2016 transition between the states of working, not working, and dead with the probabilities as observed over 13 waves of HRS, the survivors to age 94 will have worked 12.8 years. If they work to reach their stated P62 and P70 on average, they will have worked 12.3 years. The reduction is directly a consequence of the fact that P70 is less than the simulated rate based on past transition rates in the HRS (Table 7.3). This is not a large difference, but possibly more important than the magnitude of the decline is that we do not predict an increase as one might predict from the long secular increase in the frequency of working at older ages as shown in Figure 7.1.

TABLE 7.4 Simulated number of years working by survivors from ages 51 to 94 (inclusive) before and after adjustment to P70, and expected number of years not working, working, and dead after adjustment, 2033 cohort

	Simulations based on past transition rates in the HRS	Simulations based on past transition rates in the HRS adjusted to match probability of working at 70/71 to P70					
	Survivors	Survivors	All				
	Years working	Years working	Years not working	Years working	Years dead	Years alive	Ratio of years working to years alive
All	12.8	12.3	17.9	11.0	15.1	28.9	0.381
Men	14.6	13.7	15.2	11.8	17.0	27.0	0.437
Women	11.5	11.1	20.2	10.3	13.5	30.5	0.338
Education							
Less than high school	8.8	9.0	18.2	7.6	18.2	25.8	0.295
High school graduate	11.6	10.9	19.1	9.7	15.3	28.8	0.337
Some college	13.3	12.7	18.3	11.5	14.2	29.8	0.386
College graduate	16.4	14.2	18.5	13.3	12.2	31.8	0.418
Race/ethnicity							
White non-Hispanic	13.5	13.2	17.5	12.0	14.5	29.5	0.407
Hispanic	11.1	11.9	19.5	10.6	13.9	30.1	0.352
Black non-Hispanic	11.5	10.4	17.0	9.0	18.0	26.0	0.346
Men	13.3	11.5	14.1	9.6	20.3	23.7	0.405
Women	10.4	9.4	19.2	8.4	16.4	27.6	0.304

Note: "Years working" by survivors refers to the expected number of years (out of 44) that a person age 51 will be working conditional on survival. "Not working, working, or dead" refer to the expected number of years (out of 44) that a person age 51 will be where the simulated frequency of working at age 70/71 has been adjusted to equal the average stated P70 among 51- to 55-year-olds in HRS 2016. HRS, Health and Retirement Study.

The next columns show the number of years on average predicted to be spent in each of the states not working, working, and dead by the population initially age 51. Of the 44 years simulated, 17.9 years will be spent alive but not working, 11.0 will be spent working, and 15.1 years dead. Thus, 38.1 percent of the years alive will be spent working. Men are predicted to have longer work lives than women. From Table 7.4, which just shows outcomes for the 2033 cohort, we cannot directly compare the predicted work lives of the 2033 cohort with the actual work lives of the 2016 cohort. To make that comparison, we will assume that the work lives of the 2016 cohort were approximately the same as work lives of the 2033 cohort without adjustment for P70. The simulations in Table 7.3, which show both, provide strong support for that assumption. Based on that assumption, the simulations adjusted for P70 suggest that while both men and women in the 2033 cohort will have shorter work lives than adults in the 2016 cohort, men are predicted to experience a greater reduction. The variation in work life by education is substantial: those with a college education have a predicted work life after the age of 51 that is almost twice that of those who did not graduate from high school. However, those without a high school diploma are predicted to experience a small increase in work life across cohorts, whereas college graduates are predicted to experience a large decrease, 2.2 years or 13 percent.[5] Hispanics are predicted to increase work life by 0.8 year across cohorts. Black non-Hispanic individuals have a shorter predicted work life than other race/ethnic groups, and Black non-Hispanic men in the 2033 cohort are predicted to reduce work life by 1.8 year or 14 percent compared to the 2016 cohort.

Our simulations use mortality rates based on actual observed mortality in the HRS, and they are specific to the demographic groups shown in Table 7.4. Consistent with known survival differentials, women tend to live longer than men, and the better educated tend to live longer than those with less education. The magnitude of the gradient by education is notable. Those lacking a high school degree are expected to live 25.8 years after age 51, whereas those with a college degree are expected to live 31.8 years, or 23 percent more years. The last column shows the ratio of the number of years expected to be working to the number of years expected to be alive. Overall, about 38 percent of the years from ages 51 to 94 are predicted to be spent working. There is large variation across groups. For example, our predictions suggest that the ratio of years working to years alive increases steadily with education from 30 percent for those without a high school degree to 42 percent for college graduates. While standard life-cycle models would predict that those with greater life expectancy would work longer, they would not necessarily predict such relative variation. The variation could be induced by a number of factors: the less educated are more reliant on Social Security, and possibly feel that additional low-wage work is not worth the effort given their relatively high level of benefits; they are less healthy, which is reflected in their shorter lifetimes, and which makes working more onerous; or they may have less rewarding jobs.

5. Summary and Conclusions

The long-term upward trend in working at older ages, which began in about 1990, was interrupted by the Great Recession of 2008. Although some groups in the older population are working at a greater rate than before the recession, more generally by 2018 the rates have not recovered, particularly at the preretirement ages. For example, among 50- to 54-year-old men the rate of working in 2007 was 83.8 percent, but it was just 82.8 percent in 2018. Similarly, 50- to 54-year-old women worked at a lower rate in 2018 than in 2007.

The central question of this chapter is whether the long upward trend in employment prior to 2008 will resume or whether the cessation of the trend after the recession is likely to be permanent. A second question is heterogeneity in the trend. We observe increasing inequality in a number of determinants of working and wonder whether they will lead to increasing work inequalities. For example, there has been a general trend toward worse health in the preretirement population, but the health trend has not been the same for all groups: among men, as measured across education strata, health inequality has increased, but not among women. Economic inequality has increased (Schaeffer 2020), which, because retirement is affected by economic circumstances, should also lead to changes in retirement behavior. But basic economic theory does not predict whether increasing wage differentials would lead to greater or smaller retirement differences.

The rate of working at older ages is determined by the balance of many elements. The demand side is important, as shown by the drop from 2008: among men ages 65 to 69, from 1998 to 2008 the rate of working increased by 5.8 percentage points; from 2008 to 2010 it decreased by 0.4 percentage point (Figure 7.1). The supply side is also important: the health of individuals, which we have emphasized; the financial aspects, which we have not emphasized, but which are important because of the substantial variation in economic preparation for retirement; and possible mismatches between jobs and skills, which may increase with age and over time with emerging technologies.

Rather than to attempt to quantify how supply and demand may interact to determine the rate of working in the future, we used the subjective probabilities of future work reported by 51- to 55-year-olds in 2016 to forecast the rate of working. The value of adults' own reported expectations as a forecasting tool is based on the fundamental assumption that individuals have private information about their future work that they can convey in a quantitative manner. The fact that the subjective probability of working increased as the actual employment rate increased provides some reason to be confident about that assumption.

Using data gathered before the COVID-19 pandemic, we predicted that the employment rate of the 2016 preretirement population when it is 70 or 71, almost 20 years onward, will be 4 percentage points less than the employment rate of 70- or 71-year-olds in 2016. At the population level, this difference translates into a reduction of 0.5 year of work from age 51 to the end of life. We interpret this to mean that the past upward trend, which was interrupted by the Great Recession, will not resume.

As for subpopulations, we predict that the employment rate will decline for most, but the rates of decline will be uneven. For example, the rates for Blacks, both men and women, are projected to decline more than for all men and women, which would lead from a negligible difference in 2016 between Blacks and the total population to a substantial difference in 2033. But possibly the most surprising result is a predicted decline among the college educated: a reduction of 2.2 years of work after age 51 on a base of 16.4 years, or 13.4 percent. Possible explanations that warrant further investigation include declining health among women: our health index for female college graduates declined to such an extent that by 2016 it was lower than the index of high school graduates in 1992. By contrast, the health index of college-educated men was just slightly lower in 2016 than in 1992. However, because the index of the less educated groups declined significantly, health inequality increased among men. Compared to earlier cohorts, college graduates have benefited from higher wages, they have more savings, and they participated in a sharply rising stock market. Thus, the more educated may be anticipating earlier retirement because they are better off financially than the preceding generation (today's 70-/71-year-olds).

Our predictions about a narrowing of the difference between the work lives of the least and of the best educated are based on the elicitation of P70 prior to the COVID-19 pandemic. The pandemic affected subpopulations whether classified by education or race/ethnicity differently, with those who are the least well-off experiencing the greatest hardship. How this will affect retirement differences is uncertain: health effects would signal increasing retirement inequality, whereas economic shocks would signal a reduction in retirement inequality due to worsening economic preparation for retirement among the less well-to-do.

Because we have modelled mortality, we could find the fraction of the rest-of-lifetime that is projected to be spent working. That fraction increases with education, suggesting a complex interaction between survival, health, and economic circumstances that we cannot address in this chapter. For example, due to the progressivity of Social Security, less-educated workers may feel that the combination of an income replacement rate close to 1.0 combined with not working is better than the financial reward from working at a low-paid job.

In summary and in conclusion, our results do not support a projection of a continuing trend toward extended work lives in the older population.

Notes

1. We will use the terms "working" and "employed" interchangeably. Both terms include the self-employed.
2. The RAND HRS Longitudinal File is an easy-to-use dataset based on the HRS core data. This file was developed at RAND with funding from the National Institute on Aging and the Social Security Administration.
3. P70 was added to HRS in 2012 so the follow-up is not yet long enough to compare expectations to subsequent actual work status for P70.
4. Because the HRS did not ask about any work after age 62, we use P62, the subjective probability of full-time work to anchor at age 62.
5. The fraction of the older population with a college degree increased substantially between 1992 and 2016, which may have contributed to this change. However, when we classified by education quartiles, rather than by degree of education, the decline remained large: 11 percentage points.

References

Banerjee, Sudipto, and David Blau. 2016. "Employment Trends by Age in the United States Why Are Older Workers Different?" *Journal of Human Resources* 51 (1): 163–199. https://doi.org/10.3368/jhr.51.1.163.

Blundell, Richard, Jack Britton, Monica Costa Dias, and Eric French. 2017. "The Impact of Health on Labour Supply Near Retirement." Working Paper W17/18. London: Institute for Fiscal Studies. https://doi.org/10.1920/wp.ifs.2017.W1718.

Bosworth, Barry, Gary Burtless, and Kan Zhang. 2016. *Later Retirement, Inequality in Old Age, and the Growing Gap in Longevity between Rich and Poor*. Economic Studies at Brookings. Washington, DC: The Brookings Institution. https://www.brookings.edu/wp-content/uploads/2016/02/BosworthBurtlessZhang_retirementinequalitylongevity.pdf.

Chernew, Michael, David M. Cutler, Kaushik Ghosh, and Mary Beth Landrum. 2017. "Understanding the Improvement in Disability-Free Life Expectancy in the U.S. Elderly Population." In *Insights in the Economics of Aging*, edited by David A. Wise, 161–204. University of Chicago Press. http://www.nber.org/chapters/c13631. Accessed June 02, 2022.

Coile, Courtney C. 2003. "Retirement Incentives and Couples' Retirement Decisions." Working Paper 9496. Working Paper Series. National Bureau of Economic Research. https://doi.org/10.3386/w9496.

Coile, Courtney C. 2015. "Economic Determinants of Workers' Retirement Decisions." *Journal of Economic Surveys* 29 (4): 830–853. https://doi.org/10.1111/joes.12115. Accessed June 02, 2022.

Coile, Courtney C., and Phillip B. Levine. 2010. *Reconsidering Retirement: How Losses and Layoffs Affect Older Workers*. Washington, DC: Brookings Institution Press. http://muse.jhu.edu/book/356.

Hurd, Michael D. 1990. "The Joint Retirement Decision of Husbands and Wives." In *Issues in the Economics of Aging*, edited by David A. Wise, 231–254. A National Bureau of Economic Research Project Report. Chicago: University of Chicago Press.

Hurd, Michael D. 2009. "Subjective Probabilities in Household Surveys." *Annual Review of Economics* 1 (1): 543–562. https://doi.org/10.1146/annurev.economics.050708.142955.

Hurd, Michael D., and Susann Rohwedder. 2011. "Trends in Labor Force Participation: How Much Is Due to Changes in Pensions?" *Journal of Population Ageing* 4 (1–2): 81–96. https://doi.org/10.1007/s12062-011-9042-8.

McGarry, Kathleen. 2004. "Health and Retirement: Do Changes in Health Affect Retirement Expectations?" *The Journal of Human Resources* 39 (3): 624–648. https://doi.org/10.2307/3558990.

RAND HRS Longitudinal File 2016 (V1). Produced by the RAND Center for the Study of Aging, with funding from the National Institute on Aging and the Social Security Administration. Santa Monica, CA.

Sasson, Isaac. 2016. "Trends in Life Expectancy and Lifespan Variation by Educational Attainment: United States, 1990–2010." *Demography* 53 (2): 269–293. https://doi.org/10.1007/s13524-015-0453-7.

Schaeffer, Katherine. 2020. "6 Facts about Economic Inequality in the U.S." Pew Research Center. February 7, 2020. https://www.pewresearch.org/fact-tank/2020/02/07/6-facts-about-economic-inequality-in-the-u-s/.

Woolf, Steven H., and Heidi Schoomaker. 2019. "Life Expectancy and Mortality Rates in the United States, 1959–2017." *JAMA* 322 (20): 1996–2016. https://doi.org/10.1001/jama.2019.16932.

PART III

Lived Experience

The Role of Occupations, Employers, and Families

8

Dying with Your Boots On
The Realities of Working Longer in Low-Wage Work

Mary Gatta and Jessica Horning[1]

1. Introduction

In 2014, the satirical online newspaper *The Onion* ran a story with the headline "More Americans Putting off Retirement until Final Moments before Death." The article read, "Retirement is different for everyone—some people finish up working and then live off Social Security benefits for a few moments before passing on, while others may be able to lead active lives that last a whole afternoon. After a lifetime of working tirelessly to support themselves and their families, being able to enjoy several dozen seconds of retirement is a much-needed reward for most Americans."

The satire highlights a concerning reality. For many workers, retirement, in the traditional sense of a financially secure period of leisure after a lifetime of work, is elusive. Many older Americans, particularly those who have spent decades in low-wage work, are too young to die but too poor to retire. Working indefinitely has emerged as the key strategy underlying most low-wage workers' retirement plans. This chapter examines the experiences of low-wage older workers who try to stay employed—both for the ready cash and in order to increase their Social Security benefits by delaying claiming—and the economic consequences for those who stop working.

The United States' increasingly fragile do-it-yourself retirement system puts the burden on individuals to figure out their own retirement. With the decline of defined benefit pension plans and the increase of "gig" work, American workers have increasingly been asked to plan for their retirement themselves, while dealing with a diminished social safety net during their work lives. Neoliberal political ideology "celebrates risk and uncertainty as self-reliance" (M. Cooper 2014, 38). The New Deal social contract, which had as its cornerstone that individuals had clear social rights, has been replaced with a free-market approach that minimizes the role of government in individuals' lives.

The individual responsibility framework for retirement security puts low-wage workers in a bind. On the one hand, because they are unlikely to be able to save much for retirement and their Social Security benefits are small, they may be unable to make ends meet when they stop working. On the other hand, lower-wage workers face disproportionate challenges in remaining employed as they age. These challenges include failing health and disability, physical job demands, and age discrimination. Much research has focused on retirement and working longer among high-earning Americans—from encore careers and finding one's passions after retirement, to delaying retirement as long as possible. We know remarkably little about how aging lower-wage workers balance these challenges as they attempt to work longer and be economically secure.

These gaps in our knowledge are important because more than half of over-65s living alone and more than a quarter of those living in couple households lack basic economic security (Mutchler, Li, and Xu 2016). And while the situation for current retirees is alarming, the picture is worse for those who are approaching retirement age. In 2022, 52 million Americans—32 percent of the workforce—earned less than $15 an hour in low-wage sectors including hospitality, retail, childcare, and health care (Henderson 2022). Low-wage positions rarely offer retirement savings plans, leaving retirees dependent on Social Security benefits.

The COVID-19 pandemic amplified the problems with a working-longer strategy for low-wage workers. Older workers were more likely to develop serious complications from the virus; they were overrepresented in high-risk, front-line positions such as janitors and home health aides; and many held jobs in hard-hit sectors like retail and hospitality (Agovino 2020). During the pandemic, unemployment rates for workers over the age of 65 rapidly outstripped rates for younger workers. A global pandemic notwithstanding, working longer requires adults to be healthy enough to stay employed past traditional retirement age in jobs that are often characterized by intense physical demands. Understanding how low-wage workers negotiate precarious work and uncertain financial situations is increasingly important in an aging society.

We address three questions. First, how economically secure would low-wage older workers be if they no longer worked, and how does this security vary across career income levels, cohorts, and age of claiming Social Security benefits? Second, what challenges are most crucial for low-wage workers as they age? Finally, what strategies do older, low-paid Americans use to make ends meet at and beyond traditional retirement ages?

To answer the first question, we combine quantitative data from the Census Bureau on median and minimum wage earnings for two cohorts—those who reached their Social Security Full Retirement Age (FRA) in 1999, and those who reached the FRA in 2017—with data from the Elder Index on the level of income required for basic retirement security. We simulate several wage scenarios to examine how the adequacy of older Americans' Social Security benefits changes if they are able to work longer and thereby delay claiming Social Security. To answer the second and third questions, we draw on qualitative interview data. We share stories of older restaurant workers (part of a larger ethnographic study by Gatta [2018]) to better understand the challenges they face and the strategies they deploy.

We find that for low-wage workers, retirement is elusive. Workers who worked a full-time minimum-wage job their entire careers cannot ever "afford" to retire on Social Security alone, even if they own their own homes. The inadequacy of Social Security benefits stretches far up the income distribution: even median-wage men who own their homes outright have to work well beyond the earliest eligibility age for Social Security (age 62) for their Social Security benefits to clear the Elder Index benchmark. Women who own their own homes, along with both men and women who rent, are in a worse financial position. Moreover, the degree to which minimum-wage workers' Social Security benefits fall short of economic sufficiency has grown worse during the past two decades.

Worrying as these numbers are, our simulations probably underestimate the extent of the problem. Our models assume that workers' careers were spent in the formal work economy without any employment breaks. Real careers, by contrast, typically include months or years out of the labor force due to unemployment or caregiving. Some low-wage workers also find themselves working in the informal economy. Either working off the books or taking time out of the labor force reduces the Social Security benefits workers can expect.

Our qualitative data show, however, that working longer may not be a viable strategy for older low-wage workers who face physically demanding jobs, age discrimination, or the demand for "aesthetic labor." Some older workers find that their bodies are unable to perform the work as they had in the past. And ageism may surface when workers—especially those in customer-facing jobs in hospitality and retail—do not fit the "look" that employers desire. These challenges are barriers to continuous work across the life course, and they intensify during traditional retirement years.

Finally, we identify three types of strategies that older low-wage workers use for economic survival. The first is *letting it ride*: committing to working longer and taking a gamble by hoping for the best. Often in this strategy workers held the explicit expectation that they will work till they die. The second is *powering through*: working through pain and health problems, even if it means shifting from low-paid work to even lower-paid work. The third is *knitting their own safety net*, relying on friends or family to share health care, retirement savings, or housing in order to supplement an inadequate government safety net. Our interviewees described how they attempted to put highly individualized patchworks of solutions together with great innovation but not always with great success.

For many of the workers we highlight in this chapter, and the millions like them, a financially secure retirement is out of reach. They need to continue working in order to meet their basic economic needs. Yet working longer is not a simple proposition. And for workers who cannot work because of age discrimination, illness, or a lack of available jobs, their future is often quite uncertain.

2. Too Poor Not to Work

What is it like to be aging in the low-wage labor market? The experience of Diane, a 69-year-old waitress in New Jersey, highlights how working longer does not equate to economic security. At age 18, Diane began waiting tables at a coffeehouse/diner in a small New Jersey town. She worked five nights a week from 7 p.m. to 6 a.m. For each shift she earned a base pay of $6.50 a night, plus tips. Diane worked at the restaurant for nearly 20 years. In 1985, at the age of 35, she was the oldest person working at the diner: "I remember thinking what an old waitress I was then . . . and I was just 35. But in the field even then that was old."

Over the next few years she bounced from restaurant to restaurant, trying to find a good job with a sense of family and collegiality. In 1989, she found a job as a hostess and waitress at another local family-owned restaurant. Diane loved her work; she took great joy in serving her customers and felt it was a calling for her. She was making $125 a night, including tips, as a banquet server. It was good money and she had good coworkers. As she said, "I thought I would die there." She did spend a decade working there, but the owners—whom she considered family—sold the restaurant, and the new owners bankrupted it. At age 50, Diane found herself unemployed again. For the first 30 years of her career, Diane worked "off the books," meaning that she never paid into Social Security and had no health insurance or retirement benefits. Diane worked diligently for decades and had no savings, pension, or Social Security contributions to show for it.

Over the next 20 years she continued to work in restaurants (sometimes on the books, sometimes off the books). Work was slow in the winter months, so she used credit cards to pay her rent and purchase groceries. After years of a cyclical work schedule, she was unable to catch up with the debt. Diane claimed bankruptcy at age 68. She found that working harder, more hours, and more jobs on low wages was simply not a winning bet. Far too often workers are told that if they just work harder, they will achieve the American Dream. Yet this individualistic perspective often leads to an American nightmare as one ages.

Less than a year after declaring bankruptcy, Diane was again unemployed. She had lost her hostess job because of an injury at work. She had climbed a ladder to clean the blinds at the restaurant, fell, and broke her wrist. When her wrist healed, her job was no longer available to her. She was still actively searching for work, applying everywhere she could: retail stores, beach clubs, and restaurants. She even posted an ad on Craigslist to pet-sit for local families.

When Diane talked about the future, she began to cry. She never owned a home, was never able to save, and had very little in Social Security payments each month. She was two months behind in rent and her greatest fear was homelessness. Her plan—if she lost her apartment—was to live in her car with her cat. Indeed, her one ray of hope, if she could not find work, was that she would get a settlement from the restaurant where she fell and broke her wrist, and that settlement would carry her until she found work or died.

3. Who Are Today's Older Low-Wage Workers?

Of course, Diane is not alone: a substantial and growing number of older Americans are working for low wages. In 2018, according to our calculations based on the American Community Survey, more than 40 percent of Americans 55 years and older, and approximately 20 percent of those 65 years and older, were still working. Among those workers, more than one-tenth had incomes under 200 percent of the federal poverty threshold. During the past four decades, the average age of low-wage workers has risen; in recent years, more low-wage workers were age 55 or older (15.3 percent) than were teens (10.7 percent) (D. Cooper 2015). Among older workers, growth in unstable and low-wage jobs has outpaced growth in jobs offering decent pay or stable employment. By 2015, nearly one in four workers aged 62 or older were in "bad" jobs, defined as alternative work arrangements (on-call, temp/contract, and gig jobs, excluding independent contractors) or low-wage traditional jobs (paying less than $15,000 per year) (Ghilarducci, Webb, and Papadopoulos 2018). Such data belie assumptions that low-wage workers are predominately teenagers working for extra money or stepping-stones to advancement.

The lack of economic mobility that characterizes so many workers' lives highlights the lack of routes out of elder poverty. Economic mobility—even for workers with college educations—has decreased from the 1980s. In other words, "The probability of ending where you start has gone up and the probability of moving up from where you start has gone down" (Semuels 2016). Part of the explanation is that the number of jobs at the bottom of the labor market is increasing. People work but stay poor.

Although most low-wage workers have low-income retirements, some do not. Before the COVID-19 pandemic, more than a third of low-earning baby boomers were expected to escape poverty in old age (Butrica and Toder 2008). This group could move up the income ladder in one of two ways: by continuing to work or by living with other individuals (such as friends or adult children) who support them financially. Notably, these strategies rely on individual health, skill, relationships, and luck.

In America, a secure retirement involves the accumulation of wealth. And the reality is that for many Americans voluntary savings and home ownership are not part of their retirement wealth. A 2015 Government Accounting Office (GAO) report found that nearly 29 percent of American households with members age 55 or older have neither retirement savings nor traditional pension plans. Among those nearing retirement who do have some savings, the sums are often woefully inadequate. Median savings for all households with individuals aged 55 to 64 is $104,000, which translates to a projected annuity of roughly $310 a month. Moreover, labor market inequities are magnified in retirement. Racism and segregation in housing and employment opportunities hamper the ability of Americans of color to accumulate wealth: only 41 percent of Black families and 26 percent of Hispanic families had retirement account savings in 2013, compared with 65 percent of white non-Hispanic families (Morrissey 2016). And women remain economically vulnerable in retirement. They earn less than men during their working years, generally live longer than men, and are more likely to outlive their savings.

4. Low-Wage Older Workers and Retirement Security

Many Americans depend on Social Security as their main, and often only, source of guaranteed income in retirement. Approximately a quarter of Americans aged 65 or older rely on Social Security for at least 90 percent of their family income (Center on Budget and Policy

Priorities 2020). Can a retired low-wage worker live off their Social Security and have economic security? To answer this question, we need a measure of economic security for older Americans who are no longer working. The Elder Index (elderindex.org) is a measure developed by the Gerontology Institute in Massachusetts and Wider Opportunities for Women to measure the minimum amount of retirement income a person needs for a bare-bones budget. The values vary for singles or couples and the household type (renter, owner with a mortgage, or owner without a mortgage). The Elder Index is calculated for Americans who are fully retired. The transportation line item does not include travel to and from work, and the budget does not include income taxes, assuming that all income is coming from retirement savings or pensions. It does not include any frills like dining out, taking vacations, or giving birthday presents. The Elder Index is calculated at the county, state, and national level and is updated annually. What can the Elder Index tell us about older low-wage workers' prospects of retirement?

The Elder Index budget (Table 8.1) is sparse. In the best-case scenario, for a couple who own their home mortgage-free, the average basic monthly budget in 2017 required slightly less than $1,300 per person ($2,548 for the couple). Other scenarios require substantially more money to meet basic needs, up to $2,581 per month for a single elder with a mortgage. Notably, the average monthly Social Security benefit, which in 2017 was less than $1,500 for newly retired workers, is inadequate to satisfy the Elder Index budget under most of these scenarios (Social Security Administration 2018, 16).

Home ownership is a major component of elder costs. Compared to those who own their home outright, the average sums required for housing are nearly $300 more per month for renters and nearly $1,000 more per month for those who are still paying mortgages. In 2018, the plurality of U.S. residents aged 65 and older (49 percent) lived in homes owned outright, another 28 percent lived in homes with mortgages, and 21 percent were renters. Renting is substantially more common among older Americans with lower incomes than among those with higher incomes: among those who live in households with incomes less than twice the federal poverty line, 32 percent are renters (U.S. Census Bureau 2018).

Based on the Elder Index, how economically secure would older workers be if they no longer worked, and how does this security vary across career income levels, cohorts, and age

TABLE 8.1 National Elder Economic Security Index, 2017 dollars

	Single elders			Elder couples		
	Own w/o mortgage	Rent	Own w/ mortgage	Own w/o mortgage	Rent	Own w/ mortgage
Housing	516	791	1,425	516	791	1,425
Food	256	256	256	470	470	470
Transportation	231	231	231	357	357	357
Medical	390	390	390	780	780	780
Miscellaneous	279	279	279	425	425	425
Monthly total	$1,672	$1,947	$2,581	$2,548	$2,823	$3,457
Annual total	$20,064	$23,364	$30,972	$30,576	$33,876	$41,484

of claiming Social Security benefits? To answer these questions, we calculate the projected Social Security benefit amounts for workers in two different cohorts, one that reached the Full Retirement Age (FRA) in 1999 and one that reached the FRA in 2017. The FRA is the age at which workers can claim their full Social Security benefits, and it is increasing gradually because of legislation passed by Congress in 1983. We assume that adults in both cohorts start work at age 25. Those in the 1999 retirement cohort were born in 1934, started work in 1960, and worked for 40 years until their FRA at age 65. Those in the 2017 retirement cohort were born in 1951, started work in 1977, and worked for 41 years until their FRA at age 66.

We compare the 1999 and 2017 retirement cohorts in order to investigate how flat wage growth has impacted retirement security among Americans in the bottom half of the national income distribution. During the past four decades, the purchasing power of average hourly American wages has remained essentially unchanged (DeSilver 2018), while the federal minimum wage has fallen in real terms by about a quarter (D. Cooper 2015). While the federal minimum wage has remained stagnant since 2009, by 2021, 30 states and the District of Columbia and 45 localities had implemented higher minimum wages (Economic Policy Institute 2021). Local minimum wage increases have contributed to relatively few workers relying on an hourly wage equal to or less than the federal minimum wage. In 1999, after nearly a decade of unprecedented economic growth, 3.3 million workers, 4.6 percent of all hourly workers, earned no more than the federal minimum wage (National Economic Council 2000). In 2017, after a long period of job growth following the Great Recession, 1.8 million workers, 2.3 percent of all hourly workers, earned no more than the federal minimum wage of $7.25 per hour (U.S. Bureau of Labor Statistics 2018). The federal minimum nonetheless remains an important floor under wage levels.

We calculate monthly Social Security benefits for three stylized groups of workers: men who earned the median male wage each year of their careers, women who earned the median female wage, and workers who earned the federal minimum wage. Because continuous employment across four decades is not the norm, especially for women who spend time in unpaid family caregiving and lower-wage workers in precarious jobs, our simulations represent best-case scenarios for workers at a given wage level.

We use data published by the U.S. Census Bureau from 1960 (the earliest year for which median wage data by sex are available) to 2017. We use wage data adjusted to 2017 dollars using the Consumer Price Index Retroactive Series (CPI-U-RS) and manually adjust the federal minimum wage to 2017 dollars using the National Average Wage Index, which is the inflation adjustment used by the Social Security Administration (U.S. Census Bureau 2019; Social Security Administration 2020).

Next, we calculate expected Social Security benefits by taking the 35 years with the highest indexed earnings, adding them together, and then dividing by 420 months to find the Average Indexed Monthly Earnings (AIME). AIME is converted to a Primary Insurance Amount (PIA), which is the benefit workers would receive if they begin to claim benefits at their FRA. A progressive formula is used to compute the PIA, so that lower-income workers see a greater proportion of their income replaced by Social Security: monthly benefits are 90 percent of AIME before a first threshold, or "bend point," 32 percent between the first and second bend point, and 15 percent after the second bend point. The bend points change from year to year based on Americans' average wages. The year the worker turns 62 is used to determine the bend points for their PIA calculation (see Chapter 12). In our simulation, while the extra year the second cohort works does not itself make a difference to the benefits calculation, it does allow one more year of potentially higher earnings to be taken into account.

We then examine the adequacy of Social Security benefits by comparing the Social Security benefits we calculate for various scenarios to Elder Index budgets. Although costs of a basic budget vary geographically, for simplicity, we use the 2017 national average Elder Index.

We investigate whether delayed claiming of Social Security benefits would enable workers to earn benefits that reach the Elder Index threshold. In an effort to encourage workers to delay retirement, workers who begin claiming benefits earlier than their FRA receive less per month than their primary insurance amount, while those who begin claiming later receive more. Workers who claim Social Security at age 62 receive about 30 percent less per month, while those who claim at age 70 receive about 25 percent more (see Chapter 12, Table 12.1).

4.1. Benefit Changes across Cohorts

Across cohorts, monthly Social Security benefits increased modestly for median-wage men and women but fell for minimum-wage workers (Figure 8.1). Median-wage men in the 2017 retirement cohort can expect just $58 a month more in inflation-adjusted benefits than their counterparts in the 1999 cohort. And gender plays a critical role in determining retirement prospects. Due to dramatic changes in women's workforce participation since 1960, inflation-adjusted median wages for women increased 77 percent between 1960 and 2017 (U.S. Census Bureau 2019). Correspondingly, median-wage women's monthly Social Security benefit is more than $100 per month greater than that of their counterparts in the 1999 cohort,

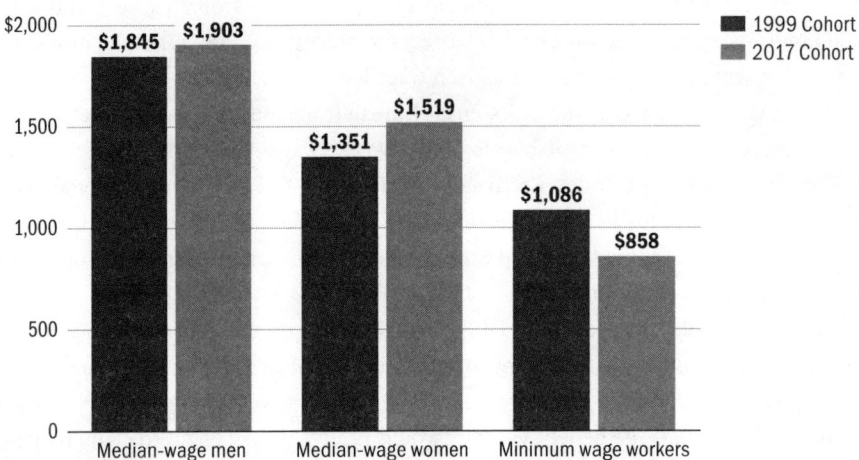

FIGURE 8.1 Monthly Social Security benefit amounts, by wage scenario
2017 dollars
Note: Simulated benefit amounts for men who earned the median male wage, women who earned the median female wage, and adults who earned the federal minimum wage every year of their career. Cohorts reaching the Social Security Full Retirement Age (FRA) in 1999 and 2017.

although it still falls well short of men's benefits. Median-wage women retiring in 2017 had an earned Social Security benefit that was nearly $400 per month less than median-wage men's benefits. Further, the absolute gap between men and women's Social Security benefits will grow every year in retirement as they each get a percentage cost-of-living increase dependent on the base benefit.

Four decades of work at the median wage still produces Social Security benefits too low to provide economic security under many Elder Index scenarios. Recall from Table 8.1 that single retirees need, on average, about $1,950 a month if they rent their home in retirement. Among median-wage earners, neither men's nor women's Social Security benefits reach this mark. Americans at the median wage or below who begin claiming at their FRA cannot rely on Social Security benefits to keep them economically secure in retirement.

It is worth noting that the benefits we model are higher than *actual* average Social Security benefits because we assume that adults work continuously at a given wage level, compared to the reality in which workers experience years of illness, caregiving, unemployment, or underemployment. In 2017, the average monthly benefit was $1,244 for retired women and $1,565 for retired men (Social Security Administration 2018, 20), roughly $300 less for both men and women than the medians we compute. Social Security is less adequate for retirement security even than our simulation suggests.

Figure 8.1 also shows that even as median-wage workers' real Social Security benefits held steady or increased slightly across cohorts, benefits fell substantially for full-time workers making the federal minimum wage each year. Among minimum-wage workers, the 2017 cohort had an earned benefit of $858 per month, approximately $200 less than the benefit for the 1999 cohort, a result of the decrease in the real value of the minimum wage. The benefit for the 1999 cohort is still nearly $600 less than the Elder Index for a single worker who owns their home without a mortgage, the lowest bar for economic security.

4.2. Working Longer and Benefit Adequacy

Can low-wage workers earn adequate Social Security benefits if they work longer? Tables 8.2 and 8.3 show how the adequacy of Social Security benefits changes across claiming ages for median-wage and minimum-wage workers in the retirement cohorts of 1999 and 2017. We compare the inflation-adjusted Social Security benefits to the 2017 national average Elder Index.

Table 8.2 represents the best-case housing scenario: adults who own their home outright and do not have a mortgage or rent payment in retirement. However, even with that asset, workers who have earned the median full-time wages throughout their careers may find that their Social Security benefits do not meet the modest level of economic security represented by the Elder Index. Median-wage men's Social Security benefits met the Elder Index (single homeowner) standard if they began claiming benefits at age 64 in the 1999 cohort or at age 65 in the 2017 cohort. In contrast, median-wage women's benefits cleared that threshold only if they worked to age 69 in the earlier cohort or to age 68 in the later cohort—several years past traditional retirement ages.

As Table 8.2 shows, workers who have spent decades in minimum-wage jobs will never meet a basic level of economic security in retirement if Social Security benefits are their only

TABLE 8.2 Monthly Social Security benefits by wage scenario as compared to the Elder Index for a single elder who owns without a mortgage, 2017 dollars

Wage scenario	Benefit if retired at . . .								
	62	63	64	65	66	67	68	69	70
Median-wage men, 1999	−196	−73	49	173	283	394	505	615	726
Median-wage women, 1999	−592	−502	−412	−321	−240	−159	−78	3	84
Minimum-wage worker, 1999	−804	−731	−659	−586	−521	−456	−391	−326	−261
Median-wage men, 2017	−245	−150	−23	104	231	383	535	687	839
Median-wage women, 2017	−533	−457	−356	−255	−153	−32	90	211	333
Minimum-wage worker, 2017	−1,029	−986	−929	−872	−814	−746	−677	−609	−540

Note: Difference between simulated benefits and the Elder Index for cohorts reaching the Social Security Full Retirement Age (FRA) in 1999 and 2017. The FRA was 65 for those who retired in 1999 and 66 for those who retired in 2017.

income, even if they own their home outright. At every claiming age, the situation is worse for the 2017 cohort than for the 1999 cohort. In the 1999 cohort, minimum-wage workers who claimed Social Security benefits at age 62 would fall more than $800 per month short of the Elder Index; their counterparts in the 2017 cohort would fall more than $1,000 short. Even those who delay claiming until age 70, thus maximizing their monthly Social Security

TABLE 8.3 Monthly Social Security benefits by wage scenario as compared to the Elder Index for a single elder renter, 2017 dollars

Wage scenario	Benefit if retired at . . .								
	62	63	64	65	66	67	68	69	70
Median-wage men, 1999	−471	−348	−226	−102	8	119	230	340	451
Median-wage women, 1999	−867	−777	−687	−596	−515	−434	−353	−272	−191
Minimum-wage worker, 1999	−1,079	−1,006	−934	−861	−796	−731	−666	−601	−536
Median-wage men, 2017	−520	−425	−298	−171	−44	108	260	412	564
Median-wage women, 2017	−808	−732	−631	−530	−428	−307	−185	−64	58
Minimum-wage worker, 2017	−1,304	−1,261	−1,204	−1,147	−1,089	−1,021	−952	−884	−815

Note: Difference between simulated benefits and the Elder Index for cohorts reaching the Social Security Full Retirement Age (FRA) in 1999 and 2017. The FRA was 65 for those who retired in 1999 and 66 for those who retired in 2017.

benefits, would be well beneath the Elder Index. Those in the 1999 cohort would fall about $260 short; those in the 2017 cohort would fall more than $500 per month short. Even if the 2017 cohort cut miscellaneous and transportation costs to zero, they would still have to cut approximately $50 per month from food, housing, or medical care.

Retirement security is more precarious for those who are not homeowners. Many lower-wage workers do not own a home. Table 8.3 shows how the modeled Social Security benefits compare to the Elder Index for a single elder renter. None of the wage scenarios allows a worker to meet their basic financial needs if they stop working and begin claiming Social Security benefits at their FRA. Median-wage men in both cohorts would need to delay claiming at least one extra year in order to clear the Elder Index benchmark—to age 66 for the 1999 cohort and to age 67 for the 2017 cohort. Median-wage women in the 1999 cohort would never be able to meet their needs. Even if they delayed claiming until age 70, they would still fall nearly $200 short every month. Women in the 2017 cohort can earn enough Social Security benefits to meet basic economic security if they delay claiming until 70 years old. If a woman in this category needs to begin claiming benefits earlier, she faces a monthly deficit ranging from $64 if she starts claiming at age 69 to $808 if she starts claiming at 62.

As Table 8.2 shows, minimum-wage workers can never meet the Elder Index with Social Security benefits alone even if they own their home. Table 8.3 shows that renters face a financial situation that is more dire and has worsened over time. If minimum-wage workers in the 1999 cohort delayed claiming until age 70, they would still have a monthly shortage of more than $500. They would need to cut all their budget for incidentals and transportation and then carve an additional $25 from their food or medication budget. If minimum-wage workers in the 2017 cohort delayed claiming until they were 70 years old, their monthly budget deficit would still be more than $800, higher than the entire renter index monthly housing cost.

How much would minimum-wage workers have to work to fill the gap between their Social Security benefits and economic sufficiency? Among workers who claimed Social Security at their FRA and continued working at minimum wage, workers in the 1999 cohort would need to work 27 hours every week to make an additional $10,000 per year to meet the Elder Index. Minimum-wage workers in the 2017 cohort face a shortage of more than $13,000, requiring them to work at least 33 hours per week, every week, until they die. (Older workers who collect Social Security benefits while continuing to work face penalties if their earnings exceed certain benchmarks, but these sums are well below the exemption thresholds.) If workers in this situation cannot keep working, they may be unable to meet their basic needs and require significant assistance to avoid homelessness.

Social Security was never intended to support workers on its own. Eighty-five years after it was passed to provide additional income to those with low pensions, approximately 25 percent of American seniors rely on the program for at least 90 percent of their income. As our modeling shows, the benefits for workers who made the median wage their entire careers still fall short of economic security as measured by the Elder Index. While some workers can boost their Social Security benefits over the Elder Index line if they delay collecting their benefits, minimum-wage workers can never afford to retire. Even if they delay collecting benefits until age 70, minimum-wage workers would need to continue working nearly full-time in order to afford rent, medical care, and food.

5. In Their Own Words

As the Elder Index data make clear, many low-wage workers have to work longer to survive economically. But is this a reality? In this section we focus on understanding the experiences of working longer for lower-wage workers. Specifically, we highlight the challenges that older workers face in low-wage work and the strategies they use to try to mitigate them. We share ethnographic data compiled by Gatta, who spent several years interviewing restaurant workers throughout the country and conducted in-depth interviews with 31 restaurant workers, as part of a larger study on aging and low-wage work. The restaurant workers' ages ranged from the 30s to the 70s, and they represented various jobs within the restaurant industry. In all cases, the workers viewed their restaurant work as their careers.

5.1. The Challenges of Working Longer in Low-Wage Work

A naïve observer might assume that low-wage workers would be eager to leave jobs that are widely regarded as "bad jobs." This was not the case. As Diane's story earlier in the chapter highlights, many of these workers loved their work. For instance, Henry, a 73-year-old bartender from New York City, fell in love with it the first time he mixed drinks behind a bar. Henry spent 30 years tending bar in Manhattan, Coney Island, and Brooklyn—including many iconic New York City bars like the Old Homestead Steakhouse, and Marylou's in Greenwich Village. As Henry recalled, "It was amazing being behind the bar in New York City; you had the whole world coming to your bar. I had a stage." This sentiment—taking pride and enjoying the work—was shared by many of the workers. And while they had to work longer for financial reasons, they also wanted to work longer because they enjoyed the work.

Yet for many of them, working longer was difficult or impossible. We found that restaurant workers described two main challenges: declining health in the face of physical job demands and age discrimination. Ironically, the older Americans who most need to continue earning money as seniors are those who are least able to do so.

5.1.1. Physical Demands of Low-Wage Work

Physical demands are remarkably common in older workers' jobs. Among workers ages 58 and older, 44 percent—about 10.2 million Americans—have jobs with physical demands or difficult working conditions including handling and moving objects; spending significant time standing, walking, or running; labor outdoors or exposure to abnormal temperatures; and body movements such as kneeling, crouching, bending, and twisting (Bucknor and Baker 2016). Extended work in these jobs can lead to back and neck pain along with ergonomic problems from use of machinery (such as vacuums for hotel housekeepers). Many workers report severe symptoms and impairments at work that spill over into their quality of life (Krause, Scherzer, and Rugulies 2005; Lipscomb et al. 2007). And as workers age in these fields, the work demands are coupled with aging-related physical changes that often cause occupational injury and restrict activities at work (Delloiacono 2015).

Older restaurant workers in Gatta's ethnographic study said that physical expectations restricted the work they could do and reduced their pay. For instance, Don, a line cook in his early 50s, worked in restaurant kitchens for over 20 years, with a brief stint working as a cashier in a fast-food restaurant. He noted that as he aged it was harder to perform the physical demands of the job and he had to find less strenuous work. Previously, Don spent several years cooking at the concessions at stadiums throughout New York City. He enjoyed the work but found it to be an extremely unstable source of income coupled with very intense work demands. "It's very physical, the overall standing, moving around, sometimes you've got to lift certain amounts of stuff, 40 pounds of sugar, ice, big cans. Lot of bending over, lot of stirring, strenuous work." He left the stadium work for a job as a cook at a nonprofit homeless agency in Manhattan partly because it appeared less strenuous.

Another waiter, Jim, from Pennsylvania, also saw that his health was deteriorating and work more challenging. "It's a young man's game—it's hard to keep up with the physical demands. The plates are not light and I am constantly carrying heavy loads." He noted that during his 30s, at one of his jobs he had to navigate two steps in the dining room. However, because the restaurant was busy, he would try to "jump" the steps to save a few seconds on each trip from the kitchen to his tables. That jumping years ago eventually led to an Achilles heel problem. Each night after his shift he felt his feet ache as he tried to go to sleep. Jim questioned how long he could do this work. "I am coming up on 60 years old. I don't think I can keep it up. I don't know how much longer I can do my job. At my restaurant everything is refillable—bread, soda, soup, salad, pasta—it's like Whack-a-Mole. I just run my entire shift." And despite all this running, he has no idea when he will have a good night financially. "There is no steady income; my paycheck is minimal, maybe $15 a week. I am totally dependent on tips."

Other workers had similar concerns for their future. Bert, a 57-year-old restaurant worker, said that arthritis in his knees and back made each day of work painful. His employer noticed his pain and "demoted" him to serving lunch instead of dinner because he was "not fast enough" for the dinner rush. Without the dinner tips he's been accustomed to earning, this change meant a clear pay cut. He kept working but got poorer.

5.1.2. Age Discrimination and Aesthetic Labor in Low-Wage Work

It was not just their health that concerned the restaurant workers; many reported that they faced age discrimination in the workplace. Age discrimination is a particular problem for hospitality workers who are often expected not only to perform the work duties but also to look the part. When employers hire workers based on their personal appearance to promote their company brand, they are requiring employees to provide "aesthetic labor" (Nickson, Warhurst, and Dutton 2005). As individuals grow older, they may not fit the desired aesthetic.

As she aged, Tanya, a long-time restaurant worker, was told that older women don't look professional in the restaurant. In essence, she had less and less of the aesthetic labor needed to bartend and serve tables. At a fine-dining restaurant where she worked, the owner, despite the good work she was doing, would repeatedly tell her that men all look the same as they age, they all look professional, and women don't. She felt this was illegal, but she was economically vulnerable. She needed the work to pay bills. Like so many women and older workers, she was trapped in a cycle of discrimination. Eventually she left the fine-dining restaurant and had a hard time finding another job. She did a summer job working as a caterer at a large outdoor concert venue—where she worked with a number of older workers, including a 90-year-old waitress—but that job was only seasonal. She noted, "The older you are, the harder [it is] to get a job."

Although age discrimination tends to be especially intense for women, some men also face age discrimination. Recall Henry, the New York City bartender we met earlier in the chapter. In his 70s, he looked for a bartending job but found that many New York bars were looking for younger bartenders. "There was a time in the '70s and '80s where people were looking for mature bartenders," he said, describing his predicament. "Now they want the youngest, newest model."

In some instances, age discrimination meant transitioning into even lower-paid work in the service industry. Restaurant workers shared that some of the more lucrative jobs in the restaurant industries (such as bartenders) were harder to secure as they aged. These are often "front-of-the-house" customer-facing jobs that may hire on aesthetic labor (how a potential worker fits the "brand" being sold), in addition to skills. Annie, a restaurant worker for decades, found that as she aged, it was harder for her to get the front-of-the-house bartender jobs. She opted instead for back-of-the-house kitchen work—but often at the expense of higher earnings. Annie felt that "jobs in the back of the house are more dignified. It is easier to get that type of work as you get older if you are a woman. In the front of the house, women get viewed on their looks. I feel like I could continue to bartend until I am in my 70s, but it is too hard to find work as you get older. There are hundreds of young girls who would get a bartending job over me. In fact, I was told at 33 years old that I was too old to bartend. That is why I stay in the back-of-the-house jobs now." While Annie enjoys bartending, the nexus of sexism and ageism creates subtle (and not so subtle) barriers to staying in that job.

5.2. Unpacking Workers' Strategies

As the stories of older workers highlight, the reality of low or no savings, and the need to meet daily economic needs, has forced them to make difficult choices. Workers whose health is still good may be able to work longer. However, for many the challenges of physical strain, health failings, and age discrimination lead to other strategies, as we explore in this section—highlighting not only the strategies but also the individualistic nature of those strategies.

5.2.1. Letting It Ride

For some workers, working longer was the only strategy that was available. That was very much the case for a New Jersey bartender named Joan. Gatta met with Joan in her living room just a few hours before Joan was set to begin her bartending shift at a bar about a 30-minute drive from her home in rural New Jersey. This was a commute that the 66-year-old woman made six nights a week—arriving for her 5 p.m. shift and often leaving the bar well after midnight to head home. This grueling work schedule was not new to her. Joan had entered the restaurant business 37 years earlier when she realized that her family needed extra income. However, her work options were limited because she needed to work a job at night. Her then-husband, a roofer, worked days. She and her husband needed to split work shifts to manage the childcare.

Over three decades later, Joan was still behind the bar. After a divorce, she met her second husband working there. Ralph was a bartender, so while he also made cash each night, he had no health insurance or retirement savings. They were married for 30 years, and got by economically. And they even put a little money away in a savings account. But then Ralph got sick and was diagnosed with terminal cancer. He could no longer work; he did not have access to paid sick days or private disability insurance. They faced challenges paying their medical expenses and daily bills with the loss of Ralph's income. It was then up to Joan to make ends meet as a bartender, and they exhausted what little savings they had. In fact, two years after Ralph's death, Joan was still getting his medical bills. "All I can do is write back and say, 'He's deceased and there is no estate.'" What becomes clear from Joan's story is how her husband's diagnosis shattered her precarious economic security puzzle. Joan and Ralph could keep it together when they both were working and in good health; however, they were unprepared for the economic impact of Ralph's cancer.

As she aged in the restaurant industry, Joan decided to move in with her daughter and four grandchildren in order to help with a "split shift" caregiving schedule (similar to the one she shared with her first husband over 30 years ago). She babysat her grandchildren all day while her daughter worked, and then Joan headed to her bartending job Monday to Saturday nights. She had no savings left or retirement tucked away. "I can never stop working. I have four grandkids that I have to help take care of. There is no retirement. I am hoping I can keep doing what I can do. Maybe if I can't bartend any longer, I can go to work at Wegmans." Joan qualified for Medicare, but the supplemental insurance cost her about $1,200 a month—something that represented a significant portion of her budget. Her future? "Getting sick is my greatest fear. I've told my daughter, if I get sick I'll jump off a bridge." So far Joan's been lucky. She has remained healthy, with just some tendinitis in her elbow. However, she fears her luck will run out—and the only contingency plan to working longer she can come up with is death.

5.2.2. Powering Through and Downshifting

Some workers try to power through as long as they can. Declining physical abilities and inability to meet the demand for aesthetic labor do not always prevent low-wage workers from having a job *of some sort*, but these challenges may push them down the wage scale. Some workers chose to "power through" their work day and worked through pain. Despite the hard work, Jim (a waiter we met earlier) kept going. "I had a rotator sprain injury last year and I just worked through the sprain. I had no choice—if I didn't work, I didn't get paid." He tried to find ways to deal with the constant pain. He started going to the gym to try to get in shape, but so many of his injuries were cumulative, caused by years of hard physical labor. How long the working-longer strategy can last is quite uncertain.

For some, powering through may require switching to lower-wage work. In hospitality work, this can take several forms. Remember Bert was demoted to less lucrative shifts when arthritis made the dinner rush difficult. This had a direct impact on his earnings. As a tipped worker, he earned the federal subminimum wage ($2.13 per hour) as his base rate, and customers' tips were a significant part of his income. However, tips are based on the total meal check, as customers often calculate a percent of that check for the tip. Because the lunch menu has lower-priced food items than the dinner menu, the corresponding tips are also less. Other workers took lower-paying jobs in the industry, like Don (who left stadium work to cook at a nonprofit homeless agency) and Annie (who moved to back-of-the-house jobs where age discrimination was less intense). So while they continue working, they are downshifting to even lower-wage work.

5.2.3. Knit Your Own Safety Nets

One way that workers who spent careers in low-wage work found some semblance of economic security was by relying on family and friends to provide a safety net. Tricia was a 55-year-old restaurant worker from Illinois. She started in the restaurant business at age 14. "My family knew the owners and they gave me a job as a salad girl—I would make the salads and dressings." By the time Tricia was 16, she was promoted to a hostess. "I was hooked on restaurant work." She then worked her way through high school and college as a waitress. After college she moved to Chicago and got a restaurant manager job. She then worked over the next 20 years in restaurant management as she raised her family. Then in her late 40s she was diagnosed with cancer and got very sick. For over four years she was treated for cancer and could not work. She went on permanent disability and Medicare. Her husband had both health insurance and retirement savings to which she had access.

Without her husband's savings and income, Tricia did not know how she would have been able to survive after cancer without work. "If I had to live off my disability payments, I think I would be so scared." In fact, Tricia has seen the impact of retirement insecurity in her own life. "My father lost his job years ago, but in his retirement he needed to work to pay the Medicare supplement. So at 76 years old I got him a job in one of the restaurants I worked rolling silverware. He worked there until he died at 82 years old. He needed the money to pay for health insurance." Tricia also notes, "I don't know anyone who retires voluntarily from restaurant work. I know general managers in their 70s who are still working. I've heard colleagues wonder where they will live after retirement."

Sue, a 53-year-old restaurant worker from Maryland, started her career as a fast-food worker in high school, and like Tricia she worked her way up the restaurant ladder. She loved working in the food industry and found the flexibility of hours very helpful as she raised her children. "I would work nights and my husband would work days. At the time I saw the flexibility as worth more than a 401(k)." And like Tricia, she had a husband with retirement savings and health insurance. "I was lucky, my husband had the job with the benefits. I couldn't have survived without him." While Sue was happily married, she acknowledged that divorce was her greatest fear. "I wouldn't have anything for the future." And her situation was not that different from others in the industry: "I know far too many great chefs without benefits." The restaurant business took another toll on her life. As she aged in the business, she started getting ill, beginning with premature contractions in her heart. After a series of doctors and tests, it became clear that the stress of the food business—she routinely worked 72 hours a week—was too much for her body and she found herself retired on disability. And without the income from her husband, she would not have been able to survive financially. Tricia's and Sue's partners provided the opportunity for them to knit their safety net during their working years and supplemented the disability and Medicare they received when they stopped working. Without their families' knitted safety net, both women would not have had the additional income they needed to cover their costs as they were forced into early retirement because of illness. Neither woman could continue to work; neither had the savings on her own to get by despite decades of successful work in a low-wage industry; and disability benefits, while valuable, were not enough to make ends meet. Social Security Disability Insurance was an important part of the story for Tricia and Sue, but they could not make ends meet on it alone.

Even for workers who continued working, homemade safety nets mattered. The knit-it-yourself safety net provided important supplemental support. Recall Bert and Tanya from earlier in the chapter. They offset their low incomes by sharing housing. Both Bert and Tanya reported that without each other to share life expenses, they would be homeless. Yet even with their cohousing arrangement, Tanya and Bert felt insecure about the future.

Another waitress, Anita, shared her knit-it-yourself strategy to get by. Anita expected to depend on the restaurant community to help her with the aging process. "I know my kids can't help me. My daughter is barely getting by with her kids and my son moved to Las Vegas, but I always thought the community of the restaurant would be there." In fact, over the years she saw how the workers took care of each other. She relayed the story of Brenda, a waitress who had a stroke at age 75. "The owner let her stay and hostess—she needed the money. She was slow but we would help her out." Anita and her coworkers took food to Brenda's home and helped her with cleaning. "We took care of her." Anita felt that some type of "Golden Girls" community of friends would be a buffer for her when she needed it.

Some of these workers aimed to knit their own safety nets by forming intentional communities—a modern-day "Golden Girls"—to support a precarious retirement future. This is part of a wider trend that is emerging as more retirees choose to live communally to take care of each other—emotionally, physically, and financially. These communities create the social infrastructure to address food insecurity, home health care, transportation, and belonging. The strategy makes sense in the face of inadequate public supports and unaffordable housing, assisted living, and health care. These older Americans depended on each other to help knit their own safety nets. Yet without institutional or governmental support, no matter how hard they tried, there were always holes in their safety nets.

6. Conclusion

For the workers in this chapter, along with millions of other workers in the United States, low-wage work is not a stop along the path to economically secure careers, nor it is work that they do not value or experience great pride doing. Instead, many workers not only enjoy their work, but thrive in it. However our labor market structures and systems of rewards, along with public policy predicated on individual risk and responsibility, contributes to a reality in which many workers spend years in low-wage industries only to find themselves financially unable to retire while also perhaps physically unable to continue working. In addition, many workers may face increased levels of age discrimination, often coded in constructions of aesthetic labor demands of many hospitality and retail jobs.

This leaves low-wage older workers with few strategies to economically survive. As demonstrated in this chapter, they can *let it ride*: commit to working longer and hope for the best with the explicit expectation that they will work till they die. The second is *power through*: work through pain and health problems, even if it means shifting from low-paid work to even lower-paid work. The third is *knit their own safety net*: rely on friends or family to share health care, retirement savings, or housing in order to supplement an inadequate government safety net. All of these strategies are far from effective.

While working longer and encore careers can be a successful strategy for segments of the older workforce, they are not panaceas. Instead, we need to bring forward the realities of all older workers, the challenges and joys they face in the work, in order to formulate collective responses that value all work and workers. If not, as long as we focus on individual response (work more, save more, live with family), we do not have to address the larger structural constraints (such as labor market discrimination, decreasing real value of wages, and low incomes in working years leading to lower Social Security payments and little ability to save). The weak social safety net has had a drastic impact on economic security, and even low-wage workers who can save typically lack access to good retirement vehicles since many employers do not offer plans. Working longer may certainly work for some older Americans, but it is not a panacea to raise all workers out of poverty. One bartender reflected on his older colleagues and cringed. His friend Charlie was still bartending at 78 years old. "Charlie is struggling, like so many of the older guys. So many of them are going to go out of work in a coffin."

Note

1. Mary Gatta designed and conducted the qualitative study which is chronicled in Gatta (2018). Jessica Horning designed and conducted the quantitative analysis in this chapter.

References

Agovino, Theresa. 2020. "COVID-19 Deals a Dual Threat to Older Workers." SHRM. July 18, 2020. https://www.shrm.org/hr-today/news/all-things-work/pages/covid-19-deals-a-dual-threat-to-older-workers.aspx.

Bucknor, Cherrie, and Dean Baker. 2016. "Still Working Hard: An Update on the Share of Older Workers in Physically Demanding Jobs." Washington, DC: Center for Economic and Policy Research. https://cepr.net/images/stories/reports/still-working-hard-2016-03.pdf. Accessed June 03, 2022.

Butrica, Barbara, and Eric Toder. 2008. "Are Low-Wage Workers Destined for Low Income at Retirement?" Washington, DC: Urban Institute. https://www.urban.org/research/publication/are-low-wage-workers-destined-low-income-retirement.

Center on Budget and Policy Priorities. 2020. "Top Ten Facts about Social Security." https://www.cbpp.org/research/social-security/top-ten-facts-about-social-security.

Cooper, David. 2015. "Raising the Minimum Wage to $12 by 2020 Would Lift Wages for 35 Million American Workers." Briefing Paper 405. EPI Briefing Paper. Washington, DC: Economic Policy Institute.

https://www.epi.org/publication/raising-the-minimum-wage-to-12-by-2020-would-lift-wages-for-35-million-american-workers/.

Cooper, Marianne. 2014. *Cut Adrift: Families in Insecure Times*. Berkeley: University of California Press. https://www.ucpress.edu/book/9780520277670/cut-adrift.

Delloiacono, Nancy. 2015. "Musculoskeletal Safety for Older Adults in the Workplace: Review of Current Best Practice Evidence." *Workplace Health & Safety* 63 (2): 48–53. https://doi.org/10.1177/2165079915570299. Accessed June 03, 2022.

DeSilver, Drew. 2018. "For Most Americans, Real Wages Have Barely Budged in Decades." *Pew Research Center*. August 7, 2018. https://www.pewresearch.org/fact-tank/2018/08/07/for-most-us-workers-real-wages-have-barely-budged-for-decades/.

Economic Policy Institute. 2021. "Minimum Wage Tracker." Accessed. August 3, 2021. https://www.epi.org/minimum-wage-tracker/.

GAO. 2015. "Retirement Security: Most Households Approaching Retirement Have Low Savings." Government Accountability Office. https://www.gao.gov/assets/gao-15-419.pdf.

Gatta, Mary. 2018. *Waiting on Retirement: Aging and Economic Insecurity in Low-Wage Work*. Studies in Social Inequality. Stanford, CA: Stanford University Press.

Ghilarducci, Teresa, Anthony Webb, and Michael Papadopoulos. 2018. "The Growth of Unstable and Low Wage Work among Older Workers." Policy Note Series. New York: Schwartz Center for Economic Policy Analysis and Department of Economics, The New School for Social Research. https://www.economicpolicyresearch.org/images/Bad_Jobs.pdf.

Henderson, Kaitlyn. 2022. *The Crisis of Low Wages in the U.S.* Washington, DC: Oxfam America. https://www.oxfamamerica.org/explore/research-publications/the-crisis-of-low-wages-in-the-us/.

Krause, Niklas, Teresa Scherzer, and Reiner Rugulies. 2005. "Physical Workload, Work Intensification, and Prevalence of Pain in Low Wage Workers: Results from a Participatory Research Project with Hotel Room Cleaners in Las Vegas." *American Journal of Industrial Medicine* 48 (5): 326–337. https://doi.org/10.1002/ajim.20221. Accessed June 03, 2022.

Lipscomb, H. J., C. A. Epling, L. A. Pompeii, and J. M. Dement. 2007. "Musculoskeletal Symptoms among Poultry Processing Workers and a Community Comparison Group: Black Women in Low-Wage Jobs in the Rural South." *American Journal of Industrial Medicine* 50 (5): 327–338. https://doi.org/10.1002/ajim.20447. Accessed on June 03, 2022.

Morrissey, Monique. 2016. "The State of American Retirement: How 401(k)s Have Failed Most American Workers." Retirement Inequality Chartbook. Washington, DC: Economic Policy Institute. https://www.epi.org/publication/retirement-in-america/.

Mutchler, Jan, Yang Li, and Ping Xu. 2016. "Living below the Line: Economic Insecurity and Older Americans Insecurity in the States 2016." Center for Social and Demographic Research on Aging Publications, September. https://scholarworks.umb.edu/demographyofaging/13.

National Economic Council. 2000. "The Minimum Wage: Increasing the Reward for Work." Washington, DC. https://clintonwhitehouse4.archives.gov/WH/EOP/nec/html/doc030800.html.

Nickson, Dennis, Chris Warhurst, and Eli Dutton. 2005. "The Importance of Attitude and Appearance in the Service Encounter in Retail and Hospitality." *Managing Service Quality: An International Journal* 15 (2): 195–208. https://doi.org/10.1108/09604520510585370.

Semuels, Alana. 2016. "Poor at 20, Poor for Life." *The Atlantic*. July 14, 2016. https://www.theatlantic.com/business/archive/2016/07/social-mobility-america/491240/.

Social Security Administration. 2018. "Fast Facts & Figures about Social Security, 2018." 13–11785. https://www.ssa.gov/policy/docs/chartbooks/fast_facts/2018/fast_facts18.pdf . Accessed June 03, 2022.

Social Security Administration. 2020. "National Average Wage Index." https://www.ssa.gov/oact/cola/AWI.html.

U.S. Bureau of Labor Statistics. 2018. "Characteristics of Minimum Wage Workers, 2017." U.S. Bureau of Labor Statistics. March 2018. https://www.bls.gov/opub/reports/minimum-wage/2017/home.htm.

U.S. Census Bureau. 2018. "2018 American Community Survey 1-year Public Use Microdata Samples, Custom Table Tool." https://data.census.gov/cedsci/. Accessed December 28, 2021.

U.S. Census Bureau. 2019. "Table P-38. Full-Time, Year-Round Workers by Median Earnings and Sex." Historical Income Tables: People. https://www.census.gov/data/tables/time-series/demo/income-poverty/historical-income-people.html.

9

Ad Hoc, Limited, and Reactive
How Firms Respond to an Aging Workforce

Peter Berg and Matthew M. Piszczek

1. Introduction

In aging societies, workplaces that provide opportunities for older workers to engage and be productive will be critical to maintaining economic growth, worker well-being, and public pensions. Much research has discussed the implications of the individual aging process for work and the implications of aging populations for public pension systems and retirement decisions. But less is known about the role firms play in promoting or inhibiting participation of older workers. This omission is unfortunate because the economic and social consequences of population aging depend in large part on how employers respond to an aging workforce.

Much research about firms and workforce aging offers aspirational solutions to potential problems, making a case for what management and labor organizations—the crucial organizational actors within workplaces—*should* do to help older workers. However, we have remarkably little evidence about what management and labor are *actually* doing to respond to and manage an older workforce (Finkelstein et al. 2015). Even the extent to which organizations consider workforce aging in designing policies and practices remains unclear. In some cases, organizational leaders may be actively discouraging working longer for at least a subset of older workers.

Specifically, we know too little about how firms view older workers from a human capital perspective, the practices they implement in response to an aging workforce, which stakeholders benefit from or are harmed by these practices, and the role of labor organizations in shaping these practices. As a result, it is unclear how firms' approaches to aging workers affect inequalities by industry, occupation, and worker skill level. We also lack evidence about how the national-level institutional context shapes the responses of managers and labor organizations toward an aging workforce. Better answers to these questions should enable researchers, advocates, and policymakers to design more realistic responses to our aging workforce.

We present new cross-national evidence of how managers and labor organizations respond to workforce aging. We use information from a qualitative study of manufacturing firms in the United States and Germany, along with previous evidence from survey data in both nations. Although the two countries are at similar stages of economic development, their employee representation systems, social policy, and common human resource planning models are very different. Our comparison of the United States and Germany sheds light on how institutional systems shape firms' approach to older workers. A mixed-methods approach allows us to understand in detail the approach firms are taking toward older workers. Our interviews with managers and labor representatives give us insight into the motivation behind decisions to implement particular practices, while survey data set the in-depth qualitative work in a broader context. We draw on previous survey research about age-related human resource practices in the United States, and we pair this evidence with new analysis of a large, nationally representative survey of German firms. We focus our qualitative study on the manufacturing sector because it has many older workers and many physically demanding occupations that may be difficult for older workers. Manufacturing therefore provides a case study of a sector in which the organizational response to workforce aging is especially important.

We offer three main findings. First, in both the United States and Germany, firms do relatively little to address workforce aging proactively. In some cases we observed, firms actively move older workers out of their jobs because of health problems, high salaries, or perceived productivity decline. This reality is in sharp contrast to organizational research that advises firms what actions they should take to retain older workers, which implicitly assume that firms want to retain older workers and would welcome advice about how to do it.

Second, in both the United States and Germany, firms' ad hoc, reactive approach to older workers has especially negative effects for lower-wage or lower-skill workers. Higher-skilled workers can leverage their knowledge to structure opportunities for working longer. Less-skilled workers tend to lack these options. A piecemeal approach to workforce aging at the firm level tends to increase socioeconomic inequalities in working longer.

Third, institutional differences between the United States and Germany affect the approach of firms to workforce aging. In Germany, labor organizations and social policy have been instrumental in encouraging phased retirement schemes that provide workers with alternatives to abrupt retirement. In the United States, where labor organizations are weaker and social policy rarely addresses older workers' issues, firms have more discretion to segment their treatment of older workers based on skill. In addition, the German approach to working time allows for more flexible, less-than-full-time work for older workers compared to the United States, which links benefits and other privileges to full-time work.

The implications of these findings for the future of working longer are that firm decisions are critical to the ability of older workers to extend working life past traditional retirement age. Given that firms view older workers as part of a human capital pipeline that determines the mix of skills at the workplace, they typically seek to retain some older workers (highly skilled and more productive) and not others (lower skilled and less productive). This increases inequalities in how older workers experience work both within and across firms. Compared to Germany, U.S. firms are doing few things to increase the flexibility of work in ways that benefit older workers or ease the challenge of working longer. Inequalities associated with later-life employment are exacerbated in the United States because of a lack of worker representation and social policy targeting older people at work. Firms that create practices to facilitate working longer typically do so out of economic need. Either firms cannot fill skills in their recruiting pipeline and need to retain older workers, or they have an older customer base that likes interacting with older, more experienced workers (e.g., financial services). Visionary leaders who understand the importance of age diversity in their workforce are not widespread. Instead, managers often focus narrowly on the retention of highly skilled and experienced older workers rather than a general program of enhancing successful or productive aging.

2. Organizations: The Missing "Meso" Level

Research on workforce aging tends to focus on one of three levels: the "micro" individual level, the "meso" organizational level, or the "macro" level of society as a whole. Most research examines either the micro or macro level, while the meso level is less well explored. These three perspectives, which have developed in separate disciplines, are often in tension with each other because each has a different view of the role of firms in response to workforce aging. Broadly speaking, individual employee (micro) research is concerned with *how the aging process affects employees* and discusses how organizations should seek to redesign work and adopt policies to accommodate a heterogeneous aging experience and promote successful aging. Society-level (macro) research is concerned with *maintaining social protections* for older citizens by keeping social insurance funds solvent and argues that organizations should adopt practices that encourage longer working lives to maintain contributions to public pension systems, protect the workplace rights of older workers, and enable more financially secure retirements. Organization (meso) research emphasizes that organizations are driven by *business needs such as performance and survival*, which may include benchmarking against competitors, complying with union contracts and legislation, or finding a strategic competitive advantage in the management of human capital (Ollier-Malaterre et al. 2013). Each lens suggests different actions for organizations to take. In many cases, these prescribed actions are inconsistent.

The tensions among these goals raise important questions: How and why do organizations differ in their responses to workforce aging? How are various stakeholders affected by these different responses? How do institutional forces shape firms' responses? Though meso-level research discusses specific organizational problems and solutions potentially associated with workforce aging, it often lacks a broader, holistic perspective on what organizations are actually doing to respond to workforce aging, why, and to what effect.

Under certain conditions, the interests of individuals and society can align with those of organizations, producing practices that sustain working longer, promote age diversity, and contribute to productivity. Well-structured national institutions of employee representation, retirement norms, and social policy can encourage the alignment of interests. This might take the form of encouraging age-specific practices, such as phased retirement, flexible scheduling arrangements, or training for older workers. However, institutions that reflect a more laissez faire approach to regulation encourage firms to prioritize their own immediate interests with respect to managing older workers. While the COVID-19 pandemic complicated labor market issues, broader demographic changes ensure that the global workforce will continue to age. To the extent younger workers become relatively more scarce and competition for them increases, firms will need to recruit and retain older workers.

Fundamentally, the business case for age-related practices and the willingness of organizations to hire and retain older workers depend on the extent to which organizational leaders view older workers as holders of critical human capital and the extent to which workforce aging threatens organizational human capital needs.

A human capital perspective explains why firms treat older workers differently based on skill, facilitating the exit of less-skilled workers and investing resources in retaining higher-skilled workers or those involved in strategically important processes.[1] Age-neutral practices, such as training, flexible work arrangements, or various forms of leave, affect workers regardless of age. Such practices can have positive effects on workers of all ages and do not stigmatize older workers by singling them out. Age-related practices target older workers specifically, offering phased retirement, training, or flexible schedules. Much research on aging workers has advocated for age-related practices (Posthuma, Wagstaff, and Campion 2012; Berg et al. 2017; Stirpe, Trullen, and Bonache 2018). These practices can be beneficial to older workers. Both age-neutral and age-specific human resources (HR) practices may be applied differently to more- and less-skilled workers in order to retain workers of value to the firm. It is with this human capital perspective in mind that we next investigate what organizations are actually doing to respond to workforce aging and the consistency of their actions with the interests of various stakeholders.

3. Evidence

It remains largely unclear what organizations are doing to address workforce aging and why. Are they acting consistently with individual- and society-level perspectives that recommend age-specific HR practices that would benefit workers and potentially society, or are such practices unattractive to organizations? Alternatively, are firms considering other practices driven more by organization-level needs? Or are they not responding to workforce aging at all? Diving deeper, what leads an organization to adopt one of these approaches over another?

We draw from multiple sources of data in the United States and Germany to explore the extent to which organizations are actually acting in line with the individual and societal perspectives. First, we examine evidence from survey data in both nations that shed light on the prevalence of age-related HR practices. Second, we analyze our own interview data from U.S. and German manufacturing firms. These rich, qualitative data shed light on the differences in organizational responses to workforce aging from an institutional perspective. In examining these streams of information, we explore what organizational and institutional characteristics might make organizations more likely to adopt age-specific practices that might benefit older workers and society more broadly.

3.1. Evidence from Survey Data

Despite evidence of workforce aging, organizations in both the United States and Germany have been slow to adopt formal policies to respond to it. In this section, we discuss previous survey-based research about organizational practices in the United States and compare those findings with new analysis of German survey data.

In the United States, a recent survey conducted by the Transamerica Center for Retirement Studies (Collinson 2018) found that only 20 percent of employers offered phased retirement, 21 percent had options for reduced-demand work, and 23 percent included age in their formal diversity policies. This report suggests that the U.S. response to workforce aging is very limited and focused primarily on financial benefits like 401(k) programs rather than on adaptations to day-to-day work. Similarly, a U.S. Senate report (2017) describes the lack of holistic organizational response to workforce aging as a form of structural lag, implying that organizations may eventually reorganize around an older workforce as the business need increases.

Conflicting perceptions of U.S. employees and employers may partly explain the lack of action on age-related policies. One study found that employees think their employers view age-related practices as a low priority, while organizational leaders think their workers are not interested in such practices (Armstrong-Stassen 2008). However, other evidence suggests many employers may simply be uninterested in attracting and retaining an older workforce. Some employers appear to be responding to workforce aging by pushing older workers out of the organization. Despite making up an increasing proportion of the workforce, the hire rate of workers 55 and over has dropped over the last 20 years due to employers' concerns about accommodating older workers' needs (Allen 2019). Counter to the recommendations of individual- and society-level research reviewed above, organizational-level evidence suggests that U.S. firms are not prioritizing older workers or changing work to suit the needs of an older workforce.

As Germany has shifted in recent decades to a heavier reliance on private pensions, research on older German workers has tended to focus more on pension provision and less on organizational HR practices. We therefore analyze data from the IAB Establishment Panel, which provides insight into the changing prevalence of age-related HR practices in Germany over time. The IAB Establishment Panel is a nationally representative annual survey conducted by the German federal government.[2] Approximately 16,000 establishments participate each year, with an "establishment" being a single facility or site that could be either a stand-alone operation or part of a bigger organization. Questions about age-related HR practices appeared in survey years 2002, 2006, 2008, 2011, and 2015.

Table 9.1 shows the trends in six practices and the trends in the proportion of establishments with no practices. Despite the increasing age of the workforce over this timespan, the prevalence of several practices has remained stable or decreased. Partial retirement was a popular practice in Germany in 2002 due to social policy incentives that proliferated such policies through industry-level collective agreements (as we discuss further below), with 36.7 percent of establishments having such a practice in place. But by 2015 that proportion had dropped by more than half to 15.3 percent. Additionally, the proportion of establishments reporting no specific age-related HR practices is increasing over time, from 51.3 percent in

TABLE 9.1 Prevalence of age-related human resources practices in Germany, 2002–2015

Year	N	Partial retirement	Special equipment for older workers	Lower performance requirements for older workers	Mixed-age teams	Advanced training inclusion of older workers	Targeted training for older workers	No practices
2002	12,549	36.7%	4.6%	5.2%	17.5%	16.8%	1.7%	51.3%
2006	12,551	33.1%	4.8%	4.3%	13.6%	15.7%	1.7%	56.8%
2008	12,887	29.5%	5.9%	4.0%	14.0%	17.5%	1.9%	59.1%
2011	13,378	23.8%	8.1%	9.7%	16.4%	20.8%	2.9%	60.7%
2015	13,854	15.3%	8.3%	10.1%	14.1%	16.9%	2.4%	65.2%

Source: Authors' calculations from the IAB Establishment Panel from the Research Data Centre (FDZ) of the German Federal Employment Agency (BA) at the Institute for Employment Research (IAB). Percentages indicate proportion of establishments reporting a practice.

2002 to 65.2 percent in 2015. While some practices have increased in prevalence, such as special equipment and lower performance requirements for older workers, they remain uncommon (10 percent or fewer establishments) and the increases in prevalence are small. By 2015, the most common practice was purposefully including older workers in advanced training opportunities—an age-neutral practice—and was only observed in 16.9 percent of establishments. As in the United States, trends in Germany suggest little movement among organizations to adopt HR practices that address workforce aging.

3.2. Evidence from Interviews

Previous research and survey data indicate that organizations are not proactively responding to workforce aging. Without such a response, many older workers affected more strongly by the aging process may find it difficult to continue working, challenging their ability to age successfully and work later in life. To help explain how and why organizations react to workforce aging, we conducted interviews between 2015 and 2017 in eight manufacturing facilities in the United States and Germany as part of a broader project on organizational responses to workforce aging. We chose manufacturing because it includes a wide variety of occupations, some of which involve physical demands that may be difficult for older workers. The facilities were parts of three large organizations with a physical presence in both the United States and Germany. We visited two German sites and two U.S. sites of a U.S.-owned chemical manufacturing company, two U.S. and one German site of a U.S.-owned electronic component company, and one German site of a German-owned auto part supplier. In each facility, we spoke with the site's top manager, an HR manager, two unit supervisors, one to three employee representatives, and a focus group of older employees.

Our findings from these interviews highlight the overall lack of a holistic, systematic response to workforce aging among manufacturing firms and instead indicate a more ad hoc, reactive approach by organizations in both nations. Given that employees in manufacturing are likely to be among the most deleteriously affected by aging processes due to the physically demanding, repetitive, and all-day nature of work in the industry, the lack of response may be even stronger in other industries less affected by workforce aging.

3.2.1. Overall Attitudes toward Older Workers

We found little evidence that top organizational leaders were concerned with age diversity or the differential impact of age-neutral policies on older workers—except to the extent that they concerned age discrimination and potential legal action. For example, when we asked the facility manager of one of the U.S. chemical manufacturing sites whether there were any initiatives to promote or manage age diversity, he said, "Other than what the law requires the company to do, I'm not aware of anything as it relates to age diversity."

On the contrary, we found some evidence that fear of legal retribution made it more difficult to enact strategies related to workforce aging. For example, the HR manager of the German auto manufacturer explained that there was no strategic effort to recruit older workers, as it would be illegal. Despite the fear of legal issues and the demographic trends suggesting it will become more important to recruit and retain older workers as younger workers become relatively more scarce and competition for them increases, she explained that some supervisors openly discriminate against older workers. "They discriminate in their heads. They say to the old person: they're already 50: we won't take that one. The dummies tell me that! They say: 'He's already 50.'" A supervisor in a U.S. chemical facility explained that, due to concerns about discrimination, he does not know the ages of his employees. "Probably about two to three years ago they have removed the access of all leaders to the age of employees. So I do not know the age of employees anymore. So you know the service years, but you do not know the age. . . . It is almost impossible to do any study on my level on age distribution." Other interviews also indicated that this made it very difficult to predict and plan for retirements. Supervisors only knew of upcoming retirements with whatever notice employees were willing to give.

Our data provide further evidence that organizational policymakers generally believe that age-related challenges are not prevalent enough to warrant a proactive approach. We found that top leaders in all facilities acknowledged that the workforce was aging, but they were largely unconcerned with workforce aging as a major challenge and believed they were responding adequately with what we describe as a reactive, piecemeal approach. For example, the top manager at a U.S. chemical facility explained that they did not consider the collective age of their workforce when instituting a hiring freeze, leading to a gap in middle managers. "You know at one time it was good that you had different levels. You had the seniors, and then you had the way juniors, and you had the middle people. And then now you've got the experienced guys and then you've got the junior guys, and there's not—there doesn't seem to be that many people in the middle anymore." They used existing practices to address loss of human capital as it occured rather than pursuing a proactive, systemic approach to managing worker retirements through, for example, formal skill tracking and knowledge transfer initiatives or the reorganization of work to meet the needs and preferences of an older workforce. As a site director in a major U.S. chemical company said, "I was just down in [location], I have responsibility down there, and they put a slide up that said, you know, '50 percent of our people are eligible to retire.' And I said, 'You know, guys, I've been hearing this for 20 years now, and this tsunami just doesn't seem to happen.' It trickles out. Is there ever gonna be this tsunami? I don't know."

One potential explanation for this general attitude is a lack of awareness of the true impact of workforce aging. Despite there being some concern about managing human capital, our evidence suggests organizational leaders are not systematically tracking the human capital exiting their establishments via the retirement of older workers. Though firms tracked retirement attrition and eligibility, they did not track the actual skills of retiring and retirement-eligible workers to understand what human capital was being lost. Of our eight facilities, only one had a thorough skill-tracking program in place. This U.S. electronic component manufacturer assigned a numerical score to each position based on both its importance and the redundancy of knowledge and skills in the organization if the person currently in that role should leave via retirement or some other means. This practice was lauded by all in the facility and was even adopted by other facilities across the organization due to its success, and because it was not based on specific retirement plans but rather a variety of factors, including retirement eligibility, it was not viewed as potentially discriminatory. For the most part, however, facilities were engaged only in basic skill tracking such as which employees held which certifications, and these metrics were not generally linked to retirements or the corresponding flow of human capital.

3.2.2. Age-Related Human Resources Practices

Despite the lack of a systemic, establishment-level response, we observed a wide variety of age-related HR practices. Consistent with the lack of top management buy-in, however, many of these practices were informal, inconsistent, and implemented only at the unit level.

In both nations, we found that some sites had initiatives in place to document important employee knowledge and skills and facilitate knowledge transfer to younger employees following retirements. In other words, most practices we observed were related to managing human capital rather than helping older workers age successfully or work longer. These unit-level initiatives could involve pairing older and younger employees into mixed-age teams, videotaping work tasks, or writing down processes and procedures depending on the formality of the documentation program, the resources available, and the willingness of employees to participate. In most cases, we found that supervisors were able to leverage only existing resources toward knowledge transfer as they did not have resources from leadership for more formal, costly initiatives. For example, we asked a U.S. chemical plant supervisor whether he was able to have older workers train newer employees before they retire. He explained, "I'll tell you it's not done systematically . . . And this deals with the whole budget constraint. If we know someone's going to retire, it would be nice to say, 'Okay, I'm going to hire someone and let you work along with that person so you can come up to speed.' Uh, that's rarely the case."

Supervisors reported positive outcomes of mixed-age teams to help facilitate knowledge transfer, but these were only possible when the existing organization of work allowed for such teams to occur. A supervisor in the German auto plant explained that about half his teams could be considered mixed-age, but constraints around team structures and the ability to move people across them sometimes made mixed-age teams impossible. "Where personnel movement exists, effectively enacted, then we've provided for it. When there isn't personnel movement in a group, then we don't have any opportunity." Otherwise, lack of financial resources prevented mixed-age teams as a formal knowledge transfer mechanism. Again, work was not being changed to accommodate an older workforce; supervisors were simply fitting older workers into the existing organizational structure to the best of their ability.

Another example of a reactive practice we observed was moving older employees to less physically demanding positions that focus on technical expertise. In several facilities, supervisory technical positions were frequently filled by skilled older workers. These positions were generally day shift only, free of repetitive or physically difficult work tasks, and had more schedule flexibility. Consistent with lifespan psychology research, the design of such positions is more amenable to the needs of older workers. However, these positions were part of the existing organizational job structure and not part of a work redesign for an older workforce. A U.S. electronics manufacturing supervisor explained how this process worked in his facility: "In manufacturing we have two shifts. You're either working 7:00 to 3:30, or 3:30 to midnight. But we do have jobs in shipping that are on alternate schedules. So if you really need a little bit of flexibility, then when the time comes you bid on a job in shipping where you can work 9:00 to 6:00 if that's appealing to you." More attractive positions were extremely limited in availability, and many older workers remained in positions with rotating shifts and relatively repetitive physical tasks.

We also observed some formal age-related HR practices, particularly in Germany. Consistent with previous institutional research, Germany had stronger employee representation mechanisms via works councils and industry-level collective bargaining agreements. These mechanisms, discussed in more detail below, provided for practices such as formal partial retirement options and the ability to use banked hours in working time accounts for early retirement. Interestingly, and consistent with our arguments regarding the overall lack of concern with workforce aging, using banked hours for early retirement was described by leadership as a policy used more for the recruitment of younger workers than the accommodation of an aging workforce. Partial retirement enrollment was typically capped at around 4 percent of the workforce and was used to incentivize older workers who had difficulty meeting productivity standards to phase out of the workforce. Our interview findings are consistent with the IAB data, which show that partial retirement practices have decreased substantially in prevalence over time.

Importantly, the use of many of these practices was strongly contingent on the human capital of the affected older worker. Efforts to extend working lives via less-taxing jobs or contract work were reserved for workers who were productive and relatively high-skill or involved in strategically important processes. However, low-skill workers or those who had injuries or health problems were encouraged to take partial retirement to arrange a predictable exit.

3.2.3. Institutional Forces

National-level institutional contexts help to explain the cross-country differences in responses to workforce aging. Hall and Soskice (2001) identify key institutional differences between Germany and the United States in their "varieties of capitalism" framework. They distinguish between coordinated market economies (CME), such as Germany and Sweden, in which actors rely on relationships and trust; and liberal market economies (LME), such as the United States and United Kingdom, in which actors rely more on market transactions. The differences in Germany's coordinated market economy and the United States' liberal market economy are manifested through institutions which affect the types of practices facilities adopted in each country. For example, worker representation in Germany was critical in setting up a process for partial retirement at the workplace. In addition, the use of working-time accounts in Germany allows workers to bank hours worked beyond the standard workweek (usually 36–38 hours). This provides workers with more paid time off, more schedule flexibility, and the ability to use banked hours to retire early. Working-time accounts are largely a result of institutionalized worker representation through works councils and industry-level collective bargaining agreements. One focus group participant in a German chemical plant explained how older employees under the collective bargaining agreement had access to partial retirement and shortened workdays. "In the [noncontract] area, there is nothing specific—no agreement with the works council for this work group. For [contract] work, it is really regulated and in their last years we have very good opportunities to make use of these things."

Other facilities in Germany also show the importance of these workplace institutions in influencing practice adoption. Consistent with the nationally representative German data in Table 9.1, our interview data show that partial retirement had been commonplace in Germany, and all the German facilities we visited had formal partial retirement programs as part of their collective bargaining agreements. In contrast, none of the U.S. facilities we visited had partial retirement programs. Partial retirement was popular in Germany partly because it was proliferated through institutional mechanisms. In 1996, the German federal government offered partial retirement subsidies to organizations as a matter of social policy in order to help extend working lives and maintain public pension solvency, and these partial retirement programs were quickly formalized through industry-level collective bargaining agreements (Berg et al. 2020). The HR director at a German chemical plant recognized the effect of these institutional forces in the adoption of HR policy. "I don't know whether if we had not had those laws and collective agreements, I don't know whether we would have come with those ideas."

In contrast, policy in the United States is typical of a liberal market economy, less reliant on relationships and driven more by market mechanisms. For example, given that health care and other employee benefits are costly in the United States, we found that organizations sometimes brought retirees back as independent contractors in order to keep their human capital in the organization longer rather than formally extend working lives through employment via partial retirement. The director of a U.S. chemical plant explained this practice: "Would you be willing to come back as a contractor and work three days a week? And quite often the answer is, 'Oh I'd love that, that'd be great 'cause it wouldn't get in the way of my fishing on the weekend!' Okay, so we got a deal. So we look at alternatives like that that work well for individuals that also serve the needs of the company. And that's a stopgap." For firms, independent contracting works similarly to partial retirement, but it avoids many of the costs of formal employment.

Thus, companies in both the United States and Germany offered flexible forms of retirement, but the forms were very different. In Germany, the employee representation and social policy institutions incentivized and legitimized formal, highly structured partial retirement schemes that appealed to both businesses and employees. In the United States, where such institutional forces are much weaker, companies negotiated short-term contracts with particularly skilled retirees to slow the exit of human capital from the organization. These two mechanisms are consistent with the institutional approaches in the two countries. The United States is characterized as a liberal market economy that emphasizes market transactions over longer-term relationships among stakeholders, which is more common in coordinated market economies such as Germany. Employee representation mechanisms play a bigger role in the German workforce and result in more formal age-related workplace policies as employee representatives such as works council members play a more active role in the day-to-day management of the business.

Another institutional difference comes from the differing models of HR planning we observed in the United States and Germany. U.S. firms used a headcount model while German firms preferred a more flexible full-time equivalent model. The headcount model treats each employee as a full-time worker with a set amount of costs regardless of how much they work. In contrast, the full-time equivalent model allows employee costs to be prorated based on hours worked, so leaders can budget for less-than-full-time work more easily. An electrical component facility in Germany struggled with the headcount model imposed by its U.S. owners because it limited flexibility. The HR director explained headcount issues with regard to both flexible work and knowledge transfer. "We are flexible if somebody comes to us and wants to reduce maybe the working hours. We are really working hard on that to make it possible, though it is a problem with the headcount." With regard to the use of mixed-age teams for knowledge transfer, she explained: "We are not doing this because so far it doesn't work because we do not have the headcounts to let somebody work only as an expert. We really need them on their jobs."

Despite these differences, we also noted a few similarities in the organizational response to workforce aging through institutions. In both the United States and Germany, social policy makes age-based employment discrimination illegal. In both countries, it was difficult for organizations to engage in workforce planning because they felt unable to broach the subject of retirement plans for older employees near the age of retirement eligibility for fear of accusations of discrimination. We observed that these concerns were especially strong in the United States. As one chemical manufacturing unit supervisor explained, "I have never heard that discussed. And maybe because age is one of the, you know, it's protected from the EEOC [Equal Employment Opportunity Commission]. I mean, it's, it's almost taboo. We don't discuss age."

A fear of discussing aging makes it a difficult issue to address for organizational leaders and unit supervisors alike. The perceived inability to ask about retirement plans combined with the significant heterogeneity in the needs and productivity of older workers may make organizational leaders more hesitant to hire older workers, ironically contributing further to age discrimination. Because age discrimination in hiring is widespread in the United States (Allen 2019), antidiscrimination laws are an important component of social policy to protect older workers. However, being unable to discuss age and retirement plans in the workforce can make it difficult for organizational leaders to plan for the needs of an older workforce, and it may in part explain why many facilities we visited had few formal initiatives for older workers. We found HR practices that directly addressed age (such as partial retirement and reduced hours for older workers) only in Germany, where such practices were suggested or negotiated by employee representatives and thus unlikely to trigger claims of discrimination.

4. Implications: Firms Are Falling Short

All in all, the quantitative and qualitative evidence reveals a lackluster response to an aging workforce from organizations in both the United States and Germany that is largely driven by managing human capital through informal, ad hoc practices designed to meet organizational needs rather than to address the well-being and longevity of older workers. Our interview data showed that top leaders were largely unconcerned with workforce aging as an organizational issue, and they believed that any challenges were being handled adequately through existing age-neutral mechanisms within the facility. The quantitative evidence showing relatively low prevalence of most age-related HR practices suggests such attitudes are widespread. Organizations thus appear to be focused mostly on the business case for the adoption of these practices and may only be adopting one or two practices—if any—best suited to their specific challenges.

4.1. The Business Case

A surprising but important takeway is the lack of movement toward a proactive organizational response to workforce aging. Firms largely do not perceive a business need for a systematic response to workforce aging. Survey data show a hesitancy to adopt formal practices designed to respond to workforce aging, and our interview data suggest that this is in part due to the perception by decision-makers that the threat of workforce aging to human capital is overblown. Research suggests that establishments will need to redesign work as well as HR practices to accommodate an older workforce, but we found little evidence that this is happening.

We characterize the organizational response to workforce aging as being almost entirely reactive. Rather than proactively adopting practices based on anticipated human capital needs or redesigning work to accommodate an older workforce, organizations are adopting practices to meet specific challenges resulting from workforce aging in a piecemeal fashion as they emerge within the organization. Our interview data suggest that organizational leaders do not see their workforces as retiring in unmanageable numbers because longer working lives have also increased variability in retirement age. This means the number of retirees at any one time may not become overwhelming.

Within organizations, unit supervisors often had a clearer view than management of the risks of losing talent to retirement. The top leaders we interviewed were mostly concerned with managing worker headcount as opposed to maintaining quality of human capital. In contrast, unit supervisors were concerned about losing high-quality human capital to retirement without having other employees sufficiently trained to take over the roles. In some cases, the position might not even be filled at all.

By reducing headcount and allowing high-quality human capital to disappear through retirement attrition without sufficient investment in employee development to capture it for future employees through knowledge transfer, firms may sacrifice long-term productivity for short-term reductions in labor costs. Firms must be careful not to lose experience in business processes where such experience is critical to success. Our interview data also suggest that firms that have undergone hiring freezes will be more likely to suffer skill shortages as a result of workforce aging as they have few middle-aged workers available to move into roles vacated by retirees. Hiring freezes create bimodal age distributions with few middle-aged employees available to step into vacated leadership roles, creating a major problem in succession planning.

We found that better HR planning systems encouraged investment in knowledge transfer practices, even if these practices were still largely informal. As an exception, the leader of one firm in our study took HR planning seriously and implemented a skill-tracking system that considers retirement eligibility of key skill-holders. This quantified the need for managers to act regarding older workers' human capital and prevented skill gaps.

4.2. Macro-, Micro-, and Meso-Level Concerns

Our study demonstrates that what management and labor organizations *actually* do to help older workers typically falls far short of what previous research on workforce aging suggests they *should* do. As we observed, organizations (the meso level) do not always act in their own best interests when it comes to human capital management. Moreover, ad hoc, reactive organizational responses to workforce aging neither help individual workers age successfully (the micro level) nor extend working lives in systematic ways (the macro level). Instead, we see supervisors scrambling to avoid losing their most important workers' skills through largely informal methods, with longer working lives and worker well-being a sometimes coincidental outcome. We found evidence that some employers discriminate against older workers in hiring and actively push older workers, whom they perceive as less productive, out of organizations.

Our findings highlight the tensions between age-specific practices and age-neutral practices. Our evidence suggests organizations should adopt appropriate age-related practices while being acutely aware of the age-specific effects of age-neutral practices on individual workers. Age-related practices such as partial retirement may be necessary to respond proactively to workforce aging, but the evidence shows they are relatively rare. Moreover, ostensibly age-neutral practices may affect older workers differently than younger workers, for better or worse. On the negative side, for example, long-term skill development programs may be less accessible to older workers due to stereotyping or a perception that such investment will not be recouped over time. On the positive side, work redesign that alleviates physically demanding, repetitive work design or shift-based work may benefit older workers more than younger workers. Both age-specific and age-neutral practices affect employee work attitudes and well-being as well as work outcomes like absenteeism and productivity.

Organizational leaders must be careful to consider such issues even if they do not see the business need to adopt age-specific practices.

4.3. The Skill Divide

Organizations are driven by costs and benefits, viewing workers as sources of human capital. High-skill older workers with unique skills are likely to retain their value as they age. More vulnerable are low-skill older workers or older workers with failing health who are unable to maintain such a value proposition to their employer. Older workers with more widely available skills are easier to replace and often work in more physically demanding jobs in which productivity declines with age may be steeper (Ilmarinen, Tuomi, and Klockars 1997).

Since the business case for working longer favors high-skill older workers, this results in the occupational segregation of retirement flexibility. Lower-skill workers are paid less than higher-skill workers, which can put financial pressure on them to work longer in order to afford retirement regardless of personal preference. However, they are also least likely to receive organizational support to work longer. They are the most likely to be pushed out of organizations should their productivity decline and the least likely to be accommodated with work reorganization, such as lower performance requirements or ergonomic equipment, as these initiatives may not be cost-effective for lower-skill positions. These workers are thus at the greatest risk given the observed patterns of organizational practices. By contrast, high-skill workers may be more likely to afford to retire, but organizations may seek to keep them working longer in order to facilitate productivity and knowledge transfer. Low-skill older workers cannot afford to retire but may be pushed out—while high-skill older workers are less likely to need to work longer but more likely to have the option available.

Opportunities to work longer are not evenly distributed, and such opportunities are not available to all those who want or need them. In the current organizational environment in both the United States and Germany, employee options for working longer are largely dependent not on individual need but rather occupation and corresponding job design as well as variation in institutional forces such as employee representation, access to flexibility, and public pension systems; and employers' perception of older workers and need for their experience and skill.

Other forms of heterogeneity are also important. Industry- and job-specific characteristics dictate what types of practices are plausible, the extent to which high-quality human capital is needed, and the degree to which older workers possess that human capital. In manufacturing, we found that older workers had important firm-specific experience and knowledge (e.g., they had production experience with a product that was still supported but no longer actively produced). However, in other industries and occupations, older workers may be less likely to hold such valuable human capital relative to younger workers. For example, stereotyping of older workers in service industries makes them less likely than younger workers to be assigned to customer-facing positions, which may encourage an early retirement from the organization (Gatta 2018). Workers who may need the most help from organizations—those in low-wage, precarious, or physically demanding jobs—are also the least likely to receive it.

4.4. Institutional Forces

A final implication of our work is that country-level institutional differences play a critical part in shaping the experience of older workers. In particular, we find evidence that worker representation can generate broader access to worker-friendly age-related policies and practices that otherwise would not have been adopted due to inconsistency with organizational interests. While the organizations we studied in both the United States and Germany generally took a reactive, piecemeal approach to managing workforce aging, the role of worker representatives is stronger in Germany and has noticeable results.

The use of working-time practices and partial retirement is more prevalent in German manufacturing, while the use of retirees as independent contractors is much more prevalent in the United States. These differences in practice can be explained by differences in worker representation: German work councils and labor unions are stronger advocates for age-related policies and practices than U.S. labor unions are.

An important implication of national differences in worker voice is that more older workers in Germany had access to age-related practices regardless of skill level. Worker representatives advocate for practices based not on the business need for human capital, but rather on the individual need of workers to age successfully. For example, we saw the opportunity to cash out working-time accounts for early retirement and reduced work hours for older workers negotiated through work councils and collective agreements in Germany. These applied to all workers, not just those with strategic importance to the firm.

4.5. Policy Considerations

Our international comparisons demonstrate the power and potential of policy choices. Social policy and worker representation have resulted in fewer options for older workers in the United States than in countries like Germany. Even as retirement has become more financially precarious, making paid employment more important for many older adults' economic well-being, workers in the United States depend for their continued employment on their perceived value to employers. Retirement for many is not a free choice, but a choice made for them by employers or by their health. Workers who want—or need—to work longer must ensure that their skills remain valuable and relevant to employers. However, for many, this may not be plausible. While our study suggests collective representation can help improve access to options for older workers, unions in the United States are typically more focused on wages and health care than on age diversity issues. Our study shows that German workers working under German institutions have more options to encourage working longer (e.g., flexible schedules, longer paid time off) and to ease into retirement (e.g., partial retirement schemes, long-term working-time accounts).

Institutionalized practices also may have age-specific effects that will continue to be important to consider. In the United States, we have seen an increase in work-life flexibility policies, such as the right to paid family and medical leave in some states, but nothing in the area of age-related HR practices. Nevertheless, older workers benefit from paid family and medical leave policies when they have access to them. As such, age-neutral social policy initiatives may benefit older workers as well as younger workers.

4.6. What's Next?

Looking to the future, we argue that U.S. organizations' current reactive practices can only address specific challenges faced by small numbers of older workers. Stronger pressure from the labor market, from unions or other forms of worker voice, or from regulation will be needed to prompt more holistic strategies by organizations to meet the needs and preferences of the broader older workforce. There are reasons for pessimism. High unemployment rates in the wake of the COVID-19 pandemic reduced the labor market pressure needed to promote a work environment that benefits older workers, especially those with low wages and less education. High variation in retirement ages may also prevent firms from facing an unmanageably large number of employee retirements, and thus reduce firms' incentives to change their practices. Reactive, piecemeal approaches to managing employee retirements may be sufficient to manage human capital and meet most business needs of organizations in the current environment. But there are also reasons for optimism. Labor markets will recover, and as older workers continue to make up a growing proportion of the labor force, they may receive more attention from employee representatives in unions and work councils and thus may negotiate more age-related HR practices through these institutionalized mechanisms.

Notes

1. We use the term "skill" to mean workers' capabilities that are valuable to a specific employer, which may be gained through formal education, on-the-job training, or other experiences. Those whose skills are both scarce and necessary to businesses are likely to be paid more than those whose skills are more commonly available in the population. Educational attainment, wages, and skills are correlated but not identical.
2. We use the absolutely anonymous Campus File of the Panel Study "Linked Personnel Panel (LPP)" project #1246. Data access was provided via a Campus File supplied by the Research Data Centre (FDZ) of the German Federal Employment Agency (BA) at the Institute for Employment Research (IAB). Data documentation is available from Frodermann, Grunau, and Wolter (2017).

References

Allen, Steven G. 2019. "Demand for Older Workers: What Do Economists Think? What Are Firms Doing?" Working Paper 26597. Cambridge, MA: National Bureau of Economic Research. https://doi.org/10.3386/w26597.

Armstrong-Stassen, Marjorie. 2008. "Human Resource Practices for Mature Workers—And Why Aren't Employers Using Them?" *Asia Pacific Journal of Human Resources* 46 (3): 334–352. https://doi.org/10.1177/1038411108091755.

Berg, Peter B., Mary K. Hamman, Matthew M. Piszczek, and Christopher J. Ruhm. 2017. "The Relationship Between Employer-Provided Training and the Retention of Older Workers: Evidence from Germany." *International Labour Review* 156 (3–4): 495–523. https://doi.org/10.1111/ilr.12031. Accessed on June 03, 2022.

Berg, Peter, Mary K. Hamman, Matthew Piszczek, and Christopher J. Ruhm. 2020. "Can Policy Facilitate Partial Retirement? Evidence from a Natural Experiment in Germany." *ILR Review* 73 (5): 1226–51. https://doi.org/10.1177/0019793920907320.

Collinson, Catherine. 2018. "Striking Similarities and Disconcerting Disconnects: Employers, Workers and Retirement Security: 18th Annual Transamerica Retirement Survey." Research Report. Transamerica

Center for Retirement Studies. https://www.transamericacenter.org/docs/default-source/retirement-survey-of-employers/tcrs2018_sr_employer-retirement-research.pdf.

Finkelstein, Lisa M., Donald M. Truxillo, Franco Fraccaroli, and Ruth Kanfer. 2015. An Introduction to Facing the Challenges of a Multi-Age Workforce: A Use-Inspired Approach. In *Facing the Challenges of a Multi-Age Workforce*, edited by Lisa M. Finkelstein, Donald M. Truxillo, Franco Fraccaroli, and Ruth Kanfer, pp. 3–22. New York: Routledge.

Frodermann, Corinna, Philipp Grunau, and Stefanie Wolter. 2017. "Lpp—Linked Personnel Panel Arbeitsqualität Und Wirtschaftlicher Erfolg: Längsschnittstudie in Deutschen Betrieben. Campus File (Lpp-Cf 1215_v1); Version 1." 201709. *FDZ Datenreport. Documentation on Labour Market Data*. FDZ Datenreport. Documentation on Labour Market Data. Nuremberg: Institut für Arbeitsmarkt- und Berufsforschung, Nürnberg. http://doku.iab.de/fdz/reporte/2017/DR_09-17.pdf.

Gatta, Mary. 2018. *Waiting on Retirement: Aging and Economic Insecurity in Low-Wage Work*. Studies in Social Inequality. Stanford, CA: Stanford University Press.

Hall, Peter A., and David W. Soskice, eds. 2001. *Varieties of Capitalism: The Institutional Foundations of Comparative Advantage*. Oxford: Oxford University Press.

Ilmarinen, Juhani, Kaija Tuomi, and Matti Klockars. 1997. "Changes in the Work Ability of Active Employees as Measured by the Work Ability Index over an 11-Year Period." *Scandinavian Journal of Work, Environment & Health* 23 (1): 49–57. https://www.sjweh.fi/article/212.

Ollier-Malaterre, Ariane, Tay McNamara, Christina Matz-Costa, Marcie Pitt-Catsouphes, and Monique Valcour. 2013. "Looking up to Regulations, out at Peers or down at the Bottom Line: How Institutional Logics Affect the Prevalence of Age-Related HR Practices." *Human Relations* 66 (10): 1373–1395. https://doi.org/10.1177/0018726713478244. Accessed on June 03, 2022.

Posthuma, Richard A., María Fernanda Wagstaff, and Michael A. Campion. 2012. "Age Stereotypes and Workplace Age Discrimination." In *The Oxford Handbook of Work and Aging*, edited by Jerry W. Hedge and Walter C. Borman, 298–312. New York: Oxford University Press. https://doi.org/10.1093/oxfordhb/9780195385052.013.0104.

Stirpe, Luigi, Jordi Trullen, and Jaime Bonache. 2018. "Retaining an Ageing Workforce: The Effects of High-Performance Work Systems and Flexible Work Programmes." *Human Resource Management Journal* 28 (4): 585–604. https://doi.org/10.1111/1748-8583.12205. Accessed on June 03, 2022.

U.S. Senate Special Committee On Aging. 2017. "America's Aging Workforce: Opportunities and Challenges." Washington, DC. https://www.aging.senate.gov/imo/media/doc/Aging%20Workforce%20Report%20FINAL.pdf.

10

How Caregiving for Parents Reduces Women's Employment
Patterns across Sociodemographic Groups

Sean Fahle and Kathleen McGarry[1]

1. Introduction

As the United States population ages, our health care system faces enormous pressure in providing care for the elderly population. The popular press is replete with stories noting shortages of home health care workers (e.g., Gleckman 2019), and both home care and institutional care are extremely expensive. Home health aides cost an average of $22 per hour, or $45,000 per year for eight hours of care per day—although individuals suffering from dementia likely need even more intensive care. Nursing homes, which do provide around-the-clock care, typically cost over $100,000 per year (Genworth 2021). Perhaps surprising to some, neither Medicare nor Medigap insurance plans provide coverage for custodial care.[2] Medicaid, the means-tested health insurance program for low-income elderly and disabled people, does cover such care and is the primary payer of formal long-term care in the United States. However, to qualify for Medicaid coverage, one needs to have very low income and few assets other than a home. Individuals with too many resources to qualify for Medicaid coverage can opt to purchase separate long-term care insurance policies, but such policies are not widely held. Only 10 to 15 percent of older individuals have such coverage (Finkelstein and McGarry 2006). Given the costs of formal long-term care and the lack of insurance coverage for most, much of the care received by the elderly is provided informally by family members.

This burden of care falls unevenly across the working-age population. Research on caregiving has nearly uniformly found that women are significantly more likely to provide personal care than are men. Among those providing care for a spouse, the preponderance of female caregivers is not surprising. Women tend to live longer than men and to marry men who are older than they are. Thus, while husbands often receive care from their wives, the reverse is less likely. Care for parents is also divided along gender lines: daughters are far more likely to provide care than are sons.[3]

While much attention has been paid to these gender differences in caregiving, somewhat less is known about the distribution of caregiving and its consequences across sociodemographic groups in the U.S. population. Given the potential for caregiving to impact negatively a caregiver's employment and financial status, it is vital that we understand who is most at risk of needing to provide this care, particularly the extent to which this need varies across sociodemographic groups. If the burden of care is being disproportionately shouldered by the least advantaged members of society, any adverse impacts from caregiving could compound existing precarities and heighten inequality.

This chapter investigates differences in caregiving responsibilities and the related effects on employment and financial status of women from various sociodemographic groups. We examine patterns both by socioeconomic status (SES), as proxied primarily by education and wealth, and by race and ethnicity. Because much of our interest lies in the relationship between caregiving and work, we focus on the provision of personal care by prime-age women to their elderly parents and parents-in-law. While caregiving for spouses occurs most frequently when the caregiver is beyond the typical retirement age (Fahle and McGarry 2018), caregiving for parents occurs earlier in a woman's life and thus potentially has a greater effect on labor market behavior. Any negative effect on market work during these prime working years could exacerbate the elevated risk of poverty faced by elderly women relative to men.

Although we anticipate that caregiving and its impacts will likely vary by SES, it is not clear a priori which groups are most at risk of providing elder care, or which groups are most likely to experience diminished labor market outcomes when they do provide care. On the one hand, many factors suggest that a greater burden will be borne by those with fewer resources. First, and perhaps most obviously, low-income families are unlikely to be able to afford to pay for formal care or to have private long-term care insurance that would cover the cost. Second, the typical argument for the preponderance of female caregivers is that the opportunity cost of time, as measured by foregone wages, is lower, on average, for women relative to men. Extending this argument to examine differences in caregiving across SES, a lower opportunity cost of time may lead to those with lower earnings selecting into caregiving at greater rates. Unfortunately, these women likely also have less retirement savings and a lower probability of pension or health insurance coverage, adding to the precariousness of their financial situation. Third, there will be differences across the population in the probability of being "at risk" of having a parent or parent-in-law who needs care. In particular, rates of functional limitations are likely to be higher for low-income elderly, indicating a greater likelihood that a parent will need care.

On the other hand, lower-SES women may be protected in some ways. First, while the ability to pay out-of-pocket for formal care will be less, low-income and low-wealth parents will be more likely to qualify for Medicaid, which covers home health and nursing home care—making formal care more affordable for the family and providing a ready substitute for care from a child. Second, low-income parents have shorter life expectancies on average. From the perspective of their daughters' employment, the effect could be either positive or negative: it could reduce the number of years during which a daughter needs to provide care, or it could more negatively affect long-term employment if the need to provide care arises earlier during the prime working years. Third, there may be differences by SES in the number of siblings or siblings-in-law, potential substitutes for the respondent herself in the caregiving realm.

There are also numerous reasons to expect caregiving differences by race and ethnicity. For example, older Hispanic adults face higher rates and earlier onset of diabetes and higher rates of obesity than non-Hispanic white adults (Aranda and Knight 1997). Similarly, there may be differences in cultural attitudes toward caregiving that affect the probability of providing care and/or the associated stress. Research suggests that Hispanic adults are more likely to rely on family care than are non-Hispanic white or non-Hispanic Black adults (e.g., Rote and Moon 2018; Pinquart and Sörensen 2005), while non-Hispanic Black adults may feel less emotional stress when caring for an elderly family member. Furthermore, demographic forecasts indicate that the fraction of populations of color that is ages 65 or older is increasing even faster than the share of the overall population that is ages 65 or older—suggesting that, all else constant, pressure on non-white and Hispanic daughters to care for an elderly parent is likely to grow more rapidly. Finally, when they do provide care, there is evidence that Black and Hispanic caregivers appear to be more likely to reduce hours of work than are other groups (Covinsky et al. 2001).

This chapter takes a closer look at the differences in caregiving across sociodemographic groups, highlighting differences by education level, wealth, and race/ethnicity. We draw on panel data from the Health and Retirement Study (HRS) to examine the effect of caregiving on employment for a cohort of women in their prime earning years. We use data over a 10-year window to examine the concurrent effects of caregiving on work as well as longer-term effects.

Perhaps unsurprisingly for those who have followed articles in the popular press or who have first-hand experience with caregiving, we find little evidence of a single type of caregiver. Most caregiving is predicated on the need of the parent and the lack of alternative caregivers. The strongest predictors of caregiving are the number of unmarried parents, their age, and the absence of sisters. Contrary to expectations informed by models of opportunity cost, but in line with earlier results (e.g., McGarry 1998), there is no evidence that caregivers are drawn from the population with weaker attachment to the labor force. If anything, the reverse is true: the caregivers in our sample tend to have stronger attachment to the labor force, more education, better jobs, and greater economic resources. Caregivers are also marginally more likely to be white and non-Hispanic. In part, these results can be explained by differences in life expectancy and family structure across sociodemographic groups: more advantaged women are simply more likely to have living parents and fewer alternate caregivers. Yet, even when we focus exclusively on women who have living parents or parents-in-law and are thus "at risk" of needing to provide care, we find that higher-SES women are more likely than lower-SES women to be caring for parents. We conjecture that greater resources and perhaps greater job flexibility enable more advantaged women to provide elder care.

While more advantaged women appear to provide care at greater rates, we find that women with lower levels of education and non-white women report more time-intensive caregiving conditional on providing care. The differences are most pronounced in the upper tail of the distribution of time spent providing care, with less educated and Hispanic women providing considerably more hours than other groups. Less advantaged women are also far more likely to struggle with the cost of formal care for their parents. Replacing family care with formal care for the average non-white, Hispanic caregiver would cost more than one-third of her family income. Overall, our evidence paints a complex picture of the inequalities in the distribution of caregiving across older women in the United States, with data on the extensive and intensive margins of caregiving providing different perspectives on the burden of care.

However, regardless of a woman's sociodemographic group, our results indicate that caregiving has a significant negative relationship with labor market activity; it is associated with a lower probability of work, fewer hours of work, and lower earnings. These effects are felt concurrently with caregiving but also appear to persist years into the future. Following the women in our data over a 10-year period, we see that women who were caregivers during our window of observation have worse outcomes than noncaregivers at the end of the period. We find similar effects across the sociodemographic groups that we examine. Taken together, this evidence suggests that caregiving can reduce women's employment during their prime working years and beyond. Caring for elderly parents may thus be a potentially important force reducing the likelihood of working longer among women across a broad array of sociodemographic groups.

2. Caregiving Rates Are High and Rising

The need for long-term care is already pervasive, and the demand is expected to increase sharply with the aging of the population. It is estimated that 69 percent of elderly individuals will need help with the activities of daily living (ADLs)—tasks such as bathing, eating, dressing, and toileting—at some point during their lives (Kemper, Komisar, and Alecxih 2005). For the vast majority of individuals, this care will come from family members, primarily from daughters or wives. Among the noninstitutionalized population receiving help with ADLs, 66 percent receive help exclusively from family members while another 26 percent receive assistance from both family (informal) and paid (formal) care providers; only 9 percent rely solely on formal care (Doty 2010).[4]

This reliance on informal care means that a large fraction of nonelderly adults will provide care at some point, and caregiving for parents peaks among individuals in their 50s. The Bureau of Labor Statistics (2017) estimates that in 2015–2016, 21.3 percent of those 45–54 and 24.3 percent of those 55–64 provided care at some point, but other estimates suggest higher rates. Increased longevity, lower fertility, and changes in disease-specific mortality all point to expected sharp increases in these numbers. Attempts to assess the cost of this informal care are "back of the envelope" calculations at best because we do not know what caregivers would be doing with their time were they not providing care. Whether caregivers are leaving highly paid jobs, cutting back on hours at these jobs, or foregoing leisure has important implications for estimates of the true cost of informal care.

Both direct reports regarding the impact of care on work and effects inferred from correlations in panel data suggest that caregiving has a negative impact on employment. The National Association of Insurance Companies/American Council of Life Insurers finds that more than a third of caregivers report reductions in paid work as a result of caregiving: 10 percent cut back on hours worked, 6 percent left paid work entirely, and 17 percent took a temporary leave of absence from their jobs. An additional 4 percent turned down promotions, directly reducing wage growth in the near term and perhaps future opportunities for promotions as well. Other studies have similarly found a negative correlation between labor market participation and caregiving—with either a reduction in the probability of working (e.g., Ettner 1996; Bolin, Lindgren, and Lundborg 2008; Carmichael, Charles, and Hulme 2010; Van Houtven, Coe, and Skira 2013) or a reduction in hours worked (Johnson and Lo Sasso 2006).

3. The Health and Retirement Study Data

We use data from the Health and Retirement Study (HRS), a panel survey that follows individuals from their 50s until their deaths, with interviews conducted every two years. When appropriately weighted, the sample is approximately representative of the U.S. population ages 50 and older.[5] Respondents in the initial cohort were first interviewed in 1992 when they were between ages 51 and 61. Spouses or partners of sample persons were included in the survey regardless of age. New cohorts consisting of respondents ages 51 to 56 are added every six years to refresh the sample and keep it approximately representative of the older population. Because the probability of caregiving for a parent peaks in one's 50s, this sample is ideal for our study.

Our analysis focuses on the role of women in providing care, so we limit our sample to women. Because there are likely to be differences in the age at which individuals provide care that may be correlated with their sociodemographic group (e.g., due to variation between groups in the health and longevity of parents or the age difference between parents and their adult children), we seek to maximize the age span over which we observe our respondents, while maintaining an approximately representative national sample and allowing for multiple observations per respondent. Specifically, we require that respondents be interviewed at least once between the ages of 50 and 57, and we take the observation within that interval that is nearest to age 51 as our starting point regardless of the year in which that interview occurs.[6] We then examine patterns of caregiving over the subsequent six interview dates, requiring that all respondents in our sample be observed for this complete window of time. Because the survey is fielded biennially and asks about care since the previous interview, we observe our respondents for approximately 10 years after the first interview, with respondents followed until they are approximately ages 60–67.[7]

Caregiving in our sample is defined as answering "yes" to the question:

Did you (or your husband / wife / partner) spend a total of 100 or more hours (since the previous wave / in the last two years) helping your (parents / mother / father) with basic personal activities like dressing, eating and bathing?

Follow-up questions ask who provided the care and the number of hours. We include caregiving provided to either the respondent's own parents or to her parents-in-law.[8] In the discussion that follows, we define individuals who provide care at any point during our window of observation as caregivers, and we distinguish these caregivers from the remaining women in our sample who we do not observe providing care during the sample period. For those respondents who were initially providing care, we do not know when caregiving commenced or their labor market status prior to the provision of care. When we exclude these women, our conclusions are substantially unchanged. Finally, because our interest is in the distribution of caregiving across the population and its impact on the employment of older women in the United States, we intentionally do not limit our sample to the subset women who had living parents or parents-in-law during the sample period.

4. Descriptive Results on the Distribution and Cost of Caregiving

4.1. Who Is More Likely to Be Caring for Parents or Parents-in-Law?

As the descriptive statistics in Table 10.1 show, individuals who are caregivers at some point during the sample period tend to be more advantaged than those who never report providing care. Nearly a third (31 percent) of our sample provides care at some point, and care commences, on average, around age 53.[9] At the beginning of our period of observation, compared to noncaregivers, caregivers are significantly younger, more likely to be married, more educated, and in better health. On the financial front, caregivers have significantly greater household wealth and household income, are more likely to have an employed spouse (conditional on being married), and the earnings of any employed spouses are greater. The differences in household wealth are large, with caregivers averaging approximately 13 percent more total wealth: $434,925 (in 2014 dollars) versus $383,824 for noncaregivers.[10] There are smaller differences by race and ethnicity, with white women more likely than non-white or Hispanic women to be caregivers; these differences are not significantly different from zero but are consistent with caregivers tending to have more advantaged backgrounds.

Figure 10.1 provides further detail on some of the associations between caregiving, SES, and race/ethnicity. The results indicate that differences in rates of caregiving are very large between socioeconomic groups, as measured by educational attainment or household wealth, and smaller by race and ethnicity. The first panel shows that the probability of caregiving increases strongly with education. About 23 percent of women with less than a high school diploma provide care, compared to about 36 percent of those with college degrees. The second panel shows a similar gradient by wealth. Those in the lowest quartile are the least

TABLE 10.1 Demographic and financial characteristics

	All (n = 5,834)		Ever care (n = 1,705)		Never care (n = 4,129)	
	Mean	SE	Mean	SE	Mean	SE
DEMOGRAPHIC CHARACTERISTICS						
Ever provided caregiving 0/1	0.31***	0.006	1.00	0.00	0.00	0.00
Age	52.54***	0.027	52.28	0.048	52.65	0.033
Married 0/1	0.71***	0.006	0.74	0.011	0.69	0.007
Years of schooling	12.97***	0.037	13.33	0.065	12.82	0.045
Number of children	2.90	0.025	2.86	0.044	2.92	0.029
Non-white and non-Hispanic 0/1	0.14	0.004	0.13	0.008	0.14	0.005
Hispanic 0/1	0.07	0.003	0.07	0.006	0.08	0.004
Fair/poor health 0/1	0.19***	0.005	0.18	0.009	0.20	0.006
HOUSEHOLD FINANCIAL CHARACTERISTICS						
Household income (2010 dollars)	95,034**	1,464	99,846	2,518	92,866	1,793
Household wealth (2010 dollars)	399,724**	11,108	434,925	22,679	383,824	12,528
Median wealth	166,273	—	189,893	—	155,387	—
Husband works (if married)	0.82***	0.006	0.84	0.011	0.81	0.008
Husband's earning (if working)	71,920*	1,384	75,337	2,751	70,247	1,571

Notes: Stars indicate if the differences between the ever and never care groups are significant at the *** 1, ** 5, or *10 percent level. The sample is all those observed at least once between the ages of 50 and 57 and interviewed at least six times after the first such observation. The statistics in the table are computed using data from each individual's first interview and are weighted to be nationally representative.

likely to provide care, while there is little difference among the other three quartiles.[11] The third panel shows that non-Hispanic white women are more likely to provide care (31.5 percent) than non-white or Hispanic women (approximately 29 percent), but these differences are much smaller in absolute terms than the differences by education and wealth.

Table 10.2 indicates that, in addition to belonging to more advantaged sociodemographic groups, caregivers also have stronger labor market attachment than do noncaregivers. There is no difference between the groups in employment status (working 0/1) at the first interview, and full-time work shows greater participation by caregivers than noncaregivers, although this difference is not significantly different from zero. However, conditional on working, caregivers work significantly more hours and have significantly greater earnings, $42,407 versus $38,416. These differences in labor market attachment appear to be long-term in nature. Caregivers have significantly more labor market experience and greater tenure on both their current job and on their longest job. Caregivers can also anticipate receiving greater Social Security payments at full retirement age, based on a measure of expected Social Security wealth available from the University of Michigan public-use files. Because Social Security benefits are a function of lifetime earnings, this measure captures well the lifetime employment history of respondents.

Perhaps unsurprisingly given their greater work experience and earnings, Table 10.2 also suggests that other dimensions of job quality are at least as good for caregivers as for

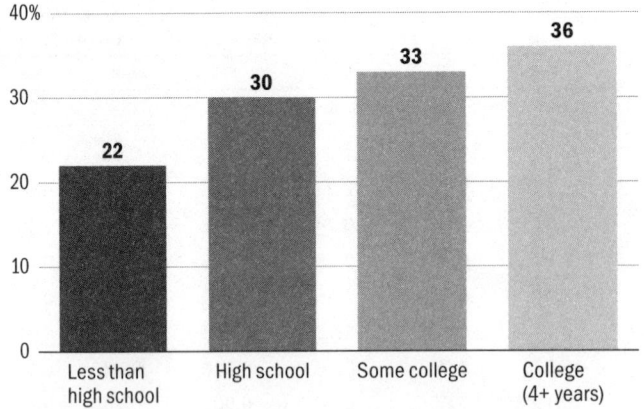
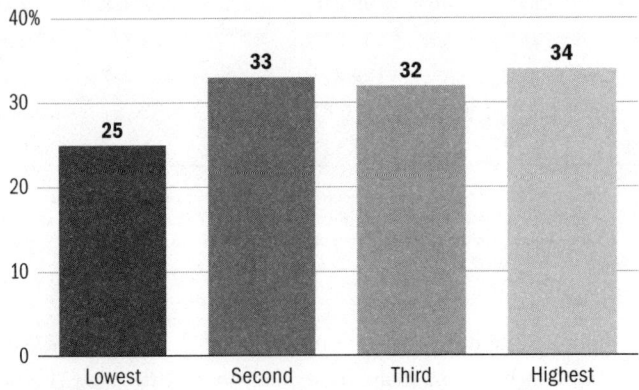
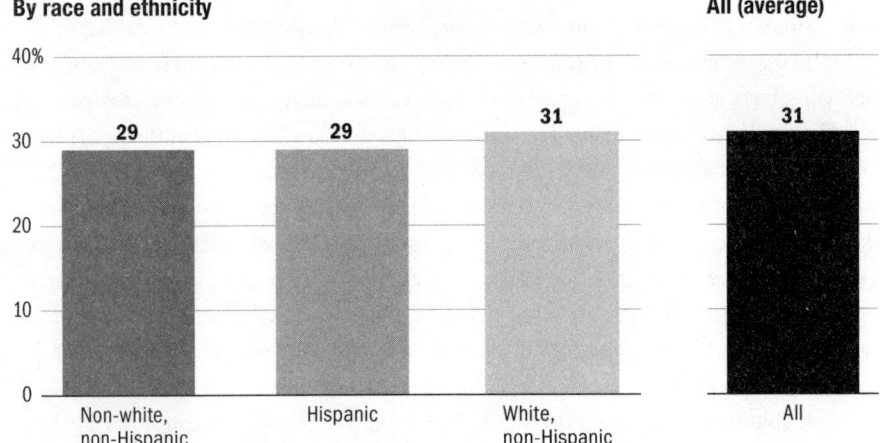

FIGURE 10.1 **Proportion of women providing care to parents or parents-in-law**

TABLE 10.2 Labor market characteristics

	All (n = 5,834)		Ever care (n = 1,705)		Never care (n = 4,129)	
	Mean	SE	Mean	SE	Mean	SE
LABOR MARKET PARTICIPATION						
Working 0/1	0.72	0.006	0.72	0.011	0.72	0.007
Work full-time 0/1	0.59	0.006	0.60	0.012	0.58	0.008
Work part-time 0/1	0.12	0.004	0.11	0.008	0.12	0.005
Hours (if working)	38.23***	0.204	39.17	0.388	37.81	0.24
Earnings (if working)	39,679***	588	42,407	1,115	38,416	688
Experience (years)	24.13*	0.148	24.51	0.266	23.96	0.177
Tenure in current job (years)	11.02***	0.152	11.86	0.290	10.65	0.178
Tenure in longest job (years)	17.58***	0.136	18.40	0.251	17.21	0.162
Expected Social Security wealth at full retirement age (2010 dollars)	86,369***	693	89,182	1,306	85,067	816
JOB QUALITY						
Pension on current job	0.59***	0.008	0.63	0.014	0.57	0.009
Health insurance on current job	0.58	0.008	0.59	0.014	0.58	0.009
Vacation days	14.23	0.342	14.77	0.623	14.00	0.410
Sick days	9.21	0.426	9.80	0.879	8.93	0.476

Notes: Stars indicate if the differences between the ever and never care groups are significant at the *** 1, ** 5, or *10 percent level. The sample is all those observed at least once between the ages of 50 and 57 and interviewed at least 6 times after the first such observation. The statistics in the table are computed using data from each individual's first interview and are weighted to be nationally representative.

noncaregivers. Caregivers are significantly more likely to have jobs with pension benefits, and although the differences are not significantly different from zero, they appear to have a slightly greater number of vacation and sick days. To the extent that caregiving causes these women to quit their jobs, they will be leaving positions at least as attractive as those held by their noncaregiving peers.

Why might these patterns exist? Table 10.3 provides some indication. Overall, caregivers are simply at greater risk of needing to provide care. Caregivers have significantly more living parents than noncaregivers, an average of 1.8 versus 1.1, as well as a greater likelihood of having an unmarried parent (who would not have a spouse on whom they could rely for help). Caregivers' parents tend to be older than the parents of noncaregivers: the age of the oldest parent as measured at the respondent's first included interview is 81.1 for caregivers and 78.6 for noncaregivers. There are similarly large and significant differences in having a parent who lives within 10 miles, and in having a parent who is worse-off financially than the respondent herself.[12] Noncaregivers are also twice as likely as caregivers to have at least one parent or parent-in-law living in another country. This is especially likely to be the case for many Hispanic respondents, making hands-on care difficult if not impossible.[13] Not only

TABLE 10.3 Family characteristics

	All (n = 5,834)		Ever care (n = 1,705)		Never care (n = 4,129)	
	Mean	SE	Mean	SE	Mean	SE
MEASURES OF CAREGIVING RISK						
Number of living parents/in-laws	1.31***	0.013	1.73	0.021	1.12	0.016
Any unmarried parent/in-law (0/1)	0.57***	0.006	0.76	0.010	0.49	0.008
Age of oldest living parent/in-law	79.57***	0.147	81.13	0.141	78.55	0.221
Any parent living within 10 miles	0.13***	0.005	0.17	0.009	0.11	0.006
Any parent worse-off than respondent	0.44***	0.007	0.47	0.012	0.42	0.009
Any parent living abroad	0.06***	0.004	0.04	0.005	0.08	0.005
Father's education (years)	10.01***	0.056	10.25	0.100	9.90	0.068
Mother's education (years)	10.25***	0.049	10.52	0.087	10.13	0.060
Spouse's father's education (years)	9.37	0.075	9.17	0.142	9.33	0.091
Spouse's mother's education (years)	9.66	0.066	9.76	0.124	9.62	0.080
SIBLINGS						
Number of sisters	1.60***	0.021	1.50	0.037	1.64	0.026
Number of brothers	1.50	0.019	1.48	0.034	1.50	0.023
Number of sisters-in-law (if married)	1.49***	0.024	1.38	0.034	1.54	0.030
Number of brothers-in-law (if married)	1.43	0.023	1.41	0.042	1.43	0.028

Notes: Stars indicate if the differences between the ever and never care groups are significant at the *** 1, ** 5, or *10 percent level. The sample is all those observed at least once between the ages of 50 and 57 and interviewed at least 6 times after first such observation. The statistics in the table are computed using data from each individual's first interview and are weighted to be nationally representative.

do caregivers appear to be better-off than their noncaregiving counterparts, but their parents may be better-off as well. Both the mothers and fathers of caregivers have more years of education than the parents of noncaregivers, though how this fact might affect the need for care is ambiguous.

In terms of potential substitutes for care, caregivers have significantly fewer sisters or sisters-in-law than noncaregivers, but there are no differences in the number of brothers or brothers-in-law. These figures suggest that sisters may substitute as caregivers while brothers typically do not.

Recognizing that many of the correlates of caregiving in Table 10.3 are also likely to be associated with the sociodemographic group to which one belongs, we next examine whether between-group differences in these factors can explain the higher rates of caregiving among relatively more advantaged women that we document above. For this task, we utilize the framework of a multivariate regression to calculate the partial correlations between caregiving and each of the variables in Tables 10.1–10.3 while controlling for all of the remaining variables.

The results (not shown) indicate that, with a few exceptions, many of the correlations documented above are robust to conditioning on other individual and household characteristics. Family structure remains a key predictor of caregiving: having more living parents or parents-in-law, more unmarried parents, older parents, and parents living nearby are all correlated with a significantly greater probability of providing care, while sisters are associated with a significantly lower probability. There remains no relationship between caregiving and the number of brothers.

In an interesting contrast to the simple correlations in Table 10.1, the multivariate regression results reveal a reversal of the associations between caregiving and race/ethnicity. Conditional on family structure and the other variables in Tables 10.1–10.3, non-white non-Hispanic women are significantly *more* likely than white or Hispanic women to provide care, and the difference in rates of caregiving between the latter two groups disappears. These shifts suggest that the small racial/ethnic differences that we observe at the population level are in large part a result of the fact that non-Hispanic white women are more likely than other groups to have parents in need of care.

Conversely, even after accounting for between-group differences in family characteristics, we continue to see that labor force attachment and some measures of SES are positively associated with caregiving. Respondents with more work experience, those who are currently employed, and those with higher levels of education are more likely to provide care than those who have fewer years of work experience, those who are not employed, and those with lower levels of education. These results challenge the perceived wisdom among economists that caregivers are likely to be drawn from those with weaker attachment to the labor force, for whom caregiving is likely to be easier and less costly than it would be for those who have a full-time job. Similarly, among those who are working, the financial cost of a reduction in hours worked, measured in dollar terms of foregone earnings, is largest for those with the highest wage. The partial correlations described above and the descriptive results in Tables 10.1 and 10.2 seem to belie this idea. Instead, the consistently better financial status of caregivers suggests that they may have come to their role because they have the financial wherewithal to manage the responsibilities of caregiving while providing for themselves and their families. Among those who are working, it is likely that more advantaged women have jobs which afford them greater flexibility to take time off to provide care.[14]

4.2. Hours of Care

The effect of caregiving on a woman's labor force participation is likely to depend on how much time she spends on it. In Table 10.4, we highlight some statistics on the total number of hours of care provided among those providing at least some care. For these statistics, we first aggregate the hours reported by each individual over all of their six interviews. (Recall that hours of care in the HRS survey are measured over the time between interviews, a period of approximately two years.) The average cumulative number of hours of care across interviews is 1,359. The median, 504 hours, is substantially smaller. This skewness is due to the long right tail of the distribution: some respondents who co-reside with a care recipient report giving care 24 hours per day. Unfortunately, while we know the total number of hours of care provided between one interview and the next, we do not know when that care was provided; it could represent a few intense months of caregiving or caregiving spread out over a two-year period. The most we can say in this regard is that the average number of interviews at which some care was reported is 1.7. Given a two-year gap between most interviews, this

TABLE 10.4 Time spent providing care among women ever providing care (N = 1,705)

	Mean	SE
Total hours of care provided over period of observation (approx. 10 years)	1,359	54.6
25th percentile	200	—
50th percentile	504	—
75th percentile	1,552	—
90th percentile	3,500	—
Age at first reported caregiving	56.2	0.09
Number of interviews at which reported caregiving	1.67	0.02

corresponds to 3.4 years or 177 weeks.[15] This back-of-the-envelope calculation thus suggests an average of close to eight hours per week if care were spread uniformly over the period. This is certainly substantial enough to affect labor market behavior.

A breakdown of caregiving hours by sociodemographic group reveals that, while more advantaged women are more likely than less advantaged women to provide *some* care for parents or parents-in-law, less advantaged caregivers are more likely to provide time-intensive care. These patterns can be seen in Figure 10.2, which presents the distributions of hours separately by education, wealth, and race and ethnicity. The bars show the mean, median, and 90th percentile of the number of hours of care for those providing a positive amount.

Considering differences first by SES, we find that those with the least education provide the greatest number of hours. Although the medians are similar between education groups, the distributions are much more right-skewed for the least educated. For example, the 90th percentile of hours among those with less than a high school degree is a striking 5,000 hours, compared to 2,900 for those with a college degree. To put these figures in perspective, 5,000 hours of care amounts to 28 hours per week using the average number of weeks shown above. In contrast to the results by education, there is less variation across wealth quartiles and little, if any, discernible pattern.

The patterns by race and ethnicity are similar to those by education. White women report providing fewer hours, with lower means, medians, and 90th percentiles than the other groups. Hispanic women provide the greatest amount of care, as demonstrated by the very high value for the 90th percentile, approximately 5,000 hours, of their distribution. In results not shown, we also find that Hispanic women provide care for more waves on average (1.81) than white non-Hispanic women (1.64) or non-white non-Hispanic women (1.65).

4.3. The Cost of Replacing Family Care with Paid Care

The high cost of formal care is likely to be a major factor in families' decisions about caregiving. While roughly equal fractions of older adults say they prefer care from family members and care from formal caregivers (Brown, Goda, and McGarry 2012), formal care comes with a steep cash outlay. Using the average hourly wage for a home health aide in 2014 (Genworth 2021) of $20, we can estimate the cost of replacing family care with paid help. We

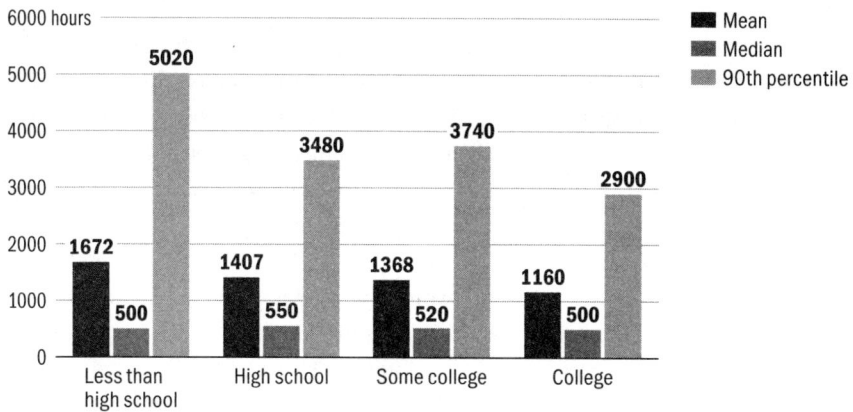
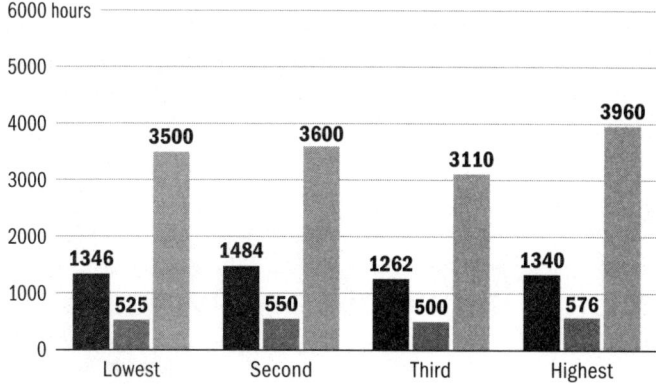
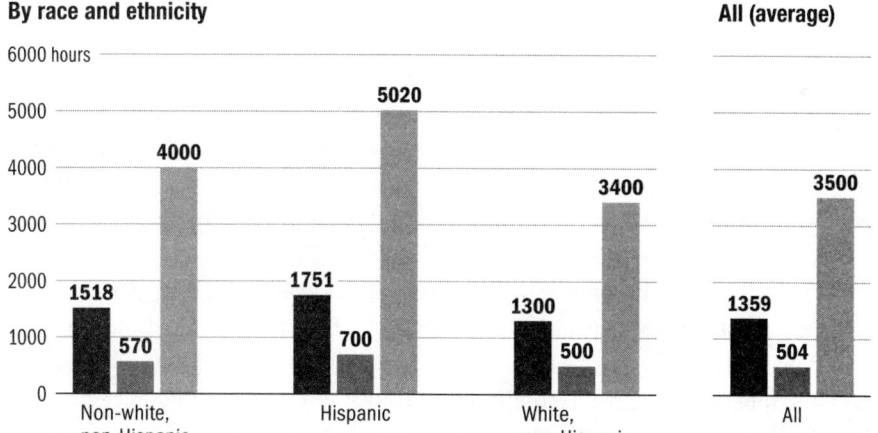

FIGURE 10.2 Total hours of care across interviews
Note: Hours of care in the HRS survey are measured over the time between interviews, a period of approximately two years. Total hours of care across interviews refers to the total over six such two-year periods.

then take the ratio of this replacement cost to caregivers' annual family income and average within each of our demographic groups.

The results, seen in Figure 10.3, reveal large disparities between groups in the relative financial burden of replacing family care with paid care measured in terms of the fraction of family income it represents. By this measure, formal care is far more "costly" for less educated and lower wealth groups, with prohibitively high replacement costs for those with fewer resources. For those with assets above the median (those in the upper two wealth quartiles), the cost of formal care is equivalent to approximately 10 percent of family income. While large, such an expense may be possible to maintain for a year or two. In contrast, for those with incomes below the median, the cash cost of formal care would be nearly 40 percent of family income. Similar differences are evident by race and ethnicity with costs ranging from 37 percent for Hispanic families, 30 percent for non-white non-Hispanic families, and 13 percent for non-Hispanic white families. These results suggest that women from disadvantaged sociodemographic groups are providing care partly because they have no other options.

The analysis to this point reveals a complex picture of the sociodemographic patterns of caregiving. While more socioeconomically advantaged women are more likely to provide care, women from less advantaged economic and racial and ethnic groups tend to provide more time-intensive care, care that has a much higher economic value when measured as a percentage of their household income. These disparities, as well as differences across groups in other economic resources and job characteristics, are likely to shape the extent to which these women are negatively impacted by providing needed care.

5. The Relationship between Caregiving and Work

Much prior research has shown that, compared to noncaregivers, caregivers are less likely to be employed and tend to work fewer hours if they are employed (e.g., Van Houtven, Coe, and Skira 2013; Johnson and Lo Sasso 2006). We now examine this relationship for the women in our sample. To isolate better the causal effect of care on work, we limit the sample here to those who were not initially providing care. We further limit our sample to those who are "at risk" for providing care in that they have a living parent or parent-in-law at the second observation in our sample of six interviews, and could thus potentially face the need to provide care.

We estimate the relationship between work, hours worked, and earnings as functions of caregiving and a number of standard control variables.[16] Both hours worked and earnings are measured unconditionally. For each dependent variable, we estimate both an ordinary least squares (OLS) regression and a fixed-effects model that leverages the multiple observations we have for each respondent. The OLS model compares observably similar caregivers and noncaregivers; the fixed-effects model compares women to their earlier or later selves, examining how women's labor force participation changes when their caregiving status changes.

Across all three outcomes and both types of empirical specifications, we find that caregiving has a significant and negative effect on work. The results appear in Table 10.5, panel

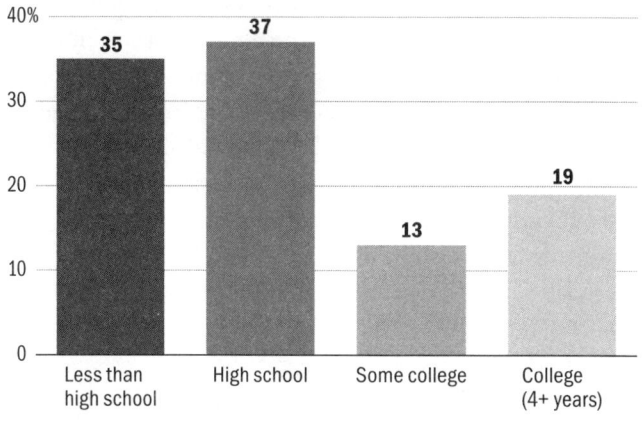
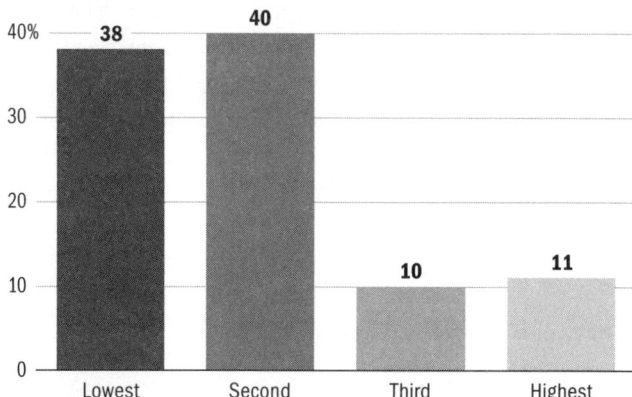
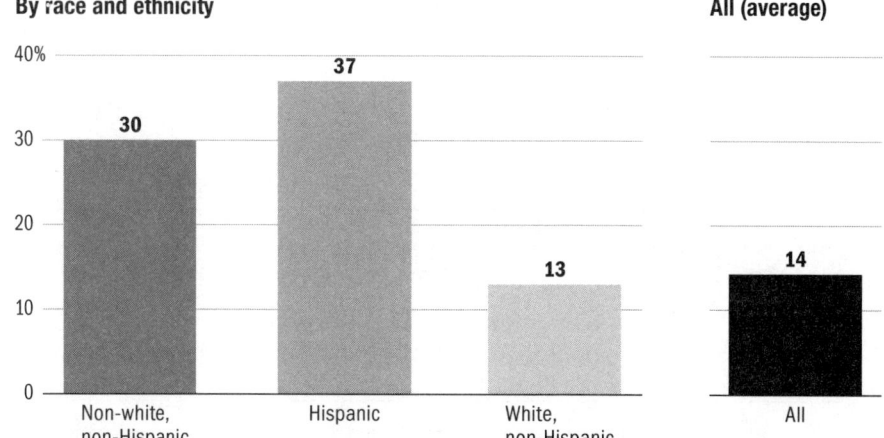

FIGURE 10.3 Relative cost of replacement care
Note: The cost of replacing family care with paid care is measured in terms of the fraction of family income it represents.

A. In the OLS model, caregiving reduces the probability of working by 4 percentage points on a base of 58 percent, or 7 percent. The effect falls by half when controlling for fixed effects, but it is still substantial, with a reduction of 2.2 percentage points, or 3.7 percent. In terms of hours worked, caregiving again has a significant negative effect, equivalent to 2 hours per week in OLS, or 9.5 percent, and 1.2 hours in the fixed-effects model. Finally, caregiving is found to be associated with a reduction of $2,104 in annual earnings in OLS, and $915 in the fixed-effects model. Thus, among those not caregiving when first observed, the take-up of caregiving is associated with significantly reduced labor market behavior.

The consequences of caregiving for a woman's financial security in retirement depend in part on whether her reduced labor force participation is temporary or long-lasting. As noted earlier, the average number of interviews at which care is reported is 1.7. If caregivers return to work after this period of providing assistance, they may be able to recoup some of their lost earnings or at least improve their financial picture in retirement. To assess the extent to which any labor market effects are "permanent," we examine work outcomes near the end of the traditional work life. Specifically, we look at the same collection of labor market outcomes measured at age 65. For each respondent, we select the observation that is closest to age 65. We require that the individual be at least 63 to avoid the large difference by age in employment at this point in the lifecycle.[17] We compare women who cared for a parent or parent-in-law at any point over the 10-year window of observation to those who were never caregivers. Because we have only one observation per respondent, we cannot undertake a fixed-effects analysis.

TABLE 10.5 Relationship between caregiving and work

	Work (0/1) OLS	Work (0/1) Fixed effects	Hours OLS	Hours Fixed effects	Earnings OLS	Earnings Fixed effects
A. CURRENT WORK OUTCOMES						
Caregiving	−0.040***	−0.022***	−2.01***	−1.17***	−2104***	−915***
	(0.012)	(0.010)	(0.482)	(0.381)	(7,621)	(645)
Observations	19,521		19,370		19,521	
Mean of dep. var.	0.58		21.0		19,935	
B. WORK OUTCOMES AT AGE 65						
Caregiving ever	−0.062***	—	−1.90***	—	−1,766***	—
	(0.018)		(0.670)		(681)	
Observations	3,678		3,635		3,678	
Mean of dep. var.	0.425		13.5		11,964	

*** $p < 0.01$, ** $p < 0.05$, * $p < 0.10$. In addition to the measure of "caregiving," the regressions in the top panel include age, race/ethnicity, categorical measures of schooling, marital status, number of living parents, number of own children, age of youngest child, household wealth, spousal employment and earnings (if married), health status, and job characteristics measured at the first observation (employment, pension, health insurance, years of experience). The first observation is omitted from the regressions. In the bottom panel the regressors are similar but are measured at the first interview. OLS, ordinary least squares.

As is apparent from the results, which appear in Table 10.5, panel B, we see strong and statistically significant negative relationships between caregiving and various long-term measures of work, with results that are similar in magnitude to the short-term effects. Ever caregiving is associated with a 6.2 percentage point reduction in the probability of working at age 65, or a 15 percent reduction. There is a decline of almost two hours per week in hours worked—very similar to that observed for the short term, although smaller in percentage terms. Finally, the negative relationship between care and earnings is again similar to the short term, with caregiving at any point over the 10-year window of observation associated with a decline of nearly $1,800 in annual earnings.

Caregiving thus appears to have potentially significant negative effects on average employment in both the short and long term.[18] Interestingly, the relationship between caregiving and long-term employment is quite consistent across sociodemographic groups, as Figure 10.4 shows. Despite the differences across groups in the probability of providing care shown in the earlier figures and the expected differences in resources and job opportunities, within each group defined by education, wealth, or race/ethnicity, caregivers are less likely to be employed at age 65 than noncaregivers. Regardless of the demographic group, caregiving is associated with a reduction in work in the later years.

6. Conclusions

This chapter provides a detailed look at the relationship between caregiving and work, with a focus on the different patterns observed by educational attainment, wealth, and race/ethnicity. Perhaps surprisingly to many readers, the results provide clear evidence that caregivers are not disproportionately drawn from those with weaker attachment to the labor market. Rather, those women who provide care to a parent or parent-in-law tend to have higher earnings, more labor market experience, more education, and greater financial resources than noncaregivers.

We find that one of the most powerful predictors of care is family composition. A larger number of living parents increases the risk of having to provide care, particularly if the parent or parent-in-law is unmarried and thus does not have a spouse who can provide care. Because more advantaged adults tend to live longer, middle-aged women with higher socioeconomic status are more likely than lower-SES women to have parents or parents-in-law who are still alive and thus at risk of needing care. In this sense, the gradient of elder care—in which more advantaged women are at higher risk—runs in the opposite direction of most of the inequalities discussed in this book. Women with greater resources in terms of education, work experience, and family wealth may be in a better position to care for their parents or parents-in-law. It is also plausible that their jobs offer more benefits and flexibility that improve their availability to provide care.

However, some of the disadvantages of caregiving for labor force participation fall disproportionately on women with fewer resources. While women with lower levels of education and non-white women are actually less likely than more highly educated women and white women to provide care during our window of observation, those who are caregivers provide

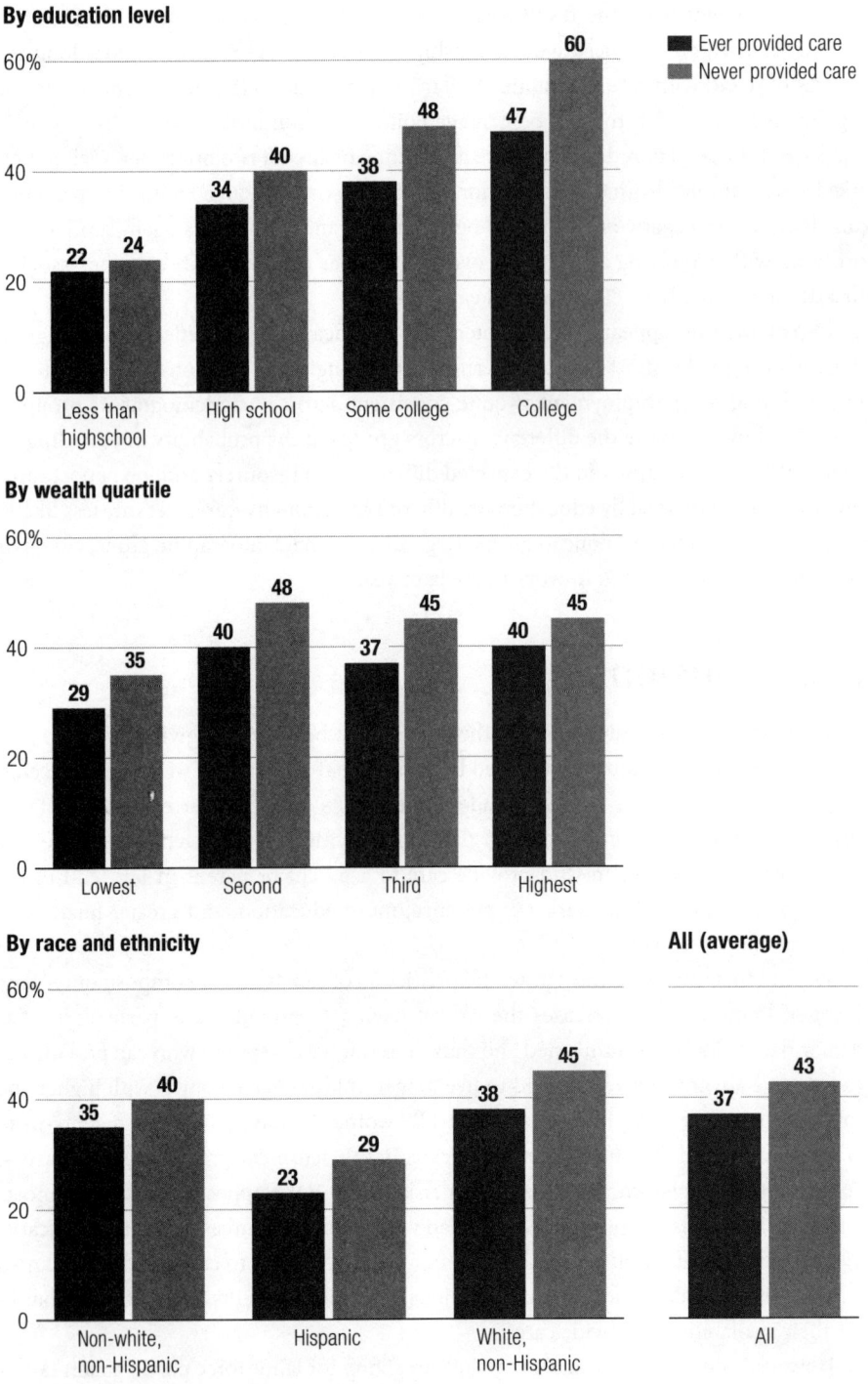

FIGURE 10.4 **Proportion of women working at age 65**

more hours of care, particularly in the extreme upper end of the distribution. Moreover, in assessing the value of the care provided relative to income, those with fewer resources are faced with an average replacement cost that represents over one-third of their annual household income, suggesting that they are likely to be unable to afford to purchase substitute care. Finally, because the parents of women with fewer resources are similarly likely to be of less advantaged sociodemographic groups, they are likely to be in poorer health for much of their lives and may need greater care, albeit at a younger age. We are restricted by the data from examining caregiving earlier in the lives of our respondents, but they may have indeed provided care as early as their 40s.

Importantly, this chapter is among the first to show that caregiving appears to have long-term consequences on work. We find a strongly significant and negative association between ever providing care to a parent or parent-in-law and being employed at age 65. Moreover, the effects of caregiving on long-term employment appear to be remarkably consistent across groups defined by education, wealth, and race/ethnicity. Caregiving is associated with a reduced likelihood of working longer among women from all sociodemographic backgrounds.

We close by exploring what our results could portend for the future of elder care in the United States and its impact on the work lives of older American women. To begin with, there are several reasons to expect that the burden of care will increase for future cohorts. First, the aging of the U.S. population and increases in life expectancy are likely to increase the demand for care. As individuals survive to later ages and face changing mortality risk from various causes, they may also spend more time in need of custodial care. Indeed, the U.S. Centers for Disease Control and Prevention forecasts that the share of the U.S. population with Alzheimer's disease and related dementias will rise from 1.6 percent in 2014 to 3.3 in 2060, with the fastest increases occurring within minority populations (Matthews et al. 2019). Caring for those with cognitive issues is likely to be particularly time-intensive and may lead to even greater negative effects on work than those shown here. Second, these same forces, combined with higher rates of divorce and smaller family sizes, will reduce the supply of potential caregivers. The American Association of Retired Persons predicts that these supply-and-demand factors will reduce the caregiver support ratio—the ratio of the population ages 45 to 64 to the population ages 80 and older—from 7.2 in 2010 to just 2.9 by 2050 (Redfoot, Feinberg, and Houser 2013). Thus, the burden of caregiving is potentially poised to become both larger and more concentrated, and because caregiving is highly gendered, the growing burden is likely to fall disproportionately on women. Our results suggest that these demographic changes may intensify the challenges of combining caregiving and paid employment for upcoming generations.

Coupled with these important demographic changes are likely longer-term changes in work patterns and other behaviors accelerated by the COVID-19 pandemic. The high infection rates in nursing facilities may lead families to eschew institutionalization for elderly relatives and, instead, assume the burden of this care themselves. Meanwhile, if the increased prevalence in "working from home" or telecommuting continues, individuals may have more flexibility in when and where work is performed and be better able to balance work and care.

How these changes will impact the relationship between caregiving and work is an important question for future research.

The role of public policy in managing these trends remains one of the largest question marks on the horizon. On the one hand, if concerns over fiscal deficits trigger a retrenchment of government spending, the result could be the paring back of a safety net that was already porous to begin with in its coverage of long-term care. Such a reaction could put more pressure on families to provide care and exacerbate existing inequalities in the burden of providing care. On the other hand, for many, it has also become increasingly clear that the United States has an inadequate infrastructure for providing care, leading to renewed calls for reform and for expanded public provision of these services. How this debate will unfold in the coming years remains to be seen.

In light of the many challenges, we end by stressing that the importance of caregiving is only likely to grow in the future, and we call for more research in this critical area.

Notes

1. We gratefully acknowledge financial support from the Alfred P. Sloan Foundation, grant number G-2015-14131.
2. Medicare covers skilled long-term care for a limited period of time. Medigap policies, or Medicare Supplemental Insurance Plans, are separate insurance policies designed to cover the "gaps" in Medicare.
3. Coward and Dwyer (1990) report that daughters are three times more likely to provide care than sons, while McGarry (1998) finds that 70 percent of child caregivers are daughters. Perhaps unsurprisingly, the higher propensity for women to provide care is also evident outside the United States (OECD 2019) and holds even in countries where parents have traditionally relied on sons for old-age support. In these cases, it is the daughters-in-law (rather than the sons) who assume the lion's share of caregiving duties (Jang, Avendano, and Kawachi 2012).
4. One might speculate that the preponderance of family caregiving would indicate a preference for such care. However, Brown et al. (2012) find that when given a hypothetical choice, nearly equal fractions of respondents prefer care from family members and care from formal caregivers. In examining these data anew for this paper, there do not appear to be strong differences in preference by socioeconomic status.
5. We use weights in our descriptive statistics but do not use weights in the regression analyses.
6. Our "first" interviews range from 1992 to 2004. The modal year is 1992, and the median is 1994.
7. If individuals in our sample miss an interview but are recontacted at the next interview, we keep them in our sample as long as we have six full interviews for them. Our results are qualitatively unchanged if we follow respondents for as long as they remained in the data or if we use fewer observations per person.
8. The first wave of the HRS, fielded in 1992, asked about assistance provided in the preceding 12 months while later interviews asked about care in the time elapsed since the previous interview, a period of approximately two years. We do not make any adjustments for the different time period covered by the first interview.
9. If care is reported at the first interview, we use the age at that time. We do not know if the respondent provided care at some point earlier in her life and ceased doing so before the first interview, or the age at which care commenced for those initially providing care. In not observing care prior to the survey, we necessarily miss care given to parents whose deaths preceded the individual's first interview. In addition, our measure of care excludes care provided to grandparents—although such care is far less common than care to parents. Finally, we intentionally omit care to spouses because much spousal care occurs after traditional retirement ages and is thus unlikely to affect labor market behavior. (For statistics on spousal care in the HRS, see Fahle and McGarry [2018]]).

10. Differences in other components of wealth are similarly large. The difference in financial wealth—which excludes real estate and business wealth, among other categories—is 28 percent, or $124,190 versus 96,650 (not shown).
11. We use wealth rather than income because income is more strongly associated with current labor market behavior, which itself may be affected by caregiving.
12. The HRS does not ask about the income or wealth of parents, just whether the respondent believes that her parents are worse-off or better-off than the respondent herself.
13. In our sample, approximately one-third of Hispanic women report having at least one living parent in another country at some point in the survey.
14. Ideally, we would like to have some measure of the flexibility of hours on the job. The HRS asks respondents whether they can reduce hours on their job, but it does not ask whether they have flexibility in when the hours are worked. Many white-collar jobs have a workload that does not allow for a reduction in hours, but they may allow a great deal of flexibility, including the option to work from home.
15. Statistics from the Bureau of Labor Statistics (2017) show that just over one-half of all women who provide care do so for less than two years, a number consistent with the patterns reported here.
16. In addition to the variable for "caregiving," the regressions include age, race and ethnicity, categorical measures of education, marital status, number of living parents, number of own children, household wealth, spousal employment and earnings (if married), health status, and job characteristics (pension, health insurance, years of experience) for those employed.
17. The very youngest in our sample thus do not contribute to these regressions.
18. Approximately 7.7 percent of our sample is providing care at the "age 65" observation. If we exclude these women from our regression sample, the results are similar and still significantly different from zero. The magnitude of the coefficients on caregiving in the regressions for working (0/1), hours and earnings change from –0.062 to –0.055, –1.9 to –1.7, and –1,766 to –2,152, respectively.

References

Aranda, M. P., and B. G. Knight. 1997. "The Influence of Ethnicity and Culture on the Caregiver Stress and Coping Process: A Sociocultural Review and Analysis." *The Gerontologist* 37 (3): 342–354. https://doi.org/10.1093/geront/37.3.342.

Bolin, K., B. Lindgren, and P. Lundborg. 2008. "Your Next of Kin or Your Own Career?: Caring and Working among the 50+ of Europe." *Journal of Health Economics* 27 (3): 718–738. https://doi.org/10.1016/j.jhealeco.2007.10.004.

Brown, Jeffrey R., Gopi Shah Goda, and Kathleen McGarry. 2012. "Long-Term Care Insurance Demand Limited by Beliefs about Needs, Concerns about Insurers, and Care Available from Family." *Health Affairs* 31 (6): 1294–1302. https://doi.org/10.1377/hlthaff.2011.1307.

Carmichael, F., S. Charles, and C. Hulme. 2010. "Who Will Care? Employment Participation and Willingness to Supply Informal Care." *Journal of Health Economics* 29 (1): 182–190. https://doi.org/10.1016/j.jhealeco.2009.11.003.

Covinsky, Kenneth E., Catherine Eng, Li-Yung Lui, Laura P. Sands, Ashwini R. Sehgal, Louise C. Walter, Darryl Wieland, G. Paul Eleazer, and Kristine Yaffe. 2001. "Reduced Employment in Caregivers of Frail Elders: Impact of Ethnicity, Patient Clinical Characteristics, and Caregiver Characteristics." *The Journals of Gerontology: Series A* 56 (11): M707–M713. https://doi.org/10.1093/gerona/56.11.M707.

Coward, Raymond T., and Jeffrey W. Dwyer. 1990. "The Association of Gender, Sibling Network Composition, and Patterns of Parent Care by Adult Children." *Research on Aging* 12 (2): 158–181. https://doi.org/10.1177/0164027590122002. Accessed on June 03, 2022.

Doty, Pamela. 2010. "The Evolving Balance of Formal and Informal, Institutional and Non-Institutional Long-Term Care for Older Americans: A Thirty-Year Perspective." *Public Policy & Aging Report* 20 (1): 3–9. https://doi.org/10.1093/ppar/20.1.3.

Ettner, Susan L. 1996. "The Opportunity Costs of Elder Care." *The Journal of Human Resources* 31 (1): 189–205. https://doi.org/10.2307/146047.

Fahle, Sean, and Kathleen McGarry. 2018. "Women Working Longer: Labor Market Implications of Providing Family Care." In *Women Working Longer: Increased Employment at Older Ages*, edited by Claudia Goldin and Lawrence F. Katz, 157–181. Chicago: University of Chicago Press. https://www.nber.org/books-and-chapters/women-working-longer-increased-employment-older-ages/women-working-longer-labor-market-implications-providing-family-care.

Finkelstein, Amy, and Kathleen McGarry. 2006. "Multiple Dimensions of Private Information: Evidence from the Long-Term Care Insurance Market." *American Economic Review* 96 (4): 938–958. https://doi.org/10.1257/aer.96.4.938.

Genworth. 2021. "Cost of Care Survey." July 21, 2021. https://www.genworth.com/aging-and-you/finances/cost-of-care.html.

Gleckman, Howard. 2019. "A Shortage of Paid Caregivers Is Raising the Cost of Home Care." *Forbes*, October 18, 2019. https://www.forbes.com/sites/howardgleckman/2019/10/18/a-shortage-of-paid-caregivers-is-raising-the-cost-of-homecare/.

Jang, Soong-Nang, Mauricio Avendano, and Ichiro Kawachi. 2012. "Informal Caregiving Patterns in Korea and European Countries: A Cross-National Comparison." *Asian Nursing Research* 6 (1): 19–26. https://doi.org/10.1016/j.anr.2012.02.002.

Johnson, Richard W., and Anthony T. Lo Sasso. 2006. "The Impact of Elder Care on Women's Labor Supply." *INQUIRY: The Journal of Health Care Organization, Provision, and Financing* 43 (3): 195–210. https://www.jstor.org/stable/29773256.

Kemper, Peter, Harriet L. Komisar, and Lisa Alecxih. 2005. "Long-Term Care over an Uncertain Future: What Can Current Retirees Expect?" *INQUIRY: The Journal of Health Care Organization, Provision, and Financing* 42 (4): 335–350. https://doi.org/10.5034/inquiryjrnl_42.4.335. Accessed on June 03, 2022.

Matthews, Kevin A., Wei Xu, Anne H. Gaglioti, James B. Holt, Janet B. Croft, Dominic Mack, and Lisa C. McGuire. 2019. "Racial and Ethnic Estimates of Alzheimer's Disease and Related Dementias in the United States (2015–2060) in Adults Aged ≥65 Years." *Alzheimer's & Dementia* 15 (1): 17–24. https://doi.org/10.1016/j.jalz.2018.06.3063. Accessed on June 03, 2022.

McGarry, Kathleen M. 1998. "Caring for the Elderly: The Role of Adult Children." In *Inquiries in the Economics of Aging*, edited by David A. Wise, 133–166. The Economics of Aging. Chicago: University of Chicago Press. https://www.nber.org/books-and-chapters/inquiries-economics-aging/caring-elderly-role-adult-children.

OECD. 2019. *Health at a Glance 2019: OECD Indicators*. Health at a Glance. Paris: OECD Publishing. https://doi.org/10.1787/4dd50c09-en.

Pinquart, Martin, and Silvia Sörensen. 2005. "Ethnic Differences in Stressors, Resources, and Psychological Outcomes of Family Caregiving: A Meta-Analysis." *The Gerontologist* 45 (1): 90–106. https://doi.org/10.1093/geront/45.1.90.

Redfoot, Donald, Lynn Feinberg, and Ari Houser. 2013. "The Aging of the Baby Boom and the Growing Care Gap: A Look at Future Declines in the Availability of Family Caregivers." 85. Insight on the Issues. Washington, DC: AARP Public Policy Institute. https://www.aarp.org/content/dam/aarp/research/public_policy_institute/ltc/2013/baby-boom-and-the-growing-care-gap-insight-AARP-ppi-ltc.pdf.

Rote, Sunshine M., and Heehyul Moon. 2018. "Racial/Ethnic Differences in Caregiving Frequency: Does Immigrant Status Matter?" *The Journals of Gerontology Series B: Psychological Sciences and Social Sciences* 73 (6): 1088–1098. https://doi.org/10.1093/geronb/gbw106.

U.S. Bureau of Labor Statistics. 2017. "Unpaid Eldercare in the United States—2015-16: Data from the American Time Use Survey." News Release USDL-17-1292. Washington, DC: U.S. Department of Labor. https://www.bls.gov/news.release/archives/elcare_09202017.pdf.

Van Houtven, Courtney Harold, Norma B. Coe, and Meghan M. Skira. 2013. "The Effect of Informal Care on Work and Wages." *Journal of Health Economics* 32 (1): 240–252. https://doi.org/10.1016/j.jhealeco.2012.10.006.

PART IV

Politics and Policy

Where Population Aging Meets Rising Inequality

11

Working Longer in an Age of Rising Economic Inequality

Gary Burtless[1]

1. Introduction

As the populations of rich countries grow older, voters and political leaders increasingly worry their societies will find it hard to support a rising number of older men and women. When the percentage of a population past age 65 rises, the cost of paying for public pensions and health insurance will also rise. One way to reduce the financial cost of an aging population is to change workers' retirement expectations and behavior by encouraging them to delay their exit from the workforce and postpone claiming a pension. Indeed, most the world's richest countries have reformed their public pension systems to curtail future outlays, often raising the entitlement age for an early or full pension (OECD 2007, 2017).

For society as a whole, a higher eligibility age for pensions is a plausible partial solution to the fiscal challenge posed by an aging population. It does not follow that delaying retirement is a feasible or desirable response for every worker who faces a higher pension eligibility age. Even if life expectancy is rising and average population health in old age is improving, some workers do not benefit from either trend. Lower-income and less-educated Americans have seen smaller gains in life expectancy compared with higher-income and better-educated Americans. Furthermore, some workers past age 55 face real hardship finding or keeping a job. Even though age discrimination laws theoretically give older workers equal access to well-paid jobs for which they are qualified, U.S. employers are much more likely to offer job interviews to younger applicants than to older applicants who have the same qualifications (Neumark 2018). This means that older unemployed workers must look for jobs longer and often with less success than younger workers who have the same credentials. For a 63-year-old worker who is dismissed from her job or who experiences a chronic disease, it is little comfort to know that improvements in longevity and health have *on average* increased the span of years in which it is feasible to work. In many individual cases, delayed retirement is difficult or impossible. In sum, even if working longer is a sensible solution to the society-wide challenge of population aging, it is not necessarily a feasible strategy for older people who face formidable barriers to remaining employed.

In the United States, population aging has coincided with a sharp increase in earnings inequality, which eventually affects the distribution of income received by retired adults. That is because Social Security benefits and workplace pensions are ultimately determined by breadwinners' covered wages during their working years. Social Security payments and other defined-benefit pensions are explicitly linked to prior wages through benefit formulas. Families' retirement savings are affected by breadwinners' capacity to set aside part of their earnings in a retirement nest egg. Workers who earn high wages or who remain steadily employed for many years are more likely to accumulate a big nest egg than workers who earn less.

It is plausible that widening inequality among wage earners and working-age families will translate into worsening inequality among the population past working age. This depends in part on the generosity of the social safety net in protecting the incomes of low-income older adults. It also depends on the willingness and capacity of breadwinners to work longer in order to offset the effect of low or erratic earnings when they were younger. The trend toward later retirement may itself contribute to rising old-age inequality if it is concentrated among breadwinners with more schooling and higher preretirement earnings, in other words, among those most likely to accumulate a sizeable nest egg. Although retirement delays have occurred among workers with limited formal education as well as among those with advanced degrees, in absolute terms, the increase in old-age employment has been bigger among workers who have more schooling (Burtless and Gary 2013). This means the increase in old-age earnings has added more to the incomes of older Americans who would have been affluent, even without later retirement.

In this chapter, I consider how the trend toward working longer has affected inequality, both within the population over age 65 and between the populations over 65 and under 65. Using wage and income data from administrative sources and household surveys as well as the findings of previous research, I describe trends in the well-being of older Americans compared with younger Americans and evaluate the link between retirement trends and income inequality among over-65s. Interpreting the raw data is not always straightforward. Popular income measures are incomplete, and some important sources of old-age income are very poorly reported in household surveys. What can the existing data tell us about the distribution of economic well-being, both within the older population and across older and younger groups? How has later retirement affected these trends? And how are current trends likely to affect the economic status of tomorrow's elderly, especially the retirees who struggled economically during their working years?

I find that, on average, the economic well-being of Americans age 65 and older improved considerably from the mid-1960s through 2019. Poverty rates fell, median incomes rose, and the income gap between adults under age 65 and those over 65 shrank. Social safety net programs for retirees, especially Social Security, have helped to protect the incomes of low-income older adults, improving both their absolute incomes compared to earlier generations and their relative economic position compared with low-income families headed by working-age breadwinners.

Conclusions about economic trends rely on accurate measurement of incomes. Unfortunately, U.S. income data are far from perfect, and the problems with income data have different implications for the young and the old. I find that the positive trends in the relative incomes of older adults are more evident when we use better measures of income than the standard money income statistics on which much research relies.

Not all older adults have benefited equally from improvements in average economic well-being. Economic inequality among older Americans has increased, though it has increased more slowly among over-65s than among under-65s. Social Security and means-tested government transfers compress the income distribution among older adults. Incomes from workplace pensions and savings, however, are closely linked to career earnings and have tended to boost old-age inequality as earnings inequality has grown. Trends toward working longer also increase old-age earnings inequality. Disparities in life expectancy between the rich and the poor have risen in parallel with rising income inequality. Notwithstanding the social protection and universal health insurance available to low-income older Americans, the accumulated effects of inequality in earlier stages of life may be denying low-income seniors full participation in the trend toward a longer, healthier old age.

Though the absolute and relative well-being of older adults has improved, even at the bottom of the distribution, there are several reasons for concern. First, the money income gains in the middle and at the top of the old-age income distribution have been fueled by increases in earnings from working longer and larger accumulations in workplace retirement plans. Low-income older adults have so far derived little benefit from these trends. Further, some of the apparent gains of low- and middle-income older adults come with an asterisk, since they are the result of steadily climbing outlays on health care. If one is skeptical of the value of the extra health spending, one may doubt whether the well-being of low- and middle-income older adults has improved as much as the statistics imply. Finally, the money income of low-income older adults has risen in large measure because Social Security pensions have been protected. If Congress does not fix Social Security funding problems, leading to cutbacks in future benefits, low- and middle-income older adults will be particularly vulnerable, because so much of their retirement income is derived from this critical source.

2. The Economic Well-Being of Older Americans Has Improved

The real incomes and living standards of older Americans have improved over the past 20, 40, and 60 years. In absolute terms, the income poverty rate of older adults has fallen and their median incomes have improved. In relative terms, the income gains of middle-income older households have substantially outpaced the gains experienced by middle-income, working-age households. Improvements in economic well-being among older adults have been driven by increases in the real value of Social Security pensions, the maturation of workplace retirement programs, broadening insurance protection under Medicare and Medicaid, improvements in average health status, and, in the decades since 1990, rising employment rates and increases in the real earned incomes of older Americans. In the recent past, rising earned

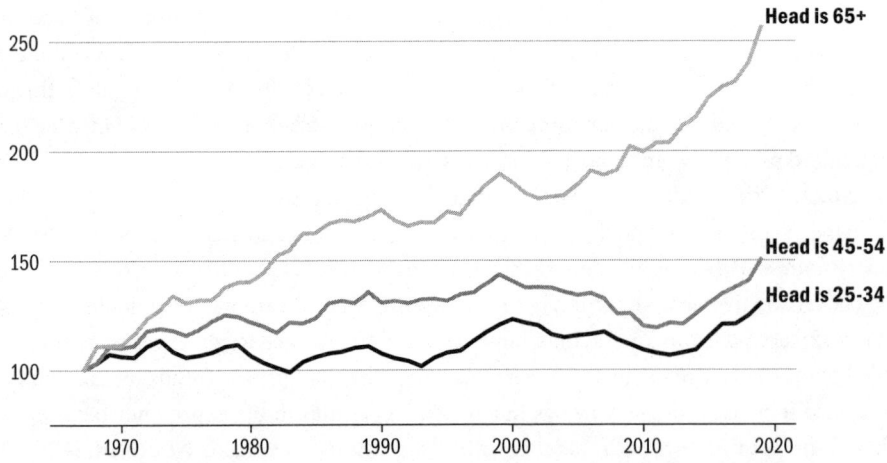

FIGURE 11.1 Trends in median real income of households headed by young, middle-aged, and older adults, 1967–2019
Real median income in 1967 = 100
Note: Census Bureau estimates of median income within each age group are converted into 2019 constant dollars using the CPI-U-RS price deflator.
Source: Author's calculations based on U.S. Census Bureau (2020) tabulations of March CPS and ASEC files.

incomes and increasing annual payouts from workplace retirement plans have been important drivers of the rising real incomes of the nation's middle- and high-income adults over age 65 (Bosworth and Burke 2012; Bee and Mitchell 2017). It is uncertain whether these positive trends will continue for future cohorts, as I discuss below.

In combination, these trends have helped boost the average well-being of older adults. Figure 11.1 shows the trends in median real income in households headed by young, middle-aged, and older householders. Between 1967 and 2019, the median income of households headed by the oldest adults increased faster than the incomes of other age groups. The median income of households headed by someone age 65 or older increased 156 percent compared with increases of 51 percent in households headed by someone between 45 and 54 and just 31 percent in households headed by an adult between 25 and 34. To be sure, the median income of the oldest households remains below those of most other age groups. However, households maintained by older adults are smaller than those maintained by working-age heads. This means smaller incomes are needed to achieve the same income per family member.

The economic fortunes of older Americans near the bottom of the distribution have also improved. In 1959, when the official poverty rate was first calculated, the poverty rate for Americans past age 65 was over 35 percent, far higher than that of any other age group. By 1970 it had dropped to 25 percent. By 2019 the poverty rate for over-65s was less than 9 percent, lower than that of 18- to 64-year-old adults and more than 5 percentage points below that of children under 18 (Semega et al. 2020).

3. Unequal Gains

Though the broad picture of economic well-being among today's older Americans is encouraging, compared both to earlier generations and to the situation of today's younger adults, in recent decades the distribution of income gains among older adults has been unequal. For example, the trend toward later exit from the workforce has lifted the incomes of some older adults, but far from all of them. The maturation of workplace retirement programs has boosted the average income of Americans past age 65, but this development has conferred little benefit on retirees who were in the bottom half of the earnings distribution when they were at work. Relatively few workers in this part of the earnings distribution are enrolled in retirement plans, so few of them accumulate pension rights or much of a retirement nest egg while at work.

American workers who earn low wages continue to receive crucial protection under Social Security and public health insurance. Unlike the situation in the first 35 years after World War II, however, neither Social Security nor Medicare is nowadays growing much more generous. In fact, the 1983 Social Security amendments gradually raised the age at which workers can claim an unreduced pension from 65 for workers born before 1938 to 67 for those born in 1960 and later years. For workers claiming retirement benefits at the earliest eligibility age, 62, this reform effectively reduced the annual pension by 12.5 percent compared with what it would have been under the old formula. Despite the increase in the age for full retirement benefits, the average monthly payment to retirees continues to increase slowly, reflecting the slow rise in workers' career earnings and the decision by many retirees to claim benefits at a later age. One major concern is the future funding of public pensions. The Social Security Trust Funds are expected to be depleted by 2035. If that occurs and Congress does not change the current law, benefits will be cut by an additional 20 percent for all beneficiaries.

The comparatively good news for older Americans comes against a backdrop of rising income inequality. Between 1979 and 2019, Census analysts estimate that the Gini coefficient of income inequality increased from 0.365 to 0.454, or about 0.5 percent a year among all U.S. families. However, inequality has increased much more rapidly among working-age families than among older families. Between 1979 and 2012, the Gini coefficient for family income inequality increased by about 0.9 percent a year among families headed by a person under 62 and by 0.3 percent a year among families headed by someone 62 or older (Bosworth, Burtless, and Zhang 2016). In 1979, inequality was substantially higher among families with an older householder than among younger families; by 2012, however, the situation was reversed. Census statistics on family income suggest that since 2012 income inequality among working-age families has remained roughly unchanged while money income inequality in families headed by older adults has continued to edge up. Nonetheless, the Gini coefficient of income inequality remains slightly lower among older families than among families headed by someone below age 65.

4. Career Earnings Inequality Has Risen

One source of income inequality in old age is inequality during breadwinners' working years. Gaps in earned incomes translate in retirement into gaps in pensions, in private retirement savings, and in Social Security benefits. Both annual labor earnings and hourly wages grew increasingly unequal after 1979, with much faster rates of annual gain among top earners compared with workers in the middle and at the bottom of the distribution (Burtless 1995; Acemoglu and Autor 2011).

More relevant to retirement security, however, is inequality in earnings over a longer span of years, say, over workers' entire 35- or 40-year working careers. Recent analysis of the Social Security earnings files by Guvenen et al. (2017) makes it plain that the trend in lifetime earned income inequality has mirrored the trend in annual earnings inequality. Career workers with low earned incomes have seen much slower improvement in their lifetime earnings than workers with a high rank in the distribution. Guvenen and his colleagues calculated the total, inflation-adjusted wages of earners in their sample over a 31-year career that begins at age 25. The oldest cohort in the data attained age 25 in 1957; the youngest reached 25 in

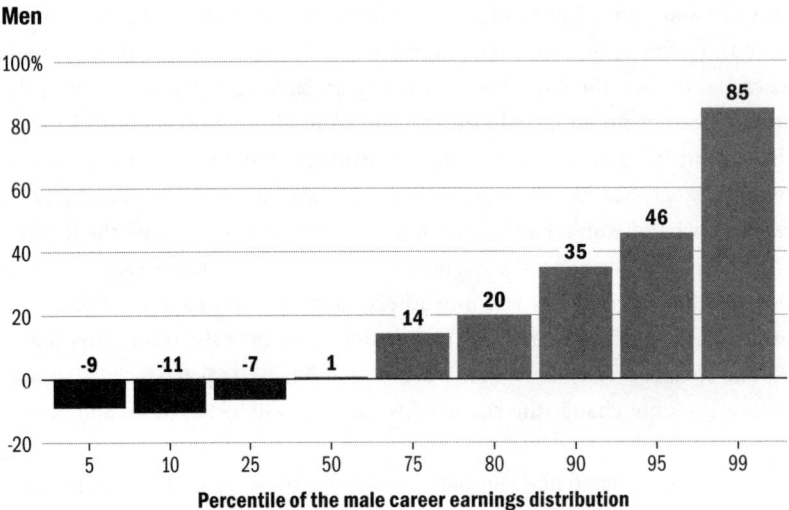

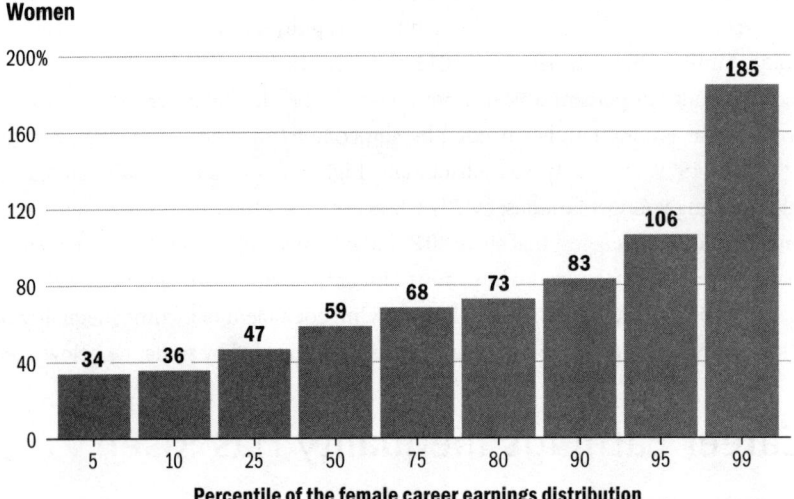

FIGURE 11.2 Percent change in real career earnings between cohorts who entered the workforce in 1957 and 1983
By position in the earnings distribution
Note: Career earnings consist of wage and salary income earned between ages 25 and 55 and converted to constant dollars using the PCE deflator. For a worker entering the workforce in 1957, career earnings consist of wages earned from 1957 through 1987.
Source: Author's calculations based on Guvenen et al. (2017) Tables A.1 and A.2.

1983 and turned 55 in 2013. Figure 11.2 shows how real career earnings changed at selected points in the career earnings distribution between the 1957 and 1983 cohorts. The top panel shows changes for men; the lower panel shows changes for women. Among men at the 50th percentile, real career earnings increased just 1 percent. At lower points in the distribution, real career earnings actually fell. In contrast, career earnings improved in the top half of the male distribution. At the 99th percentile, real wages for top male earners increased 85 percent. Women fared better than men. Even at the bottom of the female distribution, real career earnings improved over time, because women's real wages increased and women spent more years in paid employment.

In one respect the pattern of earnings gains for women and men is identical. Earners at the top of the female distribution enjoyed much faster income gains than earners in the middle and at the bottom. The shrinking earnings gap between women and men means that career earnings inequality among all workers, including both sexes combined, increased more slowly than inequality among either sex viewed separately. At the top of the distribution, however, the outsize earnings gains of high-ranking men and women have clearly driven up inequality. The rise in earnings inequality is the best known and documented source of increased income inequality. The analysis of Guvenen et al. shows the rise is not solely due to wider earnings disparities in a single year but is also evident in rising inequality across workers' full careers. Because workers' saving capacity and pension accumulations are closely linked to how much they earn over a career, this kind of earnings dispersion will carry over into wider disparities in old-age income.

5. Implications for Old-Age Inequality

If workers' retirement incomes depended solely on their earnings between 25 and 55 and if there were a strict proportional relationship between career earnings and retirement income, the notable rise in career earnings disparities would have major implications for the inequality of retirement incomes of American workers reaching their 60s. The availability of Social Security and means-tested benefits, however, has tempered the rise of inequality at the bottom of the distribution.

5.1. Social Security Decreases Inequality

A major source of old-age income is Social Security retirement and survivor benefits. For low-income older Americans, Social Security payments account for three-quarters or more of total cash income. The benefit formula used to calculate workers' basic pension is based on workers' average career earnings. While higher-earning workers receive higher Social Security benefits, the monthly pension replaces a much higher *percentage* of lower-earning workers' earnings.[2] The benefit formula at least partly protects the retirement incomes of the workers who earn low wages. Because the benefit formula is linked to average wages and because average wages have climbed faster than the wages of low earners, a rising proportion of low earners' wages are replaced at the most favorable rate in the benefit formula.

One feature of the benefit formula is advantageous to high-income recipients. Workers receive higher monthly benefits for every year they delay claiming (up to age 70). For example, workers born between 1943 and 1954 were entitled to claim their full Social Security pension when they reached age 66, the so-called full retirement age. If instead they claimed their pensions at 62, their monthly benefit was cut 25 percent below the basic pension. If they delayed claiming until they were 70, their monthly benefit would be increased 32 percent above the basic pension available at the full retirement age. This formula offers workers an upward adjustment of between 6.5 percent and 8.3 percent in monthly benefits for every one-year delay in claiming. For workers with average and above-average life expectancy, this is a good deal (Shoven and Slavov 2013). However, only about 6 percent of claimants wait until 70 to claim benefits (Social Security Administration 2020, Table 6.B5.1). Those who do postpone benefit claiming typically are able to work longer or have enough liquid resources to pay for consumption while they wait for their pension to begin (Bosworth, Burtless, and Zhang 2016, Figure II–5). Low-wage workers postpone benefit claiming less often than workers with higher incomes, since they tend to stop working earlier than better-paid workers. In addition, many low-wage workers lack the liquidity or savings to postpone collecting pensions after they stop working. By taking advantage of the favorable terms available to pensioners who delay benefit claiming, higher-income workers are partially undoing the redistributive tilt of the basic monthly benefit formula, which itself is highly favorable to low-wage workers. Nonetheless, the distribution of monthly Social Security retirement pensions is far more compressed than the distribution of average lifetime monthly earnings.

5.2. Pensions and Savings Increase Inequality

In addition to Social Security, retirees also receive income from workplace pensions, make withdrawals from workplace saving plans and IRAs, and draw down savings accumulated outside of retirement plans. It seems reasonable to expect that growing inequality in earnings during workers' prime working years will be reflected in greater inequality in retirement savings and the old-age consumption financed by these savings.

About 55 percent of American workers participate in a workplace retirement plan (U.S. Bureau of Labor Statistics 2020, Table 2). Participation rates are higher for workers further up the wage distribution. The past 40 years have seen a sharp trend away from defined-benefit (DB) pension plans and toward defined-contribution (DC) or 401(k)-style plans. One crucial distinction between the two kinds of plan is that DB pensions are guaranteed by the employer, who bears the risk that the contributions might be too small or the rate of return on investments too low to pay for promised benefits. In a DC plan, the employer guarantees only a schedule of contributions, often linked to the worker's own voluntary contributions. The risk of poor investment outcomes is borne by the employee, not the employer. Nonetheless, DB pensions are not always the better choice for low-wage workers. DB pensions can be attractive to workers who are confident they will enjoy long careers in the same firm. For workers who have a sequence of short-duration jobs, a sensibly designed DC plan holds greater promise of delivering decent income in old age.

The distinction between DB and DC plans is important because the shift away from DB plans and toward DC plans occurred at the same time as the long-term rise in wage inequality. In 1979, 84 percent of private-sector workers covered by an employer pension were enrolled in a traditional DB plan, possibly in combination with a supplementary DC plan. Just 16 percent of pension-covered private employees were enrolled solely in a DC plan. By

2011, the fraction of private-sector workers enrolled in a retirement plan who were enrolled solely in a DC plan had soared to 69 percent, while less than a third of pension-covered workers in the private sector were enrolled in a DB plan, possibly in combination with a supplementary DC plan (Burtless and Koepcke 2018).

Worker decision-making now plays a much bigger role in determining the value of retirement plan accumulations when workers reach old age. Workers enrolled in 401(k)-type plans must decide whether to save in the plan, how much of their pay to contribute to it, how to allocate their savings across different investment options, and how quickly or slowly to make withdrawals from their account balances when they retire. If workers lack the knowledge, discipline, or capacity to make good decisions, they will reach old age with too little savings to enjoy a comfortable retirement. Because higher-wage workers are more likely than lower-wage workers to have access to pension and savings plans at work and to be able to contribute regularly to them, well-paid workers tend to accumulate much bigger nest eggs than poorly paid workers.

5.3. Means-Tested Programs Are Too Narrow to Reduce Inequality Very Much

Retired workers without many resources may qualify for assistance under Supplemental Security Income (SSI), the Supplemental Nutrition Assistance Program (SNAP), and other means-tested programs. SSI applicants over age 65 who have no other income and meet the program's asset test can collect monthly cash benefits worth about 75 percent of the poverty line ($794 per month in 2021) for a single individual and 81 percent of the poverty line ($1,191 per month) for a couple. Payments are higher in the minority of states that top up the basic federal benefit. In combination with SNAP benefits, the total amount of means-tested benefits available to otherwise destitute older people might bring their monthly incomes close to the U.S. poverty line. About 4 percent of the nation's over-65s collect SSI. Unfortunately, many indigent older adults do not meet the SSI program's strict asset test. Single people with more than $2,000 in countable assets and couples with more than $3,000 are excluded from the program. If the SSI asset limits had been increased to reflect price inflation since the inception of the program, they would be about four times higher than their current level. In view of the strict asset limits and the reluctance of many older Americans to apply for government assistance, SSI is not a very effective antipoverty program. While SNAP benefits are not as generous as SSI, they are received by a larger fraction of older adults (about 7 percent), in part because the program has a more lenient asset test.

6. More Accurate Measures of Income and Well-being

As noted, the Census statistics on median income and poverty show clear improvement in the economic status of older Americans, both absolutely and relative to younger groups. The statistics have limitations, however. The first problem is conceptual. The Census Bureau's definition of money income provides an incomplete picture of families' capacity to consume out of their current resources. A second problem is underreporting of income. Both problems are likely to produce biased statistics on the absolute well-being of older adults, the relative status of older and younger adults, and income inequality among older adults.

6.1. Money Income and Its Limitations

The conceptual problems of the Census Bureau's definition of money income have long been known. The Bureau's definition counts cash payments to households in the form of wages, net self-employment earnings, interest, dividends, pensions and withdrawals from workplace retirement plans, and cash government transfer benefits. The measure focuses on gross (pretax) money flows. It makes no adjustment for the income and payroll taxes paid by respondents (and typically withheld from their pay). It does not count the flow of housing services that homeowners derive from occupying a dwelling that they own. Nor does the money income definition reflect costly employer fringe benefits, such as employer-sponsored health insurance, which are valuable to most workers. Finally, the Census definition excludes the value of noncash government benefits, including Medicare, Medicaid, SNAP, and housing assistance.

These omissions seriously bias any assessment of the relative well-being of older and younger adults or of higher and lower earners. Compared to younger Americans, older adults benefit more from public health insurance programs, have higher rates of homeownership, and are more likely to own their homes free and clear of a mortgage, which reduces their cost of housing. The exclusion of noncash fringe benefits leads to an understatement of the total compensation received by workers who have generous benefit plans. The omission of SNAP and housing assistance benefits leads to an understatement of the resources available to low-income families, regardless of the age of the head. On balance, the omissions produce a bigger understatement of the resources available to families headed by an older adult (Bosworth, Burtless, and Anders 2007; Burtless and Svaton 2010). Under the Census Bureau's money income definition, older households have lower incomes than working-age households. Under more comprehensive income definitions, the gap shrinks or even reverses.

6.2. Misreporting Income

Respondents do not always report their income accurately on household surveys. No one expects perfection, of course, but we can hope that response errors will be similar over time and comparable in magnitude across different categories of income and different classes of respondent. There is mounting evidence this is not the case for some of the nation's most important income surveys (Meyer, Mok, and Sullivan 2015). Census Bureau analysts recently compared income reports of CPS respondents with reports of the same five data items recorded in Social Security Administration (SSA) and IRS administrative files (Bee and Mitchell 2017). The analysis is especially relevant here, because it focuses on income items of special relevance to older Americans, namely, earned incomes (wages and net self-employment earnings), Social Security benefits, SSI payments, interest and dividends, and income from retirement plans. Bee and Mitchell found that income reports from respondents between ages 18 and 64 were far more accurate than those from respondents over age 65 because a larger percentage of younger respondents' total income was derived from labor earnings, an item that is accurately reported by both younger and older respondents. Sources that comprise a larger fraction of old-age income—including SSI benefits, interest and dividends, and workplace retirement plans—were severely underreported by both young and old respondents. As a result, reporting errors produce a larger understatement of income for older than for younger adults.

Using corrected income information, the Gini coefficient of old-age income inequality increases about 3 percent. Despite the small rise in inequality, the estimated old-age poverty rate declines about 2 percentage points, falling from 9.0 percent when the poverty rate is estimated using the original CPS responses to 6.9 percent when incorrect data are replaced with information from SSA and IRS records. Thus, estimated hardship is lower even though estimated inequality is slightly greater.

According to the Census Bureau analysis, the most important source of error in measuring old-age incomes is misreporting of income from workplace retirement plans. This is unfortunate, because national income statistics suggest the taxable payouts from workplace retirement plans are both rising over time and considerably larger than the benefit payouts from Social Security (Burtless and Koepcke 2018). Figure 11.3 compares Social Security and workplace retirement plan income across the income distribution. The dark bars show average 2012 income amounts reported by respondents to the CPS survey. The lighter bars use more accurate information from SSA and IRS records. The misreporting errors for Social Security are small, as noted above. The errors are much bigger in the case of income derived from workplace retirement plans, especially among more affluent workers. In the 4th quintile, for instance, survey respondents report receiving $13,000 from retirement plans, which is substantially less than the $21,400 they report receiving from Social Security. The

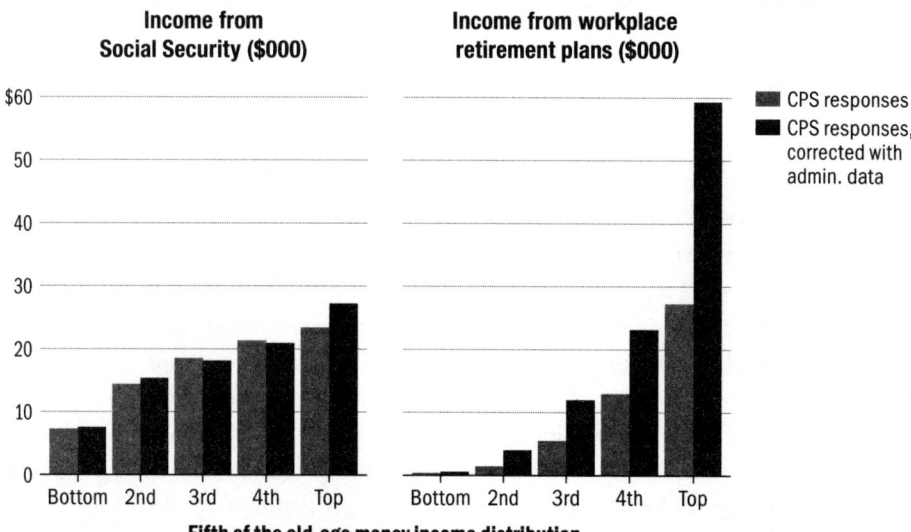

FIGURE 11.3 Social Security and retirement income reported on CPS and in administrative records for Americans 65 and older
Income from indicated source in 2012 ($000)
Note: "CPS responses" are derived from the Annual Social and Economic Supplement of the Current Population Survey.
Source: Bee and Mitchell (2017) and author's calculations.

IRS records suggest adults in this quintile on average received $21,300 from workplace retirement accounts, or slightly *more* than they collected in Social Security benefits ($20,900).

The corrected income estimates displayed in Figure 11.3 show that private retirement benefits are vastly more unequally distributed than Social Security. The average reported Social Security benefit in the top income group is 3.6 times the average Social Security benefit reported in the bottom group. In contrast, the average payout from workplace retirement plans in the top income group is almost $60,000, more than 100 times the size of the average payout in the bottom income group. Clearly, workplace savings plans play a much bigger role in supplying income to older middle- and high-income families than implied by household survey statistics.

Both the CPS responses and corrected information from the IRS and SSA files show that Social Security benefits are the most important single source of money income for families in the bottom three-fifths of the old-age income distribution. They are overwhelmingly dependent on the benefits they receive from Social Security. If benefits in that program were cut, these families would suffer the biggest proportional income losses.

6.3. Relative Status of Older Adults under More Comprehensive Income Measures

The corrected numbers just described refer solely to families' cash incomes. They ignore the contributions to well-being of home ownership, good health insurance, and other in-kind benefits. More than 75 percent of Americans over age 65 own the dwelling they live in. Virtually all of the population past 65 is covered by generously subsidized Medicare, and a large percentage of low-income older adults is also insured under Medicaid. When the values of these omitted items are included in the definition of income, the pretax incomes of Americans up and down the income distribution tend to rise. In many cases, the income increase is sizeable. Using data from the Health and Retirement Survey (HRS), Bosworth, Burtless, and Zhang (2016, Figure III–2) calculated measures of family income under a standard income definition similar to that used by the Census Bureau and under a comprehensive measure that included the value of health insurance and the annuitized value of income flows from the family's wealth holdings. They found that older Americans at the bottom of the distribution see smaller proportional drops in income after they reach age 65 than do people who are further up the distribution. They also found that between 1997 and 2011, the economic gap between people over age 65 and those aged 55 to 64 diminished, with the largest improvements in relative well-being toward the bottom of the old-age income distribution. The relative improvement in the economic status of low-income older adults is even greater when we use a comprehensive income definition to measure it.

The increasing value of health insurance helps to explain these trends. The dollar value of good health insurance has increased over time as health care costs have risen. For people entitled to a small Social Security pension, it is quite likely that the expected dollar cost of providing Medicare is greater than the dollar cost of the pension. The dollar cost of providing health insurance rises with the age of the insured, so when we add the value of health insurance to our estimate of family income, we tend to raise the incomes of older compared with younger adults, even when the two populations are covered by identical insurance policies.

The U.S. safety net provides generous health protection to older adults that it does not provide to most younger adults.

There are two caveats to these positive trends. First, *absolute* living standards of older Americans toward the bottom of the distribution may still be poor even as their *relative* incomes improve. Second, as noted above, working-age adults at the bottom of the income scale have experienced meager gains in their earned incomes (and among low-income men, actual losses) compared with earlier generations (Guvenen et al. 2017). The relative income gains of low-income older adults therefore reflect both positive trends among older cohorts and adverse trends among younger cohorts.

6.4. Shifting Position of Over-65s in the Income Distribution

Under a comprehensive income definition, older Americans have moved up in the overall income distribution during the past 40 years. The Congressional Budget Office (CBO) has combined taxable income reports, data from the CPS, and administrative records to measure household income (CBO 2014, Appendix). Its estimates begin in 1979, just before the onset of the rising tide in U.S. inequality. I use CBO's most comprehensive definition of households' after-tax income. It includes most of the noncash benefits that are excluded from the Census money definition, such as estimates of employer contributions to employees' health insurance plans and estimates of the value of government subsidies to people who are insured under Medicaid and Medicare, although it excludes the value of housing services derived from homeownership.[3]

When incomes are measured using this definition, what percentage of older adults can be found in different parts of the overall income distribution? Figure 11.4 displays evidence on this question for 1979 and 2017, the first and last years covered by CBO's analysis. The chart shows the percentage of Americans 65 and older who are in each of the five quintiles of the overall income distribution. In the figure, people are ranked by their household's income under CBO's most comprehensive income definition. One-fifth of the total population is placed in each quintile based on that definition. The figure shows the percentage of people age 65 and older who are in each quintile. In 1979, 28 percent of older adults were in the bottom income category; 23 percent were in the next-lowest quintile. Older adults were underrepresented in the top three quintiles. By 2017, the percentage of older adults in the bottom quintile plunged, falling from 28 percent to just 13 percent. By contrast, the percentage in the top quintile increased from 18 percent to 25 percent.

The increased value of Social Security and publicly subsidized health insurance helps to explain the drop in the fraction of older adults who are in the bottom income quintiles. The rise in workplace retirement benefits and old-age earnings helps to account for the rising representation of older adults in the top income categories. Of course, the statistics in Figure 11.4 reflect changes in older Americans' incomes *relative* to those of the general population. According to the CBO estimates, the incomes of households in all parts of the income distribution have improved over time. Under its most comprehensive income definition, among Americans of all ages, real income adjusted for family size increased 67 percent in the bottom one-fifth between 1979 and 2017, and it increased 55 percent in the next one-fifth.

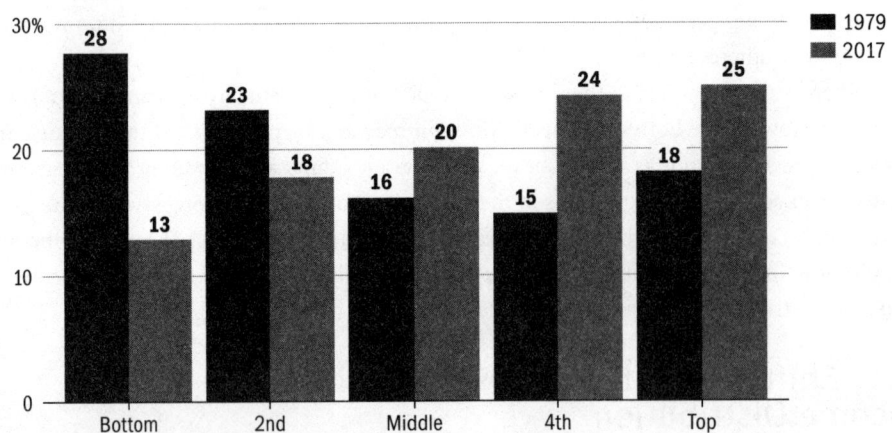

FIGURE 11.4 Percent of the population past age 65 in each fifth of the U.S. income distribution under CBO's comprehensive income definition, 1979 and 2017
Percent of persons 65 and older
Source: Author's calculations based on Congressional Budget Office (2020).

Net incomes rose even faster among households in the top 10 percent and especially among those in the top 1 percent, increasing by 137 percent and 253 percent, respectively. Not only did real incomes at the bottom of the distribution rise, but the position of low-income older adults improved compared with that of working-age adults and children.

Some observers may object that part of the relative improvement in the position of older adults is a byproduct of rising health care costs. It may not reflect any genuine improvement in the relative well-being of older Americans, especially those with low incomes. Low-income older adults may look better off because the government pays more for their health care, not because their health or economic well-being has improved in line with the more expensive subsidies for their health insurance. Further up in the distribution, this cannot explain the relative gains of older adults, because the increase in health insurance subsidies explains very little of their income gains. For the low-income elderly, however, a substantial share of the apparent improvement is traceable to the greater expense of government subsidies for their health care.

7. Future Prospects

The past 60 years have featured good news for most older Americans. Between 1960 and 2019, the real incomes of older adults improved both absolutely and relative to those of younger adults. The income poverty rate of over-65s likewise declined sharply, both absolutely and compared with rates seen among the under-65s. Health insurance coverage of older adults soared in the 1960s after enactment of Medicare and Medicaid, which provided low-income older adults better access to affordable health care than their working-age counterparts. Using comprehensive income measures and more reliable sources of information about personal income, the income gap between older and younger adults appears even smaller than it does when the gap is measured using traditional money income statistics.

However, as disparities in career earnings have increased, income inequality among older adults has grown, though more slowly than it has among families with a nonaged breadwinner. Pensions, savings, and income from working longer—all of which disproportionately benefit high earners—exacerbate income inequality among older Americans. Inequality would be even greater without Social Security, Medicare, and means-tested government transfers. These benefits compress inequality among over-65s much more than government programs do in the case of Americans under 65.

Income is important not so much in its own right but as an indicator of well-being. As the incomes of older adults have risen, we would anticipate that indicators of old-age health, especially old-age mortality, would have improved over time for rich and poor alike. While life expectancy has improved, and continues to do so for the population past 65, life expectancy has grown more unequal when we compare Americans with different educational attainments and in different parts of the income distribution. The life expectancies of better educated and higher income Americans have risen much faster than those of the less educated and less affluent (Bosworth, Burtless, and Zhang 2016; Chetty et al. 2016).

The differential trends in life expectancy, with much slower gains for low-income adults, should give us pause. Older Americans in the top half of the income distribution enjoy higher incomes and longer life spans than earlier generations at the same stage in life. It is less clear how much the well-being of low-income older adults has truly improved. Small increases in life expectancy among low-income Americans suggest that despite the social protection and universal health insurance available to low-income older Americans, the accumulated effects of inequality in earlier stages of life may be depriving low-income Americans of one of the key benefits of greater affluence.

One reason for pessimism about the future prospects of low-income older adults is the cloudy financial outlook facing Social Security and Medicare. Current forecasts suggest both programs will deplete their financial reserves before 2035. In the case of Social Security, the exhaustion of the program's reserves will mean all currently scheduled pensions, including those to low-income beneficiaries, will be cut about one-fifth when the reserves run out. Cutting benefits this much would dramatically reduce low-income beneficiaries' monthly incomes and significantly boost old-age inequality. For that reason, it is unlikely Congress will permit the cut to occur. It is more probable Congress will act before the reserve fund is exhausted and phase in gradual reforms that boost taxes and scale back future promised benefits. This can be accomplished without much risk to future low-earning workers. Early retirement benefits for low-wage workers who make steady Social Security contributions for 35 or 40 years could be left unchanged. Congress could trim benefits for other classes of retirees as needed in view of the tax hikes voters are willing to accept. While this comparatively benign outcome is certainly achievable, it is by no means certain. A key determinant of the well-being of the future elderly, especially the low-income elderly, thus depends on a political choice of U.S. leaders and voters.

Notes

1. The author gratefully acknowledges generous research support from the Alfred P. Sloan Foundation and helpful comments from John Shoven, Lisa Berkman, and especially Beth Truesdale on earlier

versions of this chapter. The views expressed are solely those of the author and do not represent those of the Sloan Foundation or the Brookings Institution.
2. For a retiree, the Social Security benefit formula is based on the highest 35 years of average indexed monthly earnings (AIME). For workers who reach the full retirement age in 2021, the formula for a basic pension at that age is as follows: 90 percent of the first $996 of AIME plus 32 percent of the AIME between $996 and $6,002 plus 15 percent of the AIME above $6,002.
3. CBO has published spreadsheet files summarizing its results and allowing users to perform analyses of its results: https://www.cbo.gov/system/files/2020-10/56575-table-builder.xlsm, accessed October 3, 2020.

References

Acemoglu, Daron, and David Autor. 2011. "Skills, Tasks and Technologies: Implications for Employment and Earnings." In *Handbook of Labor Economics*, edited by David Card and Orley Ashenfelter, 4b:1043–1171. Amsterdam: Elsevier. https://doi.org/10.1016/S0169-7218(11)02410-5.

Bee, Adam, and Joshua Mitchell. 2017. "Do Older Americans Have More Income Than We Think?" *Proceedings of the Annual Conference on Taxation and Minutes of the Annual Meeting of the National Tax Association* 110: 1–85. https://www.jstor.org/stable/26794437.

Bosworth, Barry, and Kathleen Burke. 2012. "Changing Sources of Income among the Aged Population." Working Paper 2012-27. Chestnut Hill, MA: Center for Retirement Research at Boston College. https://doi.org/10.2139/ssrn.2181632.

Bosworth, Barry, Gary Burtless, and Kan Zhang. 2016. *Later Retirement, Inequality in Old Age, and the Growing Gap in Longevity between Rich and Poor*. Economic Studies at Brookings. Washington, DC: The Brookings Institution. https://www.brookings.edu/wp-content/uploads/2016/02/BosworthBurtlessZhang_retirementinequalitylongevity.pdf.

Bosworth, Barry P., Gary Burtless, and Sarah E. Anders. 2007. "Capital Income Flows and the Relative Well-Being of America's Aged Population." Working Paper CRR WP 2007-21. Chestnut Hill, MA: Center for Retirement Research at Boston College. http://hdl.handle.net/2345/4367.

Burtless, Gary. 1995. "International Trade and the Rise in Earnings Inequality." *Journal of Economic Literature* 33 (2): 800–816. https://www.jstor.org/stable/2729029.

Burtless, Gary. 2013. "Who Is Delaying Retirement? Analyzing the Increase in Employment at Older Workers." In *Closing the Deficit: How Much Can Later Retirement Help?*, edited by Henry J. Aaron and Gary Burtless, 11–35. Washington, DC: The Brookings Institution.

Burtless, Gary, and Eric Koepcke. 2018. "The US Tax Preference for Retirement Savings." In *The Taxation of Pensions*, edited by Robert Holxmann and John Piggott, 257–295. Cambridge, MA: MIT Press.

Burtless, Gary, and Pavel Svaton. 2010. "Health Care, Health Insurance, and the Distribution of American Incomes." *Forum for Health Economics & Policy* 13 (1), 1–39. https://doi.org/10.2202/1558-9544.1194.

Chetty, Raj, Michael Stepner, Sarah Abraham, Shelby Lin, Benjamin Scuderi, Nicholas Turner, Augustin Bergeron, and David Cutler. 2016. "The Association between Income and Life Expectancy in the United States, 2001–2014." *JAMA* 315 (16): 1750–1766. https://doi.org/10.1001/jama.2016.4226.

Congressional Budget Office. 2014. "The Distribution of Household Income and Federal Taxes, 2011." Washington, DC: Congressional Budget Office. https://www.cbo.gov/publication/49440.

Congressional Budget Office. 2020. "The Distribution of Household Income, 2017." Washington, DC: Congress of the United States. https://www.cbo.gov/publication/56575.

Guvenen, Faith, Greg Kaplan, Jae Song, and Justin Weidner. 2017. "Lifetime Incomes in the United States over Six Decades." Working Paper w23371. Cambridge, MA: National Bureau of Economic Research. https://doi.org/10.3386/w23371. Accessed on June 02, 2022.

Meyer, Bruce D., Wallace K. C. Mok, and James X. Sullivan. 2015. "Household Surveys in Crisis." *Journal of Economic Perspectives* 29 (4): 199–226. https://doi.org/10.1257/jep.29.4.199.

Neumark, David. 2018. "Experimental Research on Labor Market Discrimination." *Journal of Economic Literature* 56 (3): 799–866. https://doi.org/10.1257/jel.20161309.

OECD. 2007. "A Decade of Pension Reforms: The Impact on Future Benefits." In *Pensions at a Glance 2007*, 55–75. OECD Pensions at a Glance. OECD. https://doi.org/10.1787/pension_glance-2007-4-en.

OECD. 2017. "Recent Pension Reforms." In *Pensions at a Glance 2017: OECD and G20 Indicators*, 15–40. Paris. https://doi.org/10.1787/pension_glance-2017-4-en.

Semega, Jessica, Melissa Kollar, Emily A Shrider, and John F Creamer. 2020. "Income and Poverty in the United States: 2019." P60-270. Current Population Reports. Washington, DC: U.S. Census Bureau. https://www.census.gov/library/publications/2020/demo/p60-270.html.

Shoven, John B., and Sita Nataraj Slavov. 2013. "Recent Changes in the Gains from Delaying Social Security." Working Paper 19370. NBER Working Paper Series. Cambridge, MA: National Bureau of Economic Research. https://doi.org/10.3386/w19370.

Social Security Administration. 2020. "Annual Statistical Supplement to the Social Security Bulletin." 13-11700. Washington, DC: Social Security Administration. https://www.ssa.gov/policy/docs/statcomps/supplement/2020/index.html.

U.S. Bureau of Labor Statistics. 2020. "National Compensation Survey: Employee Benefits in the United States, March 2020." Bulletin 2793. https://www.bls.gov/ncs/ebs/benefits/2020/employee-benefits-in-the-united-states-march-2020.pdf.

U.S. Census Bureau. 2020. "Table H-10. Age of Head of Household by Median and Mean Income." Historical Income Tables: Households. https://www.census.gov/data/tables/time-series/demo/income-poverty/historical-income-households.html.

12

How Does Social Security Reform Indecision Affect Younger Cohorts?

John B. Shoven, Sita Nataraj Slavov, and John G. Watson

1. Introduction

Social Security is the primary source of retirement income for many Americans. The Social Security Administration (2020) estimates that around half of married couples and 70 percent of singles receive at least half their retirement income from Social Security. The importance of Social Security is even greater for a significant minority of households: 21 percent of married couples and 45 percent of singles receive at least 90 percent of their retirement income from Social Security.

Most realistic estimates suggest that the Social Security trust fund will be exhausted by the early-to-mid 2030s.[1] Current law specifies that when the trust fund is exhausted, benefit payments must be restricted to available revenue. Options to accomplish this include cutting benefits across the board or delaying benefit payments.[2] The Social Security Trustees estimate that in 2035, the year in which they project the trust fund to be depleted, revenues will be sufficient to cover 79 percent of promised benefits (OASDI Board of Trustees 2020). However, some policy change is likely to be undertaken either before or at this date. Frequently discussed options include cutting benefits in a way that increases the system's progressivity, or raising payroll taxes, either across the board or at higher income levels. The funding shortfall could also be financed by issuing more debt, which could delay the tax increases or benefit cuts required to restore solvency to the system, perhaps beyond the lifetimes of today's adults.

Each of these policy options has direct implications for Americans' financial well-being. For example, our simulations suggest that an increase in the full retirement age (FRA) to 70 costs an average-earning woman $123,942 if she was born in 1970, and $147,750 if she was born in 1990. Other reforms have different distributional impacts across income groups and birth cohorts. The direct cost of the reforms required to close Social Security's financial shortfall is unavoidable. It can be distributed across different income groups and birth cohorts, but it must be paid sooner or later. In contrast, the main focus of our paper is on a cost that is entirely avoidable: the cost of government indecision regarding which reform to implement. That indecision creates uncertainty for young and middle-aged workers who are planning for retirement. An individual who assumes that a particular reform will occur—and is surprised by a different reform—has made a costly mistake. Knowing in advance which reform will be implemented allows for better planning and therefore has value. The government could resolve that indecision by deciding today what steps it will take to close Social Security's shortfall.

We aim to calculate the value of having accurate information about which Social Security reforms will be implemented in the future. We measure the value of early awareness by calculating the amount of money an individual requires at the policy start date to compensate for not knowing the policy in advance. That amount depends on an individual's birth cohort, gender, and earnings profile. For example, consider a woman born in 1975 with average earnings who plans for no policy changes but is surprised by a 20 percent cut in Social Security benefits in 2035. Now suppose the government instead announced in 2020 that the 20 percent benefit cut would occur 15 years in the future. We find that the value of becoming aware of the policy 15 years in advance is approximately $8,964 (measured in 2020 dollars) or about 1.52 times her average monthly earnings. This awareness value is distinct from the cost of the policy itself. The new policy—the 20 percent cut in benefits—directly reduces the individual's benefits by an annuitized equivalent of $128,106. However, if the policy remains in flux until it is actually implemented—and the individual operates under the mistaken assumption that there will be no change—then there is an additional indecision cost of $8,964. Although the early awareness value is modest compared to the direct impact of the reform, we emphasize that this cost is entirely avoidable (unlike the direct cost of the reform, which can only be redistributed).

A growing body of research examines how uncertainty over the form or timing of Social Security reforms affects the well-being of younger individuals (Bütler 1999; Benítez-Silva, Dwyer, and Sanderson 2006; Gomes, Kotlikoff, and Viceira 2012; Kitao 2014; Caliendo, Gorry, and Slavov 2019; Nelson 2020). The contribution of this chapter is to model the cost of indecision about specific, realistic reform plans in a simple and transparent way, providing illustrative calculations that can be helpful to individuals, financial planners, and policymakers. Individuals and financial planners can use the information to determine which mistakes are most costly or to rank changes that are most critical. Knowing the cost of indecision can prompt policymakers to act sooner to avoid that cost. Moreover, it can allow policymakers to assess the value of agreeing to a reform plan now versus hoping for a future political path to a more preferred reform. It can also help policymakers understand which types of indecision are most costly and how those costs are distributed across income groups and cohorts.

While the options to close Social Security's financial shortfall are relatively simple, decisions about how to distribute the cost are politically difficult, which makes policymakers reluctant to tackle the problem. Indeed, the Clinton, Bush, Obama, and Trump Administrations have already failed to deal with this matter. Our work suggests that government indecision is costly, and that a great deal has already been lost in not coming to grips with Social Security's financial shortfall 20 or more years ago. The problem was already known, and adjustments made decades ago would have been less sudden and allowed for a longer planning horizon. However, our work also suggests that there is still is an opportunity to take action before the Social Security trust fund becomes insolvent and thereby give Americans some time to prepare for the adjustments. At present, a generation of workers is facing increasing and unnecessary uncertainty about their retirement financing.

2. Current Law and Reform Options
2.1. Current Law

Social Security benefits are based on the average of the highest 35 years of earnings, indexed for economy-wide average wage growth through age 60. (Additional years of earnings count at their nominal value.) This measure, converted to a monthly amount by dividing by 12, is called average indexed monthly earnings (AIME). Monthly benefits are based on applying a progressive formula to AIME. That formula establishes two bend points, or thresholds, for AIME. If benefits are claimed at full retirement age (FRA, equal to 67 for the stylized individuals in our model), monthly Social Security benefits are 90 percent of AIME below the first bend point, 32 percent of AIME between the first and second bend points, and 15 percent of AIME above the second bend point. This amount is known as the primary insurance amount (PIA).[3] Cost-of-living adjustments are applied to PIA after age 62. These cost-of-living adjustments are based on the consumer price index for urban wage earners and clerical workers (CPI-W). Social Security taxes are based on covered earnings, or earnings below a taxable maximum (the "cap") that is also indexed for economy-wide wage growth. The total (employer plus employee) payroll tax rate for old age and survivors insurance (OASI) is 10.6 percent. Actuarial adjustments are applied to PIA to determine the monthly benefit amount for claims made either before (as early as 62) or after (as late as 70) FRA. For individuals in our model, claiming at age 62 results in a monthly benefit equal to 70 percent of PIA, and delaying to age 70 results in a monthly benefit equal to 124 percent of PIA.

What does this mean for Social Security benefits in dollar terms? To answer this question, we turn to the stylized earnings profiles that we use throughout this analysis. We construct these earnings profiles using the 2016 Outgoing Rotation Groups file from the Center for Economic Policy Research's Uniform Current Population Survey (CPS) Extracts. This dataset contains a consistent hourly wage variable (rw_ot) for each worker. (The construction of this hourly wage measure is detailed in Schmitt [2003].) To obtain a measure of full-time annual earnings, we multiply this hourly wage measure by 2,000. We then calculate the mean, 10th, and 95th percentiles of earnings at each age. This gives us the 2016 age-earnings profile for three groups: low-income (10th percentile), average (mean), and high-income (95th percentile). A worker whose earnings are in the 95th percentile at each age exceeds the taxable maximum starting in his or her late 30s. We divide each of these earnings profiles by the mean economy-wide earnings level (across all observations in the dataset). This gives us an age-earnings profile for each group relative to the economy-wide average in 2016. These relative age-earnings profiles are not smooth, so we fit a 5th degree polynomial to

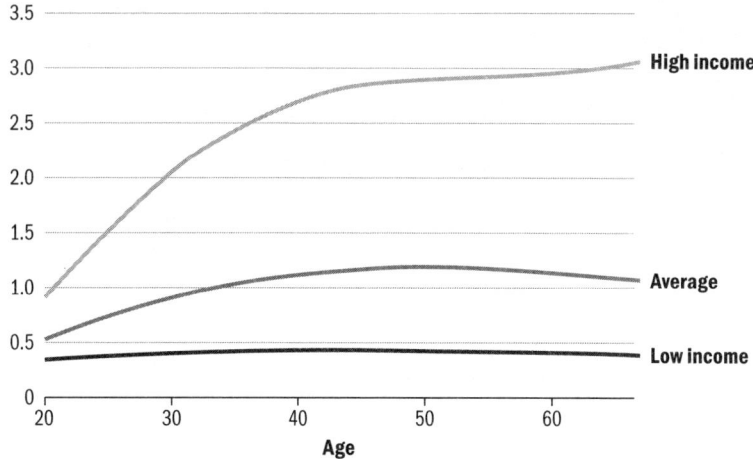

FIGURE 12.1 Relative age-earnings profiles
Earnings relative to economy-wide average
Source: Authors' calculations based on 10th, mean, and 95th percentile earnings in CEPR's CPS Outgoing Rotation Group Extracts (2016).

obtain the predicted relative wage at each age. The relative age-earnings profiles are shown in Figure 12.1.

We simulate the experience of stylized workers in multiple birth cohorts multiplying the predicted relative wage at each level by the Social Security average wage index (AWI) for that year.[4] Thus, each worker's wage growth over his or her lifetime incorporates both relative shifts due to aging and economy-wide wage growth. We use the historical values of AWI for years 1951–2018 and forecast subsequent years assuming a 3 percent growth rate. Using the wage profile and AWI, we estimate a worker's AIME. Note that Social Security's taxable maximum wage is a function of AWI, as are the bend-points of the PIA formula. Hence, the wage profile and AWI are sufficient to calculate nominal wages, PIA, and the nominal Social Security benefit a worker receives at any claiming age. Nominal wages and benefits are converted to real dollars using the CPI-W and reported as 2020 dollars. It is important to note that while these stylized earnings profiles are intended to allow simple illustrations about the cost of government indecision, they do not capture all the realities of individual labor market experiences such as differences in hours worked or labor force participation.

Table 12.1 shows monthly Social Security benefits—based on these earnings profiles— for the stylized workers in our model under alternative claiming ages. All values are denominated in 2020 dollars. There are four important aspects of these values. First, monthly benefits are modest. Among workers in the 1975 birth cohort who retire at the FRA, the monthly benefit is $1,356 for workers at the 10th percentile of the earnings distribution, $2,542 for workers at the mean, and $3,756 for workers at the 95th percentile. Second, although the progressive AIME formula means that low-income workers see a larger proportion of their earnings replaced by Social Security than high-income workers do, high-income workers enjoy substantially greater Social Security benefits in absolute dollar terms. Third, promised Social Security benefits (setting aside potential future benefit cuts) have risen across cohorts

TABLE 12.1 Monthly Social Security benefit by claiming age

Birth year	Claim at 62	Claim at FRA	Claim at 70
LOW-INCOME			
1960	$811	$1,171	$1,465
1965	$852	$1,230	$1,538
1970	$895	$1,292	$1,615
1975	$940	$1,356	$1,696
1980	$987	$1,424	$1,781
1985	$1,036	$1,495	$1,870
1990	$1,088	$1,570	$1,964
AVERAGE-INCOME			
1960	$1,485	$2,196	$2,778
1965	$1,559	$2,306	$2,916
1970	$1,638	$2,421	$3,063
1975	$1,720	$2,542	$3,215
1980	$1,806	$2,670	$3,376
1985	$1,896	$2,803	$3,546
1990	$1,991	$2,943	$3,723
HIGH-INCOME			
1960	$2,207	$3,235	$4,072
1965	$2,324	$3,406	$4,287
1970	$2,440	$3,577	$4,503
1975	$2,562	$3,756	$4,727
1980	$2,690	$3,942	$4,963
1985	$2,826	$4,141	$5,212
1990	$2,967	$4,349	$5,473

Notes: Authors' calculations based on wage profiles in Figure 1 (10th, mean, and 95th percentile earnings) and Social Security benefit rules. FRA, full retirement age.

for workers at all income levels. Among workers at the 10th percentile who claim at age 62, the expected monthly benefit has risen from $811 for the 1960 birth cohort to $1,088 for the 1990 birth cohort; among workers at the 95th percentile who claim at age 70, benefits have risen from $4,072 to $5,473. Finally, workers who are able to delay claiming to 70 receive benefits nearly twice as great as those who claim at age 62. Delayed claiming—for those who can afford to wait—is a strong strategy for improving retirement security (e.g., Shoven and Slavov 2014).

2.2. Reform Options

We consider a range of potential changes to benefits and taxes, and we assume that these changes go into effect in 2035 when the trust fund is exhausted.[5]

1. *Issue debt (DBT)*. This option implies that our stylized workers escape reform. Any tax increases or benefit cuts are passed on to future generations.

2. *Across-the-board benefit cut (CUT 20.0%)*. In this scenario, benefits are cut by 20 percent across the board once the trust fund is depleted in 2035.
3. *Increase full retirement age to 70 (FRA 70)*. In this scenario, an individual can receive their PIA only if they claim at age 70. Actuarial reductions are applied for earlier claims. We assume that any benefits claimed early before age 70 are reduced based on the current formula (by 5/9 of 1 percent for each month up to 36 months, and by 5/12 of 1 percent for each additional month). We apply this change to any individual claiming Social Security benefits in or after 2035.
4. *Switch to chained CPI (C-CPI-U)*. In this scenario, the cost-of-living adjustment (COLA) for benefits is calculated using the chained CPI, which grows more slowly than the CPI-W.
5. *Across-the-board payroll tax increase (no change to cap) (TAX + 3.1%)*. In this scenario, the payroll tax is increased by 3.1 percent of taxable wages. The taxable maximum remains unchanged.
6. *Increase progressivity of PIA formula (PIA 5.0%)*. In this scenario, the benefit formula is altered to pay 5 percent (versus 15 percent) of AIME above the second bend point. This change cuts benefits only for high earners.
7. *Remove the payroll tax cap (CAP 10.6%)*. In this scenario, the taxable maximum ($137,700 in 2020) is no longer in effect, and all earnings above the current maximum are subject to a 10.6 percent payroll tax. No additional benefits are paid on these earnings.

Individually, many of these reforms do not restore actuarial balance, though there are various combinations that do. In the analysis below, we assume that the government issues debt to finance the remainder of the shortfall (and that the tax increases or benefit cuts necessary to pay off the debt occur after our stylized workers die).

2.3. Effect of Reform on Individual Benefits

Setting aside option 1—issuing debt—each of these reforms either reduces an individual's Social Security benefits (options 2, 3, 4, and 6) or increases her preretirement taxes (options 5 and 7). Reforms 2 through 5 affect individuals across the board. Reforms 6 and 7 target high-income individuals. To calculate the impact of each reform on individuals, we project lifetime Social Security benefits for the individuals in Table 12.1 using the historical values of CPI-W for years 1974–2019 and forecast subsequent years assuming a 2 percent growth rate. We model chained CPI or C-CPI-U as CPI-W less 0.25 percent. Nominal wages and benefits are converted to real 2020 dollars using CPI-W. To calculate the present value of these benefit streams, individuals are assigned the mortality rates for their gender and birth cohort based on the cohort mortality tables underlying the intermediate projections in the 2013 Social Security Trustees Report.[6] The risk-free interest rate is set to 0 percent, reflecting the persistent low real interest rates experienced during the past decade.

Table 12.2 shows the reduction in lifetime benefits, or the increase in the lifetime taxes (both discounted to the present), for stylized workers at different levels of earnings under reform options 2 through 7. The table shows results for women; results for men are similar but slightly lower due to higher male mortality. The 20 percent benefit cut has the largest impact on the present value of benefits: a low-income woman born in 1990 would need an extra $79,000 today to make up for a 20 percent cut in Social Security, while her high-income

TABLE 12.2 Impact of reform on present value of benefits and taxes

Birth year	CUT 20.0%	FRA 70	C-CPI-U	TAX+ 3.1%	PIA 5.0%	CAP 10.6%
			LOW-INCOME FEMALE			
1960	$42,087	$0	$4,962	$0	$0	$0
1965	$55,999	$0	$7,958	$0	$0	$0
1970	$66,022	$66,102	$11,982	$1,583	$0	$0
1975	$68,335	$68,371	$14,104	$5,738	$0	$0
1980	$71,380	$71,348	$14,823	$10,175	$0	$0
1985	$74,854	$74,795	$15,638	$14,842	$0	$0
1990	$78,844	$78,871	$16,567	$19,737	$0	$0
			AVERAGE-INCOME FEMALE			
1960	$78,957	$0	$9,309	$0	$0	$0
1965	$104,984	$0	$14,919	$0	$0	$0
1970	$123,781	$123,942	$22,464	$4,334	$0	$0
1975	$128,106	$128,106	$26,440	$15,676	$0	$0
1980	$133,842	$133,777	$27,795	$27,836	$0	$0
1985	$140,351	$140,351	$29,321	$40,717	$0	$0
1990	$147,803	$147,750	$31,057	$54,241	$0	$0
			HIGH-INCOME FEMALE			
1960	$116,311	$0	$13,713	$0	$93,470	$0
1965	$155,038	$0	$22,032	$0	$125,631	$0
1970	$182,869	$182,789	$33,188	$9,904	$148,327	$7,203
1975	$189,245	$189,281	$39,058	$35,083	$153,476	$23,993
1980	$197,666	$197,666	$41,049	$61,234	$160,208	$39,895
1985	$207,345	$207,374	$43,317	$88,464	$168,216	$55,610
1990	$218,361	$218,361	$45,883	$117,117	$177,060	$70,809

Notes: Authors' calculations. Figures based on female mortality rates. Figures for males are similar and available upon request. CUT 20.0%, across-the-board benefit cut; FRA 70, increase full retirement age to 70; C-CPI-U, switch to chained consumer price index; TAX +3.1%, across-the-board payroll tax increase; PIA 5.0%, increase progressivity of primary insurance amount formula; CAP 10.6%, remove the payroll tax cap.

counterpart would need an extra $218,000 today. Bhutta et al. (2020) report that median net worth was $121,700 in 2019, and that mean retirement savings among individuals with employer-sponsored defined contribution pensions or individual retirement accounts was $269,600. Compared to these amounts, the impact of cutting Social Security benefits across the board is large.

Raising the FRA to 70 is similar to a 20 percent benefit cut, in the sense that both policies have an almost identical impact on affected individuals who claim at the FRA. The reason for this result is illustrated in Figure 12.2. The solid line shows the relationship between monthly benefit and claiming age under current law. Individuals claiming at age 62 get 70 percent of PIA, individuals claiming at the FRA (67) get 100 percent of PIA, and individuals claiming at age 70 get 124 percent of PIA. Increasing the FRA to 70 implies that the "full" benefit—100 percent of PIA—could be claimed only at age 70. This change is depicted by the horizontal arrow. Benefits are then reduced according to the actuarial formula, depicted by the dashed line, which shows that the benefit payable to age 67 claimers is 80 percent of PIA.

A 20 percent across-the-board benefit cut reduces benefits at every claiming age by 20 percent. This change is depicted by the vertical arrow. For age 67 claimers, therefore, the 20 percent benefit cut results in the same monthly benefit as increasing the FRA to 70. Thus, for affected cohorts (born in 1970 and later), the impact of raising the FRA is almost identical to the impact of cutting benefits by 20 percent. Cohorts born in 1960 and 1965 are unaffected by an increase in the FRA, as they will have retired by 2035.

Table 12.2 also illustrates that the impact of other reforms is smaller, and that tax increases have a disproportionate effect on younger cohorts while leaving older cohorts (who have already retired) unaffected. In addition, average and low earners are not affected by the policies that cut benefits or raise taxes for high earners.

The dollar amounts shown in Table 12.2 reflect the direct impact of the policies. In Section 3, we examine the *additional* cost imposed on individuals when policy decisions are delayed.

2.4. Effect of Reforms on Social Security Solvency

These policies also have different impacts on the financial stability of the Social Security system. Table 12.3 shows the effectiveness of seven policies analyzed by the Congressional Budget Office (CBO) in restoring the 75-year financial balance of the Social Security system. The seven CBO polices are not precisely the same as the policies we evaluate, but they are closely related.

The first row of the table shows that the actuarial deficit of the Social Security system over the next 75 years is projected to be 1.5 percent of GDP over that period. The second row shows that an across-the-board 20 percent cut in benefits in 2020 would roughly eliminate the 75-year shortfall. Under this change, all current and future beneficiaries would immediately suffer a 20 percent reduction in benefits relative to current law. This policy was not scored by CBO, as it is not something any politician has advocated. However, we consider this option as a benchmark. The 2020 Social Security Trustees Report suggests that a 21 percent across-the-board benefit cut in 2035 would bring payable benefits in line with revenues for that year. While the benefit cut would need to be increased to 27 percent in the future to keep benefits in line with revenues, we would expect a 20 percent benefit cut to reduce the actuarial balance to close to zero. We also note the contrast with survey evidence, which

TABLE 12.3 Effects of Social Security reform options on 75-year actuarial balance as percentage of GDP

Issue debt (do nothing)	−1.5%
Cut benefits by 20%	0%
Raise FRA to 70	−1.1%
Switch to chained CPI	−1.3%
Increase payroll tax by 1% of wages	−1.2%
Reduce top PIA factor to 5%	−1.4%
Impose payroll tax on earnings above $250,000	−0.5%

Source: Congressional Budget Office (CBO) calculator, available at https://www.cbo.gov/publication/54868, and OASDI Board of Trustees (2020). Assumes implementation in 2020 for changes to the benefit formula and 2023 for the FRA increase.
FRA, full retirement age; CPI, consumer price index; PIA, primary insurance amount.

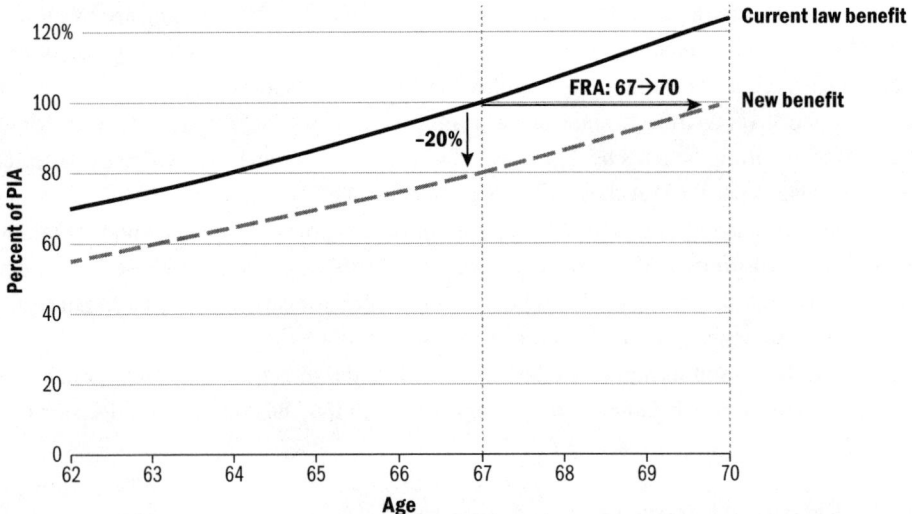

FIGURE 12.2 Raising the FRA to 70 is equivalent to cutting benefits by 20 percent for cohorts born in 1970 and later
Notes: Authors' depiction based on Social Security benefit rules. FRA, full retirement age; PIA, primary insurance amount.

suggests that individuals under the age of 35 anticipate getting only around half the benefits promised to them under current law (Luttmer and Samwick 2018). In other words, young workers are probably more pessimistic about their future Social Security benefit than the system's finances suggest.

Figure 12.2 showed that a 20 percent cut and an increase in the FRA to age 70 are essentially identical for new beneficiaries. However, raising the FRA to 70 is much less effective in closing the 75-year shortfall than an across-the-board 20 percent cut. The reason is that raising the FRA affects only new beneficiaries and leaves existing beneficiaries unaffected.

Switching to a chained CPI to calculate COLAs contributes a relatively small amount to alleviating the financial shortfall. Similarly, raising the payroll tax by 1 percent of wages is far from sufficient, but raising the rate by 3.1 percent would have a larger impact. The Social Security Trustees estimate that in 2035, the program's costs will exceed income by about 3.4 percent of payroll, with the difference growing thereafter.

The sixth row shows that changing the progressivity of benefits by lowering the top PIA factor to 5 percent is relatively ineffective in solving the financial shortfall facing Social Security. There are three reasons for this. First, relatively few beneficiaries have an AIME greater than the second bend point (the only ones affected). Second, the conversion between AIME and PIA after the second bend point is already low (15 percent), and lowering it further does not reduce benefits much. And, finally, this policy would only affect new beneficiaries and not existing claimants, meaning that the total benefit reduction is not very large.

Imposing payroll taxes on earnings over $250,000 would close about two-thirds of the money shortfall, but only if there was not a corresponding increase in future benefits.

3. The Impact of Indecision

We turn now to the main analysis of this paper: quantifying the cost of policy indecision. To see the intuition behind our analysis, suppose an individual formulates a retirement plan under the assumption that no policy change will occur. However, she is surprised by a policy change in 2035. How does her well-being in this scenario compare to her well-being in an alternative scenario in which the policy change is announced—for example—15 years in advance? In other words, what is the value of knowing about the policy change in 2020 versus 2035? This value is the cost to the individual due to government indecision. Alternatively, suppose an individual formulates a retirement plan under the assumption that benefits will be cut by 20 percent across the board in 2035. However, unexpectedly, the government decides to issue debt and pass the cost of any adjustment on to future generations. That is, the individual faces no benefit cut. Even though the surprise is a positive one from the individual's perspective, knowing about it ahead of time is valuable as it allows advance planning.

To be more specific, we consider an individual who uses a life cycle model at the start of her career (age 20) to formulate a financial plan based on a particular expectation about what will happen in 2035 when the trust fund is exhausted. We vary this expectation: in some cases, the individual assumes that there will be no change to current law benefits (debt will be issued to pay full benefits). In other cases, the individual assumes benefits will be cut. This baseline financial plan is represented in Figure 12.3 by the top timeline labeled "Individual's Plan." It shows that the individual's plan is formulated in 2020, and the plan assumes current law will be in place until 2035, after which it will be replaced with "Policy A." Policy A may be a continuation of current law, or it may be some alternative.

However, the individual's expectation turns out to be wrong. We consider two alternative scenarios. Under one scenario, the individual follows her plan and is surprised when a different policy—Policy B—is both announced and implemented in 2035. This scenario is represented by the second timeline in Figure 12.3, labeled "Scenario 1." In Scenario 1, the individual is surprised by Policy B in 2035 and must adjust her plans accordingly. Under the second scenario, the government announces in advance that Policy B will take effect starting

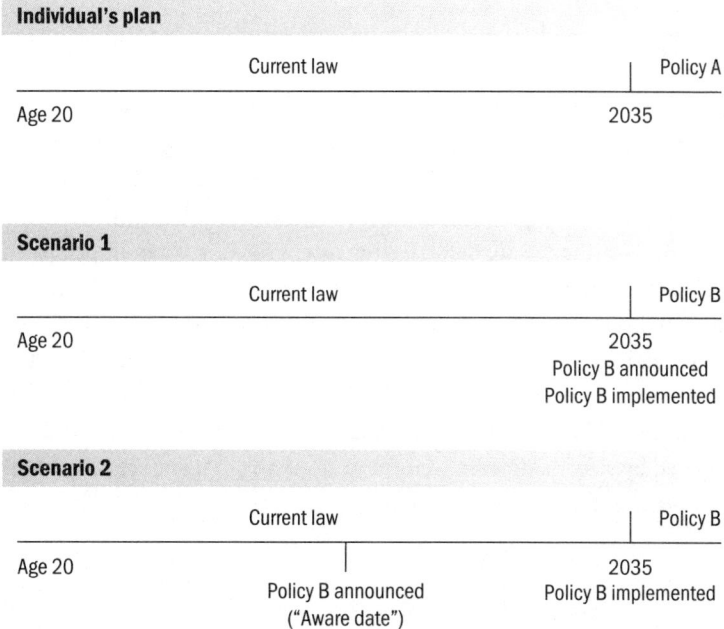

FIGURE 12.3 Alternative timelines for individuals planning for retirement

in 2035. As soon as the announcement is made, our individual can adapt her plan to these impending changes. This scenario is represented by the third timeline in Figure 12.3, labeled "Scenario 2." In Scenario 2, the government announces at some date before 2035 that policy B will take effect in 2035. We refer to the date of this announcement as the "aware date." Once the announcement is made, the individual adjusts plans.

We compare the individual's well-being under Scenarios 1 and 2. For example, consider an individual who plans for no change to current law (in other words, Policy A is a continuation of current law). However, there is actually a 20 percent benefit cut (Policy B) starting in 2035. In Scenario 1, the individual does not learn of this change until 2035. In Scenario 2, she learns of the impending policy change ahead of time, perhaps in 2020 or 2025.

4. Model

To model the value of this early awareness, we solve a standard life cycle model for stylized individuals from different birth cohorts and with different earnings profiles.[7] We assume individuals start work at age 20, retire and claim Social Security at age 67, and live for up to 110 years. Individuals choose each period how much to save and consume. There is no labor supply choice; that is, individuals work full time between ages 20 and 66 and are fully retired thereafter. Borrowing is restricted to one year of income. We assume individuals have a constant relative risk aversion (CRRA) utility function with a coefficient of relative risk aversion of 3. (To test sensitivity, we also consider alternative levels of risk aversion.) We assume a subjective discount rate for utility of 3 percent. Individuals earn the risk-free interest rate, zero percent, on any wealth. We consider workers in different cohorts with different lifetime earnings profiles, as introduced in Table 12.1, with Social Security benefits and mortality projected using the methodology underlying Table 12.2. We assume individuals retire and claim Social Security at 67.

We begin with a baseline in which individuals optimize under the assumption that there will be no changes to Social Security for the rest of their lives; that is, they assume that Policy A (in Figure 12.3) will reflect policy (1) from the list above, and the government will issue debt so that any cost of reform is passed on to future generations. Under Scenario 1 (see Figure 12.3), they are surprised in 2035 by one of the other reforms discussed above and must adjust their plan at that point. Under Scenario 2 (see Figure 12.3), they learn about the change in advance—at the "aware date." In this case, individuals can implement a new plan that anticipates the new policy. We calculate the amount of additional wealth ("compensating wealth") that—if received at the policy start date—would leave individuals indifferent between the scenario in which they are surprised and the scenario in which they know in advance (at the aware date) what change will occur. We also consider alternatives in which an individual assumes that a particular reform (e.g., a 20 percent benefit cut) will occur in 2035 and are surprised by either a different reform or no change. Again, we calculate the value of knowing the correct reform at the aware date.

5. Results

5.1. Cost of Indecision When Individuals Assume No Change

We first consider an individual who assumes that no change will occur in 2035; in other words, the government will issue debt and pay all promised benefits. Figure 12.4 shows the path of spending for an average income female born in 1975 who assumes that there will be no changes to Social Security during her lifetime. The first dotted vertical line indicates the year 2020, when the worker is aged 45. Past consumption (before age 45) is somewhat bumpy as we have assumed the economy-wide average wage grew in line with its historical levels; a smooth growth rate is assumed for the future. Starting at age 45, there are two possible scenarios. In Scenario 1, illustrated by the dotted line, the worker continues down the planned path and is surprised by a 20 percent benefit cut in 2035 (indicated by the second vertical dotted line labeled "Policy Start"). At this point, her consumption decreases, reflecting the lower benefits that she receives. In Scenario 2, illustrated by the solid line, the government announces in 2020 that benefits will be cut by 20 percent starting in 2035. In this case, the worker may be able to make an immediate adjustment. The ability to make an immediate adjustment hinges on whether the individual has already started saving for retirement—in which case saving can be adjusted in response to the announcement. Our stylized 45-year-old began saving for retirement in 2017 and is therefore able to adjust. Consumption drops in 2020 and continues along a smooth path even when the policy change occurs in 2035. This decrease in consumption is subsequently followed by an increase in savings to offset impending benefit cuts.

Figure 12.5 shows compensating wealth by aware year for the four policies that affect women earning the average wage in the 1965, 1970, 1975, 1980, and 1985 birth cohorts. The

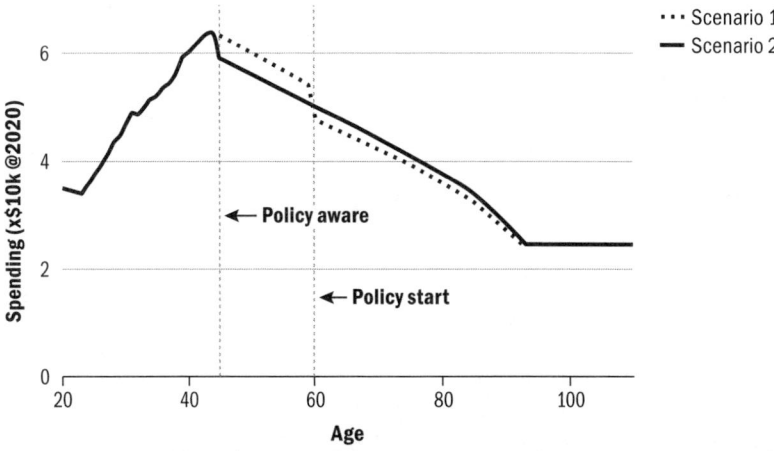

FIGURE 12.4 Annual consumption spending under alternative policy scenarios
Stylized woman with mean earnings born in 1975
Notes: Authors' calculations of consumption path for female with mean income under alternative scenarios. Based on female mortality rates and mean earnings. Results for males are similar and available upon request.

four panels correspond to policies 2, 3, 4, and 5, that is, cutting benefits across the board by 20 percent, changing FRA to 70, changing to the chained CPI, and increasing payroll taxes by 3.1 percent. Generally, policies 6 and 7—changing the PIA formula and removing the Social Security wage maximum—do not affect average earners. Note that the vertical scales of the top two panels (CUT and FRA) are multiples of $10,000 and the bottom two panels (C-CPI-U and TAX + 3.1) are multiples of $100. For an individual who retires at 67, a cut in benefits by 20 percent is nearly identical to changing her FRA to 70. However, whereas a 20 percent cut affects all cohorts, changing the FRA to 70 affects only cohorts that begin claiming benefits in 2035 or later, that is, cohorts born in 1968 or after. Similarly, changing to chained CPI for COLA affects all cohorts, but increasing payroll taxes only affects cohorts that are still working in 2035—workers born in 1969 or after.

For all curves in Figure 12.5, compensating wealth is a nonincreasing function of the aware year and goes to zero at 2035, the common start date for all new policies. Clearly,

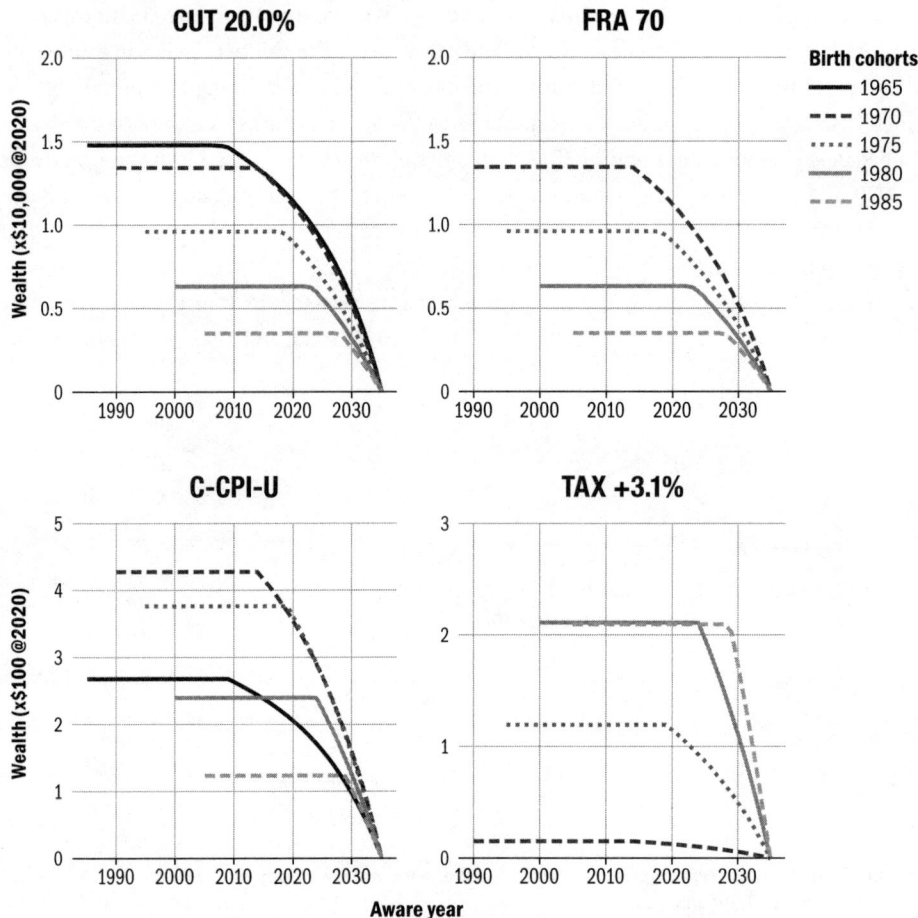

FIGURE 12.5 Compensating wealth vs. aware year
Reforms affecting average earners
Notes: Authors' calculations. Figures based on female mortality rates. Figures for males are similar and available upon request. CUT 20.0%, across-the-board benefit cut; FRA 70, increase full retirement age to 70; C-CPI-U, switch to chained consumer price index; TAX +3.1%, across-the-board payroll tax increase.

having more time to plan is better than having less. However, if the knowledge doesn't have an immediate impact on spending or saving, then it doesn't increase compensating wealth. This is the explanation for the initial flat regions of these curves, which begin for each cohort at the year the individual begins work at age 20 and remain flat to around age 40. In these years, our cohorts' wages are relatively low, and they are borrowing as much as they can. This inflexibility means that any information about future reform cannot be acted on immediately. Indeed, Table 12.4 shows the earliest age and year at which information about reform would affect consumption or saving choices in the life cycle model. This age/year is roughly the time when the individual finds it optimal, given her anticipated future wages and Social Security benefits, to finish paying down debt and start saving for retirement.[8] Any knowledge received in advance of these dates does not have any additional value. The ages shown in Table 12.4 are roughly consistent with the observation that participation in and contributions to employer-sponsored retirement plans increase with age (see, e.g., Vanguard 2021). That is, many individuals ramp up saving during middle age when incomes are higher. Variation across cohorts is driven by differences in income and mortality. Younger cohorts generally have higher incomes and lower mortality (i.e., a longer retirement to plan for).

The cross-cohort patterns observed in Figure 12.5 can be explained by when the policies begin to affect the cohorts. For example, consider the policy of changing the FRA to 70. This policy reduces an individual's retirement benefit but isn't felt until an individual actually retires at age 67. Thus, the cohort born in 1970 first feels the policy's effect in 2037, the cohort born in 1975 first feels the policy's effect in 2042, and so on. Since the policy change affects cohorts at a certain age versus in a certain year, younger cohorts have more time to prepare. In effect, the policy start date is extended and awareness is less valuable. As a result, the compensating wealth curves for changing FRA to 70 are nested—the curve for the cohort born in 1970 lies above that for 1975, which is above the curve for 1980, and so on. The 1965 cohort is not affected as individuals born in this year have already retired. In contrast, consider the CUT policy. The argument in the previous paragraph still applies to preretirement cohorts; indeed, the two policies are essentially equivalent for them. However, the 1965 cohort is affected by this policy change.

TABLE 12.4 Age/date when information begins to affect choices

Year of birth	Low-income	Average-income	High-income
1960	48/2008	41/2001	38/1998
1965	48/2013	41/2006	38/2003
1970	47/2017	43/2013	39/2009
1975	46/2021	42/2017	39/2014
1980	46/2026	42/2022	39/2019
1985	46/2031	41/2026	39/2024
1990	44/2034	41/2031	39/2029

Notes: Authors' calculations. Figures based on female mortality rates. Figures for males are similar and available upon request.

Figure 12.6 shows the impact of the two policies—6 and 7—that affect only high earners. The impact is depicted for high-earning women in different cohorts. The reduction in the top PIA factor has a similar pattern as the across-the-board benefit cut.

We now present our primary results in tabular form, which gives us the space to add results for low and high earners (in addition to average earners), and the 1960 and 1980 cohorts (in addition to those depicted in Figures 12.5 and 12.6). Table 12.5 reports how valuable it would be to inform individuals of each reform in 2020 rather than when the cut takes place in 2035. The top number in each cell indicates the monetary amount (in 2020 dollars) that they would pay to be aware of the cut in 2020. The lower number, in parentheses, indicates the monetary amount relative to their average monthly earnings (AIME). We emphasize that Table 12.5 shows only the cost of government indecision (announcing the policy in 2035 versus 2020) and goes beyond the direct impact of the policies on individuals (which was shown in Table 12.2).

The first column of Table 12.5 shows that an average-earning woman born in 1960 would pay $9,664, or 1.9 months of earnings, to be informed of an impending 20 percent cut in 2020 rather than in 2035. For low-income women born in 1960, the figure is $3,793, or 2.0 months of earnings. High-earning women would pay more in absolute dollars to be informed early ($14,042), but the amount they would pay is a smaller multiple (1.27) of their AIME. The compensating wealth of the 1965 birth cohort is higher than that of the 1960 birth cohort. Both of these cohorts are already retired when the policy change goes into effect. Thus, both cohorts first feel the change at the same time—in 2035—but at different ages. The younger cohort therefore makes better use of early awareness. For the remaining birth cohorts, which have not yet retired, compensating wealth declines for younger cohorts, in line with the results in Figure 12.5. Becoming aware early has the lowest value for the 1990 birth cohort. Learning about Social Security benefit cuts at age 30 instead of at age 45 is of marginal value because individuals have only recently started to save for retirement (see Table 12.4).

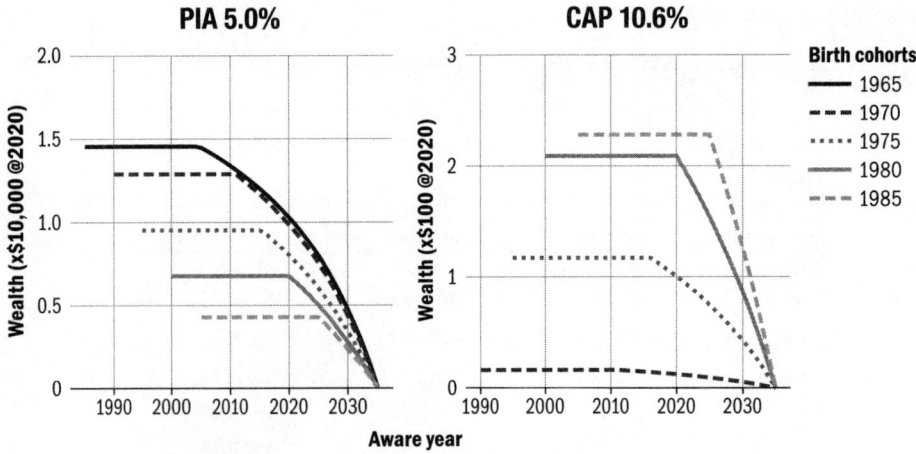

FIGURE 12.6 Compensating wealth vs. aware year
Reforms affecting high earners only
Notes: Authors' calculations. Figures based on female mortality rates. Figures for males are similar and available upon request. PIA 5.0%, increase progressivity of primary insurance amount formula; CAP 10.6%, remove the payroll tax cap.

TABLE 12.5 Compensating wealth in 2020 dollars (and relative to AIME)—Aware in 2020 versus 2035

Birth year	CUT 20.0%	FRA 70	C-CPI-U	TAX+ 3.1%	PIA 5.0%	CAP 10.6%
			LOW-INCOME FEMALE			
1960	$3,793	$0	$8	$0	$0	$0
	(2.01)	(0.00)	(0.00)	(0.00)	(0.00)	(0.00)
1965	$5,307	$0	$37	$0	$0	$0
	(2.68)	(0.00)	(0.02)	(0.00)	(0.00)	(0.00)
1970	$5,359	$5,372	$86	$6	$0	$0
	(2.57)	(2.58)	(0.04)	(0.00)	(0.00)	(0.00)
1975	$3,427	$3,431	$70	$42	$0	$0
	(1.57)	(1.57)	(0.03)	(0.02)	(0.00)	(0.00)
1980	$1,751	$1,749	$31	$53	$0	$0
	(0.76)	(0.76)	(0.01)	(0.02)	(0.00)	(0.00)
1985	$341	$340	$0	$5	$0	$0
	(0.14)	(0.14)	(0.00)	(0.00)	(0.00)	(0.00)
1990	$0	$0	$0	$1	$0	$0
	(0.00)	(0.00)	(0.00)	(0.00)	(0.00)	(0.00)
			AVERAGE-INCOME FEMALE			
1960	$9,664	$0	$100	$0	$0	$0
	(1.90)	(0.00)	(0.02)	(0.00)	(0.00)	(0.00)
1965	$11,397	$0	$205	$0	$0	$0
	(2.13)	(0.00)	(0.04)	(0.00)	(0.00)	(0.00)
1970	$11,157	$11,186	$354	$12	$0	$0
	(1.99)	(1.99)	(0.06)	(0.00)	(0.00)	(0.00)
1975	$8,964	$8,964	$361	$115	$0	$0
	(1.52)	(1.52)	(0.06)	(0.02)	(0.00)	(0.00)
1980	$6,326	$6,319	$240	$211	$0	$0
	(1.02)	(1.02)	(0.04)	(0.03)	(0.00)	(0.00)
1985	$3,497	$3,497	$123	$209	$0	$0
	(0.54)	(0.54)	(0.02)	(0.03)	(0.00)	(0.00)
1990	$980	$979	$23	$72	$0	$0
	(0.14)	(0.14)	(0.00)	(0.01)	(0.00)	(0.00)
			HIGH-INCOME FEMALE			
1960	$14,042	$0	$291	$0	$9,195	$0
	(1.27)	(0.00)	(0.03)	(0.00)	(0.83)	(0.00)
1965	$15,479	$0	$464	$0	$10,296	$0
	(1.32)	(0.00)	(0.04)	(0.00)	(0.88)	(0.00)
1970	$14,857	$14,844	$693	$23	$9,859	$12
	(1.21)	(1.21)	(0.06)	(0.00)	(0.80)	(0.00)
1975	$12,168	$12,173	$699	$214	$8,027	$100
	(0.94)	(0.94)	(0.05)	(0.02)	(0.62)	(0.01)

(continued)

TABLE 12.5 Continued

Birth year	CUT 20.0%	FRA 70	C-CPI-U	TAX+ 3.1%	PIA 5.0%	CAP 10.6%
1980	$10,243	$10,243	$588	$489	$6,750	$209
	(0.76)	(0.76)	(0.04)	(0.04)	(0.50)	(0.02)
1985	$6,575	$6,577	$370	$574	$4,291	$228
	(0.46)	(0.46)	(0.03)	(0.04)	(0.30)	(0.02)
1990	$3,225	$3,225	$177	$425	$2,067	$156
	(0.22)	(0.22)	(0.01)	(0.03)	(0.14)	(0.01)

Notes: Authors' calculations. Figures based on female mortality rates. Figures for males are similar and available upon request. CUT 20.0%, across-the-board benefit cut; FRA 70, increase full retirement age to 70; C-CPI-U, switch to chained consumer price index; TAX +3.1%, across-the-board payroll tax increase; PIA 5.0%, increase progressivity of primary insurance amount formula; CAP 10.6%, remove the payroll tax cap; AIME, average indexed monthly earnings.

The second column shows results for raising the full retirement age in 2035. Individuals born before 1968 gain no value in learning about this change early since they will be retired before 2035 and unaffected by the policy. However, for those born after 1968, the effect of raising the full retirement age to 70 is nearly the same as reducing benefits across the board by 20 percent. As discussed earlier, these policies are equivalent for all cohorts affected by them. The equivalence of cutting benefits and raising the FRA is well known among public finance economists. However, policy discussions more often focus on raising the FRA than on cutting benefits, perhaps because the public is less aware of their equivalence.

The value of advance knowledge for the final four reforms is small. We saw in Table 12.3 that switching to a chained index would close only a small portion of the financial shortfall of Social Security. The third column of Table 12.5 shows that knowing about the switch 15 years in advance has similarly low stakes. A sizable 3.1 percent increase in the payroll tax would reduce the net wealth of workers, but the fourth column of Table 12.5 indicates that knowing about it in advance would not be that valuable. Older generations would largely escape. The tax hike would cost the 1990 cohort the most (see Table 12.3). However, learning about the change 15 years in advance appears to have only modest value given that individuals in that cohort would not alter their behavior until sometime between 2029 (for the high-income group) and 2034 (for the low-income group). The fifth and sixth columns of Table 12.5 show results for the two policies affecting only high-income individuals. The fifth column shows that knowing in advance about reducing the top PIA factor is of considerable value to our high earners, but it is of less value than knowing about a potential 20% across the board cut in advance. The sixth column shows that learning in advance about removing the tax cap is not very valuable.

5.2. Cost of Indecision When Individuals Assume Policy Change

We now turn our attention to situations in which the individual assumes a particular reform (Policy A) will occur in 2035 and is surprised by a different policy (Policy B). In each of these cases, we hold initial wealth constant by starting the life cycle model in 2020 and endowing the individual with the wealth they would have at their current age if they had initially optimized under the assumption of no change. For this analysis, we focus on the 1975 birth cohort. Table 12.6 shows the compensating wealth for an aware date of 2020 under each combination of assumed and actual policies. The rows of the table represent the policies that individuals assume will be adopted in 2035. The columns represent the policies that are actually adopted. The highlighted rows correspond to the case in which individuals assume that debt will be issued and are surprised by one of the other policies. The compensating wealth figures in this row are the same as those presented in Table 12.5. The other rows correspond to cases in which individuals assume a policy change will occur in 2035 and are surprised by a different outcome. For example, the number in the second row and third column ($5,198) represents the compensating wealth of advance knowledge when a low-income individual assumes that benefits will be cut across the board in 2035 (CUT) but is surprised by no change (debt, or DBT). Along the diagonal, all compensating wealth amounts are zero because the actual policy adopted in 2035 is the same as the assumed policy when the individual optimizes in 2020. The last column of the table indicates the maximum compensating wealth in each row; that is, for the policy assumed in the row, it indicates the surprise that would be most valuable to know about in advance.

The results in Table 12.6 suggest that advance knowledge about benefit levels is more valuable than advance knowledge about taxes. For example, when the low-income or average-income individual assumes a future in which benefit levels will not change (DBT, PIA, CAP, or TAX) or a future in which benefit levels will change only slightly (CPI), being surprised by a large drop in benefit levels (CUT or FRA) is very costly relative to knowing in advance. Similarly, when the low-income or average-income individual assumes that benefits will be cut significantly (CUT or FRA), being surprised by no change to benefits (DBT, PIA, CAP, or TAX) or a small change to benefits (CPI) is very costly. Note that advance information has value even for positive surprises that increase the present value of benefits because knowing benefit levels in advance allows individuals to adjust consumption earlier.

Thus far, we have assumed CRRA utility with a coefficient of relative risk aversion of 3. While this value is often used in modeling, some empirical evidence suggests that it could be significantly lower, on the order of 1 (Gourinchas and Parker 2002; Hurd 1989). Our sensitivity analysis suggests that policy indecision has a lower cost when individuals are less risk averse. For example, when the coefficient of relative risk aversion is 1, an average-income female who assumes no change (DBT) values advance knowledge of a benefit cut (CUT) at only $937, or about 16 percent of average indexed monthly earnings. However, the pattern remains similar: being surprised by a change in benefits has a greater cost than being surprised by a change in taxes.[9]

6. Discussion and Conclusions

Knowing in advance about any benefit cuts or increases in the FRA that will be enacted to address the depletion of the Social Security trust fund can be very valuable. The value of receiving the information in 2020 rather than in 2035 can be as high as 2.5 months of earnings. Advance knowledge about payroll tax increases is much less valuable. There are also important distributional effects. If the value of advance knowledge is measured relative to earnings, then the stakes are actually higher for low-income workers than high-income workers. Low

TABLE 12.6 Compensating wealth of alternative policy combinations—Aware in 2020 versus 2035

LOW-INCOME FEMALE

Plan/actual:	FRA	CUT	DBT	PIA	CAP	TAX	CPI	Max. of row
FRA	$0	$0	$5,206	$5,206	$5,206	$4,153	$3,717	$5,206
CUT	$0	$0	$5,198	$5,198	$5,198	$4,146	$3,711	$5,198
DBT	$3,431	$3,427	$0	$0	$0	$42	$70	$3,431
PIA	$3,431	$3,427	$0	$0	$0	$42	$70	$3,431
CAP	$3,431	$3,427	$0	$0	$0	$42	$70	$3,431
TAX	$2,829	$2,826	$43	$43	$43	$0	$4	$2,829
CPI	$2,656	$2,652	$74	$74	$74	$4	$0	$2,656

AVERAGE-INCOME FEMALE

Plan/actual:	CUT	FRA	DBT	PIA	CAP	TAX	CPI	Max. of row
CUT	$0	$0	$11,939	$11,939	$11,939	$9,422	$7,515	$11,939
FRA	$0	$0	$11,939	$11,939	$11,939	$9,422	$7,515	$11,939
DBT	$8,964	$8,964	$0	$0	$0	$115	$361	$8,964
PIA	$8,964	$8,964	$0	$0	$0	$115	$361	$8,964
CAP	$8,964	$8,964	$0	$0	$0	$115	$361	$8,964
TAX	$7,256	$7,256	$118	$118	$118	$0	$72	$7,256
CPI	$6,010	$6,010	$386	$386	$386	$75	$0	$6,010

HIGH-INCOME FEMALE

Plan/actual:	FRA	CUT	DBT	CAP	PIA	TAX	CPI	Max. of row
FRA	$0	$0	$14,986	$12,391	$519	$11,281	$8,606	$14,986
CUT	$0	$0	$14,980	$12,386	$518	$11,275	$8,602	$14,980
DBT	$12,173	$12,168	$0	$100	$8,027	$214	$699	$12,173
CAP	$10,235	$10,231	$102	$0	$6,444	$22	$275	$10,235
PIA	$500	$499	$9,504	$7,500	$0	$6,660	$4,694	$9,504
TAX	$9,392	$9,388	$219	$22	$5,767	$0	$144	$9,392
CPI	$7,355	$7,351	$735	$284	$4,172	$148	$0	$7,355

Notes: Authors' calculations. Figures based on female mortality rates. Figures for males are similar and available upon request. FRA, increase full retirement age to 70; CUT, benefit cut; DBT, no change (debt); PIA, increase progressivity of primary insurance amount formula; CAP, remove the payroll tax cap; TAX, payroll tax increase; CPI, switch to chained consumer price index.

earners rely more on Social Security, so it comes as no surprise that advance information about future policies would be proportionately more valuable to lower-income individuals.

It is important to emphasize that the value of early awareness of future policy change represents a pure efficiency gain. Policymakers are well aware that the trust fund will be exhausted in the early 2030s, and the policy options that will be available at that time are known now. Our findings suggest that simply deciding now what policy will be followed when the trust fund runs dry, rather than waiting until 2035, can be the equivalent of giving people a bonus of between 1 and 2.5 months of earnings. These gains represent a "free lunch" in the sense that they can be realized just by making a decision about a problem that will have to be faced in the near future. Failing to do so complicates people's retirement plans. Thus, government indecision has a real cost.

We have shown that in the absence of an early policy announcement, people can make two kinds of mistakes, both costly. They could assume that benefits will be maintained even after the trust fund exhaustion and then be surprised that benefit cuts are enacted, or they could assume that they will face benefit cuts only to find out in 2035 that they won't. Either mistake is possible in the absence of the government making an early decision, and both mistakes are roughly equivalently costly. These costly mistakes would be avoided if the government made a decision today about what it will do when the trust fund is exhausted. The failure to realize the awareness gains that we calculate represent the cost of Washington failing to come to grips with the Social Security solvency issue.

Notes

1. For example, the 2020 Social Security Trustees Report—which did not take into account the impact of the COVID-19 pandemic—projected that the trust funds for the retirement and disability programs would be exhausted in 2035 (OASDI Board of Trustees 2020). Similarly, the Congressional Budget Office's (2019b) Long Term Budget Outlook projected a trust fund depletion date of 2032 for the retirement program. Reflecting the impact of the COVID-19 pandemic, the Congressional Budget Office's September 2020 estimate moved that depletion date to 2031 (Congressional Budget Office 2020), while Gladstone and Akabas (2020) presented alternative scenarios with depletion dates as early as 2026. More recently, however, the Congressional Budget Office (2021) returned to its projection of a 2032 trust fund depletion date for the retirement program, reflecting stronger than anticipated economic growth.
2. Huston and Morton (2019) provide a review of the legal issues and payment options.
3. The bend points in the PIA formula are indexed for economy-wide average wage growth. AIME and PIA are calculated during the year in which the worker turns 62, using the bend points that are in effect for that year; however, they can be subsequently updated to reflect additional years of work. In 2020, the bend points (applying to workers who turned 62 in 2020) were $960 and $5,785, and the taxable maximum was $137,700.
4. This assumption abstracts from the possibility that the earnings of different income groups may grow faster or slower than the economy-wide average. In particular, it abstracts from growing earnings inequality driven by faster growth at the upper end of the earnings distribution.
5. Many of these reforms are based on the options available at the Congressional Budget Office's online calculator (2019a), https://www.cbo.gov/publication/54868.
6. In reality, mortality varies by income level (see, e.g., Chetty et al. 2016). Adjusting mortality by income level would lower the lifetime value of Social Security benefits—as well as any changes to benefits—for

low earners relative to higher earners. However, we would not expect it to affect our main finding that the cost of indecision is significant for those planning for retirement.
7. Details of the model can be found in Scott et al. (2019).
8. To be more specific, in most cases, the individual begins to save for retirement in the year following the one indicated in the table; for three cases (the low-income 1970 cohort, the average-income 1975 cohort, and the average-income 1980 cohort) the individual begins saving for retirement in the same year.
9. Full sensitivity analysis results are available from the authors upon request.

References

Benítez-Silva, Hugo, Debra S. Dwyer, and Warren C. Sanderson. 2006. "A Dynamic Model of Retirement and Social Security Reform Expectations: A Solution to the New Early Retirement Puzzle." Working Paper 2006-134. Ann Arbor: Michigan Retirement Research Center. https://mrdrc.isr.umich.edu/publications/papers/pdf/wp134.pdf.

Bhutta, Neil, Jesse Bricker, Andrew C Chang, Lisa J Dettling, Sarena Goodman, Kevin B Moore, Sarah Reber, Alice Henriques Volz, and Richard A Windle. 2020. "Changes in U.S. Family Finances from 2016 to 2019: Evidence from the Survey of Consumer Finances." *Federal Reserve Bulletin* 106 (5): 1–42. https://www.federalreserve.gov/publications/files/scf20.pdf.

Bütler, Monika. 1999. "Anticipation Effects of Looming Public-Pension Reforms." *Carnegie-Rochester Conference Series on Public Policy* 50: 119–159. https://doi.org/10.1016/S0167-2231(99)00024-X.

Caliendo, Frank N., Aspen Gorry, and Sita Slavov. 2019. "The Cost of Uncertainty about the Timing of Social Security Reform." *European Economic Review* 118: 101–125. https://doi.org/10.1016/j.euroecorev.2019.05.008.

Center for Economic and Policy Research. 2016. "CPS ORG Uniform Extracts, Version 2.1." Data Set. Washington, DC. https://ceprdata.org/cps-uniform-data-extracts/cps-outgoing-rotation-group/cps-org-data/.

Chetty, Raj, Michael Stepner, Sarah Abraham, Shelby Lin, Benjamin Scuderi, Nicholas Turner, Augustin Bergeron, and David Cutler. 2016. "The Association Between Income and Life Expectancy in the United States, 2001–2014." *JAMA* 315 (16): 1750–1766. https://doi.org/10.1001/jama.2016.4226.

Congressional Budget Office. 2019a. "How Changing Social Security Could Affect Beneficiaries and the System's Finances." https://www.cbo.gov/publication/54868.

Congressional Budget Office. 2019b. "The 2019 Long-Term Budget Outlook." 55331. Washington, DC: Congress of the United States. http://www.cbo.gov/publication/55331.

Congressional Budget Office. 2020. "The 2020 Long-Term Budget Outlook." 56516. Washington, DC: Congress of the United States. http://www.cbo.gov/publication/56516.

Congressional Budget Office. 2021. "The 2021 Long-Term Budget Outlook." 56977. Washington, DC: Congress of the United States. http://www.cbo.gov/publication/56977.

Gladstone, Nicko, and Shai Akabas. 2020. "COVID-19 May Deplete Social Security Trust Funds This Decade." *Bipartisan Policy Center* (blog). April 22, 2020. https://bipartisanpolicy.org/blog/covid-19-may-deplete-social-security-trust-funds-this-decade/.

Gomes, Francisco J., Laurence J. Kotlikoff, and Luis M. Viceira. 2012. "The Excess Burden of Government Indecision." In *Tax Policy and the Economy*, edited by Jeffrey R Brown, 26:125–163. National Bureau of Economic Research Tax Policy and the Economy. Chicago: The University of Chicago Press.

Gourinchas, Pierre-Olivier, and Jonathan A. Parker. 2002. "Consumption over the Life Cycle." *Econometrica* 70 (1): 47–89. https://doi.org/10.1111/1468-0262.00269.

Hurd, Michael D. 1989. "Mortality Risk and Bequests." *Econometrica* 57 (4): 779–813. https://doi.org/10.2307/1913772.

Huston, Barry F., and William R. Morton. 2019. "Social Security: What Would Happen If the Trust Funds Ran Out?" CRS Report RL33514. Washington, DC: Congressional Research Service. https://crsreports.congress.gov/product/pdf/RL/RL33514/29.

Kitao, Sagiri. 2014. "Sustainable Social Security: Four Options." *Review of Economic Dynamics* 17 (4): 756–779. https://doi.org/10.1016/j.red.2013.11.004.

Luttmer, Erzo F. P., and Andrew A. Samwick. 2018. "The Welfare Cost of Perceived Policy Uncertainty: Evidence from Social Security." *American Economic Review* 108 (2): 275–307. https://doi.org/10.1257/aer.20151703.

Nelson, Jaeger. 2020. "Welfare Implications of Uncertain Social Security Reform." *Public Finance Review* 48 (4): 425–466. https://doi.org/10.1177/1091142120923640.

OASDI Board of Trustees. 2020. "The 2020 Annual Report of the Board of Trustees of the Federal Old-Age and Survivors Insurance and Federal Disability Insurance Trust Funds." Washington, DC: Social Security Administration. https://www.ssa.gov/oact/tr/2020/tr2020.pdf.

Schmitt, John. 2003. "Creating a Consistent Hourly Wage Series from the Current Population Survey's Outgoing Rotation Group, 1979–2002." Working Paper. Washington, DC: Center for Economic and Policy Research (CEPR). http://ceprdata.org/wp-content/cps/CEPR_ORG_Wages.pdf.

Scott, Jason, John G. Shoven, Sita Slavov, and John Watson. 2019. "Retirement Implications of a Low Wage Growth, Low Real Interest Rate Economy." Working Paper w25556. NBER Working Paper Series. Cambridge, MA: National Bureau of Economic Research. https://doi.org/10.3386/w25556.

Shoven, John B., and Sita Nataraj Slavov. 2014. "Does It Pay to Delay Social Security?" *Journal of Pension Economics & Finance* 13 (2): 121–144. https://doi.org/10.1017/S1474747213000309.

Social Security Administration. 2020. "Fact Sheet: Social Security." Washington, DC: Social Security Administration. https://www.ssa.gov/news/press/factsheets/basicfact-alt.pdf.

Vanguard. 2021. "How America Saves: 2021." https://institutional.vanguard.com/content/dam/inst/vanguard-has/insights-pdfs/21_CIR_HAS21_HAS_FSreport.pdf.

13
The Biased Politics of "Working Longer"

Jacob S. Hacker and Paul Pierson

1. Introduction

The other chapters in this volume have amply documented the strains facing older Americans. These strains not only distinguish the United States of today from that of the relatively recent past; they also distinguish the United States of today from the current experience of most other rich democracies. Compared with their foreign counterparts, older Americans receive less generous pension benefits, they are more likely to have to work to support themselves after 65, they die younger, their overall health is poorer, and they are more likely to be in poverty.

Contemporary social policy debates in the United States rarely acknowledge these stark cross-national differences. Nor do they grapple with the obvious implication: a major part of the distinctive experience of older Americans must be due to factors specific to the United States. After all, affluent nations across the globe have faced destabilizing demographic and economic changes—indeed, if anything, the United States has experienced *less* pressure from globalization and aging because of its large internal market and high immigration rate. Yet other rich democracies have not seen comparably adverse outcomes. What explains this divergence? Why does the United States, once a leader with regard to the well-being of older adults, increasingly look like a laggard?

In this chapter, we address this puzzle by focusing on a set of U.S.-specific factors often neglected in contemporary analysis: those related to American politics. The American experience is distinctive, we argue, because American public policy is distinctive, and American public policy is distinctive because the nature of American politics is distinctive.

In pointing to politics and policy, however, the puzzle in some ways deepens. If there's one thing widely known about U.S. social policy, it's that it is relatively generous toward older adults. If there's one thing widely known about generational disparities in American politics, it's that older adults are organized and engaged compared with other segments of the electorate. And if there's one thing widely known about organized and engaged older voters, it's that they have become an important source of electoral support for the Republican Party. Indeed, the Republican Party has held the upper hand in Congress since the 1990s and occupied the White House for three-fifths of the period between 2000 and 2020 (despite winning the national popular vote only once in this interval).

These trends pose two related puzzles: First, if many of the rising strains facing older Americans are a product of politics and policy, how do we explain the lack of responsiveness to an historically influential constituency that is pivotal to the power of an electorally formidable party? Second, why are older voters themselves willing to support a party that has done relatively little to relieve the strains facing older Americans, particularly older Americans without a college degree and those facing the increasing dislocations experienced in rural and small-town regions?

To address these puzzles, we draw on a perspective we call "organized political economy." In this perspective, fundamental social outcomes are rarely the product of economic forces alone. Rather, it is the interplay of politics and economics—how elected officials respond or fail to respond to these broad forces—that determines ultimate outcomes. The "organized" in the label emphasizes that politicians' responses emerge out of political contestation in which organized political actors often play a dominant role. The most important of these organized actors are political parties, and the actions of these parties reflect in considerable part the balance of power among organized groups, such as labor unions and business lobbies. Electoral competition creates some incentives to respond to the preferences of ordinary voters, but their influence in the politics of organized contestation is often muted.

This perspective helps explain the puzzling patterns we see. In general, American voters—and even Republican voters—are opposed to cutbacks in existing protections and supportive of new measures to address insecurity. Elected politicians, however, have proved much less supportive. Three major biases in the organized political economy account for this disconnect: a bias toward economic elites; a bias toward gridlock on pressing issues; and a bias toward economic conservatism within the Republican Party.

As inequality has grown dramatically in the United States over the past generation, organized power has shifted toward corporations and the wealthy. This shift in the balance of political power has pulled policy to the right. Meanwhile, as America's two major parties have become more polarized, legislative gridlock has prevented the updating of crucial social and economic policies to reflect changing realities. Finally, the Republican Party has become more conservative, more obstructionist, and more willing to use incendiary, often racialized appeals and hardball tactics to stay in power. These biases have greatly contributed to America's worsening outcomes.

Finally, while we show that these biases emerge primarily out of organized contestation within America's distinctive political institutions, we also note—and provide a tentative explanation for why—older white voters have become more skeptical of redistribution even as other demographic groups in the United States and older voters in other country have not.

Before delving into these biases, however, we need to step back and see just how distinctive the experience of older adults in the United States really is.

2. Why Are Older Americans Facing Such Serious Strains?

In cross-national perspective, the American welfare state stands out for its unusual focus on older Americans. The United States is the only rich democracy to limit its national health insurance program, Medicare, to the elderly and disabled. (The joint federal-state Medicaid program also provides coverage to the elderly, particularly residents of nursing homes, as well as to younger Americans with limited incomes.) Compared with other affluent nations, the United States also spends a disproportionate amount on transfers to older citizens—mainly through the nation's most popular program, Social Security. Indeed, the "age bias" of social spending in favor of over-65s is greater in the United States than in virtually any other rich country (Lynch 2006).

The distinctive age orientation of the American welfare state is, in turn, both a cause and consequence of high rates of political engagement among older adults. In part because of the ample resources and positive conceptions of government conferred by Social Security and Medicare, older Americans are substantially more likely to vote and to participate in politics in other ways. In 2016, according to Census data, more than 70 percent of citizens 65 years of age or older reported voting, compared with less than 47 percent of voting-age citizens younger than 30 (File 2017). Equally important, participation with regard to Social Security—contacting public officials, contributing to or voting for candidates based on their stance on the program—is not marked by the usual "income gradient" in which higher-income citizens participate more. To the contrary, participation related to Social Security is higher among *lower*-income older citizens—in part, no doubt, because the program provides more than 90 percent of income for one in four beneficiaries (Campbell 2003; Center on Budget and Policy Priorities 2020).

Older Americans not only participate individually at higher rates; they are also represented by one of the nation's few major cross-class membership organizations, the AARP. Over the last 50 years, many large-scale political groups, from private-sector unions to fraternal organizations, have atrophied. The decline has been particularly steep for private-sector labor unions—once vital to encouraging political participation and engagement among the middle class, as well as advocating for nonaffluent working families in Washington. Yet the AARP has remained one of the largest and most influential voluntary organizations in the nation, with almost 40 million members in 2018.

These two distinctive realities—an age-biased welfare state and a politically active and organized aged population—would seem to imply that older citizens might have it much better in the United States than in other affluent nations. As already noted, however, they do not. According to major cross-national indicators, they are comparatively disadvantaged, and this disadvantage appears to be growing. These indicators can be broken into four broad categories: (1) poverty and inequality, (2) labor market participation and retirement, (3) social policy generosity, and (4) health and mortality. Since the other chapters have documented many of these challenges, we focus here on providing comparative context for these findings.

Before jumping into the cross-national evidence, however, we want to clarify what it tells us. For the most part, it does not say as much as might be assumed about *current* policies. That's because a major set of such policies—public and private pensions—tend to affect older citizens only 40 years or more after they are put in place. In the United States, for example, defined-benefit pensions that provide a guaranteed fixed benefit in retirement used to be common in the private sector; now they are vanishingly rare. Yet many Americans reaching retirement today were vested into such pensions during their working lives, so defined-benefit payouts remain a major part of the income of today's retirees. Similarly, cuts in Social Security made in the early 1980s had little effect on those nearing retirement at the time. Their full effects are only now becoming apparent, and they will continue to lower benefits for retirees into the future.

In short, when we look at the situation of today's older Americans, we are, in key respects, assessing the policy choices of decades ago. In the presentation to come, therefore, we try to provide a picture not only of how those currently nearing retirement are faring but also how Americans who will near retirement in the next few decades are likely to fare. In general, what we find is that today's middle-aged Americans are likely to face *even more severe strains*. In other words, the policy choices of the past couple of decades—what elected officials have done, as well as what they've chosen not to do—have generally reduced the economic security that today's middle-aged Americans can expect when they are older.

2.1. Absolute and Relative Poverty

Poverty was once much higher among over-65s than among younger Americans. With the massive expansion of both public and private pensions after World War II, the share of older Americans living below the federal poverty line plummeted. With justification, Social Security is described as the nation's most effective antipoverty program, lifting some 15 million elderly Americans above the federal poverty line (Center on Budget and Policy Priorities 2020). Alongside Social Security, employment-based defined-benefit pensions also offer guaranteed retirement supplements for roughly half of retired Americans.

Yet poverty among older Americans remains a pressing problem. It is useful here to distinguish between two common definitions of poverty: *absolute* poverty—household income below some fixed threshold, such as the official federal poverty line or the supplemental poverty measure (SPM)—and *relative* poverty, which is usually defined as an income below some share (generally 50 percent) of a nation's median income.

Absolute measures are particularly useful for examining the consequences of policies, since they allow an apples-to-apples comparison of policy effects over time. According to both the official poverty line and SPM—which takes into account medical costs and regional cost of living, among other factors—poverty fell dramatically among adults over age 65 in the decade after 1967 and less quickly but still substantially in the two decades after that. Yet the rate of the decline has slowed considerably since. Almost half the decline in absolute poverty occurred just between 1967 and 1977. In recent years, by contrast, the trend has been close to flat. More important, the SPM shows that absolute poverty among older Americans remains a widespread problem, affecting roughly one in seven older adults in 2018—a higher poverty rate than seen among the rest of the population. This higher-than-average rate reflects the SPM's factoring in of medical costs, which, despite Medicare, are higher for over-65s than for other age groups (Sherman, Parrott, and Trisi 2014; Fox 2020).

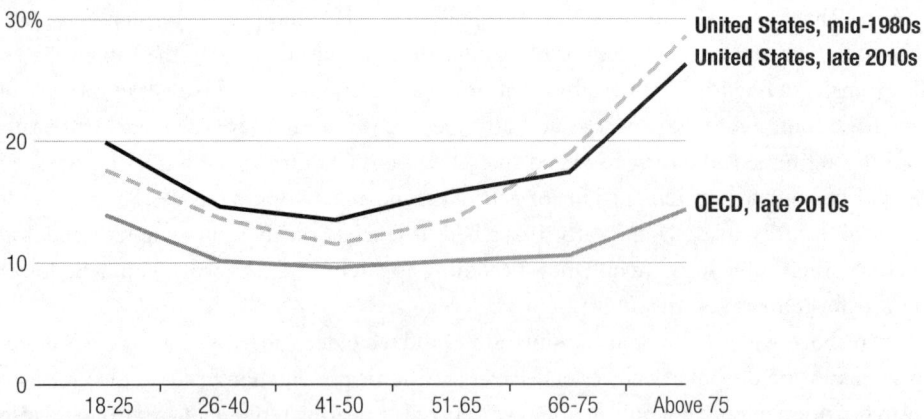

FIGURE 13.1 Relative poverty (below 50 percent of median income) by age, United States vs. OECD
Source: OECD (2018), Figure 1.1

Relative poverty measures are better at showing how the standard of living of a group compares with that of the rest of society. And what these measures show is that relative poverty among older adults is very high in the United States and rises substantially with age. As Figure 13.1 shows, the relative poverty rate for older Americans has barely budged since the mid-1980s, though it has declined slightly among adults above the age of 65 and risen slightly among those in their 50s and early 60s. More important, it is much higher than relative poverty in peer nations in the Organization for Economic Cooperation and Development (OECD), and in fact, it is roughly twice the OECD average among those older than 75. Put another way, inequality is very high among older adults, with those in the bottom strata relatively quite disadvantaged.

2.2. Labor Market Participation and Retirement

Inequality is also a salient feature of older Americans' experiences with work and retirement. Figure 13.2 shows the age of "effective labor market exit"—that is, permanent exit from the labor force due to retirement, inability to work for health reasons, or involuntary unemployment—for the top and bottom thirds of the income distribution, as well as the national average. The gap between the top and bottom is a measure of class disparities in the timing of labor market exit.

As the figure makes clear, higher-income Americans leave the workforce much later than lower-income Americans, and the average age of exit is comparatively high. Indeed, Japan—where the average life expectancy is roughly five years longer—is the only nation that has a higher effective age of labor market exit or a comparable gap between high-income and low-income workers.

This figure might be taken to suggest that working longer is mostly a choice—one that the affluent embrace and lower-income workers decline. Yet, as other chapters in this volume show, many older Americans who leave the labor force do so because of poor health, family caregiving responsibilities, or job loss. Moreover, given high poverty rates among older

The Biased Politics of "Working Longer" | 281

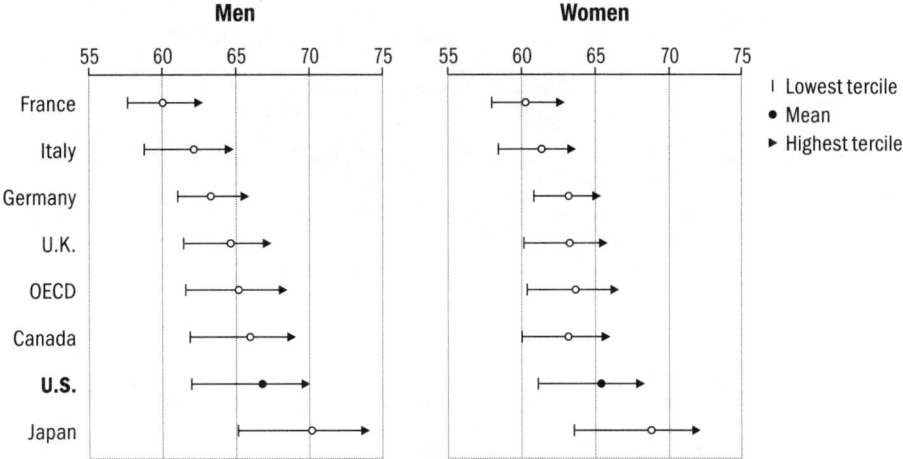

FIGURE 13.2 **Age of labor market exit for older workers by income, selected nations**
Note: The OECD average does not include Australia, Estonia, Finland, Hungary, Iceland, Norway, and Sweden.
Source: OECD (2018), Figure 1.7

Americans, it's clear that many of those who do continue working do so mainly because their pension incomes are insufficient in the absence of work. As Figure 13.3 shows, Americans are more likely than citizens in any other OECD nation to combine work and pension benefits between the ages of 60 and 69.

2.3. Social Policy Generosity

A major reason that so many older Americans continue working as long as they can is that America's public pensions are comparatively ungenerous, as Figure 13.4 indicates. The

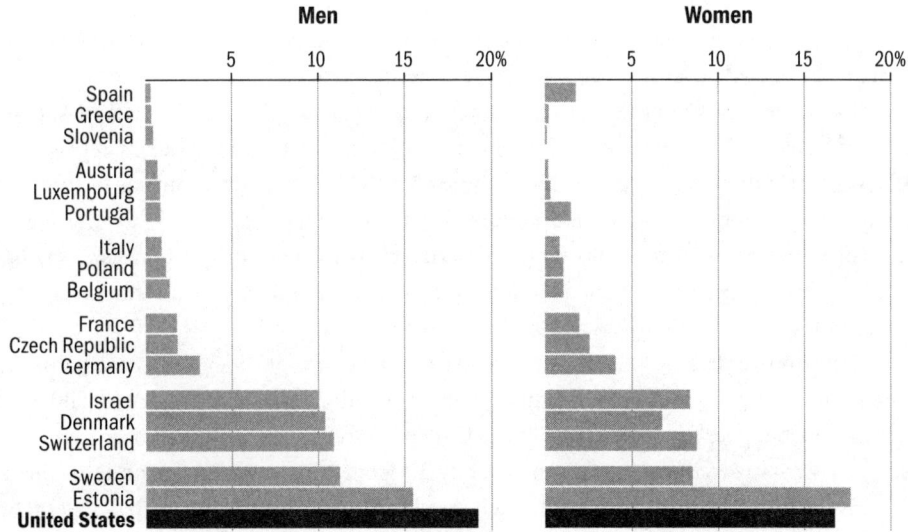

FIGURE 13.3 **Percentage of 60- to 69-year-olds combining work and pension income, 2014/15**
Source: OECD (2018), Fig 1.17

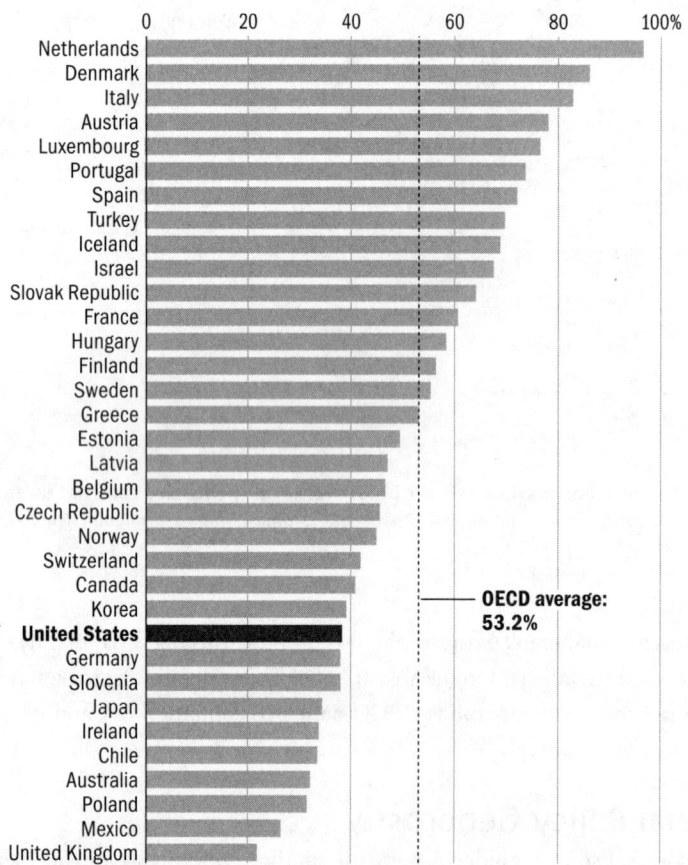

FIGURE 13.4 Public pension benefits as a share of earnings for the average worker
Source: OECD (2019), Figure 5.1

amount of prior earnings replaced by Social Security is well below the OECD average, and dramatically below the levels seen in the most generous nations.

Historically, these low replacement rates were justified by the prevalence of supplementary employer-based pension plans. These plans, however, have been largely replaced by defined-contribution plans, such as the ubiquitous 401(k). Although the effects of this shift remain muted among current retirees, future cohorts look much more likely to fall short of the income needed to retire comfortably (Ghilarducci 2010). Since private plans and savings play a much smaller role in other rich nations, these stark trends, too, are distinctive to the United States.

Comparative data on the generosity of health coverage for older adults are harder to come by, but there is good reason to think that, even with Medicare, uncovered health care costs are much higher for older adults in the United States than in most other rich democracies. A 2017 survey of adults aged 65 and over by the Commonwealth Fund found that financial considerations were perceived as a much greater barrier to care in the United States than in 10 other affluent nations. Nearly a quarter of American respondents reported having problems obtaining needed treatment because of the cost, compared with 10 percent of Germans,

9 percent of Canadians, and 4 percent of Brits (Osborn et al. 2017). Out-of-pocket spending by older Americans has also been rising as a share of income, and it is projected to rise further in the future. According to estimates by the Kaiser Family Foundation, total out-of-pocket spending (including Medicare premiums) equaled 41 percent of elderly Americans' Social Security income, on average, in 2013, and will rise to 50 percent by 2030 if current trends continue (Cubanski et al. 2018).

2.4. Health and Mortality

One reason that older Americans spend more on health care is that they are, in general, less healthy than their counterparts in other rich nations. In the Commonwealth Fund Survey just referenced, for example, older Americans reported they were dealing with substantially more chronic health conditions than did their peers in the other 10 nations surveyed. Life expectancy in the United States is comparatively short, and it has been falling farther and farther behind the international norm, as Figure 13.5 shows.

What's more, the gap in life expectancy between higher- and lower-income Americans has been growing, increasing the disparity in lifetime Social Security benefits and in the effects of higher expected retirement ages. Comparing those born in 1930 with those born in 1960, life expectancy increased among Americans in the top half of the earnings distribution, while those in the bottom half of the income distribution experienced no longevity gains whatsoever (National Academies of Sciences, Engineering, and Medicine 2015). In recent years, even before the COVID-19 pandemic, death rates actually began to rise among some demographic groups—first among middle-aged white Americans without a college degree, and subsequently among all racial and ethnic groups (Woolf and Schoomaker 2019; Case and Deaton 2020). In the modern history of affluent nations, such sustained and broad-based

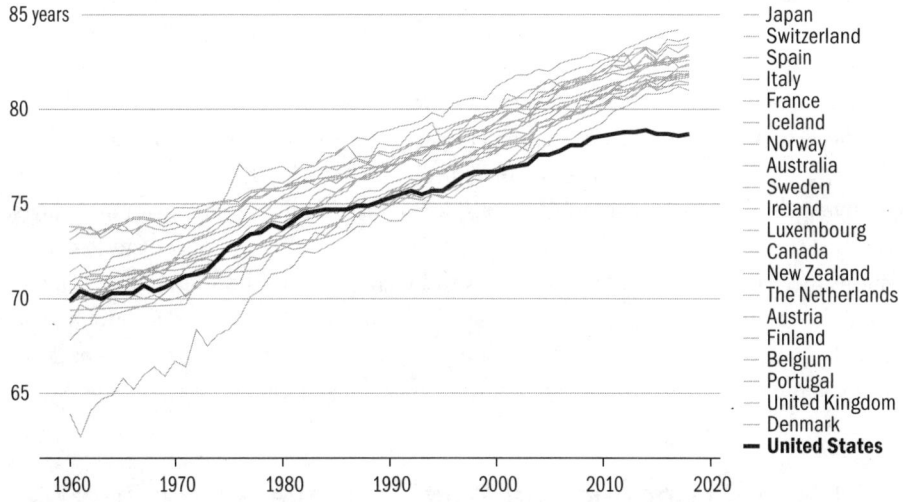

FIGURE 13.5 Life expectancy at birth in 22 OECD countries, 1960–2018
Country names are in order of life expectancy in 2018
Source: OECD (2021).

increases in death rates are virtually without precedent, and these increases likely reflect the acute economic dislocations faced by many who will soon be entering the ranks of the U.S. elderly.

To sum up, older Americans have faced increasing strains, and these strains are likely to get worse in the future, due to rising inequality and declining pension generosity. In their severity and frequency, these strains are also distinctive to the United States. Although global economic and social trends have threatened the health and economic security of older citizens in many rich nations, U.S.-specific policy choices have uniquely exacerbated these pressures, resulting in distressingly poor outcomes among a group once well protected.

3. Why Have U.S. Policymakers Done So Little to Help?

These poor outcomes raise a political puzzle. Why has there been so little policy response to a group rightly seen as possessing unique political resources due to its higher rates of participation and unusual level of political organization? In fact, the puzzle is even more specific, because those most adversely affected by these trends are, in general, closely aligned with the contemporary Republican Party. White Americans older than 50 who lack a college degree and live outside major urban centers have become the core of the GOP electoral base. They have helped Republicans retain an advantaged position in Congress for much of the past two decades, and they were integral to the election of President Trump. And yet they are among the segments of American society that have most directly confronted the loss of economic and health security signaled by the trends just discussed (Case and Deaton 2020).

In this section, we consider why political elites in general, and Republican political elites in particular, have largely failed to respond to the increasing challenges discussed in the last section. We identify three growing biases that have constrained and channeled elected officials' response to the dislocations experienced by older Americans—biases that reflect stark disparities in organized political power in an increasingly unequal society.

The first is a bias toward economic elites, whom, we shall see, are much less favorable toward generous social policies than are ordinary citizens. The second is a bias toward legislative gridlock on pressing public issues, including those associated with an aging society. The third is a bias within the Republican Party toward highly conservative economic positions. Because these economic policy stances enjoy relatively little support even among Republican voters, the Republican Party has increasingly emphasized noneconomic issues (particularly those revolving around race, immigration, and conservative religious backlash), while exploiting features of American political institutions that favor them despite the close parity between the parties.

3.1. Rising Economic and Political Power at the Top

Over the past generation, the distribution of American economic rewards has changed fundamentally. Between 1980 and 2016, the share of national income accruing to the richest 1 percent of households *doubled*, increasing from just over 10 percent to more than

20 percent. Over the same period, the share of national income accruing to the bottom half of households declined by *half*, from (roughly) 20 percent to 10 percent (Alvaredo et al. 2018). In other words, the income shares of these two groups—the top 1 percent and the bottom 50 percent—switched places. The top now has what the (50 times larger) bottom used to have.

These trends look very different from those in most other rich nations. In Western Europe over the same period, the share of income received by the top 1 percent has risen from 10 percent, on average, to around 12 percent, while the share enjoyed by the bottom half has fallen from roughly 24 percent to 22 percent (Alvaredo et al. 2018). In short, the rewards at the top are bigger in the United States, and they have become more concentrated more quickly. Meanwhile, the relative standing of the middle and bottom has fallen much more in the United States than in other rich nations.

The sharp increase in economic inequality in the United States has gone hand in hand with two other fateful transformations: a big increase in the relative political power of those at the top and a big divergence between the views of these more powerful actors and those of the rest of Americans.

Since the 1970s, there has been a staggering increase in the role of money in politics. One important form this has taken is organized political action by conservative business groups. American corporations greatly expanded their political capacities in the late 1970s and early 1980s. Deploying the now-familiar tools of professionalized advocacy—think tanks, PACs, DC lobbying houses—they out-muscled their organized opponents and helped reset the agenda of Washington, pulling both parties toward their newly aggressively conservative stances on taxes, regulation, and the role of unions (Hacker and Pierson 2010).

Along with powerful corporations, individual millionaires and billionaires also became more active in organized politics. This greater activity not only reflected the growing ranks of the superrich but also the declining regulatory barriers to political spending, the decreasing transparency of that spending, and the growing divergence of interests and preferences of the very wealthy from the bulk of Americans. In contrast with business leaders, these antigovernment investors focused less on immediate influence and more on enduring ideas. Some of the most persistent and ideologically extreme think tanks and intellectual networks of our day entered the scene in the 1970s and early 1980s—the Heritage Foundation (1973), the Cato Institute (1978), the Federalist Society (1982)—while others, such as the American Enterprise Institute, grew dramatically. These new intellectual organizations focused on making the case for relatively unpopular policies that were previously seen as excessively conservative, such as rolling back environmental protections, abolishing the Estate Tax, and turning Social Security into a system of individually managed accounts.

As these organized efforts played out, the role of campaign donations from the rich also expanded. Not only did the amount of money spent on Americans elections dramatically increase; more and more of this money came from the biggest donors. In 1980, around 10 percent of all donations to federal campaigns were made by the top 0.1 percent of donors; by 2018, the share of the (much greater) total that came from the top 0.1 percent of donors was roughly half (Bonica et al. 2013; Bonica 2019). Notably, these estimates exclude rapidly expanding independent "dark money" expenditures, which rely heavily on contributions from the very wealthy (Grumbach and Pierson 2019).

Not all of those who took advantage of these trends were on the ideological right, of course. But the most influential of these increasingly powerful players certainly were. The very rich and corporate groups invest much more heavily in the Republican Party than in the Democratic Party. This conservative tilt is even more pronounced when we focus on the most organized political actors, including influential networks of donors and powerful business groups. And it's even more pronounced when we consider the myriad nonpublic ways in the superrich and corporations can support politicians and lobby for their causes, such as "dark money" (unreported campaign and lobbying expenditures), hidden contributions to interest groups, and advocacy spending laundered through nonprofits (Grumbach and Pierson 2019).

The economic priorities and preferences of these political actors are, on average, far to the right of those of the American public. There is, of course, ideological diversity within the top decimal places of the American economic distribution, and the views of the superrich do not always align with their material self-interest. Still, we now have strong evidence that those at the very top of the economic ladder tend to hold much more conservative positions on economic issues than those lower on it, and to place higher priority on causes associated with those conservative positions, such as rapidly reducing the national debt. We have evidence, too, that the wealthiest and most politically active are farthest to the right, and that the growing economic segregation of the rich from ordinary citizens reinforces these distinctive attitudes. In short, the growing sway of wealthy donors and organized business groups has increased the pressure on elected officials to pursue conservative economic and social policies that have limited popularity among most Americans (for a full set of citations, see Hacker and Pierson 2016, 2020; Thal 2017; Hertel-Fernandez, Skocpol, and Sclar 2018; for evidence of differential responsiveness to the opinions of the affluent, relative to those of more modest means, see Bartels 2008; Gilens 2012; Gilens and Page 2014).

The sharpest opinion differences concern taxes, regulation, labor unions, and the relative importance of fiscal restraint versus spending to safeguard economic security. The wealthy are much more conservative on average: more antitax, more antiregulation, more opposed to unions, more concerned about deficits, and less supportive of programs like Social Security. Indeed, many of these conservative positions are surprisingly prevalent even in the more "liberal" wings of the plutocracy. A recent survey of big donors in Silicon Valley, for example, finds that executives in the generally liberal tech sector are more opposed to government regulation and organized labor, on average, than are Republican voters (Broockman, Ferenstein, and Malhotra 2019).

Consider just a few of the stark differences between average voters and the wealthy, which come to us thanks to an intensive effort by a team of political scientists to get a sizable sample of very wealthy Americans to respond to a set of standard survey questions (Page, Bartels, and Seawright 2013). The survey asked whether government had a responsibility to reduce income differences between rich and poor. In prior surveys, 46 percent of Americans had said government had that responsibility. In the focused survey of the very wealthy, just

13 percent of respondents did. In prior surveys, 61 percent of citizens expressed support for universal health insurance; only 32 percent of the very wealthy did.

The biggest gap, however, concerned spending on Social Security. By a 33-point margin, the very wealthy wanted to cut back the program (in other words, the share supporting a spending cut was 33 points greater than the share supporting a spending increase). Among the public, the gap was in the opposite direction and larger: the share of the public that wanted to *increase* Social Security was 46 points greater than the share that wanted to cut it. This stark divergence drives home the extent to which the influence of corporations and the very affluent creates pressure for more conservative social policies. Moreover, this gap is particularly large on issues related to pensions, the length of expected work years, and health care. For example, raising the Social Security retirement age is a staple of elite discussions of the program—supported not just by centrist and conservative think tanks but also by leading Republican candidates during presidential campaigns. Indeed, the journalist Ezra Klein (2015) has noted that "if establishment Washington has a platform, raising the Social Security retirement age is squarely at its core." Among the broader public, by contrast, raising the retirement age is massively unpopular—one of the ideas that is most corrosive to public support for packages designed to deal with Social Security's funding gap (Walker, Reno, and Bethell 2014).

The views of economic elites aren't just far to the right of the general public; they are well to the right of ordinary Republican voters. A very large 2012 survey looked at support for two central GOP policy aims of the period: the extension of the early-2000s Bush tax cuts, even for the richest Americans; and House Republican Paul Ryan's ultra-conservative budget (Kuo and McCarty 2015; for discussion, see Hacker and Pierson 2020). (The basic features of each bill were neutrally described.) It is important to emphasize how fundamental these two Republican aims were to the issues just discussed. The tax cuts—estimated at the time of their passage to cost three times as much as *permanently* fixing the fiscal shortfall in Social Security (Hacker and Pierson 2005)—posed a huge threat to the capacity of the federal government to finance programs for older Americans. The Ryan proposal would have cut several of these programs—most notably, by turning Medicare into a voucher program. It then proposed to add on top of the Bush tax cuts enormous additional tax cuts, funded through massive spending reductions in programs particularly beneficial to less affluent older Americans, such as Medicaid and Supplemental Security Income.

Did Republican voters support these two central plans of the GOP fiscal agenda? Figure 13.6 has the answer. Among all voters, the complete extension of the Bush tax cuts had just 25 percent support, while the Ryan budget commanded an even more dismal 19 percent support. Among Republican voters, the results were better but still bad: 42 percent and 32 percent, respectively. In other words, each fell well short of majority support among the party's own voters—in the case of the Ryan budget, spectacularly short. This low support is especially striking in our era of polarization and tribalism, when voters aligned with a party are generally highly receptive to its positions. Tellingly, there was only one group within the electorate for whom support topped a majority for both proposals: GOP donors with incomes in excess of $250,000 a year.

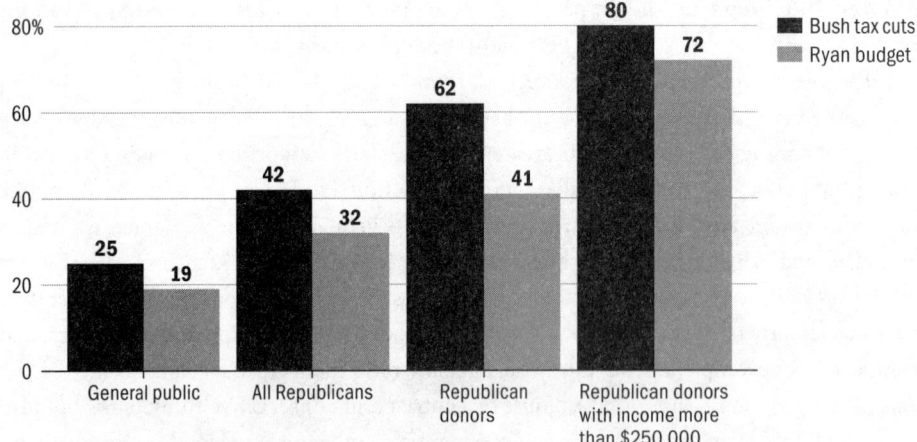

FIGURE 13.6 The stark divide between GOP elites and the party's voting base
Share of the public, Republicans, Republican donors, and wealthy Republican donors (more than $250,000 annual income) supporting the Ryan budget (gray) and extending the Bush tax cuts even for the rich (black). Only among wealthy Republican donors do majorities support both policies.
Source: Stein and Rowell (2016), Figure 1

3.2. Political Gridlock and Policy Drift

The second bias we discuss is a bias toward gridlock. By gridlock we mean stalemate on policy fronts, including those where addressing social problems requires government action. In general, gridlock has protected social provision from aggressive efforts (like the Ryan Plan) to scale back the American welfare state. For example, despite the strong support of antideficit organizations associated with the superrich, President George W. Bush's 2005 effort to partially privatize Social Security ultimately failed in the face of strong public opposition. Groups like AARP have played an important role in blocking such retrenchment.

Yet the American welfare state has nonetheless significantly eroded in the face of changing economic and social circumstances, a process we call "policy drift" (Hacker, Pierson, and Thelen 2015). Much of American social provision relies on a combination of private provision with public subsidies and regulation. If these public rules are not updated as private arrangements change, the social safety net may be effectively eroded. To continue with the example of pensions, even as Social Security has remained intact, private defined-benefit pensions have essentially disappeared in the private sector, worsening the retirement security of all but the affluent. In a host of policy areas, gridlock in the face of changing economic and social realities has produced pervasive policy drift that has eroded the economic security of older Americans.

Two aspects of American politics and policy make drift particularly common and consequential. First, to a degree unmatched in other democracies, our political institutions create multiple veto points, where opponents of action can block change. As polarization between the parties has increased, the level of agreement necessary for active governance has proved increasingly elusive, especially at the national level. Policy drift has been the result.

It is important to note that those who designed America's constitutional order did not intend for it to be so prone to inducing gridlock. They believed that the fragmentation of governing authority would not only *require* compromise but also *facilitate* it by creating cross-cutting cleavages within society. Rising polarization, changing norms, and the shifting impact of long-standing rules have challenged these expectations. For example, a major source of gridlock today is the Senate filibuster, which requires that 60 of 100 senators vote to advance legislation on most topics. The filibuster is not part of the Constitution; it is an element of Senate rules, and it played a circumscribed role in the past. As Congress has polarized, however, filibusters have become much more common. At the same time, the malapportionment of the Senate caused by the granting of two Senators to every state irrespective of population has become much more extreme. Today, Senators representing just a sixth of the U.S. population have the power, with the filibuster, to block legislation (Tucker 2019). Moreover, the malapportionment has become more consequential as the division between populous and less-populous states has become more correlated with the divide between the parties.

The second reason why policy gridlock and drift are so important in the United States is that the distinctive structure of the American welfare state makes them particularly consequential for social protection. Uniquely among rich democracies, the United States came to depend on workplace benefits as the primary source of economic security for working-age adults (Hacker 2002). Even in the wake of the Affordable Care Act, the majority of American workers receive their health benefits through employment. As already noted, workplace pension benefits also remain a vital, if declining, source of retirement security.

This job-based benefits system, however, is coming undone. The unions that once negotiated and defended private benefits have lost tremendous ground. Meanwhile, employers face strong incentives to reduce the burdens they took on during more stable economic times. At the same time, they no longer place as much value on the long-term relationships with workers that these arrangements reflected and fostered.

Moreover, the workplace is not the only site of heightened insecurity. Americans are also at greater risk because of changes within families. Although median wages have essentially remained flat over the last generation, median-income families have seen stronger income growth. Yet the whole of this rise is because women are working many more hours outside the home than they once did. Indeed, without the increased work hours and pay of women, median family incomes would have *fallen* over the last generation (Boushey and Vaghul 2016). As a result, families with two earners now rely on continuous work by both partners to maintain a middle-class standard of living. This heightens the potential for disruption when they need to take time off to care for children, parents, or themselves; when they face unexpected expenses; or when their partnerships end in divorce or separation. Of course, many of these risks are even greater for the substantial minority of parents who are raising children on their own.

In all these ways, the new world of work and family has undermined key pillars that helped limit economic insecurity in the mid-twentieth century. This "Great Risk Shift" (Hacker 2019) is not, for the most part, due to successful political efforts to undermine public protections. Rather, it is because there has been so little response to the ongoing erosion of an increasingly outdated system. In short, policy drift has had a major impact. And once again, these effects have been particularly pronounced in the areas of greatest importance for those aging into Medicare and Social Security: health care, retirement security, and job security.

3.3. Asymmetric Polarization and the Role of the Republican Party

The final bias that has worsened the strains facing older Americans concerns the Republican Party. Historically, moderate Republicans were a key part of the bipartisan coalitions that constructed generous social protections. Not only did they often support social policy enactments and updating; they also put pressure on business leaders to accommodate an enlarged role for government. Of course, Republicans were, on average, substantially more conservative than Democrats. But for a large and critical group within the party that conservatism did not always preclude support for more generous social policies and the taxes necessary to fund them.

Standard political science models suggest that rising inequality and economic insecurity should encourage political parties to support increasing social provision, because the share of citizens likely to benefit from redistribution will grow and parties face electoral incentives to satisfy the demands of the "median voter" (Meltzer and Richard 1981). Instead, however, as inequality has grown dramatically, the Republican Party has become much more economically conservative than it once was. It is also much more conservative on economic issues than center-right parties in other affluent democracies. Scholars and journalists are often reluctant to acknowledge this fact, because to do so sounds partisan. But there is really no ambiguity about what the evidence shows. The dramatic polarization of political elites over the last generation has not been symmetrical. Republicans have moved much farther right than Democrats have moved left. This asymmetry can be seen not just in congressional voting patterns but also in the relative positions of presidential and vice-presidential nominees, as well as in the relative positions of each party's judicial nominees. It can also be seen in the polarization of state-level elected officials (Hacker and Pierson 2015).

Nowhere is this asymmetric polarization clearer than in economic and social policy. Political scientists have developed rigorous measures of the ideological position of elected officials, and they all show that Republicans became sharply more conservative on the full range of economic issues in the 1990s, 2000s, and 2010s. Over this same period, no comparable leftward movement can be seen among Democrats. According to one widely used measure, for example, in 1990 about 1 in 5 congressional Republicans and a similar share of congressional Democrats were "ideologically extreme," according to their congressional voting patterns. By 2000, 3 in 5 Republican members of Congress were, with no change in the Democratic share. A decade on, more than 4 in 5 Republicans in Congress were—again, without any parallel movement among Democrats in Congress (Ingraham 2015).

It is important to emphasize that this shift does not appear to be rooted in voter attitudes. On major measures of economic policy preferences, public opinion as a whole has generally trended left since the mid-1990s. According to one commonly used indicator of "policy mood," general public views are more liberal today than at any point since the 1960s (Stimson 2019). Even Republican voters have not, in general, become markedly more conservative on economic issues. Indeed, because Republicans have had to attract more and more support from white Americans to stay in power as the country grows more diverse, they have actually come to rely more and more on white voters without a college degree—the so-called white working class. These less affluent white voters are generally to the left on economic issues, at least when the focus is public benefits identified with white Americans, such as Social Security and Medicare. On these issues, they are certainly well to the left of affluent donors and influential organizations allied with the Republican Party (Kuo and McCarty 2015; Drutman 2017).

As already noted, the growing influence of these deep-pocketed allies is a major reason for the GOP's right turn. As conservative donors and organizations gained greater power, what had been a relatively mainstream conservative party came to embrace positions far to the right of both its historical stances and the positions of conservative parties abroad. Analyses based on systematic coding of the campaign platforms of leading parties show that the Republican Party is an outlier relative not just to center-right parties in other nations, but in some cases to right-wing parties that place themselves well to the right of mainstream conservatives, too (Hacker and Pierson 2020).

Consider just two examples: health care and taxation. In the debate over President Bill Clinton's health plan in 1993 and 1994, more than half of Senate Republicans backed a competing, market-oriented approach advocated by the Heritage Foundation. The Heritage blueprint later became the guiding vision for a health plan passed in Massachusetts with the support of GOP Governor Mitt Romney. Yet when these same principles became the template for President Obama's health plan in 2009, every national Republican, including Romney, denounced it in the most apocalyptic terms. Of course, GOP opposition was so intense in part because Obama's name was on the plan, but Republicans sustained their extreme rhetoric and proposals even after the law was passed. We have already mentioned the Ryan budget proposals of the early 2010s. In. 2017, Republicans came within a few votes of repealing core elements of the Affordable Care Act (ACA) and dramatically scaling back Medicaid—a package that, had it passed, would have been the most substantial and regressive retrenchment in the history of U.S. social policy (Hacker and Pierson 2018).

Even more revealing, the effects of the GOP "repeal and replace" health bills would have been particularly devastating for the white working-class voters so crucial to Donald Trump's victory in 2016. Courting these voters during the campaign, Trump had outflanked "establishment" Republican opponents by vowing to protect not just Social Security and Medicare but also Medicaid—an increasingly vital source of protection for many of the party's white working-class voters. Residents of rural and rustbelt regions were not only disproportionately insured under the ACA's Medicaid expansion; they were also more likely to benefit from the law's support for substance abuse treatment. All the GOP bills would have curtailed most of these benefits. The new and much less generous funding formulas in the GOP bills also permitted higher premiums for older Americans. Losses would have been especially large in rural areas, and among those over the age of 50 living on moderate incomes—that is, precisely those voters who had rallied behind Trump (Hacker and Pierson 2018).

Similarly, the Republican Party once worked closely with Democrats to restrain the growth of federal health spending without reducing benefits by using Medicare's bargaining leverage to hold down provider charges. (In fact, Presidents Reagan and George H. W.

Bush each spearheaded new payment controls, with substantial GOP support in Congress.) Beginning in the 1990s under House Speaker Newt Gingrich, Republicans renounced these once-bipartisan efforts to control costs within the health care industry. Instead, GOP leaders focused their proposals on cuts in benefits, even ones that would in practice have little impact on overall costs. They advocated turning Medicaid into a limited "block grant" to the states. They proposed to raise the eligibility age for Medicare and transform it into a voucher-style system in which the federal government made a fixed contribution to the cost of private plans, shifting the risks of rising health spending from the federal government onto beneficiaries. The Republican abandonment of health care cost control is one more reason why policy drift has reigned, letting health care prices rise to ever more exorbitant levels with little government pushback.

The Republicans have also turned right on issues related to taxes. Ronald Reagan and George H. W. Bush agreed to raise taxes on several occasions, maintaining the established bipartisan formula for handling budget deficits: modestly cut spending and moderately raise taxes. After 1990, however, Republicans refused to support any tax increases in budget packages. Indeed, they sometimes insisted that "deficit reduction" agreements include (deficit-raising) tax cuts. At the same time, Republicans increasingly focused on tax cuts for the highest income groups: cuts in the estate, dividends, corporate, and capital gains taxes, as well as the top marginal income tax rate. This focus on tax cuts for the affluent reached its apotheosis (to date) in the "Trump tax cuts" of 2017, which delivered over 80 percent of their long-term benefits to the richest 1 percent (Tax Policy Center 2017). This skew is all the more striking because opinion polls consistently indicate that voters' biggest complaint about the tax system is that the rich do not pay their fair share (Sawhill and Pulliam 2019).

The rightward movement of the GOP has made it exceedingly difficult to construct new social policies that attract broad support among lawmakers. But ideological shifts have not been the only barrier to an effective response to the increased strains facing older Americans. In addition to moving right, Republicans have become much more confrontational and resistant to compromise (Hacker and Pierson 2015). Even when out of power in Congress or the White House, Republicans have been able to exploit the ample opportunities for obstruction created by our distinctive political institutions to block bipartisan solutions or renovate outdated policies.

While national lawmaking institutions have become more sclerotic, two other venues have become much more important—the courts and the states. Both are highly favorable to the Republican Party. The courts are GOP-friendly because of the combination of the Electoral College (two elections where Republicans won the White House while losing the popular vote), rural bias that has made the Senate favorable ground for the GOP, and the party's hardball efforts to stack the federal bench (witness Senate Majority Leader Mitch McConnell's unprecedented willingness in 2016 to block President Obama's nominee to fill Justice Antonin Scalia's seat on the Supreme Court, versus his also unprecedented willingness in 2020 to race President Trump's nominee to fill Justice Ruth Bader Ginsburg's seat through confirmation just days before a presidential election). The states have proved to be GOP-friendly because of the GOP advantage in the South and in sparsely populated states and because of more successful and sustained efforts at partisan gerrymandering. Republican "trifectas"—control of a state governorship and both houses of the state legislature—are more common than in the past and more common than Democratic trifectas, and, in recent years, they have resulted in a sharp move of policy to the right (Grumbach 2018).

Perhaps the most consequential success for Republicans in the courts and the states has been labor law. After decades without real movement on the issue, Republicans in states that did not have union-hostile "right to work" laws began to pursue them once again, as well as to put in place measures to limit the reach and power of public-sector unions. Meanwhile, the Supreme Court—in a series of conservative-led rulings—has hobbled unions' capacity to require dues from workers who benefit from collective bargaining, and it has expanded the power of businesses to require that workers participate in politics in ways favorable to employers' political preferences. Unions support good benefits and wages in the workplace; they are also one of the few broad middle-class advocacy organizations active in American politics. They align more closely with the opinions of the middle class and poor on economic and social policies than almost any other group (Gilens 2012). Their weakening has thus made drift that hurts broad majorities more likely to persist, and it has reduced the pushback against inegalitarian policy changes, such as tax cuts for corporations and the affluent.

In short, an increasingly conservative Republican Party has hindered an effective response to the growing strains facing older Americans. Not only have Republicans pursued policies that have either worsened or threatened to worsen these problems—ranging from large unfunded tax cuts, to measures weakening labor unions, to cutbacks in Medicare, Medicaid, and Social Security. They have also largely failed to take affirmative action that would address these serious problems. The effects of these stances are limited where strong social policies are in place and protected against erosion by automatic updates (such as indexation to price levels). But the rightward movement of the GOP has proved much more consequential where policies require regular updating and especially where existing policies increasingly fall short because of changes in the world of work and family and the erosion of private benefits. In these highly important areas—ranging from wage and labor laws to health care and pension policies—drift has eroded the economic standing of older Americans.

3.4. Putting the Pieces Together

We return, then, to our starting puzzle: Why have older voters—who are comparatively well organized, participate at high levels, and constitute a vital element of the GOP's electoral coalition—not put more of a check on these often-unpopular policies?

Each of our three biases has played an important role. First, the decline of traditional organizations representing the middle class has increased the relative power of groups representing the affluent. The near-collapse of private-sector unions has been particularly important, since unions have traditionally been a key force encouraging voters to focus on economic issues and pressuring politicians to be responsive to those voters. Second, opponents of robust response to these trends have exploited the growing tendency of our political system toward gridlock. The failure to respond to citizens' economic demands, in turn, has made Americans more skeptical of government and more willing to support extreme politicians.

Third, and finally, these economic and political trends have moved the Republican Party sharply to the right. The party has not paid a big price, however, for the relative unpopularity of its stances on economic issues. For one, Republicans have been able to use distrust of government and divisive issues of identity to retain their electoral standing among white voters. For another, they have benefited from features of the American political system that accentuate the influence of those supporters—features that they have made even more consequential by actively working to change electoral rules to discourage voting by Democratic-leaning segments of the electorate and to magnify the influence of Republican-leaning segments.

Here we come to one feature of American public opinion that we *do* think is important to the largely organizational story we tell. According to new opinion research, over the last generation older white Americans have become notably less supportive of government redistribution and public efforts to ensure economic opportunity (Ashok, Kuziemko, and Washington 2015). Crucially, the same is not true of younger white voters, or indeed of Americans as a whole. Nor is it true of older voters in other rich nations. Even more puzzling, it has occurred without a general shift among these voters to the right. Rather it is the use of government to reduce income differences and provide opportunity that distinctively appears to elicit older white voters' antigovernment instincts. Since these are high-turnout portions of the electorate that have leaned Republican, this opinion shift almost certainly has muted the pushback against GOP policy priorities and thus requires explanation.

The jury is still out on why older white voters buck the more general trends, but there is suggestive evidence that two concerns loom large. First, older white voters are the group most likely to be opposed to universal health insurance. In the 2009–2010 fight over the Affordable Care Act, Republicans successfully portrayed the ACA as a threat to Medicare (most notoriously, with the fake charges that the Affordable Care Act contained "death panels"). Today, support for Medicare for All is lowest among those who are actually on Medicare today.

Second, older white voters are also most likely to harbor what political scientists call "racial resentment"—a belief that Black Americans are getting more than their fair share. Older white voters, especially white men, are also the hotbed of anti-immigrant sentiment in the United States. Interview-based and survey work by political scientists and sociologists finds again and again that fear about losing social benefits and fear of demographic change are linked in these voters' minds. Put bluntly, many fear that a coming non-white majority will bring not only a loss of status but also a reduction in guarantees of economic security they believe they've earned, as those with a different skin color demand a larger share of the pie. In fact, simply telling white respondents that the United States will become "majority-minority" nation shifts them to the right on a range of issues, from those related to race (affirmative action, immigration) to those not about race but clearly racialized (health care, taxes) (Craig and Richeson 2017).

We want to make clear that we do not think Americans have suddenly become more racist. Rather, what has increased is the incentive for Republicans to deploy strategies grounded in racial resentment. To counter the growing non-white share of the electorate—a set of voters who lean strongly Democratic—Republicans have come to depend on winning outsized margins among less affluent older white voters. Yet, among Republican-favorable segments of the electorate, these downscale white voters are at once the *least* supportive of conservative economic policies and the most prone to racial resentment, making strongly racialized appeals an effective strategy for increasing their allegiance to the GOP and their likelihood of turning out.

Of course, such "right-wing populist" appeals are becoming more common worldwide. In general, conservative parties intensify such appeals when they are faced with rising economic inequality and there are alternative racial or religious cleavages that can easily be exploited. Yet right-wing populists in other rich nations are generally called "welfare chauvinists," demanding more generous benefits for white citizens. Republicans, by contrast, have continued to pursue policies that mostly benefit the affluent even while courting less affluent white voters.

America's electoral system helps explain why this "plutocratic populism" is possible (Hacker and Pierson 2020; Rodden 2021). The unique American electoral system substantially advantages Republicans, allowing them to concentrate on rallying their base. It combines a Senate highly biased toward less populous, more rural states (a bias that partially carries over to the Electoral College, which decides the presidency) with single-member, winner-take-all districts. This system naturally rewards parties that are broadly distributed across large swaths of sparsely populated territory. It also makes it much easier for such parties to gerrymander districts to maximize their ability to translate votes into seats, especially because they are likely to control state governments (and hence redistricting) in less populous states. Increasingly, as urban areas have become more Democratic and rural areas more Republican, the party that has been rewarded by this system is the GOP.

This Republican electoral edge has provided insulation that has, ironically, heightened the party's audacity in pursuing upwardly redistributive policies that will be devastating in many of the areas of the country where Republican voting strength is greatest. Electoral insulation means that Republicans can adopt more extreme stances with less fear of backlash from moderate voters. Meanwhile, it increases their fear of primary challengers from their right flank as opposed to general-election opponents. The conservative "outrage industry" (Fox News, Breitbart, conservative social media) has added to this insulation, fostering a GOP electorate strongly motivated by "affective partisanship"—that is, party allegiance based substantially on hatred of the other side. Like the American political parties, the American media environment has become asymmetrically polarized, with conservative media far more extreme and isolated than media sources on the U.S. left (Benkler, Faris, and Roberts 2018). The power of conservative media to define issues and identities on the right is another highly distinctive feature of the American context.

We want to emphasize again that the core sources of the GOP's asymmetric shift to the right lie in the institutional biases and organizational imbalances emphasized throughout this chapter. However, the GOP's intensified exploitation of racial backlash is a key reason why there has been so little effective electoral pushback against what are, in the main, unpopular economic stances. Given the centrality of older white voters to the party's electoral coalition, the ability of Republican candidates to attract these voters without responding to their social policy preferences has proved crucial to the political marginalization of responses to the economic strains they face. Geographic and media isolation have worked in tandem to intensify the opposition of the GOP base to government, the Democratic Party, and more effective and generous social policies seen as giveaways to racial and ethnic minorities. And because these voters are given extra weight in our electoral system, the capacity of Republicans to (so far) ignore or pay only lip service to these voters' more left-leaning economic priorities has had an outsized effect on the recent course of American politics.

4. Might Policymakers Begin to Respond?

We have argued that politics and policy are a major reason why older Americans have experienced more adverse outcomes than older citizens of other rich democracies. The flip side of our argument is that a different kind of politics, leading to different policy choices, could do much to help these very same Americans. What are the prospects for such a politics?

The past generation has taught us that the structure of partisan conflict and the electoral system mediate voters' responses to insecurity. Vigorous clarifying and mobilizing efforts by groups are particularly crucial if voters are to recognize their economic interests and act on behalf of them. Without serious efforts to rebuild groups representing workers and other diffuse constituencies, efforts to respond to rising insecurity are likely to be anemic, episodic, and vulnerable to backsliding.

Another barrier that must be confronted is the fragmented, veto-ridden structure of political authority in the United States, and the degree to which it empowers those seeking to stop, rather than enable, government activity. As we have emphasized, the status-quo bias of American political institutions—coupled with the asymmetric polarization of the parties—has stood in the way of comprehensive national efforts to address insecurity. We would add that, because of this gridlock as well as the success of Republicans in confirming conservative judges, battles in the federal courts will be fundamental.

Still, there are opportunities. For one, economic rewards are now so concentrated at the very top that substantial new policies could be financed largely through highly progressive taxation. For the first time in modern history, the wealthiest 400 families pay a lower rate of overall taxes than any other income group in the country (Saez and Zucman 2019). Reformers could use redistribution from the very top to provide visible and concrete benefits to the overwhelming majority of Americans. Raising taxes on the superrich and spending the proceeds on programs that provide tangible and widespread benefits would send a powerful message of how government can help working families.

Such policy breakthroughs face high hurdles. Although from 2020 Democrats controlled the White House, House, and Senate—the last by the slimmest of margins—their ability to make substantial progress was hampered by the Senate filibuster. (Eliminating the filibuster for ordinary legislation would have required complete Democratic unity.) Moreover, many of the organizational realities we've discussed are likely to change only slowly, if they change at all. The Supreme Court's conservative majority is young; the bias of the Senate toward low-population states is hard-wired into the Constitution; the organizational advantages of business relative to labor are deeply embedded. In this context, political and policy reforms must be designed to be self-reinforcing, starting small and growing bigger over time, with features that reduce the chance of backlash and reversal (Hacker and Pierson 2019).

The country's best hope is that the vicious circles that have appeared on the right—in which the Republican Party has moved ever farther toward the conservative pole—will give way to a more virtuous cycle. Meaningful economic reforms can lay the foundation for further reforms, strengthening supporters and weakening opponents. Progress that voters can recognize will place increasing pressure on conservative elites and organizations to address the acute economic challenges facing ordinary Americans.

Political reform could reinforce this dynamic, and Democrats have put these reforms near the top of the House and Senate agendas. Opening doors to more democratic participation and ensuring fairer elections would not only engage more citizens and ensure their votes counted; in fostering greater partisan contestation, it would change the incentives for Republicans, pushing them to build a bigger tent. Similarly, reducing the sway of money could also help replace a vicious circle with a more virtuous one.

Again, younger and non-white voters hold more progressive positions than the older white voters who form the electoral bedrock of the GOP. So long as vibrant democratic contestation remains in place, Republicans will thus face growing pressures to adapt. To date, the party has found ways to reduce this pressure, increasing turnout among their core voters, pulling in less affluent white Americans, and engaging in various forms of electoral manipulation (gerrymandering, voter restrictions, and so on). But, without intensification and extension, these strategies will become less effective over time. The big question is whether Republicans will find new ways to reduce the pressures for adaptation—and whether our democracy will remain robust despite them.

One conclusion, however, is clear: To succeed over the long term, those who seek greater security for American workers, retirees, and their families will have to tackle directly the negative political dynamics showcased in this chapter.

References

Alvaredo, Facundo, Lucas Chancel, Thomas Piketty, Emmanuel Saez, and Gabriel Zucman. 2018. "World Inequality Report 2018: Executive Summary." Paris: World Inequality Lab. https://wir2018.wid.world/files/download/wir2018-summary-english.pdf.

Ashok, Vivekinan, Ilyana Kuziemko, and Ebonya Washington. 2015. "Support for Redistribution in an Age of Rising Inequality: New Stylized Facts and Some Tentative Explanation." Brookings Papers on Economic Activity. Washington, DC: Brookings Institution. https://www.brookings.edu/bpea-articles/support-for-redistribution-in-an-age-of-rising-inequality-new-stylized-facts-and-some-tentative-explanations/.

Bartels, Larry M. 2008. *Unequal Democracy: The Political Economy of the New Gilded Age*. New York: Russell Sage Foundation; Princeton University Press.

Benkler, Yochai, Robert Faris, and Hal Roberts. 2018. *Network Propaganda: Manipulation, Disinformation, and Radicalization in American Politics*. New York: Oxford University Press. https://doi.org/10.1093/oso/9780190923624.001.0001.

Bonica, Adam. 2019. Twitter Post. https://twitter.com/adam_bonica/status/1136067959858712576.

Bonica, Adam, Nolan McCarty, Keith T. Poole, and Howard Rosenthal. 2013. "Why Hasn't Democracy Slowed Rising Inequality?" *Journal of Economic Perspectives* 27 (3): 103–124. https://doi.org/10.1257/jep.27.3.103.

Boushey, Heather, and Kavya Vaghul. 2016. "Women Have Made the Difference for Family Economic Security." Washington, DC: The Washington Center for Equitable Growth. https://equitablegrowth.org/wp-content/uploads/2016/04/Women-have-made-the-difference-for-family-economic-security-pdf.pdf.

Broockman, David E., Gregory Ferenstein, and Neil Malhotra. 2019. "Predispositions and the Political Behavior of American Economic Elites: Evidence from Technology Entrepreneurs." *American Journal of Political Science* 63 (1): 212–233. https://doi.org/10.1111/ajps.12408.

Campbell, Andrea Louise. 2003. *How Policies Make Citizens: Senior Political Activism and the American Welfare State*. Princeton, NJ: Princeton University Press.

Case, Anne, and Angus Deaton. 2020. *Deaths of Despair and the Future of Capitalism*. Princeton, NJ: Princeton University Press.

Center on Budget and Policy Priorities. 2020. "Top Ten Facts about Social Security." https://www.cbpp.org/research/social-security/top-ten-facts-about-social-security.

Craig, Maureen A., and Jennifer A. Richeson. 2017. "Information about the US Racial Demographic Shift Triggers Concerns about Anti-White Discrimination among the Prospective White 'Minority.'" *PLOS ONE* 12 (9): e0185389. https://doi.org/10.1371/journal.pone.0185389.

Cubanski, Juliette, Tricia Neuman, Anthony Damico, and Karen Smith. 2018. "Medicare Beneficiaries' Out-of-Pocket Health Care Spending as a Share of Income Now and Projections for the Future." Menlo Park, CA: The Henry J. Kaiser Family Foundation. https://www.kff.org/report-section/medicare-beneficiaries-out-of-pocket-health-care-spending-as-a-share-of-income-now-and-projections-for-the-future-report/.

Drutman, Lee. 2017. "Political Divisions in 2016 and Beyond." Research Report. Washington, DC: The Democracy Fund Voter Study Group. https://www.voterstudygroup.org/publication/political-divisions-in-2016-and-beyond.

File, Thom. 2017. "Voting in America: A Look at the 2016 Presidential Election." The United States Census Bureau. May 17, 2017. https://www.census.gov/newsroom/blogs/random-samplings/2017/05/voting_in_america.html.

Fox, Liana. 2020. "The Supplemental Poverty Measure: 2019." P60-272. Current Population Reports. Washington, DC: U.S. Census Bureau. https://www.census.gov/content/dam/Census/library/publications/2020/demo/p60-272.pdf.

Ghilarducci, Teresa. 2010. "The Future of Retirement in Aging Societies." *International Review of Applied Economics* 24 (3): 319–331. https://doi.org/10.1080/02692171003701511.

Gilens, Martin. 2012. *Affluence and Influence: Economic Inequality and Political Power in America*. Princeton, NJ: Princeton University Press.

Gilens, Martin, and Benjamin I. Page. 2014. "Testing Theories of American Politics: Elites, Interest Groups, and Average Citizens." *Perspectives on Politics* 12 (3): 564–581. https://doi.org/10.1017/S1537592714001595.

Grumbach, Jacob M. 2018. "From Backwaters to Major Policymakers: Policy Polarization in the States, 1970–2014." *Perspectives on Politics* 16 (2): 416–435. https://doi.org/10.1017/S153759271700425X.

Grumbach, Jacob M., and Paul Pierson. 2019. "Are Large Corporations Politically Moderate? Using Money in Politics to Infer the Preferences of Business." Working Paper. Berkeley: University of California, Berkeley.

Hacker, Jacob S. 2002. *The Divided Welfare State: The Battle over Public and Private Social Benefits in the United States*. New York: Cambridge University Press.

Hacker, Jacob S. 2019. *The Great Risk Shift: The New Economic Insecurity and the Decline of the American Dream*. 2nd ed. New York: Oxford University Press.

Hacker, Jacob S., and Paul Pierson. 2005. "Abandoning the Middle: The Bush Tax Cuts and the Limits of Democratic Control." *Perspectives on Politics* 3 (1): 33–53. https://doi.org/10.1017/S1537592705050048.

Hacker, Jacob S., and Paul Pierson. 2010. *Winner-Take-All Politics: How Washington Made the Rich Richer—And Turned Its Back on the Middle Class*. 1st ed. New York: Simon & Schuster.

Hacker, Jacob S., and Paul Pierson. 2015. "Confronting Asymmetric Polarization." In *Solutions to Polarization*, edited by Nathaniel Persily, 59–73. New York: Cambridge University Press.

Hacker, Jacob S., and Paul Pierson. 2016. *American Amnesia: How the War on Government Led Us to Forget What Made America Prosper*. New York: Simon & Schuster.

Hacker, Jacob S., and Paul Pierson. 2018. "The Dog That Almost Barked: What the ACA Repeal Fight Says about the Resilience of the American Welfare State." *Journal of Health Politics, Policy and Law* 43 (4): 551–577. https://doi.org/10.1215/03616878-6527935.

Hacker, Jacob S., and Paul Pierson. 2019. "Policy Feedback in an Age of Polarization." *The ANNALS of the American Academy of Political and Social Science* 685 (1): 8–28. https://doi.org/10.1177/0002716219871222.

Hacker, Jacob S., and Paul Pierson. 2020. *Let Them Eat Tweets: How the Right Rules in an Age of Extreme Inequality*. 1st ed. New York: Liveright.

Hacker, Jacob S., Paul Pierson, and Kathleen Thelen. 2015. "Drift and Conversion: Hidden Faces of Institutional Change." In *Advances in Comparative-Historical Analysis*, edited by James Mahoney and Kathleen Thelen, 180–208. Strategies for Social Inquiry. Cambridge: Cambridge University Press. https://doi.org/10.1017/CBO9781316273104.008.

Hertel-Fernandez, Alexander, Theda Skocpol, and Jason Sclar. 2018. "When Political Mega-Donors Join Forces: How the Koch Network and the Democracy Alliance Influence Organized U.S. Politics on the Right and Left." *Studies in American Political Development* 32 (2): 127–165. https://doi.org/10.1017/S0898588X18000081.

Ingraham, Christopher. 2015. "This Astonishing Chart Shows How Moderate Republicans Are an Endangered Species." *The Washington Post*, June 2, 2015. https://www.washingtonpost.com/news/wonk/wp/2015/06/02/this-astonishing-chart-shows-how-republicans-are-an-endangered-species/.

Klein, Ezra. 2015. "Raising Social Security's Retirement Age Is a Disaster for the Poor." Vox. April 22, 2015. https://www.vox.com/2015/4/22/8463843/social-security-retirement-age-increase-poor.

Kuo, Didi, and Nolan McCarty. 2015. "Democracy in America, 2015." *Global Policy* 6 (S1): 49–55. https://doi.org/10.1111/1758-5899.12228.

Lynch, Julia. 2006. *Age in the Welfare State: The Origins of Social Spending on Pensioners, Workers, and Children*. Cambridge Studies in Comparative Politics. Cambridge: Cambridge University Press.

Meltzer, Allan H., and Scott F. Richard. 1981. "A Rational Theory of the Size of Government." *Journal of Political Economy* 89 (5): 914–927. https://www.jstor.org/stable/1830813.

National Academies of Sciences, Engineering, and Medicine. 2015. *The Growing Gap in Life Expectancy by Income: Implications for Federal Programs and Policy Responses*. Washington, DC: The National Academies Press. https://www.nap.edu/catalog/19015/the-growing-gap-in-life-expectancy-by-income-implications-for.

OECD. 2018. *Ageing and Employment Policies: United States 2018: Working Better with Age and Fighting Unequal Ageing*. Ageing and Employment Policies. Paris: OECD. https://doi.org/10.1787/9789264190115-en.

OECD. 2019. *Pensions at a Glance 2019: OECD and G20 Indicators*. Paris: OECD. https://doi.org/10.1787/b6d3dcfc-en.

OECD. 2021. "Life Expectancy at Birth (Indicator)." doi:10.1787/27e0fc9d-en.

Osborn, Robin, Michelle M. Doty, Donald Moulds, Dana O. Sarnak, and Arnav Shah. 2017. "Older Americans Were Sicker and Faced More Financial Barriers to Health Care Than Counterparts in Other Countries." *Health Affairs* 36 (12): 2123–32. https://doi.org/10.1377/hlthaff.2017.1048.

Page, Benjamin I., Larry M. Bartels, and Jason Seawright. 2013. "Democracy and the Policy Preferences of Wealthy Americans." *Perspectives on Politics* 11 (1): 51–73. https://doi.org/10.1017/S153759271200360X.

Rodden, Jonathan. 2021. "Keeping Your Enemies Close: Electoral Rules and Partisan Polarization." In *Who Gets What? The New Politics of Insecurity*, edited by Frances McCall Rosenbluth and Margaret Weir. Cambridge: Cambridge University Press. https://www.cambridge.org/us/academic/subjects/politics-international-relations/american-government-politics-and-policy/who-gets-what-new-politics-insecurity.

Saez, Emmanuel, and Gabriel Zucman. 2019. *The Triumph of Injustice: How the Rich Dodge Taxes and How to Make Them Pay*, pp. 129–160. 1st ed. New York: W. W. Norton & Company.

Sawhill, Isabel V., and Christopher Pulliam. 2019. "Americans Want the Wealthy and Corporations to Pay More Taxes, but Are Elected Officials Listening?" *Brookings* (blog). March 14, 2019. https://www.brookings.edu/blog/up-front/2019/03/14/americans-want-the-wealthy-and-corporations-to-pay-more-taxes-but-are-elected-officials-listening/.

Sherman, Arloc, Sharon Parrott, and Danilo Trisi. 2014. "Chart Book: The War on Poverty at 50." Washington, DC: Center on Budget and Policy Priorities. https://www.cbpp.org/research/chart-book-the-war-on-poverty-at-50-section-1.

Stein, Harry, and Alex Rowell. 2016. "How the House Budget Sides with the Wealthy over Everyone Else—Even Republican Voters." Center for American Progress. March 15, 2016. https://www.americanprogress.org/issues/economy/news/2016/03/15/133350/how-the-house-budget-sides-with-the-wealthy-over-everyone-else-even-republican-voters/.

Tax Policy Center. 2017. "Distributional Analysis of the Conference Agreement for the Tax Cuts and Jobs Act." Washington, DC: Urban Institute & Brookings Institution. https://www.taxpolicycenter.org/publications/distributional-analysis-conference-agreement-tax-cuts-and-jobs-act/full.

Thal, Adam. 2017. "Class Isolation and Affluent Americans' Perception of Social Conditions." *Political Behavior* 39 (2): 401–424. https://doi.org/10.1007/s11109-016-9361-9.

Tucker, Todd N. 2019. "Fixing the Senate: Equitable and Full Representation for the 21st Century." Race and Democracy. New York: Roosevelt Institute. https://rooseveltinstitute.org/publications/fixing-the-senate-equitable-full-representation-21st-century/.

Walker, Elisa A., Virginia P. Reno, and Thomas N. Bethell. 2014. "Americans Make Hard Choices on Social Security: A Survey with Trade-Off Analysis." Washington, DC: National Academy of Social Insurance. https://www.nasi.org/wp-content/uploads/2014/11/Americans_Make_Hard_Choices_on_Social_Security.pdf.

Woolf, Steven H., and Heidi Schoomaker. 2019. "Life Expectancy and Mortality Rates in the United States, 1959–2017." *JAMA* 322 (20): 1996–2016. https://doi.org/10.1001/jama.2019.16932.

14
What Is the Way Forward?
American Policy and Working Longer

Lisa F. Berkman, Beth C. Truesdale,
and Alexandra Mitukiewicz[1]

1. Introduction

The U.S. population, like populations worldwide, is getting older. Changes in the age distribution affect every aspect of our society—including the way we organize our working lives and our expectations for retirement.

Demography matters. But demography is not destiny.

Policy responses to aging populations are a matter of choice. In this chapter, we propose a framework for designing policies that respond to the needs of a society that is both aging and unequal. Our central argument is that policies affecting *work*—those that shape American labor markets for workers of all ages—must be considered in tandem with policies affecting *retirement*.

Working longer—remaining in paid employment beyond traditional retirement ages—has many potential advantages. In particular, more people need income for more years of life, and working longer is one way to provide it.

But for many Americans, high and rising economic and social inequalities put working longer in jeopardy. Working for pay until age 67 or 70 or beyond is a good choice for *some* Americans[2]—disproportionately those with college degrees and stable career jobs. But as many of the chapters in this book demonstrate, working longer is neither feasible nor desirable for everyone. Physically demanding or unstable jobs, poor health, major caregiving responsibilities, and pervasive age discrimination can make working longer a daunting proposition. For the large minority of Americans who are no longer in the labor force in their late 50s, it is unrealistic to think that job opportunities will appear for them and that they will be able to rejoin the workforce in their older years. As a result, policies that raise formal retirement ages, such as those attached to Social Security benefits, fall hardest on those who are already disadvantaged.

Rising inequalities make it much harder to respond effectively to the heterogeneous experiences of subgroups of our population as we age. Large gaps in economic and social conditions—gaps defined by socioeconomic position (SEP), race/ethnicity, gender, family configuration, geography, and more—mean that one size will not fit all when it comes to work and retirement. And while disadvantaged households face particular difficulties, problems with the way work and retirement are organized are widespread and to some extent impact all workers. The diversity of American workers, American jobs, and American retirements calls for a set of policy options that work for a heterogeneous population.

In this chapter, we emphasize policies that are both broad in scope and likely to reduce the heterogeneity of work and retirement outcomes that result from social and economic inequalities. For instance, many workers would benefit from safer workplaces. But because people of color and lower-SEP adults are overrepresented in hazardous work environments, addressing workplace safety should reduce racial and SEP inequalities. Similarly, strengthening the Social Security system would benefit Americans across the board. But it has particular value for women, who rely more heavily on Social Security than men since they tend to have lower retirement benefits and longer life expectancies. The wide-ranging policies we outline here should be seen as an essential foundation for responding to diverse American needs.

In designing such policies, work and retirement are two sides of the same coin. Frequently, retirement policies (such as those governing Social Security, pensions, and private savings) are considered in isolation from labor force policies (such as those governing wages and working conditions, unemployment insurance, and workforce training). Looking at both domains together provides a better chance to design policies that engage more workers in meaningful, remunerative work as they grow older *and* support all Americans' financial security, leisure, and health in older age.

We bring a life course approach to both work and retirement. That is, we consider the needs of both today's older adults and today's middle-aged cohorts. For the purpose of this book, we set aside policy interventions in childhood and adolescence. While conditions in early life clearly shape work opportunities and well-being at older ages, our focus in this volume is on what we as a society can do in the next two to three decades. Because everyone who will be 60 by 2050 is currently more than 30 years old, we focus on policies that affect adults.

We need to attend to the immediate needs of those in jeopardy now as well as keeping an eye out for the next generation. On the one hand, many adults in the second half of life need support now. On the other hand, U.S. workers currently in their 30s and 40s are the retirees of the future, so policies that affect their work lives and retirement savings now will have ramifications for their chances of working longer and retiring with financial security in the decades to come—and relatively small investments now could avoid major social costs down the line.

We also conceive of these policy domains broadly: social and economic policies that on the surface have little to do with retirement or working longer can have an important impact. Better social provision of health care, childcare, eldercare, family and medical leave, and sick leave are rarely counted among working-longer policies. But they likely do have a virtuous impact on Americans' capacity to work longer and have a secure retirement.

In both work and retirement domains, our laws frequently lag behind current conditions. During the past four decades, the service sector has grown, some jobs have become more insecure while others have become more intensive, technology has changed the tasks people do, and traditional pensions have diminished, among other changes. In many cases, our laws do not match the stressors that workers and retirees face today. As Chapter 13 by Hacker and Pierson sets out, collective efforts to update these laws and respond to the strains facing older Americans depend on political actors and political institutions. A functioning democracy is the base on which all effective policies rest.

We offer five main conclusions:

1. *Working longer is an important (but incomplete) response to population aging.* Working longer—remaining in paid employment beyond traditional retirement ages—is a viable option for *some* Americans. Keeping more older adults in the labor force could potentially benefit individuals' financial security and health, employers' access to experienced workers, and the economy at large.
2. *High and rising social and economic inequalities put working longer in jeopardy.* Working longer is not feasible or desirable for everyone. Poor health, caregiving responsibilities, precarious or hazardous jobs, and age discrimination push many Americans out of the labor force in their 50s. Because employment rates reflect deep inequalities in our society by class, race, gender, disability, and geography, delayed retirement is concentrated among advantaged groups. As a result, policies that imagine longer working lives as the primary route to retirement security are likely to increase inequalities in old age.
3. *Robust retirement and disability policies are essential complements to working-longer policies.* America must shore up programs that guarantee financial security for adults who are not in the labor force, including retirees and those whose health prevents them from working for pay. In addition, labor force policies can work alongside retirement/disability policies; for instance, early interventions that help injured or ill workers remain employed would reduce the number of Americans who need to apply for federal disability benefits or retire early.
4. *Working longer is supported by "good jobs" policies.* Working-longer policies should promote not only employment at older ages but also employment in jobs that meet workers' needs. Policies should not force older workers to choose between trying to stay in bad jobs and retiring into poverty. Moreover, better wages and working conditions can lead to better health and more consistent work history for younger and middle-aged adults, putting them in a better position to work longer as they age.
5. *Responses to population aging should take into account the needs of Americans of all ages.* Our work and retirement policy framework takes a life course perspective. Policy should respond to the immediate needs of today's older adults (such as job search support for older workers who have lost their jobs and government backing for private pension plans that would otherwise fail). At the same time, investments now in today's middle-aged and

younger adults (such as universal retirement savings plans and better workplace protections) will have long-term benefits over the next two to three decades.

There is broad consensus among the authors in this book for many of the issues we identify in this chapter. As happens when any large group of interdisciplinary thinkers comes together, perspectives vary on how best to design solutions. As authors of this chapter, our goal is not so much to resolve all these reasonable differences as to draw attention to both the promises and pitfalls of working-longer policies and their alternatives. The purpose of this chapter is to outline several specific U.S. policy areas where progress is needed. Interested readers should consult the endnotes for examples of detailed policy proposals.

2. The American People Need a Secure Retirement

America is already facing a retirement crisis. Although estimates vary according to how adequacy is defined, even the more optimistic estimates suggest that around 30 percent of Americans in their late 60s are *not* financially prepared for retirement (Hurd and Rohwedder Forthcoming). The figures are substantially worse for women than for men, for single people than for married people, and for people with less education than for people with college degrees.

The retirement situation is more concerning still for upcoming generations. As Burtless describes in his chapter, older Americans' incomes and living standards have improved on average over the past 20, 40, and 60 years, while poverty rates have declined, but there is no guarantee these improvements will continue. Indeed, many of the chapters in this volume set out reasons to think that retirement security will become more elusive for the cohorts now in middle age.

Fundamentally, we believe that all adults deserve a secure retirement. As Gatta and Horning illustrate in Chapter 8, dying with your boots on, which is the stated expectation of many low-wage workers, should not be a policy goal. In this section we outline three key policy solutions to improve financial security among older Americans who are not working for pay because of retirement or disability: strengthening Social Security, creating universal retirement savings programs, and improving support for people with disabilities.

2.1. Making Social Security Sustainable

The top priority for U.S. retirement policy is to put Social Security on a secure long-term footing. Nearly 9 out of 10 people age 65 and older receive benefits, and a sizeable minority rely on Social Security for nearly all their retirement income (Social Security Administration 2021b). But as the U.S. population has aged, funding shortfalls have increased. Current estimates suggest that the combined Social Security trust funds will be able to pay scheduled benefits until 2034. At that point, if Congress does nothing, revenues will cover only 78 percent of promised benefits (Social Security Administration 2021a). Given that benefits are already modest, further cuts would be catastrophic for many older Americans.

Successive administrations have failed to seize the opportunity to put Social Security on a steady footing. To close the funding gap, benefits must fall, revenues must rise, or there must be some combination of the two. As Chapter 12 by Shoven and colleagues describes, there are several options for Social Security reform. One possibility is to raise the full retirement age from 67 to 70. Financially, this is equivalent to a 20 percent cut in benefits for younger cohorts. Raising the full retirement age places an outsize burden on those who are unable to work longer and delay claiming their Social Security benefits.

We are not necessarily opposed to all increases in the age at which people can claim pension benefits. As described in Chapter 3 by Börsch-Supan and colleagues, compared to the United States, many European countries have earlier retirement ages, better population health, and more robust safety nets for people who are unemployed or disabled. In these contexts, higher pension ages may be appropriate. In the U.S. context, however, raising the Social Security full retirement age would likely exacerbate deep existing inequalities in retirement security by race, SEP, gender, and other dimensions discussed in this book.

We support raising Social Security revenue through taxation. Strong possibilities include gradually raising the payroll tax cap for Social Security contributions and extending the tax to net investment income.[3] Such proposals are increasingly mainstream. American voters across the political spectrum broadly prefer raising Social Security taxes to cutting Social Security benefits. Almost 80 percent of U.S. adults said that Social Security benefits should not be reduced, even if it meant raising taxes (Walker, Reno, and Bethell 2014). During the 2020 presidential campaign, all the Democratic candidates not only avoided proposing cuts to Social Security but many proposed substantial expansions in benefits (Smith, Johnson, and Favreault 2020). Because Social Security is the core of retirement security in the United States, putting it on a stable footing should be a top policy priority.

2.2. Universal, Portable, and Automatic Retirement Savings Plans

Essential as it is, Social Security does not provide fully adequate retirement income for most Americans. Because it was intended to complement other sources of income for retired workers, benefits are modest; in 2021, average benefits were around $18,700 a year (Social Security Administration 2021b). Americans need to be saving for retirement across the life course outside of Social Security.

In the United States, retirement savings have largely been tied to employers either through defined benefit (DB) pension plans or defined contribution (DC) savings plans. Both DB and DC pathways have provided secure retirements for some, disproportionately higher-income workers; neither meets the needs of many current and future retirees.[4] Crucially, about half of all American workers do not participate in any employer-based retirement plan—a number that has remained remarkably steady during the past three decades (Center for Retirement Research at Boston College n.d.). Even savings vehicles that are better designed than the ones we currently have will fail at a population level if they do not reach the majority of the workforce.

To provide adequate retirement savings for the current middle-aged and younger generations, we need a savings reform now. This savings plan should have certain essential qualities: it should be *universal*, covering contingent work, self-employment, and part-time work as well as full-time employment; *portable*, following the worker across jobs and employers; and *automatic*, with mandatory or opt-out enrollment. Other desirable features include government or employer matches, restrictions on early withdrawals, professional management, and annuitization at retirement so retirees know what their incomes will be for life.[5]

Retirement savings accounts that follow workers from job to job are especially important because of the rise of contingent work. The current employer-focused retirement system was designed for full-time, permanent employees, leaving out a substantial and growing number of Americans in nonstandard work arrangements, including independent contractors, day laborers, seasonal workers, temps, and people working through online platforms (Gale, Holmes, and John 2020).

A universal, portable, and automatic retirement savings program could boost savings for individuals toward the bottom of the income distribution, who are disproportionately excluded from access to employer-based plans, and would thereby reduce income insecurity and poverty among retirees. Lower-wage workers tend to change jobs and employers more often than higher-wage workers, so decoupling retirement savings from a single employer is particularly attractive.

There are legitimate concerns that mandatory savings could have negative impacts on the consumption and well-being of some lower-income workers. Program design will need to address these concerns. More broadly, however, the fact that lower-income workers may not be able to afford to save shows how labor force policy and retirement policy are connected. Access to a well-designed savings vehicle matters—but so does having enough income to save for retirement. Higher wages toward the bottom of the income distribution (which we discuss below) would make universal, portable retirement savings plans substantially better at improving retirement security.

2.3. More Flexible and Responsive Federal Disability Programs

Most Americans retain the physical and mental abilities they need to hold some job into their older years, as Chapter 5 by Berger and colleagues describes. But for an important minority, disability intervenes. One study estimated that about 20 percent of 55-year-olds in the United States have a potentially disabling condition; by age 64, the proportion has more than doubled (Johnson, Favreault, and Mommaerts 2010). Poor health sharply increases an individual's likelihood of workforce exit (Bound, Stinebrickner, and Waidmann 2010).

Social Security Disability Insurance (SSDI) and Supplemental Security Income (SSI) are the core of the federal disability programs, providing benefits to 12.6 million disabled working-age Americans.[6] The same strict disability definition applies to both SSDI and SSI, but eligibility for SSDI requires substantial work history, while SSI is restricted to adults with extremely limited resources. Both provide important support for those whose mental or physical health makes them unable to work before retirement age, but there is substantial room for reforms that support both the work capacity and the financial well-being of Americans with disabilities. We highlight three priorities.

First, we need better early intervention programs. There is extensive evidence that, for workers who experience a serious new illness or injury or a worsening health condition, the best time to intervene is early—ideally while people are still connected to an employer. Basic workplace accommodations (often cost-free or inexpensive) have been shown to help keep workers with temporary or permanent disabilities employed. These accommodations include job-protected medical leave; better coordination among the employer, the worker, and health care providers; and adaptations to schedules, equipment, and work tasks (Smalligan and Boyens 2018, 2020).

A major stumbling block, however, involves the systems to connect at-risk workers with early interventions.[7] A program of national paid family and medical leave (PFML)— which we discuss further in the section on work below—would not only provide workers with the ability to take time off from work to treat an illness or injury without having to quit their job but also provide a mechanism to identify workers at risk of long-term disability and to provide them and their employers with appropriate interventions while the employment relationship is still intact.[8]

Second, reducing the length of the disability application process could help some applicants remain closer to the workforce. The typical application process takes months to years.[9] Long delays create unnecessary insecurity for applicants. Delays may also erode remaining work capacity among applicants who are eventually denied, who comprise about half of all applicants. Unsurprisingly, the longer applicants are out of the labor force while waiting for a decision, the harder it is to return to work (Autor et al. 2015).

Previous efforts to improve long wait times for decisions and other aspects of the determination process have foundered, in part, because of administrative funding constraints (Smalligan and Boyens 2019). Adequate funding for the Social Security Administration (SSA), for example by moving funding for state disability determination services from the discretionary to the mandatory side of the budget, is needed to allow the SSA to invest in administrative capacity and improve the speed and reliability of the disability application process.[10]

Finally, we need to update the safety net for Americans whose health prevents them from working. In particular, SSI does not do what it was meant to do. It both disincentivizes work and keeps recipients in poverty. SSI recipients can earn only $65 per month before benefits are phased out, a limit that has not been adjusted since 1972, when the program was introduced. They cannot have more than $2,000 in assets as singles or $3,000 as couples, a limit that has not been updated since 1989. And the maximum federal SSI benefit for an individual is less than $10,000 a year, well below the federal poverty line (Altman 2020). We support modernization of SSI to raise benefits, ease restrictions on recipients to allow saving for emergency needs, and encourage part-time work. Polls show that most Americans, including a majority of Republicans, support such reforms (The Century Foundation and Data For Progress 2021).

Disability policy is not often discussed in the context of delayed retirement. We bring it into the conversation here because if working longer is to be part of America's response to an aging population, it should be combined with policies that improve employment prospects for those who would otherwise struggle to stay employed until traditional retirement ages, and with policies that make those who can't work less vulnerable. Robust disability policy helps to address some of the most serious inequalities in our aging society.

3. The American People Need "Good Jobs"

Maintaining financial security into older age rests on two main pillars. The first, as we described above, is adequate income for adults who are no longer working for pay because they are retired or disabled. The second pillar involves creating work environments that enable middle-aged and older Americans with a broad range of skills and qualifications to remain in the workforce as long as they are able to work without risking their health and vitality—and as long as they choose.

We see good jobs as a central foundation of working longer. By "good jobs" we mean those that meet workers' needs and the needs of their families: that provide, for example, adequate pay and benefits, reasonable schedules, paid leave for illness or family needs, and a safe working environment.

Many policies to promote working longer are age-targeted—that is, they assume that the needs and preferences of older adults differ from those of younger adults. We support some age-targeted policies, such as proposals to address pervasive age discrimination in employment.[11] But in this section we highlight age-neutral policies because many labor force policies that benefit so-called prime-age adults *also* benefit older adults. This perspective brings an unusually broad range of labor force policies into view as potential working-longer policies.

In addition, today's prime-age workers are the next generations of retirees. There are no guarantees that the long-term trend toward delayed retirement will continue as these cohorts age. Indeed, forecasts by Hurd and Rohwedder in Chapter 7, based on Americans' preretirement expectations, suggest that employment rates among older workers are likely to stagnate or fall between the mid-2010s and the early 2030s. But the future is not yet written, and policy changes now could alter these trajectories. In particular, better jobs for Americans now in their 40s and 50s may improve their labor force attachment and, in turn, their chance of remaining employed as they age. As Chapter 1 by Truesdale and colleagues points out, only about half of Americans have stable employment throughout their 50s, which is concerning because stable employment appears to be an important foundation for working longer. Working-longer policies must address the needs of workers long before they approach retirement age.

To be clear, our interest in labor policy and the workplace is not only economic: we view work as a key social determinant of health. The COVID-19 pandemic illustrated this in stark terms. Both workplace health threats and job losses fell disproportionately on Black and Hispanic adults, women, and lower-wage workers, forcing millions of older adults into early retirement (Davis et al. 2021). At its best, work improves health by providing not only a paycheck but also opportunities for social engagement, learning, growth, and maintaining a sense of purpose and meaning. But in all too many cases, work is a major health hazard (Lovejoy et al. 2021).

3.1. Increasing Worker Power and Worker Voice

Pay and conditions reflect the balance of power between employers and workers. Institutions that use collective action to build workers' power—such as labor unions in the United States and works councils in Europe—strengthen workers' ability to have a say in their jobs. However, American union membership has been eroded from about 35 percent of private-sector workers to 6.4 percent between the 1950s and 2018 (Freeman 2021). Falling union membership is partly responsible for rising economic inequality and stagnating wages in the middle of the income distribution (Western and Rosenfeld 2011; Freeman 2021). Indeed, worker voice shapes both work and retirement, as Chapter 9 by Berg and Piszczek shows. Germany's social policy is more responsive to older workers' needs partly because groups that represent workers' interests are much stronger in Germany than in the United States.

Updated labor policies could protect American workers' right to organize (Block and Sachs n.d.).[12] The most basic principle is that workers should be able to organize without retaliation or interference by employers. More broadly, policies that expand the pool of workers covered by collective bargaining could reduce gender, racial, and socioeconomic inequalities in the labor market. One promising example is sectoral bargaining, which is the right to bargain at the level of the industry or sector. Under the U.S. system of enterprise bargaining, unions negotiate directly with individual firms, which leaves most workers without the protection of collective bargaining and gives firms a strong incentive to fight unionization to avoid competitive disadvantage. Sectoral bargaining would address these limitations.

Increased worker voice could substantially improve wages and working conditions. However, given the very low rates of union coverage in the United States today, we cannot rely exclusively on labor unions and other forms of collective action to create good jobs. Public policies that set and enforce minimum fair labor standards benefit workers directly and are an essential complement to policies that promote worker voice. We turn to these policies next.

3.2. Higher Wages for Lower- and Middle-Wage Workers

Adequate income is a cornerstone of good jobs, but wages in the bottom half of the U.S. income distribution stagnated during the past three decades even as the economy grew. While the main reason to address wage levels is to ensure that Americans have a living wage, higher wages also improve retirement security and may increase the likelihood of working longer.

While governments have a great deal of influence over the rules that structure economic rewards, they have relatively little direct control over wages. An important exception is statutory minimum wages. The U.S. federal minimum wage of $7.25 an hour has fallen in real terms over time and is the lowest in the developed world in terms of buying power (Howell, Fiedler, and Luce 2016). We support efforts to raise the federal minimum wage to $15 an hour, index it to the median wage, and eliminate the subminimum wage for tipped workers and workers with disabilities.[13]

The federal government also shapes labor market standards by the wages and conditions it requires from federal contractors. More than a fifth of the U.S. workforce is employed by companies that do business with the federal government (U.S. Department of

Labor 2016). Protections have historically been weak for contract workers in sectors such as building services, administrative services, security services, nursing care, and food processing (Walter 2020), but presidential administrations can raise standards using administrative and executive powers.

State and local governments also play important roles. Local labor markets—for older workers as well as younger ones—vary widely across the United States, as Chapter 2 by Coile demonstrates. Differences from place to place in education levels, industry mix, population health, and infrastructure offer opportunities for intervention.[14] While federal-level wage standards can reduce geographic inequalities, additional strategies to create good jobs can be tailored to fit the particular needs and strengths of local communities.

Wage growth funds retirement, both through Social Security and through private savings.[15] Higher taxable earnings translate directly into higher Social Security benefits, while the value of universal, portable retirement savings plans, like those we outlined above, also rises when workers' incomes improve. And when wages grow among people earning less than the Social Security tax cap ($142,800 in 2021), Social Security revenue rises, helping to pay current retirees' benefits (Morrissey 2012).

Higher wages may also improve Americans' chances of working longer. Wages that cover essential costs such as transportation, housing, childcare, and appropriate work clothing are fundamental to removing common barriers to employment. Perhaps as a result, improvements in the minimum wage appear to produce greater employment stability and labor force attachment (e.g., Dube, Lester, and Reich 2016), thus laying the groundwork for continued work later in life.

3.3. A Safer Workplace

A physically safe work environment is important for working longer—both because older workers may be particularly vulnerable to dangerous environments and because work-related illnesses and injuries sustained in middle age may have long-term consequences for work disability.

The agency responsible for ensuring that workplaces comply with safety regulations is the Occupational Safety and Health Administration (OSHA). In the half-century since OSHA was created, many jobs have become safer. However, OSHA's capacity to protect workers has been eroded over time. Between 1990 and 2019, the number of full-time employees at OSHA fell even as the size of the U.S. labor force grew. Over the same period, the number of inspections conducted by the federal agency dropped by more than a quarter (Burke 2021). The decline in OSHA's inspection capabilities leaves many high-risk worksites without adequate oversight.

Apart from the more common and well-identified hazards that workers face, including chemical and toxic exposures and mechanical and ergonomic strains, new hazards have arisen that OSHA is not well prepared to address. Infectious disease has been largely neglected in safety regulations, and especially during the early part of the COVID-19 pandemic, workers needed protection they did not receive (Kinder and Stateler 2021; Kirkham 2021).[16] Extreme heat is another neglected safety area. Exposure to high temperatures can result in illness or death for people who work outdoors in jobs such as construction and farming, or in indoor spaces without air conditioning such as warehouses.[17] As climate change produces longer and hotter heatwaves, the risks for workers will also rise.

While the particular work conditions that need to be addressed will evolve over time, the common thread is that the United States needs a federal regulatory body that has the staffing, expertise, and capacity to produce standards that respond intelligently to complex safety threats, and to enforce those standards. We support calls to allow stronger penalties for unsafe workplaces and to provide OSHA with the resources it needs to keep workers safe.

3.4. Schedule Control and Paid Leave

Many of the problems with U.S. jobs revolve around *time*: too many hours or too few, unpredictable or overly rigid schedules, and a lack of paid time off for workers to deal with illness or caregiving.

For many lower- and middle-wage jobs, a key problem is the volatile and unpredictable schedules that have resulted from "just-in-time" strategies. In an effort to be maximally efficient, employers frequently give out schedules at short notice, change schedules or cancel shifts without compensation, and cut or add both shifts and hours from week to week. These widespread practices have been shown to harm workers' health, finances, and family functioning (Lovejoy et al. 2021; Harknett, Schneider, and Irwin 2021). "Fair workweek" policies, which require employers to provide advance notice of schedules and additional predictability pay for last-minute schedule changes and on-call work, are a promising route to reduce schedule precarity.[18] Similarly, the right of employees to request a flexible schedule, which exists across a number of European countries, could help to extend working lives.

A second problem is a lack of paid time off. Almost all other industrialized nations have standards on paid parental leave, caregiving leave, medical leave, and sick days. The United States has none of these. As Chapter 10 by Fahle and McGarry shows, caregiving for elders raises the chance that middle-aged workers (especially women) will leave employment, with lasting financial consequences. For leave on the scale of weeks to months, a federal paid family and medical leave program (PFML) would benefit workers of all ages—younger workers are more likely to need time off to care for children, while older workers are more likely to need paid leave to attend to their own health needs or to provide care for their own parents.[19] As we noted above, a federal PFML program could work in tandem with return-to-work programs that provide early intervention services before a short-term illness or injury becomes a long-term work disability. For leave on the scale of days, federally mandated multipurpose earned sick leave would enable workers both to stay home when they are ill and to accommodate intermittent and urgent caregiving needs such as taking a parent to the doctor.[20]

Policies that address both schedule control and paid leave would reduce employee turnover and improve labor force attachment—paving the way for more Americans to work longer.

3.5. Building and Maintaining Social Relationships and Networks in the Workplace

Although we have emphasized public policy in this chapter, employers also have a role to play. As Beier and Davenport explain in Chapter 6 on the psychology of working longer, organizations can influence individuals' decisions to work longer by modifying the work environment.

Recent evidence has found that supportive managers and coworkers are related to better employee health and are key to a productive and healthy workforce. Interventions that enhance manager support for employees' family life and increase employees' control over their work have shown promising effects on worker well-being. For instance, Lovejoy and colleagues (2021) review a range of "work redesign" strategies that have been shown to improve workers' physical and mental health, reduce work-family conflict, and produce higher job satisfaction.

The growth of highly interdependent jobs in the twenty-first century has spawned work environments where employees must frequently interact with clients or patients and, more importantly, coordinate with each other to complete their work. Some studies in health care and social service environments have conducted experimental evaluations of strategies designed to improve relational and team dynamics, and findings are generally promising. In randomized controlled trials conducted in two different settings, an intervention to improve organizational climate led to improvements in numerous factors related to well-being, including reduced turnover, reduced emotional exhaustion and role overload, and improved morale, job satisfaction, and organizational commitment (Glisson, Dukes, and Green 2006; Glisson et al. 2012).

When employers create healthy work environments that improve retention, their organizations are likely to benefit. As Beier and Davenport point out in Chapter 6, as workers age, they tend to grow more interested in investing in relationships and mentoring others, and their job-specific and general knowledge tends to increase. Older workers' potentially valuable social skills and experience are often overlooked, however, when managers are evaluating the needs of the organization. Instead, as Chapter 9 by Berg and Piszczek shows, firms' efforts to retain older workers are often ad hoc and reactive. More work is needed to connect organizations with practices that improve work environments.

3.6. Working Conditions among Contingent Workers

Like our retirement systems, most U.S. workforce protections were designed with traditional employee relationships in mind. Many of these laws tacitly assume that there is a physical space in which work takes place (like an office, a factory, a hospital, or a store); a manager who leads on policy and practice; and a firm that is ultimately responsible for its employees' well-being. Protections and benefits are much weaker for work that does not fit this model.

Nonstandard work arrangements include short-term, ad hoc work done through online "gig" platforms, directly with employers, or in informal arrangements with customers. Many of these workers are classified as self-employed independent contractors. While contract work could be a useful source of income for older adults who want greater flexibility or who cannot find suitable regular employment (Abraham, Hershbein, and Houseman 2021), there are concerns that the rise of such work, especially via platforms and apps, may push many workers out of traditional employee jobs into independent contractor arrangements with few legal protections. A related phenomenon is "fissuring," where firms use outsourcing and subcontracting to distance themselves from the conditions of work carried out in their names (Weil 2014). For example, a large firm may outsource work that was once core to the business—such as hotel cleaning or customer phone service—to one or more smaller businesses, which subcontract portions of the work to even smaller entities, and so on. Workers in fissured arrangements may be classified as employees, but they are more vulnerable to low pay and poor working conditions than if they were directly employed by the lead firm.

For both contract work and fissuring, workers need policies to protect them against employee misclassification and to assign responsibility for workers' well-being to firms that ultimately control and direct their work. As the fight over the classification of Uber, Lyft, and DoorDash workers in California in 2020 showed, struggles between labor groups and firms are likely to continue over who counts as an employee (Conger 2020) and therefore benefits from coverage by minimum wage and overtime hours laws, unemployment insurance, workers' compensation, employers' contributions to Social Security, and employer-based health insurance and retirement plans. Our laws need to catch up with new ways that work is organized, including the evolution of online platforms.

4. Supporting Pillars: Economic and Social Policies That Spill Over into Retirement and Labor Force Policy

In this chapter, we have outlined a set of policies to (a) provide income for retired Americans and those whose disabilities reduce their work capacity before traditional retirement ages and (b) improve the labor force for Americans of all ages and increase their chances of working longer in good jobs. Our framework also calls attention to the fact that a broad range of policies—much broader than those typically considered—can support Americans' retirement security and labor force participation. For example, as Chapter 4 by Freeman points out, the COVID-19 pandemic showed how unexpected shocks can upend the best-laid plans for work and retirement. Major investments to prevent and respond to future shocks could help to safeguard the well-being of workers and retirees, even when those investments are not directly connected to either labor force or retirement policy.

In this section, we offer examples of supporting pillars in three other policy domains. However, the principle also applies across other areas we do not discuss such as transportation, housing, childcare, and education: researchers and policymakers should attend to the ways that many different economic and social policies spill over into the domains of work and retirement.

4.1. Health Care

First, our system of employer-based insurance for health care arguably results in mismatches between workers and employers. On the employer side, the cost of insuring older workers is among the reasons for age discrimination in hiring and retention (Burtless 2017; Clark and Shoven 2019; Baily and Harris 2019). On the worker side, some workers hang on to jobs they would prefer to leave because they cannot afford to lose their insurance. Expanded access to health care that does not rely on employers could improve workers' health, make older workers more attractive to employers, and improve the fit between workers and their jobs.

Universal systems, which are typical in other rich nations, fully disconnect health care insurance from employment. In the United States, the Affordable Care Act provides subsidized health care and access to Medicaid in some states. Additional reforms could reduce the age of Medicare eligibility, move eligible workers from their employers' health insurance to Medicare, and develop better health care options for part-time and contingent workers. Health care policies can be working-longer policies.

4.2. Home Care

Second, expanded access to home care for people with disabilities would take some of the strain from unpaid family caregivers. These unpaid workers are often forced to give up paid employment or better jobs to take care of family members in need. As Chapter 10 by Fahle and McGarry shows, caregiving for elderly parents reduces employment among women in their 50s. Recent evidence suggests that Medicaid home care improves the health of not only the recipients but also their caregivers (Unger et al. 2021), and broader access to such care would likely keep more family caregivers in the labor market.

4.3. Tax Policies

Third, tax policies can have beneficial effects. For example, the Earned Income Tax Credit (EITC) has long benefited working families with children but was of limited value to older workers. The American Rescue Plan Act of 2021 temporarily expanded the age range of eligible workers and increased the size of the credit for workers without qualifying children at home. A permanently expanded EITC would not only increase the incomes of working households but would likely increase older workers' labor force participation (Munnell and Walters 2019).

A broad view of work and retirement policies reveals that the boundaries around these domains are more porous than they might look at first glance. If the potential consequences of a given policy for working longer and retirement security are ignored, the overall value of policies that have positive spillover effects for older workers will be underestimated.

5. Conclusion: An Integrated Perspective on Work and Retirement

This book has probed the probable future of "working longer" in America. This final chapter aims to answer the question: Given the evidence that has been developed in this book, how should U.S. policymakers proceed?

We have proposed a policy framework that places working longer in a broader context—one that (a) integrates the domains of *work* and *retirement* and (b) takes a *life course perspective*, addressing the long-term needs of today's middle-aged and younger workers alongside the immediate needs of today's older adults.

To recap, we offer five main conclusions. (1) Working longer is an important but incomplete response to population aging. (2) High and rising social and economic inequalities put working longer in jeopardy for many Americans. (3) Robust retirement and disability

TABLE 14.1 Selected policy proposals to improve work and retirement for America's aging population

Retirement and disability policies	Good jobs policies
Improving financial security for Americans who are out of the labor force	*Improving the conditions for working longer with policies that benefit workers of all ages*
• Put *Social Security* on a sustainable financial footing by increasing revenues through taxation rather than cutting benefits	• *Increase worker voice* with policies that protect workers' right to organize and extend coverage of collective bargaining
• Create a universal, automatic, and portable *retirement savings plan* as a complement to Social Security	• *Improve wages* for low- and middle-wage workers through higher federal minimum wage standards and local place-based development strategies
• Implement *early interventions* to help newly injured or ill workers remain attached to the labor force	• Create *safer working conditions* by adequately funding the Occupational Safety and Health Administration (OSHA)
• Improve the speed and reliability of the *Social Security Disability Insurance (SSDI) application process* to minimize the insecurity and loss of work capacity that accompany long delays	• Reduce volatile and unpredictable schedules with *fair workweek* policies
• Update *Supplemental Security Income (SSI)* to raise federal disability benefits above the federal poverty level and ease restrictions on recipients	• Create federal *paid family and medical leave* and *sick leave* policies to allow workers to care for their health and their families
	• Connect organizations with practices that *improve relational and team workplace dynamics* to improve health and productivity

Supporting pillars in other policy domains
Taking a broad view of work and retirement policies

Increase awareness of how policies in domains such as health care, home care, tax policy, transportation, education, and housing affect older workers' labor force participation and retirees' financial security

---

policies are an essential complement to working-longer policies. (4) Working-longer policies must be supported by "good jobs" policies to succeed. (5) Responses to population aging must take into account the needs of today's middle-aged Americans, who are the retirees of the future, as well as today's older Americans.

We have discussed several promising policy proposals in each domain that illustrate our framework; these are outlined in Table 14.1.

Our policy target is not merely to enable Americans to work longer but also to have longer meaningful and productive work lives in a healthier work environment with better conditions and benefits and to retire with financial security. This vision is asking a lot. But we believe that our nation can achieve it, and such an achievement would lead to a more resilient and productive America.

Notes

1. We thank all the contributors to this volume, as well as John Rowe, Jack Smalligan, and Brad Hershbein, for reading and commenting on this chapter.
2. As elsewhere in this book, we use "Americans" to mean U.S. residents, not only U.S. citizens.
3. The payroll tax cap or taxable maximum (the limit on earnings subject to Social Security taxes) has been a feature of the Social Security program since its inception, but its effectiveness has been eroded over time. Decades ago, the cap covered 90 percent of taxable payroll, but rising income inequality

has pushed an increasing share of national income over the cap. In 2020, the taxable maximum was $137,700—meaning that an individual who earned $1 million from their employment paid exactly the same in Social Security taxes as someone who earned $850,000 less. Changing the cap, along with other policy proposals, would substantially boost Social Security's sustainability. See the plans proposed by Democratic candidates during the 2020 presidential campaign (Smith, Johnson, and Favreault 2020).

4. In defined benefit (DB) pensions, workers accrue benefits based on their age and tenure and are promised a set monthly benefit payment at retirement. In defined contribution (DC) savings plans, the employers and/or employees contribute a set percentage of employees' earnings toward retirement. Workers in DC plans are not guaranteed a fixed pension payment at retirement, as under DB plans. Instead, pension payments depend on the amount invested and the performance of financial markets. The share of workers with DB pension plans has declined sharply over the past three decades. In 1989, roughly a third of American workers had a DB pension; by 2016, only 13 percent did (Center for Retirement Research at Boston College n.d.). But a return to a lost age of DB pensions is not the solution, even if it were possible. As Burtless points out in Chapter 11, DB pensions typically required workers to remain with a firm full-time for several years in order to be eligible for full benefits, undermining their value to workers who changed employers. In theory, DC savings plans, which have largely replaced DB pensions, could provide better retirement incomes to workers in short-tenure, high-turnover jobs than DB plans would. In practice, however, DC plans have been inadequate for most Americans. DC plans emerged essentially by accident during the 1980s as employers learned that they could exploit an obscure section of the tax code—Section 401(k)—to shift the risk of providing retirement income from themselves to their employees. However, DC plans are voluntary for both employees and employers and allow withdrawals before retirement. In addition, few employees can devote adequate shares of their income toward savings, especially in their early careers when it matters most. As a result, relatively few 401(k) holders accumulate enough savings for retirement (Ghilarducci and James 2018).

5. See the proposal developed by Ghilarducci and Hassett (2021) to make a program akin to the Thrift Savings Plan, a defined contribution retirement plan that is currently available to federal workers, available to all workers. Alternative proposals include automatic individual retirement accounts proposed by Iwry and John (2021), which have been implemented in a few states; employer-facilitated accounts proposed by Gale, Holmes, and John (2020); and Friedman's (2015) proposals to combine various types of retirement accounts into a single account.

6. In November 2021, 7.2 million disabled working-age Americans received SSDI benefits only, 4.2 million received SSI benefits only, and 1.3 million received both (Social Security Administration 2021c).

7. Much effort in the federal disability system has focused on incentives to help SSDI recipients return to work. However, relatively few SSDI recipients return to paid work. A likely part of the explanation is that the eligibility criteria for SSDI are stringent: an impairment must be so severe that it prevents an individual not only from doing the work they did in the past but also from doing other work that exists in the economy. In a study that tracked beneficiaries for 10 years after qualifying, only about 28 percent did any paid work, and only 4 percent had their benefits terminated because of sustained work (Liu and Stapleton 2011).

8. See the proposals by Smalligan and Boyens (2018, 2020) for a program of early intervention paired with a national PFML benefit.

9. In 2018, SSDI applicants waited, on average, three to four months for an initial decision on their application, an additional three months if the application was initially denied and they requested a reconsideration, and then more than a year and a half if the application was denied a second time and they requested a hearing (Smalligan and Boyens 2019).

10. See proposals to improve the disability determination process by Liebman and Smalligan (2013) and Smalligan and Boyens (2019). More broadly, determination criteria were developed with manual labor in mind; see proposals by Maestas (2019) to modernize the criteria to reflect today's labor market and to create a system of partial benefits that could allow recipients with some work capacity to combine partial support with part-time work.

11. See proposals by Neumark (2020) such as amending the Age Discrimination in Employment Act (ADEA) to put protections against discrimination in hiring based on age on a par with those based on race, sex, ethnicity, and religion.
12. See the Clean Slate for Worker Power, a project of Harvard Law School's Labor and Worklife Program, which outlines an extensive set of proposed labor laws (cleanslateworkerpower.org).
13. See the federal Raise the Wage Act of 2021. Raising the minimum wage to $15 by 2025 would directly or indirectly benefit approximately 32 million U.S. workers, including 15 percent of workers aged 55 and over (Cooper, Mokhiber, and Zipperer 2021). For the impact of subminimum wages on people with disabilities, see the U.S. Commission on Civil Rights (2020).
14. See proposals for place-based development that reflects local needs for education and training, business services, and infrastructure development, as outlined by Miller-Adams, Bartik, and Hershbein (2021).
15. If a worker earned $15 an hour throughout their career, rather than the current federal minimum wage of $7.25 an hour, they would receive $5,000 per year more in Social Security benefits (Social Security Works 2021).
16. Workers' compensation, which pays benefits to workers who are injured or become ill from work-related causes, suffers from similar gaps in coverage for infectious disease and other modern hazards (see, e.g., Hunt 2020).
17. The Centers for Disease Control and Prevention and other groups have called repeatedly for federal safety standards to protect workers from heat. In September 2021, OSHA announced it will develop a federal rule to protect workers from heat-related illness (Shipley, Edwards, and Nickerson 2021; Wittenberg and Colman 2021).
18. See the 2019 reintroduction of the Schedules That Work Act, as well as Seattle's Secure Scheduling Ordinance (Harknett, Schneider, and Irwin 2021). In at least some cases, schedule stability benefits employers as well as workers. In a randomized controlled trial with Gap retail stores, modest improvements in the consistency and predictability of hours sharply improved business performance (Williams et al. 2018). Design and enforcement of fair workweek policies should attend to the possibility that enforcing stable schedules for employees could lead to accelerated use of contractors.
19. See proposals in the Build Back Better Act of 2021, as well as those developed by the AEI-Brookings Working Group on Paid Family Leave (2017, 2018). PFML should offer a high rate of wage replacement coupled with a pay cap and should cover all workers, including part-time and contingent workers.
20. See proposals by Maestas (2017) to expand access to earned sick leave to support caregiving.

References

Abraham, Katharine G., Brad Hershbein, and Susan N. Houseman. 2021. "Contract Work at Older Ages." *Journal of Pension Economics & Finance* 20 (3): 426–447. https://doi.org/10.1017/S1474747220000098.

AEI-Brookings. 2017. "Paid Family and Medical Leave: An Issue Whose Time Has Come." Working Group on Paid Family Leave. Washington, DC: AEI-Brookings. https://www.brookings.edu/wp-content/uploads/2017/06/es_20170606_paidfamilyleave.pdf.

AEI-Brookings. 2018. "Paid Family and Medical Leave: Charting a Path Forward." Working Group on Paid Family Leave. Washington, DC: AEI-Brookings. https://www.aei.org/wp-content/uploads/2018/09/The-AEI-Brookings-Working-Group-Report-on-Paid-Family-and-Medical-Leave.pdf.

Altman, Nancy J. 2020. "The Pressing Need to Update, Expand, and Simplify SSI." Annual Report of the Supplemental Security Income Program. Washington, DC: Social Security Administration. https://www.ssa.gov/oact/ssir/SSI20/2020_SSAB_Nancy_Altman_Statement.pdf.

Autor, David H., Nicole Maestas, Kathleen J. Mullen, and Alexander Strand. 2015. "Does Delay Cause Decay? The Effect of Administrative Decision Time on the Labor Force Participation and Earnings of Disability Applicants." Working Paper 20840. National Bureau of Economic Research. https://doi.org/10.3386/w20840.

Baily, Martin Neil, and Benjamin H. Harris. 2019. "Working Longer Policies: Framing the Issues." Economic Studies at Brookings. Washington, DC: Brookings Institution. https://www.brookings.edu/research/working-longer-policies-framing-the-issues/.

Block, Sharon, and Benjamin Sachs. n.d. "Clean Slate for Worker Power: Building a Just Economy and Democracy." Labor and Worklife Program. Harvard Law School. Accessed October 29, 2021. https://www.cleanslateworkerpower.org/clean-slate-agenda.

Bound, John, Todd Stinebrickner, and Timothy Waidmann. 2010. "Health, Economic Resources and the Work Decisions of Older Men." *Journal of Econometrics* 156 (1): 106–129. https://doi.org/10.1016/j.jeconom.2009.09.010.

Burke, Henry. 2021. "Biden's Budget Must Strengthen OSHA." *Revolving Door Project* (blog). April 2, 2021. https://therevolvingdoorproject.org/bidens-budget-must-strengthen-osha/.

Burtless, Gary. 2017. "Age Related Health Costs and Job Prospects of Older Workers." Working Longer and Retirement Conference, Stanford Institute for Economic Policy Research. https://siepr.stanford.edu/system/files/BURTLESS_Age-Related-Health-Costs_1st-Draft_Oct-2017.pdf.

Center for Retirement Research at Boston College. n.d. "Pension Participation of All Workers, by Type of Plan, 1989–2016." Accessed September 30, 2021. https://crr.bc.edu/wp-content/uploads/2015/10/Pension-coverage.pdf.

The Century Foundation, and Data For Progress. 2021. "Voters Overwhelmingly Support Strengthening Supplemental Security Income (SSI)." https://www.filesforprogress.org/memos/dfp_tcf_ssi_may_2021.pdf.

Clark, Robert L., and John B. Shoven. 2019. "Enhancing Work Incentives for Older Workers: Social Security and Medicare Proposals to Reduce Work Disincentives." Washington, DC: The Brookings Institution. https://www.brookings.edu/wp-content/uploads/2019/01/ES_20190124_Clark-Shoven-Retirement-Reform1.pdf.

Conger, Kate. 2020. "Uber and Lyft Drivers in California Will Remain Contractors." *The New York Times*, November 4, 2020. https://www.nytimes.com/2020/11/04/technology/california-uber-lyft-prop-22.html.

Cooper, David, Zane Mokhiber, and Ben Zipperer. 2021. "Raising the Federal Minimum Wage to $15 by 2025 Would Lift the Pay of 32 Million Workers." Washington, DC: Economic Policy Institute. https://files.epi.org/pdf/221010.pdf.

Davis, Owen, Bridget Fisher, Teresa Ghilarducci, and Siavash Radpour. 2021. "The Pandemic Retirement Surge Increased Retirement Inequality." Status of Older Workers Report Series. New York: Schwartz Center for Economic Policy Analysis at the New School for Social Research. https://www.economicpolicyresearch.org/jobs-report/the-pandemic-retirement-surge-increased-retirement-inequality.

Dube, Arindrajit, T. William Lester, and Michael Reich. 2016. "Minimum Wage Shocks, Employment Flows, and Labor Market Frictions." *Journal of Labor Economics* 34 (3): 663–704. https://doi.org/10.1086/685449.

Freeman, Richard B. 2021. "Ownership Cures for Inequality." In *Combating Inequality: Rethinking Government's Role*, edited by Olivier Blanchard and Dani Rodrik, 201–210. Cambridge, MA: MIT Press.

Friedman, John N. 2015. "Building on What Works: A Proposal to Modernize Retirement Savings." The Hamilton Project. https://www.hamiltonproject.org/assets/files/friedman_proposal_modernize_retirement_savings.pdf.

Gale, William G., Sarah E. Holmes, and David C. John. 2020. "Retirement Plans for Contingent Workers: Issues and Options." *Journal of Pension Economics and Finance* 19 (2): 185–197. https://doi.org/10.1017/S1474747218000288.

Ghilarducci, Teresa, and Kevin A. Hassett. 2021. "What If Low-Income American Workers Had Access to Wealth-Building Vehicles Like the Federal Employees' Thrift Savings Plan?" White Paper. Washington, DC: Economic Innovation Group. https://eig.org/wp-content/uploads/2021/03/Hassett-Ghilarducci-White-Paper-IWBI.pdf.

Ghilarducci, Teresa, and Tony James. 2018. *Rescuing Retirement: A Plan to Guarantee Retirement Security for All Americans*. New York: Columbia University Press.

Glisson, Charles, Denzel Dukes, and Philip Green. 2006. "The Effects of the ARC Organizational Intervention on Caseworker Turnover, Climate, and Culture in Children's Service Systems." *Child Abuse & Neglect* 30 (8): 855–880. https://doi.org/10.1016/j.chiabu.2005.12.010.

Glisson, Charles, Anthony Hemmelgarn, Philip Green, Denzel Dukes, Shannon Atkinson, and Nathaniel J. Williams. 2012. "Randomized Trial of the Availability, Responsiveness, and Continuity (ARC) Organizational Intervention with Community-Based Mental Health Programs and Clinicians Serving Youth." *Journal of the American Academy of Child and Adolescent Psychiatry* 51 (8): 780–787. https://doi.org/10.1016/j.jaac.2012.05.010.

Harknett, Kristen, Daniel Schneider, and Véronique Irwin. 2021. "Improving Health and Economic Security by Reducing Work Schedule Uncertainty." *Proceedings of the National Academy of Sciences* 118 (42): e2107828118. https://doi.org/10.1073/pnas.2107828118.

Howell, David R., Kea Fiedler, and Stephanie Luce. 2016. "What's the Right Minimum Wage? Reframing the Debate from 'No Job Loss' to a 'Minimum Living Wage.'" Washington Center for Equitable Growth. https://equitablegrowth.org/wp-content/uploads/2016/06/howell-fiedler-luce-right-minwage-revised.pdf.

Hunt, H. Allan. 2020. "Don't Assume Workers' Comp Will Cover COVID-19 Illness." W.E. Upjohn Institute for Employment Research. April 15, 2020. https://www.upjohn.org/research-highlights/dont-assume-workers-comp-will-cover-covid-19-illness.

Hurd, Michael D., and Susann Rohwedder. Forthcoming. "Economic Preparation for Retirement." In *Routledge Handbook on the Economics of Ageing*, edited by David E. Bloom, Alfonso Sousa-Poza, and Uwe Sunde.

Iwry, J. Mark, and David C. John. 2021. "The Automatic IRA at 15: Helping Americans Build Retirement Security." *Up Front* (blog). February 12, 2021. https://www.brookings.edu/blog/up-front/2021/02/12/the-automatic-ira-at-15-helping-americans-build-retirement-security/.

Johnson, Richard W., Melissa M. Favreault, and Corina Mommaerts. 2010. "Work Ability and the Social Insurance Safety Net in the Years Prior to Retirement." Discussion Paper 10–01. Washington, DC: The Urban Institute. https://www.urban.org/sites/default/files/publication/28276/412008-Work-Ability-and-the-Social-Insurance-Safety-Net-in-the-Years-Prior-to-Retirement.PDF.

Kinder, Molly, and Laura Stateler. 2021. "A Policy Manifesto for Paying, Protecting, and Empowering Essential Workers." Washington, DC: The Brookings Institution. https://www.brookings.edu/research/a-policy-manifesto-for-paying-protecting-and-empowering-essential-workers/.

Kirkham, Chris. 2021. "Most U.S. Firms Hit with COVID-19 Safety Fines Aren't Paying Up." *Reuters*, February 18, 2021. https://www.reuters.com/article/us-health-coronavirus-workplace-fines-ex-idUSKBN2AI1JT.

Liebman, Jeffrey B., and Jack A. Smalligan. 2013. "An Evidence-Based Path to Disability Insurance Reform." Washington, DC: The Hamilton Project. https://www.brookings.edu/research/an-evidence-based-path-to-disability-insurance-reform/.

Liu, Su, and David Stapleton. 2011. "Longitudinal Statistics on Work Activity and Use of Employment Supports for New Social Security Disability Insurance Beneficiaries." *Social Security Bulletin* 71 (3): 25. https://www.ssa.gov/policy/docs/ssb/v71n3/v71n3p35.html.

Lovejoy, Meg, Erin L. Kelly, Laura D. Kubzansky, and Lisa F. Berkman. 2021. "Work Redesign for the 21st Century: Promising Strategies for Enhancing Worker Well-Being." *American Journal of Public Health* 111 (10): 1787–1795. https://doi.org/10.2105/AJPH.2021.306283.

Maestas, Nicole. 2017. "Expanding Access to Earned Sick Leave to Support Caregiving." In *The 51%: Driving Growth through Women's Economic Participation*, edited by Diane Whitmore Schanzenbach and Ryan Nunn, pp. 93–106. Washington, DC: The Hamilton Project, Brookings Institution. https://www.brookings.edu/research/expanding-access-to-earned-sick-leave-to-support-caregiving/.

Maestas, Nicole. 2019. "Identifying Work Capacity and Promoting Work: A Strategy for Modernizing the SSDI Program." *The ANNALS of the American Academy of Political and Social Science* 686 (1): 93–120. https://journals.sagepub.com/doi/abs/10.1177/0002716219882354.

Miller-Adams, Michelle, Timothy J. Bartik, and Brad J. Hershbein. 2021. "A Moment of Opportunity: Strategies for Inclusive Economic Growth." Kalamazoo, MI: W.E. Upjohn Institute. https://doi.org/10.17848/tr21-040.

Morrissey, Monique. 2012. "Wages and Social Security." *Economic Policy Institute* (blog). July 16, 2012. https://www.epi.org/blog/wages-social-security/.

Munnell, Alicia H., and Abigail N. Walters. 2019. "Proposals to Keep Older People in the Labor Force." Washington, DC: The Brookings Institution. https://www.brookings.edu/wp-content/uploads/2019/01/ES_20190124_Munnell-Walters-Retirement-Reform_with-Reference-Material-2.pdf.

Neumark, David. 2020. "Strengthen Age Discrimination Protections to Help Confront the Challenge of Population Aging." Washington, DC: The Brookings Institution. https://www.brookings.edu/wp-content/uploads/2020/11/ES-11.19.20-Neumark.pdf.

Shipley, Julia, Brian Edwards, and David Nickerson. 2021. "The Biden Administration Is Adding Worker Protections To Address Extreme Heat." *NPR*, September 21, 2021. https://www.npr.org/2021/09/21/1039372888/the-biden-administration-is-adding-worker-protections-to-address-extreme-heat.

Smalligan, Jack, and Chantel Boyens. 2018. "Expanding Early Intervention for Newly Ill and Injured Workers and Connections to Paid Medical Leave." Washington, DC: The Urban Institute. https://www.urban.org/research/publication/expanding-early-intervention-newly-iii-and-injured-workers-and-connections-paid-leave.

Smalligan, Jack, and Chantel Boyens. 2019. "Improving the Social Security Disability Determination Process." Washington, DC: Urban Institute. https://www.urban.org/sites/default/files/publication/100710/improving_the_social_security_disability_determination_proces.pdf.

Smalligan, Jack, and Chantel Boyens. 2020. "Policies for an Aging Labor Force." Washington, DC: The Urban Institute. https://www.urban.org/sites/default/files/publication/103083/policies-for-an-aging-labor-force.pdf.

Smith, Karen E., Richard W. Johnson, and Melissa M. Favreault. 2020. "Five Democratic Approaches to Social Security Reform: Estimated Impact of Plans from the 2020 Presidential Campaign." Washington, DC: The Urban Institute. https://www.urban.org/sites/default/files/publication/103050/five-democratic-approaches-to-social-security-reform-estimated-impact-of-plans-from-the-2020-presidential-campaign_0.pdf.

Social Security Administration. 2021a. "2021 OASDI Trustees Report." Washington, DC: Social Security Administration. https://www.ssa.gov/OACT/TR/2021/index.html.

Social Security Administration. 2021b. "Fact Sheet: Social Security." Washington, DC: Social Security Administration. https://www.ssa.gov/news/press/factsheets/basicfact-alt.pdf.

Social Security Administration. 2021c. "Monthly Statistical Snapshot." November 2021. https://www.ssa.gov/policy/docs/quickfacts/stat_snapshot/.

Social Security Works. 2021. "Enacting a $15 Minimum Wage Is a Win for Social Security." Washington, DC. https://socialsecurityworks.org/wp-content/uploads/2021/02/Social-Security-Minimum-Wage-Report-February-2021.pdf.

Unger, Emily S., David C. Grabowski, Jarvis T. Chen, and Lisa F. Berkman. 2021. "Association Between New-Onset Medicaid Home Care and Family Caregivers' Health." *JAMA Health Forum* 2 (9): e212671. https://doi.org/10.1001/jamahealthforum.2021.2671.

U.S. Commission on Civil Rights. 2020. "Subminimum Wages: Impacts on the Civil Rights of People with Disabilities." 2020 Statutory Enforcement Report. Washington, DC. https://www.usccr.gov/pubs/briefing-reports/2020-09-17-Subminimum-Wages.php.

U.S. Department of Labor. 2016. "Paid Sick Leave." Washington, DC: Wage and Hour Division, U.S. Department of Labor. October 15, 2021. https://www.dol.gov/sites/dolgov/files/WHD/legacy/files/HowDoIKnow.pdf.

Walker, Elisa A., Virginia P. Reno, and Thomas N. Bethell. 2014. "Americans Make Hard Choices on Social Security: A Survey with Trade-Off Analysis." Washington, DC: National Academy of Social Insurance. https://www.nasi.org/wp-content/uploads/2014/11/Americans_Make_Hard_Choices_on_Social_Security.pdf.

Walter, Karla. 2020. "Federal Contracting Doesn't Go Far Enough to Protect American Workers." Center for American Progress Action Fund. November 19, 2020. https://www.americanprogressaction.org/issues/economy/reports/2020/11/19/179390/federal-contracting-doesnt-go-far-enough-protect-american-workers/.

Weil, David. 2014. *The Fissured Workplace: Why Work Became so Bad for so Many and What Can Be Done to Improve It*. Cambridge, MA: Harvard University Press.

Western, Bruce, and Jake Rosenfeld. 2011. "Unions, Norms, and the Rise in U.S. Wage Inequality." *American Sociological Review* 76 (4): 513–537. https://doi.org/10.1177/0003122411414817.

Williams, Joan C., Susan J. Lambert, Saravanan Kesavan, Peter J. Fugiel, Lori Ann Ospina, Erin Devorah Rapoport, Meghan Jarpe, Dylan Bellisle, Pradeep Pendem, Lisa McCorkell, and Sarah Adler-Milstein. 2018. "Stable Scheduling Increases Productivity and Sales." Hastings College of the Law, University of California. https://worklifelaw.org/publications/Stable-Scheduling-Study-Report.pdf.

Wittenberg, Ariel, and Zack Colman. 2021. "Regulators Refuse to Step in as Workers Languish in Extreme Heat." *Politico*, August 8, 2021. https://www.politico.com/news/2021/08/08/osha-climate-change-effects-workforce-heat-impact-501744.

Index

For the benefit of digital users, indexed terms that span two pages (e.g., 52–53) may, on occasion, appear on only one of those pages.

Tables and figures are indicated by *t* and *f* following the page number

AARP, 278
abilities, impact of age on, 141–42. *See also* work capacity
absolute poverty, 279–80
ACA (Affordable Care Act), 291, 294, 313–14
accommodative practices, 148–49, 307
accurate measures of income and well-being, 245–50
achievement goals, 142–43
ACS (American Community Survey), 51
activities of daily living (ADLs), 79
aesthetic labor, 189–90
affective partisanship, 295
Affordable Care Act (ACA), 291, 294, 313–14
age
   abilities, impact on, 141–42
   cohort patterns in work capacity, 131–34, 132*t*, 133*t*, 134*t*
   job loss during COVID-19 pandemic by, 99*t*, 100
   job satisfaction and, 144
   population aging, 4–6, 5*f*, 19, 303–4
   self-reported ability distributions, 121*f*
   work capacity by, 125–28, 127*t*
age discrimination
   in low-wage work, 189–90
   in organizations, 145–47, 202–3, 206–7
ageist stereotypes, 146–47
aging workforce, organizational response to. *See* organizational response to aging workforce
AIME (average indexed monthly earnings), 183–84, 256–57
American Community Survey (ACS), 51

American Rescue Plan Act (ARPA), 101
American Work Capacity and Abilities Survey (AWCAS), 116–20, 117*t*
asymmetric polarization, 290–93
attitudes toward older workers in firms, 202–3
Austria, employment rates in, 81*f*, 82*f*, 84*f*
automatic retirement savings plans, 305–6
average wage index (AWI), 257

behavioral sciences, increasing spending on, 104–5
Belgium, employment rates in, 81*f*, 82*f*, 84*f*
benefit cut (CUT 20.0%) option, Social Security reform
   cost of no policy change assumption, 265–67, 266*f*, 268–70, 269*t*
   cost of policy change assumption, 270–71, 272*t*
   effect on individual benefits, 259–61, 260*t*
   effect on Social Security solvency, 261–62
   overview, 259
biases in organized political economy
   effect on policy choices, 293–96
   overview, 277
   towards economic conservatism within Republican Party, 290–93
   towards economic elites, 284–87, 288*f*
   towards political gridlock, 288–90
Black Americans
   caregiving and, 215, 220*f*, 225*f*, 227*f*, 230*f*
   health, 6–8, 114–15
   potential earnings by age, 132–33, 133*t*
   racial resentment towards, 294–95
   self-reported ability distributions, 121*f*
   work capacity, 131–34, 133*t*

blue collar jobs, impact of COVID-19 pandemic on, 96–98, 97t
Burns, Robert, 91
Bush tax cuts, 287, 288f
business case for age-related practices, 199, 207–8

campaign donations, 285–86
CAP 10.6% (payroll tax cap removal) option, Social Security reform
   cost of no policy change assumption, 268f, 268–70, 269t
   cost of policy change assumption, 270–71, 272t
   effect on individual benefits, 259–61, 260t
   effect on Social Security solvency, 261–62
   overview, 259
career earnings inequality, 241–43, 242f
caregiving
   characteristics of caregivers, 218–23, 219t, 220f, 221t, 222t
   cost of replacement care, 224–26, 227f
   discussion, 229–32
   home care, expanded access to, 314
   hours of care, 223–24, 224t, 225f
   HRS data, 217–18
   overview, 2, 10, 19, 213–16
   paid family and medical leave, 10, 307, 311, 315t
   relationship between work and, 217, 226–29, 228t, 230f
   rising rates of, 216–17, 231
CARES (Coronavirus Aid, Relief, and Economic Security Act), 95
CBO (Congressional Budget Office), 249
Census Bureau, measures of income for, 245–50
chained CPI (C-CPI-U) option, Social Security reform
   cost of no policy change assumption, 265–67, 266f, 268–70, 269t
   cost of policy change assumption, 270–71, 272t
   effect on individual benefits, 259–61, 260t
   effect on Social Security solvency, 261–62
   overview, 259
challenge job demands, 147–48
climate trends, 91, 104
CME (coordinated market economies), 204–6
cognitive abilities, 115, 117t
   by age cohort, 125–28, 127t
   by education, 129, 130t
   by gender, 128–29, 128t
   potential earnings and, 125, 126f
   psychology of working longer model, 141–42
   by race and ethnicity, 129–31, 131t
   relationship between work capacity and, 123–25, 124t

commuting zones (CZs)
   characteristics of low- and high-employment areas, 57t
   correlation in employment patterns by education and age, 63–64, 64t
   employment differences at older ages, 52–54, 53f, 55f, 56f
   explanations for differences between, 60–63, 62t
   overview, 15, 50–51
comprehensive income measures, 248–49
computer simulations, planning for unexpected shocks with, 106
Congressional Budget Office (CBO), 249
consumer price index for urban wage earners and clerical workers (CPI-W), 256–57, 259
contingent workers, 312–13
contract work, 312–13
coordinated market economies (CME), 204–6
Coronavirus Aid, Relief, and Economic Security Act (CARES), 95
corporations, role of in politics, 285
cost of replacement care, 224–26, 227f
cost of Social Security reform indecision
   model for, 264
   under no policy change assumption, 265–70, 269t
   overview, 262–64
   under policy change assumption, 270–71, 272t
courts, Republican success in, 292–93
COVID-19 pandemic
   demographics of job loss and recovery, 98–100, 99t
   impact on labor markets, 92–96, 93f, 94t, 95f, 157
   new labor market inequality created by, 96–98, 97t
   overview, 91–92
   planning for future unexpected shocks, 103–6
   recovery, 100–1
   remote work during, 11
   Social Security and work-longer/retire-later policies, 101–3
   as unexpected shock, 16
   vulnerabilities of older workers, 151
   work challenges created by, 14
   working-longer strategy for low-wage workers and, 178
CPI-W (consumer price index for urban wage earners and clerical workers), 256–57, 259
cumulative disadvantage model, 29, 33
Current Population Survey (CPS)
   employment rates in, 34–39, 35f, 36f, 37f, 38f
   general discussion, 31
CUT 20.0% (benefit cut) option, Social Security reform
   cost of no policy change assumption, 265–67, 266f, 268–70, 269t

cost of policy change assumption, 270–71, 272*t*
effect on individual benefits, 259–61, 260*t*
effect on Social Security solvency, 261–62
overview, 259
CZs. *See* commuting zones

DBT (issue debt) option, Social Security reform, 258
defined-benefit (DB) pension plans, 244–45, 305
defined-contribution (DC) pension plans, 244–45, 282, 305
demographics. *See also specific factors*
characteristics of caregivers, 218–23, 219*t*, 220*f*, 221*t*, 222*t*
characteristics of low- and high-employment areas, 57*t*, 59
of job loss and recovery during COVID-19 pandemic, 98–100, 99*t*
population aging, 4–6, 5*f*
Denmark, employment rates in, 81*f*, 82*f*, 84*f*
developmental practices, 148–49
diabetes prevalence, 114–15
disability
employment stability and, 43*f*, 43–44
geographic differences in employment, 57*t*, 59, 63, 64*t*
policy proposals, 303, 306–8, 315*t*
rates of, 8, 9
discrimination, age. *See* age discrimination

Earliest Eligibility Age (EEA), 30
early intervention programs, 307, 315*t*
Earned Income Tax Credit (EITC), 314
economic elites, bias towards, 284–87, 288*f*
economic inequality
accurate measures of income and well-being, 245–50
career earnings inequality, 241–43, 242*f*
comprehensive income measures, 248–49
economic elites, bias towards, 284–87, 288*f*
future prospects, 250–51
impact on working longer, 303
improvement in economic well-being of older Americans, 239–40, 240*f*
income distribution, 249–50, 250*f*
increase in, 2
means-tested programs and, 245
misreporting income, 246–48
money income, limitations of, 246
overview, 237–39
pensions and savings, effect on, 244–45
Social Security, effect on, 243–44
unequal gains, 240–41
economic mobility, 181
economic policies, 313–14

economic security for low-wage workers
from Social Security, 181–84, 182*t*
Social Security benefits by wage scenario, 184*f*, 184–85
too poor not to work, 179–80
worker strategies, 190–93
working longer and benefit adequacy, 185–88, 186*t*
economic trends, 91
education
caregiving and, 218–19, 220*f*, 224, 225*f*, 227*f*, 230*f*
employment rates and, 34, 36*f*, 37*f*, 38*f*
employment stability and, 40, 41*f*
European health trends by, 76*f*, 77*f*, 78
forecasting employment, 172–73
geographic differences in employment by, 63–64, 64*t*
job loss during COVID-19 pandemic by, 98, 99*t*
past trends in health and employment by, 159, 161*f*, 161–62
potential earnings by age and, 134, 134*t*
self-reported ability distributions and, 121*f*
work capacity by, 127, 129, 130*t*
EEA (Social Security Earliest Eligibility Age), 30
Eisenhower, Dwight, 101
EITC (Earned Income Tax Credit), 314
elder care. *See* caregiving
Elder Index, 181–82, 182*t*, 185, 186*t*
electoral insulation, 295
employee representation mechanisms, 204–6, 210
employer-based retirement plans, 13, 244–45, 282, 305–6
employment. *See also* employment stability in middle-aged population; forecasting employment; geographic differences in employment; low-wage work
across life course, 29–30
caregiving and, 217, 226–29, 228*t*, 230*f*
good jobs policies, 302, 303, 308–13, 315*t*
nature of work, trends in, 10–12
past trends in, 91–92, 155, 156*f*, 158*f*, 158–62
retirement savings plans, 13, 181, 244–45, 305–6, 315*t*
trends in Europe, 69–70, 79–86, 80*f*, 81*f*
union membership, 11–12, 293, 309
voice of workers, increasing, 309, 315*t*
employment-at-will job system, 93–94
employment rates. *See also* geographic differences in employment
in Current Population Survey, 34–39, 35*f*, 36*f*, 37*f*, 38*f*
impact of COVID-19 pandemic on, 92–96, 93*f*, 94*t*, 95*f*
simulations of, for older ages, 166–71, 168*f*, 169*t*, 170*t*

employment stability in middle-aged population
    Current Population Survey data, 31, 34–39
    discussion, 44–46
    employment across life course, 29–30
    Health and Retirement Study data, 31–33, 39–43
    overview, 15, 27–29
    Steady Outs, 33, 39f, 40f, 42f, 43–44
employment transitions, 165–66, 166t
environmental factors, work-related, 140f, 145–48
ethnicity
    caregiving and, 215, 220f, 223, 224, 225f, 227f, 230f
    health inequalities, 6–8
    work capacity by, 129–31, 131t
Europe, health and employment in
    descriptive findings of health trends, 73–75, 74f
    employment trends in, 79–86, 80f, 81f
    institutional and health background, 70–71
    link between health and employment, 86
    measuring with SHARE data, 71–73
    overview, 16, 69–70
    regression analyses of health trends, 75–79, 76f, 77f, 78f
expectations of future work, 162–63
    predictive accuracy of, 163, 164t
    trends in, 163–65, 164f
expected unexpected events, planning for, 103–6

fair workweek policies, 311, 315t
family
    changes in dynamics of, 2, 10, 289
    characteristics of caregivers, 221–23, 222t, 229
    paid family and medical leave, 10, 307, 311, 315t
    role of, 18–19
Fauci, Anthony S., 92
federal minimum wage, 309
filibusters, 289
financial characteristics of caregivers, 214–15, 218–19, 219t, 220f
fissuring, 312–13
forecasting employment
    data, 158
    discussion, 171–73
    employment transitions in HRS, 165–66, 166t
    future trends, 162–63
    overview, 17–18, 155–57
    past trends, 158f, 158–62
    predictive accuracy of expectations, 163, 164t
    simulations, 166–71, 168f, 169t, 170t
    trends in expectations, 163–65, 164f
    using subjective probabilities of working, 165
401(k)-type plans, 244–45, 282
France
    age of labor market exit, 281f
    employment rates in, 81f, 82f, 84f
    public pension systems in, 70–71, 282f
    social support systems in, 71
full retirement age (FRA), 5, 287, 305
full retirement age increased to 70 (FRA 70) option, Social Security reform
    cost of no policy change assumption, 265–67, 266f, 268–70, 269t
    cost of policy change assumption, 270–71, 272t
    effect on individual benefits, 259–61, 260t, 262t
    effect on Social Security solvency, 261–62
    overview, 259
full-time equivalent employment model, 206
functional abilities
    by age cohort, 125–28, 127t
    age cohort patterns in work capacity, 131–34, 132t, 133t, 134t
    data, 116–20, 117t
    discussion, 134–35
    by education, 129, 130t
    by gender, 128–29, 128t
    overview, 113–16
    potential earnings and, 125, 126f
    by race and ethnicity, 129–31, 131t
    relationship between work capacity and, 123–25, 124t
    self-reported ability distributions, 121f
    summarizing, 120
functional limitations, 9
future prospects of older Americans, 250–51
future time perspectives, 142–43, 150

gender
    career earnings inequality, 241–43, 242f
    disability benefit receipt by, 43f
    employment rates, 34–38, 35f, 36f, 37f, 38f
    employment stability, 40–41, 41f
    European employment trends, 80f, 80–81, 81f, 82f
    European health trends, 75–79, 76f, 77f, 78f
    family dynamics, changes in, 10
    geographic differences in employment, 52–54, 53f, 56f, 61, 62t, 64t
    job loss during COVID-19 pandemic, 98–99, 99t
    labor force participation, 30
    potential earnings by age and, 132, 132t
    self-reported ability distributions, 121f
    social identities, 145
    Social Security benefits by wage scenario, 184f, 184–85, 186t
    trends in employment, 156f
    work capacity by, 128–29, 128t
geographic differences in employment
    characteristics of low- and high-employment areas, 54–60, 57t
    correlation by education and age, 63–64, 64t

data and methods, 51–52
discussion, 64–65
explanations for, 60–63, 62t
at older ages, 52–54, 53f, 55f, 56f
overview, 15, 49–51
Germany
age of labor market exit in, 281f
employment rates in, 81f, 82f, 84f
public pension systems in, 70–71, 282f
social support systems in, 71
Germany, response to aging workforce in
attitudes toward older workers, 202–3
business case, 207–8
HR practices, 203–4
institutional forces, 204–7, 210
interview data, 201–7
macro-, micro-, and meso-level concerns, 208–9
meso-level research, 198–99
overview, 18–19, 197–98
policy considerations, 210
skill divide, 209
survey data, 200–1, 201t
gig work, 11, 312–13
Gini coefficient of income inequality, 241, 247
global warming, 91, 104
goals, future time perspectives and, 142–43
good jobs policies, 302, 303, 308–13, 315t
GOP. *See* Republican Party
government, changes in role of, 12–14
gridlock, political, 288–90, 296

headcount model of employment, 206
health
cross-national differences, 69–70, 283–84
European trends, descriptive findings of, 73–75, 74f
European trends, regression analyses of, 75–79, 76f, 77f, 78f
geographic differences in employment and, 57t, 60
link between employment and, 86
past trends in employment and, 160f, 160–62, 161f
rising inequalities in, 6–8
slowdowns in improvements, 8–9
trends in middle-aged population, 9–10
work as social determinant of, 308
Health and Retirement Study (HRS)
caregiving data, 217–18
descriptive results in employment stability, 39f, 39–42, 40f, 41f
employment transitions, 165–66, 166t
forecasting employment from data in, 155–56, 166t
general discussion, 31–33
past trends in employment, 158f, 158–62
regression results in employment stability, 42f, 42–43
work history and disability patterns, 43–44

health care
cross-national differences, 282–83
geographic differences in employment and, 57t, 60
income distribution and, 249–50
policy proposals, 313–14
Republican Party and, 291–92
health deficit index, 71–72
descriptive findings of, 73–75, 74f
regression analyses, 75–79, 76f, 77f, 78f
health inequalities, 2, 6–10
health insurance, 70–71, 248–50, 294
hindrance job demands, 147–48
hiring freezes, 208
Hispanic Americans
caregiving and, 215, 220f, 225f, 227f, 230f
health, 6–8
home care, expanded access to, 314
home ownership, 182, 182t, 185, 186t, 187
hours of care, 223–24, 224t, 225f
HR practices. *See* human resource practices
HRS. *See* Health and Retirement Study
human capital
age-related HR practices, 203–4
attitudes toward older workers, 202–3
business case for age-related practices, 207–8
skill divide, 209
human capital perspective, 199
human resource (HR) practices
attitudes toward older workers, 202–3
business case, 207–8
institutional forces, 204–7, 210
interview data, 201–7
macro-, micro-, and meso-level concerns, 208–9
meso organizational level, 198–99
motivational, 148–49
overview, 196–98
policy considerations, 210
skill divide, 209
survey data, 200–1, 201t
types of, 203–4

IAB Establishment Panel, 200
IADLs (instrumental activities of daily living), 79
IBM, 97–98
income. *See also* low-wage work; potential earnings
accurate measures of, 245–50
career earnings inequality, 241–43, 242f
means-tested programs and, 245
pensions and savings, effect on, 244–45
Social Security and, 243–44
trends in, 239–40, 240f
unequal distribution of gains, 240–41
wage increases, 309–10
work capacity and, 115
income distribution, 249–50, 250f

independent contracting, 11, 205, 210, 312–13
individual attributes, 140f, 141–42
individual responsibility framework for retirement security, 177–78
industry
   geographic differences in employment, 57t, 59–60
   job loss during COVID-19 pandemic by, 93–94, 94t
institutional forces, impact on response to workforce aging, 204–7, 210
instrumental activities of daily living (IADLs), 79
intellectual organizations, role of, 285
interview-based research about organizational practices, 201–7
   attitudes toward older workers, 202–3
   HR practices, 203–4
   institutional forces, 204–7
Israel, 105
issue debt (DBT) option, Social Security reform, 258
Italy
   age of labor market exit, 281f
   employment rates in, 81f, 82f, 84f
   public pension systems in, 70–71, 282f
   social support systems in, 71

job attitudes, 143–45
Job Demands and Resources (JD-R) model, 147–48
job loss during COVID-19 pandemic
   demographics of, 98–100, 99t
   impact of pandemic on labor markets, 93–96
   labor market inequality, 96–98, 97t
job quality, of caregivers, 219–21, 221t
job resources, 147–48
job satisfaction, 144–45

Klein, Ezra, 287
knitting their own safety net strategy, 179, 192–93
knowledge abilities, 141–42

labor force participation. *See also* forecasting employment
   caregiving and, 219, 221t, 223
   cross-national differences, 69–70, 280–81, 281f
   employment versus, 31
   European trends in middle age, 79–86, 80f, 81f
   gender differences, 30
   link between health and, 86
   past trends in employment, 158f, 158–62
labor force policies, 302, 303, 308–13, 315t
labor market exit, 280–81, 281f
labor markets, impact of COVID-19 pandemic on, 92–98, 93f, 94t, 95f, 97t
labor trends, 15–16

labor unions, 11–12, 293, 309
letting it ride strategy, 179, 190–91
liberal market economies (LME), 204–6
life course, employment across, 29–30
life expectancy, 2
   cross-national differences, 8f, 8–9, 71, 283f, 283–84
   income distribution and, 251
   past trends in employment and, 159–60
   slowdowns in improvements, 8
   socioeconomic position and, 6–8, 7f
lifespan approach, 139, 140
LME (liberal market economies), 204–6
long-term care. *See* caregiving
low-wage work
   age discrimination and aesthetic labor in, 189–90
   benefit changes across cohorts, 184f, 184–85
   economic security from Social Security, 181–84, 182t
   overview, 18, 177–79
   physical demands of, 188–89
   too poor not to work, 179–80
   workers in, 180–81
   worker strategies, 179, 190–93
   working longer and benefit adequacy, 185–88, 186t

macro-level perspective on workforce aging, 198, 208–9
maintenance practices, 148–49
manufacturing industry, response to aging workforce in
   attitudes toward older workers, 202–3
   business case, 207–8
   HR practices, 203–4
   institutional forces, 204–7, 210
   interview data, 201–7
   macro-, micro-, and meso-level concerns, 208–9
   meso organizational level, 198–99
   overview, 18–19, 196–98
   policy considerations, 210
   skill divide, 209
   survey data, 200–1, 201t
maximum potential earnings, 123f, 123
MEA (Munich Center for the Economics of Aging) health deficit index, 72
means-tested programs, 245
median potential earnings, 123f, 123
median-wage workers, Social Security benefits for, 184f, 184–88, 186t
Medicaid, 213
medical leave, 311
Medicare, 278, 291–92, 294, 313–14
men
   career earnings inequality, 241–43, 242f
   disability benefit receipt by, 43f

employment rates, 34–38, 35f, 36f, 37f, 38f
employment stability, 40–41, 41f
European employment trends, 80f, 80–81, 81f, 82f
European health trends, 75–79, 76f, 77f, 78f
family dynamics, changes in, 10
geographic differences in employment, 52–54, 53f, 56f, 61, 62t, 64t
job loss during COVID-19 pandemic, 98–99, 99t
labor force participation, 30
potential earnings by age and, 132, 132t
self-reported ability distributions, 121f
Social Security benefits by wage scenario, 184f, 184–85, 186t
trends in employment, 156f
work capacity, 128–29, 128t
mental health, 79
meso-level perspective on workforce aging, 198–99, 208–9
micro-level perspective on workforce aging, 198, 208–9
middle-aged population. *See also* employment stability in middle-aged population
European employment trends in, 79–86, 80f, 81f
European health trends in, descriptive findings of, 73–75, 74f
European health trends in, regression analyses of, 75–79, 76f, 77f, 78f
health trends in, 9–10
link between health and employment, 86
mortality rates, 7f, 7
migration, 52
minimum-wage workers, Social Security benefits for, 184f, 184–88, 186t
misreporting income, 246–48
mixed-age teams, 201t, 203–4
money income, limitations of concept, 246
morbidity, 9
mortality rates, 6–8, 7f
motivation
age-based stereotypes, 146–47
job demands and resources, 147–48
organizational policies for, 148–49
overview, 17
Munich Center for the Economics of Aging (MEA) health deficit index, 72

nature of work, trends in, 10–12
Netherlands, employment rates in, 81f, 82f, 84f
nonpharmaceutical interventions, 92–93

obesity, 9
Occupational Information Network (O*NET), 113–14, 116–20, 117t
Occupational Safety and Health Administration (OSHA), 310–11

occupations
impact of COVID-19 pandemic on, 96–98, 97t
O*NET data on, 116–20, 117t
occupation-specific work capacity (OWC), 121–22
Onion, The, 177
online simulation models, planning for unexpected shocks with, 106
organizational climate, 145–47
organizational policies, 148–49
organizational response to aging workforce
attitudes toward older workers, 202–3
business case, 207–8
HR practices, 203–4
institutional forces, 204–7, 210
interview data, 201–7
macro-, micro-, and meso-level concerns, 208–9
meso organizational level, 198–99
overview, 196–98
policy considerations, 210
skill divide, 209
survey data, 200–1, 201t
organizational structures, trends in, 11
organized political economy
economic conservatism within Republican Party, bias towards, 290–93
economic elites, bias towards, 284–87, 288f
overview, 277
policy choices, effect of biases on, 293–96
political gridlock, bias towards, 288–90
OSHA (Occupational Safety and Health Administration), 310–11
overconfidence, 129
OWC (occupation-specific work capacity), 121–22

paid elder care, cost of, 213, 224–26, 227f
paid family and medical leave (PFML), 10, 307, 311, 315t
partial retirement practices, 204–5, 208–9, 210
payroll tax cap removal (CAP 10.6%) option, Social Security reform
cost of no policy change assumption, 268f, 268–70, 269t
cost of policy change assumption, 270–71, 272t
effect on individual benefits, 259–61, 260t
effect on Social Security solvency, 261–62
overview, 259
payroll tax increase (no change to cap) (TAX + 3.1%) option, Social Security reform
cost of no policy change assumption, 265–67, 266f, 268–70, 269t
cost of policy change assumption, 270–71, 272t
effect on individual benefits, 259–61, 260t
effect on Social Security solvency, 261–62
overview, 259

person-context transaction factors, 139–40, 140f, 142–45
PFML (paid family and medical leave), 10, 307, 311, 315t
physical abilities, 117t
  by age cohort, 125–28, 127t
  by education, 129, 130t
  by gender, 128–29, 128t
  potential earnings and, 125, 126f
  by race and ethnicity, 129–31, 131t
  relationship between work capacity and, 123–25, 124t
physical demands, 11
  age-related HR practices, 204, 208–9
  of low-wage work, 188–89
PIA (primary insurance amount), 183–84, 256–57
PIA formula progressivity (PIA 5.0%) option, Social Security reform
  cost of no policy change assumption, 268f, 268–70, 269t
  cost of policy change assumption, 270–71, 272t
  effect on individual benefits, 259–61, 260t
  effect on Social Security solvency, 261–62
  overview, 259
polarization, asymmetric, 290–93
policy
  discussion, 314–15
  domains, 302–4
  economic and social policies, 313–14
  good jobs policies, 308–13, 315t
  overview, 19–21, 301–4
  retirement policies, 304–8, 315t
policy, organizational, 210
policy drift, 288–90
political engagement among older adults, 278, 293–96
political gridlock, 288–90, 296
politics
  asymmetric polarization, bias towards, 290–93
  economic elites, bias towards, 284–87, 288f
  future reforms, 296–97
  inadequate policy response, 284
  overview, 20, 276–77
  policy choices, effect of biases on, 293–96
  policy drift, 288–90
  political gridlock, bias towards, 288–90
  Republican Party, economic conservatism within, 290–93
  role of government, changes in, 12–14
  strains on older Americans, 278–84
population aging, 4–6, 5f, 19, 303–4
portable retirement savings plans, 305–6
potential earnings
  by age and education, 134, 134t
  by age and gender, 132, 132t
  by age and race, 132–33, 133t
  by age cohort, 125–28, 127t
  by education, 129, 130t
  functional abilities and, 125, 126f
  by gender, 128–29, 128t
  maximum and medium, 123f, 123
  by race and ethnicity, 129–31, 131t
  work capacity and, 115
poverty among older adults, 179–80, 239–40, 279–80, 280f
powering through strategy, 179, 191–92
power of workers, increasing, 309, 315t
predictive accuracy of worker expectations, 163, 164t
primary insurance amount (PIA), 183–84, 256–57
psychologically difficult working conditions, 11
psychology of working longer
  future research, 149–51
  individual attributes, 141–42
  model for, overview of, 139–40, 140f
  organizational policies, 148–49
  overview, 17, 138–39
  person-context transaction factors, 142–45
  work-related environmental factors, 145–48
psychomotor abilities, 117t
  by age cohort, 125–28, 127t
  by education, 129, 130t
  by gender, 128–29, 128t
  potential earnings and, 125, 126f
  by race and ethnicity, 129–31, 131t
  relationship between work capacity and, 123–25, 124t
public pension systems, 86
  cross-national differences, 16, 70–71, 281–83, 282f
  eligibility age for, 237–38
public use microdata areas (PUMAs), 51

R&D (research and development), increasing spending on, 104–5
race
  caregiving and, 215, 220f, 223, 224, 225f, 227f, 230f
  employment rates and, 34, 37f
  employment stability and, 40–41, 41f
  health inequalities, 6–8
  potential earnings by age and, 132–33, 133t
  self-reported ability distributions, 121f
  social identities, 145
  structural racism, 6, 114–15
  work capacity by, 129–31, 131t
racial resentment, 294–95
reasoning abilities, 141–42
recovery of employment during COVID-19 pandemic
  demographics of, 98–100, 99t
  government efforts, 100–1

INDEX | 331

regional disparities in employment. *See* geographic differences in employment
regression analysis
  European health trends, 75–79, 76f, 77f, 78f
  geographic differences in employment, 60–63
  Health and Retirement Study data, 42f, 42–43
relative age-earnings profiles, 256–57, 257f
relative poverty, 279–80
remote work, 11, 96–98, 97t
renting, 182, 182t, 185, 186t, 187
replacement care, cost of, 224–26, 227f
Republican Party
  bias towards economic conservatism within, 290–93
  economic elites, role of, 284–87, 288f
  effect of biases on policy choices, 293–96
  overview, 276–77
research and development (R&D), increasing spending on, 104–5
restaurant industry
  age discrimination in, 189–90
  low-wage work in, 180–81
  overview, 18
  physical demands of, 188–89
  worker strategies, 190–93
retaining older workers, 18–19, 199, 200, 311–12
retirement
  coordination with working spouse, 159
  cross-national differences, 280–81, 281f
  economic security in, 177–78, 181
  effect of population aging on systems of, 5
  motivation for, 29–30
  partial retirement practices, 204–5, 208–9, 210
  trends affecting, 91–92
retirement policies, 302, 303, 304–8, 315t
retirement savings plans, 13, 181, 244–45, 305–6, 315t
Ryan budget proposal, 287, 288f

safety net for retirees, 179, 192–93
safe work environments, 310–11, 315t
schedule control, 311
sectoral bargaining, 309
Senate filibuster, 289
sensitive period model, 29, 33
sensory abilities, 115, 117t
  by age cohort, 125–28, 127t
  by education, 129, 130t
  by gender, 128–29, 128t
  potential earnings and, 125, 126f
  by race and ethnicity, 129–31, 131t
  relationship between work capacity and, 123–25, 124t
service occupations
  impact of COVID-19 pandemic on, 96–98, 97t

past trends in employment, 159
SES. *See* socioeconomic status
SHARE (Survey of Health, Ageing and Retirement in Europe), 71–73
sick leave policies, 311, 315t
simulations of employment rates at older ages, 166–71, 168f, 169t, 170t
skill divide, 209
SNAP (Supplemental Nutrition Assistance Program), 245
social determinant of health, work as, 308
social identities, 145
social inequality, 2, 303
social institutions, improving efficacy of, 105
social policies, 313–14
social relationships in workplace, 311–12, 315t
social sciences, increasing spending on, 104–5
Social Security. *See also* Social Security reform
  benefits by claiming age, 258t
  benefits by wage scenario, 184f, 184–85
  current law, 256–58
  decreased poverty due to, 279
  economic elites, views of, 287
  economic security and, 181–84, 182t
  effect on economic inequality, 243–44
  financial outlook facing, 12–13, 241, 251
  future reforms, 20
  inadequacy of, 179
  money income from, 247f, 247–48
  past trends in employment and, 159
  population aging, effect on, 5
  sustainability policies, 304–5, 315t
  working longer and benefit adequacy, 185–88, 186t
  work-longer/retire-later policies and, 101–3
Social Security Disability Insurance (SSDI)
  geographic differences, 50, 57t, 59, 63, 64t
  for middle-aged population, 28, 43f, 43–44
  policy proposals, 306, 315t
Social Security Earliest Eligibility Age (EEA), 30
Social Security reform
  cost of indecision, model for, 264
  cost of indecision, overview, 262–64
  cost of indecision, under no policy change assumption, 265–70, 269t
  cost of indecision, under policy change assumption, 270–71, 272t
  current law, 256–58
  discussion, 271–73
  effect on individual benefits, 259–61, 260t
  effect on Social Security solvency, 261–62, 261t
  options for, 258–59
  overview, 254–56
social skills, 10–11
social trajectory model, 29, 33

societal exercises, 105
socioeconomic status (SES)
    caregiving and, 214–15, 218–19, 219t, 220f, 223, 224, 225f, 227f, 230f
    employment rates by, 34
    European health trends, 77f, 78f, 78–79
    health inequalities, 6–8
    social identities, 145
socioemotional goals, 142–43
socioemotional selectivity theory, 142–43
Spain
    employment rates in, 81f, 82f, 84f
    public pension systems in, 70–71, 282f
    social support systems in, 71
SPM (supplemental poverty measure), 279
SSDI. *See* Social Security Disability Insurance
SSI (Supplemental Security Income), 245, 306, 307, 315t
states, Republican success in, 292–93
Steady Outs, 33, 39f, 40f, 42f, 43–44
stereotypes, ageist, 146–47
strategies for low-wage work, 179, 190–93
stress, work-related, 11
structural racism, 6, 114–15
subjective probabilities of working
    forecasting fraction working at older ages, 165
    overview, 162–63
    predictive accuracy of, 163, 164t
    simulations, 166–71, 168f, 169t, 170t
    trends in, 163–65, 164f
Supplemental Nutrition Assistance Program (SNAP), 245
supplemental poverty measure (SPM), 279
Supplemental Security Income (SSI), 245, 306, 307, 315t
survey-based research about organizational practices, 200–1, 201t
Survey of Health, Ageing and Retirement in Europe (SHARE), 71–73
Sweden, employment rates in, 81f, 82f, 84f
Switzerland, employment rates in, 81f, 82f, 84f

TAX+3.1% (payroll tax increase [no change to cap]) option, Social Security reform
    cost of no policy change assumption, 265–67, 266f, 268–70, 269t
    cost of policy change assumption, 270–71, 272t
    effect on individual benefits, 259–61, 260t
    effect on Social Security solvency, 261–62
    overview, 259
taxation. *See also* payroll tax reform entries
    funding Social Security with, 305
    policy proposals, 296, 314
    political support for cuts in, 287, 288f
    Republican Party and, 292

technological trends, 91
transaction factors, person-context, 139–40, 140f, 142–45
Trump, Donald, 291, 292

underconfidence, 129
unemployment insurance (UI), 94–96, 95f
unequal gains, 240–41
unexpected shocks, planning for, 92, 103–6
union membership, 11–12, 293, 309
United Kingdom, employment rates in, 81f, 82f, 84f
universal health insurance, 70–71, 294
universal retirement savings plans, 305
U.S. Census, 51
utilization practices, 148–49

voice of workers, increasing, 309, 315t
voting among older adults, 278, 294–96

wage increases, 309–10, 315t
wage scenario, Social Security benefits by, 184f, 184–88, 186t
wealth
    caregiving and, 218, 219t, 220f, 225f, 227f, 230f
    economic elites, political bias towards, 284–87, 288f
    economic security in retirement, 181
    European health trends, 77f, 78f, 78–79
welfare state, age orientation of, 278
white collar jobs, impact of COVID-19 pandemic on, 96–98, 97t
White Americans
    caregiving and, 215, 220f, 225f, 227f, 230f
    health, 6–8, 114–15
    potential earnings by age, 132–33, 133t
    Republican Party support, 290–91, 294–96
    self-reported ability distributions, 121f
    work capacity, 131–34, 133t
women. *See also* caregiving
    career earnings inequality, 241–43, 242f
    disability benefit receipt by, 43f
    employment rates, 34–38, 35f, 36f, 37f, 38f
    employment stability, 40–41, 41f
    European employment trends, 80f, 80–81, 81f, 84f
    European health trends, 75–79, 76f, 77f
    family dynamics, changes in, 10
    geographic differences in employment, 54, 55f, 56f, 61, 62t, 64t
    job loss during COVID-19 pandemic, 98–99, 99t
    labor force participation, 30
    potential earnings by age and, 132, 132t
    self-reported ability distributions, 121f
    Social Security benefits by wage scenario, 184f, 184–85, 186t

trends in employment, 156f
work capacity, 128–29, 128t
work. *See* employment
work capacity
   by age cohort, 125–28, 127t
   cohort patterns in, 131–34, 132t, 133t, 134t
   data, 116–20, 117t
   definition of, 122
   discussion, 134–35
   by education, 129, 130t
   functional abilities, 120
   by gender, 128–29, 128t
   measuring, 120–25, 124t, 126f
   overview, 17, 113–16
   by race and ethnicity, 129–31, 131t
work centrality, 144
work from home, during COVID-19 pandemic, 96–98, 97t
working conditions, 10–12
working-longer policy framework
   challenges to, 1–3
   demographic trends, 4–6, 5f
   family and workplace, roles of, 18–19
   family dynamics, changes in, 10
   future of, 3–4
   health inequalities, trends in, 6–10
   labor trends, 15–16
   national policy, 19–20
   nature of work, trends in, 10–12
   person/environment fit, 17–18
   role of government, changes in, 12–14
working-time accounts, 204–5, 210
work-longer/retire-later policies, 101–3
workplace
   accommodations, 148–49, 307
   role of, 18–19
   safety, 10–11, 310–11, 315t
   social relationships and networks in, 311–12, 315t
work-related environmental factors, 140f, 145–48